Those Good Gertrudes

Those Good Gertrudes

A Social History of Women Teachers in America

GERALDINE J. CLIFFORD

Johns Hopkins University Press
Baltimore

Johns Hopkins University Press
2715 North Charles Street
Baltimore, Maryland 21218-4363
www.press.jhu.edu

Library of Congress Cataloging-in-Publication Data

Clifford, Geraldine Jonçich.
Those good Gertrudes : a social history of women teachers in America /
Geraldine J. Clifford.
pages cm
Includes bibliographical references and index.
ISBN-13: 978-1-4214-1433-1 (hardcover : alk. paper)
ISBN-13: 978-1-4214-1434-8 (electronic)
ISBN-10: 1-4214-1433-3 (hardcover : alk. paper)
ISBN-10: 1-4214-1434-1 (electronic)
1. Women teachers—United States—History.   2. Women teachers—United
States—Social conditions.   I. Title.
LB2837.C59 2014
371.100820973—dc23   2013044630

A catalog record for this book is available from the British Library.

Special discounts are available for bulk purchases of this book. For more information,
please contact Special Sales at 410-516-6936 or specialsales@press.jhu.edu.

Johns Hopkins University Press uses environmentally friendly book materials,
including recycled text paper that is composed of at least 30 percent post-consumer
waste, whenever possible.

CONTENTS

Illustrations appear following page 120 and on page 309.

The fictitiously named Charles L. Dodgson School where Jon Carroll volunteers weekly in the library of this twenty-first-century elementary school and where he occasionally picks up his granddaughter for an after-school treat, is one of those places "where men—somehow, through no fault of their own—simply do not belong." By 9:15, when the last father has dropped his kids off, "the school is essentially a women's world. The only men I know about are the principal and one after-school phys-ed-type teacher. The parent volunteers are overwhelmingly, perhaps exclusively, women." Until granddaughter Alice meets him after the last bell, Carroll feels his estrangement from this place of learning how to learn. "The women who don't know I belong there are vaguely freaked out by . . . a solitary guy without apparent function, hanging around a school waiting for the children to come out. Heck, I'd be suspicious of me."[1]

A century earlier, Alice Freeman Palmer wrote in *The Teacher* (1908), "Never before has a nation entrusted all the school training of the vast majority of its future population, men as well as women, to women alone." Having been a teacher in Wisconsin and Michigan before becoming president of Wellesley College in 1881, Palmer was undoubtedly proud of American women for their remarkable feat in taking possession of a traditional male profession. But she may have shared wider concerns about whether it was good, for women and the educational system, that they assumed so much of the responsibility for schooling—often called this nation's "secular religion." Although women's predominance has fluctuated, in 2010 women were 84% of all U.S. teachers.

If Palmer starts us thinking about the broader phenomenon of which the "Dodgson School" is a part—the effective transfer of schools in the United States of America from men to women—we can discern something of why it happened by turning to *Leonard and Gertrude: A Book for the People,* a didactic novel written in German in 1781 by Swiss educator Johann Heinrich Pestalozzi (1746–1827).[2] In his preface to the 1885 abridged English edition, pioneer child psychologist and university president G. Stanley Hall both honored women teachers and re-affirmed a basic tenet of American political and social thought: that an educated population is a self-sufficient one, that "big education" is vastly preferable to "big government." Hall explained Pestalozzi's story as a series of metaphors:

> Thus [the village of] Bonnal is the world; the bailiff is intemperance, intrigue, and all influences which degrade society; and Gertrude is the Good Teacher by whom alone the world is to be saved, if it is to be saved at all. We shall not read this story as we ought if we forget that there are hundreds of communities in our land to-day in the same need as was Bonnal of a regeneration so radical that only these same slow methods of practical, ethical education can ever accomplish it. Such a regeneration is not be effected by endowments, legislation, or by new methods, important as they are, but, as Pestalozzi thought, by the love and devotion of noble women overflowing from the domestic circle into the community, by the good Gertrudes of all stations in life, the born educators of the race.

Thus G. Stanley Hall has given this book both its title and its focus: examining the transformative power of the idea of women as "the born educators of the race" in a social history of schoolteaching.[3] Both the "mother love" that Gertrude expressed in her cottage spinning school for the children of the poor and Pestalozzi's social philosophy became popular themes in nineteenth-century Western thought concerning school reform. Given other intersecting nineteenth-century developments—economic, demographic, political, cultural—what difference did it make, then and since, that the schoolmaster gave way to the schoolmistress?

For one thing, women from every segment of America's rich mix of cultures and nationalities have taught in America's schools: from Annie Hull and Elsa von Wintzingerode to Olympia Goldaracena, Vlasta Zoubeck, and Minnehaha Thomas. Their story includes actual as well as figurative Gertrudes, including Gertrude Baldwin (b. 1894), Gertrude Mary Heaphy (b. 1869), and her niece Gertrude ("Trudie") Robbins Fator (b. 1935). Moreover, they are all "Gertrudes": alter egos of Pestalozzi's and, more explicitly, Hall's totemic representations. Indeed, in various places throughout this work, "Gertrude" is employed in place of the more prosaic "the woman teacher" as embodying both the pedagogical significance of a transition to the woman teacher and her history-making place in American culture and society.

This book is born of a personal but reasoned decision to place in history's fickle spotlight the taken-for-granted woman teacher. Making teachers visible in history at the grass roots recovers this ill-remembered profession as it surely was:

a shifting compound of credulity and calculation, of yielding and resisting, of compassion and dispassion, of inertness and energy. I have tried not to glorify the women who taught or to give even the clearly "good" Gertrudes more credit than the record or reasonable surmise can sustain. We must not assume heroic womanhood or defer to ideological correctness on gender issues. To use the imagery of Australian scholar Jill Matthews, women teachers are to be found both among those who were "doing the squashing" and those who were "being squashed."[4]

Teachers were expected to express the values of the communities employing them, and most were probably fairly comfortably in so doing. Thus some Northern-bred teachers in the pre–Civil War South adopted and acted on the prevailing ethos of white supremacy. However, intentionally or not, the omnipresent schoolma'am was also a self-generating subversive force against patriarchy. By securing this measure of psychological and economic independence, women ultimately turned the concept of "woman's sphere" into empty rhetoric. As teachers, individual women were being equipped to enter the other historically male professions, while their instruction and example prepared and inspired legions of girls to enter the larger labor force—with significant social, economic, and political consequences.

Telling a Neglected Story

Willard Elsbree states in *The American Teacher: Evolution of a Profession in a Democracy* (1939) that every teacher should know "the conditions under which former pedagogues worked, the kind of persons they were, and the part which they played in society." In 1950, when 60% of women then in college were being prepared to teach, educational researchers across all disciplines still focused on male policy makers, institution builders, administrators, and curriculum theorists. Whether as teachers or pupils—or as professors, textbook writers, researchers, or association and union officials—women were barely noted.

Subsequently, however, all manner of people formerly "outside history" were appearing among the makers of history. This shift is reflected in a volume of original essays, *American Teachers: Histories of a Profession at Work* (1989), where William R. Johnson writes, "It seems hard to believe that only within the past decade or so have historians begun to pay much attention to schoolteachers and their preparation." Barbara Finklestein and Kathryn Kish Sklar were among the first to do so, and subsequent reference works brought selected women teachers forward—mostly neglected leaders or pioneers. Next a body of complementary studies of "ordinary women" surfaced in educational, women's, social, and labor history.

Kenneth Burke's axiom—"Every way of seeing is also a way of not seeing"—helps explain how scholars and policy makers persistently neglected women teachers' achievements, in and out of America's schoolrooms.[5] The assertion that women teachers lacked a professional's commitment to "career" is not convincing when their tutelage often linked a family's oldest and youngest siblings, and even child and parent. How can we perceive them as essentially well-meaning but passive followers of men who manage patriarchal institutions and impersonal bureaucracies when the garden-variety teacher appeared to herself, her charges, and often their parents, as a law unto herself? Or think our teachers were pitiful, man-less, ill-paid, drab, and lonely creatures, when they were the sole independent women my schoolmates and I had ever known? They were the only women who drove their own cars, traveled to distant locales every summer, dressed smartly (and certainly were never seen by their pupils in curlers, aprons, or tears)—women who made decisions rather than deferring to Papa-when-he-gets-home. (There were, of course, those teachers of either sex who tried to turn their problems over to the principal.)

Grown up, I later wondered if my school days in the 1930s and 1940s were an island in time, the exception that proved the rule to the conventional wisdom of serious historians and social scientists. Were our experiences and perceptions peculiar to unsophisticated, little-educated communities like mine: a working-class port town, heavily immigrant, perhaps too easily impressed? Yet this nation has been made up of, and made by, thousands of similar places.

This volume is a school history in being centered on those who taught children aged 5–18 in schools with formalized programs, rites, and whatever can be discerned of the incidental learning and "hidden curriculum" that schooling also imparts. While schools (and less so colleges) have never defined the whole of deliberate instruction—in that sense "teachers are everywhere"—schoolteachers' essential charge is instructing as many pupils as they receive. (This is not true of other multipurpose institutions that also educate—family, church, workplace, peer group, youth club, mass media, and now the Internet—much less the tribe or village that participated in raising children over the millennia.)

My aim has been to reconstruct a broad social history of the women who taught school and largely made it *their* work. It pursues the generic and gendered workforce and life-course issues impinging upon teachers and their schools. (Gender is understood here as a functional, normative, alterable social invention, in contrast to a biological division of human beings into the primary sexual categories of female and male.) Familiar, slighted, and misunderstood themes in the history of education are probed, especially the causes and consequences of teaching's emergence as the nation's largest profession.

To know the female teacher, one must also know her male counterpart: the men who taught and the many more who did not or did so only briefly. However, in this collective biography, males generally reside in the background: at the podium at teachers' institutes and colleges, on the school board, in the superintendent's office, at home. While men are always in women's stories, like it or not, here the "lords of creation" play second fiddle to "the gentle sex." As it must be, this is a feminist history. Feminism "postulates that woman's essential worth stems from her common humanity and does not depend on the other relationships of her life," such as marriage and motherhood.[6] The essence of feminism in the Gertrudes' story surfaces as the pursuit of equality of opportunity, competency, accountability, and responsibility—including drawing up and revising, as needed, the very rules of the game.

I strongly incline to Dale Spender's view: "there is an area—of being subordinate to men, of being defined in relation to men, of being the nurturing sex in an exploitative society—where women do share a common experience."[7] I have sought to grasp and convey what it meant to be, at once, an American and a teacher and a woman. Of course, these characteristics do not capture all that these individuals were or wanted to be. Moreover, in any given time or situation in her life, the American woman teacher's other identities—rooted in religion, social class, race, region, or domesticity—may dominate her self-consciousness and better denote her social and political place. Yet the woman teacher or former teacher is different from both the woman who has never taught and from the male teacher, their mutuality notwithstanding.

In considering what and how teaching contributed to the woman teacher's own development, the educational system, and womanhood in general, I came to accept three related propositions. First, clues to the roles that teachers play reside in many and diverse "documents." Second, teachers do not have to be "great" by any accepted definition—or popular or even effective—to be significant in individual or societal terms. Third, what Henry Seidel Canby wrote about his teachers at the all-male Yale College in the 1890s applies to the mostly female teachers of "lower" education: "We loved them, or hated them, or even despised them, but never escaped their daily presence in our thoughts."[8]

Telling a Story Differently

Antecedents of the modern schoolmistress in medieval and early modern Europe can be located in a few published works. But to write a collective biography of the woman teacher in America, in her knowable diversity, meant digging into a vast, largely untapped treasury of unpublished documents by and about teachers and their work. When my search began, around 1975, most of the relevant manuscript materials were catalogued not under "schools," "education," or "teachers" but buried within traditional archival divisions: under local and regional history; under religious and church history; by racial, ethnic, or immigrant designations; by family names; and under the temporal rubrics of the colonial period, Civil War, western movement, or frontier and pioneer history. The teacher—generally "schoolmistress" before 1850, then "schoolma'am," later the more satirical "schoolmarm"—was found in all these places, in glorious profusion, and speaking for herself and often to other teachers.

The bedrock of this book is an aggregate of personal history documents from 628 collections—gathered over a quarter century from state and local historical societies and the manuscript divisions of university research libraries: 84 repositories located in 32 states and the District of Columbia, my search guided initially by William Mathews' *American Diaries in Manuscript, 1580–1954, A Descriptive Bibliography* (1974). These ranged in scale from the Library of Congress to the History Department of the Utah Pioneer Memorial Museum, and in geography from the University of Washington Library to the Congregation of the Sisters of St. Joseph of St. Augustine (FL). (An annotated list of the more useful collections, arranged by state and archive, will be linked to Johns Hopkins University Press's website.) My research also included published letters, diaries, autobiographies, and the underappreciated journals of state historical societies that often print and contextualize long extracts from unpublished sources. Oral histories added a few early- to mid-twentieth-century teachers, and I randomly interviewed other teachers or their family members, often while traveling.

A great many teachers provided sufficient testimony to make supportable statements about the generality of teachers, in all their guises, and their variability; their school-centered motivations, experiences, careers, and achievements; and relevant elements of teachers' nonschool family, religious, and civic lives. California and the West provide more examples than usual in general works, somewhat reducing New England's dominance in the schooling story. More Gertrudes from the pivotal nineteenth century tell their stories than from the preceding or following periods. For some women (active or former) teachers, I have scores, even hundreds of pages of notes and photocopies. At the other extreme, countless women emerged as hardly more than a name and a few facts, some gathered from obituaries in local newspapers, school and college directories and alumni publications, perhaps checked or elaborated in recent years by Internet sites.

The standard historiography of American schooling runs along two sets of parallel tracks, isolating their authors and readers from one another. First is the separation of public and secular private schools from those of sectarian institutions. However, this study incorporates the nuns and lay teachers who served in the very large and significant parochial school sector of the Roman Catholic Church. A second traditional divide is that of school history from college history. While women teachers became far more numerous and indispensable in the nation's elementary and secondary schools than allowable on college and university faculties, they also bridge the histories of higher and lower education. Both as college-age students preparing to teach and as teachers returning to higher education, significant numbers of women enrolled at a crucial time: when the "old-time college" was challenged to become the modern university. For decades women also made the education field the largest program of study in American higher education, subsidizing its geographic and curricular sprawl.

The book's structure is largely topical: the chapters are thematic and roughly chronological within each of their various sections. Composite portrayals and generalizations (the aggregate of *their lives*) coexist with short case studies of a specific individual (the wholeness of *her life*.) Maxine Greene provides a language for this balancing process when she writes of "contours" (the generic) and "identities" (the individual).[9] Ideally, letting teachers tell pieces of their own stories permits the participants' own understandings and points of view to challenge historians' propensity to construct a "usable past" according to their and their readers' present prejudices, preoccupations, and language.

Using Comparative Perspectives

In one setting it is the young teacher in New Mexico forced to give up her school because a stallion killed the pony she rode the 14 miles to and from home. In another it is the Australian schoolmistress whose afternoon duties included draining the ink from her pupils' inkwells lest it attract the thirsty rats from the wheat-field stubble invading her schoolhouse each night.[10] As is now true of knowledge generally, an active international community has formed, enlisting researchers and theorists to share their interest in women in teaching. Scholarship in other English-speaking societies—especially Australia—has been important in conceptualizing this book. Subsequent conversations and exchanges of publications with European scholars also left their mark. Regrettably, much of what I explicitly detailed in earlier drafts did not survive the radical paring-down process of creating a work of publishable length.

Diverse societies have always been influenced from abroad. Colonialism did so with force. Other changes were brought through ideas. Pestalozzi's *How Gertrude Teaches Her Children* (1802) began an international stream of observers to his Rousseau-inspired schools, especially to Yverdon. Teachers themselves have also proved remarkably peripatetic; as economic opportunists, religious and cultural missionaries, or adventurers, some have planted themselves and their ways of believing and behaving in foreign soil—or brought the foreign home.

Gender aside, interchanges among educators come easily, with words, gestures, and images comfortably familiar. In *Kwanzaa and Me, a Teacher's Story* (1995), Vivian Gussin Paley relates the visit of a Lebanese educator to her kindergarten classroom at the University of Chicago's Laboratory Schools. "As we speak together I realize that the universality of school life makes it possible for us all to understand each other's experiences and expectations. . . . This is true even when, as in Majida's case, war and political strife have disrupted the general pattern of life" (p. 48).

Cross-national scholarship undermines the tendency to take one's own system for granted by showing how dissimilar means and motives can achieve similar ends. While comparative education once figured prominently in preparing historians of education, the present intensified cross-cultural exchange is different. It reflects a discernible late twentieth-century trend in historical scholarship—a conceptual revolution that has broadened the scope of inquiry of political, social, and intellectual history, rescaling events and trends into larger settings.[11]

This broad attack on parochialism and exceptionalism has been aided by various integrating developments: the Cold War's end, a worldwide feminist movement, economic globalization, an international youth culture, and shared experiences with immigration, even in formerly ethnically and culturally insular nations.[12] Worldwide demographic imbalances between men and women teachers have been influenced by varied geopolitical, cultural, or economic roots. Yet whether propelled by civil or foreign war in one nation, differential emigration in another, or religio-ideological strictures in a third, the result has usually been the same: transferring teaching primarily from male to female hands. This shift appears to be pivotal in extending formal schooling from elites to the populace and, recently, in facilitating the "knowledge economy."

The Truth in Fiction

Life and the novel often converge because diverse authors—from the Brontë sisters to Mary Balogh and Dorothy Bryant—were themselves governesses or schoolteachers and made such women their central characters. Their insider knowledge and lifelike depictions carry weight, while they bring fiction's gift of making the person whole, especially in (re)creating unseen states of mind. Those novelists not themselves teachers—Jane Austen, William Faulkner, Zane Grey, Henry James, LaVyrle Spencer, Edith Wharton—nonetheless knew teachers, as watchful pupils do. Some have crafted their teacher portraits from keen observation, diligent research, even genius—achieving truthful motivations and recognizable social situations and experiences. The schoolmistress appears widely in literature and popular fiction, even the suspect romance novels that enjoy a huge readership among girls and women.

"Susceptible readers" (meaning young people and women) have long been warned against reading novels, for fear of their influence. (Fredrika Bremer's 1865 novel *Hertha* is credited with helping change Swedish public opinion on behalf of allowing women to enter male professions, including teaching in the higher schools.[13]) Some novels have undoubtedly inspired or redirected female career choices, marriage included, by offering a yardstick against which she could measure her own surroundings, resources, and hopes. While crude stereotypes appear in fictional accounts of teachers, and distortions should be pried away from their skeletal truths, stereotypes also lurk in nonfiction—and with less implied warning to the reader. Fiction's teachers appear in these pages—without apology but with notice.

Principles of Usage

In *A Slaveholder's Daughter* (1910), published during the woman suffrage movement, Belle Kearney wrote feelingly, "The word 'woman' is strong and dignified, [while 'female' represents] the inferior position of women." Kearney's words invite some discussion of the language choices made in this study. It was generally "pupil" and "scholar" ("large" and "small"), not "student" in the eighteenth and nineteenth centuries; and "female," "lady," and "Oriental" and "colored" and "Negro" in much of the nineteenth and first half of the twentieth centuries. Language is an important element in setting historical context, and past usages are among the landmarks of the *territorium historica* contributing to the reader's feel for the "then and there," seeing things as understood by the participants. Therefore, after much reflection, I decided to employ terminology customarily used by civil, responsible speakers, writers, and members of the designated group during the historical period and in the place under discussion—however uncomfortable to the present-day eye and ear, my own included. Where terms were used interchangeably, I have generally done the same.

Where the historical actors are quoted directly, I do not insert editorial comments on their language, for example, when the generic "he" is used to refer to persons of both sexes (or even to mostly female groups such as American schoolteachers in 1920). I do not use "*sic*," finding it distracting and patronizing. To refer even to ardent early feminists as "Ms." is misguided usage. (Although I may address my women contemporaries as Ms., Susan B. Anthony was "Miss" in life and remains Miss Anthony in history.) Furthermore, we have little reason to think that current conventions of usage have more prospects of permanence than those of the past.

I have tried to be sparing in inserting modifiers (e.g., "many," "some") routinely before the great many references to "women teachers," as they are tiresome and probably unnecessary; no reader will think that any generalization describes (almost) every individual. Finally, where known I use the surname borne by a teacher while she taught, rather than any other name she acquired; the notes give both.

Notes and References

Notes are chiefly limited to printed and unpublished works and archival collections from which direct quotations are drawn or on which I have substantially depended. For every chapter the first noted citation of a published work includes author (and coauthor), editor or editors, full title, publisher, and publication date. Subsequent entries are to (first) author or editor and an abbreviated title. The first notation to an archival collection is fully referenced; subsequent citations employ a short form. Because of space limitations, no note appears when an author and work are named in the text. Important supplementary secondary sources have also been eliminated from the notes, along with ancillary biographical and related facts and opinions. Although Miss O'Rourke (see acknowledgment below) would not approve, readers are less dependent on authors for bibliographic references given the availability, accessibility, and coverage of online resources.

A brief bibliographic essay, "An Essential Reference Guide," is a concise list of published works from which I have repeatedly drawn across chapters—such as James, *Notable American Women,* and the Census Bureau's *Historical Statistics of the United States.* Such references are not included in chapter notes, except for illustrative purposes and in a truncated form. Citation errors and frustrating omissions will arise, and for these I apologize.

Acknowledgments

Many authors have contributed to this work, not least the hundreds of unsung teachers whose words and stories did not find space in the draft manuscript, much less this greatly reduced version. My thanks and profound regrets go to the archivists, family members, and others who gave me access to these still-anonymous participants in this collective history of the teaching woman.

I am greatly indebted to the archivists in rare books, manuscripts, and special collections departments and to staff members who paged and photocopied the primary sources on which this book so depends. They were knowledgeable, imaginative, resourceful, and generous. Special arrangements were made for using collections during off hours or even at other locations, such as the Pocatello Public Library, to which the late Idaho State University Librarian, Gary Domitz, transported both me and the scrapbooks of Idaho Commissioner of Education Ethel Redfield for weekend work. John White arranged after-hours use of a copy of the diary of Caroline Brooks Lilly at the University of North Carolina at Chapel Hill. Sister Eileen Ann Kelley, archivist of the Sisters of Providence at Saint Mary of the Woods (IN) kindly lent me books and searched for photographs.

The staff of the Center for American Women and Politics at Rutgers University offered valuable advice on using its resources. Allison Prentice's work on Canadian women teachers led me to the Ontario Institute for Studies in Education's archives in Toronto, and Ronald Butchart directed me to archives on teachers of the freedmen. J. Graham Gardner, head of the History Department at Swan Hill High School, arranged interviews and access to sources about teaching in his corner of Australia's Murray River country.

This type of history would not have been possible without research grants that funded travel to distant libraries, paid for photocopying, purchased dissertations, employed an occasional graduate student research assistant or translator, or extended a sabbatical leave. For most of my long tenure in the Graduate School of Education at the University of California at Berkeley, I had research support from the Academic Senate Committee on Research and two appointments as a Humanities Research Fellow. The Spencer Foundation awarded me a three-year start-up grant in the mid-1970s and made another award in the 1990s. A grant administered by Radcliffe College supported research in its Schlesinger Library on the History of Women in America. For their confidence in me, I am indebted to the staffs, officers, directors, and review committees of these entities.

Editors of the *History of Education Quarterly* kept me abreast of the latest work on teachers by assigning me manuscripts to evaluate and books to review. The annual meetings of the History of Education Society, Southern History of Education Society, and the Division on History and Historiography of the American Educational Research Association exposed progressively more engaging research on women and teaching, and I was able to obtain reactions to my work in progress at their meetings, at several Berkshire Conferences of Women Historians, and international conferences and workshops. Around 1994 Donald Warren invited me to Indiana University, where I tested my initial efforts at using popular fiction in writing about teachers.

My preliminary investigations into schools and teachers in Australia relied on the encouragement of Richard Selleck and the research of Marjorie Theobald, Alison Mackinnon, and Ailsa Zainu'ddin especially. Over two years they involved me in seminars and meetings with a wider circle of scholars or helped secure access to archives. Torsten Húsen set up a helpful meeting with scholars in Stockholm, as did Jirí Kotásek in Prague. Jaap ter Linden was generous with explanations and illustrations of Dutch schooling in earlier centuries.

America's small community of historians of education was generous in sharing work in progress, among them Joseph W. Newman, Scott Baker, Kate Rousmaniere, Katherina Kroo Grunfeld, and Joan Peterson. Joel Perlmann lent a prepublication manuscript of his massive census-based study, with Robert Margo, of women teachers. Polly Kaufman and Donald Warren supported my efforts in a number of ways, as has a group of mostly younger scholars; while some of their scholarship is specifically cited, all of them have contributed. Because they are not otherwise credited, I thank here Dr. Thea Maestre of Holy Names College for assembling a group of active, insightful Oakland teachers. Jerry Goren and Jeanni Tavlin arranged my interviews with three Los Angeles high school teachers, targets of McCarthyism.

The intellectual energy of the women's studies field has added critical momentum to the latter-day discovery of women teachers. Florence Howe helped sustain my enthusiasm for this project and pushed my efforts into new tributaries. Patricia Graham put me in touch with Katharine Lacey, who with Mary Oates, CSJ, were my chief guides to sources and insights on the educational work, community culture, and changing lives of Catholic teaching nuns. Alexa Nickliss alerted me that philanthropist Phebe Apperson Hearst once labored among the Gertrudes, prompting me to investigate the frequent but usually unremarked presence of teaching in the backgrounds of otherwise notable women.

Senior colleagues also introduced me to their students, some of whom I employed as research assistants on follow-up investigations of specific women encountered in my research; these enterprising younger researchers are credited in the notes. "Berkeleyans" Linda von Hoene, Tony Maxwell, and Edwige Gamache contributed their translations of German, Swedish, and French sources respectively, while Nina Gabelko analyzed unpublished data on women in Congress to help me establish the reach of teachers as political women over time. And Judith Warren Little assured me regularly that there were indeed readers waiting for *Those Good Gertrudes.*

Several of my former students aided this project. Suzanne Hildenbrand shared references and scholarship on women in librarianship and put her command of computerized databases at my disposal. The overlong, overwritten manuscript of my magnum opus might not have evolved into a book without the thoughtful assistance of Kimberley Tolley, whose editorial work on the first chapters set a workable model for subsequent rewriting and helped start the process of contacting publishers. And, most recently, Lana Muraskin brought forth a professional editor when I needed one: Natalie Reid, whose mantra with me has had to be the hated three-letter word: "cut." (Hugs, Natalie!)

During my research forays, shop talk with colleagues and their spouses often moved into welcoming homes and favorite restaurants. Courtney Ann Vaughn-Roberson, Craig Kridel, Polly Kaufman, John Thelin, James Guthrie, Bruce Saunders, Barbara Finkelstein, Judith Austin, Thomas Dyer, Ray Hiner, Lelon Capps, and Wayne Urban saw that my stays in their communities leavened hard work with good food, wine, and conversation. My husband, William Francis Clifford (1924–1993), gave me unfailing support and everyday assistance, both at home and on the road. I deeply regret that Bill did not live to see the completion of *Those Good Gertrudes.*

Dedication
In Particular Appreciation of the Teachers of My Youth
from Miss Marjorie M. Curtis to Miss Mary Jane O'Rourke

This history is dedicated to the memory of a tiny subsample of the veritable army of "Good Gertrudes." I had only a pupil's fragmentary knowledge of each, but it foreshadowed my construction of this broad-ranging collective portrait of the woman teacher in American history. The two women named above were among my best-remembered teachers in my first 12 years of schooling. At Cabrillo Avenue School in San Pedro (CA), Miss Marjorie M. Curtis, my second-grade teacher, shut me into her classroom's walk-in supply closet for some unremembered misdeed—likely talking too much. Forgetting about my incarceration, she took the class out at recess and returned to find that I had pulled down her neat stacks of supplies, making a general mess of her storeroom. I must have expected chastisement but received none. Did we (like other teachers and their pupils) strike a tacit agreement to ignore this example of errors in judgment on both sides?

The Curtis sisters (Miss Dorothy Curtis was my first-grade teacher) lived together, unbeknownst to me, as did several other single women among my teachers. Much later I discovered how common it has been for sisters—as for mothers and daughters, aunts and nieces—to share careers. As for Richard Henry Dana Junior High School's teachers, I dimly recall an ineffective woman, notably because we finally made her cry. More embarrassed than ashamed, we behaved better thereafter, although I suspect we drove her from teaching.

San Pedro High School in the 1940s was another matter, implanting still vivid memories of Judith Grant (Spanish), Margareth Muller (math), and Mary Jane O'Rourke, who had taught English and journalism there since 1924. Secretly known as "Lefty" in the smart-alecky circle of the school's athletes—she had somehow lost an arm—Miss O'Rourke packed another girl and me into her coupe one day and took us to an after-school meeting of Future Teachers of America. Determined then not to become a teacher, I was nonetheless impressed and highly flattered. Her ability to drive and teach one-armed did not surprise me, teachers being formidable beings in my world. Only years later did I wonder about the tortured path into schoolteaching that she surely traveled—and about those who helped her do so. Bless her! Bless them all!

Those Good Gertrudes

CHAPTER 1

"It Is Well That Women Should Be Unlettered"

Before Teaching School Was "Women's Work"

> Let the woman learn in silence, with all subjection. I suffer not a woman to teach, nor to usurp authority over a man, but to be silent.
>
> —St. Paul, 1 Timothy 2:11–12

Elizabeth Elstob (b. 1683), known around Evesham (Worcestershire) as that rare creature, a truly learned lady, struggled to survive as mistress of a small "dame school." Her letters tell of her exhaustion from instilling basic literacy in poor children for a weekly wage of one groat, worth four English pennies. "These long winter evenings to me are very melancholy ones, for when my school is done, my little ones leave me incapable of either reading, writing, or thinking, for their noise is not out of my head till I fall asleep."[1]

In 1738 she gave George Ballard a brief third-person memoir of her life, relating her early love of books, her widowed mother's forward-looking belief in educating females, and the example of a studious older brother "who very joyfully and readily assisted and encouraged" her lessons, including some Latin and Greek. She was 8 years old and William 14 when their mother died—he sent to Eton and Cambridge, and she to an uncle "who was no friend to women's learning." Allowed English books, she taught herself to read French. When her brother obtained a pastorate in London, she joined him. Although his church was poor and their lives arduous, they worked together as scholars, learning Old English, and in 1715 she published *Rudiments of Grammar for the Anglo-Saxon Tongue.*

When William died at 30, she opened a boarding school for girls in Chelsea; it failed after six months. As launching the school had taken all of her small inheritance and as the last of her family had died, Elstob was left destitute. Fearing debtors' prison, she fled without her books and papers. Ballard and his friends secured her a position as governess to the daughters of the Duchess of Portland, a position she filled until her death.[2] The duchess strongly favored educating females, but the duke regarded Elstob as unqualified to guide his daughters' education because, despite her ability to read eight languages, she could not speak French—as a gentlewoman would. Moreover, her scholarly writing was clearly inappropriate to her gender.

The Book Perhaps, but Never the Pen

In ancient Egypt a father stressed to his son that no scribe goes hungry.[3] The word "clerk" recalls that the power to write was once the near-exclusive possession of monastery- or cathedral-educated clergy. Like writing, the literary languages—in Europe, classical Latin and Greek—were functionally and ceremonially linked to important religious and civil roles reserved for men. To be called "learned" or to enter a "learned profession" was a male privilege—although Heinrich Cornelius Agrippa's *Nobility of the Female Sex* (1529) credited women with equal or superior achievement when the sexes received comparable education.

The ancient association of formal learning with the male sex was reflected in the Swedish practice of singing of "the glorious laurels" at the ceremonies awarding graduates of the boys' grammar school certification for the university. Laurel wreaths were also conferred on recipients of the doctor of philosophy degree, symbols recalling the triumphal processions of Roman warriors. In promoting female education in late eighteenth-century Russia, Empress Catherine accepted that scholarship resided in the male realm, with war and commerce, but conceded that schooling girls would nourish a reformed family life.[4] More distant cultures acted similarly. For example, during Japan's Heian era (794–1183), classical Chinese was taught in schools to wellborn males; their sisters were privately tutored in the native idiom.[5]

Women Prodigies of the Higher Learning

Women scholars did exist, if not flourish, including the lifelong scholars of the Vedic (pre-550 BCE) period on the Indian subcontinent. On the ruined walls of ancient Pompeii is a portrait of a thoughtful woman—perhaps representing Sappho, the great lyric poet of early sixth-century BCE Greece—holding a stylus, indicating full literacy. Hypatia (c. 360–416 CE) taught mathematics and philosophy in Alexandria until her death. In the early Christian era, sporadic attempts were made to confer upon women a measure of the authority of students and teachers of the written word, but efforts to encourage, record, or preserve women's words were uncommon. Although the following are just a few individual examples, they were far outnumbered by scholars of the favored other sex.

Medieval Italy had a scattering of female scholar-teachers. Trotula (c. 1075–1125) and Abella (c. 1100) taught at the University of Salerno, Europe's first medical faculty. A lecturer at the University of Bologna on philosophy, law, and medicine, Maddalena Bonsignori wrote a treatise on women under the law. Another intimation of a rising feminist consciousness appears in 1626, when self-taught Marie de Gournay argued the intellectual equality of the sexes in *Le grief des dames* (The complaint of the ladies).[6]

Like the monks in their sanctuaries of learning, before the end of the first Christian millennium a few classically educated nuns were copying the sacred texts and assembling convent libraries. Their scholarly training and accomplishments were particularly impressive in the convents of Saxony, where Benedictine abbess Hathumoda of Gandersheim (c. 840–874) and her sister nuns created a center of intellectual activity, as did Gertrude of Hackeborn (b. 1232).[7] However, because few nuns could compose in Latin or Greek, their scholarship as poets, historians, theologians, and educators was little valued until the Protestant Reformation made the written vernacular the key to biblical literacy and salvation.[8]

In the early modern era, and outside of Europe, at its height the enlightened Mughal Empire of India (1526–1707) employed "educated matrons" and elderly males to instruct aristocratic women at home—in a broad curriculum featuring the sciences, poetry, history, and theology. A retreat to Islamic fundamentalism spelled the end of the empire and its tolerance of well-educated and influential women. China had a class of itinerant women—"teachers of the inner chambers"—whose learning was a by-product of a changing economy and growing affluence in certain provinces.[9] Some were famed poets, living independent lives while teaching the daughters of the gentry.

Others must have existed, because a classic nineteenth-century Japanese text warned of the moral danger of learned women, for "if clever in their speech it is a sign that civil disturbance is not far off." While such women were probably more numerous and dispersed than surviving sources reveal, the chief importance of prodigies in a social history of the woman teacher is as a symbol of female intellectual possibilities, determination, and independence. These exemplars had the potential to inspire less extraordinary women to use their abilities, exploiting more fully whatever everyday conventions and institutions could be bent to their grasp.

The Vernacular—an Opening for the Subordinate Sex

Conservatives believed that allowing women access to writing and public speaking would increase their influence while leaving their decreed tasks undone.

Orthodox Judaism invoked the Talmud to warn against female education: "Whoever teaches his daughter Torah is as though he taught her folly," and "Let the words of the Torah rather be destroyed by fire than imparted to women." Sir Ralph Varney warned in 1690, "Let not your girle learn Latin or short hand; the difficulty of the first may keep her from that Vice, . . . but the easinesse of the other may bee a prejudice to her. Had St. Paul lived in our Times I am confident hee would have fixt a shame upon our woemen for writing as well as for speaking in church."[10]

However, in its quest for converts, the Christian church had been transcribing the Germanic and romance vernaculars into the roman alphabet. As ordinary speech in the vernacular was written down, oral societies slowly became literate ones, blurring the distinctions between sacred and secular language and between public (male) and private (female) language. Class barriers became somewhat easier to breach, opening literacy to more beneficiaries. In their native lands, French, English, Polish, and other languages would eventually replace classical studies for most students.

It was women or the family's older children who had always given young children most of their early instruction in colloquial language: caregivers helping children to understand and use everyday speech. Hence, when the vernacular first became the chief language of instruction and later a school subject itself, women gained a vital, if grudgingly provided, teaching space. Despite fears that females able to write could forge a father's or husband's signature or that learning geography could spark discontent with the boundaries of her home, females ultimately gained wider opportunities to learn and to teach outside the household. Nevertheless, most references to schooling continued to use the male pronoun for both teacher and pupils into the twentieth century, even when females were the majority in both roles.

Looking far forward, when Celia Campos became principal of Holy Family Parish School in Wilmington (CA) in 1996, her purpose in hiring three male teachers for the school's faculty of 18 was "to show the children that teaching is not only a female profession."[11] To Americans, even professional educators, the female schoolteacher is so commonly experienced and taken for granted that one can hardly accept that she was not always a *she*.[12] Nonetheless, the evidence is clear that *school*teaching was regarded (and usually practiced) as men's work, recorded in the teaching figures painted on the vases and friezes of ancient civilizations, in oral traditions and sacred writings of many societies, surviving medieval tax and census records, literature and autobiography, and the worldwide male grip on literacy and access to schools and universities.

Early Havens for the Teaching Woman

In most developed nations today, women constitute the majority of teachers in public and private elementary schools—known to older Americans as grade or grammar schools. Moreover, women have also been more than half of high school teachers in the United States since the public high school established itself firmly around 1880. Structurally (not ideologically), this male-to-female transition took place because over two millennia several niches developed in which literate females were able to instruct others. When females entered more fully into schoolrooms, first as pupils and then as teachers, theirs was an emergence from these havens.[13]

First, the most obvious haven, the household, was a place of teaching and learning where literate females—family members or governesses—could teach young children and older girls. Second, the church offered another venue by reaching into the household and taking family members into its institutions, all places of teaching and learning: cathedral, monastic, and convent schools, orphanages, even hospitals. Wherever permitted, pious laywomen and consecrated nuns labored in these religious places, under the Christian obligation to save souls. Third, schools enter this layered picture when sons, and later daughters, received formal instruction away from the household, in day or boarding schools—schools provided by entrepreneurial teachers, religious or charitable bodies, guilds, local landowners, or even early manufacturers for their workers or workers' children.

As for the schoolmistress, surviving sixteenth-century church, court, and civic records offer only scattered names, the labors of others who taught in medieval and early modern Europe likely unrecoverable. Over time the story's outline become progressively clearer, revealing the woman hired on her own, laboring in the school of a male relative, or banding with other women supporting themselves as teachers. Literary historians find teaching women when something of their writing has surfaced.[14] Few were captured in a sweep of the past by historians of education, perhaps under the presumption that women teachers were absent or inconsequential before the nineteenth century or that what they taught was of little relative value to the later story.

The School of the Family

Teaching and learning, by both example and precept, begins in and around the household, inherent in the processes of child rearing and training household help. Before the era of universal schooling, basic reading was usually acquired in literate households.[15] In Titus 2:3–4, Paul conceded a limited domestic teaching role to older women: as "teachers of honest things, they may instruct the young women to be sober minded, that they love their husbands, that they love their children." In the seventeenth century, Rembrandt painted his mother reading a large volume, perhaps a Bible. In both Catholic and Protestant states, church authorities enjoined parents to take responsibility for every aspect of their children's temporal and eternal welfare. Thus we see mothers pointing with a quill or knitting needle to the letters in a book or on a slate, their "infant scholars" struggling to call them out. Nonetheless, fathers or other adult male relatives were assumed, even mandated—first by clerics under natural law, then by judges under common law—to act as the family's instructional guide, a principle pointedly recalled whenever "the second sex" became too ambitious.[16]

One of the most repeated, ennobling, and seemingly effective reasons for gradually transferring much of the task of educating into the woman's hands was that child nurture and instruction was becoming a mother's most exalted work—a "God-given" activity. By the nineteenth century, reformers argued that females were the most desirable schoolteachers because the formal education of younger children, at least, was best when modeled upon the mother's nurturing and instructive activities. In practice, most mothers being otherwise engaged, instructing children was often delegated to the household's literate females: widows, orphans, and otherwise dependent girls and women.

Households also gave instruction under the apprenticeship system. A master was contractually obligated to provide shelter, food, and clothing along with instruction in the "mysteries" of his craft. These might involve some reading and ciphering. The use of wives and daughters to model and instruct the young apprentice, perhaps as part of their household duties, has been generally neglected. Edmund Coote's much-reprinted *The English Schoole-Maister* urged those with apprentices to promote mastery of the English language: "such men and women of trade as tailors, weavers, shopkeepers, seamsters, and such others . . . mayst sit on thy shop board at thy books, or thy needle, and nevre hinder any work to hear the scholars."[17] Rather than suppose that an indenture agreement limited the master's wife to feeding and clothing the apprentice, one may conclude that the master's wife or other female relatives participated in imparting the literacy skills being mandated in an increasingly wider array of apprenticeship contracts.

Home educators, like home nurses, often sought outside advice, as when a pious English noblewoman, Dionysia de Mountchesny (c. 1260), paid Walter of Bibbesworth to write a textbook to help her teach her daughter. Hannah Woolley's experience as governess became her text, *The Gentlewoman's Companion* (1675), and Hester Mulso Chapone (b. 1727) added her published letters "on the improvement of the mind" to the advice literature circulating in the middle classes.[18] By the mid-eighteenth century, English writers produced cheap primers and penny press pictures and verses to assist mothers and others. Anthony Benezet composed a 1788 grammar for rural Pennsylvania women: by instructing themselves, they would be prepared to teach their children. Although John Locke addressed *Some Thoughts concerning Education* (1693) to fathers, South Carolina's Eliza Lucas Pinckney wrote to England ordering an educational toy for her infant son "to teach him according to Mr. Lock's method (which I have carefully studied) to play himself into learning."[19]

Household Help: The Governess

Families with the means and inclination had long brought outsiders into the household, delegating to them some part of the parental obligation, from wet nursing to instructing their children. The male tutor and female governess represent a midpoint between the model of teaching designated members of the household—instructing the children of the resident family in the home—and that of teaching a mix of often unrelated children in an outside school.[20] A common variant was adding a few neighborhood children, the arrangement approaching that of a privately arranged "select" or "subscription" school.

Novels portray becoming a governess as the only respectable recourse of needy gentlewomen forced to earn an independent living. Miss Jane Fairfax in Jane Austen's *Emma* (1815) and several heroines of Charlotte Brontë exemplify educated women enabled to earn their own livings rather than depend on the support of a male relation.[21] Although better known through English fiction than historical scholarship, the governess was a reality: commonly a "gently born" woman employed by aristocratic families and later by lesser local elites. In the 1390s, Beatriz Galindo (b. c. 1470) tutored Queen Isabella of Castile in Latin and remained at court to teach the Spanish princesses. Stéphanie Félicité, comtesse de Genlis, governess in the family of the Duchesse de Chartres from 1777 to 1791, also published widely on education, vigorously promoting gender equality.

Maria Francesca Rossetti (b. 1827) was a governess in the English countryside when her father, Gabriele Rossetti, suffered a breakdown. To help support the family, his wife Frances became a nonresident "day governess," going daily to a family for a few hours. In this respect, she was analogous to the servant who did not live in, although of somewhat higher social status. Maria's younger sister, the poet Christina Rossetti, called herself an "escaped governess" for failing to follow the other Rossetti women into teaching.[22]

The line between governess and teacher was permeable, and nineteenth-century private schools sometimes advertised that they prepared young ladies to be either governesses or teachers. The governess title was occasionally given to the teacher of a school's youngest pupils. In *World of Girls* the fictional governess, Miss Danesbury, looked after that part of Mrs. Willis's school that the English would deem the "infant school."[23] In Charlotte Brontë's *Villette,* Miss Lucy Snowe was nursery governess until her employer promoted her to teacher of English in her girls' school, supplanting Mr. Wilson at half his wages; Jane Eyre was both a governess and schoolmistress, as Brontë (and her sisters) had been in real life.

Ruth Bowmaker, Louise Agnes Geoghegan, and Lucy Wheatley Walker each left England and her governess position for Australia and schoolteaching.[24] The governess role persisted longest in Australia's remote areas, a less costly alternative to a distant boarding school, while providing adult companionship to mothers and permitting children to continue contributing to the domestic economy. But Miss Grant's life at Courain, a sheep station in western New South Wales, also explains the declining appeal of being a tutor or governess; Miss Grant left after 18 months, hers "a lonely life, devoid of recreation outside school hours."[25]

In the tradition of craft workers, a governess secured some independence: the freedom to enter into a contract and terminate it and the freedom to control the pace and timing of her lessons. She was, however, ultimately answerable to parents' and guardians' wishes and whims, in the absence of institutional support. With autonomy came insecurity. As her pupils were often as few as one, the per-unit costs were high. Would her services be wanted, at her price, with satisfactory working conditions? Would the agreed-upon compensation be paid, fully and on time? Some of these perplexities also beset teachers in entrepreneurial and other private schools, except those operated by nuns, where a powerful church afforded protection. Still, by 1900 being a governess or tutor was essentially a relic of an ancient system where employment was customarily arranged through informal, personal contacts.

Monasticism and the Convent School Legacy

The word "nun" is rooted in European and Indic words for children's nurse, a female relative, a "little mother." It came to denote the professed woman in a religious community—"brides of Christ" who took vows of chastity in addition to the laywoman's marital vow of obedience. Marcella (b. 325) is known to have opened a refuge in her palace for other learned, well-connected Roman converts to Christianity. Pachomium founded a convent and several monasteries in southern Egypt before 346, each community practicing a rule-regulated life of consecrated work and contemplation; a sister governed her own community under rules adapted from his. By 400 there were houses of nuns in Africa, Egypt, the

Holy Land, and Italy, and 40 deaconesses (unvowed "ministers of charity") lived as a community in Constantinople.

Religious women's numbers and reach grew impressively. In 1250 Germany had more than 500 female religious communities. The double monastery also appeared, with one house of monks, the other of nuns—an abbess presiding over the whole. Each might contain its school or hospital, each sex teaching or nursing its own. Whenever permitted, active communities—as distinct from cloistered or contemplative orders—flourished, becoming the majority of post-1600 foundations. They established schools, hospitals, orphanages, prisons, insane asylums, workhouses, and refuges for the aged, destitute, blind, deaf, and mute.

At least during the early Middle Ages, convents allowed women, typically from a privileged background, a degree of independence and financial power greater than was conferred by marriage. Convent life protected wealthy daughters, spurned wives, and widows (and their estates), while giving them an opportunity to practice active Christian charity. Nuns fed the poor, nursed the sick, taught day and boarding pupils, raised surrogate daughters (the novices), hosted travelers (including princes and prelates), managed their property, and produced scholars and writers.[26] Two aristocratic Russian women rejected suitors, choosing convent life and teaching: Evfosinia of Polotsk (b. 1001) and Ianka of Kiev. A secular order, the Béguines of Flanders (f. 1184), were free from church rule, supporting their good works by teaching, nursing, and making lace.

Feminist scholars find the position of women religious better in the third and fourth centuries than later. They compare the medieval abbess to the priestess of ancient Greece, wielding civic power from the same base of wealth and family connections. Historian Mary Ritter Beard describes medieval nuns as solid businesswomen, outstanding doctors and surgeons, and great educators. "They were feudal lords operating self-sustaining estates and directing the manifold activities involved in producing goods, settling controversies as lawyers and judges settle them today, governing and participating in all the arts of social living."[27] Proliferating communities of self-governing women also aroused suspicion and envy among churchmen, bringing on recurring waves of suppression of their public works by the male church.[28] The Council of Trent recloistered nuns in 1563, forbidding them to venture outside to teach, heal, or minister to the poor.[29] Yet women religious slowly reclaimed and amplified their traditions.

Jacqueline Pascal (b. 1625) joined an order after her disapproving father's death. This younger sister of mathematician and philosopher Blaise Pascal became submistress of the novices at the Benedictine (later Cistercian) women's abbey, presiding over the education of the younger students. Her brother's educational ideas were applied and published in her book *Règlement pour les enfants de*

Port-Royal (1865).[30] Despite convent documents and histories, little is known about what was generally taught and learned. Clearly, unlike boys in monastic and cathedral schools, often preparing for the priesthood, convent-educated girls and young women were seldom taught Latin. However, this limitation better directed them into active teaching than into lives as contemplatives or penitents.

Founded in 1662, the school of the Jesuitessen in Düren functioned for 115 years—despite plagues and the town's repeated destruction by wars and earthquakes. When the Ursulines (f. 1535) moved into Cologne (1639?), they vowed to teach basic and female subjects to poor and rich girls "for all time." Their charity school for girls opened in New Orleans in 1727, the first school in then-French Louisiana.

Convent schools for girls and monastic and cathedral schools for boys represent the sex-segregated teaching and learning characterizing Catholic strongholds, even as schooling spread and became more secular. The Jesuits in nineteenth-century Italy opposed nursery schools and kindergartens for mixing boys and girls, giving women new roles, and intruding on the family's hegemony. Despite Germany's being the birthplace of the kindergarten, its schoolmen slighted the movement, associating it with women and gender equality.[31] Although many primary schools in Protestant Germany became coeducational, especially in rural areas, male teachers retained their accustomed place. As former colonies of Catholic Spain, in 1900 Mexico and Cuba had a higher proportion of male teachers (44% and 48%, respectively) than any U.S. state.

Widely dispersed across Christendom, communities of nuns had an ancient lineage in Britain. Yet England's expanding provisions for female education in the sixteenth and seventeenth centuries emerged within a canonical tradition more restrictive than that of France or Italy. As Nicholas Orme explains, "Women had little place in the educational system; their contribution to life, though indispensable, was social and economic rather than literary or scholastic." England's mostly small convents were impoverished, and, with growing anticlericalism, the estimated 3,500 nuns in English convents in 1350 declined to 1,900 by 1534.[32] As nuns lacked the knowledge of Latin grammar expected of monks and friars, bishops had an excuse to restrict their pupils to small numbers of younger girls (and sometimes boys) from wealthy families.

In 1525 Henry VIII confiscated church property that had supported about 600 schools, hospitals, and other charitable endowments and expelled the Catholic clergy. In 1609 the intrepid Mary Ward took seven Englishwomen to St. Omer in France, founding the first of several religious communities; each operated a boarding school for the daughters of English Catholics and a day school for local poor children.[33] By 1630 Ward's *Englischen Fräulein* also formed communities in

Cologne, Munich, Trier, and Vienna; expanded into rural Germany; and opened free schools in Bohemia, France, and Italy. Mistrusting these usurping "galloping girls," the Jesuits persuaded the Vatican to order them cloistered, closing their schools and houses to the public. When Mary Ward refused to comply, she was excommunicated. In 1878 Ward's followers, in the persons of the Sisters of Loreto, introduced Catholic higher education for women into Victoria, Australia.[34] Their pupils who did not become nuns were judged well equipped to teach as mothers, governesses, or schoolteachers—as circumstances dictated.

Out among the People, in Schools of Many Sorts

Among others, Francis Bacon (b. 1561) thought it "expedient that by public authority schools for women-children [girls] be erected . . . in every Christian commonweal," taught and ruled by "grave, and learned matrons . . . and that honest and liberal stipends be appointed for the said schoolmistresses."[35] Although liberal stipends were not forthcoming, women slowly came to teach both girls and boys, first younger and then older pupils. Closer to modern times, Emmanuel Lovekin wrote of schools around Tunstall (Staffordshire) in the 1820s: "I never knew but one with a man teacher."[36] In Finsbury (central London) in the 1840s, schoolmistresses outnumbered schoolmasters by nine to one, and, as boys and girls were enrolled in equal numbers, women's teaching surely extended to both sexes.

Londoner Sophia Lee (b. 1750), taught by her actor father, used the profits of her successful comedy, *The Chapter of Accidents* (1780), to open a girls' school in Bath. Assisted by her sister Harriet, Sophia was preceptress, and from 1781 to 1803 their school supported a large family. Elizabeth Mayo (b. 1793) taught in her brother Charles's school for 12 years, and they wrote popular textbooks using Pestalozzian principles. The five Åhlen sisters had a renowned girls' school in Stockholm in the late nineteenth century, another of many examples of family schools. For decades Hannah More (1745–1833) and her sisters ran, in Bristol, the best-known girls' school of its time. But they also opened 11 free reading schools held on Sundays in villages for the children of laborers and farmers, and they trained their teachers.[37]

Teaching skills were usually learned by doing, often in a relative's school. It was common in Scotland for the *dominie*—the local Presbyterian schoolmaster—to hire and train his wife or sister to assist him. Henrietta Neale was untrained for her work when she was employed in 1789 in her widowed sister's boarding school in Luton, running a Sabbath school as well. Elizabeth Caroline Duncan (b. 1798) operated a girls' school in a fashionable London neighborhood with her sister before turning to writing "penny dreadfuls" under the name of Mrs. Grey. The American Revolution caused the Loyalist Wells family to leave South Carolina for England, where daughters Helena and Louise Wells started a boarding school "for those gentlewomen of fortune who are without female relations to introduce them into life."[38]

Observing propriety, Judith Thomas instructed young ladies in writing and arithmetic in a room separate from her husband's class of young gentlemen. That Thomas Blyeth's wife taught his school for him in Kirkheaton (Yorkshire) in 1695 is known by a petition to remove him for negligence: "rarely in all that time [had he] been a person of civill behaviour or lived a regular life or diligently instructed the youth there."[39] Family schools also appeared in British Canada. After her second marriage, Kate Andrews had a day school in Liverpool, Nova Scotia, by the 1830s; when her house was large enough, she took in a few boarding pupils. A servant and a niece assisted in this establishment, which lasted a half century. Further west, the pupils of Angélique and Marguerite Nolin were probably the children of Native American women and French Canadian fur traders; the Catholic bishop of the Red River region had asked the Nolins to teach. Eliza Ruggles helped her Methodist minister husband run his school for black children, first in Canada, then the United States, and last in Africa.[40]

SNATCHING THE SCHOOLMISTRESS FROM OBSCURITY

The Icelandic sagas spoke of Ingunn, teaching at the Cathedral School of Holar around 1110. Elsewhere in Europe, Dame Tryphena was assessed taxes as a Parisian schoolmistress in 1292, as was Bietrix *la metresse,* who paid three sou in taxes; she may have been a freelance tutor or the one woman among 11 teachers laboring in schools attached to Parisian churches. A cohort of 22 French schoolmistresses and 41 masters was licensed to teach by the cantor of Notre Dame in 1380, Sersive La Bérangière and Denisette de Nérel among them. Perrette La Coupenoie was licensed to keep a school to instruct girls "in good behavior, grammar [probably limited to learning to read] and other lawful things."[41]

In Kentish English there is a reference to "the maystresse thet hath zui great schoole thet alle guoth thrin vor to lyerni." Boston (Lincolnshire) records identify Matilda Maresflete as teaching in 1404, and London documents mention "E. Scolemaysteresse" in 1408 and "Elizabeth Scholemaystres" in the Cripplesgate area in 1441. Surviving records for Taunton in 1494 show Elen Skolemastre receiving "3 shilling 3 pence" from a pupil. In 1630 the will of a Dr. Cage directed Cambridgeshire officials to use half his bequest to hire "some poor woman of the town" to instruct children to read, while a survey of 121 parish schools identified a number of women teaching in that county.[42] Other schoolmistresses are recoverable because they taught poor children placed with them by religious or secular officials, offering instruction under recorded agreements.

Teachers of advanced or ornamental subjects sometimes left their historical traces in advertisements. Mrs. Rhodes announced her intention to prepare "young ladies or Gentlewomen to read and write French to perfection" or master fancy sewing. Mrs. Jane Voyer specified instruction in French and writing, and Sarah Hay stressed an ability to read English with "the greatest correctness and propriety . . . both prose and verse." Elizabeth Ash, who taught reading and writing, would also wash and iron ladies' clothing.

A few women schoolteachers' names survive in German records dating from the Middle Ages, aside from the women's religious communities' often flourishing schools. Reports for Protestant Saxony noted several girls' schools in urban centers in the 1570s, typically run by a burgher's wife, a widow, or the wife or daughter of a male teacher. Women teachers—paid quarterly, housed free, and "given firewood and rye"—were mandated for the two girls' schools established in Berlin in 1574; they taught reading, writing, religion, sewing, weaving, and singing. The flourishing, unregulated, male-taught elementary schools of the Middle Ages, called *Winkelschulen* (alley schools) in Germany, anticipated countless "private" working-class schools of nineteenth-century England—except for the teacher's sex.

Religious schisms, the Reformation, and the multiple sects that followed gave men and women another impetus to teach. Hawise Mone and husband, Thomas, a prosperous shoemaker, ran a school in Norfolk around 1430 for the children of other members of the Lollard "heresy," a church-reform movement harkening back to a simpler Christianity. Theodosia Alleine, daughter and wife of Calvinist ministers barred from Church of England pulpits, established and taught a school of 50–60 pupils in Taunton in 1665. Her contemporary, Barbara Blaugdone (b. 1609), alternated teaching her school in Bristol with repeated imprisonment and banishment for her Quaker activities.[43]

By any standard, some teaching women were exceptional in their learning. Bathsau (Reginalda) Makin (or Makins), a classically educated Anglican from an upper-class family, published her poetry in half a dozen classical and modern languages. She headed the exclusive Putney School, before founding her own advanced school for girls at Tottenham High Cross, London, in 1663. She offered arithmetic and writing, unusual at a time when reading and "plane" or fancy needlework dominated girls' schooling. While Makin tutored Charles I's daughter, her forward-looking essays on social and educational topics were more important, arguing that educated females are a national political resource. Her *Essay to Revive the Ancient Education of Gentlewomen* (1673) may have been the earliest known work in English on female education.[44]

Aemilia Bassano Lanyer (b. 1568?) brought a more exotic background to her teaching. Daughter of a court musician and his mistress, Aemilia (also known as

Emilia Lanier) interspersed schoolteaching with courtesanship and later au-
thored religious poetry, including the feminist *Eves Apoligie in Defense of Women*
(1611). She is remembered primarily for speculation that she was the "Dark Lady"
of Shakespeare's sonnets.

Republican and Napoleonic France strongly encouraged secular versions of
convent schools. To support her family after the French Revolution, well-connected
Jeanne Louise Genet (Madam Campan) started a successful girls' boarding school
in 1795: "a feminine university to replace the abbyes and convents." Although her
pupils were the daughters and sisters of highly placed figures, she envisioned an
expansive system of inspected public boarding schools for girls, staffed by trained
women teachers.[45] Early in the nineteenth century, other wellborn, well-educated
Frenchwomen opened schools—each, presumably, "having lost due to circumstances both her rank and her patrimony."[46]

THE ENGLISH DAME SCHOOL, REVISITED

In England and its colonies, as on the European continent, the schoolmistress in
the second Christian millennium usually taught younger pupils basic literacy
and civility in small schools, sometimes called "petties" after their young students, "reading schools" after their curriculum, and "woman" or "dame schools"
after their customary teacher. These schools derived from the venerable practice
of teaching one's own or neighbors' children amid home duties. Coote's *The English Schoole-Maister* (1596) touted the ease with which beginning reading could
be taught: "and thou maiest sit on thy shop-bord, at thy loomes, or at thy needle,
and neuer hinder thy worke, to heare thy scholers, after thou hast once made this
little book familiar unto thee."[47]

Probably a great many small schools during Elizabeth I's reign (1558–1603)
were taught by women. Reformers labeled them "inferior schools," "common day
schools," or "(ad)venture schools"—for their simple curriculum, unpolished methods, homespun facilities, and usually humble schoolmasters and mistresses.[48]
Their teachers, named "abcdarians" in pre-1600 records, typically taught boys and
girls to recite the alphabet; recognize letters; spell a few words (including their own
names); memorize short verses to promote reading, moral, and religious learning;
and acquire such useful habits for later instruction and life as "to sit up straight and
treat their elders with respect . . . never throw stones, never tell a lie."[49]

The term "petty school" came into general use in the seventeenth century.
The better organized were three-year schools preparing boys for the classical
grammar schools by teaching the alphabet, the reading of English, and elements
of Latin grammar. John Brinsley was hired to teach Latin grammar to upper-
class boys and a few scholarship students preparing for college or the church. He

and his fellow grammar masters often found themselves forced to add English reading instruction to their duties. In *Ludus literarium* (1612) Brinsley complained that it was "an unreasonable thing that, the Grammar Schooles, should bee troubled with teaching A.B.C. . . . Besides it is an extreme vexation that we must be toiled amongst such little petties. . . . whereof wee can get no profit, nor take any delight in our labours."[50] Their dislike of this activity presaged a greater reliance on schoolmistresses as church and state were converted to extending basic literacy.

Brinsley also characterized schools for "these little ones" as being charitable employment to "helpe some poore man or woman, who knew not how to live otherwise, and who might doe that well, if they were rightly directed."[51] A 1759 report for the Oxford Diocese noted, "The Dean allows a poor Woman at Little Haseley forty Shillings *p. an* [per annum]. With the Liberty of living in a House Rent-free for teaching five Children to read."[52] *Our Village*, Mary Russell Mitford's astute portrait of her birthplace, Alresford in Hampshire, straddles fiction and nonfiction. Mitford (b. 1786) dates its school to 1563, founded and endowed by Lady Eleanor Lacy "for the instruction of twenty poor children, and the maintenance of one discreet and godly matron." Appointment of the schoolmistress, a "splendid piece of patronage," remained with the Lacey family, usually going to "some old dependant" of the Laceys: a retired nursemaid, the widow of a gamekeeper, an elderly lady's companion.[53]

Charles Hoole regretted that village schools relied on "poor women . . . whose necessities compel them to undertake it, as a meer shelter from beggry."[54] Nonetheless, girls as well as "lads of part" could become teachers through Scotland's parish and public schools, and woman or dame schools contributed to the remarkable extent and regular practice of literacy in eighteenth-century Scotland.[55] As for England, William Shenstone's 1736 verse, *The Schoolmistress*, recalls Sarah Lloyd, his first school dame in Halesowen (Worcestershire), as representing a familiar figure:

> In ev'ry Mart that stands on Britain's Isle,
> In ev'ry Village less reveal'd to Fame
> Dwells there, in Cottage known about a Mile,
> A Matron old, whom we School-Mistress name;
> Who boasts unruly Brats with Birch to tame:
> They grieven sore in Durance vile y-pent,
> Aw'd by the Pow'r of uncontrouled Dame;
> And oft-times, on Vagaries idly bent,
> For Hair unkempt, or Task unconn'd are sorely shent.

While likely less prevalent than Shenstone suggests—returns from Archbishop Herring's 1743 questionnaire, for example, record a dame school proper in one village in 40—women were also teaching young children and girls in a variety of schools. A few representative villages taken from the survey of the District of Riding, in Yorkshire, described their provisions for schooling that year:

E. Allerthorpe	no School in our Parish but an old woman.
N. Danby	no School kept but wt is taught by Women.
W. Dinningtonten	Children . . . taught carefully by a Widdow Woman.
W. (Leeds) Farnley	we have a petty School taught by a woman.
N. Marton	a widdow Woman teaches a few small children to read in her own house.
E. Paul	two private Schools . . . the other taught by Frances Simon.
W. Rothwell	two widows [are allowed] £1.10 each for instructing 10 of the smallest children 'till fit to be sent to the Master. . . .
N. Upper Poppleton	the Children are tautt by a School-Mistress . . .[56]

Similar references to teaching poor children become increasingly common over time and across distances. A reversal of family fortunes sent the cultured Langton family to a log cabin in British Canada, where Anne Langton's Ontario school was essentially a part-time charity school in a domestic setting. A spinster, artist, and writer, Langton (b. 1804) managed the rural household of her parents and brother, teaching children of the local poor there twice weekly.[57]

There are enough records of women teaching diverse schools before England's first American colonies were established to show New England's indebtedness to the mother country for its own dame, or woman's, schools. In contrast, most of the independent (not town) schools operating in early modern Europe, and then the American colonies, were founded, headed, and still taught by men. The Reverend Bartholomew Booth, for one, started academies—first in England and, after 1773, in Maryland—enlisting support from the wealthy Valens sisters. Although Booth's students were elite males and their teacher a man, such exclusivity of gender or social class was already weakening.[58] Other propertied men and women sponsored private girls' day and boarding schools. With an influential or rich patron, a school under either an enterprising schoolmaster or schoolmistress might acquire an uncommon success and financial stability, to survive if not prosper in a rude, often chaotic "wilderness" society. However, humble dame schools were easier to keep afloat and reproduce.

Conclusion: Borrowing the Familiar

Apart from mothers, whose teaching role was valued when modestly done, women teachers in the early modern era were akin to mammals in the age of the dinosaurs: small, discreet, humble, hidden in the fringes of public spaces traditionally, even sacredly, reserved for men.[59] The American context would hasten their emergence, for, in their own ways, the combative, virtually ungovernable settlers in these diverse colonies hoped to achieve a civilized (or at least ordered) state.[60] Borrowing and broadening the institutions of the mother country was their initial approach to that end. Furthermore, extending the reach of education and thereby the contribution of the "middling sort" met the ambitions of both colonial governors and many of the colonists—most certainly in New England where there were more of them. In honoring his native state, poet John Greenleaf Whittier (1807–1892) celebrated a nascent principle of general schooling that swelled from efforts begun over two centuries earlier:

> Yet on her rocks, and on her sands,
> And wintry hills, the school-house stands,
> And what her rugged soil denies,
> The harvest of the mind supplies.
> The riches of the commonwealth
> Are free, strong minds, and hearts of health;
> And more to her than gold or grain,
> The cunning hand and cultured brain.[61]

Every customary educational means was used, from colleges to apprenticeships. Requiring Thomas Harvey in 1695 to provide orphaned William Read with instruction in reading, writing, and the skills of his trade was the first education-promoting act of the North Carolina colony. Girls were included only in 1752, when a county court ordered Ann Stewart's master "to learn her to read and write." When widowed Phoebe Carpenter bound out her daughter Sarah to Enoch Care of Montpelier (VT) in 1803—"to dwell with" and "faithfully serve him her said master in all respects as becomes a child of her age and station"—the indenture agreement specified that he see to her acquiring "the art of a spinster, seamster and housekeeping . . . and also to instruct her or cause her to be instructed in the art of reading so that she shall understand the Word [of God]." Goodwife Care was probably Sarah Carpenter's chief teacher until age 14, when her indenture ended.[62]

"Home schooling" was still more pervasive. An extension of child rearing, teaching duties were often shared with or delegated to other household females.

Eliza Lucas was 19 in 1741, employing her "fertile brain for schemeing" to becoming an orchardist while supervising domestic duties for her frail mother and teaching her younger sister and some of the slave children.[63] In the 1820s Maria Bryan (b. 1808) used what she learned at Nathan Beman's academy to help teach her youngest sister at their Mt. Zion (GA) plantation home: "Sophia confines me very closely, and takes up a good deal of my time, for she has a number of studies, and recites long lessons." In widowhood, Maria Bryan taught Latin, French, spelling, and other English fundamentals to her nieces and nephews.[64]

How Hannah Lurvey Gilley acquired her education is unknown, but from 1812 she taught her children at the family's home on remote Baker Island (ME). The direct descendant of two presidents, Charles Frances Adams Jr. (b. 1835) was concerned that, between their mother and their governess, his twin sons (b. 1875) "have been almost wholly under female control." The remedy was Groton School, then a boys' boarding school.[65] Fanny Conant Van Blarcom (b. 1848) raised her six children alone after her husband's defection. Her daughter Carolyn, home schooled herself, was their teacher.

A descendent of the Dutch who first settled the middle colonies, Rachel Van Dyke (b. 1793) of New Brunswick (NJ) kept a diary. She had just completed her formal education at the private day school of "Mr. G" (Ebenezer Grosvenor, Yale, 1807). Afterward she and a few other girls studied Latin with him for an hour daily—an antidote, she thought, to the vapid social activities expected of young ladies of her social class. On her eighteenth birthday she unfavorably compared Miss Hay's school with those taught by classically educated men like Mr. Preston and Mr. G, on whom she had a "schoolgirl's crush." Writing of the cousin she is tutoring,

> "I can see she has learnt her lessons as I did mine at Miss Hay's—like a parrot— without understanding. . . . It is about four years since Mr. Preston taught school here, and from that time I date my improvement. . . . A new world opened to me; and I improved more in one quarter under his tuition than I have done for many years with Miss Hay."[66]

Lawrence Cremin describes schooling and teaching in seventeenth- and eighteenth-century England and America as a "blurring between households, churches, and schools all along the line."[67] In the 1640s the Massachusetts Bay Colony enacted laws compelling education but without requiring schooling. However, lawmakers and others found both that nonschool means of ensuring biblical and civic literacy were inadequate and that the colony's need for elementary instruction placed unwelcome demands on schoolmasters in the Latin grammar school. Woman's schools were one answer. A wealthy Springfield citizen, John

Pynchon, sent his children to Mrs. Pentecost Matthews's school in the 1650s. Various town records also show women teaching rudimentary "common" (i.e., public) schools by 1670 or so, usually for the same meager wages paid men.[68] In 1686 Widow Walker was employed for the year as "a school dame . . . and to have tenn shillings for her labour," the wage that Woburn's selectmen had paid earlier schoolmistresses. In 1717, Lexington had to guarantee the wives of Clark Laurance and Epheram Winship five shillings a week to secure their services for schools of fifteen weeks.[69]

Although some Massachusetts town schools recorded a mistress later than others—the first recorded in Dedham was Mary Green in 1757—a sense of New England's relative taken-for-grantedness of women as schoolteachers may be gleaned from the autobiography of Rev. John Barnard (b. 1681). Before being sent to the Boston Latin Grammar School, Barnard had formal instruction from at least three women: first his mother—"exceedingly fond of my learning, and [who] taught me to pray." Around age five he was sent to a reading school "to furnish my young mind with the knowledge of letters." He learned so well that "my mistress made me a sort of usher, appointing me to teach some children that were older than myself, as well as smaller ones; and in which I read my Bible through thrice." His parents thinking him "weakly," he spent his seventh summer in the country, "and that I might not lose my reading, was put to a school-mistress, and returned home in the fall."[70]

As chapter 2 will elaborate, from these beginnings, by the second half of the nineteenth century, a combination of females and governesses in households, nuns in church schools, and women teachers in private and public schools provided most of the basic education in most American states. In the Northeast women were already instructing both sexes among students aged 15–19. While being in school at such an advanced age was still the exception, there was no question that at least middle-class parents were allowing daughters some "advanced learning." A significant portion of these daughters would become teachers of schools: G. Stanley Hall's celebrated "good Gertrudes."

CHAPTER 2

"School Dames in Each Quarter"

America's Army of Gertrudes

A thousand years from now no building or curriculum will ever take the place of a conscientious and praying teacher.

—Roger W. Babson, *Actions and Reactions* (1935)

At their town meeting on March 2, 1783, the citizens of Framingham (MA) confirmed arrangements for the upcoming school term. "Lieutenant Drury and Eben'r Harrington to be school masters to instruct the youth of Framingham in writing; and the selectmen are appointed to settle school dames in each quarter of the town[ship], which masters and mistresses are to continue until August next."[1] Framingham hired its first schoolmaster (Deacon Joshua Hemenway) in 1706 and built its first permanent schoolhouse in 1716. As the town's population grew and dispersed, town government supported schools to varying degrees in the township's several "districts," in this case in each quadrant, bringing rudimentary learning closer to all the children.

At this point Framingham's school history reflected past English and colonial practices, such as treating writing as a special skill and selecting schoolmasters from the clergy, the militia (volunteers like Lieutenant Thomas Drury), or local families (Ebenezer Harrington, a physician). Framingham's example also points to the movement of the "school dame" or "schoolmistress" from an occasional to a regular, and then indispensable, feature in a system of common schools that started in New England and spread over the next century to every corner of the expanding nation.

In his population bulletin, *Census Statistics of Teachers* (1905), the census director explained, "The profession of teaching was selected for special consideration, partly because in the United States teachers are more numerous than any other professional class, exceeding the total number of physicians, lawyers, and clergymen, and partly because of the intimate relations between this occupation and the government."[2] In the American system, the "intimate relations" depended less on government operations per se than on the play of ideological, economic, sociopolitical, religio-cultural, and personal determinants. However, the bureau's numbers made clear that the Gertrudes were in place, prepared to effect, through the "slow methods of practical, ethical education," their envisioned work of "social regeneration."[3]

She was, and is, Teacher—"Hey, Teach!" to some of her bolder "large scholars." More often the smaller pupils slip and, in their excitement or need, call their teacher "Mom," at which she smiles benignly while the rest giggle. Like mothers, each teacher bears another identity—her name. In a sample from the 1930s, teacher surnames ranged from A (Edna Abbey, Alhambra, CA) to Z (Anna Zupet, Central City, MT). Women teachers are Cross (Mary Hannah and Lillian), Eager (Ruth), Gay (Mabel), Grim (Mary Agnes), Learned (Ella), Meek (Mary), Moody (Daphne and Eva), Savage (Alta and Carol), Strong (Mary Louise), and Sweet (Ruth). Hints of family hopes or histories appear in the names given Delight Dennett (Lewistown, MT), Lula Love Lawson (Washington, DC), America Seecombe (Yankton, SD), Empress Arrington (El Paso, TX), and Nebraska Cropsey (Indianapolis teacher and supervisor for 50 years).[4]

Thousands of teachers took religious vows and new names. In 1858, Salome Valois, Virginie Brasseur, Angele Gauthier, and Mary Lane brought western schools to Juneau (AK) as Sister Mary of the Sacred Heart, Sister Mary Lumena, Sister Mary Angele, and Sister Mary of Conception, the first of a contingent of about 300 sisters of St. Ann over the next century.[5] America's number of schoolteachers, lay and religious, tripled between 1870 (126,822) and 1900 (446,133), exceeding the growth rate of the nation's youth.[6] This increase was accompanied by a steady replacement of the schoolmaster by the schoolma'am—a movement also evident in Canada, Cuba, Ireland, and Italy. The 1900 U.S. census found that enterprising women were 80% of the teachers in cities of 25,000 or more, the places with higher salaries, better working conditions, and more evident professionalism.

Pursuing the Known, Creating the New

At Abbot Academy in Andover in 1854, an anonymous rhymester reminded those present that despite the town's Female High School (f. 1829), males were still favored: "Thus learning in this ancient town . . . The Fruits now everywhere abound. . . . But while the boys were thus cared for—The females were forgotten; The boys of yore got all the lore; The girls spun all the cotton."[7] While once generally true everywhere, a remedy resided in the arrival, with the American colonists, of the educational venues that sheltered teaching women in "days of yore." A diffusion of formal education among the colonists, evident by the later eighteenth century, created an increasing pool of potential teachers, the more willing of them female. Over time, their sex would test, transgress, and even erase traditional boundaries between male and female educational, occupational, and social spheres.

Variations on "Home Teaching"

Those attending an Episcopal convention in Philadelphia in 1856 were reminded that "from the earliest days of the Christian church many of its brightest and holiest sons have been led into the path of truth, by the gentle suggestions of a woman's teaching."[8] Along with mothers, older daughters often provided child care and instruction. Her French grandfather told Victorine du Pont (b. 1792) that the elder were obliged to instruct the younger. After the family moved to the United States, Victorine, a model pupil in a Philadelphia female seminary, encouraged similar diligence and dedication among her sisters. She also tutored her oldest brother and cousin for their admission to a Germantown academy and supervised their progress in all their studies but Latin. Widowed young, Victorine (now Bauduy) taught another family school for the youngest Du Ponts, including grandnephews and nieces. She also turned a rudimentary workers' Sabbath school into the Brandywine Manufacturers' Sunday School in 1817 and was its superintendent for 40 years. The only schooling for hundreds of millworkers and their children, it offered instruction in the *four* Rs (reading, 'riting, 'rithmetick, and religion) through advanced discussion and visual methods.[9]

In a humbler household in Franklin (MA) around 1800, Horace Mann learned his letters from his mother and his sister Rebecca, reciting from Webster's *Grammar* as Rebecca did her chores. As his sister Lydia later wrote him, "Every day of your life when with your parents and sister, at least, you were at school and learning that which has been the foundation of your present learning."[10] When six-year-old "Bennie" Mays entered the four-month Colored School near Epworth (SC) in 1900, he was thrilled to discover he knew far more than the other novices. "Susie, my oldest sister, had taught me to say the alphabet, to count to a hundred, and to read a little. Since I was the only one in the beginners' class who could do these things, I was praised and highly complimented by the surprised teacher. As we put it, she 'bragged on me.'"[11]

For children living beyond the reach of schools, mothers and older sisters stepped forward. Such were the wives of Yankee whaling captains who took their families to sea; they were perhaps a fifth of the total of whalers' wives in the second half of the nineteenth century, on voyages of three years or more. Ship mothers used familiar academic routines, modeling known school practices, setting lessons and recitations, and disciplining as best they could. Aboard the *Merlin* in 1868, Harriet Allen began teaching her son and daughter within a month of sailing. "If they will keep up their interest we shall get on finely." In the 1880s, Calista Stover also held nightly Sabbath schools and semiweekly Bible meetings for the crew of the *Daniel Barnes,* her husband's whaler.[12] Similar makeshift schooling was attempted in the endless wagon trains that rolled across the endless prairies.

Employing a governess or tutor while introducing a stranger into the household kept children and instructor under family scrutiny. In 1755 the *South Carolina and American General Gazette* informed readers of a "Middle aged woman, who can be well recommended, and understands Musick, dancing, and all sorts of Needlework, and can speak Four different Languages, . . . glad to engage as a Tutoress to Children, or, if encouraged would keep a School." In 1776 it printed the advertisement of a "young Woman of unblemished Character, and Liberal Education," ready to be governess to the daughters of a gentleman.[13]

Northern-bred women appeared more numerous, prepared, and venture-some, becoming governesses or schoolteachers in sometimes distant places. "Wants Employment: A woman who would go into any Gentleman's Family to instruct Children in Reading, Writing, and Arithmetick, also in the use of their Neddle"—so went a notice in the *New York Mercury* in April 1767. To secure a governess, Louisiana plantation families around 1800 were said to pay Yankee schoolmistresses the nation's highest teaching wages, from $700 to $1000 annu-ally. Some governesses married into local society, while others used their savings and connections to establish their own schools. When John James Audubon was studying and drawing birdlife in the South, his Pennsylvania-born wife, Lucy Bakewell (b. 1787), supported the family as a governess.[14]

Bridging Home and School

By 1825, as schools proliferated in the Northeast, the governess and schoolmis-tress roles were easily exchanged. From 1814 to 1817 Mary Lyon spent her sum-mers teaching a district school near Shelburne (MA) and her winters as a governess—until towns began hiring a woman for their "winter school" (the term that began after the harvest and ended with spring planting). Amelia Jencks Bloomer (b. 1818), among the best known nineteenth-century advocates for woman's rights, left schoolteaching in upstate New York around 1838 for a spell as a governess.[15] Both Yankees, Lucinda Hinsdale (b. 1814) and Eliza Starr (b. 1824) taught in plantation homes in antebellum Natchez (MS). Hinsdale also taught school both before and after her marriage to another educator, James Stone, while Starr went on to lecture in art and teach at St. Mary's Academy near South Bend (IN).[16]

In teaching her children to know their letters, memorize some verses, and count on their fingers, Ella Gertrude Clanton Thomas (b. 1834) may have followed her mother's example or absorbed something of pedagogy at the schools she attended around Augusta (GA). Rather than employ a governess for their further education, in 1862 she sent her firstborn to a little school in a neighbor's home. After completing her limited schooling elsewhere, Lusanar Clark opened a school in West Virginia in 1864 for her brothers, sisters, and a few neighborhood children—a typical example of ad hoc transitional institutions between home and school.[17]

Increasingly often in the nineteenth century, the combination of their own learning and some experience in home teaching led a mother (more often a daughter) into "keeping a school": in the North, usually a one-room country public school; in the Mid- and South Atlantic states, a small private school. The term "schoolkeeping" was widely used throughout the nineteenth century, especially in rural districts. It nicely captured the chief demand that the community placed on its often young and untrained teachers: that they "keep" an orderly school and instill in their "scholars" good habits and a proper respect for authority. Without apology, teachers routinely used this term to refer to their work. It was also an in-joke that teachers directed against the male "professionalizers" who railed against youthful, unprepared novices and school trustees' and parents' too-low demands.

For centuries girls and women had left home to join a "spiritual family," a sisterhood. Despite nuns' traditional nursing and social work, teaching became the primary office of the noncloistered. The Ursulines were a trusted sisterhood among German Catholics who settled in nineteenth-century Missouri, including Dr. Bernhard and Henriette Geisberg Bruns, an upper class Westphalian couple. Employing a resident tutor at times, the Bruns sent their sons to the Jesuits or to the new St. Louis public high school, and they helped establish the Young Ladies Seminary in Jefferson City. But at least one of their three daughters, Effie, attended the Ursuline Convent School in St. Louis in 1857, afterward becoming a private German instructor and public school teacher.[18]

Schools . . . and More Schools

A roughly chronological sketch of the American woman's opportunities for employment as teacher sui generis—more than the "teaching woman at home" but the *schoolteacher*—resembles a widening web of historically and naturally linked institutional forms within a correspondingly weakening domestic frame-work. Variously named "schoolmistress," "school dame," "schoolma'am," then simply "teacher" as her gender came to inhere in the role, she taught in various types of schools. Independent schools were often referred to as "pay," "venture," or "adventure" schools in colonial times and as "select" or "subscription" schools in the ensuing republic. By the mid-nineteenth century, however, these usually small, undercapitalized private schools were competing with tax-aided "common" (i.e., public) schools already spreading beyond New England with Yankee migration. After her own district school had closed for the season, a Kansas schoolmistress solicited patronage for a subscription summer school. She was told "people won't subscribe to a school when they have from 4 to 9 months publick school."[19]

Of the 10 proprietors who advertised their schools in the Pittsburgh (PA) City Directory of 1816, three were women; the number rose to 17 in 1841, the year when the city's common school system was established, presenting independent teach-ers and even incorporated private schools with new rivals for pupils and greater consumer scrutiny.[20] Entire schools altered their identity. While Nebraska's Trinity Lutheran School in Cheyenne County was unique for its expensive stamped tin ceiling, it was not unusual in becoming the local public school.[21] Mergers helped some schools to survive. In Nashville (TN), Eliza Hudson Ward and Wil-liam E. Ward's Ladies Seminary (f. 1865) merged in 1913 with Belmont College for Young Ladies (grades 1–14), founded in 1890 by Susan L. Heron and Ida E. Hood. Bought by Tennessee Baptists in 1951, it later became the independent coeduca-tional Belmont University. By the late twentieth century, hundreds of Catholic schools, unable to compete, had merged or closed.[22]

From the Colonial School Dame
to the Nineteenth-Century Schoolma'am

Colonial women worked as schoolteachers in greater numbers, for longer periods, and with more significance for themselves and society than usually acknowledged. In his 1932 compilation of schoolmasters of colonial Boston, Robert F. Seybolt admitted that "the names of women who instructed 'young ladies' and 'Misses' in reading, writing, spelling, and needlework, as well as men who taught only dancing, fencing, or singing were omitted"—omissions hardly of equal historical importance.[23] Seybolt did better with *Some Schoolmasters of Colonial New York* (1921), where 13 women are listed with 367 men. However, no women teachers appear for New Amsterdam, odd because licensed schoolmistresses were common in the private schools of Holland—which, under the Calvinists, was the most literate nation in seventeenth-century Europe, with girls actually required to attend primary schools.[24]

The English of Long Island patronized dame schools, and John Bowne of Flushing (Queens) recorded several payments to "Elizabeth Cowperthwaite, schoolmistress"; one rather startling entry in 1683 is for a "red petticoat, bought of John Broke": her wages for teaching Bowne's daughter Martha for 30 weeks. Rachel Spencer taught in Hempstead (NY) and Goody (Goodwife) Davis in Jamaica (NY), both in 1685. In 1693 Joseph Lloyd of Lloyd's Neck, Long Island, gave one shilling and sixpence to "the [school] Mistris for feast and wine," his contribution to the customary end-of-term treat.[25] Manhattan's sparse eighteenth-century records list only four schoolmistresses in New York City in the 1770s.

Quakers in the more populous Pennsylvania colony did better, partly because of their initiatives in schooling girls and Negroes. Female names appear in Chester County (est. 1682) where schoolmistresses in Quaker and Anglican schools taught reading, spelling, and sometimes writing, most commonly to girls and poor white and black children. Quaker intentionality appears in explicit calls, from the 1790s, to prepare young women "to undertake the care of not only their own connections, younger branches of their own families, but also poor children."[26] The situation was different further south. There was no record of a school in North Carolina to carry out the provision in John Ashe's will (dated November 1731), stating that his daughter "be taught to write and read and some feminine accomplishments which may make her agreeable."[27] Perhaps a governess sufficed.

The South's earliest homegrown schoolmistress may have been Mrs. Peacock, proprietress of a school in 1657 in Rappahannock (VA). The blockhouses protecting Kentucky residents during the Indian wars of the later eighteenth century housed three teachers, including Mrs. William Coomes, who "took care of the education of the young sprouts in Kentucky's earliest forts."[28] A generation later, upper-class Southern families had recourse to entrepreneurial women's schools, as Charles Coon identified 95 women school proprietors in North Carolina between 1790 and 1840.[29]

What the South lacked was the lowly dame school, so common to Old and New England, sometimes publicly funded and instrumental in the early "feminization" of schoolteaching in the Northeast. Throughout the colonial era, a literate woman of "middling origins" could be paid to teach reading in private dame schools: a school begun "on her own responsibility," without a guarantee of patronage.[30] Depending on her own learning and public demand, she might have added writing, arithmetic, and grammar—or, for girls, needlework. A school dame (perhaps church supported) was noted in an account of an Indian community near Plymouth in the 1690s; its inhabitants were taught to read and become Christians. In 1727, Experience Mayhew described the converted Mary Coshomo as "a diligent Instructor of her children."[31]

The colonies' school dames followed England's gender-based division of teachers' duties: "Good women . . . Bring little ones to read & spell," went a familiar late seventeenth-century rhyme, while "Here's men to bring them to their pen, / And to instruct and make them quick / In all sorts of arithmetic." A member of Boston's elite, Judge Sewall (b. 1652) noted that Hannah, Betty, and Sam began with the esteemed Dame Walker (d. 1695), Joseph with Mrs. Kay, and Mary with Mrs. Thair "to learn to Read and Knit." Teaching was not confined to the rich, although the smallpox epidemic of 1721 deprived Boston's poorest children of their pious, devoted teacher, Mrs. Martha Cotes, mistress of the Charity School—thus ending their schooling.[32]

Bostonian Paul Revere (b. 1735) attended a dame school, then North Writing School, until age 13, when he left to learn his father's trade.[33] Lydia Maria Child gave a quaint description of "Ma'am Betty" Francis who taught a dame school in Medford (MA) spanning the eighteenth and nineteenth centuries—"a spinster of supernatural shyness, the never-forgotten calamity of whose life was that Dr. Brooks once saw her drinking water from the nose of her tea-kettle." The untidy bedroom where she taught and her tobacco-chewing habit did not matter to her pupils, as she reportedly treated them lovingly.[34]

The Dame School as New England's Town and District School

School dames became part of Massachusetts Bay's legislated system of subsidized common schools after about 1670. Recruited by town officials, teachers were paid partly from public funds, if "rate bills"—a school fee collected from each pupil—were inadequate for securing a teacher. The wives of Allen Convar and Joseph Wright kept such schools in Woburn in 1673, and references to subsidized school dames proliferate after 1700. A town-supported elementary reading school was invariably a dame (or "woman") school from about 1730, with the schoolmistress's employment specified as to time and place. Plymouth's records for 1725 show such schools first appearing in the more distant, sparsely populated parts of a township, where the dame might be asked to teach somewhat more advanced elements of English.[35]

Being associated with statecraft, law, and commerce rather than religion and culture, writing was traditionally taught, if at all, separately from reading—these being considered discrete attainments.[36] In earlier centuries the church had forbidden women to become scribes—a term encompassing scriptural and legal interpreters, copyists, editors, and public writers—thus delaying the wider teaching of writing.[37] As scribes lost their value and status following the invention of printing in the sixteenth century, writing instruction began to be extended to nonelite males. Most pre-nineteenth-century females who could write probably learned the skill from male relatives or by sitting in on lessons not meant for them. Once they acquired this useful tool, some at least would want to share it, and some dame schools began to combine rudimentary instruction in reading with instruction in writing for both sexes.

In the American context the venerable dame school was the harbinger of the common (public) school—an instrument whereby nineteenth-century Americans would become "Americans." First, the dame school conceptually linked teaching with the domestic realm, without invariably taking place in her home or having to be fit around domestic tasks. Second, it was a subscription school, like many familiar private educational ventures that survive to the present. It catered to pupils whose parents or guardians paid a fee, typically according to the number of subjects or skills taught—with the teacher's earnings perhaps augmented by public funds. Third, like so many women's educational undertakings, closer scrutiny indicates that the dame school was a more substantial and important source of literacy, citizenship, and teacher formation for its time than is conveyed by the antiquated imagery of a mere goodwife stirring her kitchen pots, with her own babe in arms, while instructing two or three neighbors' toddlers from their hornbooks or her copy of the *New England Primer*.

Fourth, the dame school was a flexible institution, able to expand its coverage and clientele and to become first authorized and then fully subsidized by guilds or by public officials: to benefit apprentices, poor children, free blacks, or even all the younger children of a community. This transition to semipublic and then public status was evident in some American communities before 1750. For all its variability, the humble dame school represented for women a broadening of their experiences, the discovery of their powers, and their emergence into a public life; thus their absence in the South delayed much more than the feminization of teaching there.

The Proprietary School: "We Learned Our Power"

From colonial America's beginnings, small, unendowed, transitory private schools, very like dame schools in several particulars, also dispensed instruction. Some aspired to recruit older pupils and offer more advanced subjects. A lone woman, perhaps with a female relative, could operate a school with little capital, using her own domicile or a rented room. Between 1730 and 1750, Charles Town's (SC) Overseers of the Poor placed apprentices in the schools of Mr. Craig, Mrs. Bennett, Mrs. Richardson, and Mrs. Johnson. Usually little else is known of such teachers of the indigent, unlike Isabella Marshall Graham (b. 1742). A widowed mother of four, she taught and managed a school for young children in Paisley, Scotland, in

1772, then a large Edinburgh boarding school—before opening her school for young ladies in New York City in 1789.

The American Revolution caused Deborah How Cottnam (b. 1725) to leave Salem (MA) for her native Nova Scotia, where her schools were always simple affairs, run out of her house or rented room, teaching girls or small children in whatever subjects she had advertised. More grandly, Philadelphia's Madame Rivardi's young ladies' seminary offered French and English literature, history, composition, geography, natural philosophy, and fine arts. Although she probably assumed that her pupils would marry well and preside over cultured homes, some of Rivardi's former students opened their own schools. After assisting Rivardi, Antoinette Brevost opened a female seminary in Pittsburgh and adopted Pestalozzian methods.[38]

Despite the assistance of her niece, Sarah Knowles, Martha Miller was forced in 1866 to sell the Milwaukee house where she taught, "not finding the profits of teaching commensurate with the labor."[39] Some nineteenth century entrepreneurial schools labeled themselves "select" schools, with the parents' ability to pay fees often the sole basis of selectivity. Mrs. Harvey's Select School in Nevada County (CA) was one of six small woman-run independent schools that predated the first public high school in 1862. Wichita County in drought-plagued northwest Texas was settled by whites in 1879. Its first three schools were small, short-lived select schools; their teachers were Della McNinch (a "plain fashioned, modest and well educated woman"), Carrie Craig (whose school was her father's house), and Miss Harriet Seeley (who taught for a year in her bedroom before marrying).[40]

Female seminaries and academies were ordinarily refined versions of select schools, more cosmopolitan in drawing their clientele from a wider area, perhaps chartered or endowed, with older pupils studying more advanced subjects. However, some and probably many academy pupils in the antebellum period were young children learning the "common (English) branches," a necessary concession to consumers in a small or competitive market. Some survived by relocating, being more elaborate and "professional," or setting lower fees—perhaps replacing a man with a woman teacher. "Daughter institutions" operated by former teachers and graduates of Emma Willard's Troy (NY) Female Seminary or Mary Lyon's Mount Holyoke (MA) Female Seminary benefited by the reputations of the "mother institution." Schools in the Holyoke family tree ranged from Maryland's Patapsco Institute to California's Benecia Female Seminary and South Africa's Huguenot Academy.[41]

However, countless others fell victim to coeducational schools, able to double pupil numbers while keeping siblings conveniently together. If teacher or parents felt unready for full coeducation, mixed-sex schools could adopt such half measures as single-sex classrooms within a larger schoolhouse or separate seating sections, entrances, cloakrooms, and play areas.[42] As the nineteenth century unfolded, coeducation (however modified) fast became the norm for schooling Americans of all ages. For example, although some cities established a single-sex public high school as early as the 1820s, only 28 remained in 1914 primarily in New York and Pennsylvania.[43]

The fictional Waynesboro (OH) Female College, illustrates this trend in the private sector. Founded by Professor Lowery around 1850, it closed in 1875, despite the often-unpaid labors of the professor, Mrs. Lowery, their two daughters, and one or two ill-paid lady teachers hired as enrollment dictated. The school's decline and closing were fated, Mr. Lowery explained: "Our day here is past. Another few years and all young ladies in this part of the country will be going to high school and college with their brothers."[44] And so it was.

The School as a Family Business

Female-headed schools may have been fewer than those where women taught, at least initially, with a male relative—a Mr. Lowery—in charge. Assisting a husband, father, brother, uncle, or even a son undoubtedly gave work to women who could not have sustained a school on their own. A male connection was believed to give social and financial weight to an educational enterprise, even if his headship was chiefly titular. Patrons who sought schooling beyond the rudiments of an English education, the three Rs, also expected a man to teach the classics, if offered, and discipline their more fractious "large scholars."

Various eighteenth- and nineteenth-century Pennsylvania schools were family operations. The South's oldest continuous school for girls, Science Hill Female Academy, opened in Louisville (KY) in March 1825 with Mrs. Julia A. Tevis, principal, and her husband, a physician and professor of mathematics and ancient languages; they were still in charge in 1876. Mary Bouhanan first taught school alone in Texas in the 1860s, and then with her much-loved stepfather, Oliver Eraselton, a Methodist preacher. Family teaching partnerships span eras and geography, from frontier settlements to large cities. The Abercrombies had a "young ladies academy" in Nashville in 1816, when the place was Fort Nashborough. Two families largely staffed the New York City girls' boarding school that Katherine Batts attended in 1880.[45] Madam da Silva was principal, her husband handled financial matters, and her daughter and handsome son (on whom "lots of the girls mashed") were teachers. The assistant principal was Mrs. Bradford, whose own daughter and sister (Mrs. Morrison) taught in the school.

Nonetheless, women's participation in viable family school enterprises appears undervalued. Carl Kaestle found 60 men and 31 women working as teachers in New York City in 1796. The Rev. Mr. Staughton, who advertised for students in 1795, was counted—but not his wife, although she was known to have opened a girls' school that year. Kaestle concluded that his tax lists, like teacher directories and newspaper advertisements, particularly neglected females who acted both as teachers and matrons.[46] Jacob Mordecai's 1808 advertisement for his female academy in Warrenton (NC) read, "The domestic arrangement for . . . my Scholars, will be an object of primary concern, and placed under the immediate inspection of Mrs. Mordecai."[47] While it doubtless reassured parents that homesick daughters would be cossetted, it left her other duties unmentioned.

Public schools variously resemble family businesses. Teachers looked to an older female, or perhaps a respectable older male relative, for help. So, with no sister at hand when she fell ill in 1883, Carrie White rejected her brothers as her substitute in her Whatcom County school in Washington Territory: "Mother and Frank wanted me to let Art or Clarence teach for me today, but I knew the children would not do as well as with me, because they would be afraid of the boys."[48] Twins Ethel and Edith Scott constituted the entire faculty of the South Wolfeboro (NH) public school in 1919: Ethel taught grades 1–4; Edith, grades 5–8.[49]

The Evolving Mission School Tradition

From virtually their first encounters with native peoples, Christians resolved to convert these "heathens and barbarians." Catholic sisterhoods appeared early among Native Americans in British and French North America, gradually replacing the Jesuit priests and Franciscan friars as the mainstay of Indian missionary work. After declaring Indians to be wards of the federal government, from 1819 Congress funded the operation of many Indian schools and paid their teachers. Federal contracts made it possible for nineteenth-century churches to extend their work among Indians beyond their own resources—in the process widening the "woman's sphere" culturally and geographically. A precedent for employing independent, unsponsored laywomen already existed in the U.S. government's Bureau of Indian Affairs (BIA) schools when, later in the century, the BIA ended its support of church schools.

The Sisters of Saint Joseph were known in France for "elevating the tone of society" by educating the daughters of comfortable families; they also operated schools for the children of former slaves in St. Augustine (FL) and Savannah (GA). The Sisters of Charity taught girls from 1870 to 1876, before also inheriting male pupils when the Christian Brothers left Pass Christian (MS). In Indian Territory (later Oklahoma), the Benedictines taught a few German- and French-surnamed Catholic homesteaders, as well as the Potawatomie Nation. The "hard-shell Baptists" in the region, however, sent their children to the local public school.[50] In 1860, in a militantly Protestant nation, there were already 200 Catholic schools taught by nuns, brothers, and priests.[51]

After the Civil War the American Missionary Association and the American Baptist Home Mission Society sponsored many small schools for the freedmen, where girls and boys commonly studied together. As white Southerners established their new and rigidly segregated public school system, they often adopted a mission school as their first colored school, a practice followed in the Border States. In 1899, Robert Terrell spoke of his appointment as principal of segregated, public M Street High School in Washington (DC) opened in 1870 as a mission in the basement of First Colored Presbyterian Church (f. 1841). He said, "Today our children are trained by the most capable men and women identified with their pupils in blood, in hopes and in aspirations"—a claim that also applied to the colored schools in the former Confederacy.[52]

The Monitorial System as a Teaching Venue

The monitorial schools, imported to America from Britain in the early nineteenth century and seized upon as an educational panacea in many cities, is rarely considered a "woman school"—being so different from our dame school image. Conceived by industrialist Joseph Lancaster and funded by philanthropists and religious societies to deal with the "impiety, ignorance, and disorder" governing the lives of the poor, monitorial (or Lancastrian) schools used a factory production line model to instruct large numbers of pupils cheaply. Advanced students trained as monitors could multiply a single teacher efforts, as the monitors repeated the teacher's instructions and checked the work of their assigned groups (or rows) of ten or so children.

Cincinnati College originally opened in 1815 as Lancaster Seminary, a monitorial school. Within weeks it attracted 420 boys and girls; a second was quickly opened exclusively for girls, with a female teacher and monitors, and survived for four years.[53] Inspired by Johann Pestalozzi's writings about educating small children, Joanna Graham Bethune (b. 1770) taught in and managed the Lancastrian-style "infant school" she founded in 1806 for the New York Orphan Asylum Society.[54] The Boston Infant School Society and similar organizations sponsored quasi-monitorial schools for young children, usually taught by women. An 1828 article idealized a Hartford (CT) infant school for the "perfect order and harmony manifested among the little pupils, their happy countenances, and the readiness with which they obeyed every movement of the hand of the teacher, Miss Emmons."[55] Similar schools spread inland from the larger coastal town and cities, and they apparently were available in each new state.

It was said of the teacher of the African Free School sponsored by the Anglican Trinity Church in New York City that "rebellious urchins looked up to the black teacher with a confidence that proved at once that she filled the situation with dignity . . . A word from her lips struck awe in the number of noisy boys quarreling about a space of a quarter of an inch in their seats."[56] While the monitorial system is associated with Anglican and Methodist societies, the Presentation Sisters imported the Lancastrian system directly from Ireland. Their initial school in San Francisco (1869) had one large classroom with several teachers and monitors.[57]

Coming Together: The Common School and the Schoolmistress

When Florence Kelren and her sister Isabel were inducted as full members into the Massachusetts Teachers Association in 1873, the organization finally accepted the serious career woman teacher, also naming an occasional woman to its board of directors or as a contributing editor of its journal, *The Massachusetts Teacher*.[58] The reason was that during the nineteenth century, while America's public schools—generally called common (or common English) schools before about 1875—were becoming women's province, they were also becoming the dominant model of schooling for America's children. Nowhere was this truer than in Massachusetts.

Long known in a more limited way in England, the (quasipublic) school and the schoolmistress came to fruition in America, first in New England. A rich and sometimes contentious historiography exists on the "common school movement" and its most articulate and influential advocate, Massachusetts's Horace Mann (b. 1796).[59] But many of the same historical themes used for explaining "the common school triumphant" appear in the story of "the schoolmistress triumphant" that will unfold, with different emphases, in this volume. The discussion here centers on neither the ideology of the common school nor the contending interests and forces supporting and opposing public education, but on its teacher—the woman teacher, as it turns out. In making the common school her workplace, she also became the chief instrument by which it could grow into the *public's* school, spreading across the continent and into outposts of American presence and influence elsewhere in the world.

The Common School: From "Her" Summer to "Her" Winter Term

Surviving records note that Sarah Stiles, wife of a Windsor (CT) farmer and church deacon and mother of a six-year-old daughter, was hired in 1717 as the town's first recorded schoolmistress. As early as 1750, a study of four Massachusetts townships found that women were about 15% of town-paid teachers.[60] By 1825 the practice was so well accepted that many girls and women were teaching the various towns' summer schools, primarily enrolling younger children and older girls not needed at home every day. The school term that began in spring and ended before harvest was still often called the "woman's school," a name left over from dame school times. Indeed, employing "settled" women like Sarah Stiles harks back to the seventeenth-century school dames more than it forecasts the nineteenth-century's popular image of young and inexperienced schoolmarms.

In March 1826, William A. Alcott, having completed his Yale medical course, sought a teaching position in his hometown of Wolcott (CT). He was forced to price himself at the usual rate for women: $1.50 per week and "boarding 'round." This was, he mused, "a season of the year when it was not customary to employ any but female teachers in the schools."[61] Although Alcott remained close to the profession his entire life, his career also illustrates the declining and restricted demand for schoolmasters—even as the schoolmistress was widening her claim to the local schoolhouse and aspiring to seize the more daunting winter school, the term that generally began after Thanksgiving and closed as the "large scholars" left to help prepare for spring planting.

Dedham Township (MA) hired 19 schoolmistresses between 1757 and 1772. One was Susannah Brittano, teacher of summer terms for four years; on her death in 1764, her estate went to building a school and hiring a woman for Dedham Township's Third Parish. Several years earlier, in 1760–1761, Miss Mehetabel Ellis became the first woman given charge of Dedham's winter school.[62] Thereafter, women usually taught both summer and winter in Dedham—a historical milestone. By 1829 more than half of Massachusetts's common school teachers were women, partly because of a gradual, then quickening, feminization of the winter school. Extrapolations from existing records suggest that Yankee women were 13% of teachers in winter schools in 1829, 21% by 1841, and the majority before the Civil War.[63] The schoolmistress in ungraded rural and village common or public schools might even be teaching whatever of the "higher branches" of an English education vocal residents wanted—algebra, perhaps a little Latin—if only to a few pupils or even one.

Before the later nineteenth century, few women were prepared to teach the classical languages anchoring the all-male Latin Grammar School inherited from England. Hannah Adams (b. 1755), a known exception, probably learned the classics from scholars the family boarded or from her self-taught father, whose small Massachusetts general store carried books. Adams's *Memoir* (1831) gives this account: "My health did not admit of my teaching a school . . . [but] I had the

satisfaction of teaching the rudiments of Latin and Greek to three young gentlemen, who resided in the vicinity."[64] When Josephine Pearson gave the salutatory
(second highest honors) commencement address of the McMinnville (TN) private
school (c. 1868), she was "possibly the only woman, so said, ever to deliver a Latin
oration in the South."[65] Pearson was taught by her parents, Latinists and teachers.
Somehow girls were mastering Latin and teaching it in private or public schools,
so that by 1900 women had taken charge of precollegiate classics for both genders:
teaching Latin and Greek in metropolitan coeducational high schools and keeping
Latin alive in whatever passed for secondary schools in lesser places.

Consolidating and Extending Her Position

It was important to individual women, and to achieving "woman's rights," that
they teach both boys and girls, both advanced and elementary subjects, and
throughout the nation. They succeeded so well that by 1900 the United States had
325,000 women schoolteachers—73.4% of the total. Meanwhile, from 1870 to
1890, nuns went from being the minority in Massachusetts's Catholic schools
to holding a two-to-one advantage over priests and teaching brothers. A half
century later, American men briefly challenged women's numerical dominance
among high school teachers.[66] However, the 1970s saw four women to every three
men training for high school teaching. Table 2.1 shows the extent of women's
majority over 110 years.

Despite the use of the male pronoun in inspirational talks to the State Teachers'
Association of Wisconsin in August 1873, women were the majority of the Association's members and of Wisconsin's teachers since at least 1847, when female
teachers held a 301 to 223 advantage. Boys outnumbering girls as pupils meant that
Wisconsin's schoolma'ams taught both sexes. The female majority persisted despite

TABLE 2.1
Male Teachers, United States, by
Representative Decades

School Year	Total K–12 Teachers	Male Teachers, %
1880	294,000	40.8
1900	432,000	29.1
1921	723,000	16.3
1941	859,000	21.3
1960	1,408,000	16.6
1970	2,059,000	32.8
1990	3,051,000	21.9

Source: U.S. Bureau of the Census, *Historical*
Statistics of the United States. For continuations,
see statistical abstracts at http://www.census.gov
/prod/www/statistical_abstract.html.

Wisconsin's German settlers and its rural economy, which allowed men to combine farming with keeping school in the off-season (a practice evident in male teachers' average of 14 weeks of teaching per year, compared to women's 19).[67]

As elsewhere, Kansas teachers were alert to gender preferences. A Leavenworth County schoolmistress gleefully reported in 1882, "Miss Suydam has a school in the Southern part of the County where they had voted a <u>man</u> and could not get him. <u>Good</u>." The McLouth school board "also voted for a male teacher" (in 1884), but "they have hired a young lady that never taught before[;] said they could not get a gentleman." Although Mound City secured Wallace Boughton (b. 1860) as teacher for the Blue Mound School in 1884, he had to furnish his own assistant; he could only afford to hire a female, and his choice "backed square out after nearly all the good teachers were hired." For the "55 or 60 urchins" that would be her charge, Boughton found "a terrible homely old maid." However, with her 26 months' experience and a first-grade certificate (one of the county's few), he was lucky to get her.[68]

In 1900, women were the majority of teachers in every Northern and Western state except Kansas and Indiana (where men held a 2% advantage). In Wyoming they outnumbered men by four to one, and Minnie Rietz's teachers were all women until she entered the university in 1893.[69] This feminization of teaching had begun in earnest in New England. A Massachusetts law of 1789 acknowledged the presence of teachers of both sexes, and a female majority emerged by about 1830; women were 75% of the state's teachers before the Civil War. Estimates are that while about 2% of all Massachusetts women were teaching every year between 1834 and 1880, one of every four or five U.S.-born Massachusetts women had taught school at some time in her life. (The figure for men who ever taught was one in seven.)

In 1862, the president of all-male Davidson College, the Rev. Dr. Kilpatrick, gave a speech to the students of Concord (NC) Female College entitled "The Duty of Females to the Future Education Interest of Our Country [the Confederacy]." He asked, "Who is to teach the children when the bloody war shall close?" His answer was women: "for the first generation and possibly for more."[70] Although the South's devastated economy helped schools initially retain a male majority—averaging 57.6% of teachers in 1895—an annual 1% decline in male teachers had set in.[71] In 1920, North Carolina's state superintendent reported that women reached 55% of white teachers, a percentage that Wisconsin had surpassed 75 years earlier.

Within states, country districts largely operated on personal knowledge of potential teachers and the impersonal laws of supply and demand, so younger men continued to appear alongside women on rural teacher rolls well into the twentieth century. However, in larger towns and most American cities from the

1840s onward, school officials almost everywhere began to hire women by design. Cost was a factor, as was the growing supply of educated women graduating from city schools and ambitious teachers eager to leave their rural schoolhouses. There was also the hard truth that educated urban women "overchose" teaching because, relative to men, they lacked respectable and remunerative options. By 1890, when women were 72% of the nation's teachers, they averaged 92% in communities of 10,000 or more residents.[72]

European immigrants' customary preference for male teachers did not thrive in nineteenth-century America, although some cities with large German-ancestry populations initially attracted more men than the national urban average. An 1885 survey of 24 American cities showed Cincinnati (1 man to 4.2 women) and St. Louis (1:7.7) more male than the nation's urban average ratio of 1 male to 10.2 females.[73] If children left school about age 14 (the typical effective end of compulsory school attendance in most states in 1918), they may have seen men only as principals, coaches, counselors, or truant officers, or as spiritual leaders in religious schools.[74] The still small elite of pupils who continued into senior high schools found fewer men behind the teacher's desk in many subjects.

As part of E. L. Thorndike's 1909 efforts to determine the statistical relationship between the gender composition of the teaching force and boys' lagging attendance in high schools, he selected 204 medium and large high schools nationally, each coeducational and the only public high school in its community. In faculties having 6 to 16 teachers each, the mean number of teachers was 8, 3 being men. Although comparison of 1896 and 1906 data on larger high schools (12 or more teachers in 1906) revealed wide differences in the feminization of their staffs, the central tendency was clearly in the direction of adding women. Thorndike's explanation was clear, if not welcomed:

> The choice of women over men has not been a matter of sentiment, enthusiasm or theory. . . . With few exceptions, the choice of a woman rather than a man has meant, and still means, that the woman is so obviously able to do the work in question better, according to the standards of the time, that she is chosen in spite of sex prejudice. Superintendents and school boards are eager to get men to teach, but their sense of educational duty will not let them get the men who apply.[75]

Alarm at teaching's gender imbalance was most evident from the 1890s to 1920—amid the excitement of the woman suffrage campaign. During this period women's share went from 70% of all public school teachers to 85%; among high school teachers, from 58% to 65%. Despite the desperate joblessness of the Great Depression, women still commanded America's classrooms as 88.6% of elementary and 60% of secondary teachers. In the 1930s, only three states—Idaho, South Dakota, and Utah—had a slight majority of men high school teachers.[76]

Women teachers' actual participation may be even greater than these impressive numbers. Historian Elisabeth Dexter thinks that teachers were among the unrecovered colonial women of affairs, in numbers "doubtless many times as great" as those found. Much of the data on teacher sex since the Revolution are derived from the decennial federal census and other studies, where undercounting is common.[77] Census enumerators might miss a person who taught for nearly a decade. Additional distortions derive from names altered by marriage and the habit of reporting in biographical sketches and obituaries only a person's final occupation, which for many women was marriage. Turnover has persistently complicated the picture, as resignation from a particular school jurisdiction need not signify either temporary or permanent retirement from teaching.

Departures testify to such situational variables as dissatisfaction with a present teaching assignment or community, every imaginable personal and domestic issue, broader economic conditions, and even the general rootlessness in American culture, to which single women were not immune.[78] Loudovica Krause's defection seems a function of temperament and the changing market. Before 1889 she had a school in Little Rock (AK) in her home, the Albert Pike House, the site of earlier schools. Her niece, Adolphine Fletcher (b. 1882) explained, "She was a born teacher and really liked to teach. . . . Like other private schools in Little Rock, it didn't survive long, even with boarding pupils. Lou, unable to live with failure, left town by train secretly."[79]

Raising Demand and Provoking Change

Americans largely minimized Europe's social-structural separation between primary and secondary schools—and even that between secondary and higher education—permitting the feminization of high school teaching to take effect more quickly. In all but America's larger cities, "high school" initially meant a few students studying "advanced subjects" in a nominally eight-grade rural or village school with the schoolma'am—something not possible, for example, in France's *ecole primaire*. Moreover, the academic, university-bound exclusivity of France's *lycée* had no charm for many elected American school boards.

Women Teachers and the U.S. Education Market

U.S. schools were popularized more quickly than they were elsewhere by the combination of women's willingness to teach and the low cost of their labor—turning common schools that once charged parents a rate bill for some of their operations into essentially free public schools, thus raising demand. The educational landscape was rearranged, with schools and colleges proliferating (sometimes unwisely) and altering their internal operations in response to the weight of consumers' numbers, needs, interests, and influence. A certain market-driven casualness bred expectations and habits that were hard to scuttle even as tax-supported public schools and colleges became the largest item in local and state government budgets. While public alternatives to private academies and colleges may not have been essential to the Gertrudes' story, they undoubtedly eased and advanced the process.

As we have seen, well before entire systems of public schools became the nearly universal choice—of parents, students, teachers, and governments—teachers created small schools of their own, an experience arguably more important for women: an opportunity to test themselves and be tested in the marketplace. Whether short lived or long lasting, their schools underscored women's initiative, determination, and ability to learn as well as instruct and to manage as well as inspire. As consumers' needs and desires for schooling grew, the schoolmistress was both readied and ready. When enough of her pupils—and, in turn their pupils—took up teaching, the interplay of supply and demand created a cascade of consequences, some spilling beyond national boundaries.

That the overwhelming majority of women taught in lower, not higher, education mattered, for economists have shown that the greater return on investment in education flows from elementary and secondary schooling.[80] ("Return" refers both to private rates of return to the educated individual and family and to enhanced knowledge, skills, and other social goods throughout the nation-state.) Few Americans then (or later) cared that the U.S. high school (public or private) was rarely the academic equivalent of Germany's *gymnasium* or France's *lycée*. What mattered was widespread literacy and "getting ahead," both counting as social goods.

Those regions or states (e.g., Indiana) most resistant to employing women ranked near the bottom on literacy and other education indicators. The U.S. *Census Statistics of Teachers* (1905) also demonstrated that the feminization of teaching (men reduced to minority status among teachers) generally correlated positively with another education indicator: total teacher numbers pro rata. This measure speaks to class size, the availability of schools to meet existing demand (and generate more), and average teacher quality, as a small teacher supply reduces incentives for teachers to upgrade themselves. Significant differences existed among regions and states, as table 2.2 shows.

While individual cities in the South Atlantic and South Central regions might have been near or above the national average in the number of teachers relative to the school-age population, their towns and rural areas stood at about half the

TABLE 2.2

Proportion of Teachers to Persons of School Age* in Selected States and the United States, 1890 and 1900

State by Region	1890	1900	Cities of 25,000 in 1900	Towns and Rural Areas in 1900	Women Teacher Total in 1900, %
Continental United States	140	146	138	154 (est.)	78.4
North Atlantic	147	162	137	184	79.4
Massachusetts	164	188	167	218	84.2
New York	151	164	134	215	80.3
Pennsylvania	120	137	126	143	70.9
South Atlantic	79	93	155	86	69
Georgia	79	93	142	75	64.9
North Central	161	174	150	181	73.7
Ohio	166	176	144	188	64.2
Minnesota	172	181	191	178	81
Nebraska	170	206	205	206	72.2
Kansas	165	182	141	184	79.9
South Central	74	83	133	79	61.9
Tennessee	77	82	130	76	59
Western	146	181	213	171	74.4
Colorado	142	181	246	154	77.2
Wyoming	104	142	NA	142	83.4
Utah	84	136	199	122	60.9
Washington	124	189	230	174	70.3
California	176	212	203	217	77.5

Source: U.S. Bureau of the Census, *Census Statistics of Teachers,* Census Bulletin no. 23, 1905.

*Number of teachers per 10,000 persons ages 5–24.

national average. This portended high illiteracy rates, economic stagnation, poverty, and political marginality over generations. This deficit also correlated with a below-average proportion of women teachers. The most extreme difference in table 2.2 is that between Tennessee's teachers (59% female) and Massachusetts's (84%).

Some Comparative Perspective: Factors Affecting Teacher Supply and Demand

Women teachers' growing presence worldwide is a response to political and economic pressures widening a trickle of education into a broader river of opportunity. This trend appeared first in the United States and England, the Western nations where women's deployment was highest, although England resisted women teachers in mixed-gender secondary schools well into the twentieth century.[81] Sweden attained the highest representation of women teachers (78%) in Scandinavia, a marked reversal given that, from 1860 to 1910, Swedish males successfully lobbied against women becoming the majority of teachers in even the upper elementary school grades.[82] In France women so increased their majority at the primary level that the Ministry of National Education tried a quota system, reserving 25% of *ecole primaire* places for men; among France's secondary teachers, men were already outnumbered.[83]

Eventually Canada, Cuba, Germany, Italy, and Mexico found in their newly schooled populations a ready source of first primary and then secondary school-teachers, especially among females. Because secondary school teachers were expected to be university educated, increasing women's access to postsecondary education was essential, and the economies of coeducation facilitated this. The United States offers the best example, the proportion of all college women attending coeducational institutions rising from 41% in 1870 (the first statistical report) to 81% in 1920; meanwhile, by 1900, 93.6% of U.S. high school students were enrolled in coeducational high schools.[84]

Mixed-sex schooling, however, was generally resisted. In Catholic Quebec, upper schools and normal schools were organized by gender, and British Canada's gender-based schooling followed British practice; both confined women to teaching girls. However, criticisms of schoolmasters in Ontario—as "worthless scum," "ignorant and immoral persons, old soldiers, idlers of all descriptions, notorious for habits of drunkenness"—eventually extended women's role to teaching male pupils, largely in gender-mixed classes.[85]

Elsewhere in the British Empire, while most of New Zealand's rural children attended coeducational schools, the colony was slower than the mother country to employ women, explained perhaps by its primarily Scottish settlers and their Calvinist tradition of respect for the "calling" of the *dominie*—the university-educated schoolmaster.[86] White Australia's earliest recorded teacher was Isabella Rosson, a transported convict; her dame school opened in 1789 in Port Jackson (later Sydney). By 1850 the New South Wales School Board was encouraging married couples in England and Ireland to immigrate and open schools, and English organizations assisted single, unemployed schoolmistresses and governesses to settle in the antipodes. In the late 1860s an Australian teaching position, advertised in England at £15 per annum, drew 850 applicants.[87] By 1900 most teachers in both Australia and New Zealand were women.[88] Predictably, men filled the headships of the more important state schools and state bureaucracies.

Germany's high academic and scientific standing depended, it was thought, on well-educated, highly professional male teachers at all levels. (In 1900, women were only 12% of Prussia's state primary school teachers.) Although some coeducational lower-secondary schools had opened for working-class children, the strictly academic *gymnasium*—attended almost exclusively by middle- and upper-class adolescent boys—remained inviolate. Women remained less than 20% of Germany's high school teachers before 1940; nonetheless, university-educated women chose secondary teaching over other occupations—as was true in many nations.[89]

For ideological reasons, with the division of Germany after World War II, East Germany promoted coeducational and comprehensive schools rather than divide students among distinct types of secondary schools. The Soviet-dominated East European bloc also achieved an above-average female presence. In 1980, women were 79% of the elementary school teachers in Czechoslovakia, 80% in Hungary, and 98% in Estonia; the comparable Western European average was 73%.[90]

Despite roughly similar and sometimes contemporaneous developments, the effects of women teachers on institutional history appear sooner and are more significant in the United States. Foreign school systems were constrained by strong traditions of segregating the social classes and the sexes, rigid distinctions between the training of primary and secondary school teachers, and the influence of established churches on attitudes and policy, not to mention an ingrained distrust of mass schooling in circles of power and more restrictive cultural views and social practices involving females. For good or ill, these brakes on educational change were either absent or attenuated in America.

Even in essentially democratic states, centralization both stalled innovation and gave women teachers less shelter from damaging policies. For example, the Burnham pay scales of 1919 set primary teachers' salaries for England and Wales, decreeing that no woman's qualifications and experience could earn her more than 80% of a male teacher's wages. While the American schoolmistress had not reached that proportion, the decree itself would have been organizationally and politically unthinkable in America, where zeal for local control, whether in church or school, was pervasive. While the United States had and retains its own forms of standardization—for example, textbooks and commercial tests—and certainly has experienced gender discrimination, these operated in a more pluralistic, improvisational, socially inclusive, and pragmatic context—allowing females more room to maneuver.

In 1860 the United States had 150,000 public school teachers and four million students. The ratio of students to the total population was 1:5, contrasted to 1:8 in England and 1:10 in France.[91] This national advantage continued into the next century. In 1950, to compare two industrial cities, 5% of 15–17-year-olds in Birmingham, England, were still in school; in Pittsburgh (PA), the figure was 50%. An Oregon teacher, Mary Kelly, was an exchange teacher in Birmingham in 1938–1939. She discovered that most students "finished" at age 14, never entering (senior) high school. Kelly contrasted this discovery with her own experience: despite having parents of limited means, a free high school education, then "still another graduation after going through college on nothing a year," enabled her to teach. She concluded, "There was nothing more precious than democracy *and I mean the American way.*"[92] Such chauvinism would have been widely shared among Americans and those elsewhere who had contracted "America Fever."

Conclusion : Everyday, Ever-Willing Heroines Step Forward

Given the decentralization of school control and management in the United States, initiative at the local level was largely unencumbered.[93] In 1854, a combined academic and "practical" high school opened in Pittsburgh by public demand.[94] Various rural states later promoted regional high schools. The American high school would not have become so prevalent but for three connected facts: First, including a high school in a community's public school system was a local political decision, largely independent of distant policy makers.[95] Second, hiring women reduced costs to what school boards considered (politically) manageable levels. Third, attending high school led relatively easily to teaching positions for either sex, likely reducing working-class opposition to what was a tax-supported but essentially middle-class institution. Where France's teachers became national civil servants during the Third Republic (1870–1940), American teachers were employees of tens of thousands of legally constituted school districts.

Meeker (CO) was a mere village, serving an agricultural and later hunting area on what had been Ute Indian lands; the taxpayers' "wealth" lay in their farms. In 1885 a Meeker official explained (to Kansas schoolmistress Amanda Stewart) the workings of local control:

> As I am one of the School Board of Meeker, I concluded to write you and see if we could employ you to teach our school. Mr. Hosick ... was in favor of employing you for the next year if we could. Aleibrook [?] the other member of the Bord ... will be back in 2 weeks. I cant tell you yet how much school we will have as the School Laws of Colorado are not like the laws of Kansas. The Bord of directors are elected by the people and they levy a tax and choose the length of the term and pay the teacher what they chose to and we haven't met yet.... I and Hosick in favor of nine month school and as yet I havn't talked with Aleibrook I can not tell what he wishes. But he is quite a hevy tax payer and told me that we must levy a tax here enough to run a good school.... I have 2 children that needs a good teacher. if you cant come can you recommend some good teacher that can come. there is 25 familys in Meeker.[96]

Although Miss Stewart did not come, Meeker undoubtedly got its teacher, despite its remoteness; apparently no end of other Gertrudes were waiting in the wings. The essential reality is that nineteenth-century women took over schooling America's youth because their time had come. More than their brothers, they were alert to this opportunity, hungry for their chance, both patient and impatient. "Young ladies" made themselves needed, if not always wanted, and far beyond predictable levels.

Teacher-sensitive public policy worked on behalf of both the spread of popular schooling and its upgrading through higher teacher quality. That women's lower wages materially reduced the costs of secondary schooling and coeducation brought economies of scale that were decisive where low population density or competitive employment opportunities for adolescents made small, gender-segregated high schools unworkable, unsustainable, or politically untenable. Compared to European secondary schools, where per-student cost could be five times greater than in primary schools, the American ratio was closer to two to one. Virtually free secondary schooling was available to more than the local social or academic elite. When school officials excluded the working poor, they did so for other reasons, notably the racism that long withheld a public high school education from the South's black children. By the time the worldwide economic depression of the 1930s hit, America's faith in public schools was virtual dogma. Public policy and personal choice made staying in school, and even going to college, appear the wisest response to massive youth and adult unemployment.

Women teachers have also guided into practice significant changes in curriculum and pedagogy, good and bad. Hitherto, male educators—as theorists, authors, professional spokesmen, high-level administrators—have dominated the tale told and been given the credit. Where the Gertrudes are included in the retelling, blame is more often ascribed than praise. If only by their predominance, male academics charge, women lowered standards for students and, say these "schoolmen," forever fixed teaching as a semiprofession. The present study tells a different story, beginning with the next two chapters. They detail the many, sometimes discrepant, macrosocial forces and personal decisions that feminized America's teacher workforce, altering the public's schools in the process.

CHAPTER 3

"A Sisterhood of Instruction, Essential to the World's Progress"

Societal Pressures and Women's Opportunities, 1700–1900

There was no such thing as a woman teacher. It wasn't a woman's job any more than milking a cow was a man's job."

—Oliver Johnson, Indiana (1828)

Their Mississippi community was in an uproar. The school board—all Republicans—had employed Mrs. Federson, instead of the patrons' choice. This "strange lady from Maine" had arrived around 1870 to live with her sister, the widow of a Union army colonel stationed in Mississippi. "For a whole term the new teacher went to the schoolhouse, stayed the number of hours required by law, and drew a salary of $75 at the end of each month. She had only one pupil; he was her nephew." When the Democrats regained control, "the quiet dignity, and superior attainments of the Northern lady had made their impress.... The patrons who had rebelled and seceded when coercion was afoot, now selected this same teacher for the next season."[1] Mississippians, distrustful of that Yankee invention—the common school and its schoolmistress—were fully invested in the principle and practice of local control. In America, even when the ideas and teachers came from elsewhere, "the schools were indigenous."[2]

Several states to the north and east lay the mostly rural Indiana, the only Northern state with roughly equal numbers of male and female teachers when Oliver Johnson died in 1907.[3] Indiana aside, relatively rapid feminization during Johnson's lifetime was a national response to impersonal forces, acting on "all the major forms of collective life, economies, social structures."[4] Wrenching economic change, a facilitating political system, powerful demographic shifts, a multiplicity of religious loyalties and ethnic identities in an ever-diverse population, and a civil war remade the nation during the nineteenth century. Collectively these social forces also partially explain how and why teaching became (and has remained) "a woman's job" in the United States—partially, because of personal and situational factors. This chapter focuses on the (macro)social.[5]

The Economics of Women's Labor as Teachers

In 1847, W. A. Tunnell, a farmer and brickmaker, was teaching a winter school in Greene County (IL). After the county school fund ran out, his became a sub-scription (fee) school for parents wishing their children to continue. Although boys' names on his school register far outnumbered girls' (37 to 18), of the 7 who attended 90 or more days, 6 were girls. Girls were becoming less needed at home, and schooling had become a recognized investment for the average family.[6] As successively more families erected hedges against economic and other contin-gencies—by having fewer children, using public schools to care for and prepare them, and encouraging work experience even for daughters—men like Tunnell saw their female pupils succeed them at the teacher's desk. As one teacher re-minded readers of the mass-circulation magazine, *World's Work,* "Most families of a certain income fit their daughters for self-support."[7]

Women's Work and Families in Historical Time

In all societies for which iconographic, documentary, or literary evidence exists, girls and women labored relentlessly.[8] Notices in America's colonial press report widows running family businesses, from shops and notary offices to wax and pewter work. Benjamin Franklin's apprenticeship at his brother's newspaper is well known; his sister-in-law's running that business is not. Tavern hostesses were common in the colonial South, for travelers needed food, drink, and lodg-ing.[9] Nantucket Island women, their husbands and fathers whaling at sea, kept all the grocery and dry-goods shops, traveling to Boston to restock.[10]

Quaker farm wives and daughters hired themselves out to their wealthier neighbors as field hands, and they processed and sold textiles and foods.[11] Lucy Stone's mother milked eight cows the night before Lucy's birth in 1818. Until John Ise (b. 1885) and his brothers could take over field work on their Kansas farm, their German immigrant mother worked alongside her husband while tending to other farm and household industries, doing the laundry of local bachelors and widowers, serving as postmistress, selling butter and eggs. Her daughters helped—and after completing their schooling also had teaching wages to con-tribute.[12] Southern slave owners valued the field labor of slave women too much to let them care for their own children. Even the children of favored house slaves were ordinarily cared for in the slave quarters by the elderly, the infirm, or other children. A Northern governess in a Tennessee plantation household recalled a slave woman returning from the fields at sundown, a huge basket on her head holding four naked babies, tended by a young girl while their mothers hoed or picked.[13]

The earliest outpouring of American women into the paid labor force was into factory work. Industrialization came to Massachusetts in 1787 with the first cotton mill. Before 1850 New England had 800 cotton mills, with 8,000 girls working in the mill town of Lowell (MA). The *Lowell Offering's* 1840 article "Defence of Factory Girls" claimed factory hands had more benefits than domestics, seamstresses, and schoolteachers received. Moreover, of her five schoolmates now tending looms, an unidentified "Factory Girl" wrote that all continued to improve their minds, and one used her factory wages for further schooling.

For a time teaching and factory work overlapped. At one point 150 teachers were working in the Merrimack (MA) Mills, some alternating millwork with teaching their home district's summer school. Lucy Larcom (b. 1824), whose widowed mother supervised one of the first dormitories for Lowell mill girls, quit school at 11 for the factory, leaving it in 1846 to teach in Illinois and Massachusetts before settling into authorship.[14] Even the better educated and better off labored. As Nancy Cott put it, "'Middle-class' women was not a synonym for 'leisured.'" Single women "engaged in schoolteaching, domestic work, handicraft and industrial labor. When married they kept house, reared children, manufactured household goods, supplied boarders."[15] Thus, aversion to the self-reliant and wage-earning woman may have been less prevalent than social historians once thought.

Modern Women Need Work: Fitting a Daughter for Self-Support

By the late eighteenth century, however, women's customary labor and work skills were being squeezed. In 1810 cottage industries—home carding, spinning, weaving—produced 96% of all wool cloth in the United States; by 1830, half was moved into "manufactories."[16] Farm machinery reduced female labor in fields and barns, as well as the number of farm hands to be fed and boarded, while factories took over the processing and canning of many foodstuffs. Milliners, and dressmakers lost business to store-bought goods. Men were becoming hairdressers, while physicians invaded midwifery.

Industrial capitalism also weakened the household as a place for imparting job skills. The entire families that labored together in the textile mills of nineteenth-century New England and New York could offer their children neither training for a trade or profession nor social capital. With mechanization and an increasingly impersonal economic order, fewer families could either hand down their own skills or use personal connections to secure their dependents' employment. Mastering the typewriter and telephone switchboard could rarely be taught at home, whereas a private secretarial school or high school clerical course could step into the breach.[17] Thus occupational and professional networks were intruding even as traditional family networks were frayed by geographic mobility from country to town and city and from East and South toward the West.

As Dr. Emily Blackwell put it in 1883, as women's traditional jobs left the household, women must "follow their work under its new forms, or cease to work at all."[18] The work of "social reproduction," represented by instructing the young in schools, was an obvious solution to the enforced idleness of the educated daughters of the middle class and the great many in the working class aspiring to rise. A woman teacher might even earn more than a man doing dirty and dangerous work, like building canals and railroads. (Before World War II a top cowhand got $50 a month in Arizona, while Eulalia Bourne's annual salary for teaching a nine-month district school was $1125.[19])

When their father died, Mississippi's Lewis Elgar (b. 1833) prudently brought his sisters, Mary and Martha, into his own home, educated them, "and made teachers of them."[20] After the Civil War when the Bingham School's Colonel Robert Bingham spoke to 350 teachers at a convention about his several visits to Northern public schools, he noted North Carolina teachers' average annual incomes: $25 per month for a four-month school. For comparing this with what Boston paid 100 headmasters and 100 women teachers, he was berated as having "turned Yankee."[21] He responded, "If you could superinduce a set of conditions under which . . . the best man among you would have a chance at a four-thousand-dollar salary, as a free-school teacher, $1000 more than our Governor gets, and the best woman among you [has] a chance at a two-thousand-eight hundred dollar salary as a free-school teacher, $300 more than our chief Justice gets, if you could do this, you know very well that you would 'turn Yankees,' unless you have lost your senses."

"A Sacred, Not a Mercenary Employment"

When the Catholic hierarchy mandated parish schools in America in 1884, religious brothers and nuns were equally acceptable as teachers. But as teaching brothers were transferred from elementary to Catholic high schools, women religious became, by 1890, nearly two-thirds of parochial schools' teachers.[22] The reason was not that nuns were paid less than priests, although they were, but that nuns had less formal power.

That women teachers were employed alongside men and eventually supplanted most of them is often attributed to women's underselling men. For example,

Boxford (MA) paid women 41% of male rates in 1845, raised to 86% in 1880. In 1900 Harvard University president Charles W. Eliot said that, as cheap labor, women had "replaced 9/10ths of the men in American public schools." However, the low wages of teaching for both genders and women's relative lack of economic opportunity (and their proven merit), appear more important in feminizing teaching than women's "cheapness."[23] See table 3.1.

Mary Lyon suggested young women with mercenary goals become milliners or dressmakers, not teachers; teaching, for women especially, was its own reward. Women, Ohio state school superintendent Samuel Lewis asserted, were indifferent to "accumulat[ing] much property by this occupation." In 1836 he recommended to the Western Literary Institute that wages saved by employing women be used to lengthen the school term enough to attract and retain male teachers. Moreover, all teachers would benefit by having an assured eight- or nine-month income rather than subjecting themselves to the uncertainties of brief, often variable, spring–summer and winter schools.[24]

It was often repeated that women teachers could live well on less money; that male-female wage equity was unsupportable, either economically or politically; and that only inept men could be hired at women's wages. Moreover, although men teachers commonly earned 40% more than women, the discrepancies in other fields were larger, and teaching paid well compared to other women's occupations. When Miss Craft left Boston for Southern California in 1865 to teach a seven-month school for weekly wages of $12.20 and free board, Boston domestics earned $1.50 to $3 a week, and its highest paid industrial women, glass-factory workers, earned $4 to $6.[25] In 1902 Denver teachers' average annual salaries of

TABLE 3.1
Teachers' Salaries in the United States and Selected States,
by Gender and Region, 1905–1906

State	Men	Women	Men's Salaries as % of Women's
United States	$56.31	$43.80	128.6
Massachusetts	$149.02	$57.07	261.1
New York	$86.72	$86.72	100
Pennsylvania	$53.16	$39.41	134.9
Tennessee	$39.00	$35.00	111.4
Georgia	$33.83	$33.83	100
Ohio	$45.00	$40.00	112.5
Illinois	$74.57	$57.54	129.6
Nebraska	$60.78	$43.49	139.8
Kansas	$48.00	$40.00	120
Idaho	$71.00	$55.90	127
Wyoming	$77.29	$48.34	159.9

Source: U.S. Bureau of Education, 1906, 305, as given in Sumner, *Equal Suffrage,* 157.

$730 exceeded nurses' $550, while the average for 18 clerical, service, and industrial jobs was $371.[26] Teaching also appealed to women for a range of rewards only loosely coupled to economics: "the masculine privileges of professionalism, public service, scope for the intellect, relatively good pay, security of tenure, the possibility of promotion and a subsidised training."[27] None of these attributes, except the possibility of promotion, had an evident equal appeal to men.

In the classic sociological study of Muncie (IN), dubbed "Middletown," the authors speculated that an increase in men teachers—from 22% to 29% between the 1920 and 1930 censuses—"may foreshadow a condition . . . [whereby] fields like teaching, nursing, bookkeeping, and stenography will be more heavily over-run by males." They were closer to the mark, however, in, thinking the maximum paid to male teachers ($2,100) or the superintendent's salary ($4,900) "are hardly enough to tempt many of the abler men away from business in a culture in which everything hinges on money." Meanwhile, as a Muncie businessman marveled in 1935, "The girls I knew here ten years ago took up careers largely as a protection against failure to marry and similar contingencies. Now those who plan to work are nothing like so much confined to the hopeless."[28]

Politics: Government by and for "the People"

Any wishes of Massachusetts and other colonial officials to centralize their governments were thwarted by geography (sparsely settled townships and frontier conditions) as well as distrust. Political independence confirmed habits of local control, which became patriotic dogma. Even the unstable political consensus on behalf of a universal (i.e., white) literacy—uniting schoolmen with politicians, local elites, businessmen, workingmen's organizations, churchmen, and newspaper editors in thousands of communities—was achieved not by state planning but as a messy, confused social movement.[29] Cognizant of religious, ethnic, and political diversity, education's advocates concluded that the new republic's very survival required a literate citizenry, and while females could not govern or even vote, as "mothers of the republic," they too must be educated.[30] Horace Mann's coeducational Antioch College (f. 1852) pressed a reformer's faith in education and women further: "let woman . . . be educated to the highest practicable point; not only because it is her right, but because it is essential to the world's progress."[31]

Universal Literacy and Much More

While Protestant theology specified biblical literacy of each sex, colonial era memoirs, apprenticeship contracts, and public records seldom mention girls. However, as schools spread, so did taxpayer complaints about supporting schools that did not benefit their girls. Before 1800 a few New England towns began educating girls at town expense. When common schools chose a schoolmistress, more parents wished to see their daughters benefit—adding their voices, and votes, for equal access to schooling. Poorer Massachusetts towns (like Sutton) taxed themselves to educate girls, and employed women teachers a generation before wealthier towns whose leaders could school their daughters privately. Between 1809 and 1837, Sutton's teachers were Abigail Leland, her brother Jonathan, and his daughters, Silence, Catherine, and Mary.[32]

All else being equal, a growing supply generally drives down the price of what is offered, encouraging more demand, which further stimulates supply. From 1840 to 1865, Massachusetts's local school committees (boards) increased the state's number of winter schools by 55%, its pupil numbers by 54%, its teachers by 74%, and women's proportion among teachers to 88%.[33] According to Alonzo Potter's cost accounting, employing women "to a far greater extent than they have hitherto been, without any detriment to our schools," would lengthen school terms without arousing taxpayers' resistance.[34] Local boards could use the savings to add one or more high school subjects to an ungraded rural elementary school, erect new schoolhouses to relieve overcrowding, better serve a remote area, open kindergartens, or create a proper high school. Ultimately they would do all of these—and more.

Novelist Sally Pratt McLean, from a family of teachers, wrote a popular novel, *Towhead* (1888), about Lucy Bodurthas of Dymsbury (CT). She was sent to the young ladies' seminary at Mount Grimrood, "to be got kinder softened ter begin with, and ter be got kinder toned down; and then you air a goin' to be sent to high-toneder schools for to be toned up."[35] But heads of female seminaries came to scorn "toning up," added "solid subjects," and charged extra for the "strictly ornamental." Despite Milton's "one tongue is enough for a woman," by 1900 women were settling in as the typical public high school's Latin teacher. Although the classics were pressed by other subjects' claims (Latin enrollments declined from 51% of students in 1900 to 8% in 1950), other subjects with firmer places in the curriculum entered the "woman's sphere": algebra, biology, English, speech, history, music, and art.

Catharine Beecher estimated that more than two million children lacked schooling in 1850. "Were all these children placed in schools . . . it would require 200,000 women to meet the demand."[36] Along with population growth, enrollments rose as kindergartens captured younger pupils, while stronger enforcement of school attendance laws, relaxed standards, and new subjects retained more adolescents.[37] Periodic economic reversals kept even the academically unmotivated in schools and colleges. Although business upturns drew them back into the labor market, average completion levels crept upward, and the longer schooled gained a competitive advantage.

Hiring women for the winter school blurred, and then eliminated, the distinction between the woman's summer school and the man's winter school—easing the shift to a "school year," chiefly taught (as it turned out) by women. In 1861 the average young Northerner had 50–64 days of school per year, while the Southerner had 11.[38] After 1865, however, Southern youth—previously limited to "pay schools," charity schools, or illiteracy—became a sizeable new market, taught by an almost entirely new class: the homegrown public school teacher, white or colored, and usually female.

Teacher Supply and Demand: Who Will Teach These Children?

In the early American republic, schools still relied on a fluid labor force, often men paying off debts before settling into a more permanent career in commerce, medicine, law, or journalism.[39] The typically indigent, sometimes older, students who entered the nineteenth-century's many small, struggling colleges often taught during the long winter recess to cover the next term's fees. On leave from the University of Vermont in 1809, Jared Willson (b. 1786) contrasted his school-keeping with a friend's legal studies: "I must linger away a dreary winter, with a hord of snotty girls and boys; while you are tasting the sweets of Blackstone or caressing your favorite female."[40]

In the half century after the American Revolution, fewer ministerial and classics graduates showed up to teach school, even briefly, with more vacancies filled by the barely educated. John Andrew Rice's rural South Carolina schoolmaster was "just out of school, as touchy as a rattlesnake in spring, and scared," profoundly ignorant but needing the money for college.[41] These realities may have reduced public regard for the schoolmaster while enhancing public readiness for the schoolmistress. "The schoolteacher, with her neat figure and sweet smile, and a bevy of admiring little children always clinging to her skirts," was a person of consequence in poor neighborhoods—not only in New York City's Lower East Side or Chicago's South Side—and worthy of emulating.[42] In an expansive teacher labor market, ambitious children of former slaves and immigrants could hope to take her place.

Various accounts of common schools in the Northeast and Midwest speak of a "man who made a business of ploughing, mowing, carting manure, etc., in the summer, and of teaching school in the winter."[43] In an 1867 letter to a schoolmistress friend, Illinois's Clark Lewis mused, "There is no telling what a fellow would resort to when he's strapped, so I thought I would choose the least of many evils and go to pedagogueing."[44] During his three-month school at $40 per month, Lewis had to cut firewood for the schoolhouse (five miles from his family's farm) and do his farm chores. "I don't know wheather I can stand it at that rate very long or not," he admitted." He did not.

Where rural poverty and job stagnation coexisted, school terms were brief, wages low, and ill-trained teachers could find positions. In 1920 Virginia, males were 20% of the state's teachers, but in poorer, more rural, and undeveloped West Virginia, men were 47%.[45] Despite parents who did not want either their girls "toned up" or their boys "toned down" by too much schooling, education indicators rose, albeit unevenly, in population of school-age children.[46] Perhaps the most important was that, between 1890 and 1990, high school graduates (as a percentage of all 17-year-olds) increased from 3.5% to 74.2%.

The Teacher Market, School Reform, and Opportunity Costs

The schoolmaster's seat was usually vacated by a competing occupation. In 1818, Vermonter Willard Keyes supplemented his subscription school in Wisconsin by operating a saw- and gristmill. In 1836 a vein of lead near his Platteville schoolhouse caused him to abandon the school, albeit after an unusually long career.[47] When gold was discovered in 1848 along the Sacramento River, the ships in San Francisco Bay lost their crews overnight to the diggings, as did all schools in Monterey and San Francisco not taught by women. Francis Kittredge Shattuck had a teacher's certificate in his sea chest when his party reached California in 1850, but it was his sister, Mrs. Blake, who opened an Oakland school.[48] Mr. Houston "felt his misfortune very keenly" when Oakland did not renew his appointment as principal of the Piedmont neighborhood school, consoled by the fortune he brought back from the Klondike in 1900.[49]

The first teacher in Portland (OR), the ill-named John Outhouse, unloaded ships and built roads to survive on his miserable wages. His successor was a woman who did neither of those things.[50] While an offer of marriage or a better school drew young women from their schools, others were ready to take their places—which was not the case when recruiting a schoolmaster. Where the end of a country school's winter term once released men to spring planting or other work, this arrangement withered as new standards raised teaching's "opportunity costs": the time and money needed for gaining and renewing a teaching license. In return, public schools were more regularly funded, their sessions extended to the point that teachers might hope for an eight- or nine-month school year and a modest living. Pedagogy courses proliferated in high schools, normal schools, and colleges—augmented by periodic professional gatherings, called "institutes." Organized educators lobbied for basing appointments and salary scales on formal training and experience, not on the teacher's gender, the subjects taught, or the applicants' connections.[51]

While teaching's opportunity costs rose for everyone, men were predominantly affected, especially city dwellers with more occupational options. Successful with his school, Wallace Boughton was pleased that his Kansas district wanted to rehire him, but the term's end "left me without a job, until fall, so I was almost disgusted with the pedagogical profession." The Western School of Telegraphy in Sedalia (MO) had a short course "that will furnish me steady employment."[52] Enough men made similar decisions that New Jersey's commissioner of education remarked that his state added 277 new high school teachers in 1912, while its colleges graduated only five men who became public school teachers. In the 1930s during the Great Depression, however, enough men chose teaching's greater security to raise New York City's proportion of male teachers to 16%.[53]

Democracy at the Grass Roots: Decentralized Decision-Making

Virtually alone among nations, the United States lacked a national ministry of education to set hiring standards, examine pupils, or inspect schools. Citizens generally withheld authority even from their state capitals, rejecting regulations that would deprive them of decision-making power.[54] With limited and tardy intervention by state bodies and no federal presence, the nineteenth-century's functionally independent school districts improvised, imitated, and sometimes innovated. In 1831, male trustees employed Miss Charlotte Foxcroft to teach two consecutive terms (summer and winter) in their Vermont district schoolhouse, "receiving extra for languages and ornamentals." The $95 she collected that year was "quite a large sum in those days for a woman to earn."[55]

The crucial decision to hire a female for winter schools was spread through local school committees' annual reports, attesting to *her* success in "governing the larger scholars. If the consequences of hiring a schoolmistress proved positive, the practice was likely to be repeated the next year—and tried by a neighboring district. (This was even true, as in some Midwestern states around 1850, where a "district" was no more than neighbors banded together to elect trustees to hire and supervise a teacher and collect tuition fees; not a unit of local government, without taxing authority or legal claim to a share of the state school fund, such districts administered hybrids of the subscription and public school models.)

In 1839 Massachusetts had about 2,000 official school districts, a multiplicity of decision makers that might have done nothing; instead, they popularized primary and then secondary education, placing both chiefly in women's hands. Somerville (MA) was incorporated in 1842; in 1860 women were 59 of the town's

64 teachers.[56] High turnover meant the actual number of women teaching in Somerville over that period was even greater, spreading teaching and wage-earning experience and ambition more widely among families. The question of whose daughter would get the classroom was, of course, also decided locally.[57]

Over a long life, Wisconsin farmer and established seasonal teacher Jabez Brown (1825–1903) helped local youth find openings, negotiate salary and boarding arrangements, prepare for the licensing examination, and handle discipline. As a district trustee he offered to supplement the board's pay offer from his own pocket to hire a male teacher.[58] Although Brown was unusually involved, his was also a prebureaucratic time, when doing school business allowed personal discretion.

Trustees, political bosses, and mayors took bribes and bestowed favors. When a Holden (MO) school board member differed with the widowed teacher, Mrs. Carry Gloyd (b. 1846), on a minor matter, he replaced her with his niece.[59] It was frequently heard that "the Director of the District wants his daughter to teach."[60] Often a community's largest employer, school systems dispensed other school jobs—to custodians and handymen and later to secretaries, cafeteria workers, and school bus drivers. In many taxpayers' minds, public-sector jobs were entitlements or forms of charity, as when appointing a respectable indigent widow as town clerk, treasurer, or teacher.[61] But in the jobless 1930s, Mrs. Lou Byars refused to follow the custom of offering a bribe to the white trustees for the teacher's job in a Negro school in rural Caldwell County (TX). "I'm not giving [you] a nickel to let me work. . . . And they never said a word—they never said a mumbling word!"[62]

CHOOSING THE HOMEGROWN GIRL

Although schoolmasters before about 1825 were often outsiders (especially college boys on leave), locals had the edge in securing a school. They cost less to hire, room and board were at hand, and their wages might recoup some of a family's school taxes. (In New Zealand, when Frances Slater expressed an interest in attending the University of Otago to become a lawyer, her father told her that girls don't become solicitors and that if she became a teacher, "at least I'll get back my school taxes!" She taught, and he presumably recouped.[63]) Moreover, as teachers were expected to secure and compensate a substitute, having a nearby relative or friend made sense. Even in cities, magnets for experienced teachers, residents wanted their "own" given precedence. The *Atlanta Daily Herald* periodically complained of outsiders snatching positions from local girls. In 1929 a Louisville (KY) newspaper reported, "It is practically a set rule of the Board of Education that no girl is accepted as a teacher from outside . . . until all the local [normal school] graduates have been placed."[64]

Of his Missouri boyhood, where the pupils "rattled, term by term, the dry bones of reading, writing, arithmetic, and something called 'jography,'" Alexis Lange (b. 1862) remembered the inexhaustible succession of "one or the other of the daughters of the school trustee . . . and when one of his daughters stepped into matrimony, another stepped into the school—to earn her trousseau."[65] Personal connections did give laymen a familiar, if unreliable, basis for choosing from among "a crowd of candidates with hard-to-judge credentials."[66] School officials might also consider "locals" less prone to depart (except for marriage) than career-centered "cosmopolitans."

E. P. Cubberley (b. 1868), a veteran Indiana and California "schoolman," summarized district trustees' typical preferences: "the bright and attractive graduate of the last class in the local high school; the daughter of the estimable citizen; the young lady who needed to help her widowed mother."[67] When local applicants were absent or their partisans deadlocked, outsiders were hired. Wisconsin-bred Maude Frazier was chosen in 1906 as teaching principal in Genoa (NV) because her predecessor, from a nearby town, had split the board. Frazier mused, "Distance rather than qualifications had gotten me the position."[68]

Lillian Du Rocher was born on her parents' farm in Monroe County (MI) around 1888. About to enter her senior year at St. Mary Academy, she overheard the county superintendent reporting his problem—20 schools in the county without teachers for the fall term; could Lillian take one, he asked her father.[69] In the American system, nothing then prevented local officials from employing an untrained novice. Her father protested: she must finish high school. "The next day enterprising Lillian presented herself to the superintendent, reporting to her family in the evening that she had signed a contract to teach school that winter."

While state and national leaders promoted trained teachers, school trustees were obligated to fill the teacher's chair in every schoolroom at the best price possible. Thus habitual practices and ideals of proximity and local ownership governed decisions about public schooling—even as all-weather roads, the telephone, and the Montgomery Ward catalogue brought the outside world closer. No matter: the district school already had its iconic hold on the American imagination.[70]

BOOSTERISM: COMMUNITY AND INSTITUTION BUILDING

Exaggerated expressions of civic pride were common in the nineteenth century as new settlements were planted across the continent. "It was not that they loved the world less, but that they loved Keokuk more," was how Daniel Boorstin put the "community-ism" that left its stamp on many facets of American politics.[71] Even as cost consciousness kept its schoolhouse unpainted, figuratively starved the schoolmistress, and allowed the mixing of adolescent girls and boys, innumerable new institutions were founded by donations of monies, land, and labor from the residents of optimistic communities or church congregations. Swedish Lutheran communities in Nebraska jostled to host every new private or state facility. When Wahoo secured Luther Academy (later College) in 1883, it stunted nearby rival Saronville's growth. Boosterism was a way of competing with similar communities or of compensating for the lack of superior natural attractions or resources—for, just as new communities sprang up, they could also stagnate or die.

When its trustees offered the floundering Platteville Academy to Wisconsin as a state normal school site, citizens predicted large benefits to their town from the transformed institution that opened in 1866. Educating teachers for southwestern Wisconsin, Platteville acquired the character of a small college town. While land promoters might not profit as expected, females would. Coeducation, teacher education, and an occasional "lady professor" resulted from institutional proliferation—further enlarging the nation's supply of Gertrudes.

Generation and Cerebration

Colonial Quaker families foreshadowed critical nineteenth-century demographic shifts: later marriages, smaller families, and high percentages of the permanently single. Declining birthrates significantly increased prospects that a woman would live long enough to raise all her own children. Mothers born before 1788 survived the marriage of their last child by 4 years; those born during the 1880s lived for 20 years after their last child's departure from home. From 1900 to 1950 the death rate of white women fell by more than half. Cemeteries housed fewer remains of young wives, often interred with their infants, while men who buried multiple wives retreated into history. Indeed, women who survived childbirth (and men who survived childhood disease and accidents) lived nearly as long as later generations.

Higher participation in education was both a cause and a result of demographic changes affecting women and girls. Fewer pregnancies left mothers stronger and healthier, materially improving their well-being and that of their children. Their daughters' child-care and domestic duties were reduced, and their schooling prolonged. Lengthened and more regular attendance firmed up both their scholastic preparation and identification with (or dislike of) schooling. A lengthened education delayed the onset of functional adulthood, raised the age of first marriage, and reduced a woman's fecundity. These structural population changes and their sociopsychological effects are now regarded as the real American Revolution for women.

Dimensions of Demographic Change in Families

A secular trend of falling birthrates extends from the first census (1790) to the present, reversed only during the post–World War II baby boom. Among women who bore children (excluding miscarriages, abortions, and stillbirths), the U.S. birthrate fell from 7.04 live births per woman in 1800 to 3.56 in 1900 and 2.1 in 2010.[72] Called "the single most important fact about women and the family in American history," this change appeared in cities (where large numbers of children proved a heavy financial burden) and on farms (where machines reduced the need for sons' labor in the fields and daughters' in the house and yard).[73]

In the population drift from the Northeast's depleted farms, Miriam David's family left New Hampshire for Essex County (NY). Miriam (b. 1817), the 12th of 17 children, was repeatedly kept from school to help at home or with the young family of a widowed brother. She later wrote, "I could wish that my father [a tanner] was rich enough to board, clothe, and pay my tuition, somewhere at a high school. . . . [For] the height of my aspirations were to attain the position of school teacher . . . and walk to school with a score or more of little urchins calling me school-ma'am."[74]

Miriam David eventually taught, paying for several terms at an academy with her wages. At 29 she married fellow teacher William Colt. They farmed until 1856, when they joined the Kansas Vegetarian Emigration Society, one of many utopian communities. A year later, Mrs. Colt returned to New York with her daughter, leaving her husband and son in a Kansas graveyard. The life of Miriam David Colt—her later age at marriage and the smaller size of her family—are elements of the demographic shifts affecting female consciousness and behavior during and since the later nineteenth century—albeit still with the omnipresent specter of premature death.

The sometimes 20-year age gap between a family's oldest and youngest child long made school-aged girls the essential child minders and household help. Now, however, siblings were fewer and closer in age. Rules—like that in mid-nineteenth-century Boston banning school homework for girls—could be modified, then revoked, as store-bought goods, labor-saving devices, and the expanded reach of schools (themselves child-care institutions) rounded out a revolution in family life. As with maternal health, better public health and medical care raised the odds that each of a typical family's two to four children would reach adulthood, increasing the investment value of their schooling.

Creating a life space, before or during marriage, into which women could fit wage work meant that some would reorient themselves to self-development rather than family formation. In 1926, to learn "the origins of their modern point of view toward men, marriage, children, and jobs," the liberal monthly the *Nation* commissioned a series of essays by 17 women, all "feminists" born between 1868 and 1896. Mostly journalists and professional writers, 7 were or had been teachers; 6 others mentioned mothers or aunts who had taught school. Most (70%) had married—a lower figure than the national average (92%) but higher than for college-educated women of their generations. With the common theme that "mother bore too many children," only 5 of the 17 had children.[75]

When these "new women" were reflecting on their pasts, girls were 56% of U.S. public high school students, roughly 65% of high school graduates, and 47% of college and university undergraduates.[76] Would they use that education in the labor force? For those prepared to teach the probable response was yes, at least until (or if) they married. Moreover, their smaller, closely spaced families allowed more of the "marriage retired" to return to teaching when the last child reached school age or adulthood—and at a younger age.

Motivations and Mechanisms

In the 1830s Alexis de Tocqueville found himself "almost frightened at the singular address and happy boldness" of young American women. He also noted the loss of their independence with marriage.[77] In teacher-author Caroline Lee Hentz's 1856 novel, *Marcus Warland; Or, the Long Moss Spring: A Tale of the South*, Florence Delavel begs her suitor, "Let me follow my own volitions, for at least three or four years to come. . . . Let my mind soar unfettered to the heights where I wish to stand." Effie Lee Richardson viewed her humble Arizona normal school (class of 1907) as "a way to wait until I was older to marry. With a Normal education I could get a job easily, and I didn't have to marry just anyone."[78]

In her autobiography Mary Austin described the circumscribed lives of nineteenth-century small-town women, as "a world of cooking and making over . . . a world of church-going and missionary societies and ministerial cooperation." But this teacher-author also revealed women's "tiny rebellions against their 'woman nature' . . . [with] all of the care and expectancy of children overshadowed by the recurrent monthly dread, crept about by whispers, heretical but persistent, of methods of circumventing it, of a secret practice of things openly condemned."[79] A library of novels and secular and religious writings in English informed generations of English and American girls of men's nature and childbed's terrors.[80] Perhaps more important than their reading, women shared information and apprehensions in private talk and correspondence.

In widening circles women took less comfort in the consolation offered by Scripture and the church fathers on the premature death of women and children. In Utah, where Mormon orthodoxy promoted plural marriage and large families, after eight children Mary Nelson twice attempted suicide rather than endure another pregnancy. Alice Reynolds's (b. 1873) polygamous father had 32 living children by three wives. Her own mother died with her infant in childbirth at age 39, leaving 11 children motherless. Alice Reynolds taught school instead of marrying.[81]

While educated women were privy to more reliable birth-control knowledge, delaying marriage was the most effective way of limiting pregnancies. Employed women, specifically teachers, could use their work as a way to put off marriage: engaged in a respectable vocation, financially independent, yet adding to household coffers or a nest egg. An interim occupation could also become an extended, even lifelong experience—and the image of the schoolmistress saving to purchase a trousseau had to share space with that of the old-maid teacher who "gadded about." Especially between 1875 and 1915, moralists decried lifelong spinsters, the slow to marry, and mothers of small families as epitomizing the unsexing of American womanhood. With an economic interest in doctoring mothers of large families, physicians like Edward Clark warned that overexercise of the brain—the organ of "cerebration"—impeded procreation. A Canadian gynecologist described higher education as taking "every drop of blood away to the brain from the growing organs of generation."[82]

With motherhood remaining Southern women's primary source of identity and sisterhood, even higher-status white women bore above-average numbers of children.[83] However, some women from the South's plantation aristocracy refused marriage, conscious of the "moral degradation" of the master-slave relationship. Sarah Grimké and her sisters, Angelina and Mary, taught occasional schools, but Sarah remained resolutely single.[84] Like New England the South acquired a surplus of educated females, but many stayed home, increasingly to teach, rather than relocate to Western places where marriageable females were wanted.

It was rightly suspected that a feminist consciousness was incubating in peer communities. Elite women's colleges prided themselves on inspiring women to enter demanding professions and remain confidently single if they chose. But late-marrying and never-married career women were also prevalent among normal school and even coeducational university graduates. From 1880 to 1920, women went from 2.8% of physicians to 5%, from 0.1% to 1.4% of attorneys; and from 68% of teachers to 94%.[85] However, after 1910 college women's marriage rates began rising; while marrying later and having fewer children than average, women were not choosing between marriage and career but trying to have both. Schoolteaching—acceptable, accessible, and accommodating—topped most lists.[86]

Responding to Pluralism

The United States emerged as a contentiously pluralistic society: Protestants divided by sectarianism, Catholics determined to reassert themselves, "blacks" frozen in slavery, old ethnic differences aggravated by expansion into lands occupied by "brown" and "red" peoples, amid a laissez-faire immigration policy. Economic and cultural markers showed a class hierarchy—although America's "lower orders" were less deferential than Britain's, and its "social betters" less imperious. How could a unifying cultural overlay be created, and diversity made strength? Education was one response, along with an unrestrained economy and an ideology of social mobility. Women teachers turned out to be the essential instruments of the first approach and, rather surprisingly, modest beneficiaries of the second.

An 1896 editorial highlighted teachers' responsibilities in an open society: "Under our free institutions, persons born into any 'class' are privileged to pass into any other. . . . No institution in our land is so thoroughly American on this point as the free public schools, and surely their teachers can do much to send their pupils forth with ideas on this subject, so truly American as to lessen the influence of the demagogue."[87]

Religion: Deferring to Denominationalism

Despite their doctrinal and organizational diversity, Americans were heirs to the Reformation, the equally repressive Catholic Counter-Reformation, and anti-Semitism. Ireland's Catholics resorted in the eighteenth century to "hedge schools" (taught by the priest or literate laymen, sometimes held outdoors), nursing a hatred of the English and Protestantism that Irish immigrants carried to America. And when Rebecca Pennell Dean, a niece of Horace Mann, escorted some Yankee schoolgirls through Europe in 1877–1878, she dotted her detailed travel journal with sectarian prejudices. For example, the All Saints' Day mass at Notre Dame was "too absurd to be patiently endured and called Christian worship."[88]

Americans continued to view churches and their schools as both shield and weapon. To accommodate its antagonistic constituents, Detroit's Eighth Ward public school sat Protestant pupils and teacher downstairs, and the larger group of Catholic pupils and teacher upstairs. However, when Bishop Lefevere tried to secure public funds for his parochial schools, Protestants reacted. Arguing the need to equalize class size, Detroit's school board ordered 25 of the Catholic pupils downstairs and a smaller number of Protestants upstairs, causing the lay Catholic teacher to resign.[89]

As the First Amendment to the U.S. Constitution, in both its free exercise and establishment clauses, sheltered religious pluralism, a free market of faiths emerged. To preserve the faith and woo new adherents, churches (with both Catholic and Protestant women the majority of their congregants) armed themselves with seminaries, schools and colleges, Sunday schools, youth auxiliaries, publishing houses, charities, missions, and lay societies. As otherwise preoccupied husbands yielded their role as chief guardian of the spiritual well-being of the family, "a company of women" was left to assume the burden of supporting a denomination's educational, charitable, and missionary work.[90]

By 1920 nowhere was women's religious presence more evident than in the 300 congregations of Catholic women religious in the United States. Defensively militant, the Catholic Church in the United States built and staffed— especially from 1880 to 1920—the nation's largest system of church-sponsored schools: 90,000 nuns teaching in 6,000 parochial schools and 50 women's colleges. Yet this legion of Irish, French, German, and home-grown sisters was outnumbered by self-supporting Catholic laywomen teaching in public schools. An open letter in 1890 to the rector of Catholic University of America praised the "thousands of Catholic girls . . . becoming teachers . . . [who] reflect credit alike on the race that produced them, the church to which they belong, and the country which afforded them . . . the splendid opportunities which culminated in their education."[91] Although the increasing presence of Catholic teachers in public schools likely eroded Catholic-Protestant distrust in some communities, as late as the 1920s many Texas districts would not hire a Catholic teacher.[92]

As for inter-Protestant protectionism, in 1887 George Randle advised fellow teacher Edgar Strain of a vacant position in Redmond (IL), settled by Congregationalists. "Go over there and offer to take the school for $65 or $70. . . . You would have two assistants . . . both very nice ladies." When Strain (a Methodist?) was rejected, Randle sympathized: "So your religious relations have considerable to do in securing a place at Rosemond. Well I heard something of that kind before but did not know how much stock to take in it."[93]

Euphemia Strayer's late nineteenth-century description of her village of Axtel—a place without "dissensions, strife, jealousy, and unrighteous ambition," a simple, happy Kansas Arcadia—reveals a restrained toleration of diversity. "Church" could be Methodist, Presbyterian, or Catholic, coexisting in "a beautiful spirit of fellowship," allowing room for "the few outside the church." And, significantly, "there are no greater factors for developing intellect, moulding character, marshalling the forces of good against evil than well equipped *Christian* school teachers."[94]

Race and "Nationality": Seeing Our Own
on the Teacher's Platform

In the Spanish period (1769–1821), the first teacher in Los Angeles was a former soldier, Maximo Pina, who offered reading, writing, and *doctrina Christiana*. In the Mexican period, Don Ygnacio Corone was teacher of the pueblo's longest-lasting school before the "Norteamericanos" came.[95] From 1834 to 1844 he received assistance from his daughter, Soledad, the first woman teacher on record. However, Los Angeles soon lost elements of Californio culture: going from Spanish to English, from extended to nuclear families, from established Catholicism to voluntary, mostly Protestant institutions. Public schools appeared, usually with an Anglo schoolmistress.

Meanwhile an "education civil war" pitted Northern missionary societies, philanthropists, and federal agents against Southern and Border States' governments. How were 3.1 million emancipated slaves to be prepared for citizenship? Southern white officials initially preferred "colored men for the colored schools." Some colored men did teach or become principals. One was Shaw University graduate Nicholas Longworth Dillard (b. 1906), who became upper-grades teacher and principal of the Yanceyville (NC) Colored School in 1930, thereby reaffirming his parents' intentions: they had not sent him to college "so that he could 'press pants.' "[96] However, more colored women than men used even inferior schools to overcome poverty and illiteracy, ensuring the feminization of teaching in colored as well as white schools.

Colored parents protested in 1905 when Washington (DC) hired only 13 young women graduates from Miner Normal School: "the colored schools must have colored teachers, and from what source can we draw teachers better prepared and fitted than the products of our own educational system." When Mt. Clemens (MI) officials hired "four young colored women" to teach in 1937, a magazine credited Prince Drewry, a Tuskegee graduate and school board member. The civil rights movement opened far more doors, propelled by population mobility during World War II, the racist horrors of Nazism, and independence movements in the "Third World." However, as school desegregation worked its way through a still-racist society, African American students increasingly found themselves, once again, with white teachers.[97]

From the late 1830s (with the Irish) and 1840s (with Germans) and intensifying after 1880 (with Jews and Italians), immigration brought unprecedented ethnic diversity to the United States. In immigrant enclaves, children learned the English language and American customs in kindergartens and grade schools, while night schools offered adults spoken and written English, civics, history, and geography, preparing many to get their "citizen papers" and others to find a decent job or better prospects for a small family business. In 1868 widowed Jette Bruns wrote her brother in her native Germany—where most teachers were men—about her eldest daughter, Ottilie: "She told me that she would like to study to be a teacher. . . . Then she would always have something secure." By 1871 Ottilie's $600 annual salary from the St. Louis schools helped support the family. Although marriage ended her career in 1879, she resumed it when widowed.[98]

Around 1880 Estella Stevens (b. 1858) reported from Red Wing (MN), "We are the only two Americans teaching in district schools in the county[;] the rest are skandinavian."[99] The Swedish-language issue of *Till Verksamhet* for April 1886 stated flatly, "Americans send their children to high school to educate them to be teachers. . . . Our Swedish girls are wonderful hired girls. They would be just as wonderful school teachers." Community leaders, churches, labor unions, the foreign language press, and fraternal and political organizations from various nationality groups agitated for more appropriate schooling, with teachers sharing their pupils' religious, racial, or ethnic identity.

Despite anti-Semitism, the educational ambitions of Jews were admired, often emulated, and even rewarded. In describing his Brooklyn neighborhood around 1910, Samuel Tennenbaum remembered, "In Brownsville when I knew it, school was a major occupation, not only of the children alone but of the whole neighborhood. Every teacher was discussed with the minute detail a jeweler devoted to a watch." Relative to Italians, for example, fewer Jewish mothers were employed. Thus even large Jewish families did not have to divert their daughters from school, instead producing remarkably career-minded teachers.[100] The 1910 census found more than 24% of U.S. teachers had a foreign-born parent.

TABLE 3.2
Female High School Students per 100 Male Students, by Parentage

Boston, Chicago, New York City, 1908		Bridgeport, CT, 1922	
Fathers' Ethnicity	Female	Fathers' Ethnicity	Female
Native White	135	United States	134
English	161	British Empire	131
German	103	German	122
Irish	137	Irish	135
Swedish	131	Scandinavian	116
"Hebrew"-German	107	—	—
"Hebrew"-Russian	76	Russian (Jewish)	97
Polish	64	Polish	92
South Italian	48	Italian	65

Source: Michael Olneck and Marvin Lazerson, "The School Achievement of Immigrant Children: 1900–1930," *History of Education Quarterly* 14, no. 4 (Winter 1974): 453–82.

With rising family incomes and some degree of assimilation, later-arriving immigrants from Eastern and Central Europe closed the gap between them and other U.S population groups.[101] Declining fertility rates among Italian Americans during the 1920s and 1930s undoubtedly also helped narrow the remaining educational advantage that brothers had over their sisters (table 3.2). By 1950, like their fellow Catholics, Italian girls' high school graduations rates exceeded their brothers'.

Hurrying History: The Effects of Civil War

More than the nation's other wars, the Civil War was a pivot in personal and collective histories of teaching in America. In the South, new arrangements were pasted upon festering, centuries-old traditions, forcing the devastated former Confederacy and several Border States into the nation's public school mainstream—and putting the schoolmistress in place. As for the North, war accelerated the feminization of teaching, as men enlisted or took work in essential industries. In 1859 men were 80% of Indiana's teachers; by 1864, only 58%. Filling war-emptied colleges with women had enduring consequences for higher education.

"Necessity Is a Stern Master"—the End of Southern Exceptionalism

Schooling in the white South in 1850 came from a mosaic of institutional types: subscription-based schools (on the model of lending libraries and fire departments of the time) and private schools (including denominational academies, "collegiate institutes," and seminaries), catering to more advanced pupils, some furnishing one or more promising boys with public scholarships. "Free schools" were charities, like Charleston's, which gave preference "to poor orphans and the children of indigent and necessitous parents." That same year (1812) a group of Newbern (NC) women created the state's first charity for the education of "poor female children."[102] A few other tax-aided schools and state universities completed the picture.

In 1836, when soliciting funds for Georgia Female College, its founder met opposition to educating even higher-status girls. As one critic said, "I would not have one of your graduates for a wife, and I will not give you a cent for any such object."[103] Still, in 1853 Charleston's original 2 "free" schools were grown to 11, with four male and seven female teachers.[104] The longevity of these Charleston teachers—Miss Ann M. Forgartie taught from 1826 to 1856—helped legitimize the system. Mrs. Isabella Blair bested 17 applicants in being chosen teacher of Charleston's No. 6 school. Nonetheless, sectional resistance to common schools on the

New England model persisted. The new (1864) constitution of Maryland providing for public schools would have failed without the votes of Union army soldiers.

Change was forced from without, by Northerners' missionary schools for the freedmen and by federal intentions that provisions for public education appear in new state constitutions. In 1867 there were no functioning state systems of public schools in the South; by 1875, each had a state superintendent, state board of education, and state funding of local schools—usually under $1 per year per enrolled student. Atlanta's first "common school," Ivy Street School, opened in January 1872, with two men and two women—formerly private schoolteachers. Two mission schools for colored children were given over to Atlanta's school board, and more white schools opened. Within seven years Atlanta had the rudiments of a public school system, firmly segregated and meant to educate the colored race to accept its permanently inferior position.

Change also came from within, as when a daughter took paid employment, often over parental opposition. Raised by relatives in postbellum Virginia, 15-year-old Ida Stover (b. 1862) ran away from her guardians to attend high school, working for her room and board. She taught for two years before moving to Kansas with her brothers to enter the new, coeducational Lane University. Her teaching ended with marriage to a fellow student, David Eisenhower.[105]

A sample of education-related newspaper items from Tennessee's Carroll and Weakly Counties, 10 years apart, shows the persistence of antebellum practices (private schools and male teachers) and evidence of changes in where schooling took place, to whom it was given, and by whom dispensed. Relevant items from the *Carroll County Democrat* (June 9, 1893) included the fact that "Miss Kate McNeill, who has been teaching at Cumberland Presbyterian school at Lebanon, returned home" and that the University of Tennessee had concluded "to admit women unreservedly to all the privileges of the university."

The *Dresden Enterprise* (July 24 & 31, 1903) reported that Greenfield residents "Prof. H. L. Higgs and wife and Miss Georgia Shannon are attending the State Teachers Association" and further that the "accomplished daughters of Esq. G. W. Newberry and John Bragg—Misses Bera Newberry and Eunice Bragg—made excellent grades at the recent Teachers Institute." These and the region's many unnamed "Misses" took a path to independence seldom opened to daughters of the Old South. Kentucky's Eugenia Potts wrote in 1893 of the region's aversion to the independent, wage-earning woman that "for a long time no exception was made in favor of school teaching. She might trim bonnets if she kept her shop at home; or if married and abjectly poor taking a few genteel boarders might be forgiven."[106]

Four years of war changed that: the South devastated, nearly 300,000 of its men dead, others maimed, families left leaderless in a traditionally patriarchal society. Of necessity the postwar South's unmarried women, indigent wives, and widows entered the nascent public school system. In 1884, Amelia Lines (b. 1827?), a struggling veteran of the subscription school tradition, wrote to her daughter, Forrest ("Daisy") Lines (b. 1865): "If we live in Macon we shall be obliged to get in the public schools in self defense." Daisy noted that each could earn $60 dollars per month in the public schools of Mobile (AL).[107] A teacher in Georgia, Mississippi, and Florida, Daisy adopted her mother's vocation; her career was, however, shaped by the New South.

Legions of sisters and cousins and "old maids" (so considered if still unmarried at 20) were thrown on their kin or themselves for support. As Margaret Isabella Walker (b. 1824) explained, "The plantation without negroes or stock bringing in nothing, at eighteen I began my life-work, teaching, which lasted with little interruption over forty years . . . [;] the first real pleasure I had was in sending my mother the first hundred dollars I made."[108]

The social and economic disruptions experienced within kinship systems likely changed the consciousness and behaviors of women more than of men. In 1874, Mary Susan Ker's brother Willie first requested she not teach, then proposed she teach near him; she twice declined his advice. While Mary Ker remained traditional in her racial views, she came to support female suffrage and took credit for helping elect a woman school superintendent in 1921. She raised two grand-nieces, one a teacher from 1908 to 1918, who left teaching to work in a bank.[109] However, teaching school offered educated spinster-daughters far more positions than banks or law offices.

Mary Adelaide Bacon glowingly described—in *New England Magazine* (August 1894)—a Georgia normal school as a place that "brings together young women of every social position, shows them the beauty and goodness of labor, trains them for a definite work in life, reveals to them the sacredness of the teacher's calling, and sends them into the common schools of their state to lay a solid foundation for whatever noble superstructure high and aspiring effort may achieve." This "noble superstructure" eventually included coeducational public high schools in all the Southern and Border State, where women, a century after Appomattox, were the faculty majority.[110]

Womanpower on the Union's Home Front

From the war's opening salvos, the Muscantine (IA) school board showed its patriotism by denying contracts to male teachers. Women teachers became the majority in Iowa and Ohio, as "the loss of men from the ranks of teachers began when they were needed to fill up the ranks of Iowa regiments." Pennsylvania's school superintendent proudly noted the high enlistments of his state's teachers in the Union army. Virginia Penny's *Employments of Women* (1863) observed, "Thousands of women, formerly dependent on them [men now soldiers] have lost or may lose their only support. Some . . . may take the vacancies created in business by their absence—others must seek new channels of labor."[111]

Rather than close their doors as their students joined the war effort, various all-male Northern and Midwestern colleges admitted females. Their financial necessity became women's opportunity, relieving men of their near-total hold on higher education, while qualifying women to compete for better high school and even college teaching positions. Something of a male vacuum was also created by the prevailing apprenticeship approach of shop and business owners and by the emerging class of corporate leaders who asserted that a college education for men entering business was irrelevant and even unmanly.[112]

As Northern women settled into vacated places at home, others left for the vanquished South. Even before 1865, the American Missionary Association had been urging single women to go South, to bring a liberating literacy to the children of hopeful freedmen. Yankee women, especially, gave up their roles as "ornaments in their fathers' parlors" to annoy, and seemingly threaten, the erstwhile Confederacy.[113] Over the next century, their example nourished a movement of American women teachers who would take their values and cultures on a global mission.

Conclusion: Revering Motherhood While Yielding to Reality

The Enlightenment, or Age of Reason, promoted in the eighteenth century a modern Western consciousness that perceived childhood as a unique stage of life, one more profound in its implications than children's smallness or dependency. It sanctioned an ideology that enlarged the woman's role as nurturer and teacher, meanwhile placing "child-saving" responsibilities before schools, churches, workplaces, legislative bodies, and courts.[114] The nineteenth century's idealization of the family shifted its moral emphasis—from father, the breadwinner employed in increasingly impersonal sites, to full-time mother, the nurturer in the intimate domestic circle.

In mid-nineteenth-century New York, a state committee made a common distinction between the genders in guiding youth: "While man's nature is rough, stern, impatient, ambitious, hers is gentle, tender, enduring, unaspiring. . . . The woman quickly possesses herself of the affections of the children . . . and this explains the superior success of female teachers with small scholars." The audience attending opening ceremonies of Michigan's normal school in 1853 was told, "A female of practical common sense with amiable and winning manners, a patient spirit and a tolerable knowledge of the springs of human action . . . will do more to inculcate right morals and prepare the youthful intellect for the severer discipline of its after years, than the most accomplished and learned male teacher."[115]

Harmonizing Women's Work and Family Roles

While nineteenth-century feminists might have seen teaching as wholesomely engaging the female mind, the occupation was generally presented as useful, nondistracting training for home life. However, after studying the autobiographical writings of both sexes, Anna Burr concluded in 1909 that "wage earner" belonged among the modern woman's several identities, as one woman in five over age 16 was already employed, most as factory hands and domestic servants.[116] A 1913 book of vocational guidance for girls written by two high school teachers steered a middle course: "while congenial, remunerative work is open to every woman and girl who is obliged to go out into the world as a worker, fortunate indeed is the girl who is not called upon to do this, but who finds her work in her own home."[117]

Nonetheless, even during the 1950s—when intense, unremitting pressures for early marriage and large families left some ambitious women feeling wedged "between the typewriter and the toilet bowl"—women rapidly increased as a percentage of the wage labor force.[118] From 1900 to 2000 there was also a 40-fold increase in married women's employment, a significant part of which was driven by the baby-boom demand for teachers and the collapse of whatever bars to married women teachers existed. Associated demographic and lifestyle changes included a rise (after 1956) in average age of first marriages, higher divorce rates, and political pressures for birth control, wage equity, and day care.

In *What Eight Million Women Want* (1910), Rheta Childe Dorr (b. 1866) challenged the antisuffragist slogan that "woman's place is in the home": "Home is not contained within the four walls of an individual home. Home is the community. The city full of people is the Family. The public school is the real Nursery. And badly do the Home and the Family and the Nursery need their mother." Nonetheless, income-producing work has "felt" more comfortable for the individual woman and public opinion under one or more family friendly, usually overlapping circumstances.

First, history's many varieties of family businesses nudged females toward the wage economy without challenging domesticity per se. In the case of teaching, a married couple takes pupils into its home-as-school, perhaps assisted by daughters as they acquire education and competence. However, with the once-ubiquitous family school largely gone, its present-day approximation, "home schooling," essentially repudiates school.

Second, employing (middle-class) women was more easily justified if seen as a socially sanctified expression of womanly nature, exercising and strengthening those qualities of heart and mind that would enhance her transition from her family of origin to her future family (her predicted destiny). The histories of several stereotypically female professions (especially nursing, social work, and librarianship) have each displayed their own versions of this characterization, with its associated benefits and liabilities.

Third, just as the young woman could be employed in that "fallow period" between the end of her own schooling and her marriage, she could be re-employed in her "empty nest" years. Several family interests were served: finding her best marital prospect, perhaps by working in a larger community, or doing productive, paid work while a future husband is preparing to assume head-of-household responsibilities. The woman's education and training was to be as varied as the work demanded while proportionate to her presumed brief stay in the labor market.

Fourth, employment as a married woman, perhaps even a mother, was accepted as long as it contributed to her family's well-being, perhaps maintaining its integrity when personal misfortune or structural changes in the economy loomed. The woman's vocational education was to be as costly, lengthy, and theoretical as a man's if her potential contribution to the family economy was commensurate.

Each of these four conventions has helped reconcile an idealized domesticity with the economy's demands for women's labor and families' economic needs and structures in a changing America. As surrogate mothers, women schoolteachers drew to education multiple family metaphors—Gertrude included. However, teaching has not been justified for men as a contribution to fatherhood. Despite twentieth-century calls for more men in teaching, "males, typically gym teachers, fit more closely the 'big brother' or . . . 'sports idol,' than the father image." To counter the "unmanly effects" of mothers and women teachers, the Boy Scouts of America and similar organizations became unspoken surrogates for the too-absent father or vanished male teacher.[119]

The Schoolmaster: Largely Gone but Not Forgotten

When, around 1655, Watertown hired Harvard graduate Richard Norris to teach "Children to Reed and Write and soe much Lattin," this mix of duties and clientele suggested the declining status of the Latin grammar school's master.[120] The same theme played out over the next two centuries. As early as 1880, men were the minority on the high school faculties of various cities, their status degraded by the gender of their colleagues and the greater attractions of other work. Although males who were "born teachers" could look to professorships as colleges raised salaries and improved working conditions, these increased more slowly than high school positions and elementary school principalships. A state super-intendent in 1894 qualified his hope that more men would teach by saying, "I do not mean simply men, but the right kind of men."[121]

Nostalgia for an imagined time when teachers were esteemed, larger-than-life figures may have fed on the departures of the many famous or powerful men who once taught school. In concluding that "most of the distinguished men of the North and West taught school at some stage of their careers," historian Lloyd P. Jorgensen names both Wisconsin's revered Robert LaFollette and its now-forgotten three-term governor, Cadwallader Washington.[122] The Norwegian American author O. E. Rølvaag and such icons of American literature as Herman Melville, Robert Frost, and Walt Whitman once taught.[123]

The German-born son of a hard father, perhaps brutalized by poverty, John Peter Altgeld (b. 1847) first escaped home as a Civil War enlistee. Seeking respect, clean work, and good pay, he became a teacher: to "live in that other life . . . where people wore decent clothes and ate enough and seemed so happy, where small children had more learning than he did." His monthly salary of $35 from the Woodville (OH) school board helped save the family farm. Yet after a few months he shed the teacher's black coat and string tie, broke the thin cane he had affected and employed on rowdy students, took odd jobs while roaming west-ward, read law, and finally settled in Chicago as lawyer, judge, Illinois governor, and martyr to liberal politics.[124] Lyndon Baines Johnson, a product of Southwest Texas State Teachers College, taught Mexican American children in Cotulla; he later credited that experience for the education acts in his Great Society programs. Some men, of course, would enter and remain in teaching, responding to various personal or situational factors, including their own successes.

Despite men's historically poor staying power, educators have repeatedly devised schemes to recruit them. Through a concerted effort in the 1890s, Chicago officials increased male elementary school teacher numbers from 1 to 127, and from 80 to 358 at all levels; unassisted, women's numbers rose from 2,725 to 5,167. For six years after World War I, Boston paid the tuition of men who enrolled at private Boston College or Boston University in a special one-year master's de-gree program in secondary teaching—with unknown results.[125] Phi Delta Kappa, a professional fraternity, published a small book in 1939, *Teaching as a Man's Job*. It urged young men to re-enlist in this "man-sized job, one that will take all you can give of intellect, strength, enthusiasm, personality." Readers were reminded that teaching school in America began as man's work.[126]

With girls the majority of high school graduates, and more school failures among boys, in 1909 Leonard Ayres reasoned, "our schools as at present consti-tuted are far better fitted to the needs of girls than they are to those of the boys."[127]

Teachers of both genders have periodically stated that a better-balanced teaching force would be beneficial, and male preferment has remained strong among school officials and the general public. Americans have not cared to hear that the only reliable, and probably the most worthy, source of teaching manpower was womanpower. The slightest increase in male representation bred hope, even incautious predictions.

Generally speaking, motives for choosing teaching or persisting at it proved few and weak among men, while for women they were many and strong. Writing in July 1923, a *Chicago Tribune* editorial writer appeared resigned to women's predominance: "Children are impressionable and plastic. If they develop a feminine viewpoint, it will be because of the unwillingness of men to enter the teaching profession. Evidently the men of today do not care whether America is feminized or not." If a different gendered history of the teaching profession results from events in the twenty-first century, it will most likely be—as it was in the nineteenth century—largely in response to compelling, impersonal forces and events that are, in their individual and societal effects, disruptive and unwanted but also liberating and exhilarating.

CHAPTER 4

"Overflowing from the Domestic Circle"

Individual and Family Factors in Choosing to Teach

> I was the fourth youngest child, and all the others had been teachers, and I was dying to teach school.
>
> —Doris Green, Texas teacher in *Ringing the Children In*

When a New Hampshire man was given a district school in the 1830s, he jokingly referred to himself as a schoolmistress—as he well might, even at this early date. For many, Horace Mann included, it was ordained that women were inescapably drawn to teaching by their "constitution, and faculty, and temperament." Feminists, however, regarded women's employment as giving them a measure of economic and social independence and further education otherwise denied.[1] The president of Bryn Mawr College, Martha Carey Thomas, privately remarked in 1880, "I do not think there is a man who realizes that liberty and money independence and 'life work' are as much to a woman as to himself. Every time I have expressed this to a man he says . . . I always thought that a girl when she fell in love gave up all that and considered her husband's work hers."[2]

American Gertrudes' varied alter egos appeared everywhere: facing rows of restless bodies wedged behind bolted-down desks at P.S. 13 in Jersey City; sneaking a smoke with the male teachers and janitor in the furnace room of one of the nation's many James A. Garfield Schools (Garfield was a former teacher); as the new hire, transporting her teaching materials from one to another classroom at an overcrowded high school; slumped in the corridor as her class goes out for the last recess, wondering whether undoing a sensible lunch with a glazed doughnut from the teachers' lounge will bring on "the shakes" before the 3:10 bell empties the school of all its students and many teachers—the younger to "doll themselves up" for a date, the older to go home, do laundry, and prepare dinner.

Gertrude might even be abroad, answering Argentina's request to help launch its public school system by opening normal schools or helping Sandwich Islands missionaries garb the Hawaiians in Christian morals, manners, and modest dress. But whoever, wherever, and for however long she taught, the prototypical American teacher was, for 150 years, *she*—drawn into that noble profession to "contribute a little more [than the other sex] of those civilizing influences which women exert, and which cannot be estimated by arithmetic."[3]

A disappointing example is the self-described governess—a "poor desolate Exile" on a Selma (MS) plantation in the 1830s, referred to as "being deprived of parents"—although she may have left Pittsburgh after a disappointment in love. Her diary seldom mentioned her students but spoke of her holidays from the schoolroom and parading her refinements: a knowledge of French, musical accomplishments, facility at polite conversation. As for teaching, "must I to the end of my days struggle in this manner against every inclination of my nature, and day after day take up this loathed chain?"[4] In a fully commendable version she is the former teacher in Paradise (CA), saying in 1978, "I believe that the work connected with taking care of children, and the love for children, has been the sustaining force of my life."[5] Neither unique nor typical, both types come from an apparently endless reservoir of women who taught—however well or long.

Countless actual or potential teachers have left a legacy of words, if only a family tale. Laura Ellsworth followed her sister to Cornell University in 1908, without career goals. To the application question, asking her plans after college, she gave a refreshingly candid answer: "Teach." "Why?" "Because they have such long summer vacations."[6] Leavenworth (KS) teacher Ann Elizabeth "Libbie" Burbank found her "vocation" wearing thin. She wrote to a close teacher friend in 1881, wondering whether those (unlike her) who claimed to teach out of love would "have such an attachment to the school room" if the money were withdrawn.[7] Of course, articulated motives, hers included, may be partial, misleading, or even false.

Like preachers, teachers are public possessions, generally inclined to say what is expected of them, creating a story that even they may come to believe. What teachers tell us about their needs and motives is only part of their story. It is not because the historian "knows better" but rather "knows differently"—cognizant in particular of American culture and the distinctive political economy of its educational system. How and why *she* became *Teacher* is the focus of this chapter, interweaving scholars' probes with teachers' accounts, both often revealing male-like motivations and behaviors.

Deciding to Teach School

Teaching children has been lauded as a noble and ennobling calling, an inspired dedication to general enlightenment. This sentiment was nonelitist in that the gift could be "caught" from those who had it and then passed on again—perhaps a reason for its repeated appearance in some families. A Vermont-born veteran Los Angeles teacher, Blanche Wadley Bettington (b. 1901), traced her career to her father's sister, Aunt Vic, who taught their Broom County one-room school for a year—and was also named "one of the eight best teachers in the Province of Quebec." Her Compton (CA) High School teachers included "Miss Godford, one of the two great teachers of my life, [and] Miss Tuttman, Mr. McClelland, Miss Young, my goodness the quality of the teachers." Bettington was understandably proud that a nephew followed her into teaching: "Superb teacher. It's what he likes to do."[8]

Teacher interviews often refer to at least one inspiring person "who ended their somnolence, awakened them to a new way of thinking, or brought them a fresh appreciation of the familiar."[9] Helen Heffernan's address to students at San Francisco State University, probably in the 1930s, inspired one casual listener to choose rural education, teach in an isolated one-room school where her 50 students were the children of Italian immigrants and Native Americans, and adopt her mentor's teaching philosophy: "Because she believed it, because she was my teacher, and because I loved her, I also grew to understand."[10]

A fictional Samantha Yeager spoke for teachers committed to children, despite their dissatisfaction with their own teachers: "I hope I can motivate them better than I was."[11] When interviewed for a television documentary, a New York City teacher stated, "I don't remember wonderful teachers; I remember horrible, mean teachers. And so I became a good teacher—as a way of getting even."[12] Diane Natalico's initial experiences were the opposite: "I loved school, and I can remember only one teacher in all of my elementary school years that I really did not like." However, that passion faded with adolescence—her high school teachers generally "faceless and nameless"—and neither parents nor friends mentioned college.[13]

Like nurses, teachers articulate stereotypical female traits in the reasons for their career choice. Nurturing, for example: "I've always loved children." Tractable and impressionable: "I loved my own teachers and wanted to be like them." Managing: "My father had always said to me that he knew I was going to be a teacher because I used to organize the whole neighborhood [and] play teacher." Emotional: Texas teacher Gladys Peterson decided in third grade that teaching would permit her to indulge forever her love for the smell of Crayolas.[14] But others entered teaching without playing school or particularly caring about children. What Rosie Burney (b. 1921) got from the teachers in her family, her schooling, and Spellman College was intellectual curiosity and a belief in its dissemination—to give love and care was the parent's role, not the teacher's.[15]

With caution one may also explore the impetus and personal "fit" with the teacher role in those who state their firm intentions *not* to teach. Remembered as shy and studious by her Bethlehem (PA) high school classmates, Priscilla Tremper said, "[My father] programmed me on a track that I should go to West Chester State Teachers College or some equal place and become a teacher." The only surviving child of a professor at a men's college, she did not want to teach or even attend a college that prepared teachers: "I never found it particularly exciting, and I never really wanted to teach."[16] She won a partial scholarship to Vassar College in 1952, Vassar did not encourage teaching, and Tremper did not teach.

On the eve of her twenty-first birthday in October 1878, the reasoning of fictional Hilda Lessways reprises what actual women have said and written of their decisions about schoolteaching. She disdained her placid, widowed mother's life, its days "devoted partly to sheer vacuous idleness and partly to . . . everlasting cookery, everlasting cleanliness, everlasting stitchery." But Hilda's voracious reading also disclosed indiscriminate tastes and interests, and a lack of direction. "The sole vocation conceivable for her was that of teaching, and she knew, without having tried it, that she abhorred teaching."[17]

A benign form of aversion found in many self-reports was seeing teaching, initially at least, as the "default" choice. Bloomfield (NY) schoolteacher Delia Bacon (b. 1811) thought her education at Catharine Beecher's school "had prepared her for nothing except, possibly, wifehood in some misty future" or teaching, where she might "prepare other young women for nothing" but marriage and teaching.[18] "Since my home was in a rural area," Villa Fender explained, "I never had much choice other than teaching since I was a woman."[19] Although better-recognized choices existed in the mid-twentieth century, Adria Reich voiced similar resignation: "I was overqualified for stuff like factory work or non-typing clerical work. It wasn't so much that I wanted to be a teacher, but I couldn't imagine being anything else."[20]

The Unplanned, Sometimes Unwanted Choice

Stated reasons for a career choice are often matter-of-fact, thoroughly practical, even resigned or grudging. A 1900 journal article claimed, without credible evidence, that more than half of America's teachers chose teaching as the only way to secure wages, not from a liking for the work. Raised by teacher parents, "Sylvia" viewed her decision to teach as inevitable: "At first I was going to teach art, but I wasn't good enough in art, and then I was going to do special education, but I didn't get along that well with slow students. Then I went into English and all you can do with English is teach, or that's what I thought. So I guess the reason is that I fell into it."[21] "Cleo" discussed teaching with her disapproving family because "a lot of my friends were doing that."[22] Until the later twentieth century, even the eager woman teacher was easily able to explain her choice as rooted in the perception that teaching "was all educated women of my generation did," "it was something to fall back on," or "every girl I knew became a teacher."

In an earlier era, Maria Howland (b. 1836) had used the normal school to escape the near inevitability of factory work. In contrast, one of the factory women studied by the VanVorsts completed the course at the Geneseo (NY) Normal School but found teaching uncongenial: the children "made her nervous."[23] Despite wanting to be a doctor, Bess Akerson (b. 1904) "settled for" education courses and three years of teaching before marrying. By the 1970s women knew more about their options, and "Sally" took education courses so that, as a substitute teacher, she could finance a doctoral degree. She changed her goals with marriage, deciding that graduate school would "take forever," and taught instead.[24] Even longtime teachers recalled their initial resistance to teaching—certainly to its characterization as "women's work."

Doubts often disappeared. At age 10 Annie Elizabeth Johnson (b. 1826) had promised her widowed mother that she would study hard and help care for her siblings. She began teaching in Holloway (ME) in 1840 for $1.50 per week and retired as head of Bradford (MA) Academy in 1894, acknowledging, "I never would have taught if I had not been obliged to, but I have had a good time doing it."[25]

Avowedly reluctant teachers often relate various misfortunes that determined their decisions. Individuals, even entire families, were vulnerable to cataclysmic events—premature death, desertion, bankruptcy—and chronic, debilitating conditions such as ill health. The Kennedy farm in Ireland's County Meath was prosperous in 1833 when Alice Mary was born. Her father's death when she was seven, the famine in the countryside during the 1840s, and the emigration of a brother and sister to New York led her to follow in 1849. For three years Alice Kennedy supported herself with her embroidery needle while preparing to teach. She headed west in 1852, the first among her line of Kennedy women to be American Gertrudes.[26]

In 1911 an early statistical description of factors affecting decisions to teach reported that 20% of men and 25% percent of women had lost one or both parents before entering teaching. A family thus broken apart, it was claimed, "has driven the women who are in teaching to self-support harder than it has driven the men who are in teaching."[27] Four of the five daughters of Dr. E. M. Alverson became teachers. They were left without support when a train crew failed to whistle for a crossing on a bitter winter evening in Illinois in 1899 as their father was returning from an emergency call.[28]

Exploiting Other Interests

Whether brief or protracted, teaching careers often flowed from specific talents and passions. In *Women's Work* (1928), Vera Brittain remarked that specialized interests, not maternal instincts, drew many English women into teaching.[29] American high school teachers often describe themselves as "teaching biology," or some other field, rather than "teaching children." A persisting self-image as a subject-matter specialist has been statistically noted among twentieth-century secondary teachers and among those who make late decisions to teach.[30]

A major figure in Helen Hooven Santmyer's evocative novel, ". . . *And Ladies of the Club"* is Amanda, a lifelong spinster Latin teacher. "Amanda loved to teach, not because she cared particularly for young people in the mass, but because she was so thoroughly imbued with and convinced of, the importance of her subject matter . . . [of] awakening a response in someone."[31] Ruth Marantz said, "I was never one of those teachers who are born to teach. . . . I had no interest in teaching apart from French"—a passion fired by a school counselor. "I'm not really interested in kids, but I want to be the greatest teacher."[32]

By 1925 both Amanda's Latin and Ruth's French were contending with enthusiasts for a more utilitarian and purportedly democratic curriculum. Institutions like George Peabody College for Teachers were determined that music, art, drama, physical education, agriculture, and other practical and mechanical arts enter the public school curriculum. Motivated individuals drawn directly from business and industry could, through cheap and accessible summer sessions, gain the credentials to teach their skills.[33] When public education reached out to skilled craftsmen and secretarial school graduates—to teach in junior and senior high schools and junior (later community) colleges, they were attracting new recruits to teaching, notably working-class and immigrant youth. Miss Wims was her family's expert seamstress when, around 1915, she was hired for the sewing department at Tulsa's new Booker T. Washington High School.[34]

Antioch (SC) Industrial School had a faculty of one male (a lecturer in agriculture) and "eight misses" in 1915. Principal Victor E. Rector intended to alter teacher sex ratios by merging Richland County's small schools, installing a course of study to appeal to farmers and mill workers, and persuading each district to pay "a salary enough to secure a man capable of making the work a success."[35] While vocational education drew more men into secondary education, it did not alter the gender balance in the larger teacher workforce. In addition to home economics, women taught such business subjects as typing and shorthand—a combination that brought the highest enrollments in federally funded vocational education.

Some recruits were normal-school and college graduates equipped to offer the academic core subjects, however reluctantly. Parke Anderson applied in 1926 to be supervisor of public school music in Nashville, having taught in Alleghany County (VA) and all grades at the practice school at a state teachers college. But she wrote, "I . . . wish to be employed in a city system if possible for I want to continue my study in voice training and choir work."[36] Teaching generally supported diverse interests, especially in urban and secondary school settings where continuing training in one's specialty was rewarded and a public platform existed on which to display a teacher's particular talents.

David Riesman mentions a sophisticated mid-twentieth-century widow with an influential father and a "remarkable gift for exciting her pupils' interest in the theatre." She enjoyed a successful career as a high school drama teacher, "proud of her 'graduates on Broadway and in Hollywood.'" Her fellow teachers and the young principal criticized the "professionalism" she inspired and showcased in the school's auditorium—but not that of the sports coach, whose own passions seemingly aroused less ambivalence or envy among his colleagues.[37]

In the days of female seminaries, many a young woman, unmarried aunt, or widow—otherwise ill fitted or inclined to teach academic subjects—was employed, often part time, to offer lessons in fancy sewing, drawing, harp playing, singing, or Italian. Another era brought forth Ruth Appeldoorn Mead (b. 1894), a Chicago Art Institute graduate who pursued a serious career as a painter while teaching in Illinois public schools for 36 years and offering summer classes to children at the Martha's Vineyard Art Association.[38] Verda Delp majored in drama; when asked about the local performing arts groups she regularly brought into her eighth-grade English classes at Willard Middle School in Berkeley (CA), she explained that she wanted to be an actress but was too shy. "But I still love the arts, and I believe a classroom is a reflection of the teacher." Moreover, "what we do in class may be the only arts experience many of these kids will have."[39]

High school sports had become popular enough by 1900 to employ physical education teachers and coaches, and single-sex teams and programs continued to attract male teachers. While some of the first women hired by coeducational colleges taught "physical culture," women's sports programs in high schools and colleges operated on the peripheries. Nonetheless, it was sports that drew "Lee," a rebellious high-school student, to college to prepare to coach and teach. About teaching physical education and reading to younger children and teaching health and driver education to older students, she remarked, "I enjoy being a teacher, but when it comes right down to it, my total enjoyment comes from the coaching."[40]

"No Piano, No School"—the Musician-Teacher

For centuries people experienced music primarily in homes. Learning to read music and play an instrument, most commonly a keyboard, was a mark of social standing and cultural literacy. Despite her widowed mother's small income, Mary Hunter studied music in Carlinville (IL) in the 1870s, noting, "The ability to 'play a few pieces' was, for young ladies, the indispensable accomplishment." Even women "with moderate pretensions had learned to play the piano just as they learned to read, sew, and cook."[41] Around 1918 Vincent Mustacich, an immigrant carpenter supporting a family of five children in Washington State, built a house for a piano teacher as payment for his only daughter's lessons.[42]

Although the Sisters of Providence opened St. Mary's Female Institute near Terra Haute (IN) in 1841 without a piano, Mother Theodore knew that girls' schools had long promoted lady-like accomplishments—"no piano, no school"— and piano instruction appeared.[43] Music attracted many women to schoolteaching or to combining private pupils with part-time employment as a musician. The 1870 census for Burlington (VT) listed a dozen women music teachers— independent teachers, not public school employees. Among schools preparing music teachers, one in Castleton (VT), dating from 1840 to 1860, housed 50 boarders (many Southern) along with its day pupils and gave a high school diploma with an emphasis on teaching music.[44] In 1910 the U.S. census counted 85,000 women "musicians and music teachers"—behind only schoolteachers and "physicians and surgeons"—in the occupational category of professional, technical, and kindred workers. "June Recital" is Jacqueline Hoefer's poem, celebrating "the best music teacher in Monroe County" (IL), Miss Ottilia M. Baltz (b. 1893).[45]

No line existed between musician and private music teacher, and that between musician and schoolteacher was permeable. Carmen Sanabia (b. 1882) received piano lessons as a child in Puerto Rico; on her father's death she helped support the family by taking private pupils. Thereafter, she taught music in public schools, gave private lessons, and organized programs; her earnings helped her own eight children study music in Europe, and five sons became professional musicians.[46] When Eliza McCabe (b. 1886), an experienced (school?) music teacher in Louisiana and Texas, was denied a public school teaching position in 1933 in Tacoma (WA) for being black, she supported herself and her blind husband by giving private piano lessons.[47] Teachers, of course, augmented their income by taking private pupils after school and in summers.

Public performance—in high school assemblies and plays, as band director, church organist, or choral director—lent teachers extra status, visibility, and satisfaction. Although the Great Depression made private lessons a luxury, pianos remained staples in kindergartens. More than half the rural schools in Texas had a piano in 1935.[48] Yet despite a 30-year career as a high school music teacher, the protagonist in the 1995 film *Mr. Holland's Opus* still saw himself as a musician and composer. As he told his principal, teaching was "something to fall back on."[49]

Teaching School: A Public Good, and Pleasing to Domestic Harmony

In 1894 the superintendent of teacher preparation of the Louisville (KY) Free Kindergarten Association exceeded claims that teaching enhances a woman's maternal, domestic, and civic capabilities: "Regardless of whether one wishes to teach or not, it is universally conceded that a course in kindergarten training is of the greatest value to every woman." One of her students agreed: "this training can not fail to color and strengthen her whole after-life, whether she becomes a wife and mother, a schoolteacher, or one of those 'unappropriated blessings' who tender such faithful service to friends, kindred, neighbors and the community at large."[50]

In 1858, the Board of National Popular Education reported on the 481 Protestant schoolmistresses it sent west. The 75 who "defected" by marrying have supplied "good wives to . . . many gentlemen of the West"; in their new roles they would continue their ameliorative mission. In 1864 the *New York Evangelist* took the same line: "in regard to forsaking the teacher's office for domestic alliances . . . every such departure can be made good by new recruits, who will find their best friends and firmest supporters in their predecessors, settled around them as the wives and mother of the most influential members of society."[51]

Although "enhancing one's domestic capabilities" was not a likely motivator for many teachers, prevailing ideas of woman's sphere necessarily affected the private and public identities of the individual woman. Nora Stewart, herself betrothed, railed against the calumny shown those who, like her three sisters, were unmarried teachers. "I believe some get so tired of hearing their names bandied back and forth as 'old maids,' and of . . . hateful insinuations that they are willing to marry most any stick for protection."[52]

Chicago teacher Sarah Bigelow, editor of the Mt. Holyoke Class Letter, responded to a classmate's suggestion that "the unmated portion of the Class of 1851" get married, by describing permanently unmarried schoolma'ams as the biblical "saving remnant," the sea anchor of the teaching profession. As for herself, "8:45 finds her in Forest Avenue School, third floor, No. 5, where for six hours daily she dispenses knowledge to 33 incipient Lords of Creation and 30 of the gentler sex thus doing her part to forestall the nation's 'relapse into barbarism' and [to] make future teachers, most from the gentler sex."[53]

As the independent-minded daughter of a well-loved, competent mother and a problematic father, Louisa May Alcott (b. 1832) valued single women. She commented in her diary on her article: "'Happy Woman' was the title, and I put in my list all the busy, useful, independent spinsters I know, for liberty is a better husband than love to many of us." Alcott put off marriage altogether, although her novels compromised her ideals and moderated the domestic realities of most women's lives. Under the weight of received wisdom about female happiness, publishers "won't let authors have their way, so my little women must grow up and be married off in a very stupid style."[54]

E. D. E. N. Southworth (b. 1819) was a Washington (DC) teacher before her 1840 marriage. A betrayed and abandoned wife and mother who returned to teaching to support her children, Southworth published prolifically (e.g., *The Fatal Marriage, The Deserted Wife, Retribution*). Such novels advised would-be brides to "watch well the first moments when your will conflicts with his to whom God and society have given the control." Southworth's heroines, who once thought themselves man's equal, were made "little better than a bondswoman" by the marriage ceremony, each husband given "a lifelong authority to transgress over his victim-wife."[55]

To "escape a life of servitude and tedium," apparently like her own, Miss Mayhew, an experienced governess, advised her younger colleague Miss Bronwen Penny to encourage her schoolmaster suitor, who intended to marry her when his situation permitted. While "marriage itself is servitude, the recompense is better than any other employment, and the position is permanent."[56] Yet marriage itself was neither invariably fulfilling nor permanent.

When Marriages End: Death, Divorce, Desertion

Sarah Stiles—nine years married, with one child and a struggling husband—was, in 1715, the first schoolmistress in Windsor (CT). In 1735 she was succeeded by her widowed mother. Widows in Quaker records include Widow Mellor and Debby Godfrey, to whom officials may have sent some poor children as acts of charity.[57] In her autobiographical novel, *Ruth Hall: A Domestic Tale of the Present Time* (1855), popular author Fanny Fern (Sara Willis) condemns a local board of education, forever quarrelling over trifles, stymied by personality conflicts, and too distracted to judge fairly whether the widowed Mrs. Hall is qualified to teach their school.[58] Scottish-born Isabelle Moodie (b. 1844) had been a Latin teacher before her marriage to William Frost, teacher, journalist, editor, gambler, and drunkard. When he died in San Francisco in 1885, she returned to Massachusetts with their daughter and 10-year old son, Robert Lee. She first taught a fifth-grade class in Lawrence, attended by her children. In 1893, Robert Frost was teaching Latin and other subjects in "a school of rough boys."[59]

In Ohio Alice Louise Pierce (b. 1860) was boarding with Mrs. Early in 1882 while her fiancé was in Oregon, establishing himself and preparing to send for her. "Mrs. Early and I were talking . . . and I said that I should never come back. She said don't talk so[;] you may be left a widow and come here and go to teaching."[60] Suitors, husbands, and fathers who went "westering" often left their womenfolk to support themselves. William Hiller had moved his family from New York to Virginia before "gold fever" returned his wife to teaching. An established professional before her marriage in 1842, Abiah Warren Hiller (b. 1805?) and their children coped with his four-year absence. "Her truly independent spirit" was passed onto two daughters who also taught.[61] Even after premature death ceased to be an everyday event, Lucille Ellison's 1937 *Kansas Teacher* article, "When a Teacher Weds," repeated the feminist's point: "I wish marriage to play the same part in my life that it does in the life of a man, and before marriage to be prepared for a possible incompetency on the part of my husband, as well as for widowhood."[62]

From colonial times and in all regions, women initiated most divorces.[63] In Franklin County (IN), Laura Fansworth Frampton's friends applied for her divorce from her alcoholic first husband in 1832: "thus I was lawfully freed from one who had been destroyer instead of protector." Frampton supported herself and her child "by [her] needle and teaching school" until 1837, when she married Mr. Owen, "a man of steady habits."[64] The often-seen family disruptions caused by untimely deaths were, toward the century's end, precipitated by divorce. Experience, popular fiction, and government statistics—1 in every 22 marriages dissolved in 1880, 1 in 9 by 1916—confirmed the instability of marriage and family life in a society in flux.[65]

Desertion also appears in many life histories—a simpler, cheaper alternative to divorce and sometimes concealed by an acceptable fabrication. A favorite was "your husband (or father) was killed by Indians on his way home to you (us)." Lella Secor, born into a Michigan working-class family in 1887, was urged to become a teacher by her mother, a deserted wife. Instead she became a journalist, feminist, birth control advocate, and pacifist.[66]

Unwed—by Misfortune or by Design

Catharine Beecher, some of whose teaching wages may have been intended for her trousseau, returned to teaching after her fiancé's death in 1822 to prepare other young women to be self-supporting teachers: set on "the road to honorable independence and extensive usefulness" yet within "the prescribed boundaries of feminine modesty."[67] A cobbler's daughter, occasional domestic servant, and teacher in Maine, West Virginia, and South Carolina, Sarah Jane Foster (b. 1839) was one of seven surviving children in a humble but ambitious family. One brother was a minister, another a doctor, and one sister a nurse. Sarah remarked, "Families that try to rise as we have seldom do marry." She rejected "domestic slavery" for herself: she would not join in praise of "women who toil every moment and never spend an hour in self-cultivation. I will never be such a drudge."[68] Many of the unmarried, however, appeared ambivalent about the single state: both wistful and defiant.

Late eighteenth-century British feminist, George Gissing knew the plight of unwed well-educated, middle-class English women. His younger sisters, Ellen and Margaret, had "faded into bitterly religious, narrow-minded, and conventional spinsters," resigned to "sporadic and desultory attempts at teaching or working as governesses." In plotting his novel, *The Odd Women* (1893), he made the pivot Elkanah Madden's failure to ensure his six daughters' future should he die (as happened) before marrying them off.[69] Isabel became a board (state) schoolteacher, working herself into illness and suicide at age 22; Alice a nursery-governess; and Virginia a companion to an ailing gentlewoman. Two others sisters died. The youngest, Monica, made a tragic marriage rather than suffer her sisters' fates.

Mary Warner Moore (b. 1862), with a young son and pregnant again, left her husband in 1887 after his institutionalization in a mental asylum. She returned to the Missouri home of her clergyman father and, after his death, combined a small inheritance with teaching English at a Presbyterian girls' high school in Carlisle (PA). She resisted family pressures for a marital reconciliation and put her son through Yale and her daughter, Marianne, through Bryn Mawr (class of 1909). After five years of teaching, Marianne left the profession to make her reputation as poet Marianne Moore. This family history likely contributed to Moore's description of marriage as an "enterprise . . . requiring all one's criminal ingenuity to avoid."[70] In the English novel *I'm Not Complaining*, Madge, a teacher, remains single after seeing the hope ("the old, tinsel-trimmed fairy tale") contrasted with the reality ("the shoddy wreck . . . in the gray light of day").[71]

The Supportive and the Confining in Teachers' Families

Family connections have a long history in teaching. In eighteenth-century Germany, qualified widows and daughters of deceased schoolmasters were authorized to teach.[72] In some neighborhoods in late nineteenth-century London, teachers' children were 10% or more of apprenticing teachers. Margaret Berry, trained at the Dublin Normal Schools, was teaching in New South Wales, Australia, in the 1850s and later at the Brisbane Normal School, where her sister, Eliza, was being prepared. When Queensland's teachers organized, Margaret and Eliza Berry were signatories.[73]

From colonial times, devout Catholic daughters were led into a new "family," one very different from that known at home: the celibate sisterhood's well-ordered community, the mystery of the Holy Spirit, and the honor conferred by a religious vocation. Christian service fitted nuns for nursing and social work but especially for teaching, where they could also "reproduce" their replacements. Most of the 180,000 members of women's religious communities in the United States in their peak year, 1965, were teaching sisters.[74]

Teaching families were as diverse and well distributed as American teachers overall. The daughter of freed slaves, Edmonia Highgate (b. 1844) taught in Pennsylvania and the colored school in Binghamton (NY) in the 1860s, before teaching in freedmen's schools. Her teaching colleagues in Maryland, Louisiana, and Mississippi sometimes included her two sisters and her widowed mother.[75]

Occupational Inheritance

As master of the free school at Fishponds, Stapleton (England), Jacob More could not give his five daughters dowries, so he educated them as schoolmistresses. In 1757 the eldest, Mary, founded the flourishing school in Bristol at which the More sisters passed on their impressive learning to their pupils and one another.[76] As in the skilled crafts and professions generally, teaching runs in families. At one point the dame schools of Northampton (MA) were in the hands of the Parsons cousins, members of one extended family: Hannah, daughter of Jacob; Rachel, daughter of Isaac; and Prudence, daughter of Josiah—each teaching in her own home.[77]

The families of Thomas Day and his wife, Lucy Sistaire—with Joseph Neef, his wife, son, and four daughters—were the initial teachers at Robert Owen's utopian community of New Harmony (IN) in the 1820s.[78] From 1854 to 1856, Gertrude Lawrence Hoyt, a clergyman's widow, and her son, a failed gold miner and farmer, had one of the early "Anglo-era" schools in Los Angeles; her daughter, Mary Hoyt, arrived in 1856 and opened another school. For 75 years of Nevada's history, some member of the family of Mildred Bray (b. 1892) was a teacher, principal, or state superintendent.[79] At their sister Thelma Yandell's urging—she wanted someone to talk with about her work—Edith and Betty followed her to Missouri's Logan-Rogersville District; when they retired they had 111 years of teaching among them.[80]

As examples of family proclivity to teaching are many and varied—and cross-cultural—the Peabody-Mann families are unique primarily in their celebrity status. Horace Mann's older sister, Rebecca Mann Pennell (b. 1787), taught and married a teacher. When Mann went to Ohio as founding president of Antioch College, for his initial faculty of six he recruited three of Rebecca's four children: Rebecca Pennell (Mrs. Dean), Eliza Pennell (Mrs. Blake)—both early graduates of Lexington Normal School—and college-educated Calvin Smith Pennell. In turn, Eliza's son, Henry Gardiner Blake (b. 1845) taught in St. Louis and Ramsey County (MN). Various Blake descendants gave birth to teachers or married teachers—one, the father of Betty Bull Waldhauer, married three times, twice to teachers. Betty Waldhauer, who taught around raising a family, thought she saw a budding teacher or two among her grandchildren, the eighth generation.[81]

Of a Virginia farming family, James Best Dodd (b. 1807) fathered a teaching dynasty that began, Southern style, with male teachers in private and public schools, colleges, and Methodist church-education programs. His three sons taught, mostly in Kentucky and Tennessee; one, Virginius Wesley Dodd, sired a flock of teachers covering several generations. The two surviving children of James Dodd's second marriage, Flora and Lida, were spinster teachers who opened Miss Dodd's Select High School in Denver in 1895. After the Spanish American War, Flora taught Latin and mathematics at Key West Seminary, a school for Cuban children sponsored by the Methodists' Woman's Board of Home Missions.[82]

While many sons and daughters followed relatives into teaching, doing so was more significant for women. Far more mothers than fathers became teachers, and modern research shows mothers' occupation the best predictor of daughters' careers.[83] "Elizabeth" was probably typical in adopting her mother's "educational philosophy and framework for classroom actions."[84] The devoutly Catholic Zerwekh family produced six daughters, three becoming teaching nuns in Dominican or parochial schools. Women religious also modeled teaching behavior and encouraged teaching "vocations"—professed and lay—among their surrogate children.[85]

Investing in Daughters

Traditionally, education-minded families planned for their sons' education, expecting or hoping their daughters would marry or remain contented "house daughters." In Hosea Stafford's *An Astronomical Diary, Kalendar, or Almanack for 1789,* he advised fathers to marry their daughters off as soon as possible: "Daughters and dead Fish, are no keeping Wares." British author John Ruskin (b. 1819) said more generally, "If a woman can neither have a home of her own, nor find occupation in any one else's she is deeply to be pitied; her life is bound to be unhappy."[86] Nevertheless, as early as the 1840s, a nearly silent revolution was underway as women teachers reached "a higher level of self-sufficiency than practically any other group of women in their time."[87]

Families of origin have provided teachers by sufficiently schooling daughters and sons to become familiar with, and develop a taste for, the teachers' duties. As daughters of a clergyman, the three surviving Brontë sisters—Charlotte, Emily, and Ann—were schooled as a matter of course, held various teaching positions, and became published authors. In *Jane Eyre* and *Agnes Grey* respectively, Charlotte and Anne drew upon their experience as governesses. Spared her sisters' fate in dying in young womanhood, Charlotte (1816–1855) also "remade" herself, traveling comfortably in urbane British literary circles, psychologically freed of the parsonage at Haworth and the Yorkshire moorlands of Emily's *Wuthering Heights*.[88]

A Mormon, Isaiah Coombs (1834–87) was a career teacher in Illinois and Utah, fathering 20 children by three wives. He ensured that, as teachers, all could make their own ways, contribute to the family income, and help younger siblings. Of his eldest, Ida, the surviving of twin girls, and her brother, Isaiah Mark, Coombs wrote:

> April 28 (1883)—Ida came home on the train this morning. She had been in Provo attending schoolteacher's convention. Isaiah was there and gave a lecture on drawing with which Ida was dreadfully pleased. . . . Ida gave me $60.00 this morning. God bless her liberal heart.
>
> November 11—Isaiah returned to Provo this afternoon, taking Gladys with him who will enter the Academy as a student for the balance of the school year. Fanny takes care of the telegraphy off[ice] here and pays Gladys' tuition and board. Ida will clothe her. What God-like children have I.[89]

Despite Greek Americans' high regard for their Orthodox clergy, Herriclia Eliades's working-class parents, especially her mother, rejected both the conservative, gendered theology and the class-based presumptions that she would leave school early and enter a Lowell textile mill.[90] Instead, she attended Lowell Normal School, becoming the school's first Greek American woman to graduate (in 1926), a public school teacher, and a role model. Irene Shapiro Goldenberg's older siblings helped her through Brooklyn College; after graduating in 1933 she responded in turn. This was expected of educated daughters, often acting out the "unattainable desires" of their elders, especially their mothers.[91]

Ambitious families had either to see their daughters make satisfactory marriages or acquire education leading to respectable, secure employment—something that might, incidentally, also improve their marriageability. A Boston maid before her marriage and in Worcester during her widowhood, Marie Haggerty (b. 1867) told an interviewer in 1939, "Pa and I didn't have much education, but we wanted our children to so they could have a chance to become high-class people. . . . We sent Kitty, my youngest daughter to Normal School, because Pa always wanted one of his daughters to be a schoolteacher."[92]

From 1887 to 1925, at least 75%'s of Arizona's Territorial (then State) Normal School's students were females in most years. As one explained, "My father said that he knew I could always take care of myself if I could teach . . . and the pay was good for a woman."[93] In the later nineteenth century, Minnesota farmers began sending their daughters to the Winona State Normal School for sufficient schooling and training for self-support.[94] Of course, some parents undoubtedly questioned their daughters' educational ambitions, because white middle-class sons could still prosper in 1900 without attending school beyond age 14.

When Kate Leila Gregg (b. 1883) used her savings from teaching to attend the university, her father "sulked in the barnyard and refused to say goodbye. He was indignant to see me throwing away my money." When she returned three years later, she found him taking some credit for her achievements.[95] Anna Frucht (b. 1902) recalled her businessman father's response to her wish to teach. While he probably hoped to keep the family circle tight, he dwelt on Rhode Island's low salaries and Anna's diminutive stature. "Frankly, Anna, you're a little girl, and some of the kids are tough in school, and all that, and I don't think it will be good for you."[96]

Negro parents were particularly aware of the hard truths of a new economic order. In 1908, when cooks—the highest-paid domestics—earned around $200 a year, teachers in the segregated elementary schools in Washington (DC) averaged $589, while the high schools paid $984.[97] Educated Negro women were far more likely to teach than do office work, for there were more one-room country schools needing a teacher than Negro businesses able to hire a full-time secretary. Opal Seales's family was one where "putting sister through" normal school or teachers college was a family project. Her mother sold part of their Oklahoma farm to pay Opal's college expenses.[98] Teaching offered respectability, safety, and clean work. Accordingly, Negro women "overchose" teaching, even more than did the Irish. They eventually completed every level of schooling, from grade school through university degrees, at higher rates than Negro men.

A self-reliant but dutiful daughter's return to the family household, perhaps to care for an ill parent or a brother's motherless children, could be wrenching. Isabella Godding (b. 1837) first taught at Augusta and Gardner (ME) after leaving Mt. Holyoke College in 1857. Of her position at Brooklyn's scholastically elite Girls' High School, she wrote, "My associations there were with delightful women in the corps of teachers and the students were girls of most interesting Character." This ended when she was called home to care for her widowed father. "The arrangement seems to be giving him a happy old age for at 92 he has a deep enjoyment of life while I find the change in my own surroundings very limited when compared to my life in New York. . . . It was not an easy thing to do when I thus turned away from the privileges and delights which had been mine [for] thirty-three years."[99]

Teaching—a License to Roam

In 1800, when more than 90% of Americans lived east of the Appalachian range, many were already turning their faces toward the "Old Northwest Territories."[100] Yankees from worn-out farms headed west, the village-raised tried their luck in towns, and city dwellers proved an unstable population.[101] "Movement," George Pierson convincingly argues, "has always been a major ligament in our culture, knit into the bone and sinew of that body of experiences which we call our history."[102] Single women teachers roamed the continent. Although the American "heartland" (notably Indiana) was slower to convert to women teachers than was its "brain" (New England), Vermont's Miss Susan Griggs (b. 1816) presided over Indiana's Wolcottville Seminary for its 16-year existence, preparing and inspiring local girls to teach—and perhaps to venture forth. She and other Gertrudes helped increase women among Indiana's teachers: from 25% (1855) to 40% (1870).[103]

Of New England stock, Laura Ingalls's father took his family from Wisconsin to Kansas, Minnesota, Iowa, and South Dakota where, still in girlhood, Laura taught her first rural school. In 1885 she married Almonzo Wilder, and in 1894 the couple traveled by covered wagon for 55 days, settling permanently in Wright County (MO)—the journey paid for not by her teaching wages but by the dollar a day she earned at dressmaking. Countless children reading her stories of growing up in the *Little House on the Prairie* or *Little House in the Big Woods* would relive America's saga of a seemingly endless process of rerooting and uprooting.[104] While restlessness is associated with men, travel lectures were among the most popular extracurricular activities of the female majority at the California State Normal Schools—most of whose parents had, like the Ingalls and Wilders, started life elsewhere.[105]

Describing his western travels in the 1890s, Robert Louis Stevenson wrote of the unnamed schoolma'am who boarded at the Toll House in California's Napa Valley, "walking thence in the morning to the little brown shanty, where she taught the young ones of the district, and returning thither pretty weary in the afternoon. She had chosen this outlying situation, I understood, for her health." Although "the school-ma'am, poor lady, had to work pretty hard all morning: in the afternoons she subsided . . . into much the same dazed beatitude as all the rest"—sometimes, wrote Stevenson, with "other schoolma'ams enjoying their holidays, quite a bevy of damsels."[106]

Troubled family relationships sometimes prompted flight. Lucy Virginia Smith (b. 1825) and her sister left their lawyer father's cultured household in Accomac County (VA) around 1844, as they could not abide their stepmother. The sisters taught in Memphis (TN) until 1852, when Lucy married a wealthy man who was attracted to her published verse.[107] Even in happier homes, daughters were made restless—by a brother's departure, ambitions raised at school or by companions, a lack of suitable or interesting friends, or "something in the air." With three brothers in the Union army and her favorite sister teaching away from home, 15-year-old Sirene Bunten (b. 1847) viewed teaching as breaking away, even briefly, from the dullness of a too-familiar West Virginia life. "I wonder if it would be very agreeable work to teach the 'young ideas how to shoot' &c."[108]

The president of Amherst College probably did not much overdramatize the scene in nineteenth-century (and later) households where fathers would ask, "'Is not your father's house a pleasant home to you? . . . Why do you wish to leave us?' The daughter pleaded that a younger sister would be company . . . ; that she could be spared, and not much missed; that, in some other spot, she might minister to the wants of young minds; and by such considerations would win the father's consent to her departure."[109]

Gail Collins concludes that "the history of American women is all about leaving home. . . . The center of our [women's] story is the tension between the yearning to create a home and the urge to get out of it."[110] Something in their temperaments or surroundings prompted innumerable schoolma'ams to leave home. For some it was loneliness and isolation felt most by farm women—especially as farms grew larger with mechanization, and neighbors more distant. A 1912 *Atlantic Monthly* article observed that the wife and mother had once compared herself with a pioneer grandmother and felt grateful. But now, made aware of the discrepancy between town and country living standards, restless young women were part of a significant group of the country-raised, financially independent "renegades from family life" who constituted about 20% of urban employed women in 1900.[111]

When Margaret Moninger left Iowa for China in 1915 as an educational missionary, she had never been farther from home than Grinnell College and Des Moines. Alice A. Langer went to the Soviet Union to teach at a girls secondary school in Navra when the Bolshevik revolution was still fresh in memory.[112] However, an adventuresome temperament appears less common than the scarcity of nearby positions, the higher wages elsewhere, or the improvement of

one's health or comfort. Regardless, going out among strangers took initiative—
"pluck," as they called it. How ironic that her putatively conservative and cir-
cumspect occupation gave the schoolteacher a "cover" under which to travel and
live, apart from family, in distant, sometimes dangerous places.

To Taste the White Bread of Independence

The relative elasticity of America's societal norms permitted even timid women a
wider sphere of work and an unforeseen degree of self-realization through keeping school and helping create other ladies' professions. Before the Woman's Congress at the Columbian Exposition in Chicago in 1893, a twice-married Texas
teacher, superintendent, and school founder, Sue Huffman Warren Brady spoke
of a "magical uprising" and a "wide awake womanhood" whose products "eat the
white bread of independence, and who carry the lantern of hard-earned experience, lighting the way to higher, truer, broader views of life."[113]

"The Woman's Invasion" was how *Everybody's Magazine* headlined a 1908
article purporting to explain the explosive growth of employed women over
the previous quarter century. The disapproving author described three types
of "recruiting stations." One was " 'Destitution,' " where "penniless women had
been forcibly conscripted." Another was " 'Higher Standard of Comfort,' " where
women "enlisted for the purpose of supplementing the family income, because,
while their mothers were contented with bare floors and tin dishes, they themselves, with growing self-respect, demanded carpets and china." At the third recruiting station "there has been employed a full brass band, which played a tune
called 'Economic Independence,' with endless variations; and a certain number
of women . . . had been solemnly sworn in to support themselves."[114]

After gold was discovered in 1859 in the surrounding mountains, Bodie (CA)
quickly became home to 10,000 residents, 67 saloons, several brothels, a lesser
number of stores, and a schoolhouse. Whether she got as far west or as high up
as Bodie, the westering schoolma'am defied norms. Frontier histories and popular culture portray women as noble sufferers, brought along by male dreamers: submissive wives and daughters doing what their menfolk chose for them.
But American Eves, as well as Adams, went west willingly—independent, self-
realizing, and overcoming family objections if necessary.[115] Unlike Emerson's
"real Americans," however, rather than rejecting schools and libraries, laws or
government, these female rebels hastened their spread.[116]

Poised between her Keokuk (IA) school and the likelihood of being recalled
to her former position in Chicago, around 1872 Mary Julia Towne voiced an
"unwomanly" bravado in writing to her always supportive mother: "I am going
to get over all squeamishness about spending . . . my money, and get all the

enjoyment I can out of it!!" A decade later her mother advised Mary Julia (now Mrs. Redington) on how to accustom her new husband to her having been an autonomous, self-supporting teacher for 14 years. Tell him, she wrote, "You had been accustomed to using your own money as you liked and would like some now to do like wise. I presume he would be willing to give you a few doll[ar]s weekly or monthly if you proposed it. I wish you had some of your own."[117]

Despite the hard winters and remote train stops of rural Butler County (KS), Nellie Purle Cronk (b. 1883) changed her school district frequently, typically to one with higher wages. White Station District 2 paid her $35 a month in 1903; Silverton, $39 in 1904; Welcome District, $45 in 1905; and De Graft School, $60 by 1908. Only in 1917 did Miss Cronk move "to town"—El Dorado, 1930 population 10,365—teaching there until 1948.[118] After two years at the state normal school branch at Chico (CA), Laura Carman (b. 1891) first taught at Clear Creek in Butte County in 1912. Clear Creek's bachelors were happy to escort Miss Carman and Miss Harriet Cape of the Stoneman School in Roundvalley to events such as a trip to the Stirling City Hotel for dinner. However, her move to Lovelock involved her in a somewhat larger social group of the young, and with each successive move her earnings improved. For example, her school across the Oregon state line, near Lakeview, paid $125 a month, a generous amount in 1919. As Mrs. Bowles she retired from the Paradise Ridge School in 1958, eight miles from where her career began.[119]

The Yankee women leaving home in the mid-nineteenth century, in part because of an excess of teachers, had their 1970s counterparts in those who went to Victoria (Australia)—spurred by the first American teacher surplus since the Great Depression. While a few gave up tenured positions—"I'm good and I can always get a teaching job"—most were novices. About 6,000 trained American teachers from 22 states staffed schools swollen by immigration and a liberalization of secondary education. Compared to British and Canadian recruits, American teachers fared better, especially the less blasé and rural Midwesterners, who found Australia appealingly exotic. About 1,000 Americans, mostly women, settled permanently in Australia.[120] But, wherever she had taught, the schoolma'am gained financial self-sufficiency and personal discretion well before secretaries and other urbanized women workers. Importantly, their female pupils had an alternative, undomesticated model to contemplate.

Teachers Make Teachers

"You are aware that in Hawthorne's day, when great objects were to be sought it was the men who sallied out in search, in sevens, and the women (when they went at all) went in solitary ones." So began Kate Warthen's address to a high school graduation ceremony in Hamilton County (KS) around 1893. As county school superintendent, she was there—on "this day of woman's progress" before "this class of lovely, learned girls"—also to commend the one "brave hearted boy" present to receive a diploma.[121] As state and local governments funded free public high schools, more Americans were exposed for longer periods of their young lives to the influence of teachers and school culture. Economic historian Colin Burke views high schools—and the normal schools and state teachers colleges to which increasing numbers were led—as institutions with justified appeal and high relative value. Given the then-low knowledge level of most teachers, "just bringing students to the high school knowledge level was a positive and ready contribution."[122]

Girls who considered becoming teachers—or were drawn to other "well-spoken," new, and expanding female positions such as telephone operators, office workers, and department store clerks—had ample reason to persist in high school, given the economic, sociopolitical, and demographic factors previously discussed. While students of either gender might take inspiration and guidance from a male teacher, there were progressively fewer men to link school in a boy's mind with a future vocation. Even the girls who "fell in love" with a male teacher or saw him as a father figure were less likely to become teachers than those who could identify with a woman teacher.

In the 1920s, with no high school near their Texas farm, Josephine Ballard's parents boarded her in nearby Gatesville (population 2,500). When a drought upset her plans, she persuaded her family to let an elderly couple employ and board her. Rising at four each morning, she made the family's breakfast, cleaned the house, and milked and pastured the cow before walking to school. Her after-school chores were to milk the cow again, gather eggs, feed the chickens, prepare supper, and wash the dishes. Only then was she free to do her school homework. Ballard graduated in 1926, qualified to sit the examination for a third-grade county certificate—good for two years, renewable, and enabling her to teach grades 1–6.[123]

High school and normal school enrollments offered the nation's colleges and universities enormous potential for their own growth. No matter that Harvard's President Eliot warned that "generations of civil freedom and social equality" must elapse to know whether females' "natural tendencies, tastes, and capabilities" would meet collegiate standards. No matter that Harvard's Barrett Wendell thought his colleagues would suffer "mental deterioration" if they were to teach the young women of the affiliated Radcliffe College.[124] No matter that Martha Carey Thomas, the rigorously intellectual president of Bryn Mawr College, opposed practical courses, including child study and pedagogy, as softening the curriculum.[125]

Addressing a gathering of college alumnae in 1915, the dean of a university school of education pointed out that, for the young woman contemplating alternative careers, only teaching presented "the logical and familiar continuation of a smooth and well-traveled road, over which she has been passing since her first day at school. She knows the inside of schoolrooms and what teachers are likely to do or leave undone. She can easily inform herself concerning the conditions that must be met" to stand in her teacher's place.[126]

Conclusion: A Veritable Florescence of Teachers and Schools

At her Seder table in the 1980s, retired New York City teacher Frances Levy looked around at her own teaching dynasty. Of the 20 family members present, spanning four generations, 16 were teachers, and a great-granddaughter was preparing to teach. This awareness affirmed Mrs. Levy's pride and faith that "despite everything, teaching still holds an attraction for many young women."[127] These and the other women acknowledged in this volume enlisted in a movement that changed the educational landscape, bringing universal primary and secondary schooling earlier than would have been possible otherwise. Moreover, by their matriculation in normal schools, colleges, and universities, they and their female students provided a significant impetus for a more democratic higher education.[128]

Sending their children to school—and keeping them there long enough to demonstrate sufficient knowledge, desirable work habits, and some respect for persistence—was a strategy that more parents adopted. Education was the ready answer for all manner of personal contingencies and social problems. Question: what to do about the potentially delinquent children of the urban poor—"street arabs" to Americans, "apaches" to the French? Answer: enforce school attendance. Sir Arthur Conan Doyle has Sherlock Holmes describe London's big, new, working-class schools as "Lighthouses . . . Beacons of the future! Capsules, with hundreds of bright little seeds in each, out of which will spring the wiser, better England of the future."[129]

For millions of women worldwide, teaching presented multiple opportunities, challenging work, and flexibility. Individual careers spanned weeks, years, and decades. Should they chose to retire to the parlor or the nursery, they were not disadvantaged for having ventured beyond the domestic sanctuary. However protracted their careers, they widened a little the pathway for their followers. Teaching offered financial self-sufficiency if not profligacy, the opportunity to serve others, an escape from the entirely familiar. It gave women, often very young, the adult right to make choices, as increasingly more men had done since the collapse of feudalism.

Teachers were created by desperation, accident, and design. They married or did not; when married, some retired, permanently or temporarily, while others balanced wifehood, even motherhood, with a classroom life. Hometown posts satisfied some, while others were pedagogical gypsies. Those whose names brought a tear to the eye and a lump to the throat of a grateful former pupil co-existed with the quickly forgotten time servers and burned-out cases, the marginally effective, wrongly placed, or merely unlucky. Some knew too little of the teaching craft, while others commanded too much knowledge to dispense it artfully. Their variety extended from effectively independent professionals to wage slaves, from the cocky to the cowed.

Janie Richardson, an African American, and Soledad Lujan, a Filipina, were career teachers whose obituaries were printed in the same newspaper on September 4, 1998.[130] As Sister Adrian Maria, SNJM, Soledad Lujan was a professed religious, bound by the rules of her order, set within an often medieval-seeming and unremittingly patriarchal church, historically Europe's first bureaucracy. Soledad Lujan taught first grade for 52 years, nearly as long as Janie Richardson's life span. In contrast, Richardson, a public school teacher and principal, experienced the iron rule of a different kind of bureaucracy and in a particularly dysfunctional urban school setting. As chapter 5 will detail, America's Good Gertrudes were, from birth, blessed or burdened with all degrees of ethnic, racial, and class backgrounds.

CHAPTER 5

"An Honorable Breadwinning Weapon"

Who Became Teachers?

"You," she told me . . . "are going to be the teacher I could not
become." But . . . it was "teacher" and not doctor or lawyer or
engineer. Still, I am not complaining. I am one of the lucky ones.

—Florence (Rosenfeld) Howe, *Myths of Coeducation*

The *Maryland Gazette* for June 6, 1786, reported a ship unloading "Butchers,
Schoolmasters, Millwrights, and Labourers," all healthy indentured servants—
Irish men and women. Few schoolmasters continued teaching once their in-
dentures expired, as schoolteaching seldom offered year-round, well-rewarded
employment. Women were recruited to teaching more widely across the social
spectrum, even from the upper-middle classes. Several well-born French émigrés
taught schools in the new republic, women like Madame Capron, who gave lessons in French, geography, drawing, and embroidery to young ladies in 1790s
Newark. Daughter of a Schuyler and a Bleeker, Margaretta Faugeres (b. 1771) was
connected to prominent, wealthy New Yorkers. She taught schools in New Jersey
and Brooklyn to support herself and her daughter after her husband squandered
her inheritance.[1]

The genteel lady, thrust into teaching by misfortune, was a staple of popular novels. However, biographical data on the social origins of eighteenth- and
nineteenth-century women confirms teaching's early appeal to ambitious, industrious, and even successful families. John C. Edwards was governor of Missouri
in the 1840s, then a large landholder and mayor of Stockton (CA); his eldest, Emma,
taught school in frontier Idaho.[2] In the 1850s Nicholas Cheyenne Dawson—
engineer, lawyer, and member of the Texas House of Representatives—fathered
three daughters, all future teachers; an Austin school was named for Mary Jane
(Mollie), and Nancy Elizabeth (Nanny) taught high school in Austin and San
Antonio for 50 years.[3]

Many of the Sisters of the Sacred Heart traced their lineage to prominent Catholic families in France and America. In 1900, the "Schools of the Madams" (as they were known) were housed in former mansions and country estates across the nation.[4] However, teachers in Midwestern Lutheran schools, as daughters of farmers, teachers, pastors, and shopkeepers, were closer in social status to the norm for women religious; further down the class continuum were teacher-daughters of mill hands, day laborers, sharecroppers, and illiterate immigrants.[5] The fathers of Julia Tutwiler (b. 1841) and Alice Chenoweth (b. 1853) owned slaves; Susie Baker (b. 1848) and Ida Bell Wells-Barnett (b. 1862) were born to slaves.

The Relevance of Teachers' Social Class Origins for Schooling

The relationship between career choice and social class, ethnicity, race, or religious origins has long interested scholars. Teachers' social backgrounds are sometimes presumed to condition their interactions with their pupils. The poor and working-class students in Baltimore County's Miller High School in the 1950s and 1960s remembered the favoritism white middle-class women teachers showed students from backgrounds like their own, especially girls able "to please authority figures with whom they shared almost familial relations."[6] Conversely, when interviewed in the 1980s, country-raised "Chris" admitted preferring (if not favoring) her rural students—her "sixth sense" telling her that such children had better values than affluent city kids.[7] In contrast, class and cultural distinctions mattered little to Polly Bullard (b. 1881), daughter of a solid St. Paul family. She reported adjusting easily to her pupils in her first teaching job, in Mesabi Range country—her "heart going out" to these children of Finnish iron miners.[8]

In 1847, Pittsburgh officials hired Miss Sarah Cust, daughter of a locally prominent man—the first of six hired to enhance the public schools' image and appeal among families that ordinarily patronized private schools.[9] In the post–Civil War South, Ella Clanton Thomas, daughter of a ruined Georgia planter, helped support her husband and five children by teaching—one of many recruits from the white South's "better classes."[10] Such women gave public schooling a respectability previously unseen in the South, expanding public education and opening teaching to a broader spectrum of Southern womanhood.

The Providence (RI) School Committee stated in 1900 that "children coming from homes of the better class, should find ladies no way beneath those with whom they are accustomed to associate," meanwhile giving children "from lower grades of society, brilliant examples" of education's powers.[11] Local school boards were gratified when teaching attracted elite collegiate women. Between 1861 (when the first "Seven Sisters" institution was chartered) and 1918, of the 12,000 ever-employed graduates of nine eastern women's colleges, 83.5% became teachers.[12] Mary McCarthy learned something of class consciousness in the private school sector when, at age 11, she entered a Sacred Heart School near Seattle. "They were not ordinary nuns, it was scornfully explained to me, but women of good family, cloistered ladies of the world, just as Sacred Heart girls were not ordinary Catholics but daughters of the best families. And my new subjects were not ordinary subjects, like spelling and arithmetic, but rhetoric, French, literature, Christian doctrine, English history."[13]

Before her marriage Luella Smith taught high school around 1905 while her father ran the People's Bank and Trust Company in Indianapolis.[14] However, preachers' daughters were more numerous and needy, thus more likely to embrace self-support. One of seven daughters of a Methodist minister, Mary Johnson kept a country school at Springdale (TN) after Wellesley College. More fittingly, her youngest sister—"Miss Willie" (Vassar College, 1895)—taught at Higbee School for Girls, Memphis High School, and St. Mary's Episcopal School before becoming a professor of ancient languages at West Tennessee State Normal School.[15] The 10 children (all college graduates) of Rev. Delaney, vice principal of St. Augustine's College in Raleigh (NC), included Sadie, the first Negro home economics teacher in New York City's public schools. Mary Sanderson taught in an Oakland (CA) school while her minister father preached and promoted education to his and other Negro congregations.[16]

In New Orleans and Atlanta, the "black bourgeoisie" constituted a class of businessmen and professionals largely independent of the white economy, and their wives and daughters included teachers. Atlanta's political leader, John Wesley Dobbs (b.1882), was a well-paid, largely self-educated railway mail clerk, salaried head of the Prince Hall (black) Masons, and founder of the Georgia Voters League. His six daughters, graduates of Spelman College, became educators.[17]

The same held for Northern Negroes before World War I, where a "long history of free ancestry, a respectable, bourgeois style of life, and service in prominent white families or ownership of a modest business (such as a barbershop or blacksmith shop) conferred status approaching that of the handful of physicians, schoolteachers, and well-educated ministers."[18] A factory worker's daughter and career high school biology teacher, Sidney Ellwood (b. 1927) learned solid middle-class values at home. Her mother monitored her children's schooling, and there was reading aloud, reciting passages from Negro poets, discussing the news on the radio. "You were clean. . . . You had pictures on the wall and books in the household. . . . [The] children read . . . and had good manners."[19]

The daughter of a respected businessman and local public official, Edna Noble White obviously brought social capital to Danville (IL) High School and Chicago's Lewis Institute, where she taught. However, because local culture helps define social status, one cannot assume that being the daughter of a Wyoming saloonkeeper in 1910 socially injured teacher Georgia Snyder.[20] The local economy is also related to social mobility, with manufacturing and commerce more helpful to the upwardly mobile than mining and other extractive industries. There were working-class Gertrudes in industrialized Poughkeepsie (NY) by 1860.[21] While one in four students at historically black West Virginia State College in 1932 had a professional as a parent, often a teacher, the offspring of the state's many miners and unskilled workers seldom taught.[22]

Using questionnaire data from teachers in 17 states, Lotus Coffman concluded in 1910 that teachers came disproportionately from large families with low relative income.[23] Statistical studies and life histories find the social origins of women teachers higher, on average, than that of their male colleagues.[24] Thus, even though the average male teacher would gain a greater degree of social mobility than his female colleagues, proportionally fewer men made the teaching profession their instrument of social advancement.

A Cross-National Perspective on Social Status and Mobility

American education has been called "both populist and elitist, allowing ordinary people a high possibility of getting ahead through education and a low probability of getting ahead very far."[25] Using her saved wages, teacher Lucy Stone (b. 1818) represents untold numbers who entered institutions willing to admit the "calico-attired country girl of limited means"—as a Vermont newspaper put it. A century later, farm daughters were nearly half the students attending Southwest Texas State Teachers College at San Marcos; ranchers, orchardists, stockmen, and dairymen ranked next, far outnumbering professionals and businessmen.[26] Wisconsin's "Dot Miller" (b. 1922) was preparing to teach partly because the local schoolmistress dressed far better than farmers' wives and daughters.[27]

Ellen Skerrett found nineteenth-century Irish American women schoolteachers raising their own social status, narrowing the occupational gap between German and Irish immigrants.[28] It is ironic that daughters of often-illiterate Irish servants and daughters of the upper-middle class families that employed them would both become "servants of the poor" as city schoolteachers. Teaching daughters could nudge their own and some of their pupils' families from the working to the middle class or arrest a family's downward slide.

At a time when California law prevented Chinese immigrants from owning land, Locke was founded on leased property along the lower Sacramento River. This small all-Chinese town flourished from 1915 to 1952, with one Chinese school (f. 1926). Because town elders valued education, a number sent their children to the state university—threatening Locke's very existence as their educated children moved on. Retired Oakland schoolteacher Loretta Oh explained why she left Locke in 1948: "My grandmother, who couldn't read or write, always told me, 'Go for it.' And look at what we produced—doctors, engineers, teachers."[29]

In Europe, despite its more explicit class consciousness and social stratification, gender operated similarly. Britain's 1870 Education Act expanded primary school positions beyond the available numbers of clergymen's daughters and ex-governesses. England's Bessie Parkes wrote in 1865 of teaching as the place where two classes of women meet: "the one struggling up, the other drifting down."[30] The cheap pupil-teacher system attracted girls like Agnes Dawson, one of three teaching daughters of a journeyman carpenter. The rough working-class schools where they learned to teach were culturally familiar, while to middle-class girls they seemed alien, even loathsome places. Bursaries and "teacherships" helped recruit from Britain's urban upper-working and middle classes but failed Annie Barnes. Her deep wish to teach, acquired at Ben Jonson School—she "never wanted to be naughty"—could not overcome her father's need for her help in his South London fruiterer's shop after her mother's death in 1902.[31]

The proprietary or private charity schools for girls or small children, taught by Danish women of mainly lower-middle class origins, were the foundation of a public school system emerging after 1814.[32] The French government's mandate in the 1880s that lay teachers replace nuns teaching in state primary schools opened classroom doors to the daughters of artisans and white-collar workers—drawn by the new career structure, wages comparable to male teachers, and the accessible normal schools.[33]

Male reluctance to teach children persisted. Schoolboys in nineteenth-century England preferred the business office to the teacher's platform despite similar pay, because, unlike teaching, "the possibilities of business are gloriously uncertain; he may be a merchant one day."[34] Choosing the business office also freed a boy from school four years before a sister preparing to teach. Conversely, in the early twentieth century, better-off but status-anxious English parents saw teaching as their daughters' protection against downward social mobility. The mother of a Miss Cox extolled teaching as a career, praised cousins who taught, ensured that her daughter had the school subjects to pass her exams, and advanced her the college fees to make her a London teacher.[35] Nonetheless, in most nations and across time, men who chose the profession could expect promotions—more often, more quickly, and to the highest positions the educational system afforded.

In late Tsarist Russia the movement of higher-status urban women teachers into rural primary schools—the province of male teachers, largely from the peasantry—created dissension.[36] Aspiring sons of Swedish farmers and factory workers likewise saw their social mobility threatened by chiefly middle-class and urban women teachers.[37] Post–World War II Czechoslovakia's efforts to make teaching a more proletarian occupation suffered from high university dropout rates among the children of workers, compounded by teaching's weak appeal to men in a political culture that glorified manual labor. Similarly, China's Cultural Revolution (1966–1976) lauded construction workers and machinists from the more "reliable classes," as opposed to teachers who "live by selling their mouths"—depressing teacher morale and recruitment.[38]

Race, Ethnicity, and National Identity in the United States

Negro intellectual W. E. B. Du Bois (1869–1963) saw his as a time when race had become the irreducible staple of personal identity and social division: "government, work, religion and education became based upon and determined by the color line."[39] Race was also manifested in the way that education officials conceived schooling for other nonwhites—from Native Americans on reservations to Filipinos in their homeland. In the latter case, however, a half century of American influence on Philippine public education following the U.S. seizure and military occupation of the islands (1899–1920) saw Filipinas become the majority of teachers, principals, and university students.[40] By 1995, Filipina American immigrants constituted the largest Asian teacher group.

In 1900 "race" was a broadly applied term, referring also to nationality and ethnicity (the Germanic race, the Hebrew race). Eugenicists coined the term "race suicide" to remind Anglo-Americans of the dangers posed by the higher birthrates of Eastern and Southern European immigrants.[41] Coffman worried that "the intellectual possessions of the [American] race are by rather unconscious selection [being] left to a class of people who by social and economic station, as well as by training, are not eminently fitted for their transmission. . . . Training teachers who have not become thoroughly Americanized becomes increasingly momentous."[42]

The largest number of New York City's public school teachers in 1930 came from the Eastern European families of tailors, peddlers, manual workers, and retailers, particularly Jewish families.[43] Teaching drew so heavily from immigrant families that, in 1900, 27% of America's women teachers were native-born daughters of a foreign-born parent. A mere decade later, when the foreign born were less than 15% of the U.S. population, 48.5% of all kindergarten and elementary public school teachers in a diverse sample of American cities were first- or second-generation immigrants.[44] The surnames of five Sisters of Divine Providence—successive principals of the Westchester (IL) parochial school from 1958 to 1991—were Meyer, Musick, Hampton, Micka, and Simanella.[45]

The great numbers arriving, and the shift from Northern and Western to Southern and Eastern Europeans after 1880, tested the nation's laissez-faire approach to newcomers. Nativists questioned each successive group's desire and ability to assimilate. In Nebraska, where more than 50% of its country teachers were first- or second-generation immigrants, University of Nebraska teacher educators stressed that teachers be American "in sympathy, ideals, training, and loyalty."[46]

Americanization became a major concern in every nineteenth- and twentieth-century school system with a sizeable immigrant enrollment, in night school programs for adults, and even in church schools. Long after he left Seattle's Main Street School, Henry Miyatake could recall the principal, Ada J. Mahon: a "staunch American," a highly visible, relentlessly effective indoctrinator in "how to become good Americans. And she did a helluva good job."[47] The 1965 Immigration Act and the Vietnam War supplied new Asian Americans, representing both ancient literate civilizations and isolated cultures with no written language, creating further challenges for English-only language instruction.[48]

Denied entry to the United States from 1917 to 1946, south Asians arrived later but often elicited the same suspicion. While well-educated, English-proficient Indians now typically come to study engineering and medicine or teach in universities, American-born Laju Shaw was a middle school social studies teacher when she spoke at a California State Board of Education hearing in 2006. She argued that children need textbooks that tell the truth about that part of Hinduism and Indian history that consistently denied women "education, livelihood and social authority"—rights she was herself exercising.[49]

Issues of national cultures and Americanization also arose in nonpublic schools. Other Catholics questioned whether German Catholics were more loyal to their language than to the church. Irish Catholics objected in the 1880s to French nuns who staffed parochial schools in French-speaking neighborhoods in New England. In 1913, Boston's Cardinal Archbishop William O'Connell responded to the presence of "foreign teachers and traditions in Church schools" by pressuring the French Canadian Grey Nuns to conduct their elementary school classes in English.[50] Demonstrable antipathy also existed between Irish and Italian Catholics. Italian aversion to parochial schools went beyond the perceived nonsense of paying tuition for what was free in public schools. It also reflected southern Italy's historic anticlericalism, resentment of Irish dominance of American Catholicism, and the discrimination Italian Americans experienced or perceived in Catholic schools and parish life.

Teachers from America's "Subject Peoples"

As national policy, not local practice, the first initiative with the potential to broaden the racial and ethnic composition of American teachers began with the federal decision in 1819 to "School-away the Indian Problem." Once Christianized and adequately instructed, Native Americans could presumably teach their own race. Another milestone came a half century later with missionary and federal programs to educate four million ex-slaves, with even more motivation and potential for providing their own teachers. Despite increasing immigration from Mexico and their status as a long resident "involuntary minority group," Hispanics were effectively ignored.[51] Thus the initiative came later and from within—in the 1940s, with the Mexican American civil rights movement.

"Taking Up the Pencil"—Indigenous American Teachers

The earliest-known settlers in the Americas were Columbus's Indios. Christians considered American Indians to be "heathens" awaiting conversion. As with other colonized peoples, as individual Indians were reconciled or converted to the "white man's ways," some indeed became teachers—in mission, federal, and local public or private schools serving Indian children, or in adult remedial or vocational programs. During Estelle Reel's tenure (1898–1910) as general superintendent of the federal Bureau of Indian Affairs (BIA), Indians were 24% of those employed by the BIA, some as teachers, more as matrons, disciplinarians, cooks, and seamstresses.[52]

The 1900 U.S. census recorded 384 Indian teachers, from a population (above age 15) numbering 144,000. Among teachers the male proportion was higher, at 38%, than the national average and higher than it would be 100 years later. Career opportunities grew faster than the supply of even minimally prepared native teachers, and Indian men had additional prospects of becoming school principals and staff at the bureau's headquarters.[53]

But the chasm separating the cognition and beliefs of Native Americans from those of whites limited the flow of indigenous teachers, as did poverty, isolation, and social disorganization.[54] Shy 17-year-old Wendy Hopkins felt out of place at Northern Montana State College; already a mother, she quit after a year. She was 37 and a wife and mother of three on resuming her education, first at the two-year Fort Belknap College on the Gros Ventre and Assiniboine reservation where she (a Little Shell Chippewa) was raised. A bachelor's degree in biology and education, a teaching credential, life and work experiences, and an insider's perspective equipped Wendy Hopkins to teach science at the school from which she graduated.[55] When Inuit Elsie Itta started teaching at Barrow in the vast North Slope Borough School District about 1977, Alaska natives were teaching, some beginning as teachers' aides, helping preserve native languages.[56]

"The Little One Who Wanted to Be a White Man"

Around 1898, when the Hopi children of Old Oraibi were rounded up by Navajo policemen and taken to the nearby Mennonite-run, federally funded school, it was by agreement with the head of one of the two clans and without the local Hopi knowing what "school" meant. Hidden by her mother, Polingaysi Qöy-awayma was reassured by the other children's experiences: "We sit on a seat and make marks. We play in the schoolyard. When Father Sun is overhead, they give us food." Qöyawayma went to the school, was renamed Bessie, bathed, and was given the school's striped cotton ticking in place of her native dress. Bessie's schooling continued at the Sherman Institute in Southern California and Mennonite Bethel Academy in Kansas.

Passing the BIA civil service examination in 1924 and newly baptized as Elizabeth Ruth, she began teaching first Navajo, then Hopi, children. Her sandbox construction and dramatic play pedagogy reflected progressive practice; like other child-centered teachers, she met her share of skeptical parents. Qöyawayma anticipated the 1934 federal schools policy of preserving elements of traditional cultures, for example, in substituting Hopi songs and legends for "white-man stories," displeasing those who wanted their children to learn only "white-man ways." Yet she claimed that Oraibi's parents were eager to see their children "do something with their lives, as [she] did."[57]

"Colored Teachers for Our Colored Schools"

Maria Sarah Mapps Douglass taught colored children in New York City before returning to her native Philadelphia in 1828 to open a girls academy. Active in the Female Anti-Slavery Society, Douglass attended a Quaker meeting in New York City where only one person spoke to her, asking, "Doest thee go out a house-cleaning?"[58] When Douglass responded that she taught school, the other turned away. Douglass was among the first colored teachers hired for Philadelphia's public schools, around 1853.[59]

At a time when the North had a number of small schools—begun, taught, and supported by the colored race—delegates to the 1865 State Equal Rights Convention of the Colored People of Pennsylvania discussed the all-white faculty's lack of concern for the pupils at Philadelphia's public Lombard Street School. A resolution was offered: that it be "our incumbent duty, as lovers of the advancement of our race, to see to it, that our schools are under the charge of colored teachers." Agreeing that colored teachers "had the welfare of the race more at heart, knowing that they rose or fell together," Octavius Catto of the Institute for Colored Youth amended the resolution to read that colored teachers should be given preference in hiring "not by reason of their complection, but because they are better qualified by conventional circumstances outside of the school-house."[60] Thus modified, the resolution passed.

Most of the early nineteenth century's black teachers, and the bulk of the South's locally recruited teachers during Reconstruction, came from the literate portion of a free black population that—compared to a slave population of four million in 1860—numbered 220,000 in the North and 260,000 in the South. Unlike the late nineteenth-century South, white teachers ordinarily taught colored pupils in the North, but white pupils rarely saw a colored teacher. However, in Massachusetts (an abolitionist stronghold), Charlotte Forten (b. 1837) began her teaching in a Salem public school.[61] Maria Baldwin (b. 1856), principal of Agassiz School in Cambridge, headed a white faculty, and Elizabeth Smith was appointed in 1875 as Boston's first colored woman teacher in a multiracial school. In 1895, attorney T. McCants Stewart won a lawsuit allowing Susie Frazier, a colored graduate of the Normal College of the City of New York, to teach in that city's officially integrated public schools; Stewart also served on Brooklyn's school board, where he defended racially mixed schools.[62]

In the former Confederacy, whites slowly erected a racially segregated school system under their control. Initially white teachers were employed for the colored schools, often acquired from the Northern missionary societies that organized many freedmen's schools. By the 1870s the colored population was demanding its own teachers and principals. Unable to secure reappointment in Richmond's white schools, Mrs. M. C. P. Bennet was hired for a colored school in 1878. However, the patrons objected to having their children taught by white "rejects" and Negrophobes.[63]

In 1871 the commissioner of Sumter County (SC) asked the head of the colored Avery Normal Institute in Charleston to recommend two graduates for the county's colored schools: "Ladies that will popularize the work & give themselves cleverly to the work as a matter of duty would reap a rich reward."[64] By 1890 there were an estimated 25,000 Negro teachers in the South. As a vestige of their degraded status in slavery, they were listed in Memphis (TN) records without titles (Julia A. Hicks and Lulu Wilson), unlike teachers in the white schools' rosters

(Miss Anna McGinnis and Mrs. Kate E. Nevills). Despite her Spelman Seminary education, Ida Brown was fired from her Columbus (GA) position for asking a school board member to address her as *Miss* Ida Brown. Of her own experience as a teacher and lecturer, Charlotte Hawkins Brown (b. 1882) observed that "some men who occupy high places . . . feel that no negro woman whether she be cook, criminal or principal of a school should ever be addressed as Mrs."[65]

Nonetheless, the Jim Crow South witnessed a near-complete feminization of teaching—with census data showing women's share among Negro teachers rising from 52% in 1890 to 82% in 1920. Segregated schools in territorial Oklahoma gave Druscilla Dunjee Houston and other proud members of the Ida B. Wells Teachers' Association (f. 1893) careers and community roles, as did the colored and Negro schools in the Border States from Kansas to Maryland.[66]

In 1900, only 15 Negro women teachers were noted west of the Rocky Mountains—including Sara Jones, hired in 1873 and retained as a Sacramento teacher when the town's colored school became a mixed race school; she retired as its principal in 1915.[67] Ida Louise Jackson (b. 1902) was the youngest of the eight children of a Mississippi family one generation removed from slavery. Her appointment in Oakland (CA) in 1926 generated protests; it was another 13 years before the school board hired Beth Wallace.[68] Although 73% of the nation's Negro teachers worked in the South in 1940, the many such "mundane humiliations of the North" became widespread as Negro populations in the urban North and West expanded during and after World War II.[69]

"The Negro Rock of Little Rock": Charlotte Andrews Stephens

Charlotte Andrews Stephens (1854–1951) had the longest teaching career in Arkansas history—30 years in the grammar grades, 30 more teaching English and Latin at Dunbar High School and Junior College, and 10 years as its librarian.[70] Her father, William Wallace Andrews, was a favored, literate house slave and resolute Christian. In 1863, with Union troops in Little Rock, Andrews's tiny church became the first black school in Arkansas, perhaps in the South; her father was one of its two teachers. Eight decades later Lottie could see in her mind's eye the aged grandmother who asked only to "learn to read the name of Jesus." American Missionary Association and Quaker teachers built a four-room schoolhouse, giving the pupils their first school desks and a graded curriculum, which became in 1869 the first colored school in Little Rock's new public school system, with white teachers.

Her school's most advanced pupil, Charlotte Andrews first substituted for an ill white teacher, then finished her term, and then began her own at the new one-room First Ward Colored School. Thereafter, except for interludes of study at

Oberlin College, Miss Charlotte was a teacher and sometimes principal in the city's public system. She also taught in the Wesley Chapel Sunday school, played the organ at her church, and organized a united recreational program for the colored churches—all this into very old age and through marriage to John Herbert Stephens, bearing eight children, raising the six survivors, and acting as their first and best teacher.

The Hispanic Teacher

The California students counted as "Latins" on Oakland's 1910 school census forms were chiefly Portuguese from the Azores—as was San Francisco teacher Albertina Andrade. She and a Latina teacher of Mexican ancestry—or one from a long-settled New Mexican enclave of Ladino peoples (often descendants of Judeo-Spanish-speaking Sephardic Jews)—likely had less in common than Mrs. Andrade had with her non-Hispanic coworkers.[71] Like the label "Asian American" (previously "Oriental")—blanketing peoples disparate in number, racial stock, culture, history, religion, and preparation for assimilation—"Hispanic" binds Spanish-language groups with distinct histories, even contending loyalties, both recent immigrants and U.S. citizens by annexation or birthright. Incorporating Caucasians, Native Americans, Africans, and even Asians in the case of Filipinos and Peruvians of Japanese heritage—and with every conceivable admixture, "Hispanic" is a contested demographic marker.[72]

Yolanda Armijo of Las Vegas (NM) represented Hispanos: seventeenth-century Spaniards who settled in northern New Mexico and southern Colorado.[73] A descendant of Californios, Ruth Galindo was a teacher for 34 years at Mt. Diablo High School in Concord (CA), founded by an ancestor with roots in Spain and New Spain.[74] A few teachers and principals in nineteenth-century schools in southwest Texas were Tejanos: Spanish and Mexican Americans, long resident in Texas. However, most contemporary Hispanic teachers are the direct descendants of Mexican immigrants from the late nineteenth and twentieth centuries. As congressional immigration quotas exempted farm workers needed for the newly irrigated fields of the Southwest, the fewer than 500,000 persons of Mexican ancestry residing in the United States in 1890 grew to nearly five million by 1930.[75]

The first Santa Barbara County salary drawn on the new California State School Fund went to Miss Manuela Cota in 1854. Tulita de la Questa (b. 1888) taught there for many years.[76] El Paso's first "Mexican public school" was named for Oliva Villanueva Aoy, a Spaniard who opened a school in his residence in 1887 to teach English to young children and Spanish to Anglos at night. It became a public school in 1892. There were, however, no Spanish-surname school board members or school administrators at any level serving El Paso's 22 schools in 1928, and Houston did not hire Latino teachers until the 1960s.[77] Mexico-born Leonor Villegas de Magnon (b. 1876), and Texas native Jovita Idar (b. 1885) together promoted the kindergarten movement in Texas.[78] The 281 BIA schools had two Spanish-surname teachers in 1900, A. Elina Martinez at the Kiowa Agency (OK) and Fannie Benavidez at Rice Station (AZ)—although the Spanish language had been pressed on native peoples since the seventeenth century.[79]

New York City first employed Puerto Ricans as Spanish-speaking aides (substitute auxiliary teachers) in the 1940s. Among the 22 Western Hemisphere countries supplying Hispanic immigrants, Cubans offer the sharpest contrast with Puerto Ricans or Mexicans. Cubans emigrating after Fidel Castro came to power in 1959 benefitted from Cold War politics and their middle-class and urban origins. Cubans and Cuban Americans were already 16% of Dade County (FL) teachers in 1984.[80] Los Angeles County's desultory reaction to its rapidly growing Chicano population prevailed until 1969, when a Teacher Corps project placed 60 Hispanic college graduates.[81]

Schoolteachers Emerge from the "Old" Immigration

Nationality often overrode religion among American Catholics. A pupil at St. Mary's School in Madison (IL) in the 1940s, John Patrick Wathen was sure that the Polish nuns "were hard on the Irish" like him. A pupil at Our Lady of Mt. Carmel School in New York City in the 1950s, Claudia DeMonte "knew" that her Irish sixth-grade teacher loaded homework on her Italian pupils. "Then the next year we had an Italian teacher who gave the Irish kids extra homework."[82] What follows is a brief, contextualized sampling of women teachers from several distinct elements in America's population of voluntary newcomers, suggesting factors (within their own group histories and American culture) that promoted one demographic group and delayed another in becoming American Gertrudes.

For much of its history, the United States tolerated or encouraged unimpeded immigration. From the mid-nineteenth century, job seekers left Japan for Hawaii and China for California. "America Fever" often struck with the departure of a family or individual, causing Sweden, Norway, and Iceland to lose 20%–25% of their populations to the United States between 1851 and 1930.[83] This Great Atlantic Migration moved 50 million people from Europe to North America. The United States, Argentina, and Australia faced the most challenges and reaped the greatest benefits of a worldwide population shift. Meanwhile, slavery and its legacy kept most immigrants out of the South, and an immigrant population that elsewhere in the nation in 1910 comprised one in five Americans was less than 2% in the former Confederacy—with evident economic and other consequences.[84]

Census Statistics of Teachers (1905) reported, "Among females the largest proportion of teachers is found among the children of immigrants." *The Social Composition of the Teaching Population* (1911) stated that American-born daughters of foreign parentage "contributed more teachers than any other nativity class."[85] *Children of Immigrants in Schools,* 5 volumes of the 41-volume *Immigration Commission Reports* (1911) found that 48.5% of all public elementary school teachers in 30 cities were immigrants or had foreign-born fathers. A staggering 61% of San Francisco's elementary school teachers in 1910 were immigrants or their adult children, most from "old immigration" stock—especially the Irish (30%) and Germans (6%)—the two groups featured below.

Teacher appointments, salary data, and promotion lists for Chicago and San Francisco from 1867 to 1915 confirm that the larger ethnic groups, especially the Irish and Germans (18% and 8%, respectively, of U.S. teachers in 1910), secured teaching and principal positions at least equal to their share of the population, even in rural states. For example, Margaret Knapple (b. 1879) of Lexington (NE) and Bertha Knemeyer (b. 1885) of Elko (NV) were high school principals.[86]

The Interurban Association of Women Teachers of New York City chose well-connected Irishwomen for its leaders. Chicago teachers Margaret Haley and Catharine Goggin were among America's labor leaders in the early twentieth century, and Julia Riordan was a charter member of Local 89, Atlanta's teachers association.[87] By the 1930s, Indiana had so many teachers with "foreign names" that a teachers' union official feared criticism from xenophobic groups. As the seniority advantage of "old-stock Americans" eroded, immigrant-origin teachers were assigned to schools beyond their ethnic neighborhood and promoted.[88]

In a community where "a woman taught, or clerked, or cooked," a Norway-born mother opposed her daughter's plan to teach: "teaching drew one away from God because it made women domineering and self-satisfied." After her mother's early death, this unnamed woman became a career teacher near her North Dakota farm home. When Paul Knaplund left Norway in 1906, females with an eighth-grade education and one year of normal school were teaching in primary schools, likely encouraging later immigrant daughters to do likewise.[89] Janet Jipson's Swedish great-grandmother was a missionary in North Dakota, and a great-aunt taught a one-room country school at 16 before becoming a nurse. Jipson's grandmothers provided childcare while her mother alternately taught and attended normal school. By the 1880s, Swedish settlers in the upper Midwest—from Lake Michigan to the Dakotas—held most public offices, including the county commissioners who hired teachers. In 1939 Swedish voters in

Wyoming helped elect Esther L. Anderson—daughter of Swedes who settled in Kansas around 1870—as their state superintendent of public instruction.[90]

Irish Daughters Settle In

The Irish were well scattered in British North America before Ireland's Great Hunger caused more than a million Irish to enter the United States between 1845 and 1849. Given the high illiteracy rate (nearly 47% in 1850) among the Irish and long-standing religious and ethnic prejudice against them, many Irish struggled as unskilled and domestic workers. However, overpopulation in Ireland had established a pattern whereby sons and daughters left home (usually for England) to find work and younger Irishwomen became the better educated. In their unique network of female chain migration, women sent passage money to other women, typically single, who then reciprocated, replenishing and dispersing the pool. One beneficiary was Catharine Murphy, teaching in Sitka (AK) by 1870.[91] Mary McNamara (b. 1872) emigrated from Limerick at age 15 to live with an uncle in Dakota Territory and qualify to teach; she taught for 13 years, and four daughters followed her.[92]

Originally from the Gaeltacht Aran Islands, Nora Joyce of Milton (MA) remarked, "We never talked Irish to the children. . . . Two nurses, one schoolteacher."[93] Large numbers of Irishwomen quickly entered teaching, emboldened as English-speakers and sufficiently comfortable with American culture to move beyond Irish neighborhoods.[94] Boston's first Catholic woman teacher (c. 1878), Julia Harrington, was elected to the Boston School Committee in 1900.[95]

In 1908, Irish American women were the largest ethnic group at Chicago Normal School. By 1911 the Sisters of Mercy's all-girl St. James High School had produced more than 400 teachers for Chicago's public schools, where Catholics were 35% of teachers. Moreover, for a century Irish-laden sisterhoods taught the vast majority of pupils in Catholic parochial schools and academies. Margaret O'Brien (b. 1882) worked in her order's kitchen in Carlow County, Ireland, before emigrating. As Mother Mary Agnes, she opened free parochial schools in Chicago and an academy for the affluent.[96]

Two-thirds of the teachers in some Irish neighborhood schools in New York City were Irish. "The teachers were mostly Irish, and what teachers! I'll never forget Mrs. O'Connor, in the fifth grade. She taught us poetry. . . . with such animation and such joy that we ate it up. And that's what teaching should be like"— this from Mildred Tudy, an African American recalling her East Harlem schooldays.[97] In 1930 the surnames of 214 Boston public school teachers were Sullivan, Murphy, O'Brien, Kelley, or Lynch.[98] Teacher lists in New Orleans and Nashville were liberally laced with Irish names. Among the many teachers employed by the federal Indian school system were Bridget Quinn, Louise and Harriet McCarty, and Sister Macaria Murphy.

Deutscheamerikanische Lehrerinnen

As in seventeenth-century Pennsylvania, nineteenth-century Kansans referred to the Germans (Deutsche) among them as the "Dutch." "I have seventeen enrolled and those Dutch boys haven't started yet," May Stewart reported on the start of her 1887 term.[99] A century later the 1990 census counted more than 51 million Americans—one-third fully German, the remainder of mixed ancestry—one-fourth the U.S. population and larger than any other ethnic group.

Between 1848 and 1849 (following Europe's failed revolutionary movements) and 1900, Germans were America's largest immigrant bloc, ranging from liberal secularists to theologically and culturally conservative Catholics and Lutherans. When Lutheran schools could not find pastor-teachers, their patrons chose local laymen or appealed to Germany's churches rather than employ German American laywomen. Despite Germany's neglect of girls' secondary schooling and preference for single-sex schools, in reporting on the 1883 German-American Teachers' National Association annual convention in Chicago, Hermann Schuricht observed that, among the 300 delegates, "ladies outnumbered the male teachers four to one."[100]

German names appear among teachers in smaller towns and large cities, in country schools, on the frontier, in upstate New York, and downstate Illinois. In 1875, German surnames graced 80% of the population of Belleville (IL) and all its teachers (*Lehrerinnen*) and school board members.[101] Venturing farther, Maude Schaeffer and Velma Augusta Shartle relocated to Honolulu when Hawaii was still a territory to become principals at Kamahameha School for Girls and Kaahumanu School, respectively. BIA teachers included Louise Schuler at Crow Creek (MT) and Carolyn Schlattman at Morris (MN).[102]

Until 1917, high school German classes were usually required for the college bound, with German language and literature still offered in some grade schools. World War I rendered suspect everyone and everything German. Myrtle Domerhaussen became Myrtle Domer. Mary Buerger lost her teaching position in Los Angeles, her father's Civil War veteran status outweighed by her husband's German citizenship.[103] A New York City elementary school teacher, German-born Gertrude Pignol was dismissed for wearing a locket "engraved by her father and carrying the picture of the Kaiser's grandfather on one side and the cornflower on the other."[104]

Teaching Daughters Representing the "New Immigration"

About 1870, Anna Johnson's grandparents emigrated from Chaslava, Bohemia—then Austria-Hungary—settling on a remote Nebraska homestead; their American-born daughter went unschooled. However, her daughter, Anna, taught for 37 years in Wisconsin's rural schools.[105] Before and after the Austro-Hungarian Empire ended in 1918, immigrants from its constituent nationalities in Central, Eastern, and Southern Europe clustered in neighborhoods and ethnic parishes. Of probable Serbian or Croatian ancestry, Mary Gospardarić of Joliet (IL) completed college in 1926 and became a lay teacher at a Catholic school in Atchison (KS).[106] World War II service in the WAVES (Women Accepted for Volunteer Emergency Service) enabled Angeline Bratich (b. 1918) to attend college on the GI Bill, earn a credential, teach high school English to the children of American military personnel in Europe, and visit her family's natal villages in the Old Country.[107]

An unnamed 18-year-old, English-speaking teacher was hired for Goodson School in Polonia (TX) in 1922, one of several Polish school districts in Caldwell County. Boarded with a family of nine, seven born in Poland, she learned to pronounce Polish names, attend the Catholic Church on Sunday mornings, and dance the polka Sunday evenings. Initially, most Polish teachers were Jews, but Milwaukee's Mary O. Kryszak was Catholic.[108] American Catholics' quest for middle-class status eventually led conservative Polish Americans to educate their daughters longer.[109]

In 2000 nearly half of Americans were descendants of one or more of those who passed through Ellis and Angel Islands and New Orleans—especially the worrisome 12 million arriving between 1892 and 1924. A frightened Congress severely restricted the entry of these often darker-hued newer immigrants. The families of Italians and Eastern European Jews—each group constituting 20% of the foreign born in Boston, New York, and Philadelphia in 1920—were particularly affected.

Teacher Daughters of the Contadini

Small numbers of Italians settled in the United States before 1880, ranging from California grape growers to artists, musicians, and language teachers in private eastern schools and colleges. Northerners arrived first, drawn from Italy's more urbanized and industrialized regions; initially the relatively few Italian American women teachers came from this population. San Francisco hired an Italian-speaking night school teacher in 1877, after 6,000 Italians and Italian Swiss submitted a petition.[110] The daughter of an immigrant grocer from Genoa who settled in Martinez (CA) in 1857, Mariana Bertola (b. 1865) graduated from the State Normal School and taught for a decade before taking up medicine.[111]

Italian immigrants were divided by regional identity, dialect, customs, and income. Of the four million arriving between 1880 and 1920, most came from Sicily and the south—like Calabria, where 79% of adults were illiterate in Italy's 1901 census. Mario Puzo's character Lucia Santa Angeluzzi-Corbo captured the life of Italy's landless peasantry, the *contadini,* in telling her children, "I would give anything to have gone to school, to be able to read and write. Only the sons of the rich went to school. . . . At your age I was chasing goats and digging vegetables and shoveling manure. . . . School to me would have been like movie pictures."[112] Historically impoverished and often anti-clerical in their religion, denigrated by both other Italians and more devout Catholics, these latecomers nonetheless came to define how America thought of and judged Italians and Italian Americans.

Italian American youth grew up with the Old Country concept of *buon educato* (well raised): loyal to normative family and community codes of behavior, including not aspiring to surpass their fathers' achievements.[113] Family ambitions focused on family businesses, skilled trades, and labor unions, not investment in education; the few Italian men who attended college chose business, law, medicine, and pharmacy. A daughter's wages as a seamstress or silk worker were crucial in a family where Papa was an unskilled laborer and Mama and the younger children made artificial flowers or finished shirts. Not until the 1930s did most children in St. Louis's Italian Fairmount District go beyond sixth grade. High school graduation rates of second-generation daughters in Providence (RI) in 1915 ranged from 21.3% for Russian Jews to 3.2% for Italians.[114] (The figure for Yankees was 23.6%.)

Only four Italians were among the 703 women at New York City's Normal College in 1910. In 1914, when 40% of teachers and six of the 10 principals in schools in Little Israel were Jewish women, the teachers in Little Italy were Irish and German women. Around 1920, an Italian American architecture student whose sister was a factory worker expressed approval that Italian American girls did not go to college: "girls who go to college always stay single."[115] Along with poverty, rigid gender norms greatly explain why in 1973, when 20% of New York City's white residents had Italian forebears, only 10% of the city's 60,000 schoolteachers were Italian Americans.[116]

When Alice Newberry (b. 1879?) exchanged her rural Colorado school in 1909 for Denver's Webster School on the heavily Italian North Side, she had never seen a city or an Italian. Calming the "volcanic dispositions" of her fourth grade class of 50 took strenuous efforts; she named this her "campaign against the Romans."

Newberry was both fascinated and startled by children who showed their regard by placing red peppers instead of apples on the teacher's desk.[117] One of the few Italian names on Denver's teacher rolls was Della Francone (b. 1898). American born of northern Italian descent, Francone's first position was a fourth grade class in Windsor (CO) founded by German farmers from Russia.[118] Such was America.

From the Shtetl to the Teachers' Lounge

Frank McCourt's first day of teaching English as a second language began in the 1960s at Seward Park High School in the once-Jewish Lower East Side. As he wrote his name on the board, a student shouted out, "Hey, mister, you Jewish?" "No," McCourt said in his heavy Irish brogue. Another student said, "Alla teachers in this school Jewish. How come you not Jewish?"[119] The typical teacher in such Jewish neighborhoods 50 years earlier was an Irish woman, Jews then making up only 6% of New York City's public school teachers. However, in 1910 one-third of the city's public school students were first- or second-generation Jews, and by 1920 the Jewish proportion among new teachers exceeded 25%, reaching 44% in 1930 and 56% in 1940.[120]

Like Italians, America's Jews were divided, especially by religious practice, home language, occupation, and income. A small number of Sephardic Jews, most from Spain and the Middle East, had settled in British North America in the seventeenth century. A quarter million German and Central European Jews (the western segment of Ashkenazi Jews) entered the United States from 1840 to 1880, most settling in the East and Midwest. A tiny community of Eastern European Jews was established in Nashville before 1860, including Polish immigrants Jacob and Sarah Bloomstein. Their daughter, Elizabeth (Lizzie), was valedictorian of the first (1877) graduating class of the Tennessee State Normal College and immediately hired to assist two Massachusetts teachers—Julie Sears and Emma Cutter—who, with President Stearns, were the first faculty.[121] Miss Bloomstein remained at her alma mater until her death in 1927, first as a teacher of history and geography, later as the librarian of what had become the George Peabody College for Teachers.

But the hard-won, usually limited acceptance that Sephardic and German Jews had achieved, and the very image of American Jewry, appeared threatened by a third and larger wave that brought Ashkenazi Jewish refugees from rural villages in Poland, Russia, Lithuania, and Rumania: a half million between 1880 and 1925. During that period, Jews—listed as "Hebrews" in census data—were second in immigrant numbers only to Italians—making New York City the "world's largest Jewish city." Despite their centuries-long experience with anti-Semitism, these Jews were believed ill equipped for their new homeland—given their "foreign" cultural habits, diverse languages, proclivity to Orthodox Judaism, and family histories of militant unionism and socialist leanings.[122] Assimilated German Jewish teachers like Julia Richman (b. 1855)—whose career in New York City schools began at age 17 and lasted 49 years—had to yield to a pluralistic Jewry that spanned the continent. Jews were 14% of San Francisco's teachers in 1910. Jeanette Lazard and Mina Norton taught in Los Angeles in the 1890s; Elsie Myers, a Vassar graduate, in Cheyenne (WY).[123]

Among the most dramatic examples of the workings of social mobility through cultural assimilation may be schoolteachers raised in such families. When Berta Rantz began school in 1899, she spoke only Russian. Her father insisted on her mastering English and "becoming American." With the help of a sister's wages as a grocery store clerk, Berta attended a Philadelphia high school. "I didn't want to be a teacher then, but I didn't want to be a sales girl in a five-and-dime store either." A two-year normal school course led to a 62-year career, mostly in progressive schools in New York City and Massachusetts.[124] Around 1935 Florence Rosenfeld's bookkeeper mother encouraged her: " 'You,' she told me from almost the first day I set foot in school, 'are going to be the teacher I could not become.' " Soon thereafter, Florence challenged her grandmother's habit of addressing her in Yiddish: "Bubbie, speak to me in English. I'm an American and I won't answer unless you do."[125]

Later arrivals were the smaller number of Jewish newcomers displaced by Nazism or the Cold War. Rena Margulies (b. 1933) and her mother survived Auschwitz. In 1947, after her mother remarried, the family left Poland for New York. Trained as an economist, Rena worked for a public relations firm, married Benjamin Chernoff in 1957, and stayed home with their two children. She also took education courses at Brooklyn College, then taught until retirement: beginning at P.S. 58 in Brooklyn, "a good school with a wonderful principal"—a woman. Most of her pupils were Italian Americans, "respectful and easy to teach."[126]

The Personal and the Situational

Asians' historically small presence among America's teachers does not entirely explain Rodney's reaction on glimpsing his first-grade teacher at the orientation preceding his first day of school. His mother explained, "Rodney says he doesn't want to come in because he can't speak Chinese!" While this Japanese American teacher did not speak Chinese either, she knew that racial labeling explained the confusion of both parent and child. "Rodney, barely six years old, had already formed certain beliefs: first, that those with Asian physical features must be

Chinese and not American; and second that if I were Chinese I would not speak English."[127]

The abstract generalities of social status, culture, and race come together variously and meaningfully in the individual life. The black or immigrant experience is a particularly powerful lens through which to view the unfolding of personal, family, and group dreams and ambitions set amid seemingly irrepressible societal forces, ethnic stereotypes, and interethnic tensions. This chapter closes by sketching, too briefly, the lives of two such persons—one real and one fictional (but very real).

Being Japanese: Estella Takahashi

Although occasionally teachers commented on their mannerly and studious Japanese American pupils, prejudice and discrimination flourished on the West Coast long before Pearl Harbor. Estella Yorozu Takahashi was born in Thomas (WA) in 1916 to well-educated Japanese immigrants. Her mother had attended a Japanese university, wrote haiku, and studied classical dance, music, flower arranging, and the tea ceremony. When Stella was seven the family moved from their farm to Seattle, to be near the public university. Photos of the six children in cap and gown were prominently displayed.[128]

Seattle's schools were considered progressive, with the teachers engaged, civic-minded professionals, and Stella remembered George Washington School fondly. However, no Asians taught at any Seattle public school, including those where 99% of the pupils were Asian, and 45% were Nisei (second generation).[129] The Yorozus were Christians, and Stella taught in a Japanese American Methodist Sunday school, for which she received training. Her father encouraged her.

In 1934 Stella went to the University of Washington, majoring in home economics with an emphasis on textiles and fine arts. Despite there being more men than women among the perhaps 400 Japanese American students enrolled, Stella discerned no bias against girls. There she met her future husband, Yukio Takahashi, a graduate student and Canadian citizen with a premedical degree from the University of British Columbia. Stella abandoned her plans to teach when a counselor in the University's College of Education told her, "I'm sorry. It would be a waste of time. We could not get a teaching place for an Asian Teacher."[130]

Early in 1942, Stella's recently widowed mother, her maternal grandmother, and the six siblings were ordered to dispose of their possessions, taking no more than what each could carry in two hands. They went first to an "assembly center" on a fairground, where their quarters were horse stables. Stella taught fourth grade at the assembly center "school" the residents created with donated books. The family was next sent to Minidoka, a "relocation camp" in Idaho, with 10,000 other internees. The younger Yorozu children were among the eventually 30,000 Japanese and Japanese American youth schooled behind barbed wire in various remote, often desolate sites, most in the intermountain West—sites reminiscent of reservations set aside for American Indians in the nineteenth century.[131] When the University of Idaho's Education Department sent instructors to Minidoka, Stella took courses in teaching English and social studies. With practice teaching in the camp school, she earned an Idaho secondary teaching credential.

In June 1943, at her mother's insistence, Stella applied for clearance and train fare east. Stella left for Chicago with a friend whose relatives would sponsor and house them until they could get work. The large, impersonal city had its advantages; people were busy with their own affairs, and Stella—"I minded my own business"—got along. Renting a room near the University of Chicago, she read the want ads. With her art background and the wartime labor shortage, Stella readily found work at a printing company.

Stella and Yukio married in Chicago in 1949. He found work in a dry cleaning plant, but she had savings. Their daughters were born in 1950 and 1953, and the family moved to Northern California. Later, as a teacher's aide at Fair Oaks Elementary School in Redwood City, the principal asked, "What are you, a college graduate, doing as a teacher's aide? Get a teaching credential." Her husband, now a food chemist, encouraged her. With a credential from the nearby College of Notre Dame, Stella returned to Fair Oaks School. During her 15-year career, Mexican Americans took the place of many of her African American pupils. Their fathers worked two jobs, their mothers were employed, and both wanted better for their children. She was told, "You can spank them if you want," something she would not do. While neither of her daughters taught, theirs were freely made decisions—not, as in Stella's case, a dream deferred.

Anna in the Mission: Neighborhood Change in San Francisco

The fictional story of Anna Giardino reveals an American high school as a microcosm of neighborhood change as one cultural group displaces or succeeds another. Except for Chinatown, San Francisco's small neighborhoods were more mixed and fluid than ethnic enclaves in eastern cities. Mission High was an ordinary neighborhood school. Its teachers and counselors worried about chronic tardiness, high dropout rates, and occasional rumbles in classrooms and corridors—not about the effects of stressful competition on students headed to prestigious colleges, as at Lowell—the city's one academically selective "examination high school." Yet before the 1970s, Mission High sent many graduates to college or decent jobs, consistent with public education's implied promises to several generations of middle- and ambitious working-class youth, and to their assimilation-minded families.

Opened in 1890 in the city's oldest neighborhood, Mission High always served a diverse and shifting population.[132] The Mission had an Irish majority, alongside pockets of Germans, Scandinavians, Russians, and others. The Outer Mission was then open farmland, attracting Italian immigrants—distinct from North Beach, the city's original Little Italy. By 1925, Italian numbers in the Mission challenged older groups, as Hispanics did later. The city's first Hispanics were a few descendants of the Californios of the Spanish and Mexican period, augmented from Gold Rush days by Chileans, Central Americans, and some Mexicans. The Hispanic presence grew further with World War II when shipyards sent recruiters to Central America. A generation later political upheavals in Central America solidified the Mission District as a Central American *barrio,* unique among Hispanic settlements in Western cities in not having a Mexican majority. As Central Americans had good school-completion and college-entry rates, this difference likely improved the prospect that some Latino students would become teachers.[133]

Predictably, it took time for the Mission's shifting ethnic mix to be represented among Mission High's teachers and administrators. The number of Irish teachers rose from 8 (1910) to 33 (1933). Italian names appeared among male teachers by 1925, with women coming later: Miss de Ghetaldi before 1937, and Lorraine Bassadonne, Carolyn Caniglia, and Gloria Dati by 1965. No more than one or two Hispanic teachers appear at a time until 1980, when seven taught in a faculty of 130, and Teresa Hernandez Heinz chaired the math department.[134] A cross section of the city's other groups also appeared: a German and Jewish contingent from 1914, Southern and Eastern Europeans by the 1920s, and Asian and African American additions from the 1960s.

Mission High School is the basis of Camino Real High in *Miss Giardino,* a novel by Dorothy Calvetti Bryant (b. 1930), daughter of immigrants, graduate of Mission High, and high school teacher for eight years. Ann Giardino's schooling began in a mining town, where "the thin lady" teaches her to write. The family's move to the Mission District reveals the "marble palace" of a public library "with a special room for children, including Italians."[135] But Anna's defeated, embittered immigrant father opposes schooling for girls. She is saved from factory work by a visit from "a frightening, official-looking man": "I must go to school. So I am sent running down Mission Street every morning to a building only slightly less blessed than the public library. I listen amazed when the other children say they hate school and call the teachers mean and strict."

As Anna is "college material," her teachers tell her about Berkeley and scholarships. In 1928, a newly minted teacher, Anna Giardino returns to her high school, "hired when [Mr. Ruggles] retired. He had been grooming me for his job from the time he first knew me." Ruggles was more than her "connection": "I admired him. I wanted to be like him. He was a teacher. I would be a teacher. . . . I was at home in the classroom. . . . I was safe."

But some students judge her cold and unfeeling, comparing the Cs she gives their papers with their As in other classes. "My aunt used to teach English and she thought it was good." "Miss Giardino, you're so mean!" "Miss Giardino, you a racist!" She notes the irony: "When I started teaching I was looked down on and called a dago. When I ended my teaching I was looked down on and called a racist."

When she retires, Miss Giardino's replacement in the English Department is Maria Flores, a former student with whom she had clashed. Both from suspect groups, they share the experience of having been favored by their teachers as "exceptions." Anna remembers: "The teachers used to complain about the noisy Italian boys . . . [but] they assured me I was different." " 'Me too,' said Maria. 'Not like "those other Mexicans." ' " Herself an embattled teacher, Maria confesses, "This past year especially, I realized I owe you an apology. For judging you. Only three years of teaching, and do I understand!" Maria Flores had "clamped down" on her students. Although she knows the answer, Anna Giardino asks, "What happened?" "I was called a traitor to Third World people," says Maria.

Conclusion: Uncloistered Women of the World

Over a long period—even as the statistically typical American teacher was a (broadly defined) middle-class white Protestant woman of northwestern European stock—those who were not white, Protestant, or of Anglo-Saxon origins steadily diversified the teacher workforce, even as teachers became more culturally alike. In 2000, unlike the school's controversial ethnic tinkering with student admissions, it went unremarked that two social studies teachers at San Francisco's elite Lowell High were Gale Ow and Thais da Rosa.[136]

Ethnic consciousness, so integral to the first generation, usually fades or is refocused in the second and successive generations. A dominant language; economic, legal, and cultural institutions; exposure through formal education and the media to a powerful but flexible national story—these do their work. Even the stubborn divide of race is increasingly often breached in the personal and professional relations with colleagues and between pupils and teachers. When her eighth graders bullied a new student from China into the hospital with severe asthma, fictional Mrs. Bogdanovich made China the curriculum: "Where do you think paper was invented? Gunpowder? Noodles? You just raised your hand and answer 'China, China, China' and you'd be right." Mrs. B's lesson took hold: tolerance, even acceptance, checked bullying.[137]

By the late twentieth century, most public and many private schools were promoting tolerance of homosexual students, and openly lesbian and gay teachers began keeping their jobs. Legislation and greater public acceptance permitted teachers with disabilities to claim the teacher's desk. In 1921, a severed spine cost Maude L. Alverson her position as Latin teacher at Urbana (IL) High School. To support herself and her widowed mother, she sold insurance and magazine subscriptions and typed university students' papers. In 1981, the *Rosemary's* photo of Urbana High's faculty showed Bob Drew, industrial arts teacher, in his wheelchair.[138]

Although demographic distinctions among Americans waxed and waned in employment and social life, gender remained the determining (although not unchanging) social characteristic shaping experience. Gender still set different parameters for wages, teaching assignments, advancements, and expectations (not all favorable to men). In public and parochial schools, the woman still teaches, the man decides. When *his* wages were deemed inadequate, *her* more meager pay was "sufficient for her needs"—perhaps "dangerously generous." Gender restricted *her* ostensibly private life and social relationships far more than it did *his*. The conflicted imagery of teaching, its positive and negative elements, remains suffused with gender norms. Miss Giardino embodied the old-fashioned spinster stereotype; the divorced Maria Flores, a modern modality.

In 1898, Rosa Sonnenschein was blunt: "marriage is the foremost aim of the American Jewess as it was for her mother and grandmother." Already, however, a generation of Jewish women was preparing to become Gertrudes; other subcultures also offer a wealth of exceptions.[139] Thus the next chapter turns to another demographic marker: the marital status of the woman teacher and the proposition that, in her case, marriage is more than a private matter. It will become clearer how women teachers have been positioned on a shaky bridge between the market and the home and family, "expected to exhibit both the selflessness of mothers and the self-sufficiency of citizens."[140]

The "old education": an eighteenth-century German schoolroom
Paul Monroe, *"A Text-book of Education"* (1911)

The "new education": a naturalistic school
Paul Monroe, *A Text-book of Education* (1911)

The ubiquitous English dame school
Unknown source

Lined up for the county teachers examination, San Andreas (CA), c. 1893
Calavaras County Historical Society (by permission)

South Carolina Normal School students, c. 1875
University Archives, South Carolina Library, University of South Carolina (by permission)

Teachers and principals of colored schools, Tennessee, 1897
Courtesy of the Tennessee State Library and Archives

"While the children drew, Mr. Bryan would lean on Miss Jenny's desk, rearrange his white necktie, and talk to Miss Jenny."

The principal inspects the new substitute teacher.
George Hadden Martin, *"Her Book and Her Heart"* (1902)

"It was Emmy Lou's joy to gather her doll children in line, and giving out past lessons recite them . . . for her children."

Emmy Lou emulates her teacher.
George Hadden Martin, *"Her Book and Her Heart"* (1902)

Posed for a science lesson, Washington, DC, 1899
Frances B. Johnson, Going to School Series (by permission)

The ideal of the common school: an unknown California school, 1906–1907
In the possession of the late Edith Williams Clifford

Philinda Rand Anglemeyer and colleagues in the Philippines, c. 1905
The Schlesinger Library, Radcliffe Institute, Harvard University (by permission)

A teacher in paradise: Laura Bowles and friends, (1912)
Paradise (CA) Historical Society

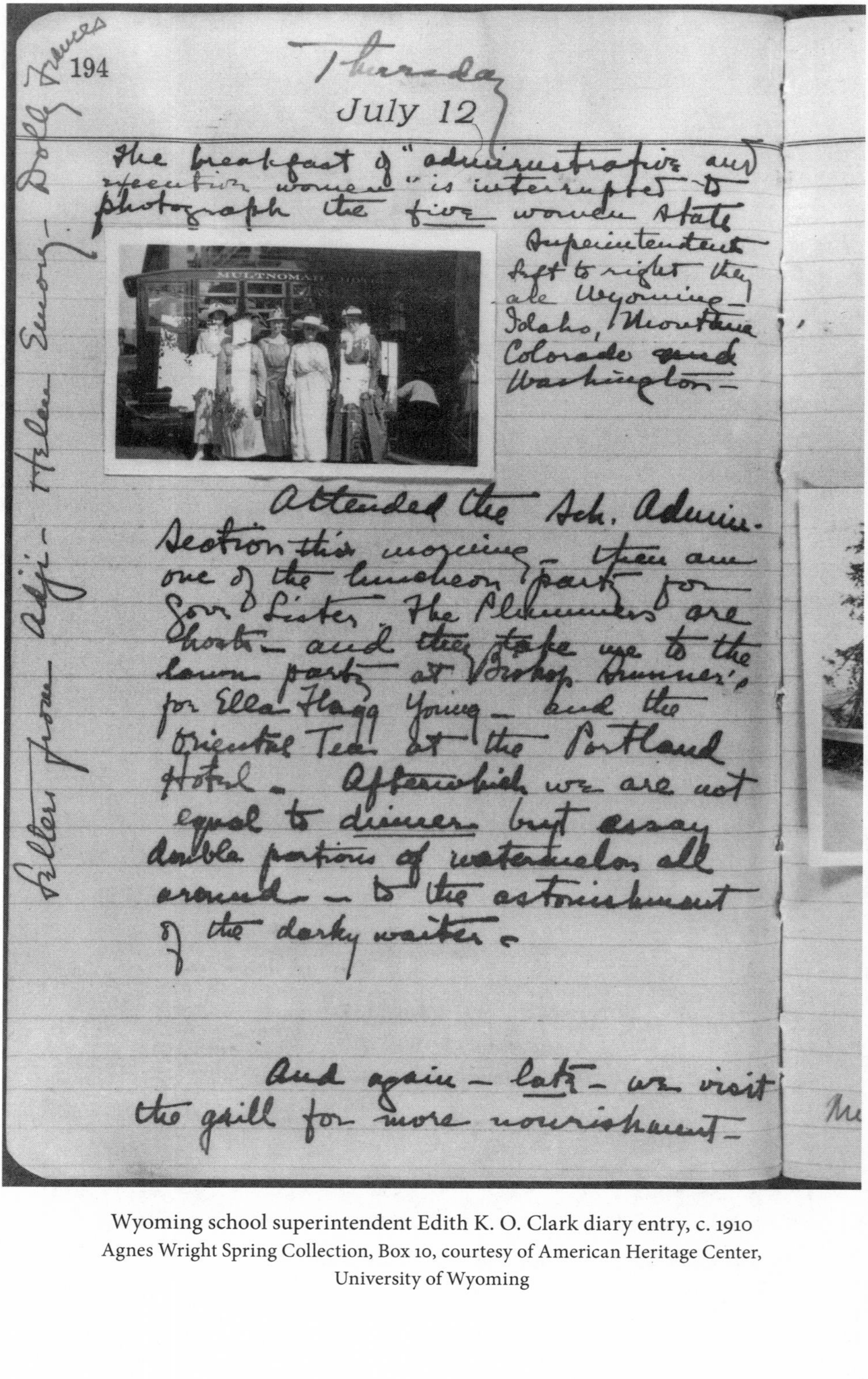

194

Thursday

July 12

The breakfast of "administrative and executive women" is interrupted to photograph the five women State Superintendents left to right they are Wyoming— Idaho, Montana, Colorado and Washington—

Attended the Sch. Admin. Section this morning— then am one of the luncheon party for Gov. Lister. The Plummers are hosts— and they take me to the lawn party at Bishop Sumner's, for Ella Flagg Young— and the Oriental Tea at the Portland Hotel— After which we are not equal to dinner but essay double portions of watermelon all around— to the astonishment of the darky waiter.

And again— late— we visit the grill for more nourishment—

Letter from Adji— Helen Emory— Dolly Travers

Wyoming school superintendent Edith K. O. Clark diary entry, c. 1910
Agnes Wright Spring Collection, Box 10, courtesy of American Heritage Center, University of Wyoming

Polingaysi Qöyawayma (Elizabeth Q. White) and her students, c. 1925
University of New Mexico Press (by permission)

Health lesson, Cemetery School, Murfreesboro, c. 1925
Courtesy of Tennessee State Library and Archives

Miss Cora Dunbar, Union City, Kentucky
Courtesy of Kathleen Schwarzschild

Frances Eisenberg and staff of "Hunter's Call," Van Nuys (CA) High School, 1947
Frances R. Eisenberg Los Angeles City Schools Loyalty Oath Collection, Department of
Special Collections, Charles E. Young Research Library, UCLA (by permission)

Labor strife: Oakland teachers, c. 1975
Photo by Nick Lammers / The Oakland Tribune (by permission)

CHAPTER 6

"The Presiding Genius of His Home and Heart"

Her Marital Status and Domestic Arrangements

> [Marital status is] the most misunderstood issue in the history of teachers and teaching. . . . The marriage bar is historians' myth.
>
> —R. Butchart et al.

The first three schoolmistresses in eighteenth-century Dedham (MA) were an unmarried woman, a wife, and a widow. Emma Hart Willard's career began as a single woman, persisted through marriage, widowhood, remarriage, and divorce. When, in 1808, her Vermont school became embroiled in denominational quarrels, local physician Dr. John Willard came to her aid. "Not many months after, [he] persuaded the successful schoolmistress, at the age of twenty-two, to become the presiding genius of his home and heart." Although marriage to a member of the local elite often ended or redirected a woman's career, this husband supported her ambitions and managed family and school finances on her returns to teaching. Many women empowered by their work found the family circle confining and sought worthy reasons to venture beyond it. "When I began my boarding school in Middlebury, in 1814, my leading motive was to relieve my husband from financial difficulties . . . [while] keeping a better school than those about me."[1]

Unmarried, Ann Lewis Hardeman (b. 1803) made her home with a married brother on his Mississippi plantation. Given, at age 46, the responsibility for the six children of a dead sister, Aunt Ann supervised their schoolwork, gained a teacher's awareness of diverse temperaments and abilities, and experienced a teacher's frustrations with bored and willful pupils. "Have had very little pleasure in hearing the children's lessons this week" went a diary entry in September 1850. Two surviving nieces—Adelaide and Bettie Stuart, "one bright, one simple,"—became teachers, forced into self-sufficiency by the loss of two soldier brothers and the family home in the Civil War. At age 22 Bettie married a widower with several children, and Adelaide married on the cusp of spinsterhood at 28. Aunt Ann could then relax, for she had prayed "they may be relieved from teaching as I fear it does not suit them."[2]

Another Mississippian, Elizabeth Ann Thompson (b. 1849), accompanied her father on his medical rounds and learned that Copiah County needed teachers. She taught for 14 years in a schoolhouse her father built for her in 1867. Although the income from her "pay school" was slight, neither marriage in 1871 nor the birth of eight children ended her career. A cradle in the schoolroom held each infant, and the older pupils helped with the toddlers, as they likely did in their own homes. As her family moved, Mrs. East taught, either at home or in a schoolhouse built by her carpenter husband. Two of her five surviving children became career teachers.[3]

Unlike the slave-holding Thompsons, Mississippi's Markham sisters and their pupils were the descendants of slaves.[4] Alice Markham Marshall (b. 1891) and Mattie Markham Vaughn (b. 1892) taught rural schools in Lincoln County. Alice married in her late thirties but resigned, as "a working wife was not [in] the plans of her husband." Mattie taught after marrying until her eight closely spaced children needed her full attention.

However, in the public mind, popular culture, and sometimes in law, the schoolmistress was single—either the young teacher waiting to marry or the spinster unable to "land her man." Over three generations, these Mississippi women present different realities while opening up other issues in teachers' work and private lives: transiency and persistence, the men teachers marry and what they bring to and gain from the union, and how wage-earning women cope with domestic demands. Employment and family, work and love, technical skills and personal obligations, the instrumental and the affective, and production and reproduction are rarely separable in women's lives. "Since women's intellectual [i.e., professional] product has been so greatly influenced by constraints on the lives of all women, the private life and the work of a woman need to be considered in close interrelationship."[5]

Career Trajectories and Marital Status

Mrs. Minnie O'Neal, a youngish Alabama widow, arrived with a 12-year-old daughter and was hired around 1914 to teach an eight-grade country school. Professionally well regarded, some also thought "she had set her cap for our community's most eligible bachelor, Mr. Marvin Peacock[;] she did get him, and there was a summer wedding."[6] Although she had taken on marriage's proverbial "School of One Scholar," the new Mrs. Peacock resumed teaching—not disqualified by her remarriage.

During the 1930s, all but one of the retired New York City Jewish women teachers interviewed by Ruth Markowitz had married, most by age 25. Most bore children, undeterred by mandatory unpaid maternity leaves and the specter of jobless husbands and other male kin.[7] While economic hardship helps explain their persistence, so does a liking for the work and access to household help or child care. A matter-of-factness characterizes teachers' own accounts, their marital status seemingly a personal and practical, not a public, concern.[8] Multiple such examples suggest that teacher selection and turnover were not as dependent on women's matrimonial status as generally believed. Not until the 1940s, however, did imagery begin to catch up with reality.

To Teach, and Then to Wed—Perhaps

Given an oversupply of schoolma'ams in the Northeast, single women were encouraged to head "Out West"—where there were reportedly too few women—to teach, "civilize," and marry; Gertrude could increase her options on each score. "Mercer Girls" was the name given Eastern women offered teaching positions on the West Coast, their ship passage paid by hopeful swains—a scheme of Seattle resident Asa Mercer. Despite the Civil War and lurid press accounts, 200 young women agreed to participate. Of the first contingent, 9 of 11 quickly married; one of the second (1866) group married Mercer himself.[9] Writing to a former student in 1885, T. B. Crisp of Girard (IL) mentioned two new "schule marms," one "a fresh importation from Boston. . . . You must come up and make her acquaintance."[10]

A shortage of females on America's successive frontiers made retaining their single women teachers difficult—made worse by bachelor school board trustees who had applicants submit their photographs or who reputedly joined the board to be first in line to court the new teacher.[11] When complaints arose in 1872 about the first teacher in Plumas County (CA)—that she crocheted as she walked the floor while teaching the Summit School—two bachelor school board members volunteered to investigate. Miss Mary Street admitted she had made 60 yards of edging on school time and would give the district's representatives the edging if they thought she had defrauded the district. One of the two, William Arms, "not only got the edging, but the teacher as well."[12]

In 1899, restless in her Illinois home, 17-year-old Edna Fay became the first teacher in Park County (MT). Six years later Miss Fay finally accepted William J. Kaiser, a homesteader, member of the Helena baseball team, "a nifty dresser and a graceful dancer." New Mexico's Pearl Barker broke her engagement to attend the normal school; she married after teaching several years. Another normal school graduate (1907), Corintha Bruce was teaching in rural Chillicothe (MO) and already "on the shelf" when rescued from spinsterhood in 1920.[13] None fits another stereotype: the young schoolma'am swept into marriage, the ink barely dry on her teaching contract.

When Michael O'Hare died in 1886 in Carson City (NV), this Irish immigrant and Civil War veteran left a widow and eight children.[14] Of their five daughters, four married men they met while teaching. A later Nevadan, Thelma Catherine Ryan was born in the mining town of Ely, on the eve of St. Patrick's Day, 1912. "Pat"—so named by her ardently Irish father—attended the University of Southern California intending to become a department store buyer; instead, she taught business subjects at Whittier High School. A little-theatre group brought her together with a young lawyer, Richard Nixon, ending her teaching career. While subsequent events made her First Lady, Pat Nixon's entrance into and exit from teaching was otherwise unremarkable.

Writing to the superintendent of Avery Normal Institute in Charleston (SC) in 1871, Commissioner J. B. Corbell requested two more "colored misses" to teach in Sumter County. He added, "Ladies too young generally have beaux upon the brain, Ladies too old are fussy and hard to please."[15] The apostles of professionalism were of several minds on both the "Green Miss" and the "Dried-up Schoolma'am." While an ever-rotating army of novices added no prestige to their profession, the "Green Miss" was indispensable: ill paid, teaching in isolated or overcrowded and underresourced schools, in the lower grades of village schools and city schools in unappealing neighborhoods. As for "old maids," these were the nation's classroom professionals: enrolling in summer pedagogy classes, earning degrees and life certificates, joining teachers associations and going to their conventions. Careerists were especially common among black women, single or married, as marriage was less often expected to retire them from the labor force. Not so the veteran teacher in California's mountainous Lassan County, traveling daily eleven miles to and from her schoolhouse while keeping house for her family, including her husband so disabled by rheumatism that she had to dress him.[16]

To Teach and Wed—and Yet to Teach

Between 1620 and 1945 far more American wives (including mothers) taught school, sometimes over a lifetime, than generally recognized. Supplementing family income was expected of most wives in colonial America; a few such schoolmistresses have been uncovered. More names appear after 1800, including Electa

Lincoln (b. 1824), a student and teacher at Massachusetts's first state normal school. As Mrs. Walton she opened a small private school for her own and neighborhood children, offered "institutes" and "summer normals" for teachers, and demonstrated reading methods at another normal school. The many married couples working in ordinary academies likely gave the antebellum South a higher than average proportion of married women teachers. Despite having five children between 1854 and 1861, Texan Rebecca Stuart Reed continued her Live Oak Female Seminary and opened another in 1876, her physician-husband its part-time science teacher.[17]

The married women and widows with young children who taught in nineteenth-century Pittsburgh's public schools "did not fit the neat little image of the school teacher as young, native born and middle class."[18] Sylvia Hunt found records of enough married women teaching in Texas between 1850 and 1940 to speak of "the myth of the single teacher."[19] Around 1916, Mary Nolan was teaching the Walnut Grove (AZ) school that enrolled her own children; during school vacations she took them across the mountains to join her husband, who ran the Columbia post office and a small store and had "stringer" gold claims. Married women were often such local residents, teaching because they were "known quantities," their small districts could not find or retain the younger single woman, or trustees were leery of alienating someone important. Tucson's superintendent issued an ex cathedra rule in the 1920s that women teachers who married must vacate their jobs—then hired Mrs. Wilson, wife of a Mormon missionary who had returned to teaching.[20]

If school officials acted inconsistently, they often had good reasons. Raised in Bennington (KS), Zenobia Boyle married and bore three children. When her husband left her, the trustees hired her despite a local understanding that teachers should be single women. She needed a job and the board needed a teacher. Moreover, because she lived with her parents, her salary went further, she had child care, and her reputation was salvaged.[21] But depersonalized city school systems also found reasons to employ or retain the wife and mother. A 1931 Pennsylvania study found married women high school teachers the most stable element in the teacher workforce.[22]

Despite claims that a mother's employment cheated both her pupils and her own family, having children was advantageous in depopulated school districts. In the 9 one-room schools of Tehama County (CA), for example, pupil numbers were so small by the 1920s and 1930s that graduation or a departing family annually threatened each school with closure. When state law required a minimum average daily attendance of 5.7 pupils, a parent took the initiative in keeping Mendocino County's Comfort School alive. One year they hired Mrs. Gowan from Ukiah as teacher, bringing her children. "The next year Mrs. Gussie Ruddock came to be teacher and brought Tom, Jerry and Mary." If necessary for maintaining the school, "County [foster] Children" were enrolled.[23]

AN EXEMPLAR: ELIZABETH MECREDY DANNER

Elizabeth Mecredy (b. 1916) grew up in the Mojave Desert where her Belfast immigrant father and her three brothers struggled to raise sheep and turkeys. When the family moved to San Francisco, Elizabeth attended Mission High School and San Francisco State Teachers College. To secure a job at the Shandon School east of Paso Robles, her fiancé drove her around to be interviewed by the trustees. One was in his dairy barn; another got off his tractor to check her credentials and references in his wheat field. The position won, a boarding place was arranged, and Miss Mecredy settled in for the expected two years of experience. Years later, the two-teacher Shandon School had been replaced by a modern building, her former pupil was district superintendent, and she was Mrs. Curtis Danner: wife, mother of four, and career teacher at Albany's Marin Grade School.[24] While the Albany board was made somewhat anxious by her teaching late into her fourth pregnancy, Elizabeth Danner had tenure and child care, the district had a maternity leave policy, and the baby boom had exhausted the available teacher supply.

When Mrs. Danner retired after 28 years of service, most of her colleagues were married women with school-age children. The single—80% of U.S. women teachers in 1930—had fallen to 23% in 1970 and to 19% in 1981. The corresponding increase of married women as a percent of all women teachers is better explained by cultural and economic factors as well as personal and family decisions than by policy changes. The equivalent of the wage-earning daughter in 1900, working to keep younger siblings in school, was the employed mother of 1975 and 2010. She was a breadwinner or second wage earner, saving to buy a home, enjoy a higher standard of living, make discretionary purchases, help aging parents, pay private school tuition, feed a college fund or retirement account, and perhaps help her children and grandchildren resist an alarming slide out of the shrinking and threatened American middle class.

CULTURE: COULDN'T YOU FIND A
NICE ITALIAN BOY, AND STAY HOME?

Although acceptance of employed wives varied by culture and social class, women of diverse backgrounds taught after marriage. Ina Beauchamp, born of white and Indian parents on the Berthold Reservation, was reportedly North Dakota's first public school graduate of Indian ancestry. After her marriage to a rancher and the birth of nine children, Beauchamp was lured back into the class-room by a temporary position that proved permanent. A Hopi, Elizabeth Qöy-awayma taught as a single woman, a wife, and a divorcée.[25]

Blanche Harris, one of the first black women sent from Ohio to teach the freedmen, taught throughout two marriages. The Negro Rural Schools Fund, sponsor of the Jeanes Teachers program—a Northern philanthropy designed to improve the training of Negro teachers—accepted married women and wid-ows.[26] Although her marriage to a physician and businessman did not retire Selena Sloan Butler (b. 1872), with motherhood she instead opened a kindergar-ten and organized the Georgia Colored Parent-Teacher Association. However, by 1960 the proportion of the married among black women schoolteachers (70%) was below that of white women teachers (80%), a consequence of the widening educational and occupational gap between black women and black men. When, rather than "marry down," the professional woman remains childless, her hard-earned cultural capital can be concentrated on the socially responsible gift of inspiring and benefitting the community's other children.[27]

If less often or later than the more liberal Protestant and Jewish subgroups, Catholic women increasingly combined career, marriage, and motherhood. Ida Stornetta, a graduate of the first class at Point Arena High School, was on Men-docino County teacher lists by 1911; married in 1916, as Mrs. Caylor she was still teaching in 1929, further defying convention by marrying outside the group.[28] May-Blossom Wilkinson also challenged norms. In 1949, when she became its first Chinese American teacher, she was warned, "The eyes of Berkeley will be upon you. If you don't do well, you will close the doors to other Orientals." Two rows of adults sat in the rear of her classroom for two months, taking notes on everything she did and said. The morning after her first date with Robert Wilkin-son, whom she later married, her colleagues asked her to consider the effects of interracial dating on students.[29]

While interethnic marriages led to estrangements in some families or excited public comment, polygamy was a national scandal, provoking heated debate and prohibitory legislation. Many Mormon teachers practiced polygamy. Emmeline Blanche Woodward (b. 1828) taught school, in New England, then in the Latter Day Saints' enclave at Nauvoo (IL), before marrying at age 16. When her husband abandoned her and Mormonism, she became a plural wife and migrated to Utah; when widowed, she taught to maintain herself and daughter. The parents of Cyn-thia Burnham Fisher (b.1866) supported her and her seven children while her wages supported her husband's first family. Their husbands' multiple families and absences as missionaries made plural wives virtual heads of households—more like widows than the more typical married woman of their era.[30]

After Congress outlawed polygamy in the 1870s, various public school officials contemplated policies to bar or regulate the ordinary married women who might apply to teach in their districts. Their response appears, however, less a reaction to Mormon transgressions than to eugenicists' and moralists' disapproval of the "over-educated" spinster, now extended to the married woman teacher. Neither would produce the large families needed to protect "the real America" from the high birthrates of its suspect immigrants.

The Marriage Bar: Public Control of a Private Matter

When most teachers were self-employed, their marital status was a private concern, but nineteenth-century Presbyterian schools, like many church-sponsored schools, refused to employ married women, trying also to limit their teachers' social contacts with single men. Historians' interest, however, has focused on public school officials who considered or enacted some version of what a Seattle teacher derided as a "medieval marriage law": an employment bar erected against the married woman.[31] New York City's Anne Kunstler refused even to contemplate matrimony, having "invested too much of my family's resources, and of myself and my dreams, not to mention money into the pension plan, for me to abandon teaching."[32] How prevalent were occupational impediments to marriage, whether dictated by church education boards, public school officials, formal rules, or informal sanctions—and how important to individual careers, lives, and American public education writ large?

The Myth versus the Realities of the Marriage Bar

Chicago's school board retained Lizzy Locke when she married in 1868; she taught through her pregnancy and was reappointed for another year. Given her weekly salary of $12 and the couple's lodgings and board bill of $14, financial need may explain the board's decision.[33] While Chicago's later school boards were not noted for compassion, they enacted no marriage bar. But Boston's school committee decided in 1880 that to marry and continue teaching required board approval. In 1900 it went further: "The marriage of a woman teacher shall operate as a resignation of her position." Was Boston's policy a job-creating concession to the young women enrolled at Boston Normal School or, perhaps, to the Catholic Church's teachings on family?[34] The answer is likely yes to both.

Official response to married teachers in the nineteenth and twentieth centuries was neither uniform nor inevitable. Married women were common among Buffalo's teachers before 1860 but prohibited later, while, in nearby Steuben County in 1899, Mrs. A. H. Watkins of North Cohocton "taught school on Friday and became a mother on Saturday." Vermont records and interviews disclose married and pregnant women, and even mothers, teaching between 1900 and 1950.[35] Rather than a response to a clear national trend, the presence or absence of a marriage bar appears a function of social, economic, cultural, or demographic variables—mediated by local conditions, idiosyncratic events, personal decisions, or chance. Whether and how it was applied, enforced, amended, evaded, or abandoned is similarly contextual.

In 1883, a California journal noted that 10% of New York City's teachers were married, there being "no rule that prevents an instructor from [keeping] her place when she has assumed hymeneal obligations . . . earning [her] living and helping [her husband] by teaching other men's children." But the mere raising of the issue shows that marriage bars were under discussion. In 1891 the *Educational Review* asked the superintendents of eight big-city districts about their married women teachers. Wives' numbers were low in Philadelphia, Cleveland, Brooklyn, and Jersey City, but not because of mandates.[36] While New York City now reported an exclusionary ruling exempting widows and teachers with disabled husbands, Denver and Chicago proclaimed that teacher-mothers were among their best teachers. In June 1900 the *Western Journal of Education* reported that Judge [W. F.] Fitzgerald ruled that a school board may vacate a teacher's position if she marries—a board discretion the Kirkwood and Red Bluff districts did not exercise, welcoming back Georgia Council and her sister, Retta Council, both married that summer.

Although New York City's 1891 strictures are often cited as evidence of a nationwide drive to regulate marriage and employment, an examination of their implementation invites caution. In 1904 a New York state court reinstated 11-year veteran Kate Murphy, rejecting the board's charge that her marrying constituted "gross misconduct." In 1915 the board reacted to its growing staff of married women by refusing them maternity leaves, making their absence due to childbirth grounds for dismissal as "neglect of duty." Bridgit Peixotto sued and won, the court ruling that a maternity leave was a legal right; the board was ordered to replace teachers on maternity leave with substitutes, thereby securing their positions. New York City's attempt in the 1930s to limit women to two maternity leaves was thwarted by Catholic opposition to birth control.[37]

If religion and ethnicity sometimes affected policy, seemingly race always did. At a time when Gary (IN) schools would not recruit married white women, Mrs. Elizabeth Lytle was hired to teach her race in a segregated Negro school. In 1931, Alice Dunbar-Nelson's superintendent used Wilmington's (DE) marriage bar as an excuse to prevent her rehiring, when speaking out against racial bias was the real issue: "a pleasant way of telling me I was permanently black listed."[38]

As in the general labor market, cities had higher proportions of married women teachers, who tended to be better educated, more experienced and qualified for tenure, older, and less tractable. In 1891 Washington (DC) officials used local teacher activist Mary Church Terrell's marriage against her.[39] Cities could save money and aggravation by eliminating or reclassifying them—for example, as substitute or night school teachers. However, teacher shortages during World War I led President Wilson to urge Washington (DC) to employ married women. In 1927 DC officials presented a referendum on a proposed marriage bar to 70 organizations (PTAs and civic groups): 57 favored married women as public school and normal school teachers, 7 voted against, and 6 were noncommittal.[40]

Elsewhere, perhaps unwilling to jeopardize their schools' reputations by gambling with personnel policies, some of the nation's other large cities—for example, Los Angeles, Chicago, Detroit, Minneapolis, Denver—either never invoked a marriage bar or had one only briefly. Cincinnati instituted one in 1890, likely influenced by its large German population's preference for male teachers.[41]

Unlike New England, Southern cities' undersupply of teachers resulted in fewer marital bars. New Orleans, however, dismissed Sarah Towles (b. 1882) in 1921 upon discovering that she was the recently widowed Mrs. Elkanah Reed. Although she regained her position on appeal and worked through the teachers' union to rescind the bar, New Orleans did not suspend its last restriction until 1950. Existing bars in Charleston (SC) and elsewhere were generally dispatched during or following World War II—and not reinstated.[42]

Teacher marriages did not ordinarily disqualify a man or restrict his career advancement. Indeed, having a wife was considered a "steadying influence," whereas having a husband was regarded as a distraction and potential threat to administrative authority. Where such opinions brought local regulations, these could be suspended in the face of activist teachers' unions, court decisions, and shifts in public opinion. As school officials had "to cover every classroom" and undoubtedly hoped the coverage was adequate, both the absence of a policy and inconsistent enforcement are understandable.

If policy decisions rested on local mores and personalized politics, court rulings on marriage bars were typically based on technical grounds, with the tenure system usually deciding the issue.[43] Between 1886 and 1940, 17 states legislated some form of tenure, usually eliminating dismissal for marriage or pregnancy. However, some school boards retaliated. A tenured California teacher who declined to resign after marrying was reassigned to teach in a tuberculosis sanatorium under her district's jurisdiction. A state court ruled in her favor in 1929, effectively ending marriage as a barrier to teaching in California.[44]

Affected teachers and their supporters did more than wait for favorable court actions. Texas teachers in prohibitory districts reported teaching while openly married or keeping marriages secret, noting principals who "simply turned a blind eye." A Texas district rescinded its marriage bar because the comings and goings of clandestine marriages scandalized the community. Despite its earlier permissive history, Utah's Cache County in the 1930s subjected married women to immediate dismissal. But there and elsewhere teachers colluded in keeping marriages secret, as they had with earlier teachers' outlawed polygamous marriages.[45]

Disentangling the Marriage Bar Knot

The marriage bar myth is the result of incorrect inferences from limited and underanalyzed data, generalized from a relatively few noncontextualized cases. The myth was perpetuated by anecdotes—"My Aunt Hattie remained single (or quit teaching) because they wouldn't let married women teach back then"—or folksy accounts that recycled the quaint 1920 teaching contract that printed "Miss" before the blank for the teacher's name and set the condition that that she was "not to get married" or "to keep company with men." Looking for marriage bars in business firms and school boards, Claudia Goldin mistakenly asserts that school boards are easier to assess and track "due to [two] comprehensive surveys of local school boards by the National Education Association beginning in the late 1920s."[46] Projecting from these same surveys, Willard Ellsbree concluded, in 1939, that "hundreds of school boards took similar action" in restricting women's freedom to marry.[47]

Such conclusions are problematic on several grounds. From the 1890s through the 1940s, the United States had not hundreds but tens of thousands of independent school districts; in 1923, after intense efforts to close or consolidate small districts, 127,931 remained. In 1925, school officials in Pasadena (CA) asked a sample of superintendents about any policies in force on married women teachers and administrators. Most of the respondents employed married women, sometimes with conditions.[48] More telling was how few school districts were queried, as with the NEA and other groups' surveys of teacher hiring and retention policies—probably because the surveys' authors already knew or suspected what a more inclusive sample would show.

Small districts (the most likely to hire locally, regardless of marital status) had already been written off as provincial, backward, unprofessional, and overdue for consolidation. In 1918 a statewide Virginia survey found one in ten rural districts and one in three urban districts (meaning towns of 2,500 population or greater) with a marriage bar. Where all of a state's local school boards were surveyed, as in Ohio in 1931, similar results were obtained.[49] Apparently only a minority of Virginia and Ohio teachers could be harmed—likely the case elsewhere.

With respect to timing, the late 1920s and early 1930s—when the two oft-cited samplings took place—was a time of financial distress and historically high unemployment. Parents even tried to unseat the half dozen married women teachers in Little Rock's Negro schools, some saying, "Turn the wives out; let their husbands support them." The effort failed when the white superintendent stated, "Married women with families make much the best teachers, especially for little children."[50]

In good times, women with employed husbands or sons were unlikely to seek work or retain their jobs—but not so during the Great Depression. The presence of openly married women teachers rose during both the 1920s and 1930s.[51] In 1931 five state legislatures heard bills to make a marriage bar the general rule, and in 1937 such bills were introduced in 26 states; none passed, except Louisiana's, which could deny a woman public employment if her husband's earnings exceeded a particular standard. These political results indicate that "ultimately married women's rights to employment had widespread support."[52] Some marital bans were undoubtedly "dead letters" from the outset: low-cost political gestures, largely irrelevant in a time when few were giving up their positions and marriage and birth rates were at historic lows.

In the never-determined number (or percentage) of districts where marriage bars appeared, exceptions may have been as common as dismissals: when a classroom had no teacher, when schools were hiring married women as daily or long-term substitutes, when the teacher had permanent tenure, or when a husband could not support his family. Like the existence, timing, and duration of marriage bars, their application varied by time, place, and personal predilections. Although policy studies seldom address the effects on individuals and their schools, life histories ground the story by sampling the varied experiences of married and single teachers in diverse school communities; at the least, for the issue of marital policies, personal history adds complexity. So does a comparative perspective.

A Cross-National Perspective on Marital Policies and Practices

Two-thirds of the teachers in the 396 schools operated by the London County Council in 1889 were women, more than a quarter of them married. By 1910 a third—and in 1926, three-quarters—of Local Education Authorities in England and Wales had a marriage bar. After the London city government extended a general marriage bar to teachers in 1923, Nan McMillan chose to live with a man sans marriage, while agitating against the policy.[53] Teacher organization activists and headmistress candidates—with their higher average ages, longer training, and richer experience—were concentrated in cities.

In Tsarist Russia a measure of local autonomy allowed St. Petersburg to impose a partial marriage bar, from 1897 to 1913; Moscow got the same results with an informal policy.[54] The incentives for these two cities were common to all cities: urban married women teachers—on average, older and experienced careerists, better paid, better connected in the community, and more politically inclined and resourceful—were costly and potentially troublesome.

Europe's Great War left large numbers of disabled and dependent veterans and fatherless children, as well as demobilization, unemployment, inflation, and disruptive boom-and-bust economic cycles. War-related mortality and morbidity, like Europe's falling birthrates, focused attention on the deleterious economic and political effects of depopulation. From the 1890s, France's response to depopulation had been to support the "maternalization" of the female labor force. As the rector of the University of Paris M. Liard declared, "My only complaint is that there aren't enough married women teachers in France." The Ministry of Education encouraged pregnant women to teach until childbirth and return immediately; a maternity leave option was reluctantly added in 1910. Among primary school teachers, the married were the majority (56%) by 1898; overall, married women increased from 17% of France's total female teaching force in 1855 to 33% in 1911.[55]

Not so in Germany. A former kindergarten teacher and socialist feminist, Luise Zietz (b. 1865) thought the economic and social trauma of military defeat and the harsh terms of the Treaty of Versailles explained the Reichstag's 1920 defeat of a legislative proposal to allow married women workers, from servants to teachers, to remain in the labor force. "Women of the Center, of the National, and of the Democratic parties polarized against us from the most diverse motives."[56]

Already into the Great Depression, in 1932 the International Bureau of Education surveyed officials in 42 nations, finding that "worldwide unemployment and governmental personnel reductions have resulted in unfavorable policies toward married women teachers in many countries."[57] During those two decades, New Zealand enforced a rule "barring every married woman from the profession of teaching," while Argentina merely cut paid maternity leaves from 60 to 45 days as a cost-cutting measure.[58] Under Canada's decentralized system, some localities imposed marriage bars, especially in the late 1920s. Jeannette Scholnick entered Montreal's teaching labor market in 1939 with a bachelor's degree from McGill, a secondary school certificate, and the near certainty that a quota on Jewish teachers would deny her a secondary school position. Her only (and realized) hope was to replace a resigning Jewish elementary school teacher.[59]

Mobilization and manpower shortages with World War II brought Canada grudging acceptance of the married woman worker. But in the Alberta community where Beverley Craine DeWinter taught, hiring a local woman teacher with a five-year-old child and an employed husband shocked public opinion. Nonetheless, a few other wives followed suit.[60] In combatant nations, wartime teacher shortages generally removed marital status and maternity as a factor in teacher hiring and retention, usually permanently. Democratic post–World War II educational reforms, notably raising secondary schools' legal leaving age, like the baby boom's effect on primary schools, brought staffing shortages that stifled efforts to reimpose marriage bars.[61]

With married women teachers the norm, in 1958 the *London Times* quoted a Mr. H. J. Weaver's complaint: "The women's staff room has become a waiting room for the bridal chamber and an anteroom for the maternity home."[62] However, Sydney Waterson, a career teacher and principal in Victoria (Australia), preferred—over any other teacher—a "lady teacher" who married into the local community. Teacher wives were local personages and "the brains" behind any number of successful local businesses, thriving farms, and community campaigns. (The local member of Parliament rushed the just-arrived home ec teacher into marriage at one of Waterson's schools.) Astute principals promoted the courtship and marriage of their women teachers and afterward catered to them, securing a well-regarded, stable workforce.[63]

John Theobald recalled his childhood, also in country Victoria, where the farmers who practiced progressive farm methods, subscribed to agricultural journals, and were active in farm organizations had usually married teachers.[64] The question arises whether American Gertrudes similarly possessed and constructively used the high relative marriageability that Sidney Waterson and John Theobald observed in Australia.

Whom Did Teachers Marry?

Throughout history a woman's standing was determined by the identity of the men in her life. In the English tradition her surname was her father's (if her birth was legitimate); with marriage she took her husband's name. Married women were sometimes listed in censuses and city directories merely as "wife of ———." Marriage to a successful, even promising, man usually elevated a woman's social standing, especially in an open society. The relationship between women teachers' occupational roles and social mobility through marriage has been little considered or researched. However, individual lives show many nineteenth- and twentieth-century women teachers "marrying up." More often than not, their husbands were themselves—or were the sons of—members of local agricultural, business, or professional elites. Others were ambitious young men making their way up.[65]

On leave from the Confederate army, Robert Randolph Cotton heeded his mother's advice to meet the young teacher boarding at his uncle's house, for she would make him a good wife. Cotton was 27 when he married 17-year-old Sallie Swepson Sims Southall and retired her from teaching. A graduate of two good female seminaries, the now Mrs. Colonel Cotton "kept up her reading," raised a large family, wrote poetry and articles, and promoted women's clubs, a state library, and the National Congress of Mothers (later the Parent-Teacher Association), all reflecting well on her astute husband.[66]

Examples abound over time and across the continent. Minnesota relatives took in Pennsylvania's Clara Hampson and her impoverished family after her soldier-father died in the Civil War. Clara was a high school teacher in 1885 when she married Andreas Ueland, the immigrant son of a prominent Norwegian family. A laborer who studied law at night, Ueland became wealthy as counsel to lumber barons and bankers. German-born Bernard Behrends left Nebraska for the California gold fields and then Alaska, where he married a local teacher in 1887; his mercantile interests flourished, and he helped bring the state capital to Juneau.[67]

W. E. B. Du Bois noted in 1914 that Negro women were using education to raise their income and occupational status and moving "quietly but forcibly toward the intellectual leadership of the race."[68] Examples of black women teachers' marriages include Georgia Camp's to an attorney, Sallie Wyatt's to a successful realtor, and Clarissa Scott's to a domestic relations court judge. Dorothy Jemison married a maintenance man and Rosa Dixon a postal worker—men doing essential but not lucrative or prestigious work.[69] When Julia Reed analyzed 1960 U.S. census data on husbands' occupation, marital stability, household income, and childbearing patterns, she concluded that, compared with their white peers, nonwhite women teachers were more culturally than socially or economically middle class.[70] (Excluding teacher husbands, 30% of nonwhite women teachers were married to professionals and other white-collar workers, compared to 49% of white women teachers.)

The unmarried teacher's life story sometimes revealed her own marital prospects. For example, Fannie McLean chose a lifetime career as an English teacher at Berkeley High School over proposals from future bankers, professors, businessmen, and judges.[71] While feminist independence kept Fannie McLean single, the teachers in a small Ohio city during the 1930s had little choice. Because they could lose their positions by marrying, they complained that their marriageability had lessened, forcing them to remain unmarried longer than they might wish.[72]

Discovering the "Marriage-Worthy" Schoolmistress

The middle-aged keeper of the stagecoach station at Coyote Holes (CA)—the Bad Man from Bodie—reputedly had nine notches in his gun. "After fifty years he began to yearn for respectability and the peace and pleasantness of his mother's home in New England." The middle-aged Yankee schoolmistress he met through a matrimonial bureau, "Mrs. Bodie, as we will call her, came on and married him sight unseen at Mojave. She brought braided rugs and a melodeon, and planted hollyhocks. . . . Sundays he shaved and put on a clean shirt, and the two of them sat on the porch rocking and singing Gospel Hymns."[73]

The teacher was believed to possess a public dowry: intellectual and educational assets; a reputation for morality, competence, authority; and teaching-related experience in managing time, tasks, and other people. A teacher in Grundy and Marshall Counties (IA) in the 1860s and a bride in 1870, Alice Money reportedly displayed "as a doctor's wife and as a mother and neighbor the same sterling qualities that had made her a successful teacher."[74] Given the strictures surrounding the schoolmistress, she largely escaped inclusion among "silly working girls" whose extravagant spending made them unfit for "men who are anxious to pay their bills and lead an honest life."[75]

In novelist John Steinbeck's *East of Eden,* Olive Hamilton exemplifies the teacher: "Not only an intellectual paragon but also a social leader and the matrimonial catch of the countryside. A family could indeed walk proudly if a son married the schoolteacher. Her children were presumed to have intellectual advantages both inherited and conditioned." But does life imitate art? Nora Stewart had barely settled into her new school in Lansing (KS) in 1883 when "a young gentleman . . . called in his broadcloth to see the new school ma'am." However, she chose to wait five years while another suitor completed his college course and became established.

During the evening dances following the 1908 Wyoming State Teachers Association convention, the young men entered en masse, wearing huge white placards announcing "NOT MARRIED."[76] In his boyhood hometown—Elgin County, Ontario (Canada)—Kenneth Galbraith (b. 1908) calls the teacher a "prime matrimonial prospect." While "the courting of a teacher had to be exceptionally antiseptic," the town's young men were "attracted by the idea of an educated wife."[77] Of his 1916 plan to recruit Eastern teachers as wives for lonely bachelors in Hayden (CO), rancher Farrington Carpenter recalled, "We had serious matrimonial intentions, and we decided that young, pretty school teachers would be the best bet of all."[78]

Despite the received wisdom that "too much schooling makes spinsters," women teachers from immigrant and other distinctly blue-collar families were acquiring cultural capital through school and employment experiences; many made advantageous marriages. A daughter of Irish immigrants and orphaned at age 16, Mary Ann Hatten (b. 1830) alternated teaching in Illinois and attending Knox College and Kansas Normal. In 1867 she married a physician, shopkeeper, and future mayor; their son, William Allen White, became the publisher of the famed *Emporia Gazette*.[79] Female graduates of Somerville (MA) High School in the 1880s thought completing high school would appeal to "status-conscious husbands seeking culturally sophisticated wives," and 80% of the school's blue-collar daughters acquired white-collar spouses.[80]

There were also the contrary cases where, by temperament or perhaps family reasons, a schoolmistress was "stuck in a backwater," unable to shop in a more promising marriage market, so "marrying across" or even "down." Nevertheless, among women workers teachers were well positioned. First, in rural and small-town America, where most people began life well into the twentieth century, the teacher was a local personage, typically respected and respectable. Second, as a specialist in children, a teacher was thought best able to give her husband's children a head start. Third, teachers were generally recruited to church work and whatever women's clubs and civic organizations existed, placing them in congenial company with the mothers, aunts, and sisters of marriageable men. Even negative elements of the teacher's image—bookish, overly serious, proper, chaste, if not sexually repressed—could become assets when a man was selecting a bride or a replacement wife and mother.

It was not that other wage-earning women lacked "bride-worthiness" but that teachers had advantages. For example, through much of the twentieth century, most "business women" were clerical workers; lacking normal school or college experience, they missed this opportunity for meeting better-educated, ambitious men at a strategic time in the life course for courting. While the education of librarians and social workers was comparable to that of teachers, their numbers were far smaller and less well distributed. Following is a further sampling of teachers' marital unions—across time, geography, and ethnicity—featuring spouses who were political figures, preachers, widowers, and other teachers.

Politicians, Preachers, and the Widower's Deliverance

Far from the White House limelight—Presidents Andrew Johnson, James Garfield, Benjamin Harrison, and Calvin Coolidge were among those marrying teachers—in 1878 Robert N. Hall married Amelia Lyon (b. 1849), a normal school graduate who taught 23 terms in New York and New England before moving to

Wyoming as the third teacher in Lander's history. While raising two children and helping her telegrapher husband succeed in ranching and three decades in the state legislature, Mrs. Hall organized a literary society, was an active club-woman, wrote for local newspapers, and boarded most of the Lyons Valley School's teachers.[81] Dorcas Calmes was teaching in Laurens County (SC) in 1917 when she married Robert Archer Cooper. Elected governor in 1919, with her encouragement he built a progressive record in education, extending the school year through seven months and reaffirming the state's controversial 1915 compulsory school attendance law.[82]

The young women at Abbot Academy's 1879 convocation were told, "It is natural for a young divine to be attracted to a scholarly woman." A quarter of Abbott's alumnae, many of them teachers, married ministers or missionaries. In the mid-1880s, Mary Austin's mother invited divinity students to tea whenever Mary came home from normal school: "like many good Christian mothers, next to having a preacher for a son, she rated having a preacher for a son-in-law."[83] A fictional Ohio mother, Mrs. Reid, thought similarly, and Amanda Reid, the town's spinster Latin teacher knew what the townspeople thought: "so suitable, just the right age and born to be a [widowed] minister's wife." She declined marriage, choosing to keep a "place in the community [that] was hers by right of her own achievement."[84]

The ministry offered black men a profession, and teacher-preacher marriages were common. The mission of racial uplift through education kept Fanny Jackson Coppin in Philadelphia as head of the Institute for Colored Youth when her bridegroom, Rev. Levi Coppin, was assigned to a Baltimore pastorate; they lived apart for five years until his transfer to Philadelphia.[85] Josephine Leavell was teaching in her native Kentucky when she married Baptist minister Allen Allensworth in 1886. After he resigned his commission as Army chaplain to a black regiment in 1908, the couple helped found Allensworth, a "race colony" near Bakersfield (CA). Its public school gave black women teaching positions in a state where such opportunities were largely closed to them.[86]

Preacher-teacher couples were especially valued for mission and government schools. A federal Indian Service agent informed the secretary of war in 1833 that Kentucky's Rev. David Lowery had "resigned the comforts of civilized life & devoted himself and an amiable partner, under great privations, to the cause of the Indian race." That partner, Mary Ann Lowery, taught at her husband's Yellow River School while he ministered to the Winnebago in the frontier settlement of Prairie du Chien (Iowa Territory).[87]

In Australia, Queensland's former premier Sir James Dickson persuaded Mary McKinlay to transfer her attention from her Brisbane girls school to his motherless 13 children.[88] One teacher described a French widower-suitor as an "aging valetudinarian who wants 'a pearl' in his home."[89] America's widowers also sought out teachers, thus securing a companion, hostess, and "seasoned" guide for their children. Wilmington (NC) merchant Aaron Lazarus had seven motherless children, including Phila, a pupil at Warrenton Female Seminary. After much persuasion, Phila's teacher, Rachel Mordecai (b. 1788), became Mrs. Lazarus.[90]

The Civil War stranded a Connecticut native, Mary Emma Hurlbut, in Vicksburg (MS) as the Lum family's governess. As General Ulysses Grant's chief of staff, General John Aaron Rawlins—a young former Illinois attorney, widower, and father—made the Lum mansion his headquarters. He removed Miss Hurlbut from her position by marrying her.[91] Although declining deaths in childbirth meant fewer widowers and motherless children, twentieth-century examples appear. In the 1920s Priscilla White, renowned for her ability to manage the bigger boys, yielded to the only widower in the vicinity of her Texas school, leaving the trustees to replace her in midterm.[92]

Not all wooers succeeded. A teacher in New Hampshire and New York since her teens, 34-year-old Abiah Warren (b. 1805) wondered about exchanging her independence for marriage to her father's business partner. She first put him off and then rejected him—no doubt influenced by her mother's remarks about his disagreeable nature and his offspring: "the worst children you ever saw and Mr. b. has not any government [over them]." When Abiah Warren married, at age 37, she chose an unencumbered former student 14 years her junior.[93]

Propinquity and Colleagueship: The Teaching Couple

In a Boston newspaper advertisement in 1718, a "certain person" offered his services to teach Latin and English "and his Wife for teaching Needle Work." For Nashville's first public school (1841), the board announced, as "it is intended to have a female assistant, the teacher's family would have a preference if qualified."[94] For practical reasons, dozens of teaching couples were recruited to help pacify the newly conquered Philippine Islands, including Mr. and Mrs. E. R. Roberts, both high school teachers in Rizal Province.[95]

The founding principal of the East Florida Seminary, Gilbert Dennis Kingsbury (b. 1825) hastily left town with the seminary's pregnant music teacher, Anna Underwood. He broke off all contact with his parents, siblings, and sweetheart in New Hampshire, married Anna, and took her to Brownsville (TX) under his assumed name, F. F. Fenn; she and their child died there. "Fenn" became Brownsville's postmaster, a Union spy during the Civil War, and a rancher and lecturer on Rio Grande history. He resumed his rightful name, reunited with his family, and married the forsaken schoolmistress who was his "first love."[96]

America's proliferating schools—with the normal schools, colleges, teachers' institutes, and association meetings that sustained their growth—offered multiple opportunities for congenial matings.[97] In South Dakota, Ethel Collins married Elias Jacobsen, her principal at the Oahe (Sioux) Industrial Boarding School. From their marriage in 1900, Margaret Elizabeth Hines and John Munsey Roberts taught together in several states, most notably at Orange Street School in Asheville (NC) in 1911: he the principal, she the sixth-grade teacher. Thomas Wolfe, her former pupil, honored Mrs. Roberts in *Look Homeward Angel* in the character of Margaret Leonard: "mother of my spirit who fed me with light."[98]

Over the centuries teaching couples appeared in all regions and demographic groups. It was noted of teaching, "There is probably no other large occupational group in which so high a proportion of both husbands and wives work in the same profession." In 1960, more than half of white male teachers with employed wives had teacher wives, and the incidence of nonwhite teaching couples was even higher. A biology teacher, the son of teachers, wrote, "I understood the lifestyle of a teacher. . . . Because I'm a teacher, I've had the time to be with my kids. . . . I've traveled all over the world. My wife's a teacher. We have this wonderful life."[99]

"A Pearl in His Home": Teacher-Wives and Teacher-Mothers

Around 1880, Alexander MacKnight began seriously courting Sadie Carpenter, a pretty, stylish schoolma'am in Madrid (NY). A niece, Helen MacKnight, remembered the conversation between her enamored uncle and his worried mother. " 'Oh Alex, son,' she had said with great tenderness, 'don't marry her, I beg of you. She is no wife for a farmer. She will squander your money, your birthright that Father and I worked so hard to get for you and Gordon.' " Alex reassured her: " 'She knows the value of money. She has taught school to earn it.' " Alas, in this case Mother was right.[100] Although many former teachers doubtless proved to be extravagant wives, careless mothers, or erratic housekeepers, the available evidence appears greater on the other side.

Berry Gordy, the son of a slave woman and her master, was a Georgia farmer when he married country teacher Bertha Fuller. Part of the post-1917 exodus of blacks from the South, the Gordys' steady progress in Detroit toward fame and wealth resulted from a protective family circle, a father's entrepreneurship, and a diligent mother's zeal for education, culture, and religion. Bertha Gordy ran her family of eight children and a grocery store, earned a business degree, founded an insurance company, and shepherded the family into business and political activism in Motown.[101]

A great many American notables were born to schoolteacher mothers whose profession provided a cultural capital reserve: attitudes, knowledge, and intellectual and linguistic skills. Eudora Welty's passion for learning was ignited by her teacher-mother, and strong women teachers figure prominently in her fiction. A Bryn Mawr College president, Mary Patterson McPherson (b. 1937) wrote, "My mother was a teacher in the girls' school that I attended, and I grew up breathing in, like fresh air, her zest for her work and her belief in its value."[102] When interviewed "Mr. Connor" said of his wife, "She's been a teacher, and she probably takes a much more active role, researching about school, talking to other parents, finding out about teachers for the upcoming year, and requesting a teacher for the next year." Other parents come to know and consult teacher-parents, thus spreading their effects.[103]

But, like other employed mothers, teachers mention their children's complaints about Mom's "homework," night meetings, and propensity to bring home "object lessons" from her classroom. Beverly De Winter's four children took the school bus going in the opposite direction from her school; none wanted to be "the teacher's kid," targeted by any bully who hated school.[104] To teenager Lauren Miller, "hell was having parents, teachers up the hill at the high school, who at three o'clock would leap into their car, drive to Walt Whitman Elementary, pick up her brother, Adam, and then come to watch her play ball."[105] And many teachers' lounge conversations have aired the mixed blessing of teaching a "teacher's kid."

Life at Home

It mattered to teachers' family and friends—and to the teacher's reputation and the school's standing in the community—that they had a decent abode, adequate (if plain) food, and a clean and appropriately garbed appearance. The schoolmaster could be "done for" by a housekeeper, cook, laundress—or a wife. Indeed, a justification for paying a schoolmaster higher wages was that he had to support a wife or pay others to do what the woman teacher could "do for herself." If she hired someone to turn up her hems, trim her hat, or iron her petticoats, her wages were assuredly too high.

The housing arrangements of a school proprietor, resident governess, or parochial school nun were implicit. Single women, teaching in in the quasifamilial context of British and American female seminaries, were expected to live in-house as mother surrogates or big sister figures.[106] As both pupils and parents expected, fashionable boarding schools employed servants. Not so schools enrolling the daughters of farmers, ministers, artisans, and proprietors of small businesses. Mount Holyoke Female Seminary's instructors cleaned their own rooms and did their own laundry and ironing—a labor-intensive chore involving hand washing long skirts and starching blouses.[107]

Bed and Board for the Schoolma'am

Rank beginners usually taught at the nearest "home" school, boarded by their own families, everyone recognizing the multiple dangers confronting young people "on their own." Teachers without nearby connections required housing, and providing it helped attract and retain respectable teachers, while households boarding the teacher ordinarily welcomed the extra income. The Presbyterians of Abilene (KS) were triply blessed: the parsonage housed two or three local teachers, the resulting income counted as part of Dr. David Townley's ministerial salary, and the teachers had companionship.[108]

While school trustees often boarded the unattached teacher, they also recommended the families of ministers, doctors, other professional men, or "solid businessmen." Alice Pierce had "good board" with the district clerk's family in Easton (OH) in 1881–1882: "I will go and wipe dishes for Mrs. Early," she wrote to her fiancé. "They are awfully kind to me the time of the snow he went down to the schoolhouse and built fire for me and broke the roads."[109] The boarding experience was common to sparsely settled areas everywhere. Teaching in the Australian "bush," Muriel Rose shared her sleeping space with the family's three daughters. Herself an only daughter, the loss of privacy greatly bothered her.[110]

Rotating the teacher among her patrons—called "boarding 'round"—was common in nineteenth-century rural districts. This "free board," a payment in kind, kept taxes lower than if a teacher was paid enough to "board herself." Not uncommonly, the rural teacher was "regularly aroused . . . for a five o'clock breakfast . . . [and] obliged to sleep in a cold room with boisterous youngsters."—provoking dissatisfaction, complaint, and the search for alternative arrangements.[111] In a 45-year career, starting in 1899 in Butler County (KS), Nellie Purle Cronk first lived at home, then boarded 'round, next moved to town and a boarding house, then shared a fellow teacher's home, and finally settled in with a widowed sister. Careful management of her teaching wages and a small income from renting her farmland enabled Alice Newberry to bring her mother and widowed sister to share her modest Denver home.[112]

In 1908 Polly Bullard and the four other teachers boarding at Mrs. Samuelson's in Eveleth (MN) rented a spare room as an upstairs sitting room for themselves and their guests. Larger communities offered business and professional women the alternatives of residential hotels and clubs, usually near streetcar lines: respectable and convenient, with space to entertain friends and associates.

In 1930s Los Angeles, Jane Bernhardt could choose between the Women's Athletic Club and the ornate, Spanish colonial YWCA.[113] Apartment buildings first appeared in larger cities, where a teacher could share space, cost, and domestic duties with sisters, colleagues, friends, or an aging parent. Small-town America appeared suspicious of the unmarried woman who rented an apartment alone. When teaching in Kirksville (MO), the widowed Mrs. Kube (Coral Adams) probably boarded, but while teaching in St. Joseph after World War I she lived in an apartment—acceptable because she had been married.[114]

A number of rural districts and small towns—mostly in the South and Intermountain West—constructed accommodations near a schoolhouse, especially the two- or four-teacher graded-school type. The land company that developed Metropolis (NV) hauled in an abandoned cabin and added shed-rooms for a "teacherage" where Eleanor Hasenkamp lived from 1917 to 1922.[115] As Washington state superintendent (1913–1928), Josephine Corliss Preston added several hundred teachers' cottages to the state's first teacherage: converted railway dining cars for teachers unable to find a boarding place.[116] Free government-approved housing for teachers was already available in England, Scandinavia, Germany, rural Australia, and to teachers in overseas U.S. and international schools catering to expatriates. Teachers working in schools for U.S. military dependents after World War II usually received housing.[117]

Later some American cities gave teachers allowances for rent and utilities, low-interest loans, or property tax credits. In 2007, New York City proposed two complexes in the Bronx, with affordable single and family-size apartments.[118] This was in response to teachers' objections to the time and expense of commuting, their surprising preference for living nearer their students, and a wish to see their own children grow up in the city where they worked. How unlike the 1950s, for example, when an unmarried teacher often preferred to drive from her city flat to her suburban school, rather than encounter students at the grocery store or movie house—or their parents at a bar. As school board paternalism lost its grip, teachers' quest for anonymity and privacy in their nonschool lives also weakened. The culture's greater informality in all social relations was undoubtedly a factor.

Domestic Arrangements for Teaching Mothers

Occupations like teaching—"work devoted to problems and concerns that the woman herself faces within the private capacity of her family"—are said to "reduce the contradictions in her self-image" arising from the contending claims of work and home.[119] The nineteenth-century school proprietor who taught in her own home, amid her own children, faced fewer and more easily managed social contradictions than do salaried employees of modern educational bureaucracies. Gertrude Thomas taught a Richmond County (GA) school in an annex to her home. Several of her seven children attended her school and looked after their preschool siblings. Augmenting her monthly wage of $35, Mrs. Thomas received $12 per month for boarding two pupils, "and not for one moment have I regretted it." Her boarders also provided companionship for her own daughter, another form of child care.[120]

After her husband's death in 1871, Euphemia "Effie" Bruns Decker (b. 1844) tried to raise three boys on a teacher's wages. In 1880, when her eldest was 12, Mrs. Decker's mother asked their kinsmen in Germany for financial help, explaining, "They are contemplating abolishing the German language in the public schools in St. Louis, and the German teachers were dismissed, Effie among them." When she was rehired at a more distant school, her family life suffered: "she does not see the boys now from breakfast time until late in the evening, and naturally she worries a great deal because of that."[121] In contrast, for 12 years Mrs. Theresa Sullivan and her two sons lived in the unusually spacious, seven-room "teacherage" in Nebraska's Hall County.

Accommodating marriage, motherhood, and employment requires strategic planning and some form of family, hired, civic, or institutional help. An Irish immigrant, Martha Spence (b. 1811) converted to Mormonism in 1848. To reach Utah, she joined the wagon train of Joseph Heywood, becoming his third of four wives in 1850. As the "sister wives" did not get along, she lived apart from them; a local girl helped care for her infants each time she returned to teaching. In contrast, Eunice Harris (b. 1860), a mother of nine, alternated teaching with caring for her own and the children of her husband's second wife (also a teacher) during their respective pregnancies.[122]

After normal school training and a year's experience on Hawaii (the "Big Island"), Jessie Lai (b. 1903) returned to Oahu and married. The newlyweds and their extended families settled in the predominantly Asian town of Wahiawa. While he worked for Dole Pineapple Company she taught elementary school almost continually. Mrs. Young's parents and other relatives cared for their two children.[123] In 1915, in Providence (RI), 60% of Italian American adults had parents, siblings, cousins, or married children resident in their own households or nearby—a boon to employed women.

In 1969 the great majority (83%) of novice women teachers—single or married—reported they planned to teach continuously or resume careers interrupted by childrearing.[124] However, the extended family of all types had declined as a mode of regular child care in middle-class America. Therefore, the congruence between a woman's work schedule and her children's schooling remains an advantage that teaching has over other careers.

Conclusion: More Than "an Amiable Partner"

The "pale schoolmistress" was still in deep mourning on joining the other boarders around the breakfast table. The group's talkative gentleman, "not infirm in point of worldly fortune," began his courtship by accompanying her on the short path to her Boston school each morning. "It was on the Common that we were walking. 'Will you take the long path with me?' 'Certainly,' said the schoolmistress, 'with much pleasure.' 'Think' I said, 'before you answer: if you take the long path with me now, I shall interpret it that we are to part no more!' . . . She answered, softly, 'I will walk the long path with you.'" He rejoiced, "The 'schoolmistress' finds her skill in teaching called for again, without going abroad to seek little scholars. Those visions of mine have all come true."[125]

In 1991, when asked what kind of woman he wanted to marry, 18-year-old Bart Stanley told *Parade* magazine that he would choose a woman "of the '90s—the 1890s": "happy simply to clean, cook, care for him and their children and watch her favorite soaps." This statement drew two published replies, both from the more traditional South. A Knoxville (TN) teacher wrote that she and her colleagues were appalled at such an opinion—"in an age where equal pursuit of happiness is an accepted (and protected) right." And to Bart's "incredibly selfish" and limited notion of what women want, a 15-year-old Louisiana girl noted, "My mother was like that until she started teaching."[126]

Sixty years earlier, district officials would blame unemployed or unmarried teachers for policies excluding married women. Along with intense job competition during economic hard times, the perception among the shrinking proportion of the self-supporting single was that marriage conferred privileges unrelated to professional competence, like being excused from extracurricular duties and being given paid maternity leaves. Teacher-mothers also tend to believe they understand their students better and are more trusted by parents than childless teachers.[127] The inference was that marriage and motherhood were normal, while spinsterhood was deviant. These contentions have largely disappeared, and the teacher's marital status receded from a civic to a personal matter. Moreover, school officials and public opinion were already adjusting to yet another social reality: the never-married mother and the same-sex household with children.

The dominant educational issues at the close of the twentieth century clustered around the teacher *as teacher*. Older expectations were reasserted: Is the teacher in charge? Does she hold and enforce high standards? Does she expect all her pupils to learn? Does the teacher *teach*? Consider a mostly African American group of parents in Richmond (CA), gathered in the late 1990s to meet their school's racially and culturally diverse but uniformly earnest teachers. The teachers, nearly all women, were reassuring the assembled parents and guardians, nearly all women, of their individual and collective caring and supportive regard for every student and their commitment to building nurturing relationships in their classrooms. A mother interrupted with a curt challenge: "The parents will take care of the loving; you just take care of the teaching."

Is this distinction a reconstituted version of the old tussle between mother and surrogate? Does it reflect a pedagogical fundamentalism in a restive minority population?[128] Was this yet another expression of ritual nostalgia for the strict, no-nonsense taskmaster of legend? Could it perhaps signal the burial of that oft-recited justification for employing women as teachers—their natural motherly qualities? Whatever these parents' idea (and ideal) of the teacher, it was not maternal. It is to the congeries of ideas and images of teachers that we next turn.

CHAPTER 7

"In the Mind's Eye"

Images and Expectations of the Teacher

"Pressed for rules and verities. . . . I recollect. . . . Scratch a myth
and find a fact."

—Phyllis McGinley, "A Garland of Precepts"

Except for their mourning-like garb, the Wardlaw sisters fit the imagery of competent, self-supporting late nineteenth-century teachers. The heir apparent of a dynasty of entrepreneurial teachers, Virginia Oceana Wardlaw (b. 1852) entered Wellesley College as a "teacher special." She taught successfully in Virginia, was teacher-principal at Nashville's Price School, and served as president of Soule Female College in Murfreesboro (TN) around 1892. By 1901, she was joined by her widowed sisters: Mrs. Caroline Martin (b. 1850?) and Mrs. Mary Snead (b. 1849?), both former teachers in New York State.[1]

Then scandal erupted. In 1909 Virginia Wardlaw was implicated in the suicide (or murder) of her niece (or "love child"). There were rumors of nighttime cemetery visits, witchcraft, and large insurance policies; the fiery death of Mary Snead's son, who assisted at their Virginia school; the death by drowning (or poisoning or starvation) of beautiful "Ocey" (Virginia Oceania) Martin in the bathtub of an unfurnished house in East Orange (NJ). This grotesque, unresolved real-life tale ended with Virginia Wardlaw's suicide by starvation while awaiting trial on murder charges and Mrs. Martin's commitment to an insane asylum. Although the sensational speculations hardly tarred their profession, the Wardlaws no longer fit familiar representations of teachers.

In general, the most familiar perspectives on teachers are amalgams: first, of assessments of who the teacher is (or was or is believed to be) and, second, of projections from what we—as students, parents, citizens, or scholars—wish the teacher to be. The resulting composite is ambiguous, contradictory, and changeable. Its dimensionality may grow with collective events (e.g., teachers waving placards at political conventions) or from dramatic, well-publicized individual actions (e.g., a married mother of four convicted of seducing her sixth-grade student and bearing two of his children between prison terms).

Social scientists and educators also contribute to the reservoir of teaching's images—some likely to discourage prospective teachers with modern sensibilities. How might a self-described "sort-of-idealist" cope with revisionist scholars' contention that teachers are, wittingly or not, agents of state-sponsored capitalism, bureaucrats slotting working class, racial minority, and female youth into inferior social and economic futures in an unjust society?[2] Or the reverse? The first frame in *The New School Teacher* (1924), an early silent film, offered this text: "This picture is dedicated to the school teacher—the doormat upon which the passing generation wipes its feet, as it moves on through the door of opportunity."[3]

Australian teacher-author Sylvia Ashton-Warner repeatedly tried to leave "the bloody profesh." Susan Griffin—poet, playwright, and feminist philosopher—wrote, "here I am / back in as the jailor, a / mother and a / teacher."[4] Schools and marriages as prisons, and the teacher as mother or jailor, are well-worn but not worn-out similes. When Atlanta (GA) kindergarten teacher, Margaret Edson, won the 1999 Pulitzer Prize for her play, *Wit,* she challenged but could not demolish G. B. Shaw's 1903 slander: "those who can—do; those who cannot—teach."

Teacher portraiture resembles a braided, even tangled, strand that runs from the positive, expected, or hoped-for to the negative and unflattering images of the job and its incumbents. With elements of the prestige and goodwill given the schoolmaster she largely replaced, the schoolmistress acquired some of the doubt and derision he also attracted. What follows is an examination of the more important or enduring elements in teacher representations, drawn from disparate sources—literature, sacred and secular homilies, films, popular culture, autobiographical accounts, and even occupational sociology. Images and stereotypes are also considered alongside the lived experiences of teachers in their time and place.

Sketching Teachers in High Art and Popular Culture

Males once dominated teacher iconography. The fifteenth-century bronze relief (representing Grammar) that Luca della Robbia sculpted for Florence's campanile shows two boys instructed by a master. Except in depictions of England's dame schools, representations of women in classrooms appear uncommon before 1800.[5] Thereafter, the generic schoolteacher is female. The models for Winslow Homer's paintings include his teacher, Adeline M. Ireson (b. 1823) of Cambridge (MA). During a 50-year career, her longest vacation was reportedly a fortnight one August.[6] Both Winslow Homer (who painted "very much American heroines") and Norman Rockwell placed the diurnal routines and contained dramas of the schoolhouse largely in women's hands.[7] For a poster celebrating Montana Territory's first capital, artist Leonard Eckel chose the schoolmistress, her pupils, and the schoolhouse: a unit, an entity, representing the essence of countless American communities and neighborhoods over long periods.

Theatre and film elaborate our mental pictures of teachers. Worthy exemplars display their character and craft in England's elite private schools (*Good-bye, Mr. Chips*, 1939), ordinary grade schools in small-town America (*Good Morning, Miss Dove*, 1955), and inner-city middle-and high schools (*Blackboard Jungle*, 1955). But in *Butch Cassidy and the Sundance Kid* (1969), the historical Etta Place throws in her lot with outlaws, explaining, "I'm 26, and I'm single, and a schoolteacher, and that's the bottom of the pit."[8] In contrast, Muriel Spark's Scottish teacher in *The Prime of Miss Jean Brodie* (1969) is proud, self-confident, and controlling.[9] Monica Sullivan wrote, "For a kid raised . . . [in] Holy Rosary Convent School in Woodland (CA), Jean Brodie seemed to me . . . the coolest teacher in the universe. Charismatic, idiosyncratic, fearless and funny . . . worshipped by her students, adored by her very married lover . . . and cordially hated by [the] Headmistress."[10]

Depictions of teachers and schools in film, radio, and television after World War II kept the teacher's moral character dominant. Film and television focused on high schools, shifting a little from situation comedies to dramas. In 1997, to gain a larger teen and young-adult audience, the television series *Nick Freno: Licensed Teacher* moved the main characters from elementary to high school, high schools presenting more adult roles for male teachers and administrators, with the male voice and viewpoint made clearer. Despite *Boston Public*'s slogan— "Every day is a fight. For respect. For dignity. For sanity"—the show (2000–2004) broke new ground only in featuring an ethnically diverse faculty.

Male teachers are overrepresented as central figures, consistent with cultural and media bias. This was appropriate in *Good-Bye, Mr. Chips* (1939) and *Dead Poets Society* (1989), set in boys' boarding schools. The male hero of *The Blackboard Jungle* (1955) reaffirms appeals for more men in teaching. Women teachers slip into what Adam Farhi calls the "super-teacher myth" in such classic vehicles as *The Corn Is Green* (1945) and *The Prime of Miss Jean Brodie*—in polar opposite types of British school communities.[11] However, in the Hollywood film *Bad Teacher* (2011), Elizabeth Halsey, the degraded antihero, is no better at teaching than at life.

Film critic Anthony Lane dreads the "teaching movie" genre largely because "the mechanics of actual teaching are sidelined in favor of a public lecture on

Ways to Inspire."[12] However, whether students are any more interested in the mechanics of teaching than are filmmakers is doubtful; what matters is the *person* of the teacher, inspiring or not. At age 85, Mont Hawthorne could still describe Miss Alice Crimes, his "first real teacher," in the log schoolhouse in Lunenburg County (VA) in the 1870s. In tobacco country, "us boys liked it best when she chewed regular leaf tobacco. . . . We'd sit there and watch her munch on it and wonder when she'd spit. . . . She was the nicest, kindest, gentlest teacher I ever had. . . . But I . . . remember a lot more about her chewing than . . . about her teaching."[13]

Many students have admired their teacher to excess. "I do love our new teacher, Miss Davis. She is a splendid lady," gushed Hattie Russell, a pupil at the Young Ladies Seminary in Benecia (CA) in 1859. "She has traveled every place nearly, and is the best teacher of Geography I ever saw."[14] Wihelmine, a 14-year-old transferred in 1883 from Miss Stewart's Kansas district school to Leavenworth's German school, wrote in her halting, heartfelt English, "I hope you can see me next winter and I want say you good by to and wont forget you and you dont forget me. I love you Teacher I love to go to school please right me some again."[15] Kathleen Jett, 73 years after she first entered Miss Cora Dunbar's Kentucky classroom in 1931, recalled, "I thought she must be perfect . . . a sort of goddess."[16]

Literary word pictures include quick sketches and expansive portraits, in great and lesser literature, serious art, and popular culture. In Shakespeare's *Love's Labour's Lost,* the pedantic schoolmaster Holofernes is a figure of ridicule, falling in and out of Latin. In Thackeray's *Vanity Fair* (1848), Becky Sharp is viperous and headmaster Dr. Swishtail ridiculous. Joyce Carol Oates's bleak novel *Foxfire* (1993) gives voice to disaffected, pitiless adolescent girls who target men who fail to practice teacherly virtues, but the high school's barely noticed women appear ineffective, remote, and lacking integrity.[17]

John Greenleaf Whittier's widely memorized poetry immortalized Arethusa Hall (b. 1802), his teacher in Haverhill (MA) and "all her kind."[18] Popular regional writer George Sturt (b. 1863), who taught for several years, remembered little of his schooling in Surry (England), except for Miss May: "she, small, already wrinkled and worn-looking—wearing plentiful dark clothes, flimsy of texture, beady, lacy—Miss May, so thin, so fragile, so inoffensive."[19] Even dead teachers are archetypal. A possible witness to a kidnapping, Elizabeth Peshman is traced to a cemetery in Sun City (AZ), her tombstone graced with fresh flowers, wilting in the heat. A guard explains, "There are some folks here who never get visitors. But this one, she gets calls from a bunch of old students."[20]

Many literary depictions blur the line between fact and fiction. Charlotte Brontë, the best-known woman teacher-author in the English canon, knew well of what she wrote, as did her sisters and Mary Wollstonecraft.[21] Even while writing (as "Miss Read") more than 35 popular novels about fictionalized English villages, Dora Jesse Saint (b. 1913) taught a village school from the 1930s. Albeit a trifle idealized, her teachers are depicted with fidelity to the realities of their work.[22] The model for the Australian boarding school in "Henry Handel" Richardson's highly popular novel, *The Getting of Wisdom* (1910), was the Melbourne secondary school she attended—its teachers utterly subordinate to the tyrannical Lady Superintendent.[23]

Keeping School: From Bath to the Badlands

A Welsh-born Canadian teacher and principal, Mary Balogh created possibly the largest gallery of teacher heroines in the modern Regency-set romance novel genre—including two who survive by prostitution.[24] Balogh's governesses and schoolteachers all marry, and very well—unlike the British government's statistical portrait of spinsters forced by age and exhaustion into retirement and perhaps the poorhouse. Yet, Balogh also uses familiar themes and idioms, each with its own germ of truth, such as the rigid spine, severe center-parted hair, and caustic, correcting voice of Frances Allard, teacher in a girls school in Bath.[25]

Balogh's Anne Jewell is a governess because her family's finances were strained by educating her brother at Eton and Oxford—a larger truth expressed in Virginia Woolf's *Three Guineas* (1938) as "Arthur's Education Fund." To protect her simple-minded pupil, Miss Jewell exposed herself to the lechery of her employer's son and heir. (The defenseless governess, taken advantage of by her employer's spouse or male relative, is a staple of the genre.) Raped and abandoned, she finds a position and a home for herself and her son at Miss Martin's School for Girls in Bath, where at least one pupil is withdrawn at the impropriety of having an unwed mother on staff. Yet Miss Jewell is the most devoted and craft-conscious teacher of an excellent faculty. "Every year I taught," she reminisced, "I would change something about the content and method of my classes, convinced that this time I would have a perfect year."[26]

The Old West is the quintessential home of the schoolmistress in American popular culture. Unlike their male counterparts—cowboys, gamblers, gunslingers, ranchers, prospectors, homesteaders, all with license to be themselves—the females come in only two packages: good (schoolma'ams) and bad (dance-hall girls). The mythic schoolma'am is typically a model of imported (i.e., Eastern) gentility, culture, and sophistication: a bearer of books and music, "the voice of civilization in a rough-and-ready world."[27] Emily Parker, an Elmira (NY) teacher visiting Dakota Territory in 1880, shows that mix of prudish goodness—"hair pulled into a spinsterish bun, . . . schoolmarm written all over her"—and sensuous longings that romance readers expect. Her creator, Allison Hayes (Lynn Codding-ton), dedicated *Spellbound* (1990) to "my mother's people, . . . the pioneers, teachers, ranchers, and especially the dreamers." Having studied local and educational history, and respecting Lakota culture, she has Emily Parker consider how Indian pupils could be taught to survive in "the white man's world" while keeping their traditions. *Spellbound* still observes the conventions of mass marketed romance novels.[28]

Farrington Carpenter's real-life story would make a worthy, if familiar, novel. Ambitious for his part of Colorado, he persuaded his neighbors to tax themselves to build a fine two-teacher stone schoolhouse in Elkhead, then sent word "back East" for two teachers. His deeper purpose, however, was to bring "eligible" young women to the area. Unaware of this plan and "fleeing privileged but unfulfilling lives in the East," Dorothy Woodruff and Rosamund Underwood agreed to come. Both Smith College graduates and "hopeless spinsters" at 29, they arrived in July 1916—and quickly found suitors. Successive waves of young teachers came and married local men—and when Eunice Pleasant arrived in 1919, Carpenter finally secured his own schoolmistress wife.[29]

Probity in Action

Seventeenth-century English and American Puritans named their daughters Patience, Content, Submit, Constant, Mercy, Hope, Thankful, Prudence, Grace, Silence—reminders of woman's sacred role to present an ennobling example and impart carefully sifted wisdom. From her mission school in India's Arracan (Burma), Massachusetts-born Sarah Davis Comstock (b. 1812) wrote to her foster father. Cognizant of having lost a father's care, counsel, and home, "yet conscience tells me that in so doing I performed a duty which I owe to myself, the heathen and my God."[30]

Mary Jane Walker wrote in her normal school journal in 1849 that "the spirit of a teacher should be of the highest, purest, and most elevated character."[31] Teachers were expected to be active believers, models of civic and social responsibility, upright family members—or in more secular times, at least "good people." In the late nineteenth century, the California State Examination Board denied a woman teacher a life diploma until her former husband and her present district sent testimonials attesting to her character and teaching.[32] In the 1920s, when the city's "apostles of school craft" agitated for higher salaries and gender equity, Milwaukee's superintendent dismissed their grievances. "Real teaching is a free will offering of the soul's essence poured out freely on life's altar for the betterment and uplift of humanity—given in the spirit of the service rendered by the garbed sisters of the cloister."[33]

Self-denial is indeed expected of the sisters, brothers, and priests who staffed hundreds of Catholic schools, taking up their work after making explicitly religious vows—"following Christ who was poor, chaste, 'and obedient unto death.'"[34] In Pérez-Reverte's novel, *The Seville Communion* (1919), Sister Gris Marsala remarks, "From the very beginning, as a novice, you're taught that in a nun's cell mirrors are dangerous."[35] Given the avowed renunciation of ego in the culture of religious communities, the historian or biographer ordinarily finds little introspective personal writing that is not confessional.

Although the growing weight of secular values weakened rigid concepts of morality and propriety and although modern-day teachers are protected by tenure, civil rights statutes, and union contracts, they may still be measured against paragons of the past—both real and imagined. A modern consciousness produces its own versions of the teacher as secular nun. One is the near-real New Yorker, Rosie Bernstein Meyers: Jewish; IQ of 145; graduate of P.S. 197, Madison High, and Brooklyn College—and a dedicated 1990s high school teacher whose husband of 25 years is murdered after he leaves her for another woman. While fleeing to escape arrest, Rosie reflects, "I did not think of the sons I was leaving behind. . . . I thought of my students and their essays, marked but not yet returned."[36]

Devotion to Duty by Those Patient "Lessons on Legs"

In 1887, 21-year old Jesse Petherbridge wrote to a fellow Kansas teacher, "We can't be too careful in our instruction. <u>One</u> word or action of ours may lead our pupils on to a high and noble avocation in life or cause them to become miserable and wretched in every sense of the word."[37] Herbert Hoover's autobiography recalls his Iowa childhood as "filled with days of school—and who does not remember with a glow some gentle woman who with infinite patience and kindness drilled into us those foundations of all we know today?"[38] If not innate, patience was "drilled into her" in the normal school and teachers' institutes she attended. The teacher must be patient for his own sake, Mary Jane Walker was told, "otherwise the anxieties and discouragements of his office will vex him and soon wear him out." The patient teacher is also the hopeful teacher, and "hopefulness is contagious"; thus the pupil responds, "thinking that he can accomplish all things."[39]

Writer Leo Rosten mixed irreverence with gratitude in recalling his English teacher at Chicago's George Howland Elementary School in the 1920s. "Miss O'Neill was dumpy, moonfaced, sallow, colorless, and we hated her." Her mission was to force grammar, syntax, diction, spelling, parsing, and diagramming, on her "runny-nosed congregation." What Rosten called Miss O'Neill's consummate professionalism, others might call a vocation. Indeed, legend had it that "she had been nudged out of her holy order for mysterious, heart-rending reasons . . . [her] punishment . . . was to teach the emphatically non-Catholic heathens" who were his classmates. From a Yiddish-speaking, working-class immigrant family, Rosten had every reason to accept all that Miss O'Neill offered: "To me, she was a force of enlightenment."[40]

In films and novels the patient, long-suffering teacher is "always right in the end," for, while students win many a battle, the teacher wins the war—by "winning over" her pupils; the (ideal) teacher's essential goodness finds and burnishes the better nature of most pupils.[41] Teachers are also expected to show tactful firmness, strength, and resilience before bothersome parents, obtuse members of the public (including school board members), and even errant colleagues. The fictional Octavia Angeluzzi studied her teachers' tailored suits, their careful speech, even how they sternly folded their lips. As the smartest girl in her high school graduating class, she was determined to join them. When Octavia told her mother, "I'll never marry. . . . I don't want your life," her mother scolded, "This is how a daughter speaks to her mother in America? Brava. You would make a fine schoolteacher."[42]

Although teachers were expected to be models—famously, "lessons on legs"— pupils often rejected or tempered their example. Catherine Ford (b. 1857) attended a small private school in California "taught by Miss Elizabeth Wheeler . . . [, who] was strong on mental arithmetic and gave us drawing and perspective and color charts etc." Thinking her ridiculous, Ford later admitted, "The reason I never would care to teach was I wouldn't want people to dislike me as I did Miss W."[43]

Callen Taylor (b. 1976) remembered Mrs. Chahine ("I never knew her first name") at La Cañada High School in Los Angeles. If not "the warmest teacher[,] . . . she was really into what she taught." Her modern world history class seemed "the one class in high school that got me ready for college." However, being merely a good student—not the "cheerleader or the 5.0 student who took 1,000 AP classes"—Callen had felt overlooked, so as a teacher she intended to "make sure all the kids know they matter." For example, Ms. Taylor met with a dozen of her students—mostly recent immigrants facing multiple challenges—for two hours on Saturdays at Morning Due coffeehouse to discuss the week's chapter from Dante's *The Divine Comedy*.[44]

In 1915, Mary McDowell's principal praised her: "she is a Quaker, and her example could not be better." However, McDowell's pacifism during the months before America entered Europe's Great War and her acting as "a silent witness for peace" became "insubordination" and "conduct unbecoming a teacher"— grounds for dismissal. At the State Teacher's Association meeting in 1918, New

York State education commissioner John H. Finley warned, "The same degree of loyalty is asked of the teacher as of the soldier."[45]

Charles Robinson credited two women—one his kindergarten teacher, Ruth Acty (b. 1913), the first black teacher in a Berkeley public school—for his decision to teach grade school—hoping to "have the positive impact on my students' lives that these teachers had on [his]."[46] However, as ethnic politics became more militant, black professionals, intellectuals, and politicians were tagged "Uncle Toms" by members of their own race, while some white radicals branded black teachers as "hopelessly middle-class." For "Wanda," growing up in a small Southern town in the 1940s and 1950s—when racist stereotypes of the Negro woman (mammy, matriarch, welfare mother, Jezebel) still flourished—her own teachers' qualities of self-discipline and organization, neatness, and good manners inspired her. A New York City teacher, with more than 20 years' experience, she felt still needed by her students for "what she was."[47]

The Teacher as "Other"

Ruth Newcomb Hastings, a Massachusetts native teaching in South Carolina in the interval between its nullification (1832) and its secession (1860), felt like a "frozen outsider." Although invited to holiday parties, she concluded that, to dedicate oneself to teaching is to "make no one happy except your scholars," as the teacher is "a cipher, in any social group not composed of teachers."[48] While Miss Hastings might have been prone to self-doubt, sociologist Willard Waller described teachers (as they describe themselves) as persons who make others uneasy, shown in "the cessation of spontaneous social life at the entry of the teacher." The teacher is a stranger: "mentally isolated by his own set of attitudes . . . , but more because the community isolates him, . . . making him the carrier of certain super-mundane values, [while] imposing upon him certain humbling restrictions."[49]

An ambiguous public regard for teachers might be inferred from an 1865 description of their workplaces in Mendocino County (CA): "One is impressed with the peculiar style of architecture exhibited in the public school-houses which he sees upon the road. . . . They are generally too small for barns, too deficient in just proportions for dwellings, and too nondescript and repulsive for anything but schoolhouses."[50] A century later the graffiti-marred, iron-barred inner-city warehouse for "at risk" students might equally be seen as demeaning teachers and their pupils—the schoolhouse and its inhabitants a pawn in the high-stakes politics of taxation.

In Frank McCourt's memoir of his 30 years as a high school teacher, "no one but my students paid me a scrap of attention. In the world outside the school I was invisible." He exercised his Irish proclivity to tell stories about himself after discovering that doing so held his students' attention long enough for him to sneak in some official curriculum. But his pedagogy raised parents' suspicions. At his second open school day at McKee Technical and Vocational High School on Staten Island (NY) around 1960, a mother challenged him: "Stick to the spelling and the words, Mr. McCurd, and the parents of this school will thank you forever."[51]

In the year that Tracy Kidder spent observing Christine Zajac's fifth-grade classroom in Holyoke (MA), she told him that she consciously tried to leave her teacher self at school. Nonetheless, she would sometimes give her husband, Billy, "step-by-step instructions . . . or she'd start wagging an index finger at him—her 'teacher finger.' "[52] Willard Willard sees the "classroom manner" reflected in teachers' voices: "dry, authoritative, . . . [with] didactic inflections." Similarly, Frances Mayes recalls watching an Italian falconer at work. His bird's "stern profile" recalled her seventh-grade teacher, back in mid-twentieth-century Georgia: "the sudden swivel of its head brings back her infallible ability to sense when notes were tossed across the room."[53] And, as was universally said of the remembered teacher, loathed or loved, "She had eyes in the back of her head!"

Teachers' "otherness" partially results from educational barriers. People with less education perceive teachers differently than do those who consider their own educational, cultural, or intellectual attainments to be greater than the teacher's, hence the stereotype of the male teacher as an unsophisticated "country bumpkin" or the schoolm'am as an "ignorant wide-eyed girl. Even older teachers are depicted as inexperienced in worldly things, particularly in sexual matters." Mistaken for a prostitute, fiction's Emily Parker has to be rescued from the attentions of drunken roughnecks in late nineteenth-century Dakota Territory; her exasperated friend says, "I think you've been a teacher too long, Emmy."[54]

Seen at a Distance

No greater distance between the teacher and the taught exists than in schools run by religious communities. "The School and the Community formed two worlds. . . . The world of the Sisters was secret, consecrated and romantic; most of them belonged to God; very little of them belonged to us," Phyllis Bottome observed about the Anglican order that operated the New York City girls boarding school she entered in 1894. "Almost any question touching on their vocation received the rebuke of silence."[55] Parochial school nuns were hardly less welcoming of pupils' overtures.

Once, in the nation's thousands of rural and village schools, "the roles of teachers were overlapping, familiar, personal rather than esoteric, strictly defined and official, the teacher . . . [being simultaneously] brother, suitor, hunting companion, fellow farm worker, boarder and cousin to the different boys and girls in the class."[56] Such intimate familiarity fades with geographic mobility, urbanism, greater cultural and class diversity, institutional bureaucracy, and certificated expertise. Distancing is also an instinctive strategy of any craft: minimizing interference with the performance of one's duties while preserving the distinction between the professional and the amateur. Teaching lore warns against becoming too friendly with one's students, lest they "take advantage," or with parents, so as to maintain impartiality.

A remembered cartoon—perhaps from Lynn Johnston's strip, *For Better or for Worse*—captures the erosion of a once-sacrosanct distancing technique, in an increasingly casual culture. In the first panel, a child at the dinner table recounts the opening day of school, disclosing his new teacher's first name, those of her husband, children, and pets, their respective ages, summer vacation travels, and hobbies. In the second panel, father turns to mother to exclaim, "In my day, teachers didn't even have first names!" Maintaining this distance has been a part of learning to become a teacher. District personnel records often give only an initial or two before the surname, making it harder for outsiders (including historians) to determine whether E. R. Parker was male or female.

In James Purdy's 1960 novel, *The Nephew*, Miss Alma Mason is an elderly retired teacher with a sound instinct for real estate investing. She encounters Mrs. Barrington, who privately believes that, "if Alma was not precisely her equal—and who was?—she was at all events a 'figure' even though only a grade school teacher, and without a doubt something of a competitor. Alma could not, in other words, be ignored."[57] In general, however, while teachers might be assumed to be morally superior, their incomes placed them close to society's "needy." Until the teacher pensions secured in the twentieth century, the widowed or spinster schoolmistress faced destitution in old age. Potential objects of charity, teachers were on the edge of becoming the "worthy" or "deserving" poor and sometimes thought of or treated as such.

The ambiguity of the teacher's social position is a recurring theme in fiction. Like the governess and tutor, schoolteachers shared the social marginality and unflattering imagery of "the hired person [set] among others' spoiled children."[58] Having experienced the indefinite position of a nineteenth-century governess, Charlotte Brontë exposed her most famous character, Jane Eyre, to both the disregard of her pupil and the snobbishness of Mr. Rochester's friends. In John Galsworthy's *The Forsyte Saga* (1906–1921), Helene Hilman is governess in the household of "Young Jolyon" Forsyte. While he recognizes her as a lady, his wife and the family's elder males regard her as "in service," a personally offensive status. Flora Thompson's memoir of Oxfordshire in the 1880s, *Lark Rise to Candleford*, finds a teacher—on the customary annual visit to the manor house with her pupils—given tea in the kitchen, not the drawing room.[59]

Assessing teachers' standing grew more complex as women became the majority of secondary school teachers in a time when high school students remained a scholastic or social elite. (The school was often the community's most impressive public building, a neoclassical offering to the upper-middle class in exchange for its support of public education.) By setting the tasks and distributing the rewards for the offspring of the community's "better families," women teachers were helping shape the character and channel the ambitions of the next generation's more powerful citizens. While mentoring older girls as someone's future wife or secretary, women teachers also exercised daily control of boys: "future kings of the universe"—to employ a popular phrase by which females ridiculed male pretensions. The "bad boys" had been left behind after the eighth grade or were sufficiently tamed, making the high school teacher's authoritativeness a less physical, more artful, and respected element in her craft.

Safeguarding Teachers' Character, Reputation, and Authority

When Charlotte Forten (b. 1839) was invited to leave the freedmen's school at Port Royal (SC) to teach the colored regiment, then stationed in Florida, she consulted her fellow teachers. "Although they do not want me to go, they cannot help acknowledging that it would be a wider sphere of usefulness than this." However, her transfer was withdrawn because "there have been of late very scandalous reports of some of the ladies down here, so of course as usual, all must suffer to some extent."[60] A well-bred, thoroughly respectable Quaker, Forten fell afoul of three realities: a general prudish, meddlesome, Victorian conventionality; the opinion that teachers' sacred calling demands special vigilance; and the prejudice that immorality characterized the colored race.

Parietal rules governing student behavior and controlling teachers' private lives were especially restrictive for colored females. Sponsoring mission societies, philanthropists, and institutional officers blamed slavery for destroying females' natural modesty, purity, and self-control; only vigilant restraint and re-education would erase the sordid legacy of "her foremother's sex role as a slave." Like other deans of women, Lucy Diggs Slowe, at Howard from 1922 to 1937, tried to limit women students' access to unsupervised housing, dance halls, and other questionable venues. Yet she protested that "when a college woman cannot be trusted to go shopping without a chaperone she is not likely to develop powers of leadership."[61] Most of Howard's women students were prospective teachers, and developing Negro teachers' potential as leaders was not a priority of males of any race.

Maintaining gentility was the watchword. Teachers must avoid doing anything, or having anything done to them, that would cause them to "lose caste and tone" in their communities.[62] The Beaver Creek (AZ) school board fired Eulalia Bourne at the end of her second year, 1910, for dancing the "one-step"—a "vulgar rag."[63] Although rules limiting the personal freedoms of males were less noted, they existed. The school trustees in the frontier mining town of Bannack (Montana Territory) warned that being shaved in a barbershop would undermine public trust in the schoolmaster. The trustees' guidelines made attending church a condition for courting a respectable young woman one night a week—best spent sitting with her and her parents in their parlor.[64]

In Massachusetts, where Cardinal William Henry O'Connell was archbishop from 1907 to 1944, ecclesiastical approval was required for nuns' visits to relatives, trips between convents, shopping, even calls on the sick.[65] Thomas Crawford of Portland (OR) was an "administrative progressive," organizing and standardizing its school system. Because teachers are civil servants, he contended that school patrons enjoy "an undoubted right to sit in judgment on the general and even particular conduct of teachers," not excepting teachers' private lives.[66] Given their formal authority to supervise, many lay boards meddled. In her unpublished memoir, Martha Frazier complained, "Women teachers suffered most of the restrictions of nuns, with none of the advantages." Wisconsin's school boards worked overtime enforcing their rules governing teachers. "She should keep [to] her place as a teacher. . . . Nobody defined exactly what a teacher's place was, but everyone knew she should keep it."[67]

There is a subset of teacher images that captures the once-patient teacher spoiled by her exertions and the demands behind them. A country girl, Carry Stewart, the "pretty, fresh-looking mistress . . . had become a pale, irritable creature, capable of striking a scholar." Her experiences in London in the late nineteenth century brought on a "fatal decline."[68] A century later such burnout was the theme at many professional conferences, possibly explaining a mid-twentieth-century Boston-area teacher saying, "I hated women teachers especially . . . always so straight and oppressive, tense and nervous." Volunteering in his daughter's California classroom in 2006, Nicholas Hoppe observed, "Her fuse is far shorter and her patience, at least in the classroom, is non-existent. Patience is not an option with these kids."[69]

Keeping Up Appearances—and Cracks
in the "Cake of Custom"

Official regulations of England's teacher-training colleges fostered a dowdy image. The Ladies' Committee of Stockwell College (f. 1861) "wish it to be distinctly understood . . . that they consider neatness and plainness of dress incumbent on those who undertake the instruction and training of the young."[70] When James Hilton's *Goodbye, Mr. Chips* was remade for public television in 2003, a critic praised casting Martin Clunes in the title role: "Clunes really does look like a guy who only manages to be at ease in life when he's in the classroom." Put more generally, "a teacher's blandness is appreciated by children and parents alike," while having an "uninteresting appearance and lifestyle" accords with being "boring and methodical in class."[71]

In 1932 Willard Waller regretted that, "whereas other women dress to emphasize feminine characteristics, women teachers dress to obscure them."[72] When the British actress Helen Mirren was interviewed about her role as Elizabeth II in *The Queen* (2006), she commented on the "frumpy clothes. Horrible tweed skirts. Very, very sensible walking shoes. . . . You know what it looked like? The sort of women who used to teach me maths at school."[73] Plain garb, however, reinforces the age-related divide between student and pupil, underscoring a teacher's authority. It is also consistent with the sexual repression expected of teachers—and expected to be reflected in what and how they taught. Lay teachers in Catholic schools could be as starchy as nuns, as a St. Luke's student recounted after a teacher found a lipstick in her classroom.[74]

"The combination of automobiles, good roads, inns, and road houses, and tourist camps," the January 1930 issue of the *Journal of Social Hygiene* reported, "has created many new sex problems the solution of which will tax the ingenuity and resourcefulness of all social agencies."[75] When a school board member took umbrage because one of his teachers had acquired a Model T, he could have been thinking about claims that the car, in the hands of the unmarried, served as a "bedroom on wheels." Just as likely, he preferred more dependent, less proud teachers. The popularity of the automobile and the movies eased the way for even the single woman teacher to enjoy herself.

By the 1930s, to raise the teacher's self-image and the positive regard of her pupil, American magazines aimed at teachers featured a modernized image: smartly dressed, energetic, even "out-doorsy." The next 50 years saw general changes in how professionals, even teachers, would dress and act. The 32 fourth graders at Commodore Stockton School in San Francisco's Chinatown in 1949 knew that Miss Briscoe differed from older, "no nonsense types"—like

Mrs. Coleman, "a meanie." Most of the teachers of that day "were literally in their suits and hats and white gloves and high heels."

Robin Briscoe, a self-described "beach bum" from Santa Monica, was "full of the energy and fresh ideas that came with being a 'leggy 28-year-old.'" Like her teaching style, her dress found disfavor with her "very formal and strict" colleagues; she did not even own a hat. She led these children of immigrants beyond the boundaries of Chinatown's tenements and the confines of the three Rs curriculum. Half a century later her former pupils could recall a visit to a modern art gallery, their amazement at seeing a house flanked by lawn, and visits to her apartment for chocolate milk.[76]

Historians (and novelists) seldom portray teachers as vamps, instead offering a schoolmistress eager to contract an acceptable marriage and directing her energies accordingly. The term "trousseau teacher," familiar for at least a century, suggests distraction, limited commitment, and a brief tenure—but not scandal. (A later-appearing version described the degree goal of a post–World War II college ed major as less the B.A. than the "M.R.S.") That she might leave teaching with both regret and a solid record or that her decision might be made easier by the knowledge that she can probably return to teaching whenever need or inclination dictate, would complicate a serviceable stereotype of women's conventionality and modest ambition. While still conservative in their views on premarital sex, like the unmarried of their generation, 1930s and 1940s Gertrudes would be followed by cohorts with perceptibly more liberal lifestyles. Before the end of the twentieth century, even a twice-divorced teacher need not fear for her job or pose as a widow.

In 1986, humorist Erma Bombeck suggested, "Maybe teachers should begin [again] to 'dress for respect,'" adding that "I don't want my tax man wearing a Hawaiian shirt with a racing form in the pocket. . . . Right or wrong, the way we look is the only yardstick we have for measuring people who want our trust, but that we don't know very well." The older black women teachers in Washington (DC) would have agreed, lamenting the "big breakdown" of standards among the district's younger teachers, including their unteacherly dress.[77]

Where Her Gender Matters Most

"Men act," John Berger writes, "while women appear."[78] Margaret Fuller (b. 1810)—American teacher, author, and intellectual—wrote at age 11, "I have already made up my mind to be bright and ugly."[79] In fiction "the strict, old-maid beady-eyed schoolmarm of the East is often contrasted with the pretty, young, fresh-from-normal-school maiden of the old West."[80] While the pretty teacher is often noted in popular culture and student comment, negative images of her appearance are legion. (A general English idiom is "she has a face like a wet weekend.")

Fashion supermodel Linda Evangelista (b. 1965), who attended Catholic schools in her native Canada, reportedly said, "It was God who made me so beautiful. If I weren't, then I'd be a teacher." In her study of "myths and musings" about physical appearance, self-image, and power, Sara Halpern places teachers in unattractive company: "Disney's witch queen looks and moves like a mean old woman, the one we saw as children in our most tyrannical teacher, our most dreadful neighbor, aunt, or grandmother, the woman we did not want to become."[81]

Moving from appearance to personality, differing perspectives and expectations are held for women and men. The 36th annual meeting of the Massachusetts Teachers Association (1880) paid tributes to deceased members, including the first woman so recognized: "Resolved, That Miss Lizzie M. Vickery, of Fall River, was an example of great enthusiasm and conscientious devotion to duty and one whose personal influence had a deep and hallowing influence upon the children of her charge."[82] Her eulogy is unlike the tributes distinguishing male teachers, emphasizing impersonal scholarly attributes and resolute traits of character. The vocational guidance literature 50 years later offers another example. The young man considering teaching was asked to appraise himself to see whether he possesses the qualities desired in a teacher. Prominent was having a sense of humor and broad interests and being alert to "opportunities for professional advancement."[83] Would this last, especially, even appear in screening the other sex?

The Spinster Schoolma'am: The Embodiment of Some Misfortune

The old-maid schoolteacher was one of society's longstanding, pervasive character types, before fading away with little apparent regret. As with other occupations devoted to attracting "the good, doing good," cynics imagined teaching in the case of the unmarried as a sublimation of her unmet marital or sexual longings. Unlike women religious, single laywomen were not shielded by the vows and mysteries of a spiritual vocation. "You a teacher? . . . I can always tell. . . . And I bet you never been married," the garrulous elderly woman crowed to the victim of her intuition.[84]

The New York City high school juniors in Frank McCourt's classes passed their branding of teachers downward to younger cohorts: "Watch out for Miss Boyd, they'll say. Homework, man, homework, and she corrects it. . . . She ain't married so she's got nothing else to do. . . . She sits there at home with her cat listening to classical music, correcting our homework, bothering us." Their advice: "Always try to get married teachers with kids. They don't have time."[85]

Miss Boyd's "looks" were not noted, but she was likely homely. In her relation-ships with the other sex, and in the competitive marriage market, a female's physical attractiveness is thought to trump other attributes: "lucky in looks, lucky in love." The woman who develops her other facets is compensating for having been dealt a bad hand by fate. But what of comely unmarried school-teachers, like Emma Hillyer, mentioned in Mary Thomas's 1873 diary? "She is so attractive; she is well educated, it is a pity anyone like her should have to teach, while a great many worthless, stupid girls seem to be the favorites of fortune."[86]

In early nineteenth-century Bath, England, a curious gentleman conjectures about Miss Susanna Osbourne: "'Do you like teaching?' he asked. 'Very much,' she said. 'It is what I would choose to do with my life even if I had myriad choices.'" He privately reasons that Miss Osbourne and her kind did not have myriad choices. "How often did one hear of a governess marrying? Yet a school-teacher must have even fewer opportunities to meet eligible men."[87] A British government school inspector concluded similarly. "Given her educated tastes and limited social contacts, "she could not marry a labourer, nor . . . a person very much above herself."[88]

A great many Gertrudes, in their diaries and conversations with other single women, jokingly referred to being "old maids"—some as if whistling in the dark. Berta Rantz (b.1893), however, was outspokenly unapologetic about her single state: "I would never marry. . . . But I have children from all over the world"— quite likely, given her 62 years in education.[89] But Estelle Reed, first woman su-perintendent of Indian Schools (1898–1910)—formerly a teacher and state school superintendent in Wyoming—advised women in BIA schools not to persist "lest they become 'cranky old maids.'"[90]

The first novel in English written for schoolgirls, Sarah Fielding's *The Govern-ess* (1749), introduces the nine pupils of Mrs. Teachum, a clergyman's wife who lost both her children within a year of her husband's death; "by the Advice of all her Friends, she undertook . . . the Education of Children."[91] In many tales, the persecution and petty tyrannies heaped on the teacher by her pupils and patrons follow from her position as a luckless virtual servant. No matter that she may be the daughter of a respectable clergyman, a "gentleman," or the second son of the landed aristocracy—some intervening misfortune must explain the need for even this respectable employment.

Popular opinion has no shortage of relatable beliefs, anecdotes, and prejudices to explain a schoolma'am's unmarried state. "She was not attractive enough to catch a man," or perhaps "she had to support her mother, and then it was too late." Or "she has too much education for her own good"—generations of young female readers heard that "if you happen to have any learning keep it a profound secret from the men who generally look with jealous and malignant eye on a woman of cultivated understanding."[92] In reality, many of England's nineteenth-century professional men of marginal incomes provided their daughters with sufficient education to teach.[93]

Around 1920 a mix of compassion and curiosity led Adolphine Fletcher Terry to invite a former classmate to the first reunion of Little Rock's Peabody High School 25 years after their graduation. "Marie," the eldest in a large, struggling family, had become a teacher. "I went down to meet her train expecting to see a sort of broken down, tight-lipped spinster teacher. On the contrary, a very well-dressed, smart-looking woman stepped off the train, wearing high heels and a becoming hat on top of hair which had a curl in it and was not gray. She had just that year been able to get her college degree after twenty-five years of service to her family and to the nation, and she was celebrating that by coming to our reunion."[94] Marie was a dedicated professional and a New Woman.

A Covert Imagery: "Sex Inversion"

The *Yale Literary Magazine* described the "attachment and intimacy" of Alice Archer and Cecilia Vaughan as "charming" in Henry Wadsworth Longfellow's new novel, *Kavanagh* (1849).[95] Social commentators generally treated intensely romantic and sometimes sensual feelings ("being in love") between young females as normal or harmless. In a "homosocial [not homosexual] environment, the spectrum of legitimate female-female behavior was broad," including acceptance of "schoolgirl crushes." Also unremarked were generations of single women teachers who lived with other women: perhaps a sister or widowed mother but often an unrelated single woman, frequently another teacher. These practical arrangements shared housing costs and domestic duties, protected one's reputation, and provided companionship and "help in doing one's buttons."[96] Oberlin College graduates Sallie Holley (b. 1818) and Caroline Putnam (b. 1826) were shunned by their Virginia neighbors not for being lifelong companions but for teaching ex-slaves.

Around the turn of the twentieth century, the term "homosexuality" appeared, and Freudianism subsequently embellished earlier suspicions of "sex inversion." Specialists' interest spread into the public and popular culture, and intimations of sexual deviancy arose in local gossip: "a normal woman will marry," or "have you noticed that she seems awfully close to Miss ——?" Lest they infect others, *The Sociology of Teaching* (1932) recommended dismissing teachers with deviant "carriage, mannerisms, voice, speech, etc." Amid murmuring about lesbianism at various women's colleges, in the 1930s a psychologist at public North Carolina

College for Women, where aspiring teachers were prepared, reportedly reassured students that any homosexual feelings would vanish once they graduated and returned to a sex-balanced environment—hardly descriptive of an elementary school's faculty lounge.[97]

In the 1930s, when Dorothy Weisselberg attended an elementary school in a New Jersey bedroom community for New York City professionals, there was no gossip about two women kindergarten teachers who lived together. When she returned in 1958 and enrolled her daughter in the same school, speculation had arisen and settled into the firm opinion that these same spinster teachers, one already retired, were a lesbian couple.[98] By the 1970s several states had passed or proposed statewide bans on gay and lesbian teachers.[99] As legislative and judicial opinion gradually shifted toward gay rights, religious fundamentalists continue to warn of a homosexual agenda targeting youth.

Not a Job for a "Real Man"?

The ancient Romans made teachers of captured Greek soldiers. In Tokugawa Japan (1603–1868), while doctors and priests might teach, farmers afflicted by one or another physical disability found their livelihoods in schoolrooms.[100] Matter-of-factly, nineteenth-century male teachers are occasionally drawn, in words and pictures, as undersized, physically frail, sickly, even consumptive— unfortunate exceptions to a robust American manhood. In 1820 Henry Sweet, a person "of delicate constitution" and schoolmaster in Dedham (MA) "was entirely disabled for three months" after trying to correct "a vicious youth."[101] Men were included among the white convicts and indentured servants sent by England to its North American colonies and later to Australia to staff schools; penniless emigrants were similarly placed.

In 1556 the town officials of Oundle, England, specified that schoolmasters and their ushers [assistants] foreswear such masculine pastimes as gambling or haunting taverns, or otherwise "give evil example to the scholars."[102] Another unmanly image arises with I. O. Snopes in William Faulkner's *The Hamlet* (1940). Teacher Snopes was accepted—but only as a woman or a preacher would be: "although they would not have actually forbidden him a bottle, they would not have drunk with him." A world of women and children, the elementary school is especially problematic for men. Mild-mannered Mr. Peepers, an early television character, becomes "more manly" as a middle school science teacher. Yet high school teacher Frank McCourt confesses to struggling for 30 years to find his way to be both man and teacher.[103]

If the nineteenth-century stream-turned-flood of schoolmistresses caused some men to avoid or abandon teaching, there is little first-person testimony to that effect. In his 1849 diary, for example, John Noyes Mead, a Harvard College undergraduate, called the teacher's life "the severest drudgery" and remarked, "I think that nothing could induce me to follow the business for life."[104] His words do not indicate that he considered teaching "unmanly." The same might be said of the accounts of numerous men who taught and then left teaching for a preferred occupation. In the 1880s David Wiggins taught for one month until a drugstore job turned up. While relinquishing his school to a grateful cousin, Minerva Coleman, other Kansans were still actively competing with women for schools in Leavenworth County.[105]

The man who teaches typically heads to the high school (where he will have some male colleagues) or for a principalship (where, whenever in the building, he will be surrounded by women). A syndicated columnist and book author, Bob Greene revisited, revised, and published a 1964 diary from his student days at Bexley (OH) High School. In Greene's student days, men were the slight majority of America's high school teachers, for the first time in living memory. As expected of schoolboys, Greene clearly related to the men, seldom mentioning women teachers, yet one wonders whether twenty-first-century men would find a positive inducement to teach in Greene's musings:

> I think of Mr. Schact sitting there in his house last night, grading all of the Algebra tests so we would have them back the day after we took them. What a way to live. I wonder what he thinks about. . . .
>
> At noon the gym teacher, Dr. DeJong, and some of the other teachers said that they didn't want Snyder and Talis to have a street fight. They said they'd fix it up so that the two of them could fight with boxing gloves after school. . . . It seemed like every male teacher in the school was . . . [present] . . . almost as if the teachers were promoting the fight. . . . The fight seemed to pick up their day. . . .
>
> Mr. Millard was the captain of the Ohio State basketball team when he was in college, and when he asks me about the [tennis] match, it's like he's acknowledging that, in a small way, we have had the same kind of experience. . . . When I made the varsity, all of a sudden I could feel the change in how the men teachers acted toward me.[106]

Men in a Stereotypically Female Field: Defamed and Underpaid

For women, "funny, you don't look like a teacher" is a backhanded compliment. For a man it is another reminder of being odd man out. Teachers are seen as bookish, cautious, reactive, rule bound, and risk averse.[107] Generally viewed as neutral or positive assets in women, these traits in men are troubling for segments of the public. This may help explain one of the few consistently observed behavioral differences in teaching between the genders: the nineteenth-century schoolmaster's greater resort to corporal punishment and, in the twentieth century, his greater tolerance of physical activity, exuberance, noise, and disorder. These qualities distinguish him from the "old battle ax" given to prissy repression. Douglas Gosse makes the point that women who teach are teachers, while men who teach are "male teachers." (In various other fields, the reverse is true, for example, in the art world where he is the artist and she is the "woman artist.")[108]

Social science and "practical schoolmen" have consistently implicated feminization for teaching's ambiguous imagery, marginal status, and nonprofessional wages. Yet long before teaching became a female-intensive occupation, the schoolmaster, and even the professor, had a contingent status.[109] Roger Ascham's classic observation on schoolmasters in his sixteenth-century England was that higher wages and more oversight were expended in training a gentleman's horses than teaching his children—producing "the tame and well-ordered horse but wild and unfortunate children."[110] Even the prestigious Latin grammar schools that prepared boys in the classics for university entrance could not hold the average master long.

In Loup City (NE), around 1875, the only man available to teach was Ming Coombs: "an awful nice fellow, excepting for being uneducated in the things he needed to know most, so the men held a meeting and figgered that since he wasn't making it farming they'd ought to elect him county school superintendent and give him a part-time job teaching children." Although Ming hung on as a teacher, the public schools' future depended on a renewable supply of young women like Mont Hawthorne's half sister Julia and his Cousin Belle. As for Mont, "I said I wasn't going to school and turn out to be like Ming Coombs."[111]

When Ruth Curryer penned the Class of 1915 prophecy for San Francisco's Polytechnic High School, she asked her muse to reveal her classmates' futures. Teaching was prophesied for several girls, including "May Maloney [who] shall teach sewing, dressmaking and millinery in a polytechnic high school." The rest would fill a mix of roles: housewifery, traditional women's jobs, and glamorous work like fashion design. Elise, a tennis player, would climb "fame's slipp'ry slope," but no medicine, law, architecture, or science appeared in these girls' futures—although women were entering these fields. None of the boys' imagined careers would be in schools.[112]

It had been generally understood over the years, if with regret and protestations, that teaching cannot offer the educated man a lifestyle comparable to men in other professions and businesses. By themselves, modest salaries do not necessarily lower public regard for a profession. Nevertheless, nineteenth-century educational leaders prepared both teachers and the public to view even secular teaching "as an act of Christian Charity" (Britain's Sir James Kay Shuttleworth) and "truly noble, truly Christian, and truly feminine employment" (Horace Mann). Self-sacrifice and intrinsic rewards have not brought enticing earnings or a compensating prestige to either sex in an increasingly materialistic society.

Under Suspicion: Male Sexuality

Well before explicit sexual language and behavior spread through the popular culture, male teachers were seen as possible moral dangers to susceptible and impressionable youth. Rachel Van Dyke (b. 1793) was clearly attracted to Ebenezer Grosvenor, a Yale graduate five years her senior—and perhaps he to her. Her last day at his school was an emotional trial for both. While his behavior thereafter was thoroughly correct, she pondered the meaning of his suggestion that they read one another's journals, and she recorded his evening visits to her family's home. "I had many things to say to him—but they all remain unsaid still . . . ," and "He will not forget Rachel I know for She can never forget him."[113]

When Gertrude Clanton attended Wesleyan Female College in Macon (GA) in the 1850s, "there was not in college a proffessor who more fully commanded my respect," she later wrote of James R. Thomas, a widower. "He is now and has been for some years married again and President of the Oxford [Emory] College, and yet Mr. Thomas loved devotedly a member of the senior class, a girl so perfect in those attributes which form the character of a woman." There was no impropriety, no scandal, for "so great a restraint did he exercise that it was not until she graduated and he the same day resigned his professors chair that he addressed her . . . with one of the noblest hearts ever offered. . . . I have been told that with the innate coquetry of her sex, but unworthy of a true woman she encouraged him and then rejected him."[114]

In contrast, Mary Richardson questioned the character of the single male present at the closing exercises of her New England district school, who then came to tea and lingered. "I suspect Mr. Potter has some object in view probably to get the school by [showing] some little attention or to get a girl by keeping the school."[115] Far worse, in William Faulkner's *The Hamlet,* schoolmaster Labove is an ambitious law student, attending "Ole Miss" on a football scholarship. With degree in hand he remains at the Frenchman's Bend school, lusting for 11-year-old Eula Varner. An attempted rape is repulsed with a shove and a scathing reference to the classic fool in American literature's gallery of teacher portraits: "Stop pawing me, you old headless horseman Ichabod Crane."[116]

Media coverage of sexual predation—together with the testing industry—have pushed the traditionally personal and warm environment of the elementary school into becoming a more impersonal and guarded place for all teachers. While "teach don't touch" is an injunction applicable to both sexes, male teachers have long fallen under more suspicion. As far as teaching children, what the culture makes easy and "natural" for one sex becomes less so for the other. Proprietors and trustees encouraged their bachelor teachers to marry, but the scarcity of male applicants and the higher salaries needed to support a family prevented most from making wedlock a condition of employment. Meanwhile, both law and public opinion included "moral turpitude" and the more vague "conduct unbecoming a teacher" as unassailable grounds for dismissal and loss of teaching licenses.[117]

A new, dark element further challenged the image of teachers as "guides into the future" when AIDS was recognized in 1981. Teachers and students at a Washington (DC) school—where the disease claimed three teachers—gained an up-close perspective on the human side of a worldwide health, social, and political disaster. A teacher described one of the memorial services for family, students, and colleagues held at the school: "the teachers and students were crying because even when he was very sick, couldn't stand, had to be supported, he sat up on the stage and sang 'America the Beautiful.'"[118]

Conclusion: In the Eye of the Beholder

Latter-day teachers (like other occupational groups) have sought safety in group power, legal contracts, collective bargaining, and bureaucratic impersonality. After 1945 public school teachers transformed most state teachers associations into unions, overcoming their middle-class discomfort with unionism. To gain the contracts they wanted meant packing noisy board meetings, picketing on public sidewalks, authorizing and supporting strikes, and doing occasional jail time in defiance of back-to-work orders. Regulations governing their dress, free-time activities, and associates vanished even as their salaries improved; at the same time some won improvements in working conditions.[119] Many in the public could not reconcile these new representations of teachers with those remembered (or misremembered) from their schooldays; it was as if they were of different species. Moreover their limited victories fed into a recurring view of teachers and other public employees as a dependent population that exploits taxpayers, property and small business owners, and the "more productive" sectors of society. Teachers have, however, retained critical elements of their own self-image.

Contesting the Teacher Image

As the political interests of Christian home schoolers, partisans of free-market economics aiming to privatize schooling and other governmental services, and philanthropic foundations with limited understanding and unlimited wealth came together, the iconography of teaching acquired yet another dimension: the conventionally prepared and tenured teacher was repainted as a time-serving obstacle to educational reform, a perpetuator of chronic inequalities in academic achievement.[120] How unlike the selfless devotion of a Daisy Dean Urch (b. 1876), nine-year teacher at Munising (MI), for whom "muddy or snowbound roads were no obstacle" as she visited every pupil's home to determine the cause of even a one-day absence from school.[121]

Teacher imagery is rooted in what teachers show of themselves and in what others think they see—determined in significant part by their own experience, status, and ideology. As English teacher Garret Keizer observes, to "the svelte mom in the Volvo, Ms. Hart is an air-headed twit . . . who probably had to write crib notes all over her chubby little hand just to get through Ho-hum State College with a C. To the burly dad in the rusty pickup truck, Ms. Hart is a book-addled flake without a practical bone in her body but with plenty of good teeth in her head thanks to a dental plan that comes out of said dad's property taxes."[122]

As the long-time president of Bryn Mawr College (founded by her father and uncle), Martha Carey Thomas (b. 1857) wanted its graduates to be something other, and more, than teachers. There are several references in her journal to teachers: in 1872—"if I can't be a doctor I'll have to be a school teacher or live at home on Father," 1875—"[although] this university [Cornell] is going to be what I want . . . the girls whom we see at the table are mostly . . . teachers and poor, struggling girls," 1883—"an ordinary teacher, or a wretchedly paid, overworked shadow of a professor at Wellesley or Smith . . . I shall never be. . . . It is not that I am ashamed of teaching or of any profession in the world. I do believe that any man or woman who does not have a large independent fortune should have one."[123]

The Quest for Perfection

One perennial element lurking in this chapter, and in the imagery of teaching, repeatedly appears in teachers' personal writing: a personal quest, a cultural disposition, and a civic tendency that is at once fugitive and hardy, so diffuse and taken for granted in thinking about teaching (and education, more broadly) as to escape labeling. Here called "the quest for perfection," it helps account for the behaviors of individuals and collectivities, figuring in both the public image and self-image of members of the profession—whether that quest is sustained by love of children, subject, learning, or performing. It spans the ambitions, values, and actions of even antagonistic persons and groups, professionals and laypersons. It links the private, subjective, and isolated world of the traditional classroom with the public, calculating, and disciplined employee organizations that emerged to represent them. It attends to the workings of gender both in classrooms and in the snare of social institutions and inflated expectations in which America's schools and colleges are caught.

This term, "the quest for perfection," is inspired by a passage from a most unlikely source: Judith McNaught's 1993 novel, *Perfect*.

> "I'm a teacher" she cried hysterically, "I teach little children! Do you think they'll let me teach children now that I'm a national scandal. . . . I've spent the last fifteen years of my life trying to be perfect. I've been so perfect. . . . And it . . . it was all for nothing! I tried so hard," she choked. "I became a teacher so they'd be proud.—I go to church and I teach Sunday school. They won't let me teach any more after this."[124]

These are the near-hysterical words of the novel's heroine, Julie Mathison, reluctantly kidnapped by an escaped convict, Zack Benedict, sentenced for murdering his wife. Julie—abandoned at birth, rescued from foster homes and school failure in Chicago, and adopted into a minister's family in a small town—is a dedicated third-grade teacher who runs athletic activities for handicapped children and a women's literacy program in her spare time. From age 11, "she had scrupulously avoided doing anything whatsoever that might bring down the censure of the gossips." Her teenage dating was confined to "school-sanctioned activities and chaste church socials" with "those few boys of whom . . . the entire town approved." She is a damaged figure, made exemplary by luck and her unremitting efforts. Following her kidnapping and during the subsequent police chase across three states, Mathison learns that she is suspected of being the convict's accomplice rather than his victim. Aghast, she rails against him for shattering the perfect life—the perfect image—that she has assiduously fashioned.

The utter propriety of Julie Mathison's life is not the remarkable element: the restrictive community expectations and even contractual obligations narrowing teachers' personal lives and curbing their freedoms are well known. Instead, the dilemma of McNaught's heroine incidentally captures the driving force in the personal psychology of many teachers and perhaps the underpinnings of public trust in (or disillusionment with) American public education: a quest for perfection. It is explicit in many teachers' memoirs and implicit in their labors. It runs through the language of beginning teachers, who likely sense how widespread among teachers is their own self-description: "a perfectionist."[125] It is also so general, so essential, to America's melioristic utopianism, as to nourish the defense of "exemplary" teachers and to fuel attacks on them in the name of some alternate version of perfection.

Following their own perfectionist vision of teaching, Blanche Bettington (b. 1901) and Frances Eisenberg (b. 1905), teachers at Canoga Park (CA) High School, never saw their profession as uncertain, self-effacing, or powerless. To these "sanction prone" teachers, to use Harmon Zeigler's term, making effective citizens of their students was an exercise of power of the most formative kind.[126] California Congressman Howard Berman said of his civics teacher, "It was Blanche Bettington who excited me about public policy, government and politics."[127] Both went far beyond most teachers in the 1940s and 1950s in "not knuckling under," first to wartime fears and tensions and second to the Cold War–fueled hunt for "un-Americanism."[128]

The family of one of Eisenberg's students alleged that both women were teaching "communistic" ideas. A Los Angeles Board of Education committee investigating the allegations quoted from a California appellate court decision, *Goldsmith v. Board of Education of Sacramento*: "The intimate personal life and habits of a physician do not necessarily affect his usefulness. . . . But the teacher is entrusted with the custody of children and their high preparation for useful life. His habits, his speech, his good name, his cleanliness, the wisdom and propriety of his unofficial utterances, his associations, all are involved."[129]

While the two women were essentially acquitted, they were separately transferred to other Los Angeles high schools where they taught until retirement. When a Canoga Park colleague tried to enlist the school's other male teachers in a unified opposition to their transfers, he found three holdouts. One saw himself vulnerable to charges of communist sympathy because he was Russian born; another said he would prefer to stay out of it; the third "felt that the safest position for him was to remain neutral and draw his pay."[130] In a 1960s study, political scientist Harmon Zeigler found that male high school teachers express greater conventionality, tension, and job dissatisfaction than their female counterparts. He concludes that sex is "key to understanding individual reactions to the teaching career. . . . In short, men teachers and women teachers are different animals." Men, even those teaching in high schools are "the underclass of the teaching profession, a rebel in a female system."[131] If so, the recruitment of more male teachers might still be desired and desirable, although men apparently have less chance than women of perceiving themselves as successful in a pursuit of perfection through teaching.

Ann Harrigan (b. 1910), a Brooklyn (NY) teacher, was not unusual in having "drifted" into a career of teaching as a way to secure some independence, contribute to family income, and gain "a certain professional satisfaction." In 1940, her diary records the dilemma of "me—the wild, untamed, Ann—struggling in the dragnet of duties of the prim school teacher trade" and looking to her faith for sustenance:

> "I tell myself, my Lord is with me always and no matter how bright and competent the other teachers are, there is some reason for this anguish, this positive dislike (based on fear) of teaching. I have made up my mind to do as perfect a job as I can—Oh Lord, help me to know & love the kids. . . . Help me to love teaching and to use my brains to the hilt in probing the secrets of teaching. . . . It is very hard to say, 'thy will be done,' when you have given a thing [teaching] a trial for 9 years and still you are not good at it. I am mediocre—not terrible, but not good—& I want to be the best—the result is a sort of mild perennial hell, chronic frustration, so to speak."[132]

Three years later, Ann Harrigan left teaching for what was essentially community development work in Chicago—still feeling a failure in the "complex job of teaching." Would, however, even the "apostles of professionalism" think her a professional failure?

The coexistence of hope ("I will make them learn") and resignation ("they will not like me for it") continues in schools—as in other human relationships. An exchange overheard at Berkeley (CA) High School in 2006 suggests as much. Student: "I really need a 'B' in this class." Teacher: "Well, I really need to lose 30 pounds. But neither is going to happen."[133] That teacher may be an idealist, but she is no innocent. In style a product *of* her times, she is a teacher *for* her times.

CHAPTER 8

"Higher Prospects for a Useful Life"

The Teacher as Trained Professional

Neither the art of printing, nor the trial by jury, nor a free press, nor free suffrage, can long exist without schools for the training of teachers.

—Horace Mann

Checking rumors of widespread fraud, in 1878 the editor of the *San Francisco Evening Bulletin* posed as a teacher and paid for—and secured—the questions on the upcoming statewide teachers' examination. On November 19, the day before the examination, the *Bulletin,* having also secured the answers, published the test. At the ensuing investigations Mary Nagle, Maggie Brady, Celia Dailey, and Mary Kennedy were among San Franciscans named as having received advance copies of the first day's questions—one having paid $100 and promising the same amount for the next set. The widely reported scandal vitiated the examination, teachers elsewhere were implicated, and a former state superintendent of public instruction lost his life diploma for his complicity.[1]

The *Daily Alta California* editorialized that the remedy for the corrupt, corrosive examination grind was issuing teaching certificates on qualifications earned at approved colleges and normal schools. In 1893, California's legislature removed licensing high school teachers from county examination boards and limited life certificates to normal school graduates. By 1902, the state board of education had accredited 17 private and public universities, exempting their graduates from licensing examinations.[2] In 1913, Illinois created a state examining board, waiving examinations for holders of a normal school diploma; a college degree granted the same privilege to high school teachers.[3] In 1920, Texas temporized: teachers could receive a temporary license by passing an examination and pledging to take a one-year course in teaching at a private or public college or university, or by enrolling in a two-year Texas normal school. Small wonder that half the students (and 90% of the women) in Texas "colleges" in 1924 were taking teaching courses.[4]

Certifying the Teacher's Qualifications

The ancient imperative that religious authorities decide a schoolteacher's fitness appeared in the American colonies in seventeenth-century New Netherlands: the Dutch West India Company only employed schoolmasters that the Dutch Reformed Church licensed. Although Massachusetts Puritans required towns to appoint schoolmasters, the Massachusetts legislature specified in 1701 that the local minister and those of two adjacent towns must approve grammar school masters. South Carolina's first (1710) free school act specified that the schoolmaster be an Anglican, with a lay board of commissioners doing the hiring.[5] However, a pronounced shift from religious to secular oversight occurred during the nineteenth century.

America tolerated competing jurisdictions in qualifying teachers. Local district and county officials prepared and administered teacher examinations, then issued or denied licenses. Meanwhile, state officials advocated centralized and standardized teacher examinations of their own devising. They also opened new institutions, staffed by experts in curriculum and pedagogy. Earned credits, diplomas, and degrees that were upgraded by ambitious, professionally minded teachers gradually replaced both local and state examination systems.

Structured teacher training in the United States effectively dates from 1839, when Massachusetts authorized a state normal school for teachers, with formal classes in pedagogy and opportunities for practicing on children in a regular or model school. Other states and some cities followed suit. Textbooks on teaching methods and educational theory, journals of educational opinion and practice, and teachers' societies supported their efforts.[6] However, an alternative individualistic tradition, popular with a thrifty, often stingy public, considered teaching school open to anyone with the basic skills of literacy and some ability to impart them—thus the long-lived examination system. It was also cheap for those unready to commit to teaching as a livelihood.

Getting Licensed: Miriam Green and Her Circle

Miriam "Mell" Green (b. 1840) of the New Garden (IN) Quaker community attended Earlham College for five months in 1861 before supporting herself by teaching and millinery until marrying at 32. Her experiences and those of her family and friends teaching in Indiana, Illinois, and Ohio amply illustrate the unsystematic means by which individuals qualified themselves to teach, state authorities' early steps to increase and standardize entry requirements, and the greater persistence of women that ultimately made them the majority of Indiana teachers.

County examiners and commissioners still tested teachers, graded the results, issued licenses, and accounted for the license fees collected, meanwhile encouraging teachers' meetings and private study to raise standards. On the day in 1864 that her examiner signed Miriam Green's county license, he wrote to her, "Friend Miriam. If you make such effort for improvement as I hope you will during the next 18 months, you can then have a certificate of the highest grade. . . . [Give] special attention to Arithmetic and Grammar."[7]

After her first week teaching at the private (but state aided) Sand Creek "Ceminary," Lizzie Parker reported her satisfaction with her pupils—"I like the apperiance of my scholars very much"—and detailed the ten-mile buggy ride down "to Collumbus . . . to get our licenses . . . but I got through all right. . . . Ten questions on reading and ten on spelling more than I ever saw at an examination there."[8] While Lizzie's highest mark could not have been in orthography, Wisconsin's Mary Stevens recalled the "smart committee man" who put a sentence on the board for the applicants to parse, misspelling four of its ten words.[9]

Finding meager success and less satisfaction in teaching, Clark Evan Lewis decided against attending normal school, writing in 1864 that he "would rather be a farmer than a school teacher, Dr, or anything else." It was otherwise for Caleb Davis. Having taught a large and successful school, "Cale has arrove at the high position of Proff of Harrisburg high school. . . . Cale says he is going to attend Normal School somewhere when his school is out."[10]

Licensing Teachers: From Examinations to Diplomas

In 1830 experienced teacher William A. Alcott served on a state examining body and found local officials ingenious in evading inconvenient state requirements. Because a district could not receive a share of the public fund if its teacher was unlicensed, in one case "she was examined by being asked how to spell a single common word, and then duly licensed! So little was the spirit of the statute adhered to, and so barefaced were our evasions of it, for the sake of peace, and our purses."[11] In 1865 Idaho's first elected superintendent of public instruction, J. A. Crittenden, proposed that county examination boards replace local trustees in licensing teachers: trustees "are not able to judge the qualifications of a Teacher or his fitness . . . [as] personal considerations frequently affect the matter to the great injury of the school."[12]

The teacher examination system colored virtually every nineteenth-century public school teacher's experience and therefore public discourse. In 1855, Lucia B. Downing appeared before Dr. Butler for a license to teach Keeler District School No. 9 near Westford (VT). Recalling the yellow slip issued by the local doctor qua school superintendent, entitling "a little girl barely fourteen," to teach for one year, she wrote, "I cannot recall any subsequent joy equal to what I felt at that moment, even a college diploma and a Phi Beta Kappa key."[13] Although May Stewart failed the Leavenworth County (KS) examination—her average score in eight subjects, 82%, was below the legal minimum—the Mt. Pleasant School Board accepted her application, presuming she would eventually present the required certificate, as she did.[14]

Like other visible performance standards, examinations are often considered "hard" in contrast to the "soft" measure of a diploma or degree. Nellie Miller likened her first examination, in Ohio in 1874, to going "through the flint mill." But examination standards were highly variable, especially in rural districts with few applicants and miserable wages and working conditions. A candidate for a Texas district school was asked two questions: how to spell "asafetida" and, more pertinent, whether she would leave quietly half way through her six-month contract if she lost the board's confidence. She failed the first question but got the job. Lillian Danton Milam was asked the same three questions by each of three Texas district trustees: What are your qualifications? What is your religious denomination? Do you play the piano?[15]

The bar was set higher for Ella Eten, earning $5 per month in 1916 as student-janitor at her school near Philo (CA). On Saturdays and after school, she and several classmates met with their teacher, Mr. Roesman, to prepare for the Mendocino County teacher' examination. Six students (most likely girls) went to the county seat for the weeklong test "to start at eight each morning and write as fast as we could until five or after, answering to the best of our abilities the question asked in the required subjects." The passing grade was 85%, and "to our surprise and to Mr. Roesman's credit, we all passed." She immediately took a position at the one-room Anderson School, at $70 per month—and was still teaching locally in the 1950s.[16]

Writing of California's Napa Valley around 1900, the vacationing Robert Louis Stevenson mentioned one Irvine Lovelands: "He prided himself on his intelligence; asked us if we knew the schoolma'am." He had put a question to her: "If a tree a hundred feet high were to fall a foot a day, how long would it take to fall right down?" Unable to solve his problem, "'She don't know nothing.'"[17] Indignant at being examined by laypersons and forced to prove themselves repeatedly to renew their licenses, teachers regularly denounced the examination system.

Of New England's "annual-examination farce," John Swett (b. 1830) confessed, "I had the cowardice, like other teachers with me, to submit to eight annual examinations . . . to determine my fitness, at each annual revolution of the sun, to teach the same school each succeeding school year. . . . Much as I honor the occupation of teaching, I am not in love with a system that tends to take all the manliness out of a man, and all the independence from a woman."[18] As California State superintendent of public instruction (1863–1867) and a San Francisco teacher and principal into the 1890s, John Swett was a reformer and a professionalizer, instituting a life certificate that exempted its holders from periodic re-examination. This incentive system, he maintained, promoted longer individual careers, bringing greater continuity and stability to public education. Swett also established a reciprocity policy that gave Katie Hall a second-grade California certificate in 1868 for having earned a diploma from a Massachusetts State normal school.[19]

Katie Hall's story embodies a national movement, initiating a transportable diploma or degree for certifying teachers. Yet Tennessee county officials were examining teaching candidates into the 1920s. Of the 47 tested in 1922, 29 passed and were authorized to teach in rural districts and villages unable to attract degree or diploma holders. For those who failed and those with no hope of higher education, Tennessee and other states retained the expedient of issuing temporary certificates to those attending a six-week "summer normal." Georgia's impoverished rural schools, black and white, accepted county licenses by local examination until 1944.[20]

Places Where Teachers Were Taught

When Atkinson citizens petitioned the New Hampshire legislature to charter their academy (f. 1787, coeducational in 1791), they noted "considerable numbers have received such education as to be now employed as instructors of youth in various parts of the state." North Carolina records show roughly two-thirds of North Carolina schoolteachers born before 1860 were products of female academies without formal work in pedagogy.[21] Many states relied heavily for their teachers on secondary schools, whether termed academy, institute, seminary, or collegiate school. One reformer acerbically referred to these as "public, academical, or collegiate establishments, often taught by obsolete methods and not pretending to deal with didactics [pedagogy] as a distinct science and art."[22] Nonetheless, equipping their students to teach was a latent function of such schools.

Driven by the market, a number of independent secondary schools introduced explicit teacher education after about 1820; as enrollments justified, their teacher preparation became more deliberate and systematic. In 1830 the classical, all-male Phillips Andover Academy added an English department (later seminary for teachers), inviting the young women of nearby Abbot Academy (f. 1829) to these classes; later Abbot began its own three-year teacher's course.[23] From 1867 to 1891, 15 independent secondary academies opened or reopened in Indiana; otherwise highly varied, most put "normal school" or "normal college" in their names, and all advertised themselves as fitting their students to teach through flexible, economical arrangements. Inconvenient distinctions between the academic and the vocational mattered little in this still rough-hewn nation, where furthering individual ambition was seen as promoting community development as well. Thus, before the Civil War, New York, Pennsylvania, Missouri, and other states helped fund a number of private coeducational academies and female seminaries claiming to prepare teachers by combining their conventional subjects with pedagogy. Their competition, the high school, did likewise.

Between 1876 and 1900, public high schools gained legal standing, funding, some popular favor, and more precise functions: to benefit youth and the nation by extending common schools upward and to compete aggressively with independent academies for the patronage and loyalty of the middle class. The public high school and normal school grew up together, both educating teachers and adopting several institutional forms. In 1855, Chicago added a normal, or teachers', department to its one high school "expressly for the qualification of young ladies to teach." Its graduates would receive preference for staffing the city's proliferating primary and grammar schools. Pittsburgh did the same at Central High School in 1868, paying its graduates higher salaries to teach in Pittsburgh.[24]

Even more important, with or without a normal course, high school graduates could usually secure teaching positions in urban grade schools—perhaps after a country school tryout—adding to high schools' appeal to girls. From 1870 to 1890, the number of youngsters graduating annually from America's high schools grew by more than 250%; in both benchmark years, girls were the majority, their share rising to 57%. If local officials were unsure of the fiscal or social wisdom of public secondary schooling—and many working-class families and some immigrant groups saw little value in it—preparing teachers "in house" appealed to ambitious youngsters and economy-minded taxpayers.

Without high schools in most regions, in 1903 the Nebraska legislature funded five geographically dispersed "junior normal schools," each operating for ten or more weeks every summer in public school buildings, using their books and equipment. These schools offered elements of the state normal school curriculum, including practice teaching, to students aged 14 and older.[25] In 1907 the state placed normal training in its accredited high schools, eventually displacing the junior normal. Various rural states passed similar laws, thereby encouraging high school formation. Meanwhile, another secondary-level institution had assumed the front rank in preparing teachers, in part because, unlike cities where high schools first took root, most state normal schools were small-town institutions, accessible to the still-rural majority of the population.

The Idea Made Real: The State Normal School

In 1850 a Houston newspaper traced Prussia's "present, perfected school system, to her Normal Schools. . . . With a population of fourteen millions she has more than forty Normal Schools."[26] However, American educators were sufficiently familiar with the normal school idea to have created a few indigenous versions. In 1818 two Baptist ministers opened Western Mission School in St. Charles (MO), providing the "common and higher branches . . . especially for the training of school teachers and aiding the preachers."[27] In 1823, Samuel Reed Hall began his Concord (VT) Academy. His *Lectures on School Keeping* (1829) made converts to the principle of trained teachers; New York's state superintendent of common schools, ordered 10,000 copies for distribution to the state's school districts.[28] Soon thereafter, fully "pedagogical seminaries" came in the form of state normal schools: places to embody and inculcate the norms, standards, patterns, models, authoritative rules, and maxims of competent and dedicated teaching. Their name derived from France's École Normale Supérieure (f. 1794); the inspiration, from Prussia.[29]

In 1827, James G. Carter's normal academy opened in Lancaster (MA), but his newspaper articles and speeches to the Massachusetts legislature mattered more: "Our ancestors ventured to do what the world had never done before, in so perfect a manner, when they established the free schools. Let us also do what they have never so well done yet, and establish an institution for the exclusive purpose of preparing instructors for them." Normal school promoters saw explicitly trained teachers as indispensable to building civic regard and patronage for public schools.[30] In New England, where common schools first took firm root, so did public normal schools—beginning with the one opened in Lexington (MA) on July 3, 1839.

Lexington's principal, Cyrus Peirce, wished to instill in his often very young students the ideals of learned professions. But a journal entry in November 1840 indicates misgivings: "How under heaven they are going to become Teachers I know not; unless it is by sitting in the school-room, and yawning like a sluggard or looking gravely like an owl, or turning about and grinning & showing the Teeth 5 or 6 hours in the day. They say nothing, know nothing and do nothing." Of the 14 original students in Lexington's first year, four or five left after the first term to take a school, worrying Peirce: "I fear the school will suffer, in the not very successful experiment which two Normalites are making in school keeping in this village."[31] But other "normalites" more than repaid Peirce's tireless efforts.

Yankees took their educational convictions west: Michigan founded the first "western" normal in Ypsilanti in 1849. In 1884 the Blue Mound (KS) district teacher wrote to teacher friends, "Two of my large girls are counting strong on entering the State Normal School as soon as school closes here. They will be the only ones from our county." Midyear he added that they had indeed gone to Emporia: "I hated to lose them from school, but at the same time felt a little proud to have them go."[32]

Like nineteenth-century college men, half or more of normal school students left before completing the course, although some portion eventually secured a diploma at the same or another place. In the 1879–1880 school year, Nashville's Baptist Normal & Theological Institute "for the Education of Colored Pastors, Preachers and Teachers" enrolled 150 male and 81 female students; a goodly number of its upper-grade students were excused to teach in colored schools, in and out of Tennessee.[33] Personal factors and demand for teachers probably explain more defections than does a low commitment to teaching, at least among females.[34] On average the 428 students in the first five classes at the Albany (NY) Normal School—founded in 1845 and modeled on Lexington—taught more than ten years each. The Missouri state normal school was founded at Kirksville in 1867; unsurprisingly, 1874 graduate Sally Thatcher was still teaching (as Mrs. McKinney) in 1917.[35]

Persistence in Teaching: A Nineteenth-Century Example

When the California State Normal School opened in July 1862, in temporary facilities at San Francisco's only high school, the applicants and the first class ("one gentleman and five ladies") were examined. The institution's history detailed the graduates and their teaching situations in 1889—at which point it had graduated 1,222 "ladies" and 221 "gentlemen." Four of that first class graduated, and those who taught were all women: "Miss Grant and Miss Baldwin are still teaching in the San Francisco schools; Miss Hart, now Mrs. Ramsdell [and mother of four], is teaching in Alameda; Miss Fink taught twelve years in San Francisco, then married . . . ; Mr. Randle is now in the office of the Southern Pacific Railroad Company in Stockton."[36]

The record of the Normal School's fourth class (1865) is remarkably similar. Just 16 when she graduated in 1865, Augusta Cameron married in 1869, bore two children, taught three years in San Francisco, and was in her 15th year of teaching in Mendocino County when she reminisced in 1889 about some of her classmates, including "Fannie Nicols whose quaint ways covered a kindly heart; [and] Cornelia, who used to declare so earnestly that she 'never would marry, but would teach all her life.'" The sole male in the class, George S. Pershin, taught for an unspecified time and then became a surveyor. Except for one classmate who "went East," the others repaid the state's investment in their training. Anna Gibbons (Mrs. William T. Garratt) taught for 14 years; Mary Perkins and Miss Campbell were both still teaching in 1889; ill health caused Fanny Nichols to leave teaching after 17 years. Of the other seven women in that graduating class, three married and reported teaching careers of between 14 and 23 years, except for Sophronia Mills Kincaid, who taught two years, married, and retired to raise seven children.

One early graduate went to the village of Mendocino around 1865, accomplishing precisely what the adherents of common schools intended: inspiring parents to abandon their makeshift private schools for the new public system. Kittie Ford recalled, "We had a young man just out of Normal School who was a splendid teacher and disciplinarian and from that time we walked a chalk line—and learned something."[37] In 1918, at her first assembly at the same normal, Ferol Marjorie Slott noted the three dozen young men in a student body of 550, "together in the two front rows as if they sought protection from the overpowering feminine enrollment."[38]

Normal Schools and Their Publics

By 1900 each of the 45 states had one or more state normal schools; in 1920 there were 172 nationwide. In 1910 Marguerite Tolbert (b. 1893) entered South Carolina's Winthrop Normal and Training School (f. 1883 and, in 1925, the nation's second-largest women's college) with a county-based competitive scholarship. Her father asked her to wait a year, it being "the time of four-cent cotton." Instead, unbeknownst to her family, she secured old county tests, followed a study plan, crammed through the July 4 celebrations, and passed the scholarship examination the next day—"the most exciting event in my life." In the 1930s, Tolbert was back at Winthrop, a junior high school teacher in its Training (or practice) School.[39]

Until public high schools spread well beyond a few large cities, many "normalites" enrolled to master high school–level subjects.[40] Indeed, for some of their histories, normal schools may have been more important in disseminating and stimulating secondary and higher education—and promoting social mobility—

than in substantially advancing teaching practice. Regardless, the inexpensive, accessible normal school represented a good public investment. A 1932 study of Pennsylvania high school teachers found normal school and teachers' college graduates having, on average, longer lives in teaching than university graduates from either academic or education departments—in part a function of social class differences between nonuniversity and university populations.[41]

Normal schools drew from the working class, farm families, recent immigrants, the lower-middle class—enrolling the offspring of families on whom a "higher education" might seem wasted. Tucson High School teacher Mary Balch suggested to Maria Urquides (b. 1908) that she take academic courses and consider becoming a teacher. Because Tempe State Teachers College offered a two-year course, Balch convinced Maria's father that his daughter could soon be self-supporting. Working as a dormitory maid and singing in a Mexican restaurant, Maria graduated with honors in 1928. "We were all equal students wanting to earn a teaching credential," her classmate, Elizabeth Fisher Wollery, remembered. "Our age group didn't have things handed to us. We earned them and were proud of doing our best."[42]

Tuition was commonly waived in exchange for pledging to teach in the common schools for an equivalent period. An unknown number reneged on their promises, were asked to pay retroactive tuition, or had their pledges waived. Wisconsin girls and their parents were reassured that the Normal's regents "promised to deal leniently with all perpetrators."[43] Soft enforcement suggests officials' willingness to admit those who wanted more schooling but had little interest in teaching, as well as leniency toward those who simply changed their minds.[44] However, by exposing young women "to discourses of professionalism," normal schools and teachers colleges likely offered their students insight into alternative futures.[45]

Westfield Normal School (f. 1839) served families of the "middling sort" in five western Massachusetts counties. Nearly 50% of its entrants around 1850 had already taught in common schools; 30% of these never did so again. Some became normal school and college instructors; others, school principals or superintendents. Several went south or west to teach.[46] Normal schools may have been the most trusted form of "higher" education in the American West, bringing culture and choice to the frontier. Of the 20 women and 13 men enrolled in Arizona's first normal school (f. 1885), only four women and one man had taught—suggesting few schools and fulsome opportunities.

Within six months of graduating from the new Colorado State Normal School (f. 1889), three women were elected county superintendents of schools. From 1890 to 1900 the normal graduated about 400 women, the newly qualified able

TABLE 8.1

Background of Public School Teachers in Providence, RI, as a Percentage of the Teaching Force

Highest Level Completed %	1882	1885	1890	1895	1900
Common School	3.5	2.5	0.8	0.2	0.0
High School / Academy	75.6	74.4	65.8	52.6	27.8
Normal School	17.0	14.6	24.3	29.6	57.3
College/University	3.9	4.9	5.9	8.4	10.5

Source: Data from *Annual Reports of the Commissioner of Public Schools of Rhode Island,* as summarized in Victoria Maria MacDonald, "The Paradox of Bureaucratization: New Views on Progressive Era Teachers and the Development of a Woman's Profession," *History of Education Quarterly* 39, no. 4 (Winter 1999): 427–53, esp. 434.

Note: From 1897 the Providence school board required certificated teachers to have a minimum of one year of normal school credits.

to compete for preferred schools and the already experienced obtaining the state's life certificate.[47] By the 1890s, the resettled Barker descendants of a North Carolina schoolmaster were supplying much of the student body for New Mexico's new normal school. Seven of Squire Barker's children graduated from the normal, five becoming teachers.[48]

In 1910 Ohio had four state normal schools, training schools run by Ohio's five larger cities, the state universities at Columbus and Athens, and 26 small church and six nonsectarian colleges, all authorized to prepare and recommend licenses for Ohio's public school teachers.[49] Providence (RI) illustrates the changing balance between different types of teacher-educator institutions (table 8.1). Each year, more than 90% of the teachers were women. Even the increasing numbers of recent immigrant descent did not slow this aspect of professionalizing teaching. While New England teachers moved ahead earlier and California's more rapidly, the shape and direction of the shifts illustrate nationwide trends.

Whether normal school students entered as novices or experienced teachers, left early or finished, most likely benefitted. Beyond the three Rs, the school's curriculum covered history, literature, natural science, geometry, and algebra.[50] It gave specific and practical pedagogical advice; modeled a variety of teaching methods; involved students in regular discussions about schooling in relation to moral issues, their communities, and the larger society; offered them systematic opportunities to practice by teaching one another and schoolchildren; attended to their moral, spiritual, and physical health; and valorized the teacher and her profession—although the male pronoun littered their pedagogy texts.

The Teachers College: A Transitional Institution

In 1891, Agnes McLean (b. 1858) was teaching in Los Angeles when she first learned of Maryland's state normal school. Founded for whites in Baltimore in

1866, it had more than 300 students, "twenty of whom only are gentlemen [and] a corps of most efficient teachers, who are bright, progressive, and not school marmy." When a friend, Helen Cole, took a leave from the normal school faculty in 1894 to study abroad, McLean was appointed to replace her on the 13-person faculty.[51] McLean gave lectures and demonstrations at city, county, and state teachers' meetings, taught Sunday school, held dramatic readings, and directed amateur theatricals to raise funds for charity. After returning to home and family, McLean still believed her vocation lay in normal school teaching. "It is more like missionary work. . . . They are many of them girls struggling to make their way in the world and I can be of reas[onable] use to them. . . . These girls are most of them away from home. . . . If I did not teach a thing of what is so important to the teachers (use of voice etc) I would feel that I fitted into this little corner."[52]

That corner, however, was moving (from Baltimore to Towson in 1915) and being renamed as its priorities changed: Towson State Teachers College (1935), Towson State College (1963), and Towson University (1988). By 1912, 85% of two- or three-year normal schools offered some college-level courses.[53] Oklahoma upgraded its normal schools to teachers colleges in 1919, including its Colored Agricultural and Normal University (f. 1897). Arizona did so in 1925 largely because California, a major employer of Arizona-trained teachers, required a college degree of all new teachers. Municipal normal schools became teachers colleges in Charleston, Columbus (OH), New York City, Philadelphia, and St. Louis, among others. Turning Boston Normal into a teachers college was part of Julia Duff's campaign to preserve its graduates' advantage in securing Boston public school openings.[54] A handful became regional, national, and even international institutions: Oswego (NY) State Normal School (f. 1861), Chicago's Cook County Normal School (1867), and Nashville's private George Peabody College for Teachers (1875).

Upgrading the normal school made high school completion an entrance requirement, lengthened the full course to three or four years, placed degree (college) courses alongside normal school work, encouraged the enrollment of men as future high school teachers and school administrators, and better accommodated institutional culture to males. Teachers colleges also more openly enrolled those without an articulated intention to teach. Institutions dedicated primarily or exclusively to teacher preparation fell from 92% in 1938 to 38% in 1956. The needs and concerns of teachers in ungraded country schools, and of elementary school teachers more generally, lost their centrality.[55]

Armed with advanced degrees from various universities, their faculties added training for counselors and deans of students, curriculum and test experts, school architects, school nurses, and system-wide managers of transportation, cafeteria, and business operations. Women students outnumbered men only three to one in the teachers colleges, compared to six to one in the normal schools. Meanwhile, the status of thousands of normal school faculty was collectively raised to instructor or professor as their institutions became colleges. Normal school faculty, like Roxanna Steele of Bloomsburg State Normal in Pennsylvania and Principal Lida Lee Tall of Maryland's Towson State Normal found their prospects improved—approaching the status and responsibilities of university professors of education like Nebraska's Lida B. Earhart.[56]

The Normal Idea in the Nation's Colleges

An unusually forward-looking Harvard College president, Thomas Hill, wrote in a national journal in 1865, without evident effect, that creation of "a Normal School in a University, and of a special course for Bachelors of Arts in a Normal School, would be steps calculated to . . . lift towards its proper dignity the high profession of teaching."[57] A feeble precedent for inserting "pedagogics" in higher education came when a state or county superintendent requested permission to hold a brief normal at a local college or the state university during the common schools' winter or spring breaks.[58] Such episodic and unconnected courses were regularized only when consumer demand and institutional self-interest converged. With rising state certification requirements for beginning teachers, underenrolled colleges and universities saw a new market, although the qualms remained. Educational theory and pedagogy perennially struggled for acceptance in liberal arts colleges and multipurpose universities, especially at research universities.

The various states' A&M (agricultural and mechanical arts) colleges and universities, founded under the federal Morrill Land Grant Act (1862), were too weak to resist pedagogy. In their early years many turned out far more teachers (and preachers) than "scientifically trained" farmers and engineers. A Virginia Polytechnic Institute professor complained, "We get a large number of students from the country who have been taught at by some 18 year old girl no more fit to teach than a pig is to count potatoes."[59] Because of underprepared students and their schools' deficiencies, education departments proliferated. By 1925 they existed in 22 private and 40 state universities and 300 baccalaureate-level colleges—ultimately awarding more graduate degrees to both sexes than any other field.[60]

The inroads made by career-oriented students new to higher education materially promoted American higher education, especially regional universities—many former teachers colleges.[61] In 1928, for the first time, one million students (12% of 18–21-year-olds) were attending America's colleges, 300,000 of these enrolled in teacher education. In 1975, traditional liberal arts colleges that once prepared a large percentage of American teachers through their general curriculum, especially for academies and high schools, enrolled less than 15% of students pursuing teacher education.[62] Instead, the multipurpose colleges and universities, especially those under public control, increasingly defined the professional education of teachers.

Even before 1900, the annual enrollment growth rate in "college"-based pedagogy courses and programs—more than 10% from 1800–1860 and 6.8% from 1870–1900—was higher than that in law, medicine, science, or theology.[63] The proliferation of colleges and some curricular diversification failed to increase nineteenth-century male enrollments beyond the population growth of college-age youth.[64] But the 80% increase from 1850 to 1890 in female undergraduate enrollments, and female preponderance within the expanding normal school–teachers college sector, set the stage for wide-ranging change in American higher education—not least women becoming the majority of the nation's college undergraduates. How odd that social scientists—who quickly recognized the direct and indirect consequences that World War II veterans and the GI Bill had for secondary and higher education and society—did not see that preparing high school graduates to teach in the public schools had similar effects, and over a much longer period.

Coming Together to Improve in Their Profession

At its 1854 meeting the Michigan State Teachers Association debated the proposal that, unless Detroit's teachers received higher wages, they should all quit. Moderates prevailed, voting to improve their qualifications and then petition for wages worthy of a professional.[65] In 1873, Indiana required county superintendents to organize teachers' institutes and inspect schools. California added a system of rural supervisors.[66] From her schoolhouse visits, deputy state superintendent Emma McVicker concluded that Utah's teachers were generally "faithful and to some degree efficient although there were marked exceptions, principally among the men teachers; some showed marks of dissipation, their schoolrooms were bare and cheerless, the recitations were conducted in a listless manner, the textbooks held in the hand and questions read from the book."[67]

Professionals are expected to hone their skills and keep abreast of new knowledge. Formal continuing (in-service) education for teachers in the nineteenth century primarily came through periodic institutes, "summer normals," teachers' reading circles, and the summer camp–like educational assemblies for adults called "Chautauquas," after the site of the first, in 1874, in New York state. Pittsburgh showed nineteenth-century Gertrudes more apt than men to attend an

increasing array of normal courses, read pedagogy texts, and subscribe to professional journals—while resisting their male colleagues' efforts to deny them roles
as institute lecturers and active teacher association members.[68]

The Ubiquitous Teachers' Institute

From the 1840s, periodic teachers' institutes became an essential approach to improving teachers' command of their work and burnishing the profession's image.
Cyrus Peirce described his teaching routines at the Massachusetts State Normal
School as "a kind of standing Teachers' Institute." Horace Mann thought of institutes as something between "an entire unpreparedness for the difficult work of
teaching, and that high degree of preparation available at a state normal school."[69]
With his state's corps of common-school teachers grown to 486 in 1858, California's superintendent Andrew Moulder's annual report urged state funding for
semiannual institutes "to impart to them the perfection of this art."[70] Even sparsely
settled Nebraska and Dakota Territories had institutes by the 1870s.[71] Some attending the September 1900 Lassen County institute rode horseback 130 miles in a
snowstorm, according to the *Western Journal of Education*. It also reported in 1910
on high participation at institutes—143 of 145 teachers in San Luis Obispo County,
and 201 of 203 in remote Humboldt County—and the few normal school graduates
with high school diplomas in 1893 had become nearly a third.

Institutes implied an "uplifting association" with (usually male) notables
as "conductors": county superintendents, normal school worthies, high school
principals, a distinguished figure passing through. At the 1863 Oregon State
Teachers Institute, Henry Cummins sardonically noted the "immense gathering
of the literati—no less than eleven men with the title of 'Professor' and fourteen
with the title of Reverend besides about fifty lesser lights." Local teachers were
called on, perhaps to demonstrate a "method" that had caught an administrator's
eye during a classroom visit. At the 1875 Leavenworth County (KS) Institute, a
novice preparing for the upcoming teachers' examination was annoyed that
"Proff. Felter is wasting a good deal of valuable breath talking to his 2nd division
in Arithmetic and while we are waiting for our class in Methods." A decade later,
this now-veteran teacher, Amanda Stewart, and her sister Nora were discussants
at the history and advanced geography sessions of another institute.[72]

For the final teachers institute of Koscuisko County (IN) in the 1881–1882
school year, Sarah Catherine Brown's contribution was a paper, "Promoting
Punctuality in Country Schools." Another participant, Harvey DeBra, thought
Miss Brown clever in luring her pupils to school before the opening bell with a
project of gathering and pasting roadside flowers into homemade individual

"books."[73] He was not the first ambitious young man to see in a promising teacher a promising wife—a not-unusual outcome of institutes' congregating young teachers during warm summer days and languid evenings.

John Ware noted approvingly in 1887 that Illinois "now allows teachers to attend 5 teaching meetings and draw pay.... A few such trips will dispel the blues."[74] Reactions to institutes varied from the wide-eyed beginner's to the case-hardened skeptic's.[75] Better-prepared, longer experienced, and more confident teachers were predictably more apt to criticize; men's apparently greater proclivity to disparage presenters also suggests status envy. Institutes undoubtedly bored some but also provided a respite from everyday teaching routines, while allowing the organizers or lecturers to display their own professionalism.

Local merchants sometimes funded prizes or medals or provided lemonade or ice cream. Railroad companies donated or discounted fares. The most geo-graphically isolated and poorly paid teachers grumbled, especially where licenses could be downgraded or withdrawn from those failing to attend. The conductor of the 1896 Stone County summer institute explained the absence of some of Arkansas teacher-farmers as their inability to forsake "the pursuit of the plow for the pursuit of knowledge."[76] Missouri's 23 "colored institutes" during the summer of 1892 drew 432 of the state's 700 colored teachers. Louisiana's summer normals, reading circles, and teachers' association meetings were similarly segregated, and invariably fewer or less accessible than those for white teachers.

As institutes tried to build citizen interest in the schools, the public was usually invited to evening sessions. Institutes often began with a prayer and concluded with a religious service, the presence of local ministers reassuring citizens of the orthodoxy of public school professionals. Henry Barnard's idea of boarding teachers and speakers in local homes was called a stroke of genius, "since the work done and to be done was sure to be talked over."[77] However, as institutes became more didactic and self-consciously professional in tone and content, public involvement eroded—although politicians continued to appear wherever women could vote. With more teachers having diplomas or college courses, par-ticipants' need for, or trust in, institutes abated.

Being professionals, John Swett intoned in 1900 that, "teachers will read something relating to modern educational psychology and practical pedagogics. They will subscribe to and read at least one weekly journal of education and one educational monthly, ... [and] the reports of the United States Commissioner of Education, whenever they can find them in the public libraries, and other school reports whenever they can get them."[78] Other educational leaders were less san-guine. Oregon legislated teachers' participation by decertifying those who had not read the designated books and journals. This provoked teacher Robert Ginter's warning, published in the *Portland Telegram* (Oct. 23, 1922): "By degrees there is being built in our state a machine among the 'aristocratic' elements of our profession that . . . will make [teachers] serfs."

Reading circles stemmed from the middle-class gatherings of friends, family, or neighbors to read printed works or their own essays and poetry. The Chautauqua Literary and Scientific Circle created a course of reading for teachers in 1878, later also organizing the reading circles that Elaine Goodale inaugurated for Indian Service teachers in the Dakotas in 1890, an "utter novelty in the Indian field."[79] Institute speakers promoted teachers' reading circles, and state teachers' associations picked up the theme, spreading the practice nationwide.

While some states had no reading circle system, others featured circles with a central board and local managers that issued certificates. These could be presented on renewing their licenses, excusing them from being examined on "the science of teaching." From 1884 Virginia's Reading Association enrolled white teachers at 50¢ per year, giving them two years to complete a reading list in education. Correspondence courses also appeared, directing independent reading through a syllabus, accompanied by textbooks selected and perhaps written by the sponsoring institution's faculty—most notably George Peabody College for Teachers.

Twentieth-Century Career Development

As with preservice teacher education, efforts to upgrade teachers' skills, enlarge their knowledge, and advance individual careers was shifting to colleges and universities. Summer sessions became a fact of life for twentieth-century teachers, as institutes had been for their nineteenth-century counterparts. Southern universities inaugurated notable summer sessions, attended primarily by women teachers. From 1883 a Tennessee camp was the site of the annual Monteagle Normal Institute and Teachers' Retreat, attended by white teachers from across the South. In 1902 the first Summer School of the South at the University of Tennessee enrolled 1500 teachers from 29 states. From 1906, teachers attending its four-week term were granted Tennessee's state certificate without examination, and in 1907 it attracted 11,000 to Knoxville with "free tuition, instruction nominal, transportation rates half-fare."[80] Meanwhile, so many Southern black teachers enrolled at Negro colleges (Tuskegee, Hampton, Florida A&M)—and at Teachers College, Columbia, the University of Chicago, and the state universities of Michigan and Colorado—that they surpassed the South's white teachers in attaining bachelor's and master's degrees.

Staff development became a central-office function of larger school systems, and participating teachers could accumulate credits used in calculating salaries. Superintendent Jesse Newlon furthered professionalism by enlisting teachers in workshops to redesign Denver's curriculum. Frances Doull, principal of the 24th Street School, developed the Denver Handwriting Scale with another principal and conducted classes for Denver teachers in methods of teaching penmanship in an era when that subject occupied a large portion of the teaching day.[81]

Miller County superintendent Elva Grow (b. 1909) made continuing teacher education in southern Georgia a cornerstone of her term (1948–1952). "Whenever the chance came up, I would arrange for workshops and training sessions, and I encouraged the many teachers who drove an hour each way on nights and weekends to take new courses and get new degrees." In Grow, these teachers had a veteran teacher who solicited active participation and valued teachers' and principals' views. "I was so proud of them, and . . . I wanted to help them to feel how serious their jobs were . . . not just to put in the hours, but to influence the lives of children."[82]

Teachers and Their Organizations

"If one attends to founding dates, then teachers might be regarded as the creators of modern professional guilds in America" with the 1794 appearance of the Society of Associated Teachers of New York.[83] Associations existed in 15 states when the National Teachers Association was formed in 1857—without women members. Its successor—the National Education Association (NEA)—held its first annual meeting in Cleveland in 1870. Charlotte Andrews, about to become Arkansas's first colored woman graduate, from Oberlin College, never forgot being introduced as her state's delegate. Her biographer friend described Andrews' reactions to "the largest crowd of which she had ever been a part, in that great splendid room, [where] she could see no other dark face. She felt accepted without question by this white group."[84] Unlike some of its state and local affiliates, the NEA did not practice racial segregation.

Although Gertrudes were not allowed to speak for themselves in early NEA assemblies, women embraced the principle of association, initially spurred by the specter of ending their careers in the poorhouse. From 1879 the Brooklyn Teachers' Association pushed its ultimately successful pension campaign; the NEA took up their cause in 1891.[85] Elizabeth Allen, teacher and vice principal in Hoboken, spearheaded New Jersey's campaign. With Arvilla DeLuce's leadership, a supportive school board, and cooperative legislators, Chicago's teachers obtained coverage in 1895. Teachers in 33 states, especially those from Ohio westward, won retirement systems by 1916, usually statewide plans with teacher contributions supplemented by state funds.[86]

State teachers associations also lobbied for child labor reform, the admission of women to state universities, tax support of public high schools, and woman suffrage. Local organizations more directly addressed matters arising from teachers' classrooms and schools, while furthering friendships and sociability.[87] "There is a Teachers Meeting tonight but it is blowing and snowing so we may not get to go," Alice Pierce wrote in 1882 from Iowa to her fiancé in Oregon. Then, "Well I went to the meeting and . . . made a short speech. . . . There is to be another two weeks hence for the purpose of organizing a teachers association."[88] However, local and county associations were not necessarily grassroots or voluntary efforts. In 1887 Superintendent L. A. Faber of Leavenworth City (KS) clarified that "all teachers in active employment in the county are considered members of the [Leavenworth County Teachers] Association, and will be expected to attend all meetings and take part in the exercises. No excuse will be received except marriage, sickness or death."[89]

The teaching profession was as divided as united. In 1900, St. Paul (MN) had 4 teachers organizations and Boston, 11. Albert Shanker, longtime president of the American Federation of Teachers, recalled the organizational disarray when he began teaching in New York City in 1953: 106 distinct groups represented the city's teachers. Most large cities had separate (woman-led) elementary and secondary teachers associations, affinity groups representing teaching specialties, and separate associations of teachers in colored schools. From 1835 to 1873, Philadelphia teacher Sarah Douglass advocated for her race through the Pennsylvania Association of Teachers of Colored Children.

The Boston Teachers' Club, with 1,500 women teachers around 1900, built alliances with Margaret Haley's labor-affiliated Chicago Federation of Teachers (f. 1897) in lobbying legislators on behalf of teachers' pensions and salary and promotion equity. To stem teachers' political activities, the Boston School Committee instituted a gag rule in 1912 (later rescinded).[90] For Edna Donley, Virginia Parks, and the other Oklahoma women in their NEA state affiliate, the gender-related issue was the declining proportions of women school principals.[91]

On the small stage of local teachers organizations, the clashing interests of their male and female members were more easily exposed. The Public School Teachers Association of Baltimore City (f. 1849) was controlled by male principals and high school teachers until 1924, when Margarietta Collins launched a militant salary campaign that led to her presidency. Under her leadership, teachers—mostly self-supporting single women—became much more involved. The association's protracted political activism provoked the mayor to recommend it be disbanded, forcing the NEA to declare, "No mayor or any other public official has the right to deny the teachers the right to organize." Collins's successors, also "imperious" white women, maintained women's control of the association until 1943.[92]

The teaching profession's gender (and racial) divides extended to honor societies, where initiates receive recognition, continuing professional stimulation, and career-building contacts. Its largest society—more than 25,000 white men in 1939—was Phi Delta Kappa: "a professional and fraternal association" that introduced men to local, state, and national leaders in public education, university schools of education, research bodies, foundations, and government. (Black men were admitted after World War II.) The small, semiformal gathering called the Cleveland Conference performed the same function for the men invited to its annual meetings.[93]

Teachers Unionize

By the turn of the twentieth century, a rival teachers union movement was beginning to coalesce. Its organizers correctly perceived the NEA as an old boy's club and a company union, promoting an ideology of the mutuality of management and labor, despite a manifest power imbalance.[94] The American Federation of Teachers (AFT), a constituent part of the American Federation of Labor, emerged as the NEA's competitor. Building on earlier labor activism, the Chicago Teachers Union (CTU) enrolled more than two-thirds of the city's teachers soon after its 1937 founding. Although the NEA was always larger, the AFT's strength lay in the Northeast and Midwest, among urban teachers of working-class origins, liberal instincts, and less anxiety than middle class teachers about being linked with ordinary, dues-paying workers.[95]

In 1937 the leader of New Orleans's white teachers (probably Sarah Towles Reed) suggested to her Negro counterpart that the latter group enlist the support of organized labor. The resulting League of Classroom Teachers (Local 527, AFT) soon enrolled 75% of Orleans Parish's black teachers, despite lingering genteel doubts about unionization.[96] In South Carolina, Septima Poinsette Clark had no doubts: "I am serving my second term on the school board of Charleston County," its first black woman. "The local teachers' union paid my fee to run the first time in 1976, because they knew that I would speak out in their behalf."[97]

The AFT's recruiting gains came during the Great Depression, when the NEA lost members, and increased in the 1950s and 1960s, when prounion sentiment and militancy rose sharply among teachers—partly from an influx of World War

II veterans into teaching. Years later Frank McCourt could remember the names of the two men and one woman who crossed the United Federation of Teachers picket line. "We called to them, don't go in . . . but they went in, Miss Gilfillan (the art teacher) weeping. The teachers who crossed the picket line were older . . . [maybe] members of the old Teachers' Union, crushed during the McCarthy witch-hunt era." Unlike his youthful experience with unions of teamsters, long-shoreman, and hotel workers, McCourt was shaken by this estrangement among fellow professionals.[98]

Aside from public schools facing court-ordered desegregation, no sector experienced more flux than Roman Catholic schools. With the liberalization of the church following Vatican II (1962–1965), many nuns left their schools. The resulting laicization of faculties and the example of unionizing public school teachers brought unsettling change. Teachers in the St. Louis Archdiocese's private high schools began collective bargaining in the 1960s, obtaining salary increases that eventually pushed other parochial school teachers to unionize. Robin Heimos, fourth-grade teacher at St. Francis of Assisi School and first president of the new union, explained that her colleagues earned two-thirds the salary of public school teachers—insufficient to send their own children to Catholic schools.[99]

Guardians of professional culture, NEA leaders urged teachers "to respect their place in the school hierarchy, to stay out of each other's classes, and most importantly, 'to be absolutely silent on school affairs.' "[100] A New York City superintendent transferred Helen Weinstein for trying to organize a union-related parade. Reminded that parading for causes was an American tradition, he said, "Not for teachers!"[101] A teacher, principal, and union activist in Elko County (NV) for 30 years, Bertha Knemeyer persisted, perhaps hardened by the discrimination German American teachers experienced during World War I.[102] Like teachers everywhere in the developed world, American teachers claimed to see little of the reputed respect once shown them. Apparently feeling they had little to lose, they were less susceptible to warnings that their standing with the public depended on their rejecting unions. The NEA itself joined the teacher union movement.

Defining Professionalism

In 1870, Illinois's chief school official celebrated the young women "crowding our normal and other professional training schools, taking the lead therein as diligent and capable students . . . and passing thence, in steadily increasing numbers to positions of large responsibility in the schools of our state."[103] However, a mounting effort to construct an "educational science" subordinated the normal school's concern with craft to the university scholar's research designs, and the practitioner's empiricism to that of the Ph.D.'s experimentalism. For example, women formerly prominent as sole or senior authors of basal reading texts (e.g., Anna Russell's *Young Ladies' Elocutionary Reader* and Miranda Branson Moore's *Dixie Readers*) disappeared from title pages by 1950—except for Catholic school series, like Ginn's Faith and Freedom books where nuns or anonymous women writers persisted. While teachers remained involved because publishers needed to refashion the researcher's knowledge to fit real classrooms, their professionalism became largely invisible.[104] The conspicuous beneficiaries were men: first, administrators (bureaucrats) and, second, college of education faculty and research and testing specialists (knowledge definers).[105]

Davis Y. Paschall—successively high school teacher, Virginia's state superintendent of public instruction, and president of William and Mary College—admired Professor Helen Foss Weeks, as masterful "in relating appropriate subject matter to the maturity levels in the growth and development of children."[106] Many studies find that teachers most appreciate the authentic, experience-based, and personalized elements in their training. Few researchers and no teacher educators should still be surprised that the ordered theories of the discipline are quickly overshadowed by an apprenticeship in the "curriculum" of everyday practice.

In *Restoration of Learning* (1955), Arthur Bestor characterizes "educationists" as "morbidly self-conscious about the standing of their profession" yet uncertain as to "the exact nature of a profession."[107] By the 1980s, feminist theorists were asking their own questions of "male-stream" analyses of "professionalism," as based largely on men's work styles and cultures.[108] Gender analysis of "the politics of knowledge," they maintain, will clarify why men "have to struggle against internal, even personal contradictions in their effort to define professional work as male, but also why women kept trying to formulate a professional ideology that included them."[109]

Promotion and Professionalism in a "Semi-profession"

Occupational sociologists have bundled up the "female intensive" fields and labeled them "semi-professions," thereby explaining the anxious state of educationists (mostly men) whose self-esteem and market value are depressed by keeping company with women and children.[110] Teaching was (and remains) the largest of several "women's professions"—all dealing disproportionately with powerless nonelites: the teacher and librarian with children or unscreened adults; the social worker with the poor, disabled, or elderly; the nurse with the ill and helpless. Little status accrues from such clients, however much practitioners are praised for their noble service.

Compared to the classically defined "learned professions," according to Bruce Kimball's reading of history, "the impermeable boundary within education was defined not by sect, institution or vocational role, as in theology, medicine, and law, but by gender."[111] The received wisdom holds that women's fields are inevitably semi-professions because of the dysfunctional competition between professional demands and biologically or culturally loaded imperatives, especially familism. Accordingly, as a class, those in female-intensive professions must repeatedly prove both their competence and their commitment to employment— unlike men in their professions.[112] Asked (presumably in the 1960s) to evaluate the women on his faculty, a college administrator complained, "The female dimension of their personalities is always dominant. Even in the most formal academic situations they behave more like housewives than skilled professionals."[113]

Amelia Turner Devenny Rathbun (b. 1889) was a New Mexico teacher whose career was interrupted by two marriages (Colfax County had a marriage bar) and resumed after two divorces. Between school terms, Amelia Rathbun returned repeatedly to Highlands University, falling two courses short of completing a bachelor's degree. She had refused to enroll in Theory and Practicum in Teaching: "after thirty years of teaching, I don't need that!" Rathbun's career was bounded by her own gender-influenced decisions about family and work, even as opportunities and constrains were defined by her era and by the state of New Mexico. Neither, however, would have a bearing on how she would answer the question, "Do you consider yourself a professional?"[114]

The school boards that first hired the schoolmistress for the winter school could not have foreseen women teachers' professionalism. Yet, as chapter 3 shows, efforts to upgrade the occupation of teaching received a more positive response from women, partly because educated women had few vocational options and, presumably, because they hoped to see its good effects on the children they taught and those they might bear. Surprisingly, women invested in themselves, and their careers lengthened and became flexible. Beginning as a one-room country schoolteacher in Tennessee in 1910, farm-bred Amanda Stoltzfus was principal of the first school in Bee County (TX), a citrus and dairy center, to offer manual training, home economics, and elementary agriculture. She then joined the University of Texas Extension Service, traveling the state promoting multiple reforms in rural education.[115]

Jennie Hubbard Lloyd was appointed Logan (UT) City Schools superintendent in pioneer Cache Valley at age 21—new or small districts being readier to promote women.[116] When two women attained the rank of big-city chiefs—Ella Flagg Young in Chicago (1909) and Susan Miller Dorsey in Los Angeles (1920)—

interest in women administrators burgeoned, with firm predictions that women would become, as in teaching, most of the superintendents.[117] However, the men closed ranks, and women lost even elementary school principalships as men largely replaced retiring incumbents. Nevertheless, as urban superintendents acquired deputies (usually men), other new administrative and supervisory positions appeared, some going (by gender ascription or necessity) to women. Former Idaho teacher Gwynne Adams Burrows was successively supervisor of music in an Idaho high school, music supervisor for the Grand Rapids (MI) district, and director of music at the North Dakota State Normal School in Minot.[118]

Normal schools and teachers colleges offered women the preponderance of faculty and administrative positions in higher education. Starting as a rural teacher in her home county, Mary Arizona (Zonia) Baber (b. 1862) was teaching in the practice school of the Cook County Normal School when noticed by some University of Chicago professors; she became their colleague and an internationally respected geography educator. It took California's Agnes Stowell only about a decade after her university graduation in 1903 to join the faculty of Brooklyn Training School for Teachers.[119] Besides pedagogy, Gertrudes appeared in colleges as librarians, instructors of "physical culture" (gymnastics and sports), and deans of women—all composing the career-teacher saga.

Nellie Angel Smith (b. 1882) was 45 years old, with pinned-up white hair, when she stepped from the train at the Alabama State Normal School at Florence as its new Latin teacher and dean of women. She had been home taught by her Alsatian grandfather before entering school in Bear Wallow (KY) at age 9. At 22 she completed high school and took a five-month school at $15 per month. Smith was teaching at Horse Cave High School when awarded a scholarship to Bowling Green Normal for her first professional training. Posts followed at high schools in Kentucky and Tennessee. After attending 17 summer sessions, Smith received a B.A. from George Peabody College for Teachers. She became the first woman with a Peabody Ph.D., followed by a Rockefeller Foundation fellowship. Hers was the only doctorate on the faculty of Memphis State Teachers College, where her summer school classes enrolled other persistent women.[120]

Teachers had ample opportunity to see how "having connections" operates, and women were not necessarily shy about exploiting that knowledge. In 1882, South Carolina teacher Charlotte Smith wrote to Hugh Smith Thompson, a former principal at Columbia Male Academy, state superintendent, recent South Carolina governor nominee, and possible relation. She cited a prominent Charleston physician: "John Forrest thinks you sh[ou]ld make me one of the Lady Superintendents of Education. I hope you will try as Gov to find something for poor women to be at—if so, do remember dear Aunt Charlotte, who is not tired of teaching but w[ould] like to do it on an enlarged scale with teachers under her supervision—& putting a little more into her pocket."[121]

Conclusion: Teaching, Where Motivation, Accountability, and Power Are Loosely Linked

In 1917, Mississippi became the nation's last state to enact compulsory school attendance—65 years after Massachusetts acted—perhaps explaining Hattie Stewart's uneven mastery of the "common branches." Yet she wished to be a more effective teacher, requesting catalogues of books and their prices for teachers, "so I can order me some of your Books as I need a compleat Algbra with questions and Ancers in it as I am teaching in a high school . . . need a new one of the Lates Stile an the Lates Plands of Algreba." Like any prudent teacher she specified that, in the teacher's copy, "Let every problem have the ancer in the Algebra that is the [correct one.] I want to have Lots of Algebras that have no ancers in them and [pupils] hafter work the ancers out."[122] Nothing more is known of the earnest Hattie Stewart: her age, race, and schooling—much less whether, despite her deficiencies, her Lincoln County pupils did indeed learn.

A half century later, California's Anne Walker planned to take the weeklong, all-day examination after her high school graduation in 1932 for the chance of obtaining a position in one of the county's several one-room schools. "The people in Greenwood [Elk] . . . changed all these plans. The Civic club raised money through their many card parties to send me off to college." Walker attended the nearest normal school (by then San Francisco State Teachers College), helping to pay her expenses as a housekeeper and salesgirl. Graduating in 1937, she was one of only two in her class of 200 with confirmed teaching jobs, in the grade school she had attended. A teacher, Alice Cooney Royce, planned to retire—but only if Annie, "local girl made good," got her position.[123]

Hilda Kean noted of schoolmistresses in early twentieth-century England that, once possessed of their ill-paid, often insecure positions, they "prided themselves on their attendance at courses, conferences, and meetings on educational theory and pedagogy."[124] American teachers' habitual, often zealous pursuit of continuing education argues that teachers have been linked, across nations and generations, by a strong pride in their craft and sense of professional responsibility. Dorothy Redus went to Halletsville (TX) in the 1930s, with a three-year temporary certificate signed by the state superintendent, a year at Prairie View College, and courses that included psychology. Understandably, she reflected, "[I] relied more on what I had seen my elementary teachers do than on what I had learned at Prairie View." However, Redus faulted her own "lack of background to accept meaningfully the offerings of the college," and periodically returned to earn her degree.

Other teachers have not been as charitable to those who trained them. Feeling ill equipped for her job in the 1980s, a first-grade Brooklyn teacher bluntly described the bulk of her training as "just garbage."[125] Magdalene Lampert—a university scholar and elementary schoolteacher, functioning simultaneously in two loosely linked worlds—offers less heat and more light: "the academician solves problems that are recognized in some universal way as being important, whereas a teacher's problems arise because the state of affairs in the classroom is not what she wants it to be."[126]

"Programs for the rehabilitation of the schools founder upon the rock of teacher resistance," Willard Waller remarked. But he concluded, "For the most part, we consider this resistance well placed. The common-sense understanding which teachers have of their problems bites deeper into reality than do the maunderings of most theorists."[127] Relatedly, when prospective teachers are compared with other college undergraduates, they are significantly more skeptical about popular "reform" ideas: the redemptive power of, for example, heavier homework, greater academic emphasis in the curriculum, more punitive standards of pupil behavior, and testing teachers' subject-matter mastery (more recently students' "high stakes" test results) to judge teachers' competence. Their views are closer to most professional opinion and, despite other differences between elementary and secondary school candidates, their positions are more alike than different.[128]

In 1915, historian Mary Beard, briefly a public school teacher, concluded, "It will be only when more women alive to the necessities of modern social life, industry, and government gain some power in the training colleges and schools that curricula will be devised to supply the needs of women teachers for the great tasks that . . . fall upon them.[129] No end of lessons flowed into the consciousness of women—as teachers and other workers, mothers, and "the second sex"—in the century since Beard's challenge. One is that power has been dispersed as well as consolidated—including the much despised veto power—the decision by a person in authority that some official rule or policy will not be observed—widely used in the absence of other power.

In the 1950s the Ford Foundation initiated programs placing graduates of mostly elite colleges, virtually untrained and noncertificated, in schools—thus repudiating, under a reform flag, the principle of professional training. Federal initiatives begun by Lyndon Johnson's Great Society programs mandated a host of changes and formally brought parents (and sometimes lawyers) into the teachers' orbit. This was also the time of foundation- and government-funded "programmed instruction," where scholar-created curriculum projects were sold as "teacher proof."[130]

Teacher bashing, which takes many forms, has many causes. As the social and economic stakes of school marks, test scores, and college acceptance mount, ubiquitous public pressure rises to new levels. At the same time the great tasks facing schools appear more gargantuan, the resources fewer, and multiple interest groups (with their often-competing agendas and political allies) more rapidly mobilized. Nor are teachers insulated from the latest manifestations of an internationalized war on women, its roots deep in diverse societies and cultural institutions.[131]

From medieval convent schools, when nuns' autonomy was curbed, to the present, teachers have seen their meager professional discretion limited by patriarchal social, economic, and political structures. Recognizing this, teachers have typically taken their subversive independence into hiding—"safe behind the doors of our self-enclosed classrooms . . . [with] the administrators' theory barred from practice, the teachers' practice barred from theory by the impenetrable barriers of resistance sustained by sexual politics."[132] In choosing to turn inward, a twenty-first-century social studies teacher sanely reasoned, "I may not be able to change the school district or to change the way the school runs, but I can change what goes on in my classroom. . . . I have the power there to do that and have it work the way I want."[133] However, many teachers will add that even that power has been eroded.

CHAPTER 9

"Laboring Conscientiously, Though Perhaps Obscurely"

Certain Realities of Being a Teacher

> Pupils watch the looks and actions of their teachers with a
> closeness of observation surprising to those unaccustomed to
> children.
>
> —Virginia Penny (1863)

"Teaching is its own reward. If you don't get pleasure out of it, you shouldn't do it. Because it's a tremendous amount of work. . . . You're on stage from the minute you come in to the minute you say goodbye to the children. It's exhausting . . . not only here, but when you're home." Home for "Mindy," was suburban New York City, a three-hour round-trip commute by train and subway to the junior high school where, in the 1980s, she was teaching a mixed-age group of able students. While their domestic routines (with a husband and three daughters 12 and younger) were as tightly organized as her lesson plans, there was never enough time.[1]

The expression "where the rubber meets the road" is here paraphrased as "where the chalk meets the chalkboard" to distinguish reality from fancy, practice from prescription, the immediately known from the theoretically abstract. It centers attention on the classroom, its regular inhabitants, and its more important material properties. (For example, in 1916 Septima Poinsette's first school had no chalkboard; she wrote on dry cleaners' bags brought from Charleston to her Sea Islands school.[2]) A school's rules, routines, and customary practices become noted, along with the longed-for incidents that, however small, interrupt the ordinary pace of the lessons, offering pupil or teacher a "re-memorable" relief from routine.

Teachers and students share an arena where quasireligious motives, quasi-technical job demands, and quasidramatic survival skills come together in a mix of the personal and the political. This chapter features teachers' (probably) candid, often contradictory words—of discouragement and satisfaction, sometimes of triumph—about relationships with their pupils, and sometimes parents, on several characteristic occasions: the first day of the school term, in disciplinary encounters, at public displays of pupils' "best work," in interactions with administrators.[3] All teachers are affected by the numbers and characters of their pupils; endure daily, sometimes deadening routines; and meet their professional obligations, often defined and always paid for by parents or taxpayers. Interacting and negotiating with pupils' families is usually the most protracted point of contact, although "showing an interest," "voicing an opinion," and the inclination to meddle flourished in the larger community, as teachers well knew.

Lives in School: Doing the Best I Can

Managing groups of children or adolescents is an unremitting test of teacher patience, imagination, energy, organizational skills, and commitment. It links teachers of all ages, male and female, urban and rural, in public and private schools—and even in novels. Meeting a nondescript suspect in a serial murder case, fictional FBI agent and psychologist Alex Cross thought she had "the beleaguered, animated quality of a public school kindergarten teacher with way too many students."[4] While today's classrooms usually house fewer pupils than many nineteenth-century schools—or public and parochial schools during the baby boom years—even 25 restless bodies may seem too many.

But the same teacher who complains of having too many students or too diverse a group—"abcdarians" mixed in with advanced "scholars"—frets when weather, illness, family need, or truancy drops the numbers of "urchins," "little angels," "polliwogs," and "tadpoles" below some felt critical mass. Thus in 1862 Charlotte Forten records a "perfectly immense school-today. 147 [for the three teachers], of whom I had 58, at least two thirds of whom were tiny A,B,C, people. Hardly knew what to do with them at first. But I like a large school. It is inspiriting."[5] Gertrude Thomas brightly noted in her diary in 1881, "I had an interesting school during last month . . . I had twenty scholars. Although I was very busy I prefer teaching that number to having a smaller school."[6]

"Never, since I've been teaching, have my scholars done so miserably as they have this week. I feel almost utterly discouraged and miserable. I will not indulge the feeling. I must not," a first-year teacher grieved in 1857, speaking for confessed multitudes.[7] In an exchange of letters in 1887 between Kansas sisters, May Stewart described two of her own misbehaving pupils—one "very near to pure meanness," while Mary was joyous at having "just the sweetest children here of anyplace. I have only one I wish I didn't have."[8] However few or many pupils a teacher has, there is often one (or several) whose absence on any day she privately celebrates. If the truant is a known troublemaker, her reprieve may safely be reviewed with colleagues. Being able to share trials and triumphs among colleagues has been a powerful attraction of multiteacher schools; the understanding, empathy, and trust flowing among those in similar situations enhances the teacher's sense of herself as a mature professional.

Trained teachers know that a pupil's absence, especially if chronic, is likely to harm the child and imperil his (usually) future—as well as reduce the school's average daily attendance funding. But, as Voltaire expressed it, "[human] nature has always had more power than education." Long before compulsory school attendance laws were in place and class size or student-teacher ratios were issues for educational researchers, reform movements, and contract bargaining, teachers spoke and wrote of their reactions to facing too many or too few pupils; to a shortage or surplus of seats, books, or other materials; to being run ragged or bored stiff.

Homework is a regularity of schooling, tiresome to both teacher and pupils. About 1874, as teacher of Greek and Latin at Ottowa (IL) High School, Alice Freeman was 19 and inexperienced. "My first week here was hard: I begin at nine in the morning and end at half-past four. Then I have my registers and class books to arrange, and so don't go home until suppertime. After that I have eight lessons to prepare for the next day, which, when I'm tired, costs some effort." She spent weekends keeping records, writing notes to parents of students with excessive absences, and reading pupils' weekly essays.[9]

In her West Virginia schoolhouse in the 1860s, 17-year old beginner Sirene Bunten found teaching "such slow work" that she wished herself back home. After a month, she rejoiced that there were "only five more weeks of school." Yet when the term closed she expressed herself "glad and sorry both." Teaching could also appear more terrifying than tedious, as it did one day in 1883 in the Hund's Station (KA) schoolhouse. As May Stewart reported to her family, "I performed the greatest feat. . . . Killed a copperhead snake three feet long. . . . The children were scared half to death, and their teacher was pretty much excited such a time as we did have."[10]

Meeting Teacher: The Pupil's First Day of School

For some children, opening day represents a private hope or a promise to parents. About her first day as a pupil at Maine's Blue Hill School around 1892, Mary Ellen Chase wrote, "On the September morning when I began my formal education I went, of course, with all the younger children into the lower [primary] room with my new slate and my new pencil box and with that vast excitement which rescues, in most minds, at least one day in childhood from oblivion." Others recall externalities, like new clothes and shoes—although in many nineteenth- and twentieth-century rural schools, children stayed barefoot until the cold weather came, and teachers might remark on their "shoeless scholars" who came through winter snows. The plight of thousands of impoverished, unshod colored children led Negro women's clubs to raise funds to buy them shoes.

If clothing was not pressed or pupils well shod, cleanliness sufficed—for it was joked that "schools were created to sell soap," so much did teachers despise dirt. A Hartford (CT) teacher was remembered for publicly washing one of her unkempt pupils. "It produced the desired effect [for] . . . not one scholar had been sent to school dirty, where there were formerly ten."[11] Promoting cleanliness was one lesson in the "hidden curriculum" that adults owed children, along with order, neatness, industry, and good work habits.

The first day of school baffled immigrant children. Writing in 1908 about teaching in the dingy basement room that housed her third grade at the brand-new Adams School in Eveleth (MN), Polly Bullard recalled her melting-pot class: "Almost every child was foreign born. . . . One little blond Russian Jewish girl had barely escaped a pogrom." Because the children did not speak Miss Bullard's language, "they sat in silence, listening, watching. Usually at the end of two weeks the silent one would burst forth into speech and take part in our talk, so happy to be one of us at last."[12] This was their real first day of school.

Getting Off to a Good Start: Setting the Teacher's Agenda

Only 14, "Miss Lucia B." was concerned most about looking the part when she met her first scholars; her mother put down all Lucia's hems to her shoe tops. In late August 1882, Lucia's father drove her to her boarding place and then the schoolhouse. Wearing her longest dress and her mother's watch, she met her first class: four children from two families. She taught from nine to noon and one to four, and, given the few books, she was hard put to fill the time each day. "And when each pupil has read and ciphered and spelled and passed the water and recessed and recessed and passed the water and spelled and had a lesson in geography and read and spelled, there was usually an hour before I dared dismiss them."[13]

Another novice, 16-year-old Catharine Wiggins began teaching in April 1890 at the Smith School near Fremont (KS): a two-month school of 10 children, paying her $20 per month, less the 25¢ per day charge for the horse she rode to and from school. Her beginners were to learn their letters; the most advanced to plod through the variety of "fifth readers" mostly inherited from parents. "Fear was still dogging me, and the night before school opened I slept very little for wondering what I would do if, when I rang the bell, the children would not come into the school house!"[14]

"On that warm September morning in 1926," wrote Susie Powers, "I drove our Model T Ford up and down the hills of a little country road in Marengo County, Alabama, and was completely happy." Armed with a good breakfast, a half-gallon jar of water, and a sack of old jelly glasses for the pupils (the school's well water and casing were untested), a globe, the paper and pencils that she suspected the parents had not supplied, and great enthusiasm, she set off with the morning's first light. "I should have been scared to death . . . because at age eighteen, I was going forth, with no experience, to teach in a small, one-teacher school consisting of five grades and eight children." Like other untrained novices she also carried images of her own school days to guide her. She hoped that she could forego the intimidating baseball bat that her first teacher had kept in reserve.[15]

On a September morning in Richmond (CA) in the early 1940s, Alice Brimhall held up a sign to collect her third-grade class from among the waiting throngs on the Nystrom School playground. All 112 of her pupils followed her into a classroom designed for 25 students, now fitted with 50 desks. "So we took turns—who would sit in the desk and who would sit on the floor—and that lasted about three days and then I got down to 60, and usually you had people absent."[16] When Evelyn Haag's school first opened in 1908, it had six or eight teachers; when she was hired in 1944, it had about 50. "The first day of school you never knew how many you were going to have," she recalled of those years that forever changed Richmond. The shipyards were recruiting men and women from Oklahoma, Arkansas, Texas, and Louisiana, running 24-hour child-care centers at some work sites. At the district's Stege Elementary School, some classrooms were sequentially occupied by four teachers a day, each greeting her students for the time that she taught, before yielding the classroom to another teacher with her own set of pupils.

Frank McCourt's first job was teaching English at a New York City technical high school in the 1950s. He has been amply warned that adolescents saw the teacher as the task- and test-master, the killjoy, the enforcer. "Sitting at the desk means you're scared or lazy. You're using the desk as a barrier. Best thing is to get out there and stand. Face the music. Be a man. Make one mistake your first day and its takes months to recover." He went to his desk as 34 students burst in, juniors with 11 years' experience with teachers. When a sandwich was thrown, McCourt reacted: "I came from behind my desk and made the first sound of my teaching career: 'Hey.' Four years of higher education at New York University and all I could think of was Hey. . . ." The kids watch as this new teacher mentally reviews his options, all meant to prove his mastery. "They had to recognize I was boss, that I was tough. . . . [So] I ate the sandwich. It was my first act of classroom management. My mouth, clogged with sandwich, attracted the attention of the class. . . . I could see the admiration in their eyes, first teacher in their lives to pick up a sandwich from the floor and eat it in full view."[17]

On Securing "Good Government" in the Schoolroom

The aim of the leader, in school as in government, is to command "not by the exercise of force, but only by the look of it"—to project "natural authority." If only drawing on her own schooldays, the typical new teacher will share the consensus opinion that an orderly classroom is a precondition to effective teaching, for, unlike tutors, teachers are engaged in "batch processing," dealing with individuals within groups.[18] Previously annoyed at the distracting behavior of two pupils, Kate Warthen had "no trouble at school today. Didn't even have to talk much about drawing pictures," because "yesterday Katie C. and Mary D. were surprised as their slates were quietly drawn away from them. Katie relinquished hers with alacrity but Mary only marred the beauty of a belle dressed in a wilderment of tucks and ruffles by drawing her moistened fingers over her in a desperate effort to literally wipe her [drawing] out of existence." Kate Warthen's quiet way of commanding her pupils brought offers of better schools, higher wages, and election to the office of county superintendent of schools.[19]

"In that little school-house, which was not more than a hut, among those rude girls and boys was learned my first real lesson in self-command," Belle Kearney remembered of her teaching in the rural, white public schools of the deep South: "In the beginning there was a fire of insubordination smouldering in the hearts of even the meekest looking of my undisciplined rabble. . . . I became Argus-eyed and learned to control my pupils by sheer will-power."[20] Promoting order and suppressing disorder before it can take hold are crucial. John Swett wrote in 1900, "The strict discipline of the public school is in itself a powerful means of indirect moral training. Pupils are trained to habits of order, silence, regularity, punctuality, industry, truthfulness, obedience, and a regard for the rights of others."[21]

Legend has it that one of Her Majesty's school inspectors, otherwise unremembered, called well-ordered schools "sit stilleries"—an expression frequently invoked in the nineteenth and twentieth centuries in the British Empire. Horace Mann articulated both a classroom reality—"order must be maintained; this is the primal law"—and a reform goal—"as soon as possible, however, the teacher must ascend from the low superiority of muscular force to the higher and spiritual one." In 1885 an Ohio educator quoted Mann as telling a gathering of teachers, "If we could import angels from heaven to supply all the schools with teachers, we might be able to dispense with the rod." Traditionalists might therefore conclude that in "the present imperfect state, it is better to control a school by the use of the rod than not to control it."[22] Indeed, the teacher's punishing ruler and the dunce cap remained as firmly in classroom imagery as the apple or the globe.

Teachers must choose whatever method works, wrote veteran teacher Millard Fillmore Kennedy: "the teacher has to have absolute power . . . to rule by 'sausion if he chose, by rough-and-tumble force if necessary."[23] At age 19, Mary Ellen Chase (b. 1887) would have appeared very mature to earlier nineteenth-century novices. But on her first day of teaching, after an achingly long 12-mile drive, her father dropped her off at the reputedly "hard" school at Buck's Harbor (ME). "It seemed to me I had never seen so many children of all ages and sizes as the number [49] which stood about in an appraising circle as I stepped from the muddy carriage. My father said good-bye, pressing as he did so an unwieldy package into my hand with a murmured command 'not to be slow in using it when necessary.' It proved to be a razor strop and, if I must speak truthfully, a veritable godsend." Her "large scholars" were boys of 18; her "babies" girls of four and five. "On that dreadful first day I could not be consoled by the knowledge that once the weather and sea improved for coast seafaring of various sorts, the oldest and most ominous of my male population would leave me in comparative peace."[24]

While women teachers probably needed and used physical punishment less than their male counterparts, or so it was believed, females also armed themselves. The schoolmistress could not rely on "ingrained male chivalry" to subdue unwilling pupils, sometimes both larger and older than her. As one victim recalled, "The worst cut I ever received from a switch in my boyhood, I took on the back of my bare calves from a woman teacher."[25]

"No Lickin' No Larning"

Colonial documents note teachers venting their frustration, even on the helpless. The youngest pupils might have their thumbs tied to the mistress's chair, be piled up and used as the master's footstool, or be pushed part way from a window and held in place by the sash across the back.[26] For the older, it was rapped knuckles, pinched ears, and whippings. Generations of students knew all the verses of "School days": "Readin' 'n writin' 'n 'rithmatick, taught to the tune of a hickory stick." The imagery of the schoolmistress as disciplinarian was treated humorously in "Willie's Essay," perhaps signaling general approval:

A schoolma'am is a verb because she denotes action when you throw paper wads at the girls. Switch is a conjunction, and is used to connect the verb schoolma'am to the noun boy. This is a compound sentence of which boy is the subject and switch is the object, first person, singular number and awful case. A schoolma'am is different than a boy, a boy wears pants, and a schoolma'am wears her hair banged all over her forehead. She puts paint on her face and some big fellows come and take her home.[27]

As a timid four-year-old, Louisa Barnes (1802) suffered repeated shame in her Franklin County (MA) schoolhouse: "Nothing grieved me more than reproof from my teacher. I remember being called up once by the mistress and placed on the dunce block, where I was kept till evening, and asked every few moments if I'd be a better child. My mortification left me no power of speech."[28] (As a teacher Barnes believed that children were not commended enough.) In Lubbock (TX), a town that expected teachers to discipline as harshly as necessary, Annie Tubbs never forgot that her first teacher, her sister, did not hesitate to crown her with the dunce's cap.[29] Was this to show she played no favorites? In mixed-sex schools, seating miscreant boys on the girls' side of the classroom was a form of humiliation employed by both male and female teachers.

Martha Cragun entered school in Utah Territory around 1858. For small offenses, her teacher's method of establishing her authority was to have the pupil stand in the middle of the floor; a repeat offender was to stand on one foot—and successive infractions added a raised arm, an arm holding a stick, and then the dunce cap.[30] Perhaps in deference to the most enlightened professional thinking of the day, "little whipping was done." Not so the teacher who confided to a teacher friend, "I have learned to <u>thrash</u> since last winter[.] If the boys need it my advice is to give them <u>all you can</u>. I hope you will get along with out it though for it is very unpleasant to whip." And Mary Petherbridge noted that the cold weather had been banished from her school: "we got 'warm' for I <u>thrashed</u> nine without stopping to rest & all girls."[31]

Half a world away, another image was stored in the memory of the pupils at the American School in Manila, a private institution. The wife of a retired army major, Beatrice Grove, was principal from 1925 to 1936. A law unto herself, Mrs. Grove used humiliation and isolation exclusively. Her instrument was the school's iron safe, standing beside her roll-top desk on the landing at the top of the school's central staircase. Children who displeased her were perched on the safe—the "punishment box," in plain sight of the elementary classes below and the high school classes on the upstairs balcony. "The children were always scandalized, for to arouse Mrs. Grove's ire to that extent they reasoned the crime must be heinous." Yet the misdemeanor might simply have been imitating their teacher's mannerisms.[32]

When a Midwestern parochial school, St. Luke's, was selected for an intensive study in the 1950s, three lay teachers were already on its faculty of 14, but all "knew" that the Sisters were stricter and thus more effective.[33] "Before 'tough love' there was Sister Patrick Mary or Sister Elizabeth Maureen. Before 'No Child Left Behind' there were behinds burnished by a swift kick from a foot that emerged without warning from under several acres of robes."[34] The stern nun and the even scarier Sister Superior are stock figures in the gallery of punishers. In Jill Eisenstadt's novel *From Rockaway* (1988), "Timmy was an altar boy up until the fifth grade, when a nun hit him over the head with his own Star Trek lunchbox and he hit back. A left hook to Sister Annunciata in the jaw." Timmy is suspended, not expelled, because his aunt, Sister Agnes, is the principal. "It was like Timmy was defending them all. Like Bruce Lee. They would have cheered if they hadn't been so terrified."[35]

American Individualism and Gender in Teacher-Pupil Competition

Johann Jakob Rütlinger, an experienced teacher from Switzerland, thought the country schools he saw in Maryland and Pennsylvania were poorly run: the product of inept teachers, high-handed children, and indulgent parents.[36] Many other eighteenth- and nineteenth-century immigrants and foreign visitors remarked on the forwardness, even insolence, of American children. The school superintendent of Monroe County (NY) thought both boys' misbehavior and schoolmasters' whippings were traceable to the larger society's admiration of individualism. "There is a spirit of independence fostered by our free institutions which prompts to high and noble bearing, but which, unguided by intelligence, and un-chastened by the moral virtues, degenerates into harshness of manners, and disregard of all law and authority."[37] This may help explain the reaction to one Sprindgdale (KS) incident in 1886, where "Powell undertook to thrash a boy and got walloped instead. Public sympathy with the boy."[38]

Novice teachers and newcomers were well warned that they should expect their authority to be tested. However, for men and boys, male competitiveness added intensity. C. J. Wimer boasted of his triumphs at his Dayton (PA) school in a letter to a former student, now a teacher as well. His whipping six pupils in the first five weeks was part of a contest of males: "I tell you it was no light whipping. . . . The boys think I have a good muscle. One boy was a little taller than I am. There were several holes cut in his pants." Nor were girls safe: "I have not whipped any girls yet, but when it is necessary, I'm going to do it. . . . I don't care if they think me <u>King</u> of the Cannibal Islands, I am going to have order."[39] About the same time an 18-year-old student in the Tarbox District near Angola (NY) drew a jackknife and cut the hand of his teacher while being whipped with a rope for refusing to change his seat.[40]

A New York schoolmaster, Lyman Cobb, knew from experience that, in exercising his rightful authority, the teacher is resisted by boys acting with that "manly independence which will elevate them in the regards of their fellows." The solution: summon the schoolma'am, for "who ever saw a young man, possessing any self-respect, pride himself upon his success in resisting the authority of a kind and respectable" female teacher.[41] "I don't believe the kids would go against a woman teacher as much as they would a man teacher," Emma Shirley said of her teaching days in Texas; "they wouldn't resent her as much."[42]

Competitiveness was compounded when young male teachers, especially the more urbane, aroused the older boys' jealousy because of their suspected appeal to the older girls. Because some in his school thought Mr. Lockwood "partial" to one of his prettiest students, he made a point of requiring her to recite in every subject. "Guess I'll get a rest on that subject now," he hoped. Meanwhile, schoolgirls might see an engaging young schoolmistress as competition for the attention of her "large scholars." Marshall Baker teased his cousin, Nora Stewart, threatening to "drop in your school & see you make the little boys stand around & then look sweet at the big ones. I don't mean to say that you do this but the most of the teachers does."[43]

"Let Gentle Means Always First Be Tried"

"Females will teach young children better than males, will govern them with less resort to physical appliances, and will exert a more genial and kindly, a more humanizing and refining influence upon their dispositions and manners," Horace Mann often reiterated. In the later nineteenth century, a general liberalizing opinion was growing among the middle classes in Western societies. "Acting out their aggressive impulses was becoming less and less attractive. In the course of years, fewer of them beat children, fewer of them maltreated servants, fewer of them exploited workers or lorded it over their wives."[44] Normal school pupils were encouraged to reject even the threat of force in governing their classes; the powerful "law of love" should prevail. The woman teacher was the antidote to the brutalizing effects—on miscreants, classmates, and teachers alike—of old-fashioned discipline and outmoded Puritanical ideas of children's evil nature.

In 1851 Connecticut's superintendent of common schools, Henry Barnard, asked Cyrus Peirce his precepts for securing order and obedience over a 50-year career. They were "that there are better ways than to depend solely or chiefly upon the rod, or appeals to fear; that much may be done by way of prevention of evil; that gentle means should always first be tried." These are "principles, truths, facts, in education, susceptible, I think of the clearest demonstration, and pretty generally admitted now, by all enlightened educators."[45] An international revulsion against the harsh methods of history's schoolmaster was growing, popular sentiment shifting in children's favor, an element of modernist thought being the inherent dignity of the estate of childhood and the individual child. Even conservative Queensland, Australia, required teachers to keep a "punishment register." Thomas Keys listed 165 incidents between 1910 and 1915; his sister, Isabella, next taught the school and used the cane twice; her four female successors not at all.[46]

Miss Bullard's third-graders, the children of exhausted mothers and of fathers daily confronting injury or death in Minnesota's mines, were easily made happy and easily disciplined. Still, the community expected occasional evidence of teacherly sternness. "At some small misdemeanor one day, a voice from the seats remarked, 'Miss Wilson has a rubber hose on her desk.' A hint was enough. I borrowed a piece of rubber hose. . . . [Now] I measured up to their requirements in this respect, too, and my standing as a disciplinarian was established."[47] Her contemporary, Eve Alper (b. 1890), faced different circumstances: a class at Brooklyn's P.S. (later I.S.) 228 reputedly full of "hoodlums" of both sexes. At 4 feet 11 inches, Mrs. Alper relied on innate personal authority and self-confidence, a sense of humor, and a subtle appeal to the boys' gallantry. And the louder they talked, the softer she spoke.[48]

Samuel Lewis (b. 1799) remembered Miss Whitney in the Grammar Department of the Elyria (OH) Union School, exemplifying the woman teacher's superior knowledge of children and a conduct toward them that "secures their confidence and love more readily than the other sex."[49] She wrote privately to a pupil, John Martin Vincent, around 1868 that she was sure that his classroom transgressions were not intended "to be disrespectful" and that her "dear Johnie" would "do so no more and it shall be right," signing herself "your loving friend M. A.W."[50] "The best ordered school I ever attended was taught by a New England lady, a Miss Cleghorn, afterwards Mrs. Gardner," Isaiah Moses (b.1834) wrote of his schooling in southern Illinois. "She was not only a good teacher, but a splendid disciplinarian. She secured the affection of her pupils and ruled them in love. No birch sticks or leather straps disgraced her schoolroom, no angry words or loud threats were heard, all was gentleness, peace, order, and with very few exceptions, hard study."[51]

However, the Wisconsin schoolmistress who "never laid hands on" her scholars made an exception if they swore at her. In getting "a couple of hedges" to use on a scholar who defied her, Mary Stewart broke her vow never to whip. Afterward she kept him at his lesson "till he wouldn't miss a question & he bawled till I thought he would never quit." While her actions worked, she was upset at herself and scornful of those who advocated the rod: "I would just like to see some of these folks that preach thrashing try it once. I've no doubt they could do it in a passion but see them try it as a duty."[52] Young women in particular confessed their loathing of both the need of punishment and its execution.

Encounters with Her Publics

Mary Walker's problems in doing her duty by her Maine pupils in the 1830s were general to teachers and general across time. "Woried most to death because I cant please every body," she lamented one day, and she reacted the next: "Heard Mrs. Binford talked a good deal went to see her. . . . Gave her as fare an understanding as I could. told here not to send her boy without books. What to get etc. . . . called at Mrs. Spencers in the morning told I herd she was put out. She said she was not. had a fare talk explained the affair as well as I could."[53] Teaching in Georgia after the Civil War, long before either free school materials and textbooks or compulsory schooling went into effect, Mrs. Gertrude Thomas had to remind parents to send and equip their children. When Charlie Wiggins's uncle complained that Charlie was using a pencil, she inquired, "'Do I understand you sir . . . to say that you prefer his using a pen and ink instead of learning to write with a pencil?' 'Yes' was his reply." Then, "Will you be so good as to see that he is supplied with them. The copy books and pencil which Charlie has used I have given to him.'"[54] In these two instances we see teachers having to deal with patrons, handle criticism of their teaching practices, and solicit family cooperation.

Along with their concerns about teachers who whipped too much, too hard, or not enough, parents by the late nineteenth century knew just enough about "germs" to worry about contagion in their often crowded, overheated, ill-ventilated, and dirty schools. They would keep their healthy children home, send the sick to school, or demand that teacher or trustees suspend the term, cancel and save funds, or reschedule—limiting teachers' income and employability elsewhere. Kansas teachers and friends Libby Burbank and Amanda Stewart exchanged health reports in 1882–1883. Libby's Leavenworth city class was "badly broken up by mumps and measles," while Amanda's spring term in Leon began a week late because of smallpox in their neighborhood, closing again two weeks later— probably permanently, as two children had died, including one who had "gone to school" to Amanda.[55]

Teacher-Parent Relations

The Methodist minister (Uncle Jack Langley) fathered the most unruly pupil of the 60 crowded into Miss Mary Wills's school in Morland (KS) around 1889.

After one incident the preacher told Frank "he must forgive and love the teacher who had whipped him." Frank replied, "Father, I can forgive her, but I can't love her." On arriving at the schoolhouse, Uncle Jack "talked very calmly to the teacher and departed with the remark, 'Well, if you have to kill him, pick up the pieces so that we can have a funeral.'"[56] Another father who would not contravene a "Lady Teacher's authority" was commended in an 1897 *New York Times* story from Joint District 12, enrolling children from Randolph and Poland (NY). Having trouble with 17-year-old Wait, Miss Benedict "told him he 'must take his books and go home or else submit to a whipping.'" He refused, "and when she attempted to punish him he dealt her a heavy blow in the face with his fist, felling her to the floor." The boy's father, "with great common sense, made the boy accompany him back to the school-house, and instructed the teacher to punish the boy, or he would. . . . Miss Benedict rose to the level of the occasion, and gave the young man a drubbing."[57]

Charles Stokes first assumed the teacher's desk in 1870, near Rancocas (NJ), with 63 scholars. His diary reveals that, after the first week, "patrons complain of my severity in schoolroom." After his trustees' visit, he "was quite cheered by their complemantary remarks about discipline etc." The threat of expulsion being more effective if no alternative schooling existed, Stokes "made a confidential agreement with Geo. Williams to maintain [support] each other in all expulsions from school. not to receive each others scholars."[58] Such arrangements were lost as the authority to accept and reject students passed from private teachers to public school boards. Nonetheless, trustees and parents often took the teacher's side. Harvel (IL) trustees asked George Randal to "write what rules [he] might need for the control of the school and approved them without a change," and they also "assured [him] that they would support [him] in enforcing the rules and in case of a suit would defend [him]."[59]

Parents frequently told teachers, "I can't do anything with him either, without lickin'; keep it up!" Mothers appeared more likely than fathers to voice their helplessness and defer to the teacher. As late as the 1960s, a teacher's unthinking call to Augie's mother about his behavior brought his father in during a lesson. He banged his son around, ignoring the teacher's protests. As the class sat in hostile silence, the teacher realized that "there's no respect for teachers who send you to the office or call parents. If you can't handle it yourself you shouldn't even be a teacher."[60] Other parents resolutely defended their offspring, questioned the teacher's impartiality, even threatened to give the teacher "a dose of [her] own medicine." In 1853 a Barnstable County (MA) schoolmistress was taken to court by the father of a boy whipped "about the arms, back, hips, and other parts of the body."[61]

Negotiating and Securing a Living Wage

Informal encounters with their several publics are important in teachers' stories—as is payday. When most teachers were independent entrepreneurs, considerable effort went into ingratiating themselves to a community and scouting for pupils. Then came their soul-withering task of collecting the agreed-on fees, sometimes having to accept only partial payment and promises. In arrears for his sons' tuition and boarding fees, G. Bull begged Moses Waddell to be patient "as our long staple cotton has bore no price at all."[62] A Northern teacher, long resident in Georgia, Amelia "Jennie" Akehurst Lines was in Macon, looking for new students and collecting the tuition fees due her. "Mrs. Brown owes me for nearly two months and will not pay. Mr. Wing was behind and the little girls who only came six weeks won't pay at all."[63] Subscription schools like hers persisted in the South after they had atrophied elsewhere. In territorial Utah, local boards of trustees appeared as settlements grew. Although trustees chose the teacher and set the tuition, the teacher still had to collect from patrons; not all paid.

When Miss Eunice Will accepted a position at the Sutherland Springs (TX) Free School in 1879 for $1.50 per pupil, two conditions were set: the contracted three-month school would end early if the public fund ran dry, and full pay depended on average daily attendance not falling below 75% of the registered pupils. Miss Nellie O'Donald was first hired in early 1882 to teach at the log cabin public school in frontier Wichita Falls (TX) as a subscription school when state funds were exhausted. The next year, "state funds paid me seventy-five per month as long as the fund lasted, then I finished the year again on private tuition. . . . I lost the tuition of but one pupil when the family moved away without paying me—but she was such a dear little girl and learned so rapidly, she more than repaid me for the lost tuition."[64]

A solid reason for a general levy to support schools was to protect teachers and their pupils from such vicissitudes. But public officials did not always pay wages either fully or on time. Teachers' incomes could be affected by declining enrollments, natural disasters, and mismanagement by school trustees. Tax authorities were known to fail to collect all taxes, overestimate revenues, and even misappropriate school funds. In the best case, teachers were anxious and uncertain; in the worst, they received discounted warrants or none at all.

In eighteenth-century Vermont, even the wealthy paid their taxes and store bills in produce. Therefore, it was an unusual concession when subscribers promised Samuel Hopkins seven pounds, four shillings to teach the three-month school in Newbury in 1781, "paid in hard money, and hard money only."[65] In territorial Utah, teachers were routinely given "country pay": wheat, eggs, fruit, or the labor of some member of the pupil's family. Parents sometimes contributed their children's labor in settling their tuition bills—in one case three dollars per month, payable in produce—by tending the teacher's garden on Saturdays or hauling in fertilizer from their home gardens.[66] Some Texas patrons contributed slave labor to settle tuition bills at the Rev. John W. P. McKenzie's institute.[67] In the summer of 1890, 16-year-old Agnes Morley received 23 dozen eggs and thanks from the scattered New Mexico Territory ranching families who hired her to "learn" their gun-toting children to read, write, and "figger."[68]

Wage discrimination—women teachers typically earned 40% to 50% of a male teacher's wage—made the self-supporting schoolma'am's situation especially perilous if her employer did not pay. In 1888, Mrs. Griswold wrote to her former boarder, Amanda Stewart, asking whether the county teachers had been paid "and to know when I shall get my money . . . I am discomoding myself in waiting though I did not intend to confess it."[69] In a December 23, 1900, editorial, "Worrying the Teachers," the *Chicago Tribune* scolded the Chicago Board of Education for not paying its teachers on time.

Paying teachers by warrants in lieu of cash or check put the holder to the trouble and uncertainty of redeeming them from a third party, with the risk of payment being deferred or depreciating in value. During hard times—including the protracted Great Depression—salary warrants were commonly issued and heavily discounted, perhaps paying 40% of face value. Everywhere in the nation the spinster teacher struggled to create a little nest egg in the days before pensions, credit unions, or other institutions aided career teachers who outlived their resources. On a tour of the Dickinson County (KS) "Poor Farm," Charlotte Laing Dahl's memories of Abilene's Garfield School in the mid-1930s were darkened on seeing Anna Dakin (b. 1875), her long-ago first-grade teacher, standing in her bathrobe with the other elderly residents.[70]

A Little Entertainment down at the Schoolhouse

As a legacy of Puritanism, eighteenth-century American schools remained in session on December 25, a Reformation tradition persisting well into the nineteenth century. Eventually Christmas Day became a school holiday, a reason for decorating the schoolhouse, the scene of parties and pageants for the pupils (and sometimes parents). Activities celebrating Thanksgiving, patriotic holidays, and Halloween usually engaged even unmotivated pupils, while testing the teacher's stamina and organizational skills.

The open examination was an established feature of nineteenth-century American schools, inherited from the public display of erudition and awards at college and university commencements dating from the Middle Ages. Poetry readings, declamations, tableaux, and musical performances were often inter-spersed with questions posed by a local clergyman, college professor, school board member, or the pupils' teacher. Over time the local school examination tended to become an "exhibition," with carefully scripted and rehearsed indi-vidual and group pieces and entertainments. Schools were also the site of other community diversions, especially debates and spelling bees, some attracting a dozen contestants and scores of onlookers. These neighborhood gatherings at school retained a sense of community, even as the self-contained community slowly collapsed under modernity.[71]

In 1834, Rev. Moses Waddel, the retired president of Franklin College (later the University of Georgia) "addressed my high approbation to a numerous Au-dience" at the examination of the pupils at Miss McQuerns's academy.[72] While few visitors, and none distinguished, came to the closing of Mary Richardson's term at a Maine district school in August 1833, her scholars were expected to perform, sometimes without warning. Her journal reads, "closed my school. There were over forty scholars present. Father[,] Dr. Whitney and Dr. Potter called on us very unexpectedly. Yet I was glad to see them my scholars were quite as orderly as I could expect."[73] Townspeople might stop by the schoolhouse dur-ing the term, unannounced, "to see for themselves." There were 64 teachers in rural Mendocino County (CA) in the 1879–1880 school year; 904 visitors were recorded.[74]

Many boys and girls first learned to think on their feet and gain confidence before an audience—if they remembered to practice. Eleven-year-old Turner Thomas of Georgia had not, as his mother explained: "[He] had been selected as one of the seven best speakers in his class to contend on the following Friday for a prize—He had forgotten it and when called upon was not prepared to go on. This he told me with tears of mortification and I believe I was as much disap-pointed as I would have been contending for first honors in college."[75] Such events were opportunities for adults to impress upon the young the honor pre-sented, the force of good habits of study, the ambitions held for them. The public was invited to Sarah Pierce's Litchfield Female Academy's once-weekly "fault-telling" sessions, surely among schools' more unusual entertainments—still per-haps comforting to adults steeped in Puritanism's zeal for self-examination or parents too gentle to correct their own daughters forcefully.[76]

Anna Peck Sill ingratiated herself and Rockford (IL) Female Seminary with the citizenry by her twice-yearly public exhibitions. An 1852 newspaper reports a breathless public following her pupils as they parsed sentences, answered questions on state history, solved algebra problems, translated Latin passages, read their compositions, recited poetry, sang songs, and played the piano or mandolin. Ultimately, however, it was Miss Sill who was being judged: Were their daughters' results worth the tuition? Was the principal capable of heading this private school?[77] Less elite but far more common were public exhibitions that informed patrons and trustees and formed or confirmed public opinion as to whether the district should rehire a teacher for another term. A 14-year-old novice with only four "scholars," from two families, drew 25 curious and entertainment-starved Vermonters in 1882—"a vast and terrifying audience having assembled—entirely out of proportion to the number of pupils. There were fond parents and grandparents and aunts and uncles and cousins thrice removed." The students, and she, "passed."[78]

Capp Jay Bird was taught at home in west Texas until a school opened nearby around 1894, when he was 11. Capp had "gotten up" his speech for Miss Janie Roberts "and thought he could say it all right" until a new worry arose: "But, Mama, what if she should call on me to say another one? What would I do?" When Mrs. Bird next wrote of a "little entertainment" at the Buck Creek School, Miss Ola Neff was teacher and Capp was a seasoned performer. "The house was packed. . . . Miss Ola had many compliments on this, as it was all her own getup. Capp received the medal."[79] In larger grade schools and city and regional high schools, new dedicated spaces were created for "the civil ceremonies of schooling": class performances, school plays, educational films, and various assemblies.[80]

Like other public festivities, those offered by the day schools on the Sioux reservation in Dakota Territory had their "hidden curriculum": furthering Indian cultural assimilation. In her memoirs, Elaine Goodale Eastman explained, "Community suppers, magic-lantern shows, and other wholesome diversions were a part of our plan, largely supplanting the native dances" thought to lead to unruly and sometimes defiant behavior. By the twentieth century, however, federal authorities were coming to accept some concessions to Indian culture and no longer forbade all native rituals and entertainments.[81]

The Turning-Out Ritual Becomes the School Picnic

"Barring-out the teacher" was an utterly different exercise or entertainment, largely gone by the later nineteenth century as women teachers became ubiquitous. This boisterous, sometimes violent contest of wills and strength between the schoolmaster and his larger pupils was brought to North America from England and Scotland, and it was most firmly rooted in Scots-Irish settlements in upper South and border colonies and states. While a more symbolic, ritualized, and usually milder form appeared in rural communities elsewhere, this custom forced New England district schools to close often enough to reinforce the trend of turning the winter schools over to women.[82]

The ritual typically began with pupils demanding a week off from school, along with "treats" from the schoolmaster, who occasionally announced in advance that no school holiday would occur on his watch. The emerging contest was to see who prevailed on the appointed day. If the teacher arrived first, the challenge was to seize and throw him out or to bar him from entering if he arrived late. In most cases, the teacher made a token resistance, capitulated, and offered refreshments—sometimes "hard drink" shared by the watchful community. However, matters sometimes got out of hand, bringing some number of teacher deaths and serious injuries on both sides.

The *Jamestown* (NY) *Journal* for February 14, 1879, reported that the Town of Poland witnessed the near demise of teacher Irving Fiske, a bachelor aged about 30. He had been teaching in District No. 6 without known trouble until the school's older and larger boys threatened to follow "the noble and time-honored plan of 'turning the teacher out.'" At the start of the school day, Charles Staples began to read aloud, unasked, then refused to stop, swore, and was being whipped when Albert Walrod, age 17, intervened, picked up an iron poker and dealt his teacher a heavy blow. Unconscious, Fiske was carried by other students to a nearby house, physicians were called, and a few days later he recovered sufficiently "to resume his place in school."

Male students found their repertoire diminished when the schoolma'am took over the schoolhouse. No longer were students able to express rebellion violently, nor was the barring-out contest condoned with a woman teacher. A notice in a 1903 Tennessee newspaper reported what was already a commonplace substitute: "Miss Nora Duke gave her school children a picnic . . . where they spent a pleasant day romping through the woods and enjoying the scenery."[83] Another benign relic—later often turned over to the school PTA or a "room mother"—was the teacher providing "treats" before the Christmas recess or the term's close.

The Gender Script on Governing Schools

In opposing the woman suffrage movement, the Rev. Horace Bushnell contrasted the "positivity" of man with the "receptivity" of woman.[84] Balancing the strengths of each sex would work well in schools: she the schoolroom teacher, he the principal or superintendent. Had not Horace Mann, among others, claimed that women teachers would remain satisfied with the company of children (and other women), not seeking to wield power or "gain further emoluments"? Was this surmise not borne out in Sallie Bethune's decision to relinquish the principalship of a Charlotte (NC) school to return to teaching first grade? Yet Bethune's 46-year career in Charlotte shows otherwise. She moved quickly from opening a private school in her own home around 1870 to teaching in Mr. Boone's large private school of 400 hundred pupils. In 1882 Charlotte's town fathers asked her to organize and then teach in the town's new public school system.[85] In 1908 she was named principal of the new Fourth Ward School, holding that office until 1920. As to her leaving it, her patrons or the school board may have tired of her, or she with "administrivia."

Critics of bringing a "female style" to public roles—whether as managers or in dispensing discipline, philanthropy, religious conversion—repeatedly recite the gender script: contrasting women's innate emotionality and indulgent qualities with the "manly, straightforward, and strengthening tone" that male leaders of private and public organizations project.[86] In modern terminology, men's role as "boundary keepers" is distinguished from women's as "relationship makers." This did not prevent women teachers expressing their skepticism about male colleagues, especially when less experienced, less qualified, or less competent. Among themselves and in their writings, nineteenth-century women teachers referred, dismissively, to the "boy principal" or volunteered to tutor him in the workings of a school.

While women's styles of leadership and administration are sufficiently different to show up in research studies, individual women could be as peremptory, irrational, and arrogant as any man. Ada J. Mahon (b.1881)—principal of Seattle's Main Elementary School and its successor institution for 30 years—was classed with her authoritarian fellow principal at George Washington School, Arthur G. Sears.[87] In the later twentieth century, several intrepid black women district superintendents—Ruth B. Love (Oakland and Chicago), Arlene Ackerman (Washington, San Francisco, and Philadelphia), and Carol R. Johnson (Minneapolis, Memphis, and Boston)—were judged "tough enough for the job." As chancellor of Washington (DC) schools (2007–2010), uncompromising Michelle Rhee—"my way or the highway"—fired 900 employees, from central office staff to teachers and classroom aides, and proposed to close or restructure a third of the District's schools.[88]

Throughout the nation, assigning the sexes their respective roles was remarkably consistent. Madison (WI), incorporated in 1855, opened a public grade school with 250 pupils and four staff members: two women teachers, one male teacher, and a male principal (also named city superintendent and principal of the high school). All the later nineteenth-century city and county superintendents mentioned in the voluminous Stewart-Lockwood Kansas Collection were men—as were most school board members. A 1905 photograph of the multiteacher public school in Nome (AK) shows a typical distribution: eight women (teachers) and one man (principal). Jettie Irving Edwards married Ernest Felps, her "first love" in 1916; in their early careers they taught in separate small schools. When teaching together in larger schools, like one in Texas, Ernest Felps was named superintendent. Her ire rose at his "making about twice my salary." He also heaped his problems on her: "If a volley ball coach was needed, I was asked to take the work, if no one could teach Spanish, I would have to manage that some way. And ever since old Adam laid all the blame on Eve when things went wrong, I got the blame."[89]

Women teachers who did secure administrative positions still lacked what their male counterparts could usually take for granted: admission into a male-only web of individual influence and organizational power that stretched across the community. She was excluded from veterans, fraternal, and sports associations and from the locker-room and boardroom bonhomie that conferred on men some degree of trust and support from local power brokers and press lords. As school systems became larger and more tightly controlled, the one administrative niche women had occupied, principal of a graded elementary school, slipped out of their grasp: 62% in 1905, women were only 20% in 1972.[90]

Beware the "Cuckoo"—the Official Visit

"My headmaster has asked me to tell your headmaster that the cuckoo is coming early this year"—the cuckoo being the HMI (His Majesty's inspector). "Tell all the teachers to check registers, weekly forecasts, exercise books, have inkwells cleaned, windows decorated with flowers."[91] Unlike the British system, where teachers were subject to announced visits by central government officials, the American system was improvisational. Still, a teacher could be rendered sleepless by the prospect of a county or district superintendent's visit, fearful that even her better pupils would forget the "9-times table"; impudence was less likely, as even the "bad boys" were in awe of official outsiders. Perhaps because he did not plan to stay in teaching, Anson O. Lockwood seemed unperturbed that "The Wise Man of Leavenworth is to visit my school on Monday. No doubt I'll get lectured. . . . But I can not think brains are necessary for a position as County Supt."[92]

Even her principal's visit could put the schoolmistress on edge, although reports of her swooning are more rare than with superintendents' visits. An experienced rural teacher in her first year (1909–1910) in the highly regulated Denver schools, Alice Newberry was pleasantly surprised: "The principal has the reputation of being very severe but she is very nice to me, and I must be very trying. There are so many things to remember and to forget! I know what my buzzer signals to me now. I know the bells and gongs."[93] Not so with "Anna Henson's" principal at a Detroit junior high school in the late 1960s. Suddenly hired to replace a teacher let go for drinking at school, she found a chaotic class. "I remember asking the principal if he at least had a list of names, so that I'd have a place to begin. But he said 'no.' He just walked me to the classroom and closed the door. I will never forget that."[94]

Hearing that County Superintendent M. J. Faber was coming to inspect her Kansas school, May Stewart "wore best dress, white apron, hair up, blacked shoes." He came—and stayed the morning, along with Director Lee and Clerk Stigleman of her school board. (Teachers often voiced their disappointment or disgust with those who failed to show up when expected.) Faber wrote, "Grading and classification of school, fair to good; order and decorum, good; program of exercises, fair; lessons well recited; industry of pupils at seats good; General interest in exercises, good." This evaluation buttressed board support when disciplinary problems arose later, and she was reassured that no fault was found with her handling the misbehavior of two boys; teachers have the right to send pupils home "and the Board will sustain you."[95]

At teachers' meetings, Little Rock (AR) superintendent "Professor" Rightsell scolded his admittedly underprepared teachers, preaching that he should find them with their books closed, not following a pupils' recitation with a finger on the passage. "I was in a classroom the other day and did not see a bit of teaching. All I saw was a teacher hearing a lesson."[96] However much his criticisms made teachers uncomfortable, Rightsell had sufficient personal experience and judgment to know what to look for in his classroom visits and to offer realistic advice— an improvement over many official visitors.

On her appointment as the Bureau of Indian Affairs supervisor for the day and boarding schools on the Sioux reservation, Elaine Goodale boasted, "It may be taken for granted that mine was no conventional call some twenty minutes long, ending in a formal handshake and an inscrutable smile"—her indirect criticism on the quality of supervision often given in both Indian and public education. "I gave no less than a full day to each little camp school at each visit, and to every boarding school a week or more. Then I offered such encouragement as I honestly could, together with a few constructive suggestions, and repeated their substance in a carefully written letter soon afterward."[97]

In her fifth year as a kindergarten teacher in an Oakland (CA) school with many non–English speaking children, Rebecca Akin emphasized pupils forming and expressing their own ideas. But, whenever a supervisor came, she admitted to switching her lesson plans for a more traditional, less time-consuming approach: "churning out volumes of work samples, racing through the curriculum and keeping busy . . . producing tangible evidence of growth and development." In a multiclassroom big-city school, she felt like her predecessors in remote one-room schoolhouses, their needs ignored until exposed to outside eyes.[98]

Individual personalities or competencies aside, teachers of both genders have consistently revealed a dismissive, sometimes adversarial, relationship with administrators.[99] A perceived failure to support teachers in a dispute with a student or parent, often over grading or disciplinary matters is often mentioned. Parents, students, and teachers highly esteemed Sister Roberta, principal and eighth-grade teacher at St. Luke's parochial school in the 1950s, even though she refused to be "top cop." Sister Roberta was "Bobby" to her teachers, lay and religious, and even to the older students. "The Principal wants to be 'everybody's friend.' She tells the teachers to handle their own disciplinary problems, and refuses to act as head disciplinarian, lest the children look on her as a 'monster.'"[100] If her fellow nuns felt no resentment, her lay teachers might.

Rosemma Burney Wallace and the "Golden Nuggets"

With a master's degree from Teachers College, Columbia, Rosemma Burney (b. 1921) taught home economics for a time at Prairie View State College near Houston—where she met and married a recent graduate, Leonard LeRoy Wallace. After teaching at Tennessee State in Nashville, another historically black college, the Wallaces moved to California. She retired to domesticity until their daughters entered school, when she earned a teaching credential. In 1951 she became an Oakland teacher and later the first African American woman to take the Oakland principal's examination.

Mrs. Wallace, raised in an environment and a social group—Atlanta's "black bourgeoisie"—where interaction with white professionals was common, if not comfortable, entered school administration at the height of the civil rights movement. From the mid-twentieth century, Oakland's school district and the city always appeared at or near the eye of some storm, usually involving race relations. Black Panthers, Black Muslims, and other factions warred for influence with black politicians and voters. Superintendent Marcus Foster, a respected reformer from Philadelphia, was murdered after one contentious school board meeting. Refugees from the Vietnam War crowded into run-down neighborhoods, bringing high educational aspirations but arousing new tensions. While most of the schools where Wallace taught or administered reflected Oakland's new black majority, she was also vice principal at Westlake, with a well-established Chinese American student majority and principal.

In her role as Oakland's executive associate superintendent for curriculum, all heads of curriculum and instruction programs reported to her. She scheduled early morning meetings so that principals would be in their schools when they opened. Described as a "people person," not a "paper person," she would be on the scene when problems arose: some trouble besetting a new principal, word of a student "rumble," angry parents, feuds between neighboring schools. "Oh! Here come the narcs," older students would call out when Wallace and another woman staffer showed up on a campus—remaining for days, even weeks if necessary, to resolve an issue.

Earlier, when Wallace left the principalship of Oakland's Castlemont High School, a group of women educators gave her a necklace with a golden nugget; in turn, she christened them the "Golden Nuggets." Rosie's sister, Anita Burney, described them—Caroline Getridge, Ellen Posey, LeeNell Jennings, Dorothy Kakamoto, among others—as Rosie's protégées. Some she met through professional interactions with teachers; others sought her out. As the door had been nudged opened for her—marked as a "comer" by Superintendents Foster and later Ruth Love—Wallace wished to open it wider for yet other women.[101] By the mid-1990s, African Americans exceeded the total of the other ethnic and racial groups among principals: Caucasian, Hispanic, Asian, and Middle Eastern. None of Oakland's six public high schools had Caucasian enrollments above 12%, and four of the six principals (three men and three women) were African Americans.[102]

LeeNell Jennings retired after long service as an administrator; Ellen Posey spent 38 years with the Oakland Unified School District, the last seven in Wallace's former position at Castlemont High School. Carolyn Getridge, one of "Rosie's diamonds in the rough," became Oakland's school superintendent. The school board's December 1996 resolution recognizing "Black English" provoked a national media furor over "Ebonics," which included hearings before a U.S. Senate committee. Having died in 1995, Mrs. Wallace was not there to advise or to see Getridge essentially driven from office.

Conclusion: Teaching Has No Place for "Spoiled and Petted Misses"

Although teaching is often chosen with starry-eyed confidence—"I love kids," "I loved my teacher," "I was a good student myself," "I was born to teach," "I can succeed at this"—teachers' idealism and faith are invariably tested. As a Belgian ex-teacher, school inspector, and educational theorist wrote in 1927, "Becoming a pupil means . . . learning to listen to someone who is older and stronger than you are, who has at his disposal unlimited power and all kinds of torments (such as writing out and copying, staying behind, bad marks, reports, exams, etc.) to keep you in check, . . . who makes you read in books about sunshine when it is raining outside."[103] This truth helps explain the proclivity to belittle formal education, as found in a study of 110 American autobiographies published over two centuries—selections, however, biased toward the self-described "self-made man."[104]

Some students will perform poorly, misbehave, or exude boredom despite the teacher's best efforts. Isobel "Belle" Osbourne (b. 1858) and her best friend Laura Eager did not dislike Miss Miller or have grievances with the school or their classmates. Indeed, Belle later wrote, "It was here in East Oakland that I enjoyed the kind of school days the poets sing about." Simply high spirited and thoughtless, they wore their teacher down: "the smart answers we had given Miss Miller that made the whole school laugh, banging the door every time we went in or out, scuffling our feet, asking silly questions and pretending not to understand the answers, each trying to outdo the other in attracting the attention of the class."[105]

Whether passive or active, student alienation is both personal and structural. For Isobel and Laura, it was temperament. But alienation is also structural, because a great many youth were, and are, in school against their will—kept there by social reformers and labor leaders (most born in the nineteenth century) who secured compulsory school attendance. As social work pioneer Florence Kelley put it in 1905, "The best child-labor law is a compulsory education law covering forty weeks of the year and requiring consecutive attendance of all the children to the age of fourteen years."[106] Compulsion was then extended through adolescence and beyond, by longer average life spans, social controllers (including churches), the compression of unskilled jobs, economic depressions, the aspirations of ethno-politicians, and the social striving of parents seeing their worth as reflected in their children's attainments.

While many teachers lived, even thrived, with the consequences, others left teaching entirely or removed to another school, community, state, or country. Researchers have asked large samples of teachers about their reasons for putting their names on intradistrict transfer lists, the simplest strategy for making a fresh start. Five years after the student composition of her school changed, one respondent could have been speaking for many: "I have had it. My parents tell me I'm becoming impossible to live with. I think it has reached the point where I am becoming emotionally disturbed. I want to do a good job, but . . . the constant tension in the classroom drains my energy."[107]

Another example is Kelly: her first teaching position in the low-income community of East Palo Alto (CA) in 2006 was "taking a horrendous toll on her well-being." To watch her struggle, her father, a once-a-month volunteer, was to see her transformed: "scanning the room with those murderous eyes, daring a kid to break the silence." He remarked that, confronting her 29 fifth graders, "my 25 year old daughter glared at them with a murderous look on her face. My sweet, fun-loving, delightful child had turned into the Wicked Witch of the West."

> It's now lunchtime, and the kids are outside, tormenting each other instead of their teacher. I've brought my daughter a salad, and she eats it while correcting spelling tests. . . .
>
> I got up to leave. "Only four more weeks until Summer," I said, giving her a hug. "Hang in there and it will all be over."
>
> She looked at me and smiled. "I can do better, you know. I've learned a lot.
>
> . . . . "I told the principal I'm coming back. I want to make some changes. I know one thing. Next year I'm starting out mean and then I'll get nicer as the year goes on, instead of the other way around."[108]

That last remark recalls the "wisdom" that student teachers a half century before shared among themselves: "Don't smile until Christmas." It didn't always work then either, and two years later Kelly was teaching at an American school in Brazil.

"As Long as It Was Teaching": A Change of Scene but Not Vocation

Teaching has portability: "the only profession that can migrate readily, that can carry its work with it, transfer it, and take it up without loss or injury anywhere that conditions are uniform," a Brown University professor noted in 1911. "Furthermore, the teacher personally is usually not so firmly rooted as his neighbor of another calling. He is used to travel during his vacations, he is adaptable, and springs with considerable facility from one abode to another."[109] If these generalizations seem less true of women, the schoolma'am has long displayed a migratory restlessness. When Massachusetts native Anna Peck Sill arrived in Rockford (IL) from a New York school in 1848, more than 60 teachers in Rockford's 21-year history had come and gone, and not necessarily into matrimony.[110] Relocation remains a given in teaching; in the 1990s roughly half of teacher turnover came from teachers on the move.[111]

For most teachers throughout American educational history, the chief, most reliable means of bettering their situation entailed a move, especially for women, for whom "promotion in place" was harder to achieve. Virtually every kind of promotional move was made by Zella Flores (b. 1894), first in her native Iowa where she taught successively in a one-room rural school, then graded schools, and finally in a high school. Next she changed states, moving to Colorado as a high school math teacher, before taking an elementary school principalship. Self-supporting women heading west usually found gender-based salary differentials were smaller or nonexistent. Vera Summers (b. 1895?) changed districts only within Utah, moving from San Juan County to Box Elder County because its teachers' "school-year" salaries were paid out over twelve months.[112] In 1935, average pay in country schools in Texas was $663 a year, thought sufficient for a young, unmarried woman; a mere $10 per month increase led women to change to otherwise comparable communities.[113]

Personal, situational, organizational, and professional variables interacted in teacher migration: leaving a one-room schoolhouse for a graded grammar school—better yet for a high school, finding within a town or city system the more satisfying schools, leaving a racially segregated system for one more integrated (or the reverse), escaping an intolerable principal or hectoring patrons, gaining more professional discretion or job security. A 1911 study of Indiana teachers in 160 accredited high schools in various-sized districts showed that a quarter to half had previously taught in an ungraded rural school or a town's grade school.[114] Larger communities drew and held far more of the experienced, with new city positions coming primarily from growth rather than turnover. Until the suburban demographic shifts following World War II, American cities typically drained surrounding communities of their better educated, more experienced, and career-minded teachers.

While some, perhaps many, were simply ready to exchange the rut of the known for the challenge of the new, other teachers stayed in place, or returned to, their hometowns, perhaps living with aging parents and offering financial or emotional support in return. Except for her studies at Susquehanna University (A.B. 1927), Maud Pritchard spent her entire career in her native Ashland (PA): beginning as a night school teacher and, at age 47, becoming its high school's principal.[115] Although the generic teacher lost some of her relative stature as an educated and cultured person as the American public became longer schooled, this was less true in smaller communities. There the local newspaper frequently reported the doings of some or another "Miss Ever Active" returning, for example, from a yet another "study trip" abroad.

The "Woman Peril" Revisited

Initially, supporters of women teachers described them as more patient and effective teachers of the very young. (In time women college instructors were found to lecture less and build more student participation into their pedagogy.)[116] Practical school boards acted on the knowledge that better-prepared teachers for the common schools could be had, and for significantly less money, by employing women as both elementary and secondary teachers, ranging from ungraded country schools to urban high schools. State-level leaders envisioned desirable pedagogical results transformed into societal benefits: more satisfied pupils and parents would "grow" schooling, raise the educational level of the general public, and enhance the nation's well-being.

However, at least since the 1890s, prominent men worried aloud at the feminization of teaching, arguing that boys would suffer. (That girls might benefit did not apparently count for much.) A New Jersey school superintendent asserted in 1911 that "the presence of women as teachers of boys [even] in the upper grammar grades . . . causes thousands of boys to become disgusted with and to leave the schools . . . because of their intense dislike of being (using their own words) 'bossed by women.'" A steady diet of women teachers, more humiliating because many were hardly older than their pupils, would force "real boys" to rebel or retreat, leaving the upper grades—and the ranks of potential future teachers— primarily to females and "feminized" males."[117]

The teacher's role once conferred on the schoolmaster the authority to exercise control over males, especially elite males, in a way not possible outside of the classroom. The schoolmistress gained that power. The most obvious change attending the feminization of teaching may indeed have been altering the relationships between the female (as teacher) and the male (as student). However much adolescent boys might have preferred and better related to men, they began staying longer in school, if only because the alternatives of earlier eras had vanished with industrial technologies. Arguably, their teachers' gender was being rendered less pertinent.

In 1915, Alice Duer Miller satirized male angst because schoolgirls so often outperformed the other sex. She wrote, "There, little girl, don't read / You're fond of your books, I know, / But Brother might mope / If he had no hope / Of getting ahead of you. / It's dull for a boy who cannot lead, / There, little girl, don't read."[118] She did read, however, and write and cipher. In the cohorts born around 1865, as around 1925 and 1957, the median years of completed schooling of females were higher. These faceless census data are personalized in high school graduation photos and programs and commencement honors. While girls' early two-to-one advantage as high school graduates shrank to a mere majority by the 1950s, from the 1970s college women were significantly broadening their participation in graduate and professional degree programs in the male bastions of law, medical, and business schools, and the twenty-first century opened with women the majority of U.S. undergraduates.[119]

Cold War–era critics in particular asserted that employing a predominantly female teaching force undermined academic values, women being less able or willing, by nature and socialization, to resist the anti-intellectualism lurking in populist movements like universal public education. Nonetheless, while "boys were found to be clearly superior to girls at solving problems" in "more authoritarian" schools, in the "modern school, which followed sex roles less closely, girls were equal or superior at problem solving."[120] A homey classroom environment; a tolerant, maternalized discipline; personalized standards; and democratized curricula have all advanced in public and many private schools. These are, some claim, not coincident with woman's arrival; they are its virtually inevitable consequences.[121]

A more balanced response to the question of whether and how teacher gender makes a difference is that it does—in a more self-limiting way. It matters because boys and girls, men and women, have both different and common experiences and expectations in the model lives toward which parents, peers, and the mass media point them. Classroom research shows, for example, that male elementary school teachers tolerate more noise and physical activity than women do. But schools are also organizations that have evolved and hardened over centuries, with structures and rules that channel individual teacher inclinations and ability to deviate meaningfully from the norm—including the belief that their role requires that students respect teacher authority and that of the "text." The ideal is reached with a given group not when it acquiesces to the teacher's cues but when it anticipates them and acts accordingly. This is as true of the boys in John Keating's *Dead Poets Society*— being instilled with the conformity of "nonconformity"—as of the classrooms that Winslow Homer inserted into the nation's collective memory.

The teacher-pupil relationship is far from a simple story of formal power in the one and dependency in the other. In her 99th year, Berta Rantz (b. 1894) recalled the rural school on Puget Sound where she began her career. "I once kept a boy after school to punish him. Then he punished me by refusing to go home. We both learned about the inherent humanity of one another. I'll never forget the experience." His behavior may have been less "sheer cussedness" on his part than an unarticulated form of devotion to what she represented. For those children of Norwegian immigrant farmers and fishermen living "unadorned" and isolated lives, their 20-year-old teacher's "knowledge of far places, real and literary," represented a wondrous greater world. Richard "was simply using the opportunity to learn to become himself," she concluded. "Going to school . . . every day became a self-replenishing spring. They thirsted, and they were refreshed. So was I."[122] While certainly not an inevitable outcome of life in schools, some hope of mutual growth has kept teachers coming back over the ages—captured, a little, in the prosaic utterance, "teaching keeps me young."

CHAPTER 10

"The Great Perplexities of the Teacher-Life"

Gertrudes Talk and Their Pupils Reminisce

> I shall be glad when I can go to teaching. I have never felt so
> happy, as I did when I was engaged in teaching the young ideas
> how to shoot.
>
> —Mary Jane Walker, normal school pupil, November 1848

Mary Gamble, a schoolma'am in rural Kansas in the 1870s, was one of Amanda
Stewart's more interesting correspondents. She left at least one school because of
feuding district officials, appealing to the state superintendent for support of her
resignation. She applied to teach at the Sac Fox Agency in Indian Territory, but
because her father was "growing old—he said no, so [she] gave it up." Although it
caused her "a severe struggle," she broke at least two engagements, having promised "out of sympathy not love—and so [for] the second time I demanded and
secured my freedom." She was also a devoted sister: "My youngest brother is my
great anxiety at present for time is passing & he has little or no education. . . . He
will farm without enough education for anything unless I can get him with me
soon." Mary also wrote Amanda in 1882, "I suppose you are still in the same old
condition of single loneliness plodding back and forth to some old school house
trying to better other folks 'jewels' when its my opinion you ought to be enjoying
your own."[1] Teasing one's friends about their respective marital states was habitual in teacherdom.

Amanda's and her friends' stories constitute what Paul Veyne calls "non-
eventworthy history"—the "local, habitual, and mundane"—but where answers
to basic historical questions often reside.[2] To understand and fully appreciate
lives, we historians and biographers must respect their individually grounded,
personally contextualized experience. This chapter gives a tiny handful of the
legion of participants in American schooling the chance to speak for themselves,
at a somewhat greater length: presenting in their own relatively unjudged (but

not unguarded) and minimally interpreted words an account of their particular involvement in the great story of women in teaching.

The author of a diary, journal, memoir, autobiography, even a letter, is not a disinterested reporter. Each selects, distorts, conceals. As in other forms of authorship, the voiceless "facts" are made to utter the writer's "truth." This selectivity extends beyond the diaries or letters home that were somehow coerced, for example, as writing exercises required in many nineteenth century schools and submitted with the expectation that a preceptress would read and grade them.

Because "writing is onerous . . . like work because it is work," the diarist's habit, especially, must be deeply ingrained or the motivation (often religious) particularly strong.[3] Cultural habit explains a great many nineteenth- and twentieth-century diaries; a surprisingly large sample, perhaps unrepresentative, have survived. For teachers, the detailing of a humdrum day or a reflection on the meaning of teaching may represent a respite from the often intense and unremitting encounter of competing wills that teaching and managing students represents. As for recollections, memory favors the vivid, often isolated and unrepresentative event, and the account also shaped by their present.

Historians and editors, by ordering their material (as I have done, here and throughout this volume), inevitably add some distortion to the participant's recording. The processes of sampling, examining, interpreting, contextualizing, and generalizing turn what was the often inchoate immediacy and messiness of the teacher's or pupil's daily existence into clues of meaning-making history: something that the participants did not know they were making and might barely recognize or even disclaim. Even if the subject of occasional, speculative gossip, the details of a teacher's personal life and nonschool experiences were to be guarded knowledge—rendering most former pupils' accounts partial, even skewed. As the excerpts are primarily chronological, the style, spelling, and topics of focus change over time. But these teachers' thoughts about teaching and the pupils' thoughts about their teachers transcend time.

"The Hand of Providence Appeared So Plain"

The oldest surviving of 11 children of a Maine farm family, until her 26th year Mary Richardson (1811–1897) lived as an ordinary schoolmistress. Her full diaries reveal, especially, her inner life and feelings about a teacher's responsibility, as a Christian, to bring children to God, and her dream of becoming a missionary. In 1836, when Richardson asked the American Board of Commissioners for Foreign Missions (ABCFM) to send her to South Africa, her unmarried status was an obstacle. The following edited diary excerpts are taken from 1833–1837, when prayerful self-examination produced a life-altering decision.[4]

(Jan. 8, 1833)—Commenced my school. [Jan. 13]—I have never before lived where prayer was not attended to in the family. I wish I knew how I would pray in my school. my schoollars are very ignorant. I mean to try and do them some good if I can. (Jan. 27)—I have now been teaching school three weeks. I like the employment very well. I think I shall prefer school-keeping to any thing else for getting a living. It affords me more time for study. (Feb. 19)—Have felt as if I were doing no thing of any amount. . . . I have a desire to engage in some next enterprise that would call all my ene[r]gies in to exercise. (June 12)—Just so wretched all the time. . . . am vexed in spirit find little reliefe. have no heart to prey much. some times almo[st] conclude to give it up entirely. . . . Yet some thin[g] seems to whisper that this may only be a suggestion of the adversary [Satan]. and so try to hold fast a little longer hoping the day may yet dawn and the day star arise in my soule. . . .

(July 4)—A very fine day I had my school house decked [out]—and spent a part of the afternoon in relating to my school the history of the United States as connected with the Declaration of Independence. They seemed attentive. (Sat. evening, twentieth)—The children went to bed for a joke and left me alone with [Mr.] Bell. . . . I felt some embarrassed but he read me his Journal and [I] then took the lamp and went to bed. (April 28, 1834)—I thought to be sure I could have this school if I wanted it. I don't see for my life why Mr. Sawyer [trustee] likes Sarah Sanborn better than me. I can think of no kind of a place where I wish to go. I want to do a thousand things yet can not do anything.

(May 14, 1836)—My attention has been called of late to the subject of matrimony. . . . I have had a fair sort of an offer don't know whether I ought think of accepting it or not. did he possess knowledge and piety I should like him. but I fear he lacks a kindred soul. could I inspire in his bosom the sentiments that expand my own. . . . Ought to bid adieu to all my cherished hopes and unite my destiny [with] that of a mear farmer with little education and no refinement. In a word shall I to escape the horrors of perpetual celibacy settle down with the vulgar I cannot do it. May a wise providence direct my way. Perhaps I have a better opinion of myself than I ought to have. . . . (Sept. 18)—My mind very much excited don't know what to do have always harbored the design of going on a mission. . . . Oh may I decide aright. (Sept. 19)—Declared to Mr. T. my thought of offering myself to the ABCFM. He rather approves and very kindly offers me all the friendly instruction I need.—And now O! God direct my decission. lead me in the path of duty. (Dec. 21)—I am much pleased with the reception and reply my proposals to the A. B. have received.

(April 10, 1837)—I have thot much of my Missionary enterprise and have frequently contrasted my present situation surrounded as I am with every comfor[t] and the attention of kind friends with what it may be some future day when I may sicken and die on some foreign shore attended by stranger hands. O how many tender emotions are excited in the mind. I recall more than ever how much I shall need a companion of my own to lean upon in sickness and trouble. . . .

(April 22)—looked out and saw two gentlemen approaching . . . one was Dr. [Rev.] Whitney. could not tell who the other was. . . . Dr. W. entered and introduced a tall and rather awkward gentleman as an old associate of his and a Bangor [Theological Seminary] student. . . . The conversation soon turned on different [mission] stations and particularly to Africa. . . . Mr. W[alker] spoke with interest of the Zoolars [Zulus]. . . . I saw nothing particularly interesting or disagreeable in the man, tho I pretty much made up my mind that he was not a missionary but rather an ordinary kind of unaspiring man. . . . I thought he took more interest in getting acquainted with me than the rest . . . [and] I felt conscious that on some account or other I was the subject of close scrutiny. . . . I could not make out my mind what to think of that man. There was something unaccountable about him. . . . I however prayed for resignation and thought perhaps he might be after all more than he seemed. But no sooner were we all up [next morning] than all in the kitchen began to discuss the merits of the strange[r]. Sister P. says well are you going to ketch him. Me ketch him no sister nevr, Phebe [you] ketch him was the reply. . . . I was tempted to leave him [Mr. W] alone [to read his bible]. But concluded it would hardly be polite.

As good fortune would have it however, I happened just that moment to think that very likely he would like to read my letters from Armstrong [ABCFM] I handed them to him and seating myself at a respectful distance. . . . began composedly to knit. As he read I remarked that they seemed to object to me very much on account of my being unmarried. When he had finished he [re]marked. . . . "I am an accepted Missionary destined etc. . . . I may as well do my errand first as last. As I have no one engaged to go with me I have come with the intention of offering myself to you. You have been recommended to me by Mr. Armstrong, & here is another letter from Thayer." Blushing, agitated & confused I took the letter confessed my surprise and retiring to the ferthrest corner of the room & attempted to read. . . .

Called on Dr. Whitneys consulted him in regard to the case in hand. . . . Begin to feel quite happy about the affair. . . . The hand of Providence appeared so plain that I could not but feel that there was something like duty about it, and yet how to go to work to feel satisfied and love him I hardly knew. But concluded the path of duty must prove the path of peace . . . altho I felt in the morning as if

I wanted to throw the bargain off on to some one else, at evening I would not willingly have given up my titles . . . with only father and mother he asked their approbation of his design. And I guess went to bed rather satisfied with his day's work.

(April 29)—that other called. Renewed his professions of attachment. I told him it was no use. Said he[,] I would rather have seen you pass on a bier than in a chaise with W. I told him I was engaged & satisfied with W. Said he, he does not love you as well as I do. Said I, I love him better than I do you and all I hope is that you will find some one that will suit you as well as he does me. He said to that people did not think I was cutting a great cheese. (May 7)—had priviledge of hearing Mr. Walker preach, for the first time. he made out full as well as I expected I feel better & better satisfied with the allotments of providence. I feel that I am used better than I deserve to be & I hope I am in some suitable degree thankful. (May 25)—Feel afraid I don't love Mr. W. as well as I ought. I wish he would treat me with a little more freedom. There certainly would be no harm in a little more affection and familiarity. I feel afraid he dont love me as he ought. I hope we shall be able to do right. . . . My wishes in regard to W. have been fully realized & the cause of his distance ascertained.[5]

Collecting Knowledge and Confidence

Like many teachers of her time, Mary Jane Walker (1828–1876) of Billerica (MA) entered the junior class at the "normalcy school" in Newton, having already taught. Principal Cyrus "Father" Peirce, a keeper of journals, required the "normalites" to do likewise, inspected them and wrote brief, encouraging notes: "Quite a good journal, the principal fault in punctuation; valuable entries; written in a cheerful spirit; your Journal shows an earnest devoted girl." How much his remarks influenced Walker's accounts is unknown, but her detailed journal entries make clear that the normal offered a serious, multifaceted professional experience.[6]

(April 12, 1848)—Today I made my first appearance in the Normal hall. . . . My class of twenty six members were examined . . . and we all passed a satisfactory examination. (April 13)—The school was opened by devotional exercises by the principal, and singing by the pupils. He then gave some instructions as regards Moral Education which were very profitable, and also spoke about securing good government in schools. The classes were then called. recited first in Practical physiology, Mr. P. teacher. after which we had an exercise in Phonography. Miss Lincoln teacher which was quite a pleasant exercise. The next class was Mental

Arithmetic, Miss Watson teacher. Like the manner in which she teaches. P.M. . . . each lesson was recited in Grammar Reading &c. . . . Mr. Peirce closed to the sentiment, Live to the truth.

(April 14)—This afternoon the school discussed the question whether public schools should be opened to receive visiters. we come to the conclusion that they should. . . . Mr. P. read an account of the Origin & History of the Normal school. He said that Normal was from a Latin word signifying Norma, which means according to rule, strictly true. (April 19)—It being stormy, our recess was spent in the Gymnasium, our amusement was dancing, & our dear Miss Lincoln joined us. After which Father P. gave us instruction about making out Promisory Notes. . . . He said every school where there are boys from twelve years of age or upward should be taught about making out orders, Receipts &c. The last half hour . . . we are to devote to punctuation.

(April 25)—Rose very early [4 am] & studied 2 hours before school. . . . The conversation was upon the subject whether teachers could be familiar with their scholars & yet possess dignity. We all thought they might and not lose their dignity. (April 28)—P.M. the teaching exercises were very good especially Miss Townsend's address to the Junior Class which was excellent. May she be a bright and shining lamp in her profession, and when she thinks of the good she is doing, may she have the satisfaction of thinking that her Normal life was not spent in vain. Miss Louisa Copeland gave a biography of Queen Elizabeth that was very interesting. Hattie M. Brigham one of my sister boarders gave a description of London thought she succeeded very well in her exercise, think she would make a good teacher.[7]

(May 2)—Conversation was upon the duties of committee [school trustees] and teachers, or how far they might carry out their own views, as regards the different modes of teaching, discipline, &c. (May 8)—I visited the Model School this afternoon at recess. . . . It is just such a school as I should like to teach. (May 22)— This afternoon Miss L. told our class how she should commence to learn small children geography. She sais she should first teach them the points of the compass. She should inform them of the sun's rising and setting, and how they could learn north and south by the sun. . . . She said she should draw the schoolroom, or model of it upon the black board, and call it a Map or a picture, and teach them the different positions of the place, and their situation from the other places.

(June)—When Father P. was reading in the scriptures this morning he alluded to the 6th verse of the CXXVI Psalm and said he thought that verse was well adapted to a teacher in troubles and discouragements He said that when a teacher goes forth to teach, she enters a new epoch in her life. She will meet with many disappointments and discouragements. I know they meet with many little troubles, but I think the happiness derived from school teaching more than balances the troubles.

(July)—I felt very lonesome all day; . . . what . . . presents such [a] sickening aspect to a school, and especially to a teacher as vacant seats? Perhaps, if some of the young ladies, knew the feelings of a teacher, when pupils are absent, I think they would avoid being absent as much as possible. (July 4)—I have been reading in the Teacher and I found several faults that every teacher should avoid. I will record them. 1st Guard again prejudice on entering a school. 2nd Do not allow your pupils to direct their own studies. 3rd Do not attempt to teach too many things. 4th Never attend to extraneous business in school hours. 5th Avoid making excuses to visitors for the defects of your school. 6th. Never compare one child with another. 7th Avoid wounding the sensibilities of a dull child. 8th. Never lose your patience when parents unreasonably interfere with your plans. 9th. Never make the study of the Bible a punishment. 10th Ride no "hobbies" in teaching. (July 24)—Examination day. About 50 visiters. Peirce told them he would continue his office for the present. he said he wanted to see before he left an examination without a single failure.

(Sept. 7)—Middle Term. Had out first recitation in bookkeeping; F.P. teaches it. undecided about taking Geometry; for that is very seldom taught in the public schools. (Sept. 13)—Sentiments given during the opening exercises of school. We praise men for fighting; and punish children. As is the teacher, so is the school. (Sept. 21)—As I entered Normal hall . . . they told me that Sarah Newhall was no more. . . . She was cut down in the midst of her labor, to prepare herself for usefulness in the world, and she was looking forward with bright anticipations to the future. . . . Father P [said] She has left us an example worthy to be imitated; of sound integrity, conscientiousness, truthfulness, and indomitable perseverance.

(Sept. 29)—This afternoon we had teaching exercises. I taught, and I feel very much dissatisfied with my performance. I did not teach at all, as I intended before I went up. As soon, as I stood in front of the school, I lost every idea I had. . . . Alice Cunningham taught admirably. . . . I wish I could acquire some of her habits of self possession. (Oct.)—I enjoy Father Ps general lessons, that he gives us in the morning. . . . He said when a teacher entered a school she should not have any assumed manners, but should appear perfectly free and easy. . . . Teachers should be careful to have the first impression made on a school be a favorable one. (Nov.)—To day has been my first in the model room. I can truly say it has been a happy one. I have had good recitations, and good order with the exception of the primer class. The children in that class appear as if they had done pretty much as they wanted to.

(Dec. 4)—I had an application when I was at home to teach a winter school in Billerica, and I almost wanted to accept, but I knew I could not. (Dec. 6)—Father P's remarks this morning were upon examinations. He said there were many objections. . . . On the whole he approved of them, said they were good stimulus to the teacher and scholars for exertion. He said the parents in the district . . . had a good opportunity to judge of the school if the examination was rightly conducted. The next time he is going to speak of the disadvantages attending them.

(Jan. 8, 1849)—I cannot realize that this is the last term of my Normal life. . . . I asked Miss Lincoln if she would let me join in the Geography class if it does not come when I am engaged. . . . I feel very desirous to teach Geography in the manner that Miss Lincoln does.

(Jan. 30)—The career of a teacher does not lead to distinction or wealth. It leads to something better than distinction—to the heartfelt honour and affectionate respect of those who feel that they have been made wiser and better by its influence.

"I Shall Be Earning Something for My Children"

The journals of Ella Gertrude Clanton Thomas (1834–1907)—Gertrude to family, friends, and teachers—opens in 1848, when, at age 14, she entered Wesleyan Female College in Macon: a self-conscious daily account of a Georgia schoolgirl, typically focusing on friendships, fashions, outings. They end 41 years later, its disillusioned author dependent on income from boarders in her late mother's house, the only remnant of her inheritance. Gertrude's husband—James Jefferson "Jeff" Thomas, a Princeton College graduate who dropped his medical studies to become a planter—proved an alcoholic and faithless husband. (Both her father and husband fathered children by slave women.) The journals reveal her deepening reflections on slavery and white-black relations, the private-public woman, and women's rights—foreshadowing her later activism in temperance and woman suffrage. From a story of great personal growth, these excerpts sample Gertrude's schooling, her thoughts on social issues, and the beginnings in 1878, in her home near Augusta, of her untrained life in teaching; she taught until 1884.[8]

(April 4, 1851)—My seventeenth birthday. I was talking with Anna Jeffers and did not prepare the Astronomy so I stayed away from recitation . . . a note [came] for me . . . from the "'Adelphian Society" . . . soliciting I should join them. I returned a note respectfully declining. To have joined I shou[ld] have been thrown into two close communion with the girl I most dislike in college Leah Goodall. . . .

(Jan. 1852)—My school days are over. . . . Saturday night a received a letter from Leah Goodal. She is engaged in teaching school. She writes a beautiful letter. (March)—Mr Thomas called. He remained until after ten o'clock. . . . We went over to Oak Hill where Jimmie [brother] is going to school, where Miss Bowdon is teaching. The sight of the school house renewed old and very pleasant associations, it being the first school I ever attended. (May)—Here I am seated in my room engaged in a new avocation teaching Mamie and Buddy [siblings]. I just commenced this morning am quite pleased. I will now hear Mamie's lesson in Geography.

(April 1856)—My . . . twenty-second year! . . . I left school when seventeen, . . . the next winter made my debut in society. . . . Mr. Thomas presented me with a most beautiful engagement ring with nine large diamonds. . . .

(Feb.? 1858)—A query—Why is it that while Dr McDonald would be considered perfectly right in refusing to take his [unfaithful] wife back to his home and heart, . . . But Mrs. Finn, [a] deserted wife . . . is expected to show her womans love (or rather her womans weakness) her all forgiving spirit and receive the wanderer back again?. . . . I am no 'Womans Rights Woman,' in the northern sense of the term, but so far as a womans being forever 'Anathema Maranatha' [i.e., cursed, excluded]—in society for the same offence which in a man, very slightly lowers, and in the estimation of some of his own sex rather elevates him. . . . I say there appears to be a very very great injustice.

(Sept. 17. 1862)—Turner will be eleven years old. . . . He drives two of his goats to school every morning, over at Mrs Carmicheals, where he is taught by Mrs Beattie. I am not pleased with his progress in education. . . . [Mary Belle] will be six years old this month. She has not learned her letters yet, but as some author has beautifully expressed it. 'Education does not begin with the alphabet. It begins a Mother's look—with a fathers nod of approbation, or a sign of reproof. . . . (Sept. 23)—The idea has gradualy become more and more fixed in my mind that the institution of slavery is not right. . . . —owning a large number of slaves as we do I might be asked why do I not free them? This if I could, I would not do, but if Mr Thomas would sell them to a man who would look after their temporal and spiritual interest I would gladly do so. Those house servants we have if Mr Thomas would agree to it I would pay regular wages . . . I can but think that to hold men and women in perpetual bondage is wrong.

(March 1865)—I strive to get away—to forget in reading or in writing or in talking the ever present, the one absorbing theme of war and thus it is thrust upon me—I make no plans for the future. . . . I have seen poverty staring me in the face when I expected [General] Sherman in Augusta and our planting interest was destroyed. . . . But even then I nerved myself and was prepared to do something if I could. . . . I look forward and asked myself what can I do? Nothing, except teach school and if I left Augusta nothing to support me with my little ones—if I remained the doubt as to wether I could procure a school unless compelled to take the oath [of loyalty to the United States]—and a new idea just now presents itself to my mind[;] I wonder if I would not be compelled to teach the young and perhaps old ideas of the Negroes how to shoot.

(June 1869)—I look round & I see worthy men who talk about their sons being indispensable in the field, "hands are so scarce" and to obtain a hand the boys head suffers and he grows up an ignoramus while negro women toil and strive, labour and endure in order that their children "may have a schooling."

(May 1871)—During our conversation Mr. [Jefferson] Davis remarked to me "that he had great faith in the Southern women, that they would train the boys right," he added placing his hand upon [his namesake] Jeffs head. "It will come out right. I may not live to see it, but it is not in the nature of God to allow the best people he ever made to remain permanently under the rule of the meanest people he ever made.". . . . President Davis has strong predjudices as the remark indicated, but he is mistaken. We are not the best, nor are the Yankees the worst nation god ever made.

(Dec. 1878)—If I can succeed in procuring a situation this time next year I shall be earning something for my children. . . . How strange life is. Mrs Carmicheal is dead and for two months past I have had charge of the county school. . . . I am grateful and contented that I have an opportunity of adding to the comfort of my family I know I will be more constantly employed than heretofore, that I will not be mistress of my own time but with that thought comes the reflection I shall be profitably engaged. . . .

(Jan. 1879)—Mr Thomas said to me the other day "Gertrude if you expect to teach school you ought to improve your handwriting." Indeed I am very conscious of my deficientcy in that respect as well as in arithmetic. . . . I feel that if I had more advanced pupils it might be necessary for me to study two[;] as it is none of my pupils are father advanced than fraction. . . . For the first month I received thirty dollars. I will not draw my second months salary until next Saturday. I expect to be paid for wood which we have furnished. My stove and eight desks and benches were furnished me by the county. . . . A few weeks after I began school I took all of my sch[o]lars in the carriage and wagon to Augusta to visit the orphan asylum. I then gave them all a street car ride from the upper end of town to the cemetery. (Feb.)—I have had my salary increased to thirty-five dollars. We sell a cord of wood for four dollars to the county for the use of the school so that I drew thirty-nine dollars.

(May 1879)—I commenced this school this winter as an experiment. . . . I intended if possible to continue it during the year. A remark Mr. Wiggins made expressed . . . [a] sentiment of many of my neighbors. "I know" said he "Mrs Thomas will not continue the school. She wasn't raised to work and she will grow tired of it very soon.". . . . What are my feelings with regard to it? Instead of being delighted with my holiday I am sorry that my school will not be continued through June. I am realy heartily interested in my school. And the income I receive is so welcome to me . . . I have bought nothing but clothing for the family since I paid the taxes on the place in Columbia. I sent home a good portion of the money for February to Mr. Thomas to settle with the [farm] hands. (Aug. 10)—It is absolutely necessary for me to remember how much I can buy for the family to give me courage to take charge of the school for another year. I wish, how I wish there was no necessity for it. Listen dear journal I will tell you what I tell no one else. I do wish I could do without teaching school. . . . When I think of ten months to listen to such small children and such restless little ones read in the 1st and 2nd reader!

(Oct. 1879)—"I did not think he [son Clanton, age 6] was very sick. . . . I remained from Sunday School with Clanton who still complained of his head. . . . The next morning I went into the school room leaving Cora Lou with him. . . . I came in, changed his clothes at recess. . . . When I came in again he did not know me [dying soon after]. Oh my God that is so hard. I was teaching other peoples children when I ought to have been with my own child.

(Jan. 1880)—I have striven conscientiously to do my duty by the children and I have earnestly requested the cooperation of the parents. I have written to Mrs Neely several times urging her to buy the children books and have them study at home. Allen Neely has been without an Arithmetic Spelling or Reading book all winter. . . . . Bessie has been without slate or pencil or a reading book until the last few weeks. . . . Sometimes I have thought I would give up the school or be glad of an excuse to give it up but I will not be compelled to give it up if I have to import children into the neighborhood or hire them to come. When I give up the school I shall do so voluntarily. (Feb.)—My school is progressing well. I have twenty scholars with the promise of several more. . . . There is something in the contact with their fresh pure young spirits which compensates me for the drudgery of teaching. (May 12)—Two weeks ago I wrote an article with regard to the improvements on our chapel, signed my name Mrs. Gertrude Thomas and it was published in the Chronicle and Constitutionalist. I am a public woman now

[and] would like for the patrons of my school to have an idea that I am capable of writing an interesting article. (May 18)—Yesterday Charlie Wiggins wore a white jacket of Clantons' which I gave to him with a pair of shoes. . . . Charley Wheeler has had his frail little body covered this winter with the same little warm coat which my little Clanton wore last winter.

(Jan. 1881)—I have five classes in Geography in my little school. . . . Class after class follow each other in rapid succession. I have no time to tell as I would like to do some incident connected with each place. I often think of what use is all my learning. . . . Why if I had a class of pupils all of them of the same grade in learning I could take a geography and with every country, city and principal river I could blend some story—some association, some fact, some legend of poetry or romance which would make the hard dry names they study become bright and blooming as a rose. This week I will place two of Geography classes together.

(Oct. 1882)—So far as I am concerned I have made up my mind that school teaching is to be my employment and if I were the only one to consult I would call my creditors together—make the best terms I could with them, try to secure some kind of support, give up every thing and work the rest of my life.

Kinship and Collegiality: A Kansas Covey

The Stewart-Lockwood Family Collection, 57 linear feet—chiefly correspondence—is richly populated with teachers: career and temporary; immediate family, cousins, and friends; mostly in Kansas, but also nearby (e.g., Missouri) and more distant (e.g., West Virginia and Oregon); women and men. The letters were mostly addressed to Amanda Stewart and her sisters Mary Jane (b. 1854), Nora (b. 1864), Olive Maude (b. 1872), and her twin, Eliza May. Amanda, Mary Jane, and Maude remained single, Eliza married late (1910?), and Nora taught until marrying teacher Anson Ovid Lockwood in 1888, being prepared for the ministry. Three of the Lockwoods' seven children taught. The excerpts include the perceptions of teachers, trustees, and patrons on the politics of hiring and paying teachers; professional issues including pupil behavior, school and class size, teacher institutes and examinations, and the job market; and gossip about family, friends, and "affairs of the heart."[9] The selections are grouped first according to their individual authors (in italics) and then chronologically. Unless noted the writers are in Kansas.

Susannah Garner (Brandonville, WV) to Amanda Stewart (Mar. 1870)[10]—My name is Susannah M. Garner. I came down on purpose of getting a school. But

I think wages are better where you live than they are [here] but as an unprofessed hand & quite young I can afford to teach for less money. I live near Kingwood, Preston County, West Virginia was raised in a family of 16 children. . . .

Susannah to Amanda (April 1871)—I am not teaching this summer from the fact that there is not money sufficient for summer schools: each District is allowed six months school in a year, and it is chiefly consumed for winter schools. Wages are varied, the highest forty five dollars per month. . . . You ask if we have Teachers Institute in Va. We have.

Sue to dear Mannie [Amanda] (Mar. 1872)—I have been attending school during the past winter, and have been compelled to practice both daily and nocturnal study. . . . I have some idea of teaching this summer but not certain. . . . I have not yet drawn any conclusion on the subject of matrimony from the very fact that fortune has not yet endowed me with means to support husbands. . . . Mannie if you still continue to teach school ten months in a year you ought to be able to marry. . . .

Cousin Sue to Amanda (July 1876)—Since I wrote you last I have taught 21 months of school. I like the profession very much. Sevilla [sister-in-law?] taught the winter [term]. She and I attended school four months last summer, at Aurora, twenty miles from home. We paid no tuition, the school being supported by the Peabody Fund. And having relatives there, we procured boarding for eight dollars per month. . . .

Chalmers Brown[11] (Gavers, OH) to friend Amanda (May 1874)—I am informed that you are now teaching at Reno. How I would like to step into your school this afternoon, and see you marching up and down in the aisle pointing at John to turn around in his seat, then to Lizzie, Maria, Jane and a lot of others. . . . endeavoring to instill into the youthful mind principles of truth, honesty, virtue, brotherly kindness and temperance. What better, nobler work could any mortal be engaged with, although we frequently feel that our labors are not appreciated[:] . . . [people saying] "what good times you teachers have there in the shade (or if in winter, in the warm [school]house, making more money than we do at home." . . . There are some you know who will talk this way, . . . but not those who have taught, who have had some thirty or forty real mischievous urchins to watch and control.

Chalmers Brown to kind friend Amanda (Mar. 1876)—Mr. Rhea [former trustee] will hardly succeed in his plan of dividing No. 11 district. Nor of getting a new schoolhouse built near him. I cant imagine what he wants a school-house near him, since his children [are] grown up and no prospects of him having any grandchildren to educate soon? . . . Were I director and his daughter apply for it in the future, my conscience would not disturb me greatly by making her as mean an offer as he did you.

Harriet "Hattie" Baker[12] to Cousin Amanda (April 1876)—The last time I went to be examined I know I deserved a certificate but I guess the examiners thought I was nothing but just a little girl too little to teach, every person say that they are partial . . . and they did not let one of their Lancaster pets fail I do not dare stop and think about it I am so anxious to teach I know I could not help but like it. *Hattie* to Amanda (May 1876)—I am glad to inform you of my successfulness. I went back to the examination received a certificate. . . . I was successful in obtaining a school but had to go [board] away from home it is 3 miles from home I come home every Friday evening you better think I am glad to see Friday. . . .

Eva & Ernest [Beebe][13] to Amanda (Nov. 1878)—I am in my school room scratching way for dear life to get started ere the bell rings . . . , then I must go and observe the boys' pranks, that being my post for the present month and 'tis any thing but a desirable position. School goes on quite smoothly so far. . . . But "miserable dictu"! we have to teach until 345 P.M. . . . it gives me so little time at home to do anything. *Eva* to Amanda (Dec. 1881)—For the last month I have been going to a reading class directly from school and don't get home until after six. Ernest generally has supper ready. . . . My school is large 45 morning attendance and from 50 to 60 in the afternoons. . . . Ernest gobbles the money into his business so fast that I don't dare spend much. *Eva* to Amanda (Aug. 1882)—We call her "May Beebe" and Ernest thinks there never was a nicer child. . . .

Ann Elizabeth "Libbie" Burbank[14] (Leavenworth) to Amanda Stewart (Sept. 1880)—In the morning paper appeared the assignments and I was to go back to my old place and I was happy. . . . as I should have such an easy time there. . . . We went to Institute in the morning and lo and behold, Prof. Fitzpatrick . . . says . . . there were some mistakes in the morning paper and instead of my being sent [back] to the Colored School, it [I] was down as 1st [top] or 10th grade, Morris School.[15] I was completely thunderstruck. The hardest and most important grade given me and I am very much afraid of it. To be sure the salary of that grade is more . . . but I told Prof. I would prefer taking the darkies, but both he and Miss Geyer talked to me. . . . I ought to feel quite complimented on having it offered to me as they are more particular about the teacher for that grade than any other. . . . What a life a "schoolmarm" leads. no wonder they get old & sour and cross and all that, is it?

Libbie Burbank to Amanda (June 1883)—Well about the city schools. . . . send a written application to the chairman of the Committee on Teachers and Salaries, and with it send all the recommendations you can get. . . . Teachers are not appointed so much here, by favor or influence as by qualifications of the person. That was all Em Gibbs did to get in at K.C. [Kansas City]. She had written recommendations from Prof. Van Eman and Mr. Sharpe, of Kickapoo, where she had previously taught. She was acquainted with not one of the Board but was appointed. *Libbie Burbank* to Amanda (Jan. 1884)—Today is my birthday and I am an "old maid." Twenty-five years old! It does not seem possible—but don't tell anyone for I am only 23(?). *Libbie* to Nora Stewart (Oct. 1884)—We have a splendid principal, a young man named Little, a graduate of the University so there are three of us in the Morris [School] from that institution.

Libbie Burbank to Amanda (Oct. 1885)—I am going to have my state certificate renewed. then I'll be free for sure, from all examinations.... Amanda, I think you did pretty well to get $50 this year. That is good for a district school. *Libbie* to May Stewart (May 1887)—Two more weeks of torment and then I will have a rest. We all have to put in an application, this Spring, something new for us. It is to bind the teacher I guess. *Libbie* to Amanda (June 1887)—Do you know I have a notion to go to Evans and take a thorough course of book keeping. I think I would like the business. I hate teaching—only the pay and short hours being the attractive features. *Libbie* to May and Amanda Stewart (Feb. 1888) ... I wish I never was coming to school again. I am so tired and cross, and the children are so lazy, what few are here. The rest is out with mumps, chicken pox and winter cholera.

Jake King [Little Walnut] to my duck of a neice [Amanda] (Nov. 1874)—We had offers of experienced Teachers to teach our school this winter at $20. per month and board themselves the district joining us on the west had employed a teacher at $15. per month but this is an exceptional year. my Nephew, J. Watson is teaching our school at $28. per month we gave him $35. last winter. . . . There may be a chance to get a situation in the El Dorado School they have a graded school there and employ a Principle with three assistants summer and winter and pay liberal wages. If you think you would like a situation there let me know and I will make application as I am acquainted with two of the members of the Board.... But I must confess I have some forebodings especially since your Aunt Lydia ... fears your present term will be you[r] last ... [as] you will commit matrimony.

Jake King to Amanda (July 1887)—The Board has "voted you out...." The teachers are Logan McClain Prin. teacher, Ass't Prin. Elmer Wiseman, Grammar Class Miss Lou Burroughs. Mrs. Butcher & Mrs. Cosner not yet assigned.... The selection of Teachers seems to have been more the sake of harmony than for qualifications.... I have already seen the Quitto director. he says they are instructed to hire a gentleman.

Jesse C. Petherbridge to Mary Ann Stewart (Jan. 1886)—In reference to the school; that he [Mr. Rogers] was in favor of you ... that Thos. wanted more than they could pay; his price being $40; that he was emphatically not in favor of Mr. Obe W, L.L.D. Prof. Esq. D.D. etc; that you write and get Mr. Ed's consent and it would be all right with him; that if you should be employed it would be between Ed & him because he (Mr. Rogers) and Mr. John W. could not agree, Mr. W. being in favor of his son, Obe; that he (Mr. R) was not going to be led around by the nose of Mr. Weishaar any longer. . . . Employ determination & perseverance.

Nora Stewart to Family (April 1885)—Mr. Moulder and his wife were there [at the Sunday school]. . . . He has been trying to get that [Eagle] school away from Miss Lee. . . . They have hired her for a month on trial, and will be sure to find fault. . . . it was only the large boys that wanted him here. . . . Lydia [Knowlton] said he was a good teacher but he didn't have no business to do [it] that way.

Colleagueship and Courtship

Alice Louise Pierce (1860–1934) of Rochester (MN) and Ira Benjamin Whitcomb (1856–1897) of nearby Bryon, met in 1879. Whitcomb's father, a successful farmer and businessman, expected his 11 children to find their own success. Accordingly, "Ben" left for Oregon Territory in April 1880, looking for good land, perhaps with his brother Moses. In Oregon he resumed schoolkeeping even as he tried to succeed in farming. Alice "Allie" left Minnesota for better-paying schools in Ohio and Iowa, where relatives lived nearby. Their correspondence began in February 1880, on the eve of his departure for the West; it ended late in 1883. The extracts below are arranged chronologically—an ongoing personal and professional conversation that also evokes other teachers' accounts of varied hopes, worries, ambitions, calculations, and experiences.[16]

Allie (Muddy Knowl district OH), to Ira (Feb. 18, 1880)—I rec'd your letter at noon to day and was very glad to receive the invitation which I except with pleasure. I can let school out by three o'clock. *Ben* (RR camp, Ritzville, OR) to Allie (March)—I suppose ere you get this I will be back at work again [after an injury] and you will be teaching. I hope you will have good luck in getting a school and God's help in teaching it. *Ben* (Oswego. OR), to Allie (Oct. 20)—You're a strong minded sensible woman and can govern yourself, as I know by experience. . . . I will tell you the starting point was your friendship with my friend Mrs. Rice. You won my confidence and respect by refusing me a kiss and lastly my love by promicing to be mine forever.

Allie (Lonesome Hollow District, OH) to Ira (Jan. 1881)—Saturday went to Eaton and was examined. I think I may pass as it was not very hard. They only examine in Reading, Arithmetic, Geog. and Grammar so it is not so difficult as in Minn. *Allie* (Greenbush, OH) to Ira (March)—I have got to teach Algebra this term and I dread it some. by the way do you think I can board at Uncle Curts and walk three miles? I am going to try. May be it will take some of the fat off which I hope it will. . . . have a notion to teach here as fall and winter wages are so much higher here than out home. *Ben* (Oswego) to Allie (April 1)—I suppose ere you receive this you will be engaged in teaching. as to that Algebra. pshw! you need not fret . . . just wade in as if you knew everything and you will have no trouble. . . . If it were myself . . . I would stay where, or go where I could make the most money. . . .

Allie (Rough Hill district, OH) to Ira (April)—I do love to be alone after school and then I have the whole time without interruption to think of you. . . . I board at Mr. Early's [district clerk] and they are very nice people. *Allie* to Ben (May 5)—I think by the time I stay here till next Spring I will be nearly weaned from home and will be better prepared to live so far from home. . . . I am getting along nicely with that terrible Algebra but will have to hump if I teach here this winter for I shall have some advanced scholars.

Ben to Allie (June 4)—[Not] a single night passes but that I pray earnestly to God that he may prosper you in your work and so direct the minds of the people that they may appreciate your work and those of your schollars that they may be in earnest after knowledge. . . . *Allie* (Eaton, OH) to Ben (June 27)—my school closed last Saturday. . . . The scholars all felt so bad because school was out and there was not one I think but what shed tears and it is needless to say that I did. . . . We closed by singing Sweet Bye and Bye and it did seem so appropriate.

Allie to Ira (Sept.)—School has been keeping one week today and I have 26 of the nicest scholars in the county I am sure. . . . My scholars are having a Jollifica-tion with French Harps and Jews Harps and it sounds nice. . . . I am going to sew for Mrs. Dillerman this week nights and morning so will save my board. *Allie* to Ira (Oct. 23)—I have an awful nice school but several more are coming in that are advanced and it makes me sick about what I am lacking in. I would give up the school if it were not for the looks of the thing and then you know I want to make my way clear and of course it will take money. . . . One of my greatest worrys and trouble is the fear that my school will not be a success. . . . Mrs. Early says to me to night "You are getting on so nice. . . . Why in the District South they are about to turn him off just on account of bad scholars and yours are having such success."

Allie to Ira (Nov. 7)—Next Friday is speaking day . . . The scholars want me to have a ciphering and spelling match and I expect I will have to as they are such good scholars and try to please me so well. I tell you 'those big boys' are gentle-men in every respect. . . . I feel as though I must teach another school [term] in this place if my luck does not turn. . . . But I never intend to teach another winter school in this country. *Ben* to Allie (Nov. 10)—I can fully understand and appreciate your condition for I have often been there my self; have lain night after night when the angel sleep would not come to my dizzy brain nor slumber to my eye lids, when my thoughts were in the school room and my mind in the books. *Ben* to Allie (Dec.)—The folks here wanted me to teach their school so I went to an examination at Independence and wrote and I came within 8/9 of a first grade [certificate]. . . . so you will see that I will be in the old business soon.

Allie to Ira (Jan. 1882)—I was called to sit up with an old lady Mrs. Harris who is 70 years old. She had a stroke of Paralysis last Saturday and as her grandson and a girl working for her board comes to my school I felt it my duty to go and sympathize with those young minds. They were both so glad to see me. Etta met me at the gate and put her arms around my neck and kissed me. Poor Ora takes it as hard about his grandma. . . . I have taken the summer school in the same place at last summer wages. A Lady in fact two came and applied for the school and they told them they wanted to hire me if I would possibly stay and I could not get away.

Ben to Allie (March 1882)—I have quit my school and I will tell you why. They let me run out of wood and did not get any more just neglect. . . . They said they would get me wood if I would only go on with the school. . . . I have taken on an other school over near Salem. I get $45.00 per month and my board costs me $2.00 a week. I am to have the school for 8 months commencing the First Monday in April.

Ben (Monmouth, OR) to Allie (June)—There is a family in the district by the name of Murphy; whose child I compelled to do some work on the black board; I, however, did nothing rough to the child. They kept it at home next day and I wrote a note to the child's mother saying that I would like to have the child back or an excuse for her absence. They sent no excuse and since then they have been working to injure me: how they have succeeded I don't know but. . . . you know such things never get any better and I would perhaps be doing myself an injury in staying. . . .

Allie (in Iowa) to Ira (Nov. 5)—I got my certificate yesterday. My average was 88% Second Grade. . . . I will get 30 dollars a month and board myself. *Allie* to Ira (Nov. 21)—I imagine you trying to enlighten some dull boy or girl about some example and I really envy you that pleasure for mine are all small between the years of 4 and 11. I do wish I had my old school in Ohio even if it did make me study to keep up with them. My schoolhouse is situated on a vast prairie and is in a poor condition. . . . I have been sewing for my board this week and will for a few more weeks. . . . The people where I board are poor and everything is out of place and inconvenient but I can stand it from Monday till Friday night.[17] *Ben* (Salem. OR) to Allie (Dec. 5)—I am getting on nicely with my school one more week of this and $200 more to add to my mean bit of the world's goods. But I am blessed with health and strength and am thankful for this.

Allie to Ben (Feb. 1883)—I have four more weeks of school and oh such a drag. Only 9 scholars [and] one family that sends four is going to move away to Minn. this week. I hate to spare them awful bad. . . . Do you remember three years ago the 14th day of February? I never can forget it I was teaching that Friday and about 2:30 p.m. you came.

Ben (Monmouth, OR) to Allie (June)—One week ago last Friday I got into some trouble with one of my big boys at school. . . . [he] paid no heed to what I said but kept on talking verry saucy and I order him to take his seat which he refused to do; I then stepped to him and told him again to take his seat and shut his mouth; at the same time slapping him twise and pushing him toward his seat. I finally succeeded in getting him to his seat when he commenced swearing violently . . . and I slapped him again this time as hard as I could, this shut him up pretty well, and he got his books together and started home. . . . In the evening his father came up past the school house . . . and wanted to know why I struck his boy, I told him, because the boy neaded it he then commenced to quarrel in which he said I might get a chance to go to Dallas. . . . Sure enough he went to Dallas [Polk County seat] swore out a warrant and on Mo[nday] noon, at school, he had me arrested for assault and battery. . . . When the trial came off which re-sulted in my vindication and acquittal and of the honnor of the whole country around; in proof of which they promised me a grand dinner and reception on the last day of school. I worried my self over it until it came pretty near making me sick; . . . am feeling much better so I resumed school again today.

Allie (Rochester, MN) to Ira (Nov. 30)—My Own Darling yours of Nov. 18 is at hand and also that invitation for me to come. . . . Your father was down to see us a week ago today and I went home with him and stayed till Monday and had such a nice time which I shall never forget. . . . I will start for Portland. . . . Dec. 5. I suppose you will have all arranged about our marriage and what pleases you will suit me only I agree with your mother in one thing and that is this that we marry as soon as possible.[18]

A Writer's Random Impressions of Her Schools and Teachers

To the memoir of her growing-up years, *Search for a Soul* (1948), Phyllis Bottome (1881–1963) brought a mature writer's burnished gifts and a psycho-analyst's training. In all, she published 50 novels, collections of short stories, and works of nonfiction. The youngest of the daughters of an Englishwoman of aristocratic family and an American-born Anglican clergyman, from February 1890 she spent six years in America. Bottome's first encounter with American education came at age nine, in Yonkers (NY) at a prototypical progressive school, next a less relaxed girls school in Jamaica (NY), and finally a High Church Anglican boarding school in Manhattan. Her schooling ended in England, where she remained except for teaching briefly in Austria and Germany. These much edited extracts from her memoir recount some of her impressions of the schools and teachers she encountered and sometimes their perceived effects on her inner development.[19]

My first American school was a day school, held in a clean, spacious, sunny wooden house, and every hour was filled by quite extraordinarily amusing work. . . . We danced, sang, moulded in clay and wielded fret-saws, while learning history and geography, and even arithmetic, in effortless ease, and with almost equal interest. Ninety per cent of the American children of my day went, in a less luxurious and more arduous manner, to public schools, and I often wonder if we should not have profited by greater exposure to the proletarian spirit. But I suppose it was felt by my parents that we needed special attention while being broken into the American scene . . . (72).

Our young and pleasant teacher, as she often did, was reading a story out loud to the whole class when my listening ear caught a palpable misstatement. I put up my hand. "Why," I demanded, "did the mother expect her baby before it came? Did God tell her it was coming in a dream like Joseph's?" There was a momentary hushed pause. The teacher to my astonishment blushed scarlet; and the whole class burst into a gale of most disconcerting laughter. The teacher stopped it at once; turning to me she said kindly, "I think we had better talk this [over] together after the school is over." When the other children had gone home, she said rather doubtfully, "I think you ought to ask your mother to tell you more about how babies come! I don't like to do it without her leave!" (86–87).

My father, after a year's extremely successful work at Yonkers. . . . was offered the choice of three livings. Jamaica, Long Island [was chosen], a rather ramshackle small town not far from Brooklyn. . . . (94). I started school at Miss King's [Select Academy for Young Ladies]. . . . It was extremely good, with young, intelligent teachers and happily instructed children. There were two charming friend-teachers called Miss Dunn and Miss Burnett. . . . I learned everything I could from them, particularly poetry. I have often hoped that their lives were half as happy as they made mine (97). We were encouraged by our teachers, even by the best of them, to shine rather than to acquire a good working knowledge of our subject. [And] we had too many subjects (156–57). Unfortunately, this very pleasant if mediocre school came to an abrupt end. . . . The close of Miss King's School threw us back into the unprepared bosom of our family.

Mary, George and myself were sent daily to an uneducated, neurotic and wholly incapable lady who wanted to earn her living and thought that imparting what she didn't know was the easiest method of earning it (164). I fell from Miss H's grace by an act of moral courage rather infrequent in my career. Miss H. slapped George with a ruler and, though I think he may have been more astonished than hurt, he burst into wild and bitter tears. . . . I threatened and stormed at Miss H. . . . Mother supported my outburst. . . . From that hour George was neither punished nor educated. As he was only five, perhaps this hardly mattered, but Miss H. saw to it that there should be a victim. All my lessons went wrong from that moment; nothing I could ever do pleased or won any further recognition from her. I was an ambitious child and felt this fall from achievement greatly (164–66).

Mother hear[d] of a boarding school run by a branch Sisterhood of St. John the Baptist [in New York City]. The thought that I could be companionated by Anglican Nuns and brought up in a High Church atmosphere, no doubt greatly influenced my mother's willingness to part with me (181). Sister Elise Monica, the Superintendent, received us, and while she kept my mother to talk to, she sent me straight to bed. At last Sister A., whose name I will not mention as she left the Sisterhood a few years later under a cloud, knocked at my door. . . . I took an instinctive and overpowering aversion to her (185). Very much younger, still a novice, Sister Agnes Maria was my religious instructress and I became extremely attached to her. . . . I fear I gave her a great deal of trouble because of the fearful persistency and awkwardness of my questioning; and my impious refusal to take 'the Church teaches' as an answer (189). Sister Elise Monica did not make any immediate or great impression upon me. She was short, brusque and severe . . . [but] a human being who, however severe and undemonstrative would never let any child down. . . . Sister Elise Monica cleared her throat loudly, and wore creaky shoes, so that she never came upon you unawares in passages (185–86).

Our [lay] teachers were keen and fresh from college. . . . [Miss Macconochie] had gorgeous, venetian red-gold hair, a pink and white complexion, and a tall and graceful presence. Sunshine came into a room with her and left at her departure. All mathematical problems took on a remarkable clarity in her presence. She also taught, and taught extremely well, "English". . . . I only wish I had had more of such teaching and over a longer period. I was, however, less fortunate in my music. . . . Nothing I did ever pleased her [Sister A.] and she gave me the lowest marks she could (190–91).

Then the blow fell. We were to go back to England (220). . . . I know now that some of my sorrow, perhaps the deepest, was in leaving Sister Elise Monica herself. . . . I left school next day, and it was the end of my education (222–23). Mary was at her former school in Bournemouth, acting as pupil-teacher. My only companions, as the windy dull days flickered past, were my books. . . . For a few weeks I went to a horrible old-fashioned girls' school where the children lay on their backs on the floor to improve their figure. I found these children morons— and rough morons at that . . . (227).

With the spring came a new offer for my father at the church of St. Peter's, Bournemouth (237). I was allowed to go to Grammar School for part-time lessons, where, to my intense surprise and delight, I found I could understand Euclid, and where I made an intense and highly educational friendship with our French teacher, Mademoiselle Mellie Darius. She was, when I was fourteen, a very handsome, intelligent and ambitious young woman of seven and twenty. She had a lovely figure and rode a bicycle like a winged angel (239). For the next few years Mellie, and all she taught me, swept over my parched life like the waters of the Nile over the barren Egyptian desert. . . . She gave me courage and taught me to believe in my own abilities . . . (240).

A Kentucky Sisterhood of Spinsters: Miss Cora and Company

Although a mere hamlet, Union City supplied a number of Kentucky's teachers. Kathleen Jett Schwarzschild (b. 1925) recalls her teachers and describes their community. She first introduces her mother, a would-be teacher who married instead, thus meeting conventional male-set norms for women living in small towns in those days. They would marry and raise good children, unlike those who taught Union City's school in the 1920s and 1930s—who also raised children. Most remained single by choice or necessity, and Cora Dunbar (1892–1979) was the most memorable of these.[20]

My mother, Martha Ann Sharp Jett (1894–1996), began school in Doylesville (KY) near her family's "bottom land" farm, then attended Union City's one-room school after the family moved to a smaller, less productive farm; my maternal grandmother, Lucy Williams Sharp, wanted to be closer to the "metropolis." I believe my maternal grandfather, Isaac Newton Sharp, was one of the men of the community who got together and hired a teacher for what mother called a "subscription school"—this around the turn of the century. The teacher, usually a man, would come for a number of months, other parents joining in to pay the teacher. My grandfather ordered some books—not textbooks, but fiction—keeping them at home. My mother said she read them all—Dickens, Thackeray, Barrie, Eliot, Austen, Cervantes—before the "school" began.

After the eighth grade, Mother returned several times to help the teacher with the little ones—not for money but because she wanted to be still in school. Her Uncle Jim [Sharp] was district attorney for northern Kentucky, took her to Cincinnati for a business course, and may have paid her tuition; she lived in a boarding home for young ladies in the few months she was there. She came home because a high school class was organized in Union City's [new schoolhouse], and she desperately wanted to be in a real school. She was about 19 when she enrolled and 23 when she completed in 1917, one of the four young women who constituted the whole first graduating class.

Now eligible for the normal school, Mother spent two terms as a boarding student and loved it. On her father's death, however, the family "elders"—her two brothers-in-law—thought her schooling too costly (fifty cents perhaps)—so they had her come home. Mother knew that nursing was less expensive, but that was decreed an improper thing for a woman to do. So, in a year or two she married Isaac Jett (b. 1894). He had been out of Madison County, even to New York, spoke somewhat better English than other locals, may have read a book, and didn't have dirty fingernails. They were divorced when I was little more than a baby, and Mother ran a general store to support us—while my father mostly sat on the porch of his family's large house on one of the area's largest farms.

One of my earliest memories is of standing by the gate in front of our house on a country road in Union City, a crossroads village in Madison County, waiting for Mary Lou Dunbar to drive by and say hello on her way to school. Miss Mary Lou was, I think, the youngest of a large family; its three unmarried daughters were schoolteachers. Miss Mary Lou was young, beautiful, and one day she took me for a few yards down the road and waited for me to walk back to my yard. My guess is that this was 1928, when I was three. Miss Mary Lou drove the seven miles each way between the Dunbar house and Doylesville's ungraded one-room schoolhouse alongside the Kentucky River, morning and night, in her one-horse, one-seat black buggy. A few years later she taught in Cincinnati, until she retired and moved back to Richmond [the county seat] in the fifties.

But now it's September 1931: my first day of school at Union City's two-story brick schoolhouse, built in 1913, with twelve grades in its four rooms; one very old woman called it "the College," so grand it seemed after the one-room, eight-grade school it replaced. My best friend across the road, Samuel Griggs, and I both have brand new matching striped trainman's coveralls. Samuel's much-older sisters, or so they then seemed to me, Rozellen and Frances, walked with us the half mile or so and delivered us to Miss Cora Dunbar's room. Rozellen had been in Miss Cora's room for four years and was then in Miss Verna's room where she would spend the next four years—after which Miss Verna went to Richmond to teach.

Rozellen says both Miss Cora and Miss Verna wore chocolate brown dresses, and that she hoped when she grew up she could have chocolate brown dresses too. Miss Cora was small, seemed very old to me—or very one-age; I thought she had always been and would always be the same. She did not smile, but she did not look angry either. Perhaps sad. Sometimes she would screw up one side of her mouth, close the eye closest to the upside of the twisted mouth, and point a finger. I don't remember what the offense was, talking probably, but even then she did not seem angry. Objectively she was not imposing: 5 feet 2 inches and 120 pounds by her own report. Still, any of us could easily recall a reprimand, rebuke, or other wounding delivered by Miss Cora. Her style was more blunt than tactful.

Miss Cora's room? Could there have been six or eight rows of iron-legged desks? The desks were pretty beaten up, though I cannot imagine how they became so carved with initials. There were ink bottle holes—just holes—and pencil holder slots. Miss Cora's always neat desk was at the left-front, the pot-belly stove at the right-front. The front and right walls were blackboard, the left's windows too high to show anything but sky. Miss Verna's room, across the hall, was pretty much the same. But upstairs in the high school there was one large room with a stage at the center front and a sliding divider to shut off one half the room and stage from the other half, making it possible for two people to teach at the same time.

Something very exciting must have been happening outside the classroom in that first year, for a lot of children were asking to be excused. "Being excused" in 1931—and until 1939, when we went to the county's consolidated school with its indoor plumbing—meant a visit to the privy, outside and down the hill—a place without lids or stalls around its three or four holes. Rozellen said that the fuss outside was that Miss Verna had a battle with one of the eighth-grade girls, and the girl threw Miss Verna's car keys down the privy! (I think Miss Cora and Miss Verna each drove her own car to school.) That incident may have been the motivation for Miss Verna to look for a city school. And, perhaps, the fact, and it never occurred to me before, that there was no teachers' toilet. They must have had to use the outhouse too. But I never saw any of the teachers either coming from or going there.

After Union City High School, my friend Rozellen Griggs (b. 1919?) went to the nearby Eastern Kentucky State Teachers College, graduated, and taught;

because of her training she could better recall some of Miss Cora's practices. One was group teaching: bringing up to the front, small groups selected by their reading ability. She also taught large groups, all [four] grades together, elements of one or another subject. Rozellen remembers the flash cards Miss Cora used; I do not, perhaps because I was already reading when I began school. Textbooks were so standard and primitive as to make one wonder about their usefulness. The main book was the reader. The only one I remember was a third reader with a picture of a French poodle which scared me, so little did it resemble what I thought of as a dog. There were thin blue spelling books, by grade, which were well used for the school spelling bee. The library was one bookcase, [where I looked] through a book about the First World War. . . . I remember, I think, pictures of gas masks which frightened me so that I had no further interest in "the library."

A few years back, I've heard, the community held a Miss Cora Day. Rozellen thinks Miss Cora taught only at the Union City school and retired when it was closed by consolidation. She had begun teaching in 1916, took time off in 1928 to attend Eastern Normal's high school division, and had earned credits—including 10 from summer sessions, at [the renamed] Eastern Kentucky State Teachers College—enough in the 1930s to hold a standard life teaching certificate. Absent tenure, she had to reapply periodically for her position. Miss Cora ran a tight ship, better than Miss Verna, who had a temper and got terribly annoyed when students could not recite the multiplication tables or the school's other memorization tasks—no matter whether or not you comprehended what you were reciting. Still, these two sisters were responsible for the educational foundations of many people, three generations in some families.[21]

Unlike my friends, who went directly home after school and had little contact with the whole community except on Sundays, I went from school to the store and six days a week saw the entire parade of locals. In the period of my growing up, Union City had, perhaps, 50–55 families, about 260 people. Local families, white and black, raised and grew most of what they needed. There were five black families. One was a tenant farmer living on the owner's land; the other families were owners. One family, parents and an unmarried daughter, had a car. This daughter, M. L. Hatton—everyone called her M. L., although I heard smart-aleck high school boys (who thought she was high falutin', or uppity) refer to her as Molly Lou—taught the black school, and she drove some of the children to school. I suppose she must have prepared in Frankfurt, where there is a black college.

There were 17 local women who were or had been teachers; six had married. Around 1939, of the 10 teachers, 6 were unmarried women, 2 of whom later married. When I think of the number of young women in that community who became teachers, it is astonishing. Surely it must have been a yearning to get out—or not to follow your mother and grandmother's pattern of marriage, babies, very hard work with no help. They must have thought, "Anything but this." If one asked, "What else could I do?" teaching was about the only way out—for there wasn't even a Woolworth's to work in. Going away to school didn't happen, even in the more literate families.

Unless they went to normal school, unmarried daughters seemed to have stayed at home with aging parents. Two of my father's three sisters, Miss Mary and Miss Lucille, lived with their mother, as did my father after my parents divorced. Others of our acquaintance, Miss Lizzy and Miss Eleanor, the two unmarried daughters of Ma Berry (Mrs. Berry to everyone but family), lived at home, as did their unmarried brother, the town drunk. Mrs. Berry, however, had been a schoolmistress before raising six or more children and caring for an ill husband while teaching in her home.

One day our new fifth-grade teacher, Mrs. Roberts, announced that we were going to Richmond the following day to a movie. My mother asked whether all the children were going, and I said no. She said she would rather I stayed in school since she thought all the children should go. (I later realized that the seven could not afford the fifteen cents for admission.) So I also did not go. That day the principal, Mr. Smith, came to be our teacher for the whole day. He was funny and fun. He pulled down a big map from the blackboard that I had never seen before; did he bring it with him from the high school? And he read us something about Russia and a place called Nizhnenovgorod, and he had us pronounce it over and over again. I suspect that no one at the movie had a better time that day than those of us who stayed behind—and I loved that man. There were four male principals during my growing-up years.

The final three grades in Union City were pretty awful—no Miss Cora. The sixth grade teacher was the unmarried daughter of a man whose father had been the Baptist minister years earlier. Seventh and eighth grades were taught by an unmarried, unhappy, mediocre local woman. When I got to high school, now removed to Richmond, I can recall six men teachers and can only think of six women that year. By the following September several of the male teachers went off to the war, so the male-female proportions changed considerably.

One day, around 1933 or '34, Miss Cora introduced a man [with] a portable, wind-up phonograph. He talked a bit, opened up his phonograph, and played the Beethoven Overture to Egmont. Some of the children giggled. Miss Cora put an end to that with her funnyface and pointed finger. Well! I thought I'd died and gone to heaven. Years later, as a high school senior I played second violin in the

All State Orchestra. The conductor was Dr. Alexander Capurso, who had first played Egmont for me. His rural school project had been a federally funded program of the Roosevelt administration. There was no school music until high school. By the time I got to high school, there was a choral teacher and an instrumental teacher. There was a pathetic high school orchestra: so pathetic that, when the teacher broke her arm in my senior year, I rehearsed the orchestra.

There were 80 or more in my freshman class and 32 in my graduating class (1943). Only three, possibly four, went to college. I majored in music at Berea College. In Cincinnati I studied music at the conservatory, took a degree in music education at the university, and did practice teaching in a public school. I was probably okay at it, but I didn't love it. I got a master's degree in voice, while teaching music two days a week at Miss Dogherty's College Preparatory School for Girls. I came to New York in 1950 with the teachers and a group of students from the conservatory's opera department. But I would not be among any conservatory's one or two people who will make it professionally. And in New York I couldn't even think of looking for a place to teach. And the rest, as they say, is history.

CHAPTER 11

"That Our Daughters May Be as Cornerstones"

Women Teachers and Messianic America

Colonization carried forward by the armies of war is vastly more costly than that carried forward by the armies of peace, whose outpost and garrisons are the public schools.

—Samuel McCune Lindsay (1909), Secretary of Education
for Puerto Rico

Late in 1822, the second contingent of 12 American missionaries to the Kingdom of Hawaii arrived at Lahaina (Maui). Among them was 20-year-old missionary Betsey Stockton, unprepared for the native Hawaiians, coming aboard from their canoes, "half man and half beast—naked—except for a narrow strip of tapa around their loins." Her more sophisticated companions were equally jarred: "The ladies retired to the cabin, and burst into tears; some of the gentlemen turned pale: my own soul sickened with me, and every nerve trembled. Are these, thought I, the beings with whom I must spend the remainder of my life!"[1] Her comfort was a Christian's certainty that "they are men and have souls."

Eighty years later the seminomadic, westernmost Sioux bands had been confined to reservations in the Dakotas—and their children in schoolhouses, for, as Annie Beecher Scoville observed at an Indian rights conference in 1901, "What gold is to the miser, the schoolhouse is to the Yankee. If you don't believe it go out to Pine Ridge, where there are seven thousand Sioux [the Oglala Lakota] on eight million acres of land incapable of supporting these people, and find planted over that stretch of territory thirty-two schoolhouses, standing there as a testimony to our belief in education. There is something whimsical in planting schoolhouses where no man can read." "Uncle Sam," she added, "is like a man setting a charge of powder. The school is the slow match. He lights it and goes off whistling, sure that in time it will blow up the old life, and of its shattered pieces he will make good citizens."[2]

If education, particularly the public school, has been America's only agreed-upon faith, its primary instrument became the woman teacher. Despite the patriarchal, often misogynic, character of churches and their sacred books, educational roles for women were being written into Christian scripts. Ecclesiastical scrutiny was extended to schoolmistresses in 1555, indicating a spread of teaching women. In 1763 Alexander Stewart informed the Church of England's Society for the Propagation of the Gospel in Foreign Parts that, along with baptizing Carolina Indians, "[I] have fixed a school mistress among them to teach 4 Indian and 2 Negro boys and 4 Indian girls to read and to work and have supplied them with books for the purpose."[3]

Mary Lyon, a Congregationalist, was intent on "urging into the field a multitude of benevolent, self-denying female teachers." In 1836 she wrote to a benefactor of her new Mount Holyoke Female Seminary, "This work of supplying teachers is a great work, and it must be done, or our country is lost, and the world will remain unconverted."[4] From its inception Mt. Holyoke nurtured teaching as an act of Christian conversion and renewal. Despite conservatives' charges, public schools were far from "godless," promoting a nondenominational Protestantism through textbooks, rituals, and the flavor, at least, of teacher discourse. In "Our State," the iconic nineteenth-century Quaker poet John Greenleaf Whittier affirmed the corrective contributions of church and school, faith and reason, to the good society: "She needs no skeptic's puny hands, / While near the school the church spire stands; / Nor fears the bigot's blinded rule, / While near the church spire stands the school."[5]

Of necessity schools and civic life slowly grew more mutually accommodating as religious pluralism intensified with the immigration of millions of Catholics and Jews and Protestantism's further fragmentation. Over time, being Catholic or Jewish rather than Protestant, or Mormon rather than Baptist or Lutheran, came to matter less on either practical or normative grounds. Churches were rented as schoolhouses, as the Poughkeepsie (NY) school board did from 1873 in leasing two Catholic churches.[6] Pennsylvania and Arizona public schools employed nuns. Where courts or legislatures did not end the practice, it disappeared with the professionalization and secularization of public schooling and the growth of a Catholic school system needing its nuns.

Meanwhile, a new, often competing "God-given" civil religion arose—love of country, loyalty to its core institutions and their sacred texts, a supreme trust in America's transcendent nature. Civic buildings, among them now public high schools and colleges, competed with churches or temples in scale and grandeur—and became increasingly socially inclusive.

This chapter shows Gertrudes in the contexts of both "that old time religion" and the "new civil religion" of Americanism: first in sectarian schools and later in ordinary nineteenth-century public schools, where Protestant teachers acquired Catholic and Jewish colleagues. Sponsored by churches or hired by the federal government to convert America's indigenous "heathens" to Christianity and the "American way of life," Gertrudes were also expected to rescue the freedmen's children from ignorance and other dehumanizing legacies of slavery. As the United States became a colonial power, American schoolmistresses "followed the flag," where the task of Christian conversion was joined by, and sometimes made secondary to, disseminating the American ethos.

The "Sisters' Schools" of Fact and Legend

The girls schools founded by Catholic orders of nuns denied an intent to proselytize, but "in the interests of discipline" they required all students to attend religious instruction and exercises—raising Protestant alarms at "papist ambitions." The three girls academies in Catholic settlements in Kentucky, present from the 1820s, provoked the *Louisville Morning Courier* to editorialize in 1844, "It is manifest, that the Roman Church proposes to secure the ascendancy in this country, chiefly by means of literary institutions of every grade . . . to bring the Protestant youth of the country under their influence."[7] The Ladies' Society for the Promotion of Education at the West was organized in 1847 to forestall Catholic advances by ushering single Protestant women from the oversupplied Northeast to the Ohio valleys and beyond to staff new common schools.

The Post-Reformation American Battlefield

Catholic-Protestant competition intensified in the later nineteenth century in cities with large immigrant populations—including Chicago, Milwaukee, Detroit, and Buffalo—where parochial schools enrolled 25%–50% of all school-age children, far above their long-term national average of about 10%.[8] The Segale family left Italy in 1854, settling in Cincinnati. Schooled by various orders, Justina (b. 1847) and Blandina (b. 1850) entered the Sisters of Charity, beginning long careers in teaching and social work, especially among Italian Americans.[9] Immaculate Conception Academy in San Francisco saw six consecutive student-body presidents enter convents, most to teach in parish schools.[10]

Viewing the United States as a mission field, historic European orders arrived, joined by indigenous American sisterhoods, beginning in 1810 with Elizabeth

Seton's little school for girls at Emmitsburg (MD). Women religious, soon numbering in the thousands, were to teach the laity, recruit and instruct their own members (most the daughters and granddaughters of Catholic immigrants), return Protestants (including blacks) to the Catholic fold, and convert Indians to Catholicism. As teaching became the largest profession of women generally, instructing children replaced much of the social work and nursing ministries practiced by nuns in earlier times.[11]

Warned of loss of faith among their children and their own perdition should they fail to build schools, Catholic parents pushed parochial school enrollments to 600,000 children by 1890, and 1.1 million children by 1915, while the number of nuns more than doubled, reaching 90,000 in the 1920s. But the church was unable to build, support, or staff sufficient parochial or archdiocesan high schools to place "every Catholic child in a Catholic school" as Catholic numbers grew. In the nation's largest Catholic city, Chicago, only 42% of its younger children were in parochial schools in 1930, and less than 15% of its adolescents in Catholic secondary schools.[12]

Catholic schools and colleges began as manifestations of a siege mentality. But with overt Protestantism declining in most public schools and secularism gaining in the larger society, twentieth-century Catholic schools acknowledged assimilation.[13] The influence of liberal prelates, the educational and social ambitions of their increasingly middle-class patrons, and the quest for social mobility and civic equality among working-class Catholics together led parochial schools to adopt "morally acceptable" features of public schools. By the 1930s, of Illinois's 121 Catholic high schools, 99 had state accreditation.[14] The Sisters' pride in instilling Americanism and patriotism, along with Catholic conservatives' complaint that parish schools overly resembled public schools, testify to the porous "wall" separating an essentially Irish American church from Anglo-American public schools. Anti-Catholic views had moved toward the margins as Catholics became represented in every line of work and outnumbered Protestants in Congress and the Supreme Court.

A Postscript: Catholic Women Teachers after Vatican II

When Marguerite Costello died in midcareer in 2004, her obituary exceeded 36 column inches in the *San Francisco Chronicle*—unusual recognition of the passing of a middle school teacher. Costello merited recognition for her teaching skills, shown over a 25-year career mentoring other teachers, leading school-wide improvement projects, and receiving honors from local and national professional organizations. Importantly, she was also of Irish extraction, a product of Catholic schools, and, briefly, a nun.[15]

The most startling development in Catholic education was the virtual disappearance of the teaching nun. Nationally, in 1950 nuns were 90% of Catholic schools' teachers, 75% in 1958, near 50% in 1970, and 3% in 2012. In 1960 a loose network of Catholic schools educated 12% of the nation's K–12 students, in 13,000 schools; in 2006 it was less than 5%, in 7,000 schools. Amid a growing Catholic population—76 million in 2005—parish officials closed schools and merged others. St. Michael's School had served Catholics in the countryside around Axtell (KS) since 1889; for a time it even had a high school department. In the 1980s the Sisters left, needed elsewhere; their convent housed the lay principal and was then torn down.[16]

Therefore, when 22-year old Dulce Aguilar Rodriguez, a native of Mexico, became a novice with the Dominican Sisters of Mission San Jose (CA)—a sisterhood that once operated 32 schools, with convents in Oregon, California, and Mexico—she knew she might be the one left to "turn out the lights." Rebecca Shinas, born during the 1950s, experienced the whirlwind of interest in "street ministry" and social work while a postulant. She asked her prioress for permission to play her guitar and sing of God to Hell's Angels motorcyclists outside a nearby tavern: "We have to be where the people are; we need to be more visible in the world."[17] When U.S. nuns made news in the early twenty-first century, it was for their collective decision to work for social justice, often outside of ecclesiastical structures, despite increasingly conservative Vatican directives.[18]

As nuns left their schools, if not their vows, the lay teacher—not necessarily Catholic or female—became the mainstay of parochial schools. Like private schools generally, laicized parochial schools experienced high teacher attrition rates and associated costs.[19] Some of the parents at "St. Luke's" parish school said, "If you don't have Sisters for the children you might as well send them to the public school." A seventh grader remarked, "Sisters to me are people who have been given a very wonderful gift and have used their talents to the utmost that the good Lord gave them. Lay teachers have nothing to give up but time, and that isn't very valuable considering it is their jobs and not their lives."[20]

Small numbers of Catholic laywomen have taught in parochial schools and academies for generations, greatly outnumbered by those employed in public schools, despite barriers parents and communities might erect. "Comparatively few public schools are willing to receive Catholic teachers," the *School Bulletin & New York State Educational Journal* noted in 1889, although it "would seem the plainest dictate of common sense to enlist these worthy Catholics upon our side."[21] With most Catholic children enrolling in public schools, it was asked, would not the presence of Catholic teachers ease Catholics' distrust of public schooling?

Ellen Buttomer (b. 1855?) was reportedly the first Roman Catholic student at Bridgewater (MA) Normal School. She was then hired, possibly to mollify Catholic parents sensitive to the religious and ethnic prejudice in Protestant-oriented public schools. On her first teaching day, the local superintendent entered her classroom, calling out, "Open the windows. I smell fish in here!" His insult drew upon references to Catholics as "fish eaters" (for their Friday dietary observances).[22] Clearly the religious affiliation of teachers, parents, and communities still mattered, as did religion in the curriculum.

The Wider Realm of Religious Education

In a 1524 sermon, "On the Duty of Sending Children to School," Martin Luther described the schoolteacher's office as "next to the ministry the most useful, greatest and best." In St. Louis in 1855, the pupils of five Lutheran schools marched to celebrate the 300th anniversary of the treaty allowing German princes to select the official religion of their respective states. While the United States never welcomed state-supported sectarian schools, most nineteenth-century private and public schools reflected the nation's dominant Protestantism, although some believed that public schools were overly secular.

Lutheran congregations opened many church schools, preferring their teachers be pastors, church organists, or choir directors. Women teachers appeared of necessity, initially for the primary grades. The ultraconservative Missouri Synod of the Lutheran Church (f. 1847) increased its first 14 schools in the Midwest to 179 by 1860. Bethany Academy (later Bethany College and Normal Institute) at Lindsborg (KS) opened as a preparatory school in 1881, and Ella Lawson taught there in 1886. Nebraska's Luther Academy (f. 1883) offered pedagogy and, in its first 50 years, graduated 85 ministers and 312 public school teachers.[23]

From its organization in Michigan in 1863, the Seventh-day Adventist Church maintained several thousand schools worldwide—from Sabbath schools and preschools to universities—as part of its missionary character and interest in health education. Relative to Adventists and Lutherans, other Protestant denominations opened few schools. The Mormons usually felt no need of them, typically controlling teaching appointments and curriculum in local public schools. Those few created were turned over to Utah and Idaho school boards in the 1930s.

Anglican sisterhoods re-emerged in Britain between 1850 and 1900, and a few opened Sisters' schools. In 1904 the Sisterhood of St. John the Baptist in New York City agreed to staff the girls school, St. Helens Hall (f. 1869), in Portland, under the auspices of the Episcopal Bishop of Oregon; it had been founded and originally taught by three laywomen: Mary, Lydia, and Clementine Rodney.[24] Other women religious served schools, colleges, orphanages, and homes for the aged and taught in home and foreign missions.

Other denominations had experiences like Indiana Quakers. While public schools almost entirely replaced Friends' Schools" in Quaker communities, it was acceptable because "many of those [public] schools are virtually under the control of Friends, as teachers, principals, or trustees."[25] The African Methodist Episcopal (A.M.E.) Church was reportedly teaching 200,000 students in day and Sunday schools by 1885, when the first African Baptist conventions began operating schools, Sunday schools, and missions. Educated in an A.M.E. school, Rosa Jinsey Young (b. 1890) taught in both A.M.E. and Baptist schools and at her secular Rosebud Literary and Industrial School. Raised an Episcopalian, she converted to Lutheranism (Missouri Synod). Called "the mother of Black Lutheranism" she opened several Lutheran mission schools and Concordia College–Selma in her native Alabama.[26]

Mary Goldsmith Prag (b. 1846) first taught at two San Francisco synagogues. Widowed, she began a second teaching career at Girls High School; retiring at age 82 as vice principal, she became the board of education's first Jewish woman member.[27] As already detailed, a great many Jewish women taught in public schools. Having placed their trust and their children in public schools, America's thousands of synagogues sponsored far more afternoon Hebrew and Sabbath schools than Yeshivas (full-time religious schools). As Fannie Neumann, founder and parent of the Brooklyn Center School (1930), observed, Jews "relied upon the Hebrew school to undo the 'mischief' of the un-Jewish environment . . . an antidote to the virus of assimilation"—although she saw no inherent incompatibility between the American and Jewish traditions.[28]

The Sabbath School and Its Extensions

The American Sunday School Union (f. 1824) early signaled a more ecumenical, less theologically divisive state in Protestant education. Hundreds of Sunday school missionaries, often theology students, went out to begin or revive Sunday schools in Midwestern and Southern states, distributing Sunday school texts, teacher magazines, teaching aids, and the tracts and pamphlets that were reading material in countless households without books and magazines.[29] Thus Cary Wimer was surprised, on taking the town school in Minneola (MN) in 1883, that, despite its Protestant church (Norwegian Lutheran), of "Sabbath schools there are none."[30]

The Louisville Free Kindergarten Association included Sunday school teachers in its training program. In 1920 the George Peabody College for Teachers began a nondenominational Christian program of courses on religious education for public and Sunday schools. President William Payne believed that serving the Sunday schools' needs was within the schoolteacher's vocation.[31] Sunday school "volunteers" were often present or former public school teachers, some with a six-day teaching week, resenting the presumption that Sunday school work was intrinsic to their positions.

Protestant outreach to America's youth used related sectarian or interdenominational organizations. The Young Men's Christian Association (YMCA) and its female counterpart, the YWCA, significantly coordinated the interests of different Protestants sects. Thus Italian Presbyterian ministers used the YMCA to try to convert Cincinnati's Italian immigrants. Under American sovereignty in the Catholic Philippine Islands, the normal school in Manila offered courses for both YWCA and Sunday school work to middle- and upper-class Filipinas.[32]

"Children Made Wise unto Salvation"

Perhaps because Sarah Pierce (b. 1767) lost both parents by age 14, the early Republic's best-known headmistress stressed the lesson of their mortality—"to die a Christian"—to the young ladies of her Litchfield (CT) school—as Catherine Van Schaack's 1809 journal testifies. Iowa teachers at an 1860 gathering were exhorted, "always to strive to implant deeply and firmly . . . the great fundamental principles upon which Christians can agree."[33] Early normal schools taught novices that teaching is less an art or science than a consecrated mission.[34] Certainly other novice teachers must have received advice like that May Stewart's mother gave her when she left home to teach: "I hope you will not undertake a day's work in the schoolroom without first asking help from our Divine Master and if you do, believing you will receive the help you will be all right."[35]

When Mary Payne (b. 1843) started school in rural Henry County (IN), the schoolmaster routinely read from the Bible before dismissing the school for the day. "On one occasion my Sister Sarah Ann refused to close her book. She was trying to solve a problem in algebra." Years later, Mary Payne Beard referred to that day in the Pleasant Hill school: "When he started to her, she left the room and School forever." She continued at another school, and when Sarah Ann became schoolma'am at Pleasant Hill, one may imagine more mathematics and less Bible were evident.[36]

Although the nearly universal practice of daily classroom Bible reading was receding from both public and private schools by 1900, Southern institutions retained opening prayers, Bible reading, their pronounced religious orientation, and censorship longer. Georgia's black and white Christian teachers shared the view that, as Christians, they were daily making God's glory manifest in their classrooms.[37] While women's institutions elsewhere promoted women's rights and suffrage, one of the South's favorite women's colleges, Agnes Scott, took pride in strengthening its students' Christian character.[38] In 1960 the Georgia-born writer, Flannery O'Connor wrote, "I think it safe to say that while the South is hardly Christ-centered, it is most certainly Christ-haunted."[39]

As religion alternately defined, united, and divided white America, it also spurred home and foreign mission organizations. The interdenominational American Missionary Association (AMA) evolved into a Congregational body, forerunner of the United Church of Christ's Board for Homeland Ministries. Before 1900, the AMA was supporting preachers and teachers in stations from Mobile to Molokai, as was the primarily Congregationalist and Presbyterian American Board of Commissioners for Foreign Missions (ABCFM).

"Chosen Daughters" and the Home Mission Field

From colonial times a millennial vision of "all mankind's acceptance of Christ's kingdom on earth," under the divinely ordained leadership of America, had left its mark on the religious, political, and popular culture of the future United States of America. Protestant churches, seminaries, schools, colleges, charities, mission societies, and publishing houses were the means of awakening and proselytizing. This "grand view of both the national and the Christian future" and its extension from personal virtue to what historian Timothy Smith calls "social holiness" inspired home and foreign teachers and missionaries "and from 1815 onward sustained various moral crusades: for Sunday schools, public education, antislavery, peace, temperance, and concern for the destitute."[40]

Deeply religious, Annie Ellicott Kennedy (b. 1839) joined the Presbyterian Church at age 15 and taught in a mission school in a derelict city neighborhood. In 1868 she married a California congressman, General John Bidwell; they settled in Chico (CA). Perhaps borrowing pedagogy from the Chico State Normal School, she used pictures and charts to teach the nearby independent-minded Maidu at Mechoopda village, becoming their minister in 1879. Frances Louisa Goodrich (b. 1856), great-granddaughter of schoolmaster-lexicographer Noah Webster, asked the Presbyterian Board of National Missions for a place to serve humanity. First assigned as a companion to a depressed teacher in a Presbyterian-run public school in Riceville (NC), she later became a teacher and social worker in isolated hamlets in the Blue Ridge Mountains. Over 18 years she raised funds for a hospital, opened and taught Sunday schools, and recruited ministerial students as volunteers to start preaching services.[41]

Hundreds of churches' aid societies and home mission organizations were active in immigrant neighborhoods and ethnic enclaves. They worked through church and public schools, priests and preachers, Sunday schools, immigrant organizations and publications, social workers, public libraries, newspaper editors and magazine writers, and popular entertainments from parades and band concerts to vaudeville and later the radio, movies, and television. At least as a sideline, they also promoted Americanism.

Although proselytizing was a central feature of Mormon life, missions to non-believers worked both ways. Seeing Mormonism as a non-Christian cult, the mainline Christian denominations sent missionary teachers to Utah and Idaho territories from the 1860s. Emma M. Coyner, Jennie Kennison, and Sarah Walker Eddy were among the 57 teacher-missionaries in 33 Presbyterian schools in Utah and Idaho in 1883.[42] Of the 44 Congregationalists teaching in Utah in 1887, "truly a light in a dark place," 37 were well-educated women, supported by the New West Education Commission (1879–1893).[43]

New Hampshire teacher and Protestant missionary Melinda Rankin (b. 1811) worked in Catholic strongholds in Texas and Mexico from 1848 to 1872. She raised funds and opened schools for Mexican children, including the Rio Grande Female Institute (f. 1854) in Brownsville. Her Unionist views in Confederate Texas during the Civil War disrupted her efforts to distribute Spanish-language Bibles and teach English and Protestant doctrine.[44]

Christianizing Native Americans: Education, Not Extinction

"Peoples of color" interested whites from their first exposure. Jesuits opened a Christian school for American Indians in Havana, Cuba, in 1568 for children of the Calusa tribe brought from Florida. In colonial Massachusetts the "praying villages" of Martha's Vineyard were considered an early success in bringing a heathen people to the Christian's God.[45] However, from his 1831–1832 travels in the United States, Alexis de Tocqueville doubted the very survival of Native Americans, given their helplessness before the territorial advance of "the most grasping nation on the globe."

Early in the Republic's history, some in the federal government concluded that the only alternative to the physical extinction of the Indian race was a converting education: teaching the "Red Man" to live and believe like whites. The secretary of war, in March 1819, prodded the U.S. Congress into a church-state collaboration that authorized federal monies—the Civilization Fund—to support missionary work among Indians. The bulk of early federal support went to missionary schools already engaged in the work of "moral and practical transformation."

In 1842 Washington supported 37 mission schools, with 85 teachers and 1,283 students; their funding ended in 1884, and most mission schools closed or became federal schools.

In 1900 about 85% of enrolled Indians were in Bureau of Indian Affairs (BIA) schools. Federal policy shifted again, partly because of ineffective teaching in both mission and federal schools. Grants went to local public schools enrolling Native American children, persuaded that the example of their white classmates would prevail: inspiring, for example, the development of "wants" in Indian youth, coaxing them "into trousers . . . with a pocket that aches to be filled with dollars."[46] By 1931 rural public schools enrolled more than half the nation's Indian students. As Creek author and professor Tsianina Lomawaima writes, "Indian education flowed far beyond academic or vocational boundaries, soaking the child's growing up in the cleansing bath of Christian labor. Tribal/community identity, primitive language, heathen religion: these pernicious influences would be rooted out and effaced in the construction of a new kind of American citizen."[47]

CONVERSION AND CITIZENSHIP—EDUCATION'S REMEDY FOR "BARBARISM"

During their nine years at the Tshimakain mission among the Spokane tribe, the two missionary couples—Cushing and Myra Eells and Elkanah and Mary Richardson Walker—failed to Christianize anyone. Instead of the spiritual joy of converting, Mrs. Walker (b. 1811) found her 16-hour days consumed with largely familiar domestic and farm duties, including teaching her own children— leaving her little time to work toward their mission's goals.[48]

Lucy Meserve Smith (b. 1817) experienced success in teaching, if not in converting. In 1844 she became the second of ultimately six wives of a well-connected Mormon. In 1847, awaiting their departure for Utah, she accepted the Pawnee mission school at Bellevue (IA) for six months, her methods bringing "many gentlemen from the East to visit my school." She taught six days a week and gave singing lessons at the Sabbath school. "They, the Missionaries, offered me double wages if I would stay longer as I had such good control over the old folks as well as the children." On her departure her pupils wrote, "You such good lady. . . . You teach us long time to read, write, and study geography and Atlas."[49]

Ray and Pearl Colglazier and Claude and Vivian Hogg Hayman taught at Chilocco Indian School for decades. Both missionary and BIA officials recruited married couples to staff their Indian schools, exemplified early by Quakers Robert and Mahalah Green among the Shawnee at Wapakoneta (OH) in 1829.[50] On a family visit to Washington Territory, Edwin Chalcraft (b. 1853) entered business while his schoolteacher wife, Alice Pickering Chalcraft, was asked to teach the first Squak Valley (later Issaquah) school. When a business recession pushed them into federal service, they taught in Oregon, Wyoming, and Oklahoma for more than 40 years.[51]

In 1900, Richard H. Pratt asked his teachers to compare their former white pupils with their present Carlisle Indian School students. Given ingrained ideas of "modesty and propriety," several noted that "it is hard work to persuade an Indian girl, in school for the first time, to stand up and recite at all in a class with boys." "Miss S." was first struck with the marked stillness, the "reposeful feeling" in a room full of Indian pupils, commending the Indian's "true eye," finding them "more patient and painstaking than white children." "Prof. B, especially, thought 'civilization' had robbed Whites of valued personal qualities." He found in Indian pupils "more genuine beauty of character." Moreover, a quality "all but universal, among them and in which they are our superiors . . . is that of personal dignity."[52]

Romanticized, Edenic images of Indians as unspoiled "children of nature" have competed with racist depictions of bestial, subhuman creatures. Christianity warned native peoples of certain damnation as heathens, offering instead the brotherhood of Christ and redemption through love. Frontier novels and later films added their own images, picturing Indians, at best, as noble "losers" in their valiant struggles against the priest, the cavalry, the cowboy, the pioneer, even the schoolmarm.

NARCISSA WHITMAN AND MARY CLEMENTINE COLLINS

Inspired by her mother's intense religiosity and a missionary's account of service in India, at age 15 Narcissa Prentiss (1808–1847) announced her wish to become a missionary. After attending Auburn and Franklin Academies, Narcissa taught Sunday school, an evening singing school for the employees of her father's mills, and district schools in her native Prattsburgh and nearby Butler (NY). In applying to the ABCFM, she learned—as had Dr. Marcus Whitman, a Presbyterian medical missionary—that it did not sponsor unmarried missionaries. She and Dr. Whitman met in 1834, married early in 1836, and immediately went west. She wrote her sister, "I have such a good place to shelter—under my husband's wings. He is so excellent. . . . Jane, if you want to be happy get as good a husband as I have got, and be a missionary."[53]

At the end of the Oregon Trail, their missionary outpost—Waiilatpu, near present-day Walla Walla (WA)—was the second Protestant mission in what became the Oregon Territory in 1848. Losing their only child to an accident, Mrs. Whitman took in several abandoned mixed-race children and the seven orphaned Sager children, mothering and instructing 11 in all. Although the Cayuse

Indian leaders requested a mission, they appeared little interested in the white man's god; instead the mission became an important way station for whites streaming onto Indian lands. "The Indians are anxious about the consequence of settlers among them," Marcus Whitman wrote in 1843, "but I hope there will be no acts of violence on either hand."[54]

In this context and during an 1847 measles outbreak—against which the Cayuse had no immunity and Dr. Whitman few remedies—13 missionaries and settlers (including the Whitmans, the two Sager boys, and the current schoolmaster, Luke W. Saunders, and his family) were killed by a small Cayuse raiding party. About 50 women and children were taken hostage; some died in captivity, and others were forced into marriages with their captors before the Hudson Bay Company ransomed them. Under military pressure the Cayuse surrendered five men, who were hung after a long, controversial trial; their spokesman claimed that, as Christ had died for his people, they were dying for theirs.

Although horrified by news of the martyred Whitmans, the home and foreign mission work continued—buoyed by faith, zeal, and its success stories. Mary Clementine Collins (b. 1846) was lauded in missionary circles as a natural-born teacher and social worker and stalwart friend of the Native American. A college graduate with a master's degree, Collins taught in her native Iowa before volunteering as a Congregational missionary and reaching Dakota Territory in 1875. She quickly learned the Lakota dialect, visited Sitting Bull, talked with him in his own language, and was adopted by his band with the name Winona (princess or daughter). In February 1890 the *American Missionary* printed one of her letters from her Grand River days, where she recounted being approached in Cheyenne (still Wyoming Territory) by "fine looking, well-dressed young Indian men" who explained, in English, that they "went to school to her" years before. "It made my heart strong to take these manly young men (whom she remembered as "dirty little long-haired, blanket Indians") by the hand and to hear them say, 'You were my first teacher.'"

Collin summarized both her motivating faith and her belief in her mission's success, writing, "I had some rich experiences, many hardships new to me, but I sowed seed which I doubt not will spring up. . . . God meant me to get into the homes and hearts of those strangers, and I had no fear but that he planned it all."[55] In a 35-year career, she taught, was ordained, preached, and "doctored" until her 1908 retirement. She then toured America, promoting Indian rights and school reform, having changed many of her original views on Indian people, their cultures, and their needs.

"To Be Useful in My Master's Vineyard"—Schooling the Freedmen

Prevented by their pacifism from enlisting, Northern Quakers followed the Union army into the South, founding missions (in freedmen's camps), providing relief supplies, opening orphanages, and supervising farming efforts to "show the Slave Oligarchy of the surrounding country here that the Negro can and will work without a driver, or a cowhide incentive."[56] Schooling soon followed. In 1863, Indiana Quakers sent Lucinda B. Jenkins and Mary E. Pinkham to help Lizzie Bond teach reading to adults and children in Vicksburg (MS), using pine boards and charcoal as slates and chalk. By 1870, there were more than 4,300 schools, with 9,000 teachers instructing 250,000 colored children and an unknown number of adults. Nearly half of the teachers were women, primarily Northern whites and Southern blacks, representing a mix of Protestant denominations and Catholic sisterhoods.

The Freedman's Aid Society branch in Chicopee (MA) raised the funds to send Bessy L. Canedy from Fall River to Norfolk (VA) early in 1865 as one of that city's 14 Yankee teachers. In March 1865, the *Freedman's Record* published a letter from Canedy, reporting that "[a] teacher in one of our schools was exceedingly mortified by the disorderly conduct of some of her pupils during a visit of some friends from the North." She later spoke with the miscreants, "asking them if that was the way to show their gratitude to the people who sent them teachers. Where-upon one of the little innocents exclaimed, 'I thought God sent us our teachers!'"[57]

African Americans were enthusiastic converts to Christianity, but Anna Julia Cooper (b. 1858), educated in an Episcopal school, repeatedly urged Christians to make common political cause with Negroes through education. In exhorting Episcopalian clergy she stressed black women as the future leaders of racial uplift: "Snatch them, in God's name, as brands from the burning! There is material in them well worth your while, . . . a staunch, helpful, regenerating womanhood on which, primarily, rests the foundation stones of our future as a race."[58]

Because of their own Christian faith and that of their sponsors, white teachers tended to report the freedmen's zeal for education as religiously directed. However, they and teachers of their own race probably saw literacy more broadly: a symbolic "good" that represented the freedom and independence long denied blacks by law and repeatedly obstructed by poverty, discrimination, intimidation, and violence. As an astute observer wrote, "The people are keen for education which they see to be necessary to their children in the future of equal rights."[59]

Like other white Northerners, Harriette Pike admired what she saw. "Old and young are eager to learn," the men and boys worked in the cotton fields "from sunrise till dark, sitting under a tree studying a Primer during the few moments of rest they are allowed after dinner."[60] Yet, despite their gratitude for Northern help, black communities sought spiritual and cultural independence, their own preachers and teachers, churches and schools.

Baltimore was home to the first sisterhood of black nuns: the Oblate Sisters of Providence, founded in 1828 by French-speaking West Indian women. The Oblates prepared many black teachers, notably for the colored schools of Washington (DC). Two additional black orders appeared: the Holy Family Sisters (f. 1852) in New Orleans and the Franciscan Handmaids of Mary (f. 1916) in Savannah.[61] Requests for their services exceeded supply, as the Bishop of Natchez (MS) found in 1873 when asking for nuns to take over the School for Colored Children in his cathedral. Throughout the nineteenth and twentieth centuries, most of the teaching of black children by religious orders was by white nuns.

Protestant-Catholic antagonism reappeared in schooling the freedmen. In an 1867 letter, Mrs. M. M. Williams, teacher in the AMA school in St. Augustine, reported, "Great dissatisfaction is felt with the Catholic schools, and the nuns are said to have tried to inculcate the old slavery dogmas, which you can imagine are not calmly received. Many of the Catholic children have already returned to us, and many more will eventually return." The AMA teachers—Mrs. Williams, Miss Cornelia Smith, and Mrs. Charlotte J. Smith, their former principal—instructed 74 day and 35 evening students, "all of whom seem eager and anxious to improve the opportunities held out to them."[62]

To weaken white opposition to its work in Louisiana, in 1864 the Board of Education for Freedmen adopted a staffing policy for its 45 schools: by "giving the preference to Southern Teachers whenever such could be obtained . . . the Board have gained an unexpectedly strong moral support to their enterprise." Edwin Miller Wheelock (b. 1829) was less sanguine. A Unitarian chaplain in the Union army, Wheelock was New Orleans's school superintendent in 1867–1868, before becoming Texas State superintendent. Although called "profoundly ignorant . . . of the nature, rights, and needs of the white people in Texas," Wheelock was credited with capably filling his office and organizing the Texas public schools. In 1868 he reminded Northern educators and politicians, "No insurgent State had a practical free school system and no loyal one was without it. The line of Free Schools divided the faithful and the rebel communities as sharply as did the contending camps."[63] Certainly the Jim Crow South's rigidly segregated, inequitable public schools fell tragically short of the common school ideal.

Ann Harrigan on Race, Radicalism, and Catholic Action

Ann Harrigan (b. 1910) began her career during the Great Depression with seven years of "subbing drudgery" in New York City schools, becoming permanent in 1937. By chance that year she discovered Dorothy Day's writings and her Catholic worker movement, and through her learned of Baroness Catherine de Hueck, a White Russian émigré, founder of Friendship House in Harlem. In 1938 Harrigan began to volunteer at Harlem Friendship House—a lay Catholic experiment in interracial and intercultural understanding—and to lecture on its behalf before Catholic groups. Also, "I guess it was because I was a teacher that I was given charge of a rough, rowdy crowd of mid- and older teenagers, of whom I was mostly scared," she later recalled.[64] In 1942, Harrigan left for Chicago, ostensibly on sabbatical leave to pursue a master's degree in sociology—a ploy to placate her mother and the New York City Board of Education. In fact Harrigan went to be codirector—with Ellen Tarry, a Catholic convert, Birmingham teacher, black journalist, and author of children's picture books—of a new, Chicago version of Friendship House.

Friendship Houses (seven in all) recruited idealistic Catholic laypersons. Mostly whites, they chose poverty and life in racial ghettos, serving and interacting as equals with poor Negroes "whose poverty was involuntary." As Harrigan wrote in 1938, in the 40 blocks of Harlem, three groups were working. "The first, Protestants built churches and launched activities serving preschoolers through the aged—"doing missionary work in Harlem before we Cath[olics] knew there was such a place." To their political left, Harrigan observed, the Communists "fight with the zeal of the first apostles for the amelioration of their oppressed brothers. . . . They live in these places and know what they're fighting for." She was impressed with their 22 centers, 3 open 24 hours, where "white and colored meet on [an] equal basis," and their enthusiastic and well-equipped teachers and counselors, emphasizing every kind of popular art and craft. "They play up all the artists . . . and bolster up their race pride which has been so stomped on; all ages get attention."[65]

As for Catholic efforts, three prominent New York priests persuaded the Baroness to open Harlem's Friendship House in 1937. She did so, de Hueck wrote, to "counteract the dynamite of communism with the dynamic of Christianity."[66] Nonetheless, Friendship House borrowed some features of the communists' programs: an employment bureau, credit union, and co-ops for adults; crafts, arts, dramatics, athletics, social activities, and a library; and something open day and night, including youth clubs. The volunteers' apostolate included confronting their own ignorance and racial prejudice in operating Friendship House, and in her unfinished memoirs Harrigan marveled at how invisible she had once found the Negroes and their neighborhoods in her daily commute on the Fulton Street car to St. Joseph's College for Women.

The 1970s prosperity of parochial schools—havens for those wishing to escape public school integration—recalled for Harrigan the racial segregation practiced in Catholic schools, colleges, and religious orders during her youth. In 1938, for example, Harlem's colored parochial school had 400 students in 250 seats because the nearby parochial school, "half white and half colored," would not take more black children to fill its vacant seats." In truth, "Negroes were expected to keep the faith or be converted by the pure, unadulterated truths of Xty!"[67] Harrigan left Chicago's Friendship House in 1948, reportedly disagreeing with the Baroness's emphasis on work among blacks being, foremost, an expression of Catholic anticommunism.[68]

America, the Christian Candle

Ignoring critics of imperialism like Mark Twain, the colonial adventures of postbellum America exploited messianic Christianity, whether by missionary or military force, while pushing the secular but "God-given" civil religion of Americanism. Protestant ideology and the relentless march into "empty space" had long since transformed Native Americans from "nature's noblemen" to a population to be "schooled and saved." Historian David Adams sums up the ideology that conflates conversion with the conquest and containment of the Indian: "by providential intention, America had a millennial destiny to impose its system onto those who stood in the path of its march to the Pacific"—a conceit expressed in subsequent military interventions and annexations.[69]

Women, the Candle Bearers in All Their Diversity

Episcopal missionaries John Henry Hill and his wife, Frances Mulligan Hill (b. 1807), gave the capital of Greece—a young republic lately freed of "the tyranny, heathenism and ignorance beneath which she had been buried" by the Ottoman Turks—its first school for girls in 1831. With two of Mrs. Hill's sisters assisting, the Hills' school began in a ruined cellar with 20 girls, some from poor families, others made destitute by the war. Within a decade they had 790 pupils, including the offspring of Greek officials who, in 1834, began sending them older pupils to be trained as public school teachers and teacher educators.

The influential editor of *Godey's Ladies Book* marveled "that such a change of sentiment should occur respecting the capacity of women to acquire knowledge and become the teachers of national schools in the country where, until twenty years ago, all learning was confined to the other sex, seems little short of a miracle."[70] Staffed by the Protestant Episcopal Board of Missions, Hill Memorial School was funded by Greece's government and, significantly, by an association of women supporters of Emma Willard's Troy Female Seminary.[71]

The second issue each year of the *American Missionary* reminded readers of the work being supported, "among four races, the white, the black, the red and the yellow . . . children of a common Father; . . . [and] the possible heirs of a common Saviour." Among the missionaries "are teachers of 'common branches' and 'higher branches.' There are teachers of industries for men and women, house-makers and home-makers. . . . Notice, also, what a large proportion of our missionary work is being done by Christian women. . . . The history of this Association [AMA] is a grand and splendid eulogy of woman."[72] Women were 49% of active U.S. mission staff by 1830.

Around 1816, while a paid slave in the home of Princeton College president Rev. Ashbel Green (a supporter of the mission movement), Betsey Stockton (b. 1798?) was converted and then emancipated. Unschooled, her education came through accompanying Green's son to Sunday school and using Green's library to teach herself. While preparing to teach colored children locally, she applied to the ABCFM to serve as a missionary in Africa. Instead Stockton was assigned to a missionary couple, Rev. and Mrs. Charles Stewart, as their domestic servant and official helper in their new mission activities in the Sandwich Islands.[73]

Intelligent and highly literate, judging by her surviving letters and journal, Stockton taught English to one of the Hawaiian princes and then taught a small class of English and Hawaiian pupils. "This, with the care of the family, I find as much as I can manage." Two years later, as a stream of missionary and lay teachers from the mainland arrived on the islands, Stockton handed her school to a new missionary and headed home with the Stewarts to a teaching career in Princeton (NJ).

Missionary teachers and evangelists were a diverse lot. Pennsylvania widow Charlotte H. White insisted on being sent to a Baptist mission in Burma. She offered to donate her land to a mission society as a bribe, and she sailed in 1815. Her sponsors were vastly relieved when she met and married English missionary Joshua Rowe in India, ending her disturbing status as a single lady.[74] Henrietta Hall (b. 1820) came from a privileged Virginia family swept by the religious enthusiasm of the day. "The sincere prayer of my heart is, Oh, that I be qualified to become a missionary of the Cross," she wrote in 1835 as she left for China with her young husband, J. Lewis Shuck. Their boarding school in Hong Kong eventually housed 32 boys and girls, as well as their own four children. On her 27th birthday, in failing health, she prophetically wrote her father, "Farewell! May you long, long be spared to your family and to the cause of God. Do what you can for China."[75]

Born to a working-class family of "tolerant Baptists" in East Rodman (NY) and graduate of the State Normal College in Albany, Adele Marion Fielde (b. 1839) was a Long Island schoolma'am in 1864 when she became engaged to Cyrus Chilcott. When she arrived at his Siam mission in 1865, she learned he had died. She remained ("I don't believe our Lord sends his servants on useless errands"), serving as a teacher and medical missionary in Bangkok and China until 1889.[76] Her Bible-teaching program trained about 500 "Bible women" as evangelists, on the principle of "each one teach one." Author of a dictionary of the Chinese Swatow dialect and *A Corner of Cathay: Studies from Life among the Chinese* (1894), she also lectured on biology in America.

In preparing and sending ministers abroad, mission organizations promoted marriages: for emotional support, as models of Christian families, and because wives did most of the literacy work in missions worldwide. They fed, clothed, and taught children, alongside their own offspring and their servants' children in many small boarding schools. In 1818 American Baptists sent Miss Philomela Thurston to Bombay, with John Nichols and Allen Graves and their wives, to teach 1600 "Jewish, Mahometan, but chiefly heathen" children and youth at 11 schools. A widower, Rev. Mr. Newell, quickly married Miss Thurston. [77] The marital record may belong to Rev. Edward Clemens Lord (1817–1880). A Baptist missionary to China, he reportedly married six times, sometimes the widows of other missionaries. His first wife (in 1846) was Lucy Lyon of the Mount Holyoke faculty; his second (in 1853), her sister, Freelove Lyon.[78]

However, the aspiring missionary no longer needed to contract a marriage. In 1861 Sarah Marston was sent to Burma by the Boston branch of the Woman's Union Missionary Society. This was one of 44 U.S. women's missionary organizations that, by 1900, sponsored only single women, thereby contributing to woman's emancipation. The proportions of single women, married women, and married men in the broader mission field later averaged about one-third each.[79]

Mission Outposts of Nineteenth-Century Educational Institutions

The missionary on furlough made the "usually mundane Sunday service become exotic and exciting, as the world beyond the United States suddenly seemed real"— while mission boxes awaited the contents of pockets and purses outside Protestant and Catholic churches and church schools across America.[80] "No churchgoer born before 1960 can forget the childhood thrill of hearing a missionary speak in church. . . . The audience sat transfixed, imagining what it might be like to eat termites in Africa, or beg on the streets in India." In an information-starved society, church congregations and Sunday school classes were enthralled. Moreover, in most Protestant denominations between 1910 and 1950, two out of three visiting missionaries were women.

While students at Mount Holyoke Female Seminary and Oberlin College may have been readied by family traditions of Christian service, an atmosphere of deep piety and reformism also permeated their schools.[81] Within two years of Mount Holyoke's opening in 1837, it sent missionaries to the Creek Nation, Hawaii, and stations in Turkey, India, and Ceylon. China received a member of the Holyoke faculty in 1840: the founder's niece, Lucy Lyon Lord. Two 1840 classmates, Prudence Richardson Walker (d. 1842) and Zeviah Shumway Walker (d. 1848), began the seminary's mournful presence in Africa at the Gaboon [Gabon] Mission. Japan's first Mount Holyoke missionary was probably Ann Eliza Clark Gulick (b. 1830); she arrived in Okayama under the great opening to Western influence during the reign of Emperor Meiji (1868–1912).

Youth at other academies, colleges, and normal schools were similarly exposed to missionary appeals. When, in 1865, Principal Anna Peck Sill decided to remain at Rockford Female Seminary, she wrote, "I asked my Heavenly Father that if I was not permitted to enter the foreign field, I might see one of my pupils go in my stead." Her first graduate, Anna Allen, married a Baptist clergyman in 1854 and as Mrs. Douglass raised their nine children in Madras, India, where she taught for 15 years.[82] Kobe Girls School—founded in 1873 by Rockford Female Seminary graduate Julia Dudley and Rockford (IL) resident Eliza Talcott—evolved into Kobe High School (f. 1891) and Kobe College (f. 1894). Foreigners founded institutions, from kindergartens to colleges before the welcome cooled early in the twentieth century.

Charlotte "Lottie" Moon (b. 1840) grew up comfortably on her family plantation. However, at Albemarle Female Institute in Charlottesville, at 18 she "found Christ" through the religious revivals sweeping the school. Her younger sister, Edmonia, went to China as a missionary in 1872, and Lottie soon followed, among the first unmarried women sponsored by the Southern Baptist Convention. While teaching 40 "unstudious children" at a girls school in Dengzou, Moon accompanied missionaries' wives on their "country visits" and found her vocation: evangelical work with Chinese women, planting churches in remote villages. She abandoned Western dress and racial prejudice, sharing her provisions with her famine- and disease-stricken neighbors.[83]

Eva Roberta Coles (1880–1902) graduated from Hartshorn Memorial College in Richmond (VA). She taught in Charlottesville's colored public schools while her fiancé, Clinton Boone, completed his studies for the Baptist ministry. While black mission boards had far fewer resources to support missionaries, they felt an intense obligation to offer Christian rescue wherever Africans lived. In May 1901 the couple arrived at the Palaballa mission in the Congo Free State.[84] She began a kindergarten and a sewing circle, and she gave occasional medical treatment. When her own baby died, the villagers mourned with the sweet young woman they called "Mama Buna," who died soon thereafter from a venomous bite.

Missionaries were particularly struck by the pervasive illiteracy among girls and women—in North Africa, much of Latin America, the Caribbean, Greece, India, and China—the largest field for American missionaries.[85] They opened and served in schools and colleges, clinics, medical and nursing schools—and even seminaries. Martha Linda Franks's 40-year missionary career in China began when, after two years as a Virginia kindergarten teacher, she spent a year at the Southern Baptist Seminary and sailed to China in 1925, supported by a Baptist Church congregation in Richmond. From kindergarten work, she ended up teaching Chinese seminary students: "Not much difference," she joked.[86]

The Presbyterian Board spoke for other mission organizations, reaffirming that "woman everywhere represents the stronger element in the religious faith of the community whether that faith be true or false." Historians agreed: "Gaining access to the people, especially to women and girls, and the overwhelming impact of 'heathen' culture outside the gates of the mission residence turned the boarding school into a building block of Asian missionary strategy."[87] Male missionaries were set aside wherever direct contact between unrelated men and girls was culturally forbidden.

Preparing Teachers on the American Model

Having known female seminaries and state normal schools at home, women missionaries were prepared to plant these familiar American institutions abroad—as they did in a great many places. Preparing native evangelists and teachers was an early and continuing objective, extending missionary (and colonialist) influence through the generations. However, a sovereign nation asking another for a delegation of experienced teachers to create a chain of normal schools was unique indeed—and a fitting application of Gertrudes' mission in a younger republic.

In 1866, President Domingo Faustino Sarmiento invited "las Norteamericanas" to Argentina to establish its first normal school, essential to realizing the 40-year-old dream of Argentina's early leaders: to sustain an independent and secular republic through free, inclusive schools. Argentina's existing schools were church run, formal, traditional, and intended for a cultured elite in this nation of immigrants. Virtually no middle class existed, and the first national census found 75% of Argentinians illiterate. Sarmiento was determined that Odisea Laica—

Argentina's epic voyage into democracy—would come through public education and reside in lay hands, hence the name he gave his movement. Sarmiento had been Argentina's consul in the United States, where he met Horace Mann, whose vision of common schools inspired him and whose wife, Mary Peabody Mann, helped recruit 67 American volunteers: the core of *Odisea Laica*. Sarmiento's minister of education, Nicholas Avellaneda (later Sarmiento's successor), gave the movement time and political support.

The first American schoolmistress to arrive was likely Mary O. Graham (b. 1843), an Ohio-born, New Mexico–raised daughter of a Baptist minister.[88] Graham attended Hamilton Female Seminary in the "Burned over District" of western New York State, where the fires of religious revivalism periodically erupted from 1800 to 1850. Hamilton's principal, Mary Anne Hastings (b. 1822), modeled the school after Emma Willard's Troy Seminary, where she had studied and taught.[89] The message that Rev. Brooks, the charismatic Baptist pastor, and Miss Hastings preached to their students—"Chosen Daughters"—was that doing God's work must override any barriers set before women by nature and society; they must create and seize opportunities to serve.

Graham was teaching Indians in New Mexico when Jeanne Smith Carr, whom she had met through Rev. Brooks, urged her to accept the offer from Argentina. Daughter of a prominent Vermont family, graduate of an upper-class Philadelphia girls school, and former teacher, Carr had a reach that reflected the workings of the social networks that educated nineteenth-century women formed during their seminary and normal school years. Similar personal and institutional connections brought nearly 100 other American teachers to Argentina by 1900, all but four being women. These American "guests" in still-Catholic Argentina were mainly evangelical Protestants, especially Baptists and Methodists—half from the Northeast.

One of the best-remembered directors of normal training was Mrs. Sara "Sallie" Chamberlain Eccleston (b. 1840), who arrived from Pennsylvania in 1883 to open a kindergarten department at Escuela Normal des Paranà.[90] Frances Armstrong, an 1878 graduate of Minnesota's Winona Normal School, arrived in 1883 and first taught at Paranà—one of 14 such schools founded by 1921. Armstrong was then sent to Argentina's cultural capital, Córdoba, to open a normal school to prepare Argentine women to teach, perhaps in "mixed" schools.[91] With its ancient university (f. 1613) of "eminently learned monks and bishops and professors of theology who taught the purest Latin under classical canons" and Jesuits "transmitting their militantly religious views to the young," Córdoba was an alien environment for secular coeducation in general and young Frances Armstrong in particular. She persisted and also opened the coeducational Normal

Escuela Mixta in San Nicholás de Los Arroyos. In the opinion of a group of normal school Argentinians 150 years later, "without that first step, the coming of American teachers, education based on a systematized methodology would have been impossible."[92]

Domesticating America's New Empire

"If your mechanic arts are unsurpassed in usefulness, if you have taught the river to make shoes, and nails, and carpets . . . let these wonders work for honest humanity. . . . I wish you to see that this country, the last found, is the great charity of God to the human race." This challenge came from Ralph Waldo Emerson in late 1863 while the Union was using its "proud catalogue of mechanic arts" on behalf of the great moral struggle of the age: to "strike off the chains which snuffling hypocrites have bound on the weaker race."[93] The industrializing North's victory in the Civil War ensured that some American leaders could imagine becoming an empire, or at least think of the United States as a world power. Soldiers seasoned in that war, and war against Native Americans and Mexicans, could be deployed elsewhere: to pacify in their own lands other peoples deemed racially and cultural inferior or, at best, "childlike."

A broad interchange of American personnel, their assumptions, and their practices similarly influenced the nation's schooling of its diverse "dependent" populations: freed slaves, Native Americans, and the indigenous or immigrant peoples of its new colonies. In 1848 Richard Armstrong was named Hawaii's second school superintendent; in 1868 his son, Samuel Chapman Armstrong, founded Hampton Institute in Virginia, a school for blacks and Indians. Dealing with illiteracy—in 1910, 56% among Native Americans and 30% among Negroes—suggested lessons for dealing with, for example, pidgin English in Hawaii. Mary Helen Fee, in 1905 the first teacher at the girls school at Capiz in the Philippines, later taught Native Americans in California.[94] Despite profound differences among the objects of their colonizing efforts, reigning ideas of race—especially white superiority—affected the thinking and actions of policy makers, administrators, and teachers.[95]

In midsummer 1901, the military transport USS *Thomas* arrived in Honolulu on its way to the Philippines, with more than 500 American teachers. Their orientation was a recital of America's experiences with Hawaiians.[96] In 1917, Agnes Crary Weaver (b. 1866), a well-connected clubwoman, offered her perspective on Caucasians' responsibilities in Hawaii. "Ten percent of us are trying to make the ninety per cent an English speaking people with the fundamental institutions of the family, property, customs and morals . . . etc after the pattern of the United

States."[97] The enculturation agenda for its Pacific Islanders strongly recalls that conceived for mainland subcultures: Mexicans, Negroes, Indians, and recent immigrants.

Soldiers in Skirts: Pacifying the Philippine Archipelago

The Philippine archipelago—7,107 islands, about 300 inhabited by peoples of diverse languages, customs, and faiths—passed into the Spanish orbit in 1564 when friars arrived to convert these "heathens" and "pagans." The Spaniards marveled at small children writing their letters in the sand or on leaves, their first steps to literacy in their native languages. Taught by tribal and perhaps family tutors, reading and writing were commonplace among Filipino adults of both sexes, especially the Tagálog with their written grammar and dictionary, as well as a grammar of the other 11 indigenous languages.

When the United States took effective military possession of the Philippines (along with Guam and Puerto Rico) in late 1898, there were seven Army schools in Manila, taught chiefly by military chaplains and noncommissioned officers. In June 1899, as fighting continued (not against Spanish troops but between American troops and nationalist Filipinos), Yale graduate Lieutenant George Anderson became the first school superintendent, overseeing 39 such schools.

In authorizing the U.S. president to govern through a Philippine commission, Congress responded to anticolonialist sentiment in the United States by reiterating that the new government must secure the islanders' "free enjoyment of their freedom, property, and religion." All cabinet officers were to be Filipinos except for the secretary of the Department of Public Instruction—a noteworthy exception. Nonetheless, a public school system for the islands would require a trained and socialized corps of Filipino teachers. If "found competent and willing to perform the duties, they are to receive the offices in preference to any others," an invitation, first to local elites, to implement the invaders' mission.[98]

On a self-congratulatory note, *A Handbook of the Philippines* stated, "It was unheard of that a mother country should extend and plan a general common-school education for the inhabitants of her colony . . . [to] afford as great opportunities to the poor as to the rich."[99] Contemporary writers attributed the schooling campaign to "the conviction of the military leaders that no measure would so quickly restore tranquility throughout the archipelago." William Howard Taft, governor-general of the Philippines, said of the educational foundation being laid, "If the same spirit continues in the [Philippine] Government, [it] will prove to be the most lasting benefit which has been conferred on these islands by Americans."[100]

Sri Lankan historian K. M. de Silva, contends that, beyond force, a general feature of colonialism is "the acceptance of the total superiority of European culture," the non-European being held "in awe and psychological subordination."[101] Hardly had the Americans landed than some 100 Filipino students matriculated at mainland institutions, succeeding despite their limited English. Dolores Eleuteria Machado's degree (1900) from the University of California was immediately put to use in Philippine education.[102] The Philippine Normal School (f. 1901) and the University of the Philippines (f. 1908) were soon equipping other Filipinos to enter American schools and colleges on equal terms with white students.

Schooling "the Little Brown Brothers"

From their August 1901 arrival in Manila, the 530 American teachers were quickly and permanently labeled "Thomasites." Mostly young, the recruits were experienced teachers with normal school or college preparation; others followed, bringing teacher numbers close to 1,000. Men were the majority of Bureau of Education teachers: 75% of the Americans and 83% of the Filipinos. For the moment American men were responding to the fact that teaching in, say, Dumaguete offered more adventure and rewards than teaching in Dubuque or Daytona. While the Thomasites initially attracted crowds, complaints soon arose that Filipino children were too easily Americanized.

The new public system increased enrollments in all kinds of schools—including the Spanish-era's private and religious schools favored by expatriate European and American families. One, Colegio de la Inmaculada Concepcion, was preparing some Filipinas to teach. Overall, the estimated 150,000 primary school pupils of 1901 grew to one million by 1920. The results appeared to validate the jingoistic *Chicago Tribune* prediction that American-style public schools would accomplish more in two or three generations than Spanish rule had in three or four centuries.[103] Governor Juan Pimontel of Ambos Camarines Province commented, "There are no stronger Americanistas than those school children who have come within the sphere of the personal influence of the American teachers. Such converts to American ways and ideas are seldom if ever lost."[104]

Americans taught in every type of school, except *barrio* (rural village) schools. Fifty English-language schools opened on Sulu and Mindanao Islands among the Muslim Moro, where Californian Laura Lorine Donnelly was teaching. Despite fears that their American and Catholic Filipino teachers would proselytize Christianity, American authorities promised Muslims religious freedom. Nervous family and friends at home, reading sensational stories of wild tribes in some areas, were reassured that Luzon's fierce Igorrotes "hewed out materials for school buildings . . . in which a lone school-teacher instructs their children in perfect security amid a population of 8,000 'head hunters.'"[105]

The 3,160 public schools of 1906 were taught by 831 American and (by one report) 4,719 Filipino teachers.[106] By mainland standards the Americans' salaries were handsome—and consistently inequitable. Massachusetts's Philinda Rand and Indiana's Thaddeus Delos Anglemyer met and married in 1906; she taught for $2600, he for $3600.[107] Filipinos' salaries were smaller, and American teachers sometimes returned part of their salaries so that Filipino colleagues could be paid when a municipal treasury ran dry. As demand exceeded the supplies of teachers and schoolhouses, Philippine class size was typically twice or more the mainland's average of 36 pupils. Rightly or not, the teacher's task was judged easier because Filipino children were "not inclined to mischief or roistering. They become intensely interested in work that they comprehend"—leaving the teacher's tasks chiefly to motivate and clarify.[108]

As Americans were reassigned to new secondary schools and supervising public schools in underserved areas, Filipinos took their places, starting with the primary schools. Sofia Medina, a provincial high school teacher, and Pilar Zamora, preparatory teacher at the normal school in Manila, exemplify how quickly Filipinas freed themselves from many conservative Spanish attitudes toward women. They acquired more literacy, teacher training, and even university degrees than their menfolk, becoming an economic and political force. In the mid-1980s, when Sally Inguito graduated from high school in suburban Manila, Filipina schoolteachers were long entrenched, Sally's high school principal was a woman, and Filipino parents typically assumed their daughters would work wherever opportunity presented itself.[109]

Colonizing in the Caribbean

A repeated element in the Americanization of its Spanish colonies was sending selected overseas students to U.S. institutions, including those specializing in assimilation: Filipinos went to Oregon's Chemawa Indian School; Puerto Ricans, to Pennsylvania's Carlisle Indian School. Carlisle's military and vocational approach was already well tested with domestic blacks and Indians and thought workable for the 800,000 blacks in the Caribbean islands, along with the largely illiterate poor among their racially mixed population. As Booker T. Washington wrote in 1900, "To tell what has already been accomplished in the south under most difficult circumstances is to tell what may be done in Cuba and Porto Rico."[110] Cubans, however, were freed of American occupation after two years.

Expansionists, like the *Chicago Tribune*'s editors, argued for a comprehensive, Philippine-like educational approach in Puerto Rico: a basically American system of secular public schools conducted in English but teaching the principles of self-government. A department of education, created in 1900, began recruiting

American teachers to bring native Spanish speakers to English fluency. Teachers were imported from higher-paying U.S. states, most leaving within two years.[111] Raising literacy above the existing 20% meant recruiting Puerto Ricans to teach, in a society without a middle class and with few lay teachers. One, Rosario Andraca (b. 1873), began teaching at age 16, under Spanish times. As Señora Timothee, she retired in 1945 as principal of Lincoln School, named for the American president she idolized.[112]

Puerto Rico's first two secretaries of education, both Americans, sent about 60 volunteers to Carlisle Indian Industrial School in 1899 and more in 1901, including Juan José Osuna, a future dean of education at the University of Puerto Rico. Some decamped, academically disillusioned or offended by being classed with Indians; others adjusted, even valuing Norte Americano contacts. Concebida Duchesne lived with an American family while at Carlisle—her descendants claim that Carlisle made her an American—and attended Bloomsburg (PA) State Teachers College, probably with her sister, Francisca. Tia Conci returned to her homeland with Tia Paquita in the 1920s as English teachers, traveling daily to rural schools on mule back. Around 1930 both settled in the United States.[113]

Maria Tomasa Cadilla y Colón (b. 1886) was the hoped-for model. After some training in the United States, she returned to Puerto Rico in 1902. Through marriage and motherhood, she built a career as a schoolteacher and university professor. The University of Puerto Rico (f. 1903) was modeled after an American teachers college; by 1924, three of every four graduates were women.[114] When Julia de Burgos left the University of Puerto Rico in 1933 with a teaching certificate, the island's superintendent was Puerto Rican, as were the majority of its teachers and administrators.[115] Spanish remained the primary language of the population, with English taught as a second language with indifferent results.

Extending America's Reach after World War II

For the schools at the ten camps to which 110,000 West Coast Japanese Americans, like Stella Yorozu and Massaye Nagao, were sent in 1942, the War Relocation Authority used teachers' and administrators' experience in schooling Native Americans, although it might have come as readily from teaching Southern Negroes, native Hawaiians, or Filipinos. The BIA loaned Lucy Wilcox Adams (b. 1898) to the authority as its first Education Section head. However, Adams's Indian Service tenure came under liberal leadership, and her anthropological perspective brought a degree of idealism and progressive thinking into the programs she directed at the Manzanar (CA) camp.[116]

The war effort and its aftermath created other teaching sites. "Marie," an Air Force wife, taught all over the United States and in Asia: "There was always a job . . . [and] I was willing to do whatever was available, as long as it was teaching." Elizabeth Rodman (b. 1921) married William Shuey while in college and taught during his Navy service; the Shueys then taught for 20 years at international schools with the U.S. Agency for International Development.[117] Such examples were dwarfed, however, by the postwar spread of American schools where U.S. forces were stationed.

Seeking Democratic Reforms in Postwar Japan and Cold War Germany

Military forces and civilian advisors occupied Japan between 1945 and 1952, intent on bringing social and political change through decentralized authority, secularized rather than "divine" power, and legal rights for women in civic and family affairs. A degree of localism did emerge in school and university governance, and the junior high school took hold. Out of necessity, coeducation crept in—as building one school for both sexes made financial sense in a war-ravaged landscape. But Japan's faith in the endurance, within altered institutions, of traditional notions of gender roles and the family's hold on sex-role socialization also remained.

Washington State University's dean of women, Lulu H. Holmes, had taught at Kobe Women's College during a two-year leave in the 1930s.[118] Her prewar contacts brought her back to Japan in 1946 as higher education advisor in General MacArthur's military occupation and pacification mission. In 1940, 1% of Japan's women had received higher education, all in normal schools and women's colleges; Holmes was to increase and diversify females' opportunities. The prewar familiarity of Westernized Japanese women with American-style education and the wider perspective of Japanese men whose wives or daughters had studied abroad contributed to some change. In 1948, the University of Tokyo (Tokyo Daigaku) admitted 20 women to a nursing education program, the first of their sex in the institution's history. A few Japanese women entered American and European universities, this time for graduate studies where Japan most resisted women's educational ambitions.

The American military pressured Japan into writing a pacifist constitution, in effect making the United States Japan's "protector." American military and naval bases were established throughout the archipelago, bringing in another round of American teachers. Meanwhile, the wartime Allies—the United States, the Soviet Union, and the United Kingdom—divided a defeated Germany in the postwar period.[119] American officials wanted structural, democratizing reforms, especially inclusive, coeducational, and secular German secondary schools. By 1947, however, even in the American Zone, planning for a structurally unified, more egalitarian secondary education system lost priority to rebuilding West Germany's economy for waging the Cold War.[120]

Public Schools for Military Dependents:
A Bit of Home and Perhaps a Beacon

An American-style system materialized early in post–World War II Asia and Europe only in U.S. Department of Defense overseas schools for the minor children of active duty military and "direct hire" civilian personnel. Before 1940, branches of the United States military operated Domestic Dependents Elementary and Secondary Schools on selected bases, chiefly in the South, for the children of officers, enlisted men, and civilian employees, although families could use local public schools. The Military Academy at West Point had an elementary school, as did Fort Knox (KY). These schools in the South were originally created "to provide service members the option to send their dependents to non-segregated schools."[121]

In 1946, 38 "public" elementary and five high schools opened. Kubasaki High in Okinawa, Japan, and Heidelberg High in Germany date from 1946, as did the elementary school at Bentwaters Royal Air Force Base in England where Mary Meniktas Thodos (b. 1924) taught before returning home to resume a long classroom career.[122] Thus began an unprecedented system of schools for military dependent minors that appeared at many of the 700 bases and facilities maintained by the United States—enrolling an annual average of 160,000 students worldwide during the 1960s. Although some Department of Defense Education Activity (DoDEA) schools were in the United States and its territories, more were found in former possessions (the Philippines), conquered and occupied nations (Japan, Germany, Italy, Austria), and such sovereign nations as France, South Korea, and Turkey. There were still 23 schools and 5,000 students in the Kaiserslautern (Rhineland-Palatinate) District, 60 years after the first opened.

Given the sheer size and longevity of the program, DoDEA offered careers. Marlene D. Koenig retired after 14 years as a teacher and 12 as a principal. Dr. Ellen Minette taught at three postings in Germany before becoming principal of Heidelberg Middle School, and she was recognized as middle school principal of the year by the National Association of Secondary School Principals.[123] Government recruiters preferred single women, hired stateside. A number requested transfers from base to base, from Europe to the Pacific, to travel and experience different cultures before retiring or returning home. Others married military or civilian personnel they met on site, continued to teach, and changed schools

as their husbands were transferred; some married foreigners, including educators. DoDEA schools sometimes coexisted with American-sponsored private schools—some founded by nineteenth-century missionaries and attended
by the children of off-post military personnel, State Department employees,
businessmen, and expatriates.

The minimum professional requirements in the 1950s—a state certificate, two
years' experience, and a master's degree—were upgraded to seven years' experience and passing a standardized test of basic skills and professional knowledge.
Many applicants offered far more. Deborah Bridges had taught for 28 years when
she joined the history faculty at Mahaffey Middle School, Fort Campbell (KY), in
1999. That year Diana Ohman brought extensive stateside experience as an elementary school teacher and principal and Wyoming county and state superintendent to her position as DoDEA's deputy director for Europe.[124] As at home,
school psychologists and counselors were recruited, as were specialists in teaching preschoolers and students with disabilities. But much would be new.

As DoDEA students became "third culture kids," so did their teachers. Teaching in Germany, "Lee" took visitors to a tiny museum at Checkpoint Charlie. "We
had," she explained, "considered ourselves politically sophisticated," until a cray-
oned depiction of the Berlin Wall in the museum's display of drawings by German
grade-school students "pierced my pseudo-sophistication, and I never forgot it." A
child's insightful caption read, "The worst thing about the Wall is that people can
get used to anything."[125] Jack, an American teacher in Germany recalled the day
in 1989 that neither teachers nor students foresaw: "You've heard the joke about
'when my ship came in, I was at the airport.' When the Wall came down, I was out
of town," with some 20 other teachers from Berlin, "on a bus somewhere in West
Germany, following the 'Fairy Tale Road' of the Brothers' Grimm."[126]

In 1992 the Philippine government declined to renew the lease on U.S. bases.
Elsewhere, annual reductions and redeployments left 8,700 teachers and 84,000
pupils in the remaining 193 DoDEA schools in 2013—67 years after the first
opened. A smaller, more focused organization brought teacher-welcomed changes:
summer schools, reduced class sizes in the primary grades, and full-day kindergartens. The system's stated mission remained "to be among the world's leaders
in education, enriching the lives of military-connected students and [significantly]
the communities in which they live."[127]

Conclusion: Educational Exchange in a Postcolonial World

At least from 1806, when Samuel J. Mills met with other Williams College students
to consider "sending the gospel to Asia," resolute individuals spread American-style

education, culture, values, and prejudices.[128] While Spain used soldiers and priests—Filipinos called them "men in skirts"—to control and convert the Philippines, Guam, Cuba, and Puerto Rico, the United States enlisted schoolteachers in the work of pacification. With or without sponsorship, American women crossed cultural, social, and geographical boundaries to study, teach, even preach. Teaching the children of white frontiersmen in the raw common schools of the territories, from Oklahoma and the Dakotas to Alaska, also exposed often-youthful Easterners to culture shock, even as their labors helped ready these rough places for statehood.

Mission schools created successive generations of Western-leaning educators, most notably in China, by 1914 the largest source of foreign students at the vast summer schools operated by George Peabody College for Teachers.[129] The new International Institute of Teachers College, Columbia University (TC) immediately recruited educators, most notably from China. The Institute (f. 1923) became an unprecedented secular exporter of the latest in American educational ideals, ideas, and practices. During its first 15 years, more than 4,000 foreign students from 50 nations studied at TC under its aegis, while TC professors, students, and researchers visited overseas sites.[130] Foreign students were offered inspiration with a reformist bent, practical and theoretical training, and advanced degrees of use at home. Despite the patriarchal conservatism of their countries and the male leadership of TC's international initiatives, an unknown number were women. For example, a 1930s-era photo of TC alumni receiving Professor Paul Monroe at Canton's Lingnan University shows as many Chinese women as men in the delegation.

Whatever their situations, the American teachers were somehow altered by their experiences. In her *The Lady and Sada San* (1912), Fannie MacCauley expressed her debt to the Japanese she hoped to serve: "My gratitude to this little country is great. . . . But for nothing am I more thankful than for the love and friendship of the young girl-mothers who were my pupils, but from whom I have learned more of the sweetness and patience of life than I could ever teach."[131] Carriers and promoters of an alien, often "unwelcomed" or disdained culture—"saviors" to some, and "despoilers" to others—many "on their mission" were neither oblivious nor insensitive to the dissonance attending their duties. A sense of personal ineffectiveness or disillusionment with their efforts, even rebelliousness, crept into the personal writings and official reports of some sojourners.[132]

With women the majority of missionaries and institution builders in many mission stations, "woman's work for women" became a byword. Isabella Hall Tobey arrived in China in 1848 to carry on her sister's work: greater than "the few children learning their lessons at her side"—encompassing "a vision of educated

Chinese womanhood, with feet unbound and minds set free." The YWCA was added to missionary campaigns to emancipate Chinese girls and reproduce in China the West's "New Woman."[133] As some (perhaps many) recognized the cultural, political, and economic imperialism embedded in their work of promoting conversion and change, missionaries' concomitant discovery of a "global sisterhood and the essential unity of humankind was a valuable corrective to patriarchal notions that valued men over women and boys over girls in many parts of the world"—their own country included.[134]

CHAPTER 12

"The Feast of Reason and Flow of Soul"

The Political Rights and Civic Duties of Women

> Nothing since the coming of Christ promises so much good to
> future humanity as the intellectual, moral and political emanci-
> pation of women.
>
> —John Hyde Braly (1912)

In March 1870, five women were impaneled to serve on a mixed grand jury in Laramie, the wives of a physician, military clerk, merchant, and the court's deputy clerk, and Miss Elizabeth Stewart, a 37-year-old schoolmistress who had arrived from Crawford County (PA) the year before.[1] The women went to and from the courthouse heavily veiled, refusing to be photographed or interviewed for an event that received wide attention elsewhere. They dealt with the usual horse and cattle rustling, illegal branding, and murders. The women's presence and the leadership of Miss Stewart reportedly inhibited the standard bad behavior of male jurors—gambling, smoking, and drinking.

The oldest daughter of a family of nine siblings, at age 14 Stewart became a surrogate mother upon her mother's death. Fourteen years later she was valedictorian of her class at Washington (PA) Female Seminary, having taught winter schools to finance her studies. In every particular but her pioneering jury service, Miss Stewart's biography as an exemplary daughter and a devoted schoolteacher tells a familiar story.

Nearly 150 years later, we might still hear, "We don't want bad girls teaching our kids, after all (no 'Lola' or 'Roxy'); we want the safe, wholesome types—both matronly and unmarried." But, added this father of a 10-year-old daughter, "I secretly hope the right kind of 'bad girl' teaches her. After all, bad girls question authority, speak up in front of Congress, occupy Wall Street, and all those other bad things."[2] Lucy Stone (b. 1818) was clearly a bad girl, her resolve as hard as her name. In 1881, she wrote, "In education, in marriage, in religion, in everything, disappointment is the lot of women. It shall be the business of my life to deepen this disappointment in every woman's heart until she bows down to it no longer." Stone paid her way into and through Oberlin College by teaching; chose the Classical (not the Ladies) Course; formed a female debating society that met in secret, often in the home of a colored woman; refused to have a male deliver her commencement essay; and created a public scandal by marrying Henry Blackwell under the condition that she retain her own name. From 1847 her sole occupation was public advocacy of woman's rights.[3]

Three faces of the public woman—campaigner for woman's rights, involved citizen, and office seeker—constitute this chapter. It begins with the woman teacher's prominent part in broad-gauged (and international) feminist campaigns on behalf of woman suffrage (the term used then, and thus in this work), temperance, and woman's rights.[4] Next comes the more conventional, accepted woman's role: devoting herself to unpaid community service, but now energized by the suffrage battle and prepared to organize. Teachers, already public persons, were a natural choice to lead other women in projects for the common good. Women's success in enfranchising their sex then made it possible for women teachers to build upon a natural constituency should they aspire to public office—as they did in large numbers, from the local school board to Congress.

"He Has Denied Her"—Teachers as Feminists

Nevada's Lucy Stone Non-Partisan Equal Suffrage League was founded at an 1891 meeting by Frances Slaven Williamson (1842) and others. Through the league this career teacher, mother, and widow of a state senator led the campaign for a state suffrage resolution. Williamson exploited the views, tactics, and organizations of the larger woman's rights movement. In 1895, Susan B. Anthony and Anna Howard Shaw spoke at the first statewide public meeting of suffragists in Reno. *The Nevada Citizen,* which Williamson published with her daughter, gave its aim as "the advancement . . . of women in the ethics of civil government, ordained in the Declaration of Independence and established in the Constitution." Williamson worked unremittingly for woman suffrage, dying the year the Nineteenth Amendment passed Congress and Nevada began its ratification process.[5]

A widely known lecturer and writer on antislavery, woman suffrage, and peace issues, Lucretia Coffin Mott (b. 1793) learned something about inequality as a 13-year-old student at the sex-segregated Friends' boarding school at Nine Partners (NY) and as an unpaid assistant teacher at 15. "My sympathy was early enlisted for the poor slave, by the class-books read in our schools, and pictures of the slave ship," she recalled. "The unequal condition of women in society also early impressed my mind. . . . I early resolved to claim for my sex all that an impartial Creator had bestowed."[6]

An experienced teacher at 18, Minnesota's Sarah Jane Christie (b. 1844) also trusted in the essential equality of the sexes as creations of the Almighty. Therefore, she took her father to task for his comments about her plan to further her own academy education:

> It really made me vexed when you said that Algebra was a "Masculine attainment" like as if I could not learn it as well as any "Masculine" I ever saw, and maybe a great deal better than some, without killing me either. . . . I guess that if the "Masculine" got the same teaching and the same ideas crammed into them which the "Feminine" get about their not being anybody, they would be just as helpless, weak, vain, miserable things as the generality of Females are.[7]

As a student at the Framingham Normal School from 1856 to 1858, Frances Merritt attended to her instructor's opinion on the Woman Question: "There is so much truth in what Mr. Stearns said to-day of women's mission. His view seems to be just the right one. Better exercise the influence God has given her over the heart, mind and will of all mankind in the most lovely and becoming manner, than to speak about women's rights, or to step out of her Heaven-ordained sphere." However, her diary also comments on Dorothea Dix, a former teacher testing prevailing notions of woman's sphere with her lecturing, debating, and political confrontation: "an unexpected visit from that noted lady and philanthropist Miss Dix occurred today . . . a woman great from good deeds."[8]

As state normal schools and avant-garde female seminaries invited women lecturers on moral and political issues of the day, questions of equal suffrage and woman's grievances intruded into females' social discourse. Their private papers show present and future teachers becoming a significant segment of the women who gathered tens of millions of signatures on thousands of petitions before full suffrage was won in 1920. An impressive number also took other public and private actions, campaigning to influence not only families and friends but also legislators, newspaper editors, college officials, and public opinion general. Some undoubtedly influenced their pupils' thinking about "woman's rights and wrongs."

Constructing a School of Equal Rights for Women

The woman's rights convention held at Seneca Falls (NY) in July 1848 became the enduring symbol of an emergent feminist consciousness.[9] Its manifesto and list of woman's grievances included mankind's "history of repeated injuries and usurpations . . . having in direct object the establishment of an absolute tyranny over her." She was deprived of "her inalienable right to the elective franchise," and the married woman was, "in the eye of the law, civilly dead." By denying her "the facilities for obtaining a thorough education, all colleges being closed against her[,] . . . he has endeavored, in every way he could, to destroy her confidence in her own powers, to lessen her self-respect, and to make her willing to lead a dependent and abject life." Of the convention's five organizers—Elizabeth Cady Stanton, Mary Ann McClintock, her sister Elizabeth McClintock Phillips, Jane Hunt, and Lucretia Coffin Mott—four had taught school.[10]

Over 75 years the movement's best known leaders—Mott, Anthony, Stanton, Stone, Amelia Bloomer, Frances Willard, Carrie Chapman Catt—repeatedly invoked the Declaration of Independence's preamble on equality.[11] Of the seven named, all born between 1783 and 1820, again all but Stanton had taught. Yet these names do not come close to exhausting the list of teachers among the "first fiddles" of the various crusades for, and by, women. The most selective list of other well-known feminists must include these other teachers: Ida Wells-Barnett, Mary McLeod Bethune, Antoinette Brown Blackwell, Lydia Maria Child, Anna Dickinson, Margaret Fuller, Sarah and Angelina Grimké, Sarah Joseph Hale, Mother Jones, Abigail Kelley Foster, Caroline Severance, Mary Church Terrell, and Emma Willard.

Unremembered but more numerous woman's rights advocates included the members of the Iowa State Teachers Association, who passed a resolution favoring woman suffrage in 1857—a dozen years before Iowa's first woman suffrage association was formed and 62 years before Iowa ratified the Constitution's Nineteenth Amendment. The army of now-obscure suffragists included Isabel M. Kelren, a teacher at the Parkman School, who acknowledged being an activist member of the South Boston Woman Suffrage Club—writing articles, petitioning, and lobbying state legislators in the 1870s.[12]

Teaching is second only to writing as the primary career in the 1,470 biographies in *A Woman of the Century* (1893), and a number did both.[13] The book's compilers, former teachers Frances Willard and Mary Livermore, were among the nineteenth century's best-known agitators. Other suffragists included schooled Easterners who went west to teach, then married, joined the early ranks of permanent settlers, and became political activists or served in quieter ways.[14] Fannie Gordon's sisters were noted suffragists, while she supported their efforts by running their joint household while she herself worked as the teacher-principal of a New Orleans public school.[15]

Even before Seneca Falls, the schoolmistress knew the injustices named by the assembled women. Fannie McLean (b. 1864?) often exclaimed, "I would rather talk to a body of teachers on the subject of equal suffrage than to any other people, for we are the most obviously and vitally interested in the matter. . . . We need the ballot for our personal advantage, for the uplift of our profession, and for the increase of our value to society"—spoken like a true Gertrude. A voteless woman presided over 83% of California's classrooms in 1910, yet while "other women are the mothers of one, two or three children; she is the mother of hundreds, nay, of thousands in her lifetime." The state's high schools graduated nearly twice as many girls as boys; girls deprived of the vote thus deprived society of the contributions of the educated.[16]

In 1915, Walter Lippmann described women's enlistment in the equal suffrage movement as "evoking a wider popular response than perhaps any political reform in history."[17] Viewed historically, woman suffrage "was the single most important democratic movement in this country, and it brought the vote to more people than any other effort to extend the franchise. But that is just the point history books do not make."[18] With teachers the majority of educated employed women, their voiced grievances received wide play in suffragist publications.[19]

WOMEN TEACHERS: "A SPECIAL FITNESS FOR THE FRANCHISE"

How can we explain the frequency of teaching experience in the lives of these and untold numbers of other activists? The answer was simple for Robert Riegel: "good family, intelligence, superior education.[20] But teacher feminists were not invariably so blessed. Was it because of their large numbers in the general population of women? In part, certainly, but far more American women never taught, even in the Northeast. The Ockham's razor Riegel invokes simply trims away too much, ignoring factors present in teachers' experiences.

Many emergent feminists found sufficient grievances within teaching to raise their hackles; at the least their situations lent concreteness to wider claims of inequality in nineteenth-century America. Harriot Hunt described herself as left "pinched, degraded, condemned, accused, weary, and miserable" by the low regard for teaching she witnessed; she practiced medicine instead and refused to pay taxes. Frances Knox was outraged when the Austin (MN) High School hired her for less than the men: "I get more and more disgusted every year at the way in which women are abused in the matter of salaries. That a [university] class mate whom I kept up with for five years whom I invariably left in the rear in Greek should get twice what I receive and do half the work makes me most righteously indignant. I think I shall put on pants and go west."[21]

As a young Pittsburgh teacher, Lizzie Wilkinson (b. 1838) devoured Jane Swisshelm's columns, tracking feminists' speeches and actions. Later, as Mrs. Elizabeth Ward—married teacher, principal, and mother of two—she put school affairs (and woman's rights issues, like divorce laws) in a critical light, writing for the *Pittsburgh Leader* as "Bessie Bramble." Of the "boy principal" in 1883, she wrote, "Our thick-headed school directors will take a young man so green the cows would eat him, and give him the highest position in a school, where he may or may not prove a success, usually not."[22]

In 1917, in the hectic final months of the campaign for nationwide female suffrage, Margaret McNaught, commissioner of elementary education in the California State Department of Education, exhorted elementary school teachers and principals, "The woman school teacher has not only a special fitness for the franchise, but a special need to make use of it." Woman suffrage was achieved in some Western states, won in part from approving communities as recognition of teachers' "arduous service." Their victory was "due largely to an unnumbered host of young women who some fifty years ago resolved to be self-supporting, self-directing and independent; who, to that end, entered schools and offices and shops and not only went to work but demanded pay for the work even as men were paid."[23]

Obligatory male missionary work and male plural marriage deprived observant Mormon women of their husbands' company, undermined notions of romantic love, and led some to a sense of sisterhood that promoted emotional independence and economic self-sufficiency. Despite national opposition to polygamy, Susan B. Anthony welcomed Utah's Mormon teacher suffragists.[24] In New York Charles Evan Hughes's presidential campaign against Woodrow Wilson was beset by women speakers and writers, reminding voters that, as governor, Hughes had vetoed a 1907 equal pay bill for teachers. Those working for that bill included 14,000 New York City women teachers.[25]

When asked to reflect upon the suffragist and pacifist activities in which she participated, architect Florence Luscomb (b. 1887) said, "Just why seeing women walk down the street in a parade should convince men to vote for suffrage is a mystery, but it did so by the thousands. Probably because it gave the visual proof that the women who wanted the suffrage were ordinary representative women— homemakers, mothers, daughters, teachers, working women—and not the unsexed freaks the anti's declared they were."[26] Luscomb spoke a probable truth, especially for teachers.

Teaching's simple requirements attracted many unexceptional women. One did not have to be exceptional to partake of the enlightening possibilities inherent in teaching; modest daring usually sufficed. How ironic that an otherwise unremarkable woman could, as teacher, act the subversive: presenting her pupils with an achievable "model for a new definition of womanhood."[27] However, rebels of another stripe also entered teaching or became radicalized. Kate Kennedy of San Francisco and Catherine Goggin of Chicago, under the respectable (and underestimated) shelter of teaching, unionized their colleagues.[28] Convents and provincial houses bred their own "winged souls" protecting their communal autonomy; defiance could hide under a wimple as well as under those large, encumbering hats that helped reassure enough voters about suffragists' residual conventionality.[29]

As female self-confidence and powers grew, so did their perceptions of the points where available power needed to be directed. Belle Kearney recalled those "days of quiet growth for me" teaching in all-white Mississippi schools: "Poor little homes were entered and parents met who had lived within two miles of our plantation since my early childhood, but who were unknown to me.... [Their] poverty and ignorance ... became a positive burden on my soul." Comfortable and cultured homes also harbored pathologies. "When the serious business of life commenced, there came a recognition of the dreadful havoc drunkenness had made in the homes about me."[30] The Louisville Free Kindergarten Association added social science to its curriculum because teachers are "social agents" and "come into immediate contact with the chief social problems of the day, especially in the free kindergarten work, and therefore require all possible information regarding cause and solution of the same."[31]

The shared experiences of the workplace brought teachers into sororal networks independent of traditional family and neighborhood associations, school friendships, and even nationalities. Women teachers forged links with others of their sex: their fellow teachers, their pupils' mothers, housewives with whom they boarded, church- and clubwomen, sometimes even pupils. These linkages, through occupational affinities, paralleled those that men historically possessed and exploited for their purposes.[32]

Teachers' voices for woman's rights and other unpopular causes came in regional accents beyond New England's. Abigail Scott Duniway was the leading exponent of woman suffrage and gender equality on the Pacific Coast; her no-nonsense, populist remark—"One-half of the women are dolls, the rest of them are drudges, and we're all fools!"—was among her least outrageous sermons against the complacency of both sexes about gendered roles.[33] Every Intermountain West and Midwest state featured teachers in local and statewide suffrage work. The antebellum American South was home ground to softer-spoken "genteel Ladies" with both feminist and antislavery views—although later white suffragists generally remained silent about civil rights and Negro suffrage.

WOMAN SUFFRAGE FOR WOMAN'S RIGHTS
AND HUMAN RIGHTS

Suffragists involved themselves in local, state, and national campaigns of reform and rescue that ranged, over time, from abolitionism, moral purity, married women's property rights, and temperance to child labor, the ten-hour day, prison and asylum reform, Indian rights, conservation, good-government initiatives, family planning, world peace, consumer protection, pure food and drug laws, and more. A growing number of liberal-minded Americans considered woman suffrage necessary, if not sufficient, to realizing any of these objectives. But more women needed to speak out. In 1881, Alice S. Pierce (b. 1860) wrote to her fiancé of her participation in a public debate while teaching in small-town Ohio: "The women are not in the habit of attending but it is my desire they should. . . . Some of the District think me queer because I am in favor of Debates but never the less I am. . . . The question for Debate tomorrow evening is Resolved that Ministers not join in Political discussions. I take the affirmative. . . . This world would amount to nix if I could not talk or write."[34]

Early on, white Southerners perceived a "symbiotic and inseparable connection" between the woman's rights movement and abolitionism.[35] A number of women abolitionists, notably Lucretia Mott and the Grimké sisters, came to view women's status as a form of slavery. Sarah Grimké (b. 1792) and Angelina Grimké Weld (b.1805) were among the first American women to speak in public; both taught school at various times and for lengthy periods. "The whole land seems aroused to discussion of the province of women, and I am glad of it," Angelina Grimké wrote in 1837. "We are willing to bear the brunt of the story, if we can only be the means of making a break in the wall of public opinion, which lies in the way of woman's rights, true dignity, honor and usefulness."[36] Abbie Hopper Gibbons and Maria Chapman were teachers, as were at least half of the feminist abolitionists.[37] Feminist abolitionists developed organizational and tactical skills, and they formed personal networks that figured in the broader woman's rights crusade, including temperance.

The attack on patriarchy was among what author John Updike later called "the cracked eggs of the feminist litany." Suffragists understood that patriarchy's "resilient persistence" included "elevating women in order to subdue them" and that the "natural laws" of a sentimental God were no less deterministic than the Catholic or Puritan versions. In praising states whose voters had enfranchised women, Georgia suffragist Rebeca Latimer Felton—born to Georgia slaveholders in 1835, a teacher remembered as the first woman appointed to the U.S. Senate—observed that Southern men "have given the Southern women more praise than the man of the West—but judged by their actions Southern men have been less sincere. Honeyed phrases are pleasant to listen to, but the sensible women of our country would prefer more substantial gifts."[38]

The political chaos of secession, the devastation of a civil war fought mostly on Southern soil, and fond references arising in the 1890s about antebellum times and the "Lost Cause," generally suppressed Southern feminism or channeled it into the temperance movement. Felton was an exception. Her indignation on behalf of teachers was widely shared: "A callow youth can vote at 21, while his capable teacher, if a woman, is forbidden to vote." She described antisuffragists as "those who prefer to hug their chains," serfs "in mind, body or estate— . . . content to allow negro men superior voting privileges to themselves." Despite her rabid white-supremacist views, Felton courageously noted aloud that "it was 'property rights in slaves' that forced on the War of Secession. It is now called 'State's rights.'"[39]

THE "COLOR LINE" IN THE WOMAN'S RIGHTS CRUSADE

Were Negro teachers also strong for suffrage? Mary Church Terrell (b. 1863) suggested why colored women—bearing "through an unfriendly world, the burden of race as well as that of sex"—might be wary of making common cause with white activists. Because many Negroes were deeply offended by the negative images of colored women left by slavery and racism, their woman's rights work was differently contextualized. It was Frances Watkins Harper's concern with domestic morality that fueled her antislavery lecturing and later writings on behalf of temperance, education, and woman's rights.[40]

Adella Hunt Logan (b. 1863) named her youngest child for white suffragists, Isabel and Emily Howland, and directed the suffrage work of the Women's Club at Tuskegee Institute where she taught in its normal and model schools. Knowing of racism within the suffrage movement, Logan often campaigned in Alabama, Louisiana, and Ohio by passing as white.[41] Mary Ann Shadd Cary (b.1823), among the best-known Negro women of her era, shared the speakers' platform with white suffragists at the 1878 convention of the National Woman Suffrage Association. When a large demonstration on behalf of the federal suffrage amendment was held in Chicago in 1916, Ida Bell Wells-Barnett (b. 1862) and other suffrage clubwomen marched with their white counterparts.[42] However, many white suffragists displayed prejudice or tactical concerns that interracial collaboration would impede the woman's rights movement.

Tennessee's antisuffrage leader, Josephine Pearson, questioned the motives of Mrs. Catt, "marching through the streets of New York, with a negro woman on either side of her! . . . thus proclaiming her ideal of the supremacy of the negro-race that threatens the South if Federal Suffrage should ever come to us?"[43]

Antisuffrage bitterness was kept fresh by Negrophobia after ratification of the Nineteenth Amendment.

"Missionaries of the Gospel of the New Democracy"

At age 15 a Midwestern schoolgirl, Julia Brown, described herself as "very strong for woman's rights, you know. I think I shall become a second Susan B. Anthony.[44] Brown labored, unremembered, for equal suffrage while teaching school and founding libraries. Her idol, Susan Brownell Anthony (1820–1906), was called "the drillmaster of the little company of soldiers in the war for female equality," its premier organizer and manager. As a schoolgirl, Anthony asked her teacher why he taught long division only to boys. He replied that girls needed to know only how to read the Bible and count their egg money. Anthony was paid a fraction of a male teacher's wages at the Friends School of Philadelphia and a rural school near Hard Scrabble (NY). Although Rochester schools paid better, her savings after 15 years of teaching and frugal living totaled only $300.

Anthony was first active in temperance work; attempting to speak at a Sons of Temperance convention in 1852, she was admonished, "The sisters were not invited to speak but to listen and learn." Walking into education conventions, "Miss Anthony, with her staid Quaker face and firm step," would take a conspicuous seat, "as if to say, Gentlemen, here I am again, to demand that you recognize as your equals, the hundreds of women . . . teachers, who sit in these conventions, without a voice or vote in your proceedings." Eventually women were admitted as full members of the New York State Teachers' Association. But, as Elizabeth Cady Stanton said, "The multiplication table and spelling book no longer enchained her thoughts; larger questions began to fill her mind." By 1865 Anthony was the militant, full-time leader of feminist legend: speaking in Negro churches, to labor conventions, to college women, in every statewide suffrage campaign—and, yes, at teachers' conventions.[45]

Another former New York teacher, Amelia Jencks Bloomer reportedly introduced Anthony to Stanton. Of the consequences Stanton wrote, "Whenever we saw a work to be done, we would together forge our thunderbolts, in the form of resolutions, petitions, appeals, and speeches, on every subject—temperance, anti-slavery, woman's rights, agriculture, education, and religion—uniformly accepting every invitation to go everywhere, and do everything."[46]

In 1880 Amelia Bloomer wrote of "woman's place" as it existed in Council Bluffs (IA): "The trustees of the public library of this city are women, the teachers in the public schools, with one or two exceptions, are women, the principal of the high school is a woman, and a large number of the clerks in the dry-goods stores are women." She committed her newspaper, the *Lily,* to "The Emancipation of

Woman from Intemperance, Injustice, Prejudice and Bigotry." It captured a widening circle of subscribers and contributors moved by her logic: "While she demands a law that entirely prohibits the traffic in strong drink, let her also obtain a right to a voice in making all laws by which she is to be governed."[47]

By the later nineteenth century many women saw, in their political nullity, a root cause of social evils. Raised in a prohibitionist family, Mary Evelyn Dobbs (b. 1870) attended Emporia State Normal School; she taught for 11 years before becoming an officer of the Kansas Woman's Christian Temperance Union (WCTU). One of the emissaries her branch sent into schoolhouses to lecture on prohibition was a Mrs. [Clara M.?] Crane. After Crane's visit to the school in Millwood (KS) in 1887, the teacher reported that "she gave the youngster some good advice if they'd a took it instead of making fun after she was gone."[48]

Thomas Wentworth Higginson described Margaret Fuller Ossoli's brief life (1810–1850), even more than her book, *Woman in the Nineteenth Century* (1845), as a work undertaken on behalf of "the intellectual enfranchisement of American women."[49] However, it was political enfranchisement that Wisconsin farm girl Carrie Clinton Lane (b. 1859) craved, worked for, and brought to fruition. She gave her first speech at a teachers' institute when she was 18, linking women's education and woman suffrage. Teaching paid her fees at Iowa State College. On graduating she was first teacher, then teaching principal at Mason City High School. Promoted to school superintendent in 1883, she was forced to relinquish her position in 1885 when she married Leo Chapman. Soon widowed, she turned to suffrage organizing and lecturing before remarrying (becoming Mrs. Catt), and taking center stage.

Representing the new professional woman—"diplomatic, and politic and shrewd"—Carrie Catt turned suffrage gatherings "from recitals of grievances to programmed discussions of the current debasement of politics by electoral corruption, and the usurpation of power by political machines," featuring progressive speakers advocating a comprehensive platform of reforms that could be achieved with women's votes.[50] She was Susan B. Anthony's choice to replace her when age and wear caused Anthony to resign as head of the National American Woman Suffrage Association. Thus in 1900 one former teacher replaced another.

In the six months before New York State's referendum on woman suffrage in 1915, women held 10,300 meetings and printed and circulated 7.5 million leaflets. Amid intense publicity the campaign culminated in a parade in which 20,000 marched along New York City's Fifth Avenue. On Election Day 6,330 women watched at the polls from 5:45 in the morning through the vote counting. The referendum lost, despite receiving 535,000 votes in an election in which no woman could vote.

Catt responded by reiterating that literate, informed, and moral women (exemplified by schoolteachers) were denied what illiterate, ignorant, and dissolute men possessed: the vote. In Rochester the male inmates of the almshouse and rescue home were taken out to vote against the amendment. Men too drunk to sign their own names voted all over the state. "I do feel keenly that the turn of the road has come," Catt wrote to Maud Wood Park in 1916. "Come! my dear Mrs. Park, gird on your armour once more."[51] The following year the New York suffrage referendum passed. With the nation's largest state captured, the forces supporting a federal measure were heartened and soon triumphant.

ANOTHER FIRST AMONG EQUALS: FRANCES E. WILLARD

Although associated with the American Southwest, the nature writer Mary Hunter Austin (b. 1868) grew up in central Illinois: in a town on a railroad line that brought political candidates (including Abraham Lincoln), temperance orators, and others seeking an audience and converts. One of her intimate memories came with "the first woman who . . . [spoke] in our church on the right of women to refuse to bear children to habitual drunkards, and my mother . . . taking my hand in one of the few natural gestures of a community of woman interest she ever made toward me."[52] But most she remembered Frances Willard.

No teacher-feminist, except her friend Susan B. Anthony, won more attention than the incomparable Frances Elizabeth Caroline Willard (b. 1838). More than 20,000 people reportedly viewed Willard's casket on her death in 1898. (It is also said that no American surpasses Willard in having schools bear her name—remarkable, if true, given the ubiquity of schools named for George Washington, Abraham Lincoln, Horace Mann, and other male worthies.) President of the national WCTU, Willard displayed zeal, oratorical flair, and strategic talents rivaling Anthony's own.

Willard's feminist consciousness bloomed early. As an adolescent in Wisconsin Territory she recalled an event that "helped to stir up my spirit into a mighty unrest": Election Day when her 21-year old brother, Oliver, in his "Sunday best," drove off with their father and the hired men. To even question the unfairness of being left behind was to be labeled the dreaded "strong minded" female.[53]

Before becoming a full-time woman's rights and temperance activist, Willard, an 1859 graduate of North-Western Female College, taught in small schools in Illinois, in Kankakee Academy, several female seminaries, and, in 1871, as president and dean of the Evanston College for Ladies. While teaching she campaigned, unsuccessfully, to have woman suffrage made part of the Illinois state constitution. To women who said they did not need the vote, that their menfolk would represent their interests, Willard scoffed that "the idea that boys of twenty-one are fit to make laws for their mothers, in an insult to everyone."[54]

Temperance and prohibition organizations were quintessentially feminist in criticizing male behavior: the drunkard symbolic of a more general male culpability and oppression. America was a hard-drinking society through the nineteenth century. Commercial and homemade spirits were plentiful and cheap, a worker's wages might include a "daily dram," and an employed woman could not withhold her wages from her drunkard husband or dispute his custody of their children. Texas teacher Edie Gist Williams fumed, "[A] woman was not even allowed to go in [a saloon] and drag her drunk husband out." Although Irish saloons, German brewers, and beer halls were favorite targets of nativists and temperance orators, intemperance was not limited to immigrants or the poor. The men of the famed Adams family, at the center of the Northeast's Protestant establishment, had an intergenerational history of alcoholism, and the Adams women dealt with the consequences.[55]

Mary Emma Smith Holmes (b. 1839) came into temperance work through her father's influence. As a Maine seaman he asked that his allowance of "grog" (rum) be paid in money, and he progressed to master of a merchant vessel whose crew all took the temperance pledge. His daughter taught school in her native Peoria (IL) for six years, freely choosing the city's poorest neighborhood. She then combined marriage and motherhood with teaching and holding office in county and state temperance and suffrage societies. Collective activism, from signing petitions to demonstrating and civil disobedience, drew such women together.[56] Another teacher, Carrie Amelia Moore Nation (b. 1846), whose physician husband died of alcoholism, became notorious for attacking saloon property with her ax.

Martha Lupher Hawthorne, married to an intemperate man, told her 12-year-old son, Mont, that she had "looked into it and she figgered the laws of Nebraska was even harder on women than the teachings of Paul. No matter how hard a woman tries she couldn't hope to rise above her husband." Mont remembered, "It wasn't just our home or our valley, neither. I've knowed of many a country school where the only children walking through the door in shoes was the ones belonging to the saloon keeper."[57] Mont pledged never to drink alcohol—except medicine prescribed by a doctor, while "Mama pinned on the white ribbon-bow of the WCTU."

The world's largest nineteenth-century organization, with thousands of local units, a quarter million members and another million adolescent girls in youth auxiliaries in the United States alone, the WCTU was organized in 1874 by anti-suffrage women from 17 states. It initially appealed to churchwomen as a "blessed antidote to the radicalism, fanaticism, and blunders of the woman-suffrage associations."[58] By 1881, however, when Susan B. Anthony attended a WCTU convention as a visitor, she was warmly greeted. Francis Willard, elected corresponding secretary at the WCTU's 1879 meeting, soon led the suffrage bloc that unseated a conservative president. Willard knew how to help women "out of their swathing femininity."[59] Without denying those who trumpeted the domestic sphere, this slight, pretty spinster gently preached women's independence. In 1882 the WCTU endorsed woman suffrage and allied itself with the National Woman Suffrage Association (NWSA).

By the late 1880s, the political link between NWSA and state and local WCTU units was perhaps the most helpful element in the white South. Mississippi's Belle Kearney (b. 1863) remarked, "For over nine years Miss Willard had been more to me than any woman who lived, except my mother." On the other side of the South's racial divide, Della Haydn was inspired to found the Virginia State Teachers' Temperance Union in 1888; it soon had 600 members.[60] The WCTU surpassed every women's reform group in the breadth of its defined mission and the relentlessness of its activities. As Willard often said, "Everything is not in the temperance movement, but the temperance movement should be in everything."

THE ANTISUFFRAGE POSITION AND JOSEPHINE PEARSON

In the University of California (Berkeley) Library's copy of Rev. Horace Bushnell's *Women's Suffrage: The Reform against Nature* (1869), an unknown reader penned this verse on a flyleaf: "O woman! in our hour of ease, / Uncertain coy, and hard to please, / And variable as the shade / By the light quivering aspen made." Beneath it and in another hand came this retort: "They are too variable to suit political bosses."[61]

Bushnell and the other men and women who opposed woman suffrage argued along three main lines. First was that it was unnecessary: men already voted women's interests—or would if all women "knew" their own best interests. Second, the very laws of nature put politics and the science of government beyond women's competency or inclination. Third, voting would coarsen women's character, increase immorality, unnecessarily divide families, and grievously undermine the male chivalry, sentimental generosity, and protectiveness that made women "the subordinate but not inferior sex."

In 1873 a group of women petitioned Congress to resist proposals for woman suffrage, giving rise to the National Association Opposed to the Extension of Woman Suffrage (NAOWS). Active and former women teachers among the "antis" included a Minnesota high school mathematics teacher, Minnie Bronson, general secretary of NAOWS.[62] Sarah B. Cooper (b. 1835), founder of San Francisco's Golden Gate Kindergarten, challenged in an 1872 article the need and worth of woman suffrage: "Prudent, well advised motherly diplomacy need not fear to cope with the keenest political machiavellian astuteness. . . . Are not all avenues of trade, and all the higher professions, now open to womanly competition?"[63] Yet Mrs. Cooper later spoke to her fellow kindergarten teachers as women workers laboring "with one arm paralyzed or bound up—very tenderly, very lovingly, but still very firmly in a sling."[64]

Mildred Lewis Rutherford (b. 1851) and Josephine Pearson (b. 1868) were two stalwart Southern opponents of woman suffrage and its supposed consequences. Briefly an Atlanta public school teacher, Rutherford was closely identified with the Lucy Cobb Institute in Athens (GA), a girls school founded by her uncle; she taught there and was its principal from 1880 to 1926. Rutherford's career and social and political views fit the Old South better than the New.[65] Teaching in private sex-segregated schools, comfortable with their "refinement" and chaperonage, and given to invoking the Confederacy and states' rights, she opposed woman suffrage.

As teacher-leader of the Tennessee State Association Opposed to Woman Suffrage, Josephine Pearson's antisuffragism also fit within a mosaic of Southern opinions.[66] The Southern Women's League for the Rejection of the Susan B. Anthony Amendment, of which Pearson was Tennessee division president, lobbied state legislatures to prevent ratification, later claiming that the ratifications were illegal. In 1920 Pearson wrote, as the "fate of white civilization in the South may hang on a few votes, let your neighbors and your representatives know where you stand in this great battle for State Rights, Honor, and the safety of Southern civilization." If men allowed suffragists to persuade them "it would be submissive Adam again succumbing to persistent Eve."

Born in Gallatin, only child of Rev. Philip Anderson Pearson and Amanda Roscoe Pearson, Josephine's formal education began with her parents and continued at the local Howard Female College, where she excelled, and the collegiate department of the coeducational Irving College in McMinnville, where her father was principal. Pearson began her career at Irving College, teaching piano and voice, before taking on her mother's courses in dramatics and literature. Except at McMinnville's public high school (1890–1894)—whose superintendent described her as "a woman of tremendous energy: quick, shrewd, and fearless"— and South Carolina's Winthrop State Normal College for Women (1897–1899), Pearson's career led through a half dozen mostly small single-sex institutions long characterizing Southern education.

Josephine Pearson linked her political and professional activities without apology: "For several years it had been my privilege, by my pen, in my class-room and on the platform, to give the best within me for the cause of Anti-Suffrage."[67] In 1909, while teaching in Missouri, she claimed to have read about European suffrage activities and traveled to several Western suffrage states—"with an open mind, to collect data." Pearson claimed her "long and unswerving steadfastness of purpose" in opposing votes for women hurt her professionally. She was not rehired by Christian (Columbia) College. Whether either intolerance of her opinions (as she claimed) or using her classrooms to proselytize the "anti" cause explain the college's decision is unknown.

Pearson viewed the suffragists who came to Tennessee in August 1920 for the ratification struggle as latter-day carpetbaggers and believed the Nineteenth Amendment threatened "utter disintegration of southern sentiments and law and order" and "complete demoralization, when the black female of the species comes into her Sable rights!"[68] Seeing younger suffragist daughters among her close friends, neighbors, and advisors, Pearson may have felt most embittered toward Southern "turncoats." Around 1916 state suffragists proposed to add woman suffrage as a plank in the platform of the Tennessee Federation of Women's Clubs. Tennessee congressmen helped pass the suffrage amendment and send it to the states to ratify or reject. The vote in Tennessee's upper house was 25 for and 4 against; in the lower house, 49–47; the majority of Tennessee's representatives had deserted Pearson's Red Rose Brigade, the 38 Tennessee legislators opposing woman suffrage.

A staunch supporter of the suffrage amendment was Charl O. Williams, Shelby County's school superintendent. During the legislature's ratification session, Williams waved a telegram from a meeting in Memphis of 250 white teachers: "Shelby County Institute met this morning. Miss you, but want you there until the amendment is ratified. We are with you. Stay on the job." As Williams explained, "I told them that every vote I got for ratification meant just that much for 20,000 school children of the county."[69] Pearson called Williams's action another assault by "the teacher force in this country." She accused the "educators' trust for suffrage" of holding Southern women teachers and college girls in thrall.[70] Williams was soon to become the National Education Association's most influential woman, first as a field secretary and then as president.

Pearson would have thought her point confirmed when President D. B. Johnson of all-white Winthrop Normal and Industrial College—in South Carolina, no less—wrote to Teachers College, Columbia, after passage of the Nineteenth Amendment. He wanted to employ "the most forward-looking suffragist, most capable, most dynamic teacher of social science[:] to come to Winthrop [to prepare students] to participate in the affairs of their state and community, to be more informed so they will vote intelligently."[71]

Enfranchising Women: An International
Community of Interest and Action

In August 1920 Tennessee, in the most antisuffrage section of the United States, became the 36th and decisive state to ratify the Nineteenth Amendment to the U.S. Constitution, 72 years after the Seneca Falls convention. Various nations had already enfranchised women, including Australia, Canada, Czechoslovakia, Mexico, New Zealand, and Russia. Although California achieved state suffrage in 1911 "in an orderly and dignified manner," Fannie McLean would not condemn those "sisters" who felt forced to act militantly elsewhere. In 1913 she predicted, "50 years from now when most of us will be forgotten, [England's] Mrs. Pankhurst will be the Joan of Arc in the history of woman's enfranchisement."[72]

Custom, law, and government everywhere created a man's world that disenfranchised an entire sex, despite historical and cultural differences among nations. "The man without a country was a tragic exception; the woman without a country was the accepted rule," Katherine Anthony (b. 1877) pointed out in 1915. "The vision of the emancipated woman wears the same features, whether she be hailed as *frau, fru,* or *woman*." An Arkansas teacher turned author, Anthony explained that enfranchising women came "too late to inculcate in them the narrow views of citizenship which were once supposed to accompany the gift of the vote." She predicted—correctly, it appears—that a "conscious internationalism" would grow from women's pursuit of these common goals.[73]

Middle-class Anglo-Canadian women teachers, like Ada Mary Brown Courtise (b. 1860), organized other women, as did Australia's Annie Montgomerie Martin (b. 1841), one of the officers of South Australia's Women's Suffrage League, and Vida Goldstein (b. 1869). An elementary school teacher, Ethel Annakin married British politician Philip Snowden and converted him to woman suffrage; like many suffragists she promoted other causes, including legalizing birth control.[74]

Reform in Victorian England by middle- and upper-class women began on behalf of England's army of ill-trained and poverty-stricken governesses, abetted by the rediscovery of *A Vindication of the Rights of Women* (1792), written by one of their number, Mary Wollstonecraft. England's suffrage movement was so identified with women teachers that they were caricatured in several popular novels, including H. G. Wells's *Ann Veronica* (1909) and Clemence Dane's *Regiment of Women* (1917). Teachers were 40% of all unmarried professional women over 45, women unlikely ever to marry—having, therefore, the greatest economic and social stake in securing gender equality in careers. Younger women, drawn to teaching by its promises of personal independence and self-support, also proved receptive to feminism.[75]

The Civic Lives of Women Teachers

In her "Teachers as Social Beings," published in the April 1876 issue of *Journal of Education,* Boston teacher Louise S. Hotchkiss (b. 1836) saw "two ways for a teacher to progress: one poring over her books, the other mingling with the world"; she advocated the second. Whether by temperament or principle, many teachers indeed mingled effectively. The authors of the women's *Who's Who in Illinois* (1927) explicitly linked civic distinction and teaching experience. Of Mary Bell Sloan, one of its many teacher subjects, they wrote, "The broad training that Mrs. Edwin Sloan had had as preparation for her career as teacher formed a splendid background when she transferred her interests to civil and social work. . . . Mrs. Sloan is proving that the education and training acquired to help one make a livelihood often becomes of greatest value to the community." Of another they claimed, "The appointment of Miss Ethel Jaynes, Principal of the Burley Grammar School, as Director of the Burley Community Center was signification of her success as a teacher and an executive."[76]

Before an acknowledged woman's movement was even recognized, the schoolmistress had already been fitted into the tight coat of "public servant-hood." Like the schoolmaster before her, she was expected to be the mainstay of church and Sunday school; to promote the free library and the lyceum, the little theatre group, and the museum; to donate her time to the "good works" for which the more affluent might be persuaded to open their purses; and to collaborate with other "good women" in service organizations. Before tenure laws, failure to identify with the community was a common reason for not rehiring a teacher.[77]

In a study of teachers' community involvements, Florence Greenhoe found most teachers to be lower-middle class Protestants with rural or small-town roots.[78] Although small towns undoubtedly asked more of their teachers, urban systems garnered good will from publicizing a teacher's service as a museum docent, unpaid sports coach, or volunteer at a charity kitchen, senior center, or vaccination drive. Of course, many teachers never taught a Sunday school or catechism class, enlisted in a cause, sponsored a youth group that was not assigned by the principal, or voluntarily joined an organization (except, perhaps, the purely private or social in nature—like the bridge clubs that attracted the lonely, socially isolated Tucson teachers whom Eulalia Bourne observed in the 1920s).[79]

Historian Mary Beard remarked, "Thousands of men may loaf around clubs without ever showing the slightest concern about the great battle for decent living conditions that is now gaining ground in our cities, but it is the rare woman's club that long remains indifferent to such momentous matters."[80] If Beard's contrast was overdrawn, a difference between the community lives of men and women teachers nonetheless appears: on average, female participation looks broader and more consistent, and women's willingness to volunteer, noticeably greater.[81]

With marriage and commuting distances, latter-day teachers likely limit their community participation, volunteer, and club work. Yet a fifth-grade teacher at Andre Lucas Elementary School at Fort Campbell (KY), a Department of Defense Education Activity (DoDEA) school, Joyce Schenck Loyd was a 26-year teaching veteran in 2004, when she won the department's Teacher of the Year award. The citation also recognized her community involvement: fundraising for scholarships, music, the March of Dimes, Paralyzed Veterans of America programs; volunteering for her church and professional organizations and tutoring at-risk children.[82]

The Women's Club Movement—The Most Political of All?

Mary Hunter's mother was part of a small group of Carlinsville (IL) women who formed a WCTU club. "How the women of our town, an important minority of them, loved that organization! With what sacred pride they wore the inconspicuous white ribbon; with what pure and single-minded ardor they gave themselves to learn to serve it, legal technicalities, statistics, Roberts's Rules of Order, the whole ritual of public procedure." Women's historic exclusion from doing the public's business made conducting a meeting a personal and group trial. "During those first years there was scarcely a meeting in which they did not more or less come to grief over parliamentary procedure, or one in which somebody was not hurt in her feelings to the point of bursting into tears. And then they would hold hands and sing a hymn and begin all over again."[83]

Convent women had "discovered the rewards and joys of friendship and work with other women" by the late fourth century, and the nineteenth and twentieth centuries' proliferating women's associations laicized this discovery.[84] In women's mission societies, choirs, clubs, book clubs, and even sewing clubs lay the potential for more radical organizations, from temperance and suffrage groups to the National Organization for Women and the Feminist Majority. Female societies in coeducational high schools, normal schools, and colleges further accustomed women to gender-specific organizations and the respite from domesticity and patriarchy they offered. In her autobiographical novel, *A Woman of Genius* (1912), Mary Hunter Austin rhetorically asks, "Does anybody remember what the woman's world was like in small towns before the days of women's clubs?"[85]

Mary Burnett graduated from Oberlin College in 1886, and like her mostly white classmates, became a teacher. She was assistant principal of Little Rock's Union High School in 1891 when she married businessman William Talbert and moved to Buffalo (NY). She worked on behalf of the women's club movement, was a president of the National Association of Colored Women's Clubs, and encouraged colored churches to become an educational force in combating discrimination. In 1905, with W. E. B. Du Bois and others, she founded the Niagara Movement, the precursor of the National Association for the Advancement of Colored People.[86]

Anne Scott concludes generally about women's institutional and organizational lives that behind their avowed purpose—educational, charitable, neighborhood improvement—"there's also the covert purpose, which is to form an acceptable framework in which women can have a public life."[87] Because men judged women's club "politics" as the pursuit of female and private, not public, interests, they were often overlooked. Nevertheless, husbands could be leery; Florida teacher and clubwoman Lucy Blackman recalled "the manly prejudice," close questioning, and grudging acquiescence, provided that "a good supper was ready, on time." This forbearance changed when "a State Federation of these new-fangled societies was proposed in 1895, calling for an absence from home of a couple of days. . . . Now that bordered on the outrageous!"[88]

Andrew Knutson's tolerance level was supposedly exceeded in 1958. His public appeal, "Coya, come home," was directed to his wife, Congresswoman Cornelia Gjesdal Knutson (b. 1912). Drawing upon her teaching and farming experience in North Dakota and in Minnesota, she was building a solid record on such relevant issues to her Minnesota district as preserving the family farm, Indian affairs, and education. A full generation after the first woman, Jeanette Rankin (also a teacher), was elected to Congress from Montana, public sympathy for Andrew Knutson showed the durability of the ideology of the women's sphere. Admittedly, however, Coya Knutson's subsequent political defeats may have stemmed more from intraparty discord than from patriarchy.[89]

The Well-Qualified Woman: Teachers as Office Holders

Perhaps the first recall election in American history occurred in 1913, when C. Louise Boehringer, the first female elected official in Arizona, replaced the male school superintendent of Yuma County. She was re-elected to a regular term the following year, running without opposition. After an arduous trip to the Cibola District, one of Yuma County's remote, never-visited schools, Boehringer found Myrtle B. Gould teaching the six-pupil school. Graduate of a California normal school and paid $75 a month, Mrs. Gould had been in her post for five years and was, in the superintendent's words, "the community leader in all social and civilizing activities."[90]

"The argument is all over," Walter Lippmann wrote in *The New Republic* in 1915. "Woman suffrage has become as plain a condition of the creation of a liberal and socialized democracy as is male suffrage."[91] School suffrage, making women eligible to vote on school matters, was already present in a number of states. In 1838 Kentucky began by giving widows with school-aged children the right to vote in elections for education offices, on the theory that such women had lost the man who could speak for her. Yet until 1984, all Kentucky's state superintendents were men. (Between 1889 and 1995 most states had zero to two women as chief state school officers except in the Intermountain West—especially Montana and Wyoming, where women doubled men's years of service in that role.[92])

When Kansas awarded all adult women school suffrage in 1859, it was reportedly women's votes that repealed their district's contract provisions prohibiting female teachers from receiving "attention and calls from their admirers" and recapturing part of their salaries if they married before a term ended. A former teacher who had retired on marrying, Mary Petherbridge Hull, faulted the Winchester (KS) school board for never having hired a woman for the winter term. "I think most any woman could excel the man we had last year. But you see I am not the schoolboard, maybe I will be part of one some day."[93] By the mid-1880s her Leavenworth County's residents began to comment that districts had a woman clerk or trustee and that a man was not invariably favored to teach the local school.

During New York's first experiment with school suffrage, the *New York Times* credited female voters with electing women to school boards in several towns in 1880. By 1894, 20 states had granted school suffrage to all adult women. The Southern and Border States, and Missouri, Arkansas, Pennsylvania, and Maine were not among them. A suffrage map of the United States in 1915 (*opposite*) indicates where and when women acquired full or partial suffrage.

Women candidates for the East Denver school board used school suffrage to agitate for full suffrage, which Governor Davis Waite then supported in his inaugural speech in 1893. In signing the initiative that year, he noted, "The heavens have not fallen and the efficiency of the public schools has been greatly improved."[94] In the five years following the ratification of the Nineteenth Amendment, the number of women serving on school boards in Pennsylvania went from 81 to 2,100. At the end of the twentieth century, women held 31% of school board seats—more than any other governmental office in the United States. This office was also a customary first step to other elective offices.

Unsympathetic to nontraditional gender roles, University of California president Benjamin Ide Wheeler disapproved the popular election of school superintendents, prompting Harr Wagner's editorial response in the *Western Journal of Education*: "Trust the people. The work of public education is not complete until every man is an expert citizen; until every community, city, and state is sufficiently expert to select its own officials." Thomas Jefferson could not have

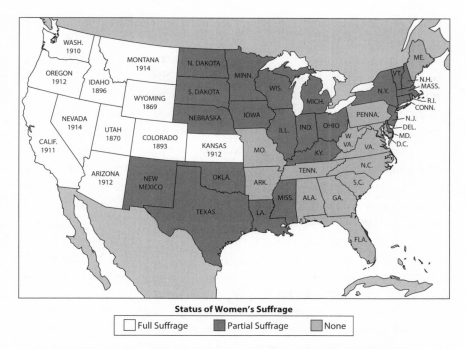

Status of Women's Suffrage

[ ] Full Suffrage   ■ Partial Suffrage   ■ None

Woman suffrage map, 1915. Full woman suffrage was mandated for all U.S. states
with the passage of the Nineteenth Amendment to the Constitution in 1920.

said it better, and Gertrudes were doing that and more.[95] Strategic, tactical,
organizational, and managerial skills used for securing woman suffrage were
required for promoting a range of causes for which women worked to become
enfranchised, and persons possessing them were needed, recruited, and promoted as decision makers. A common entry to politics was lobbying the state
legislature. One recalled, "My first personal contact with politics was when as a
high school teacher in Portland, Oregon, I went with a group of instructors to
the state capitol to lobby for the Teacher's Tenure Act."[96] She was later elected
to Oregon's legislature.

A Good Place to Start: The County School Superintendency

New York governor Alonzo B. Cornell asserted in 1889 that women, being more
likely than men to "increase the efficiency of our school management," should be
both qualified to vote and to run for education offices.[97] In Colorado, Kit Carson
County voters turned out Mr. Burnett as county superintendent, in favor of Susie
Morgan in 1895. It may have been Burnett's failure to visit schools diligently—as
Alice Newberry reported, he visited her Seibert school only once. In thousands

of rural districts the county superintendent, not a principal, was the only school administrator with whom teachers worked.

The degree of trust and the quality of the conversation between the more- and the less-experienced schoolma'ams, in their classrooms and around the kitchen table, generally determined the county superintendent's reputation and re-electability. In her Blue Earth County (MN) campaigns, Sarah Jane Christie Stevens (b. 1844) stressed her value to the mostly young and inexperienced teachers; she represented "the counsel, advice, and encouragement" of an older, more worldly woman teacher. In an 1894 statement to women voters, Stevens framed her re-election campaign in terms both familiar to supporters of other early women office seekers and novel in invoking both eligibility and entitlement. She claimed that her candidacy was a matter of principle, not politics: "Where there are ten offices for the men to share among themselves, and a competent woman is a candidate for the eleventh office, which is not political and to which she is eligible by law, no man should be a candidate against her. The women of this county are entitled to some recognition, and they should insist that they have it."[98]

As the teaching principal of schools in Kearney and Hamilton Counties in southern Kansas, Sarah Catharine Warthen (b. 1866) was described as "competent, industrious and faithful, . . . a perfect lady and accomplished teacher and . . . a valuable acquisition to any society." While canvassing for votes for county superintendent, bearing "a letter of introduction, certificate, and testimonials as to my educational qualifications," Warthen found herself well known—partly because she was also a correspondent for the *St. Louis Globe-Democrat* and wrote the Educational Department column in the local *Syracuse Journal*. She was twice elected county superintendent.[99]

Plumas County in California's rugged mother lode grew up around its mining camps. As families settled in, schools were turned over to schoolmistresses, and women were chosen as county superintendents—both before and after California passed full woman suffrage in 1911. In 1910 Mrs. Felix Hall won the office held by her husband when she was Miss Mary Leonard, teacher. Kate Mullen held the post in the 1890s and again, as Mrs. Donnelley, from 1914 to 1922, when succeeded by Mrs. Vivian L. Long (1923–1931). Women held the post almost continuously until 1963, with the post–World War II re-emergence of male teachers.[100] However, with consolidation of rural school districts, the power of the county school superintendent had declined, in Plumas County and elsewhere.

In 1946 Mildred Doyle was the first woman superintendent of Knox County (TN)—a year when men were busied in returning America to a peacetime society— but re-elected regularly until 1976. A tomboy and a college dropout with pathetic grades, Doyle taught with an emergency credential and obtained a principalship through her father's influence with the county commissioners. PTA leaders objected to her youth, her hot-tempered "cussing," and her late hours, calling her the "flapper principal." Doyle was, however, an instinctive politician, at ease in the "old-boy" Republican circles that ran things locally. She also practiced what became known as a woman's administrative style: being accessible, holding office hours on Saturdays, and talking about schools on a Sunday radio show. She named women as principals and to other administrative jobs and lived with another woman, a widow.[101]

Further Afield: State and National Capitols
Become Their Classrooms

In the first decade of federal suffrage enough women held public office, apart from education, to keep the suffrage reform promise alive: the governors of Wyoming and Texas, 149 representatives in state legislatures, two state treasurers, six secretaries of state, a dozen mayors, including Seattle's, as well as judges, city clerks, and thousands of lesser officials.[102] Teachers were, again, a disproportionate number of elected women. Indeed, teaching has appeared in the background of more women elected or appointed to public office, at all levels of government, than any other paid occupation. In these respects, the prominence that teacher feminists displayed in the nineteenth century's multifaceted woman's rights movement continued through the twentieth century.[103]

A 1983 study found about 20% of all women state senators, state house members, and county commissioners had been teachers; among a sample of women mayors, 13.3% were teachers, but among newcomers to that office teachers' representation was 38%.[104] Unlike the nineteenth century, when male teachers were common (especially in state offices), 15% of women officeholders had been teachers compared to only 5% of the men. Although women attorneys in government service were heavily concentrated in the judiciary, teachers ("generalists") in office were widely distributed.[105] As in suffrage, sectional differences remained important. In 1971, one woman was serving in Alabama's legislature, but 71 in New Hampshire's. Moreover, by 2008 New Hampshire's senate became the first to have a majority of women; the speaker of its house was Terie Norelli, a high-school math teacher when first elected.[106]

Georgia Lee Lusk (b. 1894) returned to teaching in 1919, a widow with three small sons who accompanied her daily from their ranch house to her Levington (NM) schoolhouse. Her political career began in 1924 when she was elected school superintendent of Lea County, then state superintendent of public instruction in 1931. During Lusk's first term in the state capitol, she found some unexpended mineral lease funds and persuaded the legislature to use them to buy schoolbooks for rural schools where 25 pupils might share a single reading text. Although demography influenced voters' position on women candidates, New Mexico had enough "Anglo" women to form women's clubs and a state federation for lobbying legislators. After a break from politics, Lusk ran for Congress in 1946, carrying all the "Little Texas" (Anglo) counties but none of the Hispanic ones. During her one term in Congress, like her fellow Democrats Lusk favored federal aid to public schools and a cabinet-level department of education. She returned to Santa Fe to again head the state's schools.[107]

Given that women officeholders often credit the support of women's organizations in their decisions to compete, organizational experience can hardly be overvalued.[108] In her club work, Indiana's Cecil Murray Harden perfected the skills she had developed through teaching, and she made and cultivated political contacts that led her to five terms in the U.S. House of Representatives.[109] The South's first women's club, in Atlanta, came in 1895, late in the movement—probably a factor in the region's history of women officeholders; appointing an incumbent's widow to her husband's seat was, at best, a particular expression of Southern gallantry—called "rising from her husband's ashes."[110] After graduating from the Dickson Normal College, Thaddeus Horatio Caraway and Hattie Ophelia Wyatt each taught school before he left it for the law and she to marry him in 1902. Both later became U.S. senators from Arkansas, Hattie Caraway serving first as his widow.[111]

Despite the Caraways' uniqueness, in this particular, countless women in federal offices, elected and appointed, once taught school. Among congresswomen serving between 1917 and 1964, teachers exceeded lawyers and public servants (male legislators' traditional backgrounds) by three to one; teachers were 20%; college teachers, 7%; and principals (former teachers), 3%, of women's total.[112] In one of history's ironies, the two earlier women members of Congress were teachers representing opposite poles on woman suffrage. In 1916 Montana elected a liberal Republican, Jeanette Rankin (b. 1880), to Congress before passage of the Nineteenth Amendment. But Oklahoma Republican Mary Alice Robertson, sent to Congress in 1920, was an antisuffragist whom feminists were happy to see lose after one term.

Oregon was once represented simultaneously by two former teachers: U.S. senator Maurine Neuberger (b. 1907) and U.S. representative Edith Starr Green (b. 1910). Both women wielded influence in pushing President Lyndon Johnson's Great Society education programs. The few women who sought nomination for president or vice president also included active and erstwhile teachers: Belva Ann Bennett Lockwood ran for president on the Equal Rights Party ticket in 1884; Lucy Gaston was briefly a Republican presidential aspirant, in 1920; Senator

Margaret Chase Smith was a presidential candidate at the 1964 Republican Convention; Shirley Hill Chisholm campaigned for nine months for the Democratic Party presidential nomination in 1972. Geraldine Ferraro advanced the furthest, as the vice presidential nominee on the Democratic Party ticket in 1984.

Then a two-term Congresswoman, Chisholm told a 1973 conference on black feminism, "We must get the message out that on these issues, child care, abortion and women in the labor force, white women must get in behind us."[113] While women legislators were more likely to sponsor bills in the "warm and fuzzy" areas of children, families, health, and welfare, they were as successful as men in seeing their bills become law.[114] In 1985 the female-intensive fields of teaching, nursing, social work, and clerical work produced one-third of state legislators and one-half of county and local officeholders. However, their representation, especially in federal offices, will shrink as certain male professions continue to attract women who once would have chosen such "women's work." Lawyers were 45% of all U.S. Congress members in 1993, and many women will be attracted to government, especially given the overproduction of attorneys.

Conclusion: Questioning the Feminist Critique

Virtually every theme in this chapter is captured in the lifelong professional and public life of May Eliza Wright Sewell (1844–1920). The daughter of a New England schoolmaster resettled in the Midwest, she taught school in Wisconsin, Michigan, and Indiana, before marrying Edwin Thompson in 1872. They taught together at an Indianapolis high school until his death in 1875; she stayed there until her marriage in 1880 to Theodore Sewall, headmaster of an Indianapolis boys' school. They founded the Girls' Classical School, where for 25 years she was teacher, and he principal. Despite its rigorous academic curriculum, Mrs. Sewall introduced physical education and dress reforms in her school. Well respected locally as an educator, she was more widely known as an effective organizer for woman's rights. She founded the Indianapolis Equal Suffrage Society, chaired NWSA's executive committee for eight years, testified before congressional committees, edited the *Indianapolis Times'* woman's column, and organized a school in India for child widows as part of an international community of feminist reformers.[115]

In marked contrast, Mary Little Yeargin's contribution to the Gertrude story is one of unfulfilled promise. Yeargin (1867–1893) shared Sewall's (and Willard's) expansive view of reform. When jokingly asked by a Cornell University classmate what she stood for, she replied, "I stand for reform in everything."[116] In her brief life—she died in a boating accident on Cayuga Lake—she had run her father's cotton gin to pay for more schooling, taught from age 17 with marked success, been appointed to state commissions (one requiring visiting and reporting on Northern industrial schools for girls), and borrowed on a life insurance policy to pay her way through Cornell. Among other manifold possibilities, had she lived, Mary Yeargin would almost certainly have continued her temperance activities. Accustomed to public speaking, sometimes in towns that had never heard a woman lecturer, she was tempted by the plea of South Carolina WCTU leaders that she stand for president and lead the campaign. As she wrote her parents, "I have turned the matter over to the Lord—if it pleases them to elect me at the coming convention I shall do my best. I hope you wont mind very much if the papers say any ugly things about me or the work."[117] Instead came the moving obituaries, lamenting, "Her Ambitions Cut Short."[118]

Schoolteaching, the earliest successful extension of the ideology of women's domestic sphere into the workplace, became perceived as a conservative, even reactionary, choice upon which any radical women's movement has to turn its back. Florence Howe contends that pioneer women educators were feminists who lost control of their girls schools to the male functionaries who ran the emerging co-educational public school systems. Schools were "drained of their feminist content and their commitment to change," and "women were educated to believe in their own limited capacities and in the unlimited capacities of males." (This last purported outcome, at least, is surely contradicted by the evidence in this and other chapters.)[119]

Schoolteaching, some might claim, so stifles reformist inclinations that the protest minded, like Mother Jones (Mary Harris), abandon it—as, perhaps, feminist nuns later surrendered their orders' schoolteaching mission. Moreover, no occupation so large, easily entered, diversely constituted, and of such evident transiency and brevity as teaching could contribute much: feminism was not a mass movement, and achieving reform demanded sustained devotion to the cause. (Are these not examples of elitist tendencies in feminist analysis often noted, even by feminists themselves?)

Also, how could teaching—an occupation avowedly compatible with the domestic imperative of the "woman's sphere"—be truly subversive of it? Alice Money sacrificed and studied diligently, if briefly, to prepare herself to leave the drudgery of her father's household through teaching; after four brief terms she married and settled into domesticity. A far better known Alice, onetime Michigan schoolmistress Alice Freeman, left the presidency of Wellesley College to become Mrs. Palmer, the second wife of a Harvard philosopher given to insensitively celebrating the qualities of his first wife.[120] Even teaching nuns wore wedding rings and were called "brides of Christ."

Another presumption apparently underlying the feminist critique is that—in terms of feminist consciousness, accrued political capital, or political skills—teaching children conferred little "added value." Yet, before Clarissa Barton began teaching, she had a total of two weeks' knowledge of the working world, gained as a loom hand at her brother's mill. Her autobiography paints her without dresses long enough to mark her transition from girl to woman, having no money of her own, "diffident, timid, non-committal," without faith in her capacities to rule a classroom—lacking poise or experience in using "the power of a stinging glance." Clara, however, proved good at teaching, and it made "Miss Barton" a personage of some local reputation and in demand for better-paying, more visible, and more demanding work.[121] Although Barton was undoubtedly above average in her ability to profit from experience and turn a heightened self-confidence toward new challenges, she was hardly alone in acquiring the instrumental assets that teaching could confer or strengthen—and which have been noted in previous pages.

The present study represents a different perspective on feminism, concluding that the rhetoric of a "woman's place" must be seen for the possibilities it offers, as well as for the restraints it imposes. It argues that women's portals into the male preserve of teaching school, and subsequently into other professions, were widened as part of an energizing, encompassing campaign on behalf of children, and society in general, carried forward by the traveler as well as the settler.

The women who promoted seminaries to prepare girls to become teachers—Mary Lyon, Emma Willard, Zilpah Grant, Catharine Beecher—were subversives, however much they denied intending to challenge males. Beecher's father called her "the best boy I had." In seeing teaching as a "training ground for feminists," historian Andrew Sinclair discounts much of the rhetoric Beecher used to build support for women's enlarged presence in teaching. While distancing herself from woman suffrage, Beecher dwelt not on woman's weakness but on her powers to do good, and Beecher lived a life that demonstrably contradicted her domestic rationale for the woman's excursions outside the home circle of duties.[122]

Writing of a much earlier generation of mostly Quaker "teaching daughters" in rural Pennsylvania, Joan Jensen sees their literacy as having "carried them beyond the confines of the home to a place in the public sphere, which they occupied proudly and from which they engaged in battles to extend the rights claimed by the men of the Revolution to new groups." Thus, Jensen continues, "on the crest of this new revolution, they could hardly imagine that some women might one day feel themselves trapped in teaching as earlier daughters had felt trapped in households." Often forgotten is that "teaching daughters were an essential link between Republican motherhood and feminist sisterhood."[123]

CHAPTER 13

"A Lady Well Qualified to Show the Way"

Widening Women's Work

> Many men would banish women from the editor's and author's
> table, from the store, the manufactory, the workshop, the
> telegraph office, the printing case, and every place except the
> school room, sewing table, and kitchen.
>
> —Virginia Penny, *The Employment of Women* (1863)

In 1943 the University of California (Berkeley) student newspaper advertised a work forum for women students. "The vocational problem is still a big question mark for most co-eds," and in these war years "the only sure thing is that industry needs them, business needs them, the government needs them, and education needs them. Today, at 4pm, in the Women's clubrooms of Stephen's Union, the California co-ed has a date to find out which needs her most, and incidentally, which can make her the best offer."[1] During World War II, twice as many of Berkeley's 4,294 undergraduate women entered the premedical course and mathematics department as in the prewar period, increased their share of chemistry degrees by 400%, raised numbers in engineering from 2 to 38, and responded to the war effort's manpower needs by studying economics, statistics, public administration, and the applied sciences.

America's earlier wars had also increased women's choices. The Civil War drew them into nursing and federal clerical jobs, some from their schoolhouses. Although America's 1917 mobilization for Europe's Great War was brief, women teachers' horizons widened beyond the rural districts where 60% worked. Marjorie Stinson, a Texas teacher and licensed pilot, was teaching military men to fly. Gussie Nettleton Whitcomb, a business college graduate and commercial teacher in Eaton (CO), became chief clerk of Weld County's draft board. Kansas City teacher Helen Bradley worked with injured soldiers as a U.S. Army rehabilitation aide and in 1924 was chief rehabilitation aide at the U.S. Veterans

Hospital in Kansas City.[2] Although World War II offered wider opportunities, albeit subsequently retracted, an additional half million women entered male strongholds between 1970 and 1985—as journalists, physicians, lawyers, professors, police officers, bartenders, and telephone installers. Meanwhile, 3.3 million women entered the labor force as nurses, bookkeepers, secretaries, and cashiers.[3]

However, apart from teachers, relatively few women appeared in the U.S. census category of "professional, technical, and kindred workers." From 1837 to 1887, Mount Holyoke Female Seminary graduated 2,341 women; hundreds became teachers and 21 became physicians.[4] Using 1890 census data, Western Reserve University's president—ignoring the nation's 238,397 women teachers, many of them college educated—lamented the dearth of college-educated professional women, referring to the 1,235 ministers, 208 lawyers, and 4,555 physicians and surgeons (perhaps 200 having attended a "regular" college).[5] Even as the newer fields of home economics, social work, librarianship, and nursing moved into universities, teaching remained the destination of most women graduates until the late 1970s.[6] As with teaching, these reconceived occupations did not "so much transcend gender distinctions as recast them into new forms."[7]

In 1986 the *New York Times* quoted a Harvard labor economist as saying that the critical labor force advancement of the next 20 years would be occupational shifts among women and readjusting their wages relative to men. Women teachers had won virtual wage equity and long since breached a number of the traditionally male professions, especially between 1870 and 1920. For example, of medicine's five women pioneers featured in *Eminent Women of the Age* (1873)—Elizabeth Blackwell, Harriot Hunt, Hannah Longshore, Clemence Lozier, and Ann Preston—all taught school first. Teachers also helped turn women's volunteer and charitable work into paid professional employment. Ellen Gates Starr (b. 1859) was a Chicago teacher for a decade before founding Hull House with Jane Addams and becoming especially active in industrial reform and organizing women workers. A failed South Carolina teacher, Matilda Evans (b. 1872), her state's first colored women physician, founded the first of two training schools for colored nurses in 1901.[8]

Making Career Decisions: A Sampling of Cases, Causes, and Outcomes

Between 1827 and 1833, Boston's Harriot Kezia Hunt (b. 1805) ran a school with her sister following their father's sudden death. She wrote of her teaching experiences, "My school was flourishing and I loved it. Yet I never felt it my true vocation. It seemed to be preparing me for something higher and more permanent."[9] For an unknown reason Lucy Dupey Montz (b.1842) left her schoolhouse to train at a dentist's office in Cincinnati, after which she returned home to become Kentucky's first woman dentist.[10]

Perhaps the nation's first woman police captain, Pearl L'Heureux dreamed of being a lawyer or detective while growing up in Nickerson (KS). More realistically she took bachelor and master's degrees into high school teaching and school administration. Her first step into a new career came in 1931, working with the Witchita (KS) police department as a juvenile supervisor.[11] As part of her adolescent quest to "find herself," Janis Joplin joined the Future Teachers of America at Thomas Jefferson High School, along with the Future Nurses and the Slide Rule Club. By her senior year, however, this future rock star "was doing everything possible to show her parents she would never become the Port Arthur (TX) schoolteacher of their dreams."[12]

Karen Elliott's odyssey was utterly different. In tiny Matador (TX) in the late 1940s, her interest in teaching was squelched by her father—a fundamentalist who viewed schools as riddled with godless communists. Karen Elliott became a journalist instead, starting with school news column for the local paper, then with the *Dallas Morning News,* where she covered education before becoming its Washington correspondent. From her next position, with the *Wall Street Journal* (where communists were scarce), she worked her way up to publisher.[13]

A Dallas elementary school teacher in 1971, Sandra Force defected to the upstart airline on learning that Southwest Airlines was hiring flight attendants. A Memphis native, Baptist college graduate, and occasional beauty contestant, she recalled her mother's shocked response: "Sandra, if you're going to quit your teaching job, why don't you go with a well-known airline like Braniff?" Force was still working for Southwest 35 years later, a senior flight attendant earning $100,000 annually, and a millionaire through her employee stock plan.[14]

The women met here represent the many who left the classroom for another profession and a few others with the potential to teach who never did so—both groups illustrating the range of personal, accidental, and societal factors affecting career decisions. Whatever their specific circumstances, teachers' experience with self-support, negotiation, management, and meeting the public were likely assets in their new professions. Brief accounts of these professions' respective histories expose themes developed elsewhere in these pages. They include issues of status and imagery, professional education and socialization, males protecting their preserves, and gender-linked discrimination.

Following the Men: Paths Away from the Schoolroom

A group of nineteenth-century women, more numerous even than teachers, were erstwhile teachers. This group deserves scrutiny as a larger (and better equipped) supplier of pioneer female attorneys, doctors, journalists, and preachers than colleges and universities could provide. (In 1890 colleges enrolled, but did not graduate, less than 3% of the nation's 18–21 age group.) Many women's lives show how teaching either preceded careers other than marriage or was practiced simultaneously. For some career changers, teaching was never their preference. In other cases teaching "stiffened the spine": bred sufficient mettle to attempt more lucrative or congenial work.

A traveling phrenologist had advised Clarissa Barton's mother "to throw responsibility on her. She has all the qualities of a teacher." Clara Barton (b. 1821) followed two older sisters, Dorothea and Sarah, into teaching. She proved a gifted teacher, ranging ever farther from home. Her abilities, reputation, and friendships gave her the confidence to bargain with school boards, lobby New Jersey officials, and eventually pressure the federal government to join the International Red Cross. Becoming "her own woman," Clara Barton also became the most admired woman in America.[15]

The typical late nineteenth-century schoolma'am—high school, normal school, or college educated—was several steps along the path toward other fields that might become "woman's work." Few, if any, formal requirements were needed for entering social work and much of journalism, authorship, and editing; there were, for example, more than 700 women editors in nineteenth-century America.[16] Columbia University's School of Library Economy opened in 1887 with a mere six-month course.[17] The technical elements of nursing were largely learned on the job, and law could be "read" (studied) in a law office. Savings from a teaching wage of $25 per month sufficed to send Louisa Wright (b. 1862) to Oregon Medical College and the University of Michigan; she practiced medicine in Montana and her native Clark County (WA).[18]

Path breakers already familiar in women's history include Fanny Fern (Sara Willis) in journalism, Dorothea Dix in social work, Olympia Brown in religion, Clara Barton in nursing, Elizabeth Blackwell in medicine, Belva Lockwood in law, and Ellen Swallow Richards in home economics—all former teachers. However, the brief sketches that follow are of one-time teachers—some possibly well known in their own times and places—who have slipped into "the history of the anonymous." Particularly anonymous is the unnamed young Indiana woman writing her sister in California in the 1860s for help in "getting a school." She mentioned, without enthusiasm, the possibility of studying medicine; her first choice of work was "to scribble."[19]

Teachers as "Scribbling Women"

In the seventeenth century, the Countess of Winchelsea, Anne Finch, described women authors as "intruders on the rights of men." In a 1797 diary entry, Maryland's Henrietta Neale (b. 1741) confessed her struggle against the women's sphere, for "I know not how to resign the pen for the needle."[20] Born 162 years later and half a world away, New Zealand's famed teacher-writer, Sylvia Ashton-Warner, expressed a similar need with different imagery: "as the other escape hatches edged shut about me—art, music, swimming and marriage—leaving only the bloody profesh, here was the same skylight inching open again as it had in the dark part: writing." Dale Spender claimed for literary creation that "to write was to be; it was to create and to exist. It was to construct and control a world view without interference from the 'masters.'"[21]

Those with literary tastes and the impetus to write might be attracted to teaching for its hours and seasonality, and writing was the earliest field where teachers achieved critical, popular, and economic success. However, their parents' deaths sent Ulster's Mary Balfour (b. 1755?) and her sister to operating schools, the last in Belfast. Her Anglican clergyman father likely provided Balfour the classical learning that adorned her plays and poetry on themes in Irish folklore. Poet and widow Alice Flowerdew (b. 1759) operated her own schools in London and Bury St. Edmund, both her teaching and writing reportedly done "under the severe Pressure of Misfortune."[22]

Ann Douglas looked at 30 prominent nineteenth-century literary women for her study of the sentimentalizing of America's "creed and culture"; 19 of them were teachers.[23] A number, like Kate Douglas Wiggin, managed to teach and write concurrently.[24] Farm-bred Mary Abigail Dodge (b. 1833) was an effective and popular science teacher at the Ipswich and Hartford female seminaries and Hartford High School. She also wrote poetry and eventually made her living by her pen as "Gail Hamilton," writing several books, including a biography and an informed treatise on common schools.[25] The all-inclusive, five-volume *The Vermont Historical Gazetteer* (1867–1891) is Abby Hemenway's magnum opus. Hemenway (b. 1828) kept a district school from age 14, attended an academy in 1846, and taught for three unhappy years in Michigan. Returning home, she began her explorations of Vermont with an anthology, *Poets and Poetry of Vermont* (1858).[26]

The private character of writing made women authors less visible and worrisome to gender traditionalists than the woman lawyer or preacher—although publishing beyond ladies magazines, becoming successful, or taking to the lecture circuit exposed nineteenth-century women writers to intense scrutiny. Rachel Jones (b. 1813) had taught in Cabarrus County (NC) before her 1834 marriage and moved to Charlotte, where her husband edited the weekly *Miners' and Farmers' Journal,* later the daily *North Carolina Whig.* Despite journalism being both a public and indecorous undertaking, widow Rachel Jones Holton's need to support her eleven children likely softened any criticism when she was listed as editor and proprietor of her late husband's newspaper in 1861. Despite shortages of paper, ink, and manpower, she published until 1863, her newspaper outlasting the Whig party.[27]

The newspaperwoman, warned Gilson Willets in 1903, "is obliged to approach men to whom she has never been introduced, and talk to them, [and to] interview murderers and make analytical studies of criminals of the most degraded kind." Not so for Annie Brown Leslie (b. 1870), a Mt. Holyoke graduate and teacher in three states before marrying a Pittsburgh journalist. Writing as Nancy Brown, her mature, didactic column, Experience, responded to readers' letters. Running in the *Detroit News* from 1917 to 1942, it pushed other newspapers to hire women.[28] Although assigned to cover "women's interests," more women worked as general reporters and editors. By the 1980s women reached virtual parity with men—in numbers, not influence. By that point most women in the print media and television were coming directly from college journalism and mass communications programs, where women students predominated, bypassing the earlier path through schoolteaching.

Securing racial justice drew Jessie Redmon Fauset (b. 1885?) into magazine work. She taught classical languages and French in high schools in Washington (DC) and New York City before becoming editor of the NAACP journal, the *Crisis.* She also wrote poetry, short stories, novels, and reviews and encouraged writers of the Harlem Renaissance. Over her sharecropper parents' objections, Alice Allison Dunnigan (b. 1906) gained sufficient education to teach in Kentucky's rural schools. She then earned a home economics degree and helped her small town obtain gas and water lines and mail delivery. Moving into journalism, she was the first black woman admitted to Washington press galleries.[29]

The Business of America Is Business

In eighteenth- and nineteenth-century Britain, a clerkship was an accepted route into business for males who lacked capital but had ambition and some education. In the later nineteenth century "white blouse" jobs began to open up to women: shop assistants, bookkeepers, postal and bank clerks, and telegraphers. In George Gissing's novel *The Odd Women* (1893), Monica Madden—a young, weary English shop girl—explains, "I wish now they had brought me up to something different. Alice and Virginia were afraid of having me trained for a school [teacher]; you remember that one of our sisters who went through it died of overwork. And I'm not clever, Miss Nunn. I never did much at school." Rhoda Nunn, a crusading feminist, responds, "But there are things you might manage. No doubt your sister told you how I get my living. There's a great deal of employment for women who learn to use a typewriter."[30]

Two teachers of commercial courses at Technical High School in Newton (MA) flatly asserted, "The inventor of the typewriter ought to be an honorary member of every woman's club in the land, for, to how many young women has it furnished the means of independence.[31] In 1912, Elizabeth Conrad (b. 1882), a Charlotte (NC) public school teacher, taught herself to type, took shorthand classes, and opened Conrad Advertising and Letter Shop. It catered to individuals needing a single letter or small businesses wishing to reach a large group of customers without maintaining their own clerical staff. As the business and machine worlds changed, so did Miss Conrad, becoming a virtual employment agency: training and hiring other women and recommending them to other employers. After woman suffrage she copied voter registration lists to sell to political candidates, including the first woman from the county to sit in the state legislature. Her activism extended to club work, helping to found local units of Altrusa and Business and Professional Women's Clubs.[32]

When Oklahoma's Eleanor Reser (b. 1902) mentioned her interest in secretarial work, her father said, "No girl of mine works in no man's office. Now if you want to[,] . . . I'll help you find a country school." She capitulated.[33] Nonetheless, through the 1920s and 1930s popular novels and Hollywood films called the office worker the "business girl," her image more feminine, her work life more glamorous, than the teacher's, dealing daily not with children but with men, some eligible. Educated young women were enticed to try the business office—perhaps with hopes of becoming the "executive," "private," or "confidential" secretary of a tycoon.

Being the "office wife" was also considered preparation for an advantageous marriage. The legend under the picture of a typing class in the 1950 *The Black and Gold,* San Pedro (CA) High School's annual, read, "Here are kittens on the keys dreaming of being glamorous secretaries and marrying the boss' sons." G. K. Chesterton is supposed to have quipped, "Twenty million young women rose to their feet with the cry, 'We will not be dictated to' and promptly became stenographers." By 1960, 60% of women entering the labor force directly from high school were clerical workers; women, doing most of the routine white-collar clerical work (76.6% of all clerical workers), exceeded the percentage of women (69.9%) among all college graduates who taught.[34]

Others saw office work merely as a stepping-stone, as men would: a way to learn about advertising, public relations, real estate, banking, or publishing.

Without connections or even a scintilla of secretarial skills, Barbara Zimmerman (b. 1926) headed for New York City. After beginning in publishing at Doubleday and marrying, Zimmerman (now Epstein) cofounded the *New York Review of Books* in 1963 and remained its coeditor until her death. Her Radcliffe College friend, novelist Alison Lurie noted, "Barbara's quiet brilliance was all the more striking because she hadn't had much backing at home. . . . Her parents' highest hope . . . was that she might become an elementary school teacher."[35]

The Lure of the Learned Professions

Unlike in Europe, most U.S. nineteenth-century legal, medical, and theological training took place outside of colleges and universities: by apprenticeship arrangements and in proprietary schools sometimes loosely affiliated with a "college." Working professionals, not academics, effectively controlled these venues, more effective in passing over aspiring women than most budget-minded, tuition-dependent college officials could be. Thus American women found acquiring medical or legal training much harder, for example, than securing a liberal arts or teacher education. In 1920 a mere 2,000 women were enrolled in the nation's many indiscriminate (but discriminatory) law schools, while the dearth of coeducational medical schools forced women to found their own institutions.[36]

Eva Beller had her sights set on architecture. A 1905 honors graduate of the scholastically elite Girls High School in Brooklyn, she won a scholarship to Cornell University. When her father queried New York architects about his daughter's prospects, their women employees uniformly warned him, "Firms will hire the worst man before they hire the best woman architect." After a two-year teachers' course at Brooklyn Manual Training Normal School, Beller instead began a 53-year career, mostly teaching business math to ninth graders.[37]

Anticipated breakthroughs into historically self-governing ("free") professions largely failed to appear. In 1929 women were 2.1% of lawyers and 4% of physicians. Women's participation in medicine, as in university teaching and administration, either stagnated or declined between 1910 and 1960. In 1920 women interns were not accepted by 90% of American hospitals, and influential medical and law schools set 5% quotas on women students lasting into the 1940s. However, women's share among attorneys rose, from 1% in 1910 to 4.7% in 1970.[38]

TO PERFORM THE DUTIES AND RECEIVE
THE BENEFITS OF AN ATTORNEY

Colonial American women—exercising powers of attorney, testifying before courts and legislatures, and serving as executrixes and notaries—would have been amazed that these rights vanished during the nineteenth century.[39] The first licensed female attorney, former Iowa teacher Belle Aurelia Babb Mansfield (b. 1846), studied law with her older brother. Both were admitted to the bar in 1869; she passed "a most eminently satisfactory examination" and was complimented by a liberal, court-appointed committee. However, Mansfield turned to college teaching and promoting woman suffrage.[40] Many nineteenth-century men also failed to practice, as "reading law" was appealing for its mental challenge, its supposed benefit in business and politics, and the relative brevity and ease of acquiring a license and re-entering a field that changed slowly. But men's decisions about practicing law were not gender determined.

In the 1920s Judge Jean Horton Norris predicted, "The woman lawyer of 1950 will be regarded solely in her professional capacity; we must admit, however, that sex is a handicap at the present time"—noting Harvard and Columbia Law Schools' refusal to admit women.[41] An anonymous bit of doggerel, addressed to aspiring Portias, appeared in a legal publication in 1925: "A librarian or a secretary you may be—But think not a client you can tree. If you would rise—forsake the book; Take on the stove and be a cook." The suspected author was a law professor who had eloped with his former student, retiring her from the county district attorney's staff.[42]

The bench and bar steadfastly resisted women's entry. "It would not promote justice to permit women to engage in trials at the bar," the Illinois Supreme Court ruled in 1870 in denying Myra Bradwell's admission to the state bar. Like the U.S. Supreme Court, the Wisconsin Supreme Court ruled in 1875 that admission to the bar would "tempt women from the proper duties of their sex by opening to them duties peculiar to ours." While the Wisconsin legislature overruled the decision, until the 1970s women attorneys remained a token everywhere.[43]

Daughter of freeborn blacks, Mary Ann Shadd taught for years in Pennsylvania, New York, and Canada. She had recruited colored troops for the Union army, raised money for John Brown's widow after Harper's Ferry, and helped found and edited a newspaper. She received her law degree from Howard University in 1883, at age 60. Charlotte Ray also taught school, studying nights at Howard. The first colored woman to earn a law degree (1872) and be admitted to the Washington (DC) bar, she returned to New York and teaching in 1876, unable to find enough clients to keep her law practice going.[44]

After working her way through school and teaching in Pennsylvania, Emma Gillett (b. 1852), a white woman, began attending evening law classes at Howard, graduating in 1883. Her dissatisfaction with a teacher's wages and the example of Belva Lockwood led her toward the law and years of suffrage activism in the nation's capital.[45] After teaching in Washington (DC), Sophonisba Breckinridge (b. 1866), a white woman from a prominent Southern political family, passed the

Kentucky bar in 1894 but was similarly unable to get clients. She gravitated toward social work instead.[46]

In 1920, one of the 3% of attorneys who were women, Sarah Tilghman Hughes (b. 1896) was the first female federal judge in Texas when her picture appeared in newspapers worldwide, administering the presidential oath of office to Lyndon Johnson aboard Air Force One in November 1963.[47] But, in having taught school in order to study law, Judge Hughes was among company stretching from the mid-nineteenth century.

Chicago juvenile court judge Lynne Kawamoto (b. 1951) also attended night law school while teaching. In three years of rulings on a notorious case of child abuse and neglect—involving 28 children, six mothers (five of them sisters), 22 fathers, and 22 lawyers—Kawamoto "stole the solution from her days of grading students: long yellow spreadsheets, with new developments marked in color-coded inks."[48] However, most of the post-1970 generation of aspiring women attorneys pursued legal careers from the outset, reaching 25% of new lawyers in the 1990s on their way to becoming the majority of many university law school classes.

A WANT AND NEED OF FEMALE PHYSICIANS

Discovery of Martha Ballard's diary detailing her lifelong work, delivering babies and generally tending to the sick in Massachusetts and Maine communities, recalled women's history as healers.[49] Given housewives' accumulated empiric dealings with illness and accident, they practiced "physick" and "chirurgery" (surgery) at a time when few physicians had special training, surgeons ("sawbones") belonged to the barbers' guild, and some thought women the naturally superior healers.

Despite women's history of preparing herbal medicines, midwifery, and home nursing, physicians began to steal patients from midwives in the eighteenth century. While childbirth was medicalized, infant care (later pediatrics) was left to the household.[50] One critic of the "man-midwife" observed that much training was being required "to give Men by Art, what Women attain by Nature."[51] Nevertheless, as physicians increasingly defined childbirth as a hospital-treated illness, only women with formal medical training and hospital privileges could apply their expertise.

As accredited medical schools replaced apprenticeship and proprietary schools, "regular medicine" marginalized homeopathy, osteopathy, eclecticism, and other competing "sects" through which nineteenth-century women often entered medicine. A Boston physician observed that "one of the first and happiest fruits of improved medical education in America [is] that females were excluded from practice."[52] To protect their status and future earnings, medical students in Philadelphia rioted when women sought entry. Public opinion generally followed, reproaching women physicians as unlicensed eccentrics and criminal abortionists.[53]

Utah's Martha Hughes (b. 1857) saved her wages from teaching school (from age 14) and setting newspaper type to earn a chemistry degree, medical license, and advanced pharmacy training in Pennsylvania—the lone woman among 75 students. Hughes returned to Utah in 1882, was a resident physician at Deseret Hospital, had a private practice, founded the state's first training school for nurses, campaigned for woman suffrage, and secretly became the fourth of the six wives of the hospital's director, a prominent Mormon, Angus M. Cannon.[54] In 1896 she defeated Cannon and five other Republicans for a seat in the state senate. In her first month she introduced bills to advance each of her deep interests: public health, the protection of women industrial workers, and the education of handicapped children.

When Abraham Flexner published his landmark report on American medical education in 1910, women were 6% of U.S. physicians. A significant proportion practiced around Boston, where women built a parallel power structure around their own medical colleges; in 1890, two-thirds of U.S. women medical students entered such schools. However, as mainline medical schools began admitting token women, the trustees of the 17 women's medical colleges established before 1900 closed or merged their institutions—preferring coeducation and believing that gender discrimination was vanquished. Instead, the medical profession colluded in limiting women's presence: setting quotas and denying them access to internships, medical societies, and referrals—an exclusionary system that persisted for another half century.

Obstacles to maintaining a viable private practice turned many women physicians to institutional employers—from elite private schools and public colleges to tuberculosis sanitaria, orphanages, and residential state schools (usually first named asylum or school for the blind, deaf, and dumb). Lilian Welsh, an 1875 graduate of the State Normal School at Millersville (PA) taught and was principal of her hometown high school, resigning in 1886 to enter the Women's Medical College of Pennsylvania. Unable to find an academic position in chemistry, Welsh was a physician at the Pennsylvania State Hospital for the Insane before settling in Baltimore as a physician and professor of physiology and hygiene at the Woman's College (Goucher). Annie Wells Williams (b. 1853), a Brooklyn native whose father was a forty-niner, taught in California's Monterey and Sierra Counties after graduating from normal school. She then turned to medicine, including an appointment at the Colorado State Insane Asylum.[55]

Autonomy mattered to Alice Hamilton (b. 1869): "As a doctor I could go anywhere I pleased. . . . I should not be tied down to a school or a college as a teacher, or have to work under a superior, as a nurse must do."[56] A pioneer in industrial medicine, Hamilton was appointed the first woman professor at the Harvard Medical School—on the condition that she would not march in academic processions. Former teacher Susan La Flesche (b. 1865), the first American Indian woman to become a Western-trained healer, resolved to give her people better care than the inattentive, seemingly incompetent white doctor from her childhood. In 1913 La Flesche was practicing in the Omaha Agency at Walthill (NE), where she realized her dream of a reservation hospital. She nursed her alcoholic husband—testifying in Congress for legislation banning alcohol sales to Indians—raised their two sons, ran her clinic, and paid house calls across the 450-square mile reservation as doctor, nurse, financial advisor, family counselor, and friend.[57]

SISTER VOCATIONS: TEACHERS MADE PREACHERS

Massachusetts's Puritans had banished the theologically liberal Ann Hutchinson for preaching, saying, "You have stepped out of your place, you have rather been a husband than a wife." Except among Quakers the ministry was man's province. Caroline Healey Dall (b. 1822) taught school and lectured on women's educational rights, freely chosen employment, and full citizenship—perhaps expressions of her frustrated ambition to preach: "could I have had a theological education in my youth, or had even the paths of the ministry at large been open to women, I have every reason to believe that I should be at this moment a settled minister."[58] The National Education Association's Committee on the Education of Girls concluded, in 1886, "Many of the duties belonging to the office of the ministerial profession might with entire propriety be transferred to the care of women . . . [for] to her willing hands, even now, is committed the burden of all the work of all the churches."[59] Before 1800, in addition to calling on women volunteers, the home and foreign mission fields recruited pious women, some showing "more faith and patience" than the men.[60]

The influential Rev. Horace Bushnell acknowledged woman's special affinity for an active religious life: "We have many more Christian women than Christian men; their piety ranges higher, and they have many of them higher gifts of experience, and practically speaking, a more instructed insight of the Christian truth and life. . . . [But] "the question of ministration is one thing, and the question of administration another."[61] The few nineteenth-century churchwomen who attained a pastorate faced every form of discrimination from worshipers, male or female.[62] The decline in male vocations and women's increasing numbers as religious workers likely provoked churchmen and the laity to "hold the line"—as happened in other professions confronting the increasingly aggressive "gentler sex."

In the 1850s, Ohio teacher, preacher, and future U.S. president James A. Garfield heard the pioneer Congregationalist minister, Antoinette Brown Blackwell.[63] "There is something about a woman's speaking in public that unsexes her in my mind, and how much soever I might admire the talent, yet I could never think of the female speaker as the gentle sister, the tender wife, or the loving mother." It being still uncommon for women teachers to speak aloud at formal educational gatherings, Garfield's was likely the attitude of most male teachers. Some women teachers thought similarly, including Garfield's fiancée, Lucretia Rudolph.[64]

Onetime schoolteacher Ada Burpee Bowles (b. 1836) was ordained by the liberal Universalists in 1875. After marrying Rev. Benjamin Bowles in 1858, she taught school and raised his two children and their three before accepting a pastorate. Tutored in theology by her husband, she served churches in Bradford and Easton (PA).[65] However, ordained women were more likely to find careers as missionaries or in religious education, less so as professor or dean in a theological seminary or Christian college, and least as church pastors. Women's share in the clergy ranged from less than 3% in 1880 to less than 6% a century later. Theological seminaries did not admit feminist theology into the curriculum or "church culture" until the 1960s and 1970s, under multiple pressures from the feminist, antiwar, and civil rights movements.[66]

Creating the New "Women's Professions"

When Alexis Lange addressed a meeting of women college graduates in 1915, he articulated a generous, optimistic vision of women's roles in improving society. What he meant by "social housekeeping" careers for college women was broader than social work. He spoke of "persons of broad culture specifically prepared . . . in some branches of industry, of business, of agriculture, in house and city planning, in public hygiene, in the management of the corporate and institutional affairs of city, state and nation."[67] Although narrower than Lange's grand vision, potential alternative professions to teaching or the classic "learned professions" were being created in the later nineteenth century. Women quickly became the majority of practitioners in home economics and nutrition, librarianship, social work, and nursing.

From Household Arts and Domestic Science to Home Economics

Catharine Beecher (b. 1800) opened girls schools in Hartford (CT) and Cincinnati, lectured on "righting woman's wrongs" through advanced education, wrote about religion, and recruited New England women to teach in the West. With her *Treatise on Domestic Economy* (1841), Beecher also virtually invented the field of home economics. Her intent was to elevate homemaking and teaching to equal status with men's professions.[68] As a career and a school subject, the renamed "home economics" also appealed to traditionalists as less likely than teaching to "unsex" women by taking them from the home, raising their aspirations above domesticity, and turning them into spinsters or feminists.

Columbia University's Teachers College (TC) originated in 1880 as the Kitchen Garden Association: to teach good housekeeping practices to immigrant and working-class women. TC quickly became the nation's most influential center for ambitious public school professionals, educational researchers, and reformers, while retaining a household arts department and creating the allied field of nutrition education. Forward-looking urban school districts in the early twentieth century were attracting teams of social workers, criminologists, public health doctors, dentists, and nurses—personifying a grand vision of the public school as a lever for community development, social reform, and preventive medicine. As school playgrounds and gymnasia recruited specialists in body mechanics and recreation, school cafeterias attracted home economists and nutritionists.

Many of the nation's academic and scientific women owed their positions to home economics. Although her 1904 University of Chicago Ph.D. was in pure chemistry, Nellie Goldthwaite's professorships came in home economics. After five years at Mount Holyoke and a research position at the Rockefeller Institute, she taught at various universities, helping prepare home economics teachers despite never having taught school herself.[69] Not so with Christine South (b. 1884), a South Carolina public school teacher before joining the faculty of Winthrop College. Foreseeing that teaching English had less potential for advancement than home economics, Christine South studied at TC, launching a new career in working with farmwomen in state-administered programs under the U.S. Department of Agriculture's Extension Service.[70]

Like social work, home economics could be seen through a social-reform lens or as an applied science that would anchor a respected new profession and dignify housewifery.[71] Madge Reese took her Northeast Missouri State Normal School diploma (1909) into a career as a demonstration agent for the U.S. Bureau of Education and the Department of Agriculture.[72] Between 1910 and 1926 the number of colleges, teachers colleges, and state universities with home economics electives, majors, or degrees grew from 100 to 651.

Junior and senior high schools often required home economics for girls, reflecting curriculum reformers' belief in vocational or practical skills and "hand-oriented" learners.[73] A survey of several thousand women matriculated at land grant colleges between 1889 and 1922 found that 55% of home economics graduates had been gainfully employed; 32% were teachers, more than the combined total of dieticians, home demonstration agents, food technologists and inspectors, scientists, consumer economists, and other careers imagined by pioneer home economists.[74] Here, then, was a new gender-linked profession that did not as much compete with teaching as broaden its appeal among public education's diverse constituencies.

Custodians of Books—and Hopes: Women and Librarianship

As with schools, private subscription libraries, created by and for males, preceded free public libraries. Thus in 1872 the suggestion that a woman replace the "truly gentlemanly" Charlie Herbst as head of Atlanta's recently organized dues-paying Young Men's Library Association elicited doubts about her abilities and possible inhibiting effects on patrons. Although gender conservatives prevailed in Atlanta, "lady members" were soon admitted, and female librarians quickly became a fixture virtually everywhere.[75] Women's clubs and Andrew Carnegie's philanthropy sped library growth, and high demand for library workers offered "bookish" women an alternative to teaching. Between 1920 and the 1970s, women were more than 80% of librarians, and the librarian image—formerly "timid men in rusty black suits"—became that of the bespectacled "silencer" in her grey cardigan. Combined positions also appeared in schools, colleges, public libraries, and recreation centers.

Libraries offered "book worms" a sanctuary. Moreover, librarians saw themselves as educators of the greater public, engaged in a democratic enterprise to enlighten individual patrons and entire communities.[76] Like missionaries and teachers, pioneer librarians who "went west" thought themselves a civilizing force. However, public library patrons in Pendleton (OR) "would not tolerate anyone who showed in the least degree that she felt intellectually superior"; they wanted a "good mixer" who could dance, play cards, and enjoy herself. Acknowledging popular tastes, in their recommendations library deans noted their graduates' pleasant appearance or attractive personality, along with good breeding and cultural refinement.[77]

The ideology of the woman's sphere was applied to both librarianship and teaching, thus differential wages, promotion opportunities, and specialties. Women's "tolerance for routine" and "natural affinity for detail" shuttled library women into poorly paid, low-prestige work as cataloguers.[78] Former teacher Mary Wright Plummer (b. 1856) started at the St. Louis Public Library as a cataloguer. However, she moved on: organizing and directing the Pratt Institute's library and library school in Brooklyn and becoming the founding principal of the New York Public Library's training program. At a time when many libraries would not admit young readers, Plummer's pushed collection development of childhood materials, children's reading rooms, storytelling hours, after-school programs, and training children's librarians.[79]

Other pioneer women librarians had attended normal schools or teachers colleges and taught, giving librarians and teachers common frames of reference. Milwaukee teacher, Lutie Stearns (b. 1866) captured the attention of local librarians by using public library books to augment her school's juvenilia. Her career evolved into organizing public and traveling libraries in Wisconsin's more remote communities.[80] School libraries eventually employed more women than any other library site. Educated at the two-teacher school in Paint Rock (TX), Fannie Ratchford (b. 1887) taught in rural and small-town schools for 15 years, leaving to become rare books librarian at the University of Texas. Working closely with university students and library patrons, Ratchford reportedly never lost her early identification as a teacher.[81]

Melville Dewey's first class at the School of Library Economy in 1887, a fledgling unit within Columbia College, enrolled three men and 17 women. The Pratt Institute opened in 1890, and most of its 600 students over the next two decades were women. In recommending to the president of Armour Institute "the best man in America to start the library and library school," Dewey explained, "The best man in America is a woman." A former schoolteacher and 1892 graduate of Dewey's Albany library school, Katharine Lucinda Sharp (b. 1865) saw university-based schools as the future. She moved Armour's library program to Urbana in 1897 as the Illinois State Library School (renamed the University of Illinois Library School in 1926).[82] During her career Sharp collaborated with the State Teachers Association and State Federation of Women's Clubs to promote public libraries.

Moving from a professional to an academic setting placed librarianship with other "women's fields" in the lower reaches of the prestige gradient in research-oriented universities. While women directed many pre–World War I library schools, librarianship tried to improve its status by placing men in elite positions. Like the national organizations of other female-intensive fields, in its first century 38 men and 14 women headed the American Library Association.[83] Newer libraries specializing in business, technical, scientific, medical, historical, and governmental materials sheltered the male minority.

Computerization in the last third of the twentieth century brought reference and retrieval services online, and software engineers and web page designers modernized what had passed for "library science." Subsuming librarianship under the field of "information technology" was another gender-related development.[84] Male recruits likely preferred a school of informatics to a library school.

Changes in image, critical library functions, and training requirements pushed women librarians' sphere, most obviously the school library and the children's room of the public library, to the margins. The number of library workers declined, casualties of the privatization of public-sector services and budgetary squeezes.[85] Information was being removed from the realm of the free—the open library stacks—and made a commodity for subscribers or purchasers.[86]

Scientific Charity and Municipal Housekeeping

The Freedmen's Bureau (1865–1868) is sometimes called the first federal welfare agency. However, most government social service came from feeble local entities, reliant on volunteer organizations that formed or expanded during the nineteenth century to coordinate relief and rescue work. Through churches, nondenominational moral reform societies, and charitable, ethnic, benevolent, and fraternal organizations, nineteenth-century women visited the sick and bereaved, dispensing assistance and advice to the destitute and despairing. Most of the 4,000 charity organizations' "friendly visitors" reported in 1892 were women.[87]

Frances Goodale introduced readers to the range of women's social welfare activities in 1893, maintaining that "it is Nature's inexorable law that undisciplined charity shall not bless, that unwise love shall never be beneficent." The Pennsylvania Society to Protect Children from Cruelty (f. 1877) devoted its efforts to the "worthy poor," not to "drunks, loafers, and prostitutes." The nineteenth century's prevailing emphasis on individual failings—of the illiterate, the poor, the infirm, the intemperate, the delusional, the lawbreaker, or the simply unlucky—shifted during the progressive era, adding flawed social structures to the equation.[88]

The character of the emerging social-work profession is indicated in the varied new careers of a sample of former teachers. A high school chemistry teacher for 10 years, Katharine Bement Davis (b. 1860) financed her growing interest in public health by teaching school and charity work in a troubled Philadelphia neighborhood. Thereafter she became superintendent of the Bedford Hills Women's Reformatory, commissioner of charities and correction of New York City, and head of the privately funded and directed Bureau of Social Hygiene.[89] Nebraska's Kate Barnard (b. 1875) was teaching in an Oklahoma City public school when she revived the United Provident Society to help impoverished immigrants. In 1907 Barnard was elected to fill a constitutional office created for her: commissioner of charities and corrections.[90] Josephine Chapin Brown (b. 1887) left her position at an exclusive Pennsylvania private school to organize a farm school for delinquent girls at Sauk Center (MN). In 1920 she learned casework at the United Charities of St. Paul. Brown's career focused on the theory and practice of rural social welfare, including training public relief workers for New Deal agencies and readying the field for the new Social Security system.[91]

Esther Eggertson Peterson's teaching career in Boston extended to YWCA evening sessions for women factory workers. Peterson (b. 1906) recalled the impact of learning that "the fathers of the children I taught during the day were exploiting garment workers I taught at night. . . . That experience got me started as an organizer and reformer." She became director of education and congressional legislative representative for the Amalgamated Clothing Workers of America and the AFL-CIO. Her appointments, in three presidential administrations, extended from the Department of Labor to Consumer Affairs.[92]

The premise of both education and social work is that people can improve with thoughtful instruction and good example. Her encounters with immigrant children as a teacher in Chicago's Hull House kindergarten drew Mary Eliza McDowell (b. 1854) into the coalescing social work profession. Founder of the University of Chicago Settlement (1894), she noted of moving to Chicago's meat-packing district, "No social climber ever desired more earnestly to be accepted by the elite than I wished to be accepted by my [new] neighbors."[93] The dictum of settlement staff was that to benefit the needy "we must discover and adopt their point of view, put ourselves in their surroundings, assume their burdens, unite with them in their daily effort."[94]

Settlement house staff offered teachers in heavily immigrant urban schools insights on their students' out-of-school lives, health and recreation issues, and competing cultural values. They sponsored free kindergartens and adult education programs that worked their way into public school systems. A onetime Elmira (NY) teacher, Anna Beach Pratt (b. 1867) promoted trained visiting teachers, vocational guidance, and employment services in Philadelphia schools. A major figure in launching school social work as both a practice and perspective on child welfare, Pratt championed the professionalism of social work while promoting a "whole-child" mentality among classroom teachers.[95]

Professionalism required gathering stray courses into coherent schools of social work, distilling principles and practices from an amalgam of multiple services, offered by private and public entities in settings from mountain hollows to urban tenements, for clients ranging from infants to octogenarians, from "innocent victims" to "hardened cases." Social work schools, like schools of education, served two separate, if overlapping, communities. One comprised rank-and-file agency and organization practitioners, mostly women; the other administrators, policy makers, researchers, and theorists, mostly men.[96] As the latter group expanded, while agency budgets were constricted, women dropped to 60% of all social workers by the late 1970s.

Catholic sisterhoods had a centuries-long history of maintaining orphanages, shelters for the indigent, and soup kitchens. Beginning in the 1960s, many American nuns left their inner-city and suburban parochial schools for emergent social-work sites: storefront agencies, public housing projects, homeless encampments, halfway houses, migrant workers' hiring halls, shelters for battered women, and safe houses for political refugees and immigrants. This recalls a distant past when "street work" with the helpless and troubled was the bedrock of their mission.

The New Nurse

"Every woman is a nurse" was the opening line of Florence Nightingale's *Notes on Nursing* (1860).[97] Secular nursing, one of the household arts, emerged from the home nursing done by family members, servants, and neighbors "watching" at the bedside to relieve the household. Although both sexes helped, when illness overwhelmed a family, the custom was to call on all the local women for nursing help.[98] At age 11, Clara Barton was nursing an injured brother; for two years she applied the leeches and poultices and administered his medicines. Linda Richards wrote, "Quite early in my teens I was called upon ... and I recollect with what pride I heard some one say of me, 'She will be a real born nurse some day.' "[99]

Some "practical nurses" began collecting fees from patients or charged church or public officials for nursing the poor or wounded soldiers. While practical nursing was typically a sideline of (usually) girls, spinsters, and widows known as adept "watchers," some city hospitals began hiring these self-taught nurses as aides and orderlies. Nursing might be called "a high form of spiritual discipline," but home and institutional nursing featured the most repugnant tasks of domestic service.[100] Whether they worked in their patients' homes or in pesthouses, workhouses, unregulated private infirmaries, or "voluntary" (charitable) hospitals, nurses generally ranked with the lowliest servants. Men and women—including known thieves and prostitutes—nursed as untrained assistants in the disorderly environments during hospital nursing's "dark ages." The five hospitals in the American colonies in 1776 were described as "almshouses with infirmaries for the homeless and poor, where residents nursed each other."[101]

The religious and secular women who brazenly inserted themselves into hospital and field nursing during the Civil War—unofficial, untrained, unpaid, and often unwanted volunteers—challenged the view that nursing was outside the respectable woman's sphere. Nonetheless, the status of secular nurses, as distinct from nuns, was such that the government rejected the American Nurses Association's offer of nurses during the Spanish-American War, turning instead to the untrained but genteel Daughters of the American Revolution.[102]

Apprenticeship-based hospital nursing schools in the United States effectively date from 1873. An 1877 report from one, the Bellevue Training School, anticipated a time "when the profession of a nurse for the sick will rank with that of a teacher for the young." This translated to recruiting a more refined and intelligent class of young women. In the formative decades a number of these had taught school.[103] Mary Lewis Wyche (b. 1858), at age 36 a self-described old maid schoolteacher in Chapel Hill (NC), was ready for a new career—not doctoring (as she had once hoped) but nursing: admittedly "a profession not often followed at that time by women of the highest type." In a long career in private-duty work and hospital nursing and administration, Wyche initiated training programs in several North Carolina hospitals, opened the state's first nursing school (Rex Hospital School of Nursing, 1894), founded the North Carolina Nurses Association in 1902, and served on the State Board of Examiners for Trained Nurses. Under her leadership, her state enacted the nation's first nurse licensing law.[104]

The nation's 5 hospital schools in 1900 grew to more than 2,000 in 1930. Workplaces more than schools, student nurses performed arduous, often menial labor—commonly with unbroken shifts of 10 hours daily or 12 hours at night. Their primary appeal was (and remained) to working-class girls with ambitions above domestic or factory work but without the means to progress beyond high school. "Mary Benjamin" explained, "I chose nursing by a process of elimination. For a while I considered teaching English. Most of my friends were going to teachers' college. But I wasn't that good in English. I couldn't afford a four-year program anyway." Her working-class parents were pleased: "They thought of nursing as a prestige job."[105]

In 1899 Isabel Hampton Robb and Mary Adelaide Nutting—Canadian teachers before entering nursing schools—inaugurated America's first course for graduate nurses at Teachers College: in "hospital economics" for women training to become hospital matrons. The eventual Department of Nursing Education became the largest unit within TC, offering nurses the full panoply of first and advanced degrees. Women were 93% of American nurses in 1910 and 98% in 1940. The perception that, like teaching, marriage would shorten nursing careers argued against lengthy or highly specialized training. Therefore, nursing leaders' decades-long effort to shift training from three-year diploma programs in hospital schools to four-year degree programs in collegiate schools of nursing had limited success. Instead, the community college–based associate degree program became the growth area. It was less costly, found in more institutions, operated closer to home, and fit mature and minority students better.

Male nurses served primarily as medical corpsmen and mental and military hospital staff. Unlike social work and teaching, men seldom saw nursing as a career through which to advance into supervision or administration. Few later trained as doctors—perhaps because, long before, "the healing arts branched into the medicine-giver and the care-taker," each thought to call on different human qualities.[106]

"Women's Professions" and Women's Lib

"If woman is no longer to be womanish, but a human being of powers and responsibilities, she must become militant, defiant." For Miss Barfoot, a fictional composite of British suffragettes, any "woman's profession" merely reclaims, for pay, centuries of unpaid women's work that perpetuates inequality and injustice. Addressing a small audience of young women in 1890s London, Barfoot conceded that an "excellent governess, a perfect hospital nurse, do work which is invaluable; but for our cause of emancipation they are no good; nay, they are harmful. Men point to them, and say: Imitate these, keep to your proper world."[107]

Lois Mathews, the University of Wisconsin's dean of women, seemingly agreed. She promoted not law or medicine but social work—"Christianity applied to everyday living"—pointing also to fulsome opportunities "in business, welfare work, in play-ground work, in charities and correction associations, and in all lines opened up by household economics."[108] Still, as the percentage of the 18–21 age group in college rose—from 15% (1940) to 45% (1970)—most of that increase was women earning a bachelor's or first professional degree in education. In 1972–1973, 317,254 graduates completed their preparations to teach—two-thirds of them women.[109]

For post–World War II females, Rael Issac concludes, "the goal of the earlier woman's rights movement—equality with men in the rewards, statuses, and satisfactions that come with careers—awaited a new feminist consciousness."[110] The 1970s witnessed a reawakened women's movement—its agenda Barfoot's. It even infected the ranks of the "selfless" professions, putting hospital staff nurses on picket lines and threatening strikes—although less often than teachers. Recalling her options in the 1930s, a Canadian teacher found her first choice inhospitable: "you almost had to be the daughter of a doctor before you could hope to get anywhere in medicine."[111] Women were less than 10% of first-year medical students in 1969, and 25% of the 1980 incoming class.

The U.S. Labor Department concluded in 1985 that women had displaced men as the majority in the nearly 50 professional fields that "develop, produce, distribute, and apply knowledge." From 1963 to 1973 alone, women's share of degrees in the personnel, accounting, banking, and finance specialties together went from under 10% to around 40%, with steady growth in female business school

TABLE 13.1

Changes in Racial and Sexual Representation by Occupation, per 1,000 Workers

Demographic Group	Physicians		Attorneys		Engineers		Journalists		Computer Analysts	
	1970	1990	1970	1990	1970	1990	1970	1990	1970	1990
White Men	880	653	930	710	961	787	578	443	578	591
White Women	87	147	45	211	16	68	381	445	381	247
Black Men	18	23	11	19	11	28	11	22	11	29
Black Women	4	12	2	15	1	7	10	30	10	24
Asians	—	108	—	14	—	70	—	20	—	72

Source: U.S. Bureau of the Census data, as summarized in Andrew Hacker, "Goodbye to Affirmative Action?," *New York Review of Books* 43 (July 11, 1996): 26.

graduates. By 2000 women were the significant majority entering veterinary medicine, pharmacy, and psychotherapy. Despite inequities, America had a more gender-neutral and less race-sensitive workplace culture in the professions and corporate world, as Table 13.1 suggests.[112]

Even the Sputnik-driven astronaut program made space for women: Christa McAuliffe (1986 launch), Sally Ride (1983), and Mae Jemison (1992). Admittedly, all occupied the teacher-in-space role. "They couldn't be astronauts without the alibi of being involved in education. They [NASA] wanted someone safe, someone everyone could identify with," a feminist media critic observed.[113] A small 1980 study of the feminist leanings and career satisfaction of 327 full-time, New York City elementary school teachers showed profeminist attitudes to be weak among the 21–30 age group—unlike the 31–40 group that attended college in the 1960s when the bravado of women's liberation appealed to the imagination and rebelliousness of the young.[114] The explanation given for the relative absence of younger teacher feminists was that profeminists had chosen alternative careers. Centered on inducting children into a seemingly change-resistant society, schooling looked impossibly conventional and inflexible to many feminists—and to some liberals more generally.

One of feminism's few leaders to question its disdain for teaching was Florence Howe, editor at the Feminist Press and a former teacher—although she did so with a barb. "Why is it more important to spread a thin tokendom of women through the nontraditional kingdoms," she wondered, "than to attempt a transformation of the traditional ghettos themselves—especially if one of those, the public school system, is responsible for the perpetuation of sex stereotyping and the low aspirations of women."[115] Yet *Business Week* (2003) marveled, "Girls are on a tear through the educational system. In the past 30 years, nearly every inch of educational progress has gone to them"—an accomplishment for which feminism, not teachers or public schools, got credit.[116] Feminism certainly raised consciousness, but it took schoolwork to prepare girls to become the women who could walk through those half-opened doors.

Despite a fourfold increase in teacher numbers from 1900 to 1960, teachers declined from 85% to 50% of all women professionals, explainable by steeply rising numbers of nurses. More generally, for the first time in over half a century, women's applications to alternative fields were growing substantially. Education degrees—25% of total college graduates in 1950 and 38% in 1973—fell to 14% by 1981, and less than 5% as college undergraduates said teaching was their intended field. In 1982 the alumnae magazine of Mount Holyoke College, producer of teachers for 150 years, congratulated itself that the MBA had finally surpassed the teaching credential on its graduates' résumés.

The most arresting change in the 1970s was the widespread collapse of the market for teachers. By the mid-1970s, from 5% to more than 20% of new teachers could not find positions.[117] Hardly noticed—except, agonizingly, by prospective teachers, their families, and those who taught or employed teachers—this reality appears significantly more important than feminism per se in the sudden, radical change in the plans of college women. In essence, prospective teachers were less pulled to appealing (if relatively inhospitable) alternative careers than pushed out of teaching by demography.

Closed Opportunities and Unwanted Challenges

In her discussion of women and teaching, England's Sandra Acker cautions against an explanation where "aspirations and motivations have crowded out everything else." This tendency is especially prevalent in America, where ideology emphasizes personal choice, not imposition or constraint—the American ethos having elevated an individualistic over a structural or environmental framework for explaining human behavior.[118] However, like other ostensibly personal decisions, an occupational choice is seldom freely made. An inclination or preference may be stillborn, redirected, delayed, or channeled, subject to social determiners beyond the individual's command.

For example, high and rising divorce rates heightened cynicism about marriage and motherhood—perhaps most among the educated, persons with more options. The percentage of first-year college women who agreed with the sentiment that "a woman's place is in the home" shrank from 50% in 1967 to 20% in 1974, a remarkable change in so brief a time.[119] The escalating costs of raising children to a middle-class standard were largely beyond individual control. Teaching salaries—considered adequate for the single or the two-wage earner household—were devalued when the woman was chief or sole breadwinner, as generations of men had complained. These facts, and others, affected birth rates—something individuals could better regulate, especially with the pill. Their fewer children required fewer teachers.

Students and Teachers, Demography and Politics

The "baby bust" first appeared as a lower birthrate in 1961. It slowed and then halted the building and staffing of new elementary schools, eventually closing many schools. The falling numbers of those already born pushed the problem through the grades; the high schools' 1979 senior class would be their largest for at least another 18 years. In 1968 no state reported a teacher surplus; in 1972, 22 did. The tough job market in Seattle ended Janeen Richards's childhood dream of teaching history; she filled prescriptions for 14 years, then enrolled in the social studies program at TC hoping the oft-predicted teacher shortage would finally materialize.[120]

The major producers of teachers continued through the 1970s to overproduce would-be teachers and teacher educators—seemingly on the principles of freedom of choice or "let the buyer beware." Supply shrank only when prospective teachers re-evaluated their options and colleges redirected resources from teacher preparation to computer science and business. Between 1976 and 1996, the proportion of college women earning degrees in education was halved: from 24.4% to 12.1%.[121]

Teaching vacancies were further limited as more teachers hung onto their positions. Like decisions to enter or avoid a field, decisions to leave a work setting are highly contextual.[122] Teachers, women especially, had traditionally "promoted" themselves by moving between schools and districts, seeking higher salaries, a better working environment, greater personal satisfaction, more evident success, new challenges. As the demography of retrenchment sank in, resigning became riskier. The highway of career mobility was both clogged (too much supply) and narrowing (too little demand).

Unlike in the 1930s Depression, teaching appeared less a respectable employment, with modest potential for upward mobility, than a status-losing occupation. In many districts, persistent novices spent several years on the substitute lists. Openings were disproportionately listed in schools primarily enrolling racial and ethnic minorities and with resources far below those of privileged districts.[123] With the advent in the 1990s of "high-stakes" testing, pressures on teachers and students increased—not only in schools deemed failing. Rendered accountable for the schools' "outputs," teachers had no more control of the "inputs"—students, resources, colleagues, facilities—than 50 years earlier, despite their unions.

The popular exposés of the period spoke movingly, and justifiably, of the damage inflicted on rural and urban schoolchildren by poverty, racism, troubled families, violent neighborhoods, and underresourced schools. Apart from teacher turnover in such places, school effects on teachers and their work went comparatively unmentioned—except among teachers and prospective teachers—or were underanalyzed in the popular media. In one of many jeremiads, *Newsweek Magazine* in 1981 summarized the woes of teachers: "underpaid, under-qualified, badly trained, overburdened and increasingly under pressure . . . held accountable for the decisions of everyone from the Supreme Court to unfit mothers." (What of absent fathers?)[124]

As in a number of other societies, students' and teachers' lives and work in the later twentieth century were made more difficult by polarizing, sometimes violent conflict. In Louisville, the epicenter of America's early free kindergarten movement, public school kindergartens were closed for a decade after 1956 as Kentucky officials withheld schooling rather than mix the races in desegregated schools.[125] Black Washington (DC) veteran teachers found their estrangement from parents in the black community unprecedented. Both black and white teachers were transferred in and out of New York City schools as "community control" reached its boiling point in the late 1960s. A "social revolution" was how "Berta" described the turmoil around her New York City school.[126]

"I never feared any pupil in school," nothing worse than "some backtalk," Evelyn Weiss recalled of her tough high school in the Red Hook section of Brooklyn; contemporary schools' security guards and metal detectors, stories of assaults on teachers, and gun-carrying elementary school principals horrified her.[127] Not surprisingly, then, a 1996 national poll reported that only 46% of teachers would recommend their profession to their own children or most promising students. In the same poll, discipline problems replaced low salaries as the most commonly perceived reason for leaving the field—although school discipline, by their own accounts, had been a minefield for generations of teachers and patrons.[128]

Civil Rights and Civil Wrongs

In 1975, 22% of American students were ethnic or racial minorities, previously known to many prospective teachers and their families primarily through the gritty scripts of television and film, featuring shabby schools in declining, even dangerous neighborhoods, with disrespectful or apathetic students. Black and Hispanic leaders pointed to inner-city schools, with their many novice teachers, as evidence of the continuing racism of the "white establishment." In one teacher's eyes even academic writers' characterizations of her students as "culturally deprived," "culturally different," "at risk," or "high need" was simply blaming the victims: "maybe what the teachers of the immigrants of fifty years ago had was not better kids (don't tell me babies out of Italy with the evil-eye and the garlic around the neck weren't less culturally deprived than the PR's [Puerto Ricans] today) but [teachers had] more courage, more self-respect, and a fair share of faith in their jobs and themselves and their children."[129]

In 1954, the United States Supreme Court declared racially segregated schools, where it was legally sanctioned, to be unconstitutional. Southern and Border State governments promptly legislated "massive resistance": rewriting their constitutions to eliminate public education, voiding compulsory school attendance laws, funding hundreds of new and private "segregation academies" through tuition grants to parents, and enrolling their teachers in state pension plans—all overturned by federal courts. To promote desegregation, more black than white schools were closed. Many African American educators lost their positions entirely, others were downgraded, and newly prepared black teachers were passed over.[130] A product of New Orleans's segregated schools, teacher Louise Metoyer Bouise protested the vilifying of black schools and their teachers: "I didn't feel I was getting an inferior education. In fact, I am sure I had very good teachers."[131]

In an illustrative case, black adolescents were transferred without notice to a previously all-white Maryland high school. While physically closer to their home neighborhood, they were "not at home" in a school where white students spat on them and teachers ignored their raised hands, questions, and needs. That only white girls joined the future teachers club cannot surprise.[132] St. Clair Drake wrote movingly of black students' feelings about one-way desegregation: blacks were "sent from a James Weldon Johnson High School with Crispus Attucks's picture on the wall to a Stonewall Jackson High School with the Confederate flag flying."[133] Ingrained racism, intransigence, and inequities in power, from the local school board to the U.S. Congress, determined that black institutions—and black pupils, teachers, administrators, counselors, bus drivers, and cafeteria workers—would bear most of the burden, especially in the small towns and rural districts in the South's "black belts."

Estimates are that 39,000 black teachers and principals in the South lost their positions between 1965 and 1972.[134] The effects persisted, for, in 2005, 38% of America's schools did not have a single nonwhite teacher on their faculty.[135] However, the civil rights movement also widened educated black women's options. In 1980 more than 1,000 black women practiced medicine, and their numbers on college faculties doubled between 1970 and 1990 to a modest 2.4%.[136]

The American black middle class was, with undoubted exceptions, wary and worried by the events and consequences of the civil rights movement. The sit-ins, demonstrations, and retributive violence that began in the 1950s and exploded in the 1960s put even Northern and Western cities on news broadcasts around the world, unsettled their citizens' lives, and challenged their plans for their children's futures. Rather than hearing "teaching is always a good bet for a woman," black (and white) women heard, or themselves recited, some variant on "given the way things are today, I think a woman can do better than teach."[137]

Finding Teaching Prospects Where We May

"The downside of the women's movement has been to allow those talented teachers, that is, the women who would have become teachers as they did in the early 20th century, to go into many other professions," historian Joseph Illick concluded. "I benefited enormously from teachers who could have been lawyers, doctors, etc., but for the cultural restraints that prohibited women from entering those fields. Indeed, I could name (and of course see in my mind's eye the faces of) those wonderful teachers—far better, in general, than the men who stood in front of the classroom."[138]

However, it is not clear that those talented teachers of Illick's youth would have entered professions other than teaching if encouraged to do so. Nor is it obvious that women now choosing investment banking, corporate law, landscape architecture, or computer engineering would be exemplary teachers had they chosen to teach. What appears certain is that having those women in America's classrooms could not have protected either teaching or schools from the cultural and societal turmoil of the times—especially given the tattered document that the social contract had become. As was said of Kathleen Moffatt's decision to end a 12-year teaching career, "as she got better the job got worse."[139]

Woman's True Profession (1981) is Nancy Hoffman's pathbreaking collection of women teachers' accounts of their work lives. That a similarly titled book would have currency in, say, 2035 is unlikely, considering the refusal of many daughters to follow their mothers or aunts into teaching; the decline since the late 1970s in education's share of new women college graduates; the reduced representation in teaching of black women, professed nuns, and the descendants of nineteenth-century immigrants; and the prohibition of the blatant forms of sex discrimination that historically narrowed women's career choices.

Conclusion: "All Human Knowledge
Takes the Form of Interpretation"

A compelling historical and cross-cultural case can be made that women will still command most K–12 classrooms into the indefinite future. Less obvious, but still credible, is that schoolteaching will also continue to surpass any competing profession in its ability to recruit, reward, and retain the women who choose it, teachers' choice being made for many of the same reasons that operated in the past. Moreover, as in the past, unpredictable events in the larger society, local and global, will intervene and with unknowable consequences.[140]

In the early 1970s, teaching's share of university or training college graduates ranged from Nigeria's 23% and Iran's 27% to Brazil's 79% and the Philippines' 81%. Inspired by his high school journalism teacher, Thomas L. Friedman (b. 1953) wrote in the *New York Times* (March 24, 2006), "The more I cover foreign affairs, the more I wish I had studied education in college, because the more I travel, the more I find that the most heated debates in many countries are around education." Serious educational debates, however, will not be about the gender composition of most nations' future teachers. Despite marked diversity, in 2009 women were the majority of primary school teachers in most nations (typically in the 65%–85% range) and 50%–65% of secondary school teachers in more than half the nations.[141] Women's share among teachers worldwide will rise further as less-developed countries close the male-female schooling gap. Moreover, the reservoir of teachers in training is predominantly female—across virtually every modern, non-Islamic society.

Despite salary and promotion disparities, gender inequity in teaching is smaller than in many alternative sectors. Moreover, when incumbents are questioned in various societies, teaching displays "uniformly low conflict between women's occupational and familial roles." Women teachers in South Asia report that, along with raising their social status, their work "is viewed favorably by their family and friends and has made a positive contribution to their family and marital adjustment and to raising their status vis-à-vis their husbands, children, other family members, friends, and the non-employed wives of their husband's colleagues."[142] In India, for example, women teachers were marrying men (especially professionals) with higher status than their fathers. Small wonder that most women who attend training colleges and universities in varied nations become teachers.[143] Meanwhile, educated and higher-status parents have shown an aversion to teaching as a career choice for a son.

Whether the professional woman interrupts her employment in a life course that includes marriage and child rearing or juggles competing career and domestic

demands, her obligations exceed those of her male colleagues. A mature feminism has acknowledged women who have, and value, their dual lives—as it must
when, as in the United States, the majority of children are raised in households
where both parents work or where the mother is the sole provider.[144] These realities will keep women the majority of teachers as long as schools as we know them
exist. They will help replenish teaching with an unknowable number of career
changers. Connecticut's Jayne Williams decided she "didn't want someone else
raising my children."[145] Mary Wasiak, 48, left a law firm for a Texas high school
classroom, believing she had "missed her calling."[146] Along with dropouts from
law school, the disaffected woman attorney has been there all along: restricted by
her gender in access to high-status clients, showpiece cases, or a timely partner-
ship in the firm, and "worked to death."

"When I went to school all we could think of was social work, nursing and
teaching. I was tremendously idealistic," Kathleen Moffatt said of her decision to
teach. The motivating power of idealism is recorded in each of these fields, as in
librarianship as conventionally defined, resonating across autobiography, iconography, literature, and social scientists' motivational studies. Their professional
training has aimed at imparting a holistic view of those they serve, a "humanis-
tic, interpersonally sensitive, anti-bureaucratic ideology."[147] Librarianship and
social work have resisted unionism as foreign to their service ethic, while teaching and nursing have embraced it as necessary and beneficial to the same end.

In her 37-year teaching career, Vivian Paley (b. 1927) wrote a dozen books for
teachers and children, lectured widely, and received a MacArthur Foundation
genius award. Everyone has a stake in seeing that there are more Vivian Paleys in
the pipeline. More realistic, and more important, may be that every teacher can
be heard, taken seriously, and allowed to learn from the intimate "felt knowledge" of the ever-shifting classroom. A visit from three Ohio teachers prompted
Paley to state, "I have yet to come upon any teachers who were not ready and
willing to . . . tell you what they know and push the boundaries to discover more
about the children they teach. The notion that teachers are not reflective or introspective is far off the mark."[148]

A late twentieth-century reform movement that began within the teaching
profession was the effort to create a career ladder allowing superior teachers to
remain classroom teachers while also functioning as "teacher leaders." From 1987
those who meet the voluntary program's rigorous, professionally designed, standardized, and validated criteria become National Board Certified teachers.[149] For
retention purposes the laudable National Board Certification program may be,
initially at least, a solution in search of a problem. In a 1996 poll of teachers about
their colleagues' reasons for leaving teaching, "outstanding teacher performance

goes unrewarded" and "difficulty of advancement" were at the bottom of their rankings.[150] If these teachers judged accurately, traditional incentives still operate in teaching and may continue to influence the decisions of twenty-first-century women. What cannot be predicted is whether these incentives are sufficient to ensure that teaching remains woman's "true profession," retaining its historic first-place hold on the educated class that supplies professionals.

In some measure the answer may depend upon women's success in cracking open such still-resistant male fields as engineering and architecture. More important will be women's ability to maintain and extend their participation in and satisfaction with law, medicine, and business—over the life course, probably by pressuring for more family-friendly concessions and by taking their skills into the growing universe of not for-profit organizations. More significant will be the competitive attractions of the other large, female-intensive fields that share with teaching a still relatively uncorrupted ethical base and ideal of social service.[151] Nursing, teaching, and social work each flourished for centuries within the extended family and in convents and monasteries, before becoming careers for secular, trained professionals. Elements of their shared history include viewing their work as "not merely a profession [but] a vocation; not merely a gainful occupation, but a ministry."[152] As Anna Giardino demanded to know, "Why is it better to negotiate divorces or cut out tonsils than to train healthy young minds!"[153]

Walt Whitman, "the poet of America"—once himself a teacher—effectively answered that question, at least for this author. For the inauguration of a new public school in Camden (NJ) in 1874, he ended "An Old Man's Thought of School" with these words:

And you America,
Cast you the real reckoning of your present?
The lights and shadows of your future, good or evil?
To girlhood, boyhood look, the teacher and the school.[154]

Gertrude has long been essential in realizing the teacher's part of the mutual obligation residing in these words—and so she will remain.

Introduction

1. Jon Carroll, *San Francisco Chronicle* (Dec. 5, 2007). Carroll writes a regular column for the *Chronicle*.

2. *Leonard and Gertrude,* trans. Eva Channing (D. C. Heath, 1885).

3. This text retains the eighteenth- and nineteenth-century spelling of the following as single words: "schoolteacher," "schoolkeeping," "schoolteaching," "schoolgirl," "schoolmistress," and "schoolhouse," among others. (Split words include "school board," "school committee," "school bus," and "school system.") In *Webster's Third International Dictionary of the English Language Unabridged* (G. & C. Merriam, 1963).

4. Jill Julius Matthews, *Good and Mad Women: The Historical Construction of Femininity in Twentieth Century Australia* (George Allen & Unwin, 1984).

5. Kenneth Burke, *Permanence and Change* (New Republic, 1935), 70. Neither Hannah More's nor Mary Wollstonecraft's teaching is included in such common reference works as *Webster's Biographical Dictionary* (1974) or *The Columbia-Viking Desk Encyclopedia* (1953, 2 vols.). Limitations of space appear less the explanation than a seemingly shared inability to imagine teaching as being a formative influence on a famous personage.

6. Barbara J. Berg, *The Remembered Gate: Origins of American Feminism* (Oxford, 1978), 5.

7. Dale Spender, *Women of Ideas, & What Men Have Done to Them* (Routledge and Kegan Paul, 1982), 47n1.

8. Henry Seidel Canby, *Alma Mater: The Gothic Age of the American College* (Farrar & Rinehart, 1936), 173.

9. Maxine Greene, "Identities and Contours: An Approach to Educational History" (paper presented at the Annual Meeting of the American Educational Research Association, New Orleans, Louisiana, February 25–March 1, 1973).

10. Agnes Morley Cleaveland (1874–1958), *No Life for a Lady* (Houghton Mifflin, 1941), esp. 121–26.

11. Bernard Bailyn, "How England Became Modern: A Revolutionary View," review of *1688: The First Modern Revolution*, by Steven Pincus, *New York Review of Books* (November 19, 2009): 44–46.

12. See Joel Spring, "Research on Globalization and Education," *Review of Educational Research* 78, no. 2 (June 2008): 330–63.

13. The Fredrika Bremer Association was founded in 1885 as Sweden's earliest feminist organization; in Christina Florin and Ulla Johansson, "Education as a Female Strategy: Women Graduates and State Grammar Schools in Sweden, 1870–1918," *Journal of Thought* 1, no. 2 (1991): 5–27.

Chapter 1 · "It Is Well That Women Should Be Unlettered"

1. Elizabeth Elstob to George Ballard, Mar. 15 & 27, 1753, in Todd, *Dictionary of British and American Women Writers*. The quotation that titles this chapter is from Matsudaira Sadanobu, Japan's chancellor, c. 1790, cited in Kumiko Fujimura-Fanselow and Asuko Kameda (Eds.), *Japanese Women: New Feminist Perspectives on the Past, Present, and Future* (New York: Feminist Press, 1995), 95.

2. Elizabeth Elstob in George Ballard, *Memoirs of Several Ladies of Great Britain, who have been Celebrated for their Writings or Skill in the Learned Languages Arts and Science* (W. Jackson, Printer, 1752).

3. Michael Cole, "What's Culture Got to Do with It?" *Educational Researcher* 39, no. 6 (Aug.–Sept. 2010): 461–70.

4. Catherine the Great in Carol Nash, "Educating New Mothers: Women and the Enlightenment in Russia," *History of Education Quarterly* 21, no. 3 (Fall 1981): 301–12.

5. Elene Kolb, "When Women Finally Got the Word," *New York Times Book Review* (July 9, 1989); Ronald Philip Dore, *Education in Tokugawa Japan* (U California P, 1965).

6. Marie le Jars de Gournay, *Apology for the Woman Writing and Other Works*. Edited and translated by Richard Hillman and Colette Quesnel (U Chicago P, 2002). Marie Jars de Gournay in Katharine M. Wilson & Frank J. Warnke, *Women Writers of the Seventeenth Century* (U Georgia P, 1989); Anne Echols & Marty Williams, *An Annotated Index of Medieval Women* (Markus Wiener, 1992); Vicki León, *Uppity Women of the Renaissance* (Conari Press, 1999).

7. Echols & Williams, *Annotated Index of Medieval Women*; Daniel Bornstein & Roberto Rusconi (Eds.), *Women and Religion in Medieval and Renaissance Italy* (U Chicago P, 1996).

8. Charlotte Woodford, *Nuns as Historians in Early Modern Germany* (Oxford UP, 2002).

9. Zubat Kausar, *Muslim Women in Medieval India* (Janaki Prakasshan, 1992), 145; Usha Nayar, *Women Teachers in South Asia: Continuities, Discontinuities and Change* (Chanakya, 1988); Dorothy Ko, *Teachers of the Inner Chambers: Women and Culture in Seventeenth-Century China* (Stanford UP, 1994).

10. Myra Reynolds, *The Learned Lady in England, 1650–1760* (Houghton Mifflin, 1920), 24; Kevin M. Sharpe & Stephen M. Zwicker (Eds.), *Reading, Society, and Politics in Early Modern England* (Cambridge UP, 2003), 105.

11. Celia Campos, in Tara Nakashima, "Revival at Holy Family," *San Pedro (CA) News Pilot* (Jan. 4, 1997).

12. In 1995, I began an invited address to faculty and graduate students at George Peabody College for Teachers of Vanderbilt University as follows: "*Teaching is traditionally men's work.*" Politeness kept my audience silent at this obvious "misstatement," but when I repeated it, someone asked, "Didn't you mean to say teaching is traditionally *women's* work?"

13. Elisabeth Hansot and David Tyack use "evolution" to elucidate a slow process that "blurred the distinction between home and school, between learning [and teaching] in the family or in a public place"; in "Gender in American Public Schools: Thinking Institutionally," *Signs: Journal of Women in Culture and Society* 13, no. 4 (Summer 1988): 741–60.

14. Many entries exist for British and American teacher-authors in the biographical dictionaries noted in the "Essential Reference Guide" in this volume.

15. Guglielmo Cavallo & Roger Chartier (Eds.), *A History of Reading in the West* (U Massachusetts P, 1999); Monica Kiefer, *American Children through Their Books 1700–1835* (U Pennsylvania P, 1948).

16. William Blackstone, *Commentaries on the Laws of England* (Clarendon, 1765–1769), chap. 16: "Of Parent and Child"; "In Defense of Marriage," in Steven Ozment, *When Fathers Ruled: Family Life in Reformation Europe* (Harvard UP, 1983), 1–49.

17. Edmund Coote in Paul Monroe (Ed.), *Cyclopedia of Education* (Macmillan, 1911); Echols & Williams, *Annotated Index of Medieval Women*, 386, 387.

18. *The Work of Mrs. Chapone: Now First Collected. Containing, I. Letters on the Improvement of the Mind. II. Miscellaneous . . . In Four Volumes* (Wells & Wait, 1809). In 1574 the first known nursing manual was published in Germany to assist those caring for the sick; in Richard Shryock, *The History of Nursing: An Interpretation of the Social and Medical Factors Involved* (W. B. Saunders, 1959), 161.

19. Anthony Benezet in Joan Jensen, *Loosening the Bonds: Mid-Atlantic Farm Women* (Yale UP, 1981), 169. Mrs. Pinckney in Elisabeth Anthony Dexter, *Colonial Women of Affairs: A Study of Women in Business and the Professions in America before 1776* (Houghton Mifflin, 1924), 122.

20. Edward Gordon & Elaine Gordon, *Centuries of Tutoring: A History of Alternative Education in America and Western Europe* (UP of America, 1990).

21. Mary Evans, *Jane Austen & the State* (Tavistock/Methuen, 1987).

22. Fiona MacCarthy, "Governess on Speed," review of *Christina Rossetti: A Writer' Life*, by Jan Marsh, *New York Review of Books* (Nov. 2, 1995).

23. Miss Danesbury in L. T. [Elizabeth Thomasina] Meade, *A World of Girls: The Story of a School* (New York Book, 1911).

24. Ruth Bowmaker & Lucy Walker in Marjorie Theobald, *Knowing Women: Origins of Women's Education in Nineteenth-Century Australia* (Cambridge UP, 1996); Louisa Geoghegan in Lucy Frost, *No Place for a Nervous Lady: Voices from the Australian Bush* (U Queensland P, 1984, 1995).

25. Miss Grant in Jill Ker Conway, *The Road from Coorain* (Vintage, 1990): 35.

26. Jo Ann Kay McNamara, *Sisters in Arms: Catholic Nuns through Two Millennia* (Harvard UP, 1996); Lina Eckenstein, *Women under Monasticism* (Cambridge UP, 1896); Suzanne Wemple, *Women in Frankish Society: Marriage and the Cloister 500–900* (U Pennsylvania P, 1981).

27. Mary Ritter Beard, "Woman—the Pioneer," CBS Radio Address, 1939, in Ann J. Lane (Ed.), *Mary Ritter Beard, A Sourcebook* (Schocken Books, 1977), 194.

28. Peter Green, "The Women and the Gods," *New York Review of Books* 54, no. 11 (June 28, 2007), 30n1; Mary Lawrence McKenna, S.C.M.M., *Women of the Church: Role and Renewal* (P. J. Kenedy & Sons, 1967), 147.

29. Mary Ann Dzuback, "Gender and the Politics of Knowledge," *History of Education Quarterly* 43, no. 2 (Summer 2003): 172–195; Margaret L. King, *Women of the Renaissance* (U Chicago P, 1991).

30. Jacqueline Pascal and *Rules for the Children of Port-Royal,* in Monroe, *Cyclopedia of Education.*

31. James Albisetti, "Froebel Crosses the Alps: Introducing the Kindergarten in Italy," *History of Education Quarterly* 49, no. 2 (May 2009): 159–69; Ann Taylor Allen, "American and German Women in the Kindergarten Movement, 1850–1914," in Henry Geist, Jurgen Heideking, & Jurgen Herbst (Eds.), *German Influences on Education in the United States to 1917* (Cambridge UP, 1995), 85–102

32. Nicholas Orme, *English Schools in the Middle Ages* (Methuen, 1973), esp. 52–56.

33. Ward cited in McNamara, *Sisters in Arms,* 463–64.

34. This phase of the story of the Loreto Sisters (Institute of the Blessed Virgin Mary) in Rosemary Williams, "From Isolation to Integration: St Mary's Hall, University of Melbourne, 1918–1968," *History of Education Review* 27, no. 1 (1998): 19–32.

35. Francis Bacon in Foster Watson (Comp.), *English Writers on Education, 1480–1603: A Source Book* (Scholars' Facsimiles & Reprints, 1967), 503.

36. Lovekin in Phil Gardner, *The Lost Elementary Schools of Victorian England: The People's Education* (Croom Helm, 1984).

37. Hannah More in Monroe, *Cyclopedia of Education.*

38. Lee Holcombe, *Victorian Ladies at Work: Middle-Class Working Women in England and Wales 1850–1914* (Archon Books, 1973), 25; Jane McDermid, "Wells, Helena (1761?–1824)", *Oxford Dictionary of National Biography* (Oxford UP, 2004).

39. Mrs. Blyeth in Canon J. S. Purvis, *Educational Records* (St. Anthony's Press, 1959), 103.

40. Ruggles in Alison Prentice (Ed.), *Canadian Women: A History* (Harcourt Brace Jovanovich, 1988).

41. The chief sources for this section are Orme, *English Schools in the Middle Ages,* 54–55; Echols & Williams, *Annotated Index of Medieval Women;* "Dame Schools—England"; and "Women, Higher Education of," both in Monroe, *Cyclopedia of Education;* Brother Azarias, "The Primary Schools in the Middle Ages," *Educational Review* 1 (March 1891): 220–43; and the biographical dictionaries of literary women.

42. Dr. Cage in Carl Bridenbaugh, *Vexed and Troubled Englishmen, 1500–1642* (Oxford UP, 1968), 334.

43. Echols & Williams, *Annotated Index of Medieval Women.*

44. Bathsua Makin in Monroe, *Cyclopedia of Education;* León, *Uppity Women of the Renaissance,* 70–71; Gerda Lerner, *The Creation of Feminist Consciousness: From the Middle Ages to Eighteen-Seventy* (Oxford UP, 1993).

45. Millicent Mali, *Madam Campan: Educator of Women, Confidant of Queens* (U. Press of America, 1979).

46. Linda Clark, "The Primary Education of French Girls: Pedagogical Prescriptions and Social Realities, 1880–1940," *History of Education Quarterly* 21, no. 4 (Winter 1981): 411–42; Rebecca Rogers, "Competing Visions of Girls' Secondary Education in Post-revolutionary France," *History of Education Quarterly* 34, no. 2 (Summer 1994): 147–70.

47. Coote cited in E. Jennifer Monaghan, "The Three R's: Notes on the Acquisition of Literacy and Numeracy Skills in Seventeenth-Century New England" (paper presented at the Annual Meeting of the American Educational Research Association, New Orleans, April 23–27, 1984).

48. J. H. Higginson, "Dame Schools," *British Journal of Educational Studies* 22, no. 2 (June 1974): 166–81; D. P. Leinster-Mackay, "Dame Schools: A Need for Review," *British Journal of Educational Studies* 24, no. 1 (Feb. 1976): 33.

49. From a reminiscence of a dame school student in Norwich (CT) in Walter Herbert Small, *Early New England Schools* (Ginn, 1914), 183. The term "abcdarians" (abecedario, abecedaria) was probably familiar before John Minsheu's *Guide into Tongues* (John Browne's Shop, 1617); in Monroe, *Cyclopedia of Education.*

50. John Brinsley, *Ludis literarius; or, The Grammar School,* is reproduced in Cohen, *Education in the United States,* 1:284–89.

51. Brinsley is quoted in Jon Teaford, "The Transformation of Massachusetts Education, 1670–1780," *History of Education Quarterly* 10, no. 3 (Autumn 1970): 280–307.

52. Oxford dean in Pamela Horn, *Education in Rural England 1800–1914* (St. Martin's Press, 1978), 5, 10.

53. Mary Russell Mitford, "The Village Schoolmistress" extract in Edward Eggleston, *The Schoolmaster in Literature* (American Book, 1892), 188–99.

54. Charles Hoole in John Lawson & Harold Silver, *A Social History of Education in England* (Methuen, 1973), 8. Literacy rates for both sexes may have been higher in early modern Europe than previously thought; see, e.g., Michael Van Cleave Alexander, *The Growth of English Education 1348–1638* (Pennsylvania State UP, 1990).

55. On rural Scotland see David Kent, "Libraries, Learning and the People in Enlightenment Scotland," *History of Education Review* 24, no. 1 (1995): 1–15; Jane McDermid, "Gender and Geography: The Schooling of Poor Girls in the Highlands and Islands of Nineteenth-Century Scotland," *History of Education* 32, no. 2 (2003): 30–45.

56. In W. E. Tate, "Some Yorkshire Dame Schools," *History of Education Journal* 4, no. 3 (Spring 1953): 93–96, with spellings as in the original; Horn, *Education in Rural England.*

57. In Prentice, *Canadian Women.*

58. Maurice Whitehead, *The Academies of the Reverend Bartholomew Booth in Georgian England and Revolutionary America* (Edwin Mellen Press, 1996).

59. William O. Walker Jr., "The 'Theology of Woman's Place' and the 'Paulinist' Tradition," *Semeia: An Experimental Journal for Biblical Criticism* 28 (1983): 101–12.

60. Bernard Bailyn, *The Barbarous Years: The Peopling of British North America; The Conflict of Civilizations, 1600–1675* (Knopf, 2012).

61. John Greenleaf Whittier, "Our State" (II, III), in *Songs of Labor, and Other Poems* (Ticknor, Reed, & Fields, 1850), p. 334 in 1888 edition.

62. Ruth Wallis Herndon & John E. Murray (Eds.), *Children Bound to Labor: The Pauper Apprentice System in Early America* (Cornell UP, 2009); Committee on Pioneer Women in Education, *Some Pioneer Women Teachers of North Carolina* (North Carolina Delta Kappa Gamma, 1955); Carpenter indenture in *Vermont Quarterly* 20, no. 4 (Oct. 1952): 305–6.

63. Eliza Lucas in Dexter, *Colonial Women of Affairs,* 119–22.

64. Maria Bryan Harford in Carol Bleser (Ed.), *Tokens of Affection: The Letters of a Planter's Daughter in the Old South* (U Georgia P, 1996), esp. 57.

65. Hannah Gilley in American Mother's Committee, *Mothers of Achievement in American History, 1776–1976* (C. E. Tuttle, 1976), 240; Fannie Emily Conant Blarcom in Frederick Odell Conant, *A History and Genealogy of the Conant Family in England and America* (Harris & Williams, 1887); C. F. Adams Jr. to Endicott Peabody, in James McLachlan, *American Boarding Schools: A Historical Study* (Scribner, 1970), 269.

66. Manuscript diary of Rachel Van Dyke, entries for May 29, Aug. 22, Oct. 21, Nov. 27, & Dec. 30, 1810, & May 4, 1811, Special Collections and Archives, Rutgers University Libraries. Punctuation and spelling as in the original. A published and annotated version is Lucia McMahon & Deborah Schriver (Eds.), *To Read My Heart: The Journal of Rachel Van Dyke, 1810–1811* (U Pennsylvania P, 2000). On Miss Hay, see Joan Burstyn, *Past and Promise: Lives of New Jersey Women* (Syracuse UP, 1997), 72.

67. Lawrence Cremin, *American Education: The Colonial Experience, 1607–1783* (Harper & Row, 1970), 173; Joel Perlmann, Silvana Siddali, & Keith Whitescarver, "Literacy, Schooling, and Teaching among New England Women, 1730–1820," *History of Education Quarterly* 37, no. 2 (Summer 1997): 117–39.

68. Mrs. Pentecost Matthews in Jo Anne Preston, "'He Lives as a *Master*': Seventeenth-Century Masculinity, Gendered Teaching, and Careers of New England Schoolmasters," *History of Education Quarterly* 41, no. 1 (Fall 2003): 350–71.

69. Dexter, *Colonial Women of Affairs,* 79–81.

70. Autobiography of the Rev. John Barnard in *Collections of the Massachusetts Historical Society,* 3rd ser. (John H. Eastburn, Printer, 1836), 5:177–243, esp. 178, 179.

Chapter 2 · "School Dames in Each Quarter"

1. Framingham employed women at least from 1770, when the March town meeting appointed a committee "to provide school dames." J. H. Temple, *History of Framingham, Massachusetts . . . with a Genealogical Register* (Town of Framingham, 1887), 256.

2. U.S. Bureau of the Census, *Census Statistics of Teachers,* Bulletin no. 23 (1905), 5.

3. G. Stanley Hall, introduction to Johann Pestalozzi, *Leonard and Gertrude* (D. C. Heath, 1885).

4. Teachers' names are from archival sources and published secondary sources, where cited; when a source is not given, names are from personal acquaintance; biographical data in miscellaneous obituaries and school and college alumni records; or compilations otherwise cited in in this text, including its essential reference guide.

5. Beth Hill, "The Sisters of St. Ann," *The Alaska Journal* 7, no. 1 (Winter 1977): 40–44.

6. U.S. Bureau of the Census, *Census Statistics of Teachers* (1905), 8–9.

7. The writer was Samuel Gray, a future Abbot trustee, quoted in Susan McIntosh Lloyd, *A Singular School: Abbot Academy 1828–1973* (Phillips Academy, 1979), 11, 480n16.

8. Henry Gilpin, "The American Missionaries in Greece," address at St. Luke's Church, Philadelphia, Oct. 13, 1856 (King & Baird, 1856); Mary P. Ryan, "A Women's

Awakening: Evangelical Religion and the Families of Utica, New York, 1800–1840," *American Quarterly* 30, no. 5 (Winter 1978): 602–23.

9. Mary Johnson, "Victorine du Pont: Heiress to the Education Dream of Pierre Samuel du Pont de Nemours," *Delaware History* 19 (1981): 88–105.

10. Jonathan Messerli, *Horace Mann: A Biography* (Knopf, 1972), 2. During the 1850s Lydia Mann was herself a teacher, at Myrtilla Miner's Colored Girls' School in Washington, DC; in Myrtilla Miner entry in James, *Notable American Women*.

11. Benjamin Mays, *Born to Rebel: An Autobiography* (Charles, 1971), 11. Mays' students at Morehouse included Martin Luther King Jr.

12. Margaret Creighton, "The Captains' Children: Life in the Adult World of Whaling, 1852–1907," *American Neptune* 38 (July 1978): 203–11.

13. *South Carolina and American General Gazette* (Sept. 11, 1755, & Oct. 2, 1776), cited in Julia Cherry Spruill, *Women's Life and Work in the Southern Colonies* (U North Carolina P, 1938; Norton, 1972), 256.

14. Lucy Blakewell Audubon in Mary Ormsbee Whitton, *These Were the Women: U.S.A. 1776–1860* (Hastings House, 1954).

15. Edward Hitchcock, *The Power of Christian Benevolence Illustrated in the Life and Labors of Mary Lyon* (Hopkins, Bridgman, 1851).

16. Lucinda Hinsdale Stone and Eliza Allen Starr in James, *Notable American Women*.

17. Gertrude Ella Clanton Thomas Papers, David M. Rubenstein Rare Book & Manuscript Library, Duke University Library, by permission; Lusanar Clark in Stephen Cresswell (Ed.), *We Will Know What War Is: The Civil War Diary of Sirene Bunten* (Maclain, 1993), 77 (entry for Dec. 13, 1864).

18. Adolf Schroeder & Carla Schulz-Geisberg (Eds.), *"Hold Dear, As Always": Jette, a German Immigrant Life in Letters,* trans. Adolf Schroeder (U Missouri P, 1988).

19. Johnson & Ida Butts' response to Amanda Stewart's inquiry, April 2, 1882, in Stewart-Lockwood Family Collection, Kansas Collection, Spencer Research Library, University of Kansas (hereafter SLC), by permission.

20. Marguerite Renner, "Who Will Teach? Changing Job Opportunities and Roles for Women in the Evolution of the Pittsburgh Public Schools, 1830–1900" (Ph.D. diss., University of Pittsburgh, 1981), esp. 31–32.

21. Trinity School in John Martin Campbell, *The Prairie Schoolhouse* (U New Mexico P, 1996).

22. "Organization of Ward Alumnae," clipping, Sept. 12, 1912, in Nashville Scrapbook, Tennessee State Library. On Catholic schools see chaps. 11 and 13 in this volume.

23. Robert Seybolt, "Schoolmasters of Colonial Boston," *Publications of the Colonial Society of Massachusetts: Transactions* (The Society, 1932), 27:130–56.

24. Robert Seybolt, *Some Schoolmasters of Colonial New York* (SUNY P, 1921); Reston Nelson Potts Jr., "The Dutch Schools in North America, 1620–1750" (Ph.D. diss., Rutgers University, 1973). The first school founded in the American colonies was created by the Reformed Dutch Church (1633) in New Amsterdam, followed in 1635 by the Puritans' Boston Latin Grammar School.

25. See also Ronald William Howard, "Education and Ethnicity in Colonial New York, 1664–1763: A Study in the Transmission of Culture in Early America" (Ph.D. diss.,

University of Tennessee, Knoxville, 1978), 177; Joseph Lloyd in Alice Morse Earle, *Child Life in Colonial Days* (Macmillan, 1899), 77.

26. Thomas Woody, *Early Quaker Education in Pennsylvania* (Teachers College P, 1920); Joan M. Jensen, *Loosening the Bonds: Mid-Atlantic Farm Women, 1750–1859* (Yale UP, 1988); Leonard S. Kenworthy, *Quaker Education: A Source Book* (Quaker, 1987).

27. John Ashe in Committee on Pioneer Women in Education, *Some Pioneer Women Teachers of North Carolina* (North Carolina Delta Kappa Gamma Society, 1955), 1.

28. R. E. Banta, "Learning on the River," in *Rivers of America: The Ohio* (Rinehart, 1949), 411.

29. Charles Coon in Spruill, *Women's Life and Work in the Southern Colonies,* esp. 190, 256; Committee on Pioneer Women in Education, *Some Pioneer Women Teachers of North Carolina,* 4; Kim Tolley & Nancy Beadie, "Socioeconomic Incentives to Teach in New York and North Carolina: Toward a More Complex Model of Teacher Labor Markets, 1800–1850," *History of Education Quarterly* 46, no. 1 (Spring 2006): 36–72.

30. Joel Perlmann & Robert Margo, *Women's Work? American School Teachers, 1685–2001* (U Chicago P, 2001).

31. Laura Arnold Liebman (Ed.), *Experience Mayhew's Indian Converts . . . of Martha's Vineyard* (U Massachusetts P, 2008), 270; Jennifer Monaghan, "'She Loved to Read in Good Books': Literacy and the Indians of Martha's Vineyard, 1643–1725," *History of Education Quarterly* 30, no. 4 (Winter 1990): 493–522.

32. Milton Halsey Thomas (Ed.), *The Diary of Samuel Sewall, 1674–1729,* 2 vols. (Farrar, Straus & Giroux, 1973), 1:130, 277, 338, 343; 2:983.

33. Esther Forbes, *Paul Revere & the World He Lived In* (Houghton Mifflin, 1942).

34. Account in Thomas Wentworth Higginson's biography of Mrs. Child, in Parton, *Eminent Women of the Age,* 41.

35. Joel Perlmann & Robert Margo, "Who Were America's Teachers? Toward a Social History and a Data Archive," *Historical Methods* 22, no. 2 (Spring 1989): esp. 127–28.

36. Geraldine Clifford, "A Sisyphean Task: Historical Perspectives on Writing and Reading Instruction," in Anne Dyson (Ed.), *Collaboration through Writing and Reading* (National Council of Teachers of English, 1989), 25–83.

37. The first association of professional teachers, as distinct from the priestly class, may have been the scribes; their *edubba* (tablet house) dates from c. 3000 BCE Sumeria; in R. Freeman Butts, *The Education of the West: A Formative Chapter in the History of Civilization* (McGraw-Hill, 1975), 42–43.

38. Lois K. Kernaghan, "Deborah How Cottnam," *Dictionary of Canadian Biography,* vol. 5 (University of Toronto / Université Laval, 1983); Mary Johnson, "Madame Rivardi's Seminary in the Gothic Mansion," *Pennsylvania Magazine of History and Biography* 104, no. 1 (Jan. 1980), 3–36; and Mary Johnson, "Antoinette Brevost: A Schoolmistress in Early Pittsburg," *Winterthur Portfolio* 15 (Summer 1980): 151–68.

39. From "Pages from an Autobiography, Edited by Her Son," 90, in Papers of Sarah Knowles Bolton (1841–1916), Schlesinger Library on the History of Women in America, Radcliffe Institute, Harvard University, by permission.

40. Mrs. Harvey in "All Schools Were Not Public," *Nevada County Historical* Society 16, no. 2 (May 1962): 4; Charles H. Tennyson, "History of Education in Wichita County" (master's thesis, East Texas State Teachers College, 1925).

41. Anne Firor Scott, "The Ever Widening Circle: The Diffusion of Feminist Values from the Troy Female Seminary, 1833–1872," *History of Education Quarterly* 9, no. 1 (Spring 1979): 3–25.

42. Edward Deming Andrews, "The County Grammar Schools and Academies of Vermont," *Proceedings of the Vermont Historical Society* 4, no. 3 (Sept. 1936): 117–206; David Tyack & Elisabeth Hansot, *Learning Together: A History of Coeducation in American Public Schools* (Yale UP, 1990).

43. Winifred Richmond, "Present Practices and Tendencies in the Secondary Education of Girls," *Pedagogical Seminary* 23 (June 1916): 185

44. Helen Hooven Santmyer, ". . . *And Ladies of the Club*" (Berkley Books, 1985), 285.

45. The Abercrombies in "Schools" entry in card catalogue and letter of Octavia Zollicoffer Bond (Jan. 28, 1932) in Bond Papers, courtesy of the Tennessee State Library and Archives; Mary Bouhanan Gordon Papers in Dolph Briscoe Center for American History, University of Texas Library, by permission; Katherine S. Batts Carrington, in W. E. Benjamin Collection, Rare Books and Manuscript Library, Columbia University.

46. Carl Kaestle, *Evolution of an Urban School System: New York City, 1750–1850* (Harvard UP, 1973), 38n20.

47. Mordecai leaflet reproduced in Cohen, *Education in the United States,* 3:1572.

48. Carrie White, diary entry for Jan. 12, 1883, in Special Collections Division, University of Washington Library, by permission.

49. James Wallace, "Achievements and Anxieties: Twins Complete a Second Year of Teaching in a New Hampshire Village School, 1920–1921" (unpublished paper, 1994, courtesy of Professor Wallace, Lewis and Clark College).

50. Other examples are in Campbell, *Prairie Schoolhouse.*

51. Frank H. Bredeweg, C.S.B., "Catholic Schools and Their American Roots," in Mary Mahar (Ed.), *Catholic Schools in America* (Fisher, for National Catholic Educational Association, 1979), ii.

52. Terrell (1857–1925) remarks in the *Evening Star* (June 13, 1899) in Robert Heberton Terrell Papers, Manuscript Division, Library of Congress. Gender is treated only incidentally in Howard Rabinowitz, "Half a Loaf: The Shift from White to Black Teachers in the Negro Schools of the Urban South, 1865–1890," *Journal of Southern History* 40, no. 4 (Nov. 1974): 565–94.

53. *History of Cincinnati and Hamilton County, Ohio* (S. B. Nelson, 1894), 98.

54. Joanna Graham Bethune in Ohles, *Biographical Dictionary of American Educators,* 1:122.

55. Boston example in David Nasaw, *Schooled to Order: A Social History of Public Schooling in the United States* (Oxford UP, 1979), 22–23.

56. Graham Russell Hodges, *Root & Branch: African Americans in New York and East Jersey 1613–1863* (U North Carolina P, 1999), 218.

57. Catherine Ann Curry, "Shaping Young San Franciscans: Public and Catholic Schools in San Francisco, 1851–1906" (Ph.D. diss., Graduate Theological Union, Berkeley, 1987), 71.

58. "Full Text of 'Abstract of the Proceedings of the Massachusetts Teachers Association 1845–80'" (typescript volume in UCLA Library).

59. Carl Kaestle, "Victory of the Common School Movement: A Turning Point in American Educational History," in *Historians on America* (U.S. Department of State, 2008), 22–29.

60. Linda Auwers, "Social Meaning of Female Literacy: Windsor, Connecticut, 1660–1775," *Newberry Papers in Family and Community History 77*, 4A (Newberry Library, 1977); Walter Herbert Small, *Early New England Schools* (Ginn, 1914).

61. In "Dr. William A. Alcott," in Barnard, *Memoirs of Teachers,* 51–64. His autobiography was first published as *Confessions of a Schoolmaster* (Gould, Newman and Saxton, 1839).

62. Dedham in Elizabeth Dexter, *Colonial Women of Affairs: Women in Business and the Professions in America Before 1776* (Houghton Mifflin, 1924, 1931), 82. Mehetabel Ellis in *Dedham Historical Register* (Dedham Historical Society, 1892), 3:116.

63. Tolley & Beadie, "Socioeconomic Incentives to Teach," 65; Joel Perlman, Silvana Siddall, & Keith Wisecarver, "Literacy, Schooling and Teaching among New England Women, 1730–1820," *History of Education Quarterly* 37, no. 2 (Summer 1997): 117–39.

64. Hannah Adams, *Memoir* (1832) extract in Mary Beard (Ed.), *America through Women's Eyes* (Macmillan, 1933; Greenwood Press, 1969), esp. 175.

65. Josephine Pearson, Student Work File, in Box 12, Josephine Pearson Papers, courtesy of Tennessee State Library and Archives.

66. U.S. Bureau of the Census, *Historical Statistics of the United States*; National Center for Educational Statistics, *Teachers in Public and Private Elementary and Secondary Schools, by Selected Characteristics: 1993–1994* (NCES, 1994).

67. "School Report of the Secretary of the Territory for the Year 1847," in Lloyd P. Jorgenson, *The Founding of Public Education in Wisconsin* (Wisconsin State Historical Society, 1956), 161, 202–3.

68. Mary Petherbridge to Nora Stewart, Oct. 15, 1882 (emphasis in original); Di Magill to Mary J. Stewart, Feb. 19, 1884; & Wallace Boughton to May Stewart, Aug. 18 & Oct. 16, 1884; in SLC.

69. Estelle Reel, "Educational Advantages: Wyoming," in Estelle Reel Collection; Minnie A. Rietz, "Wyoming Schools from 1882–1894," 12, WPA Project typescript, both in Wyoming State Archives.

70. Committee on Pioneer Women in Education, *Some Pioneer Women Teachers of North Carolina.*

71. Judith Joyner, *Beginnings: Education in Colonial South Carolina* (Museum of Education, University of South Carolina, 1985); U.S. Bureau of the Census, *Census Statistics of Teachers,* Census Bulletin no. 23 (1905).

72. Keith Melder, "Woman's High Calling: The Teaching Profession in America, 1830–1860," *American Studies* 13, no. 2 (Fall 1972): 19–32; James Boykin, "Women in the Public Schools," *Educational Review* 18 (Sept 1899): 138–43; Willard Elsbree, *The American Teacher* (American Book, 1939).

73. Disaggregated from tables in Kay Hodes Kamin, "The Woman Peril in American Public Schools: How Perilous?" (Unpublished paper [Rosary College] presented at the Berkshire Conference on the History of Women, Cambridge, MA, 1974).

74. H. R. Bonner, "Compulsory Attendance Laws," *American School Board Journal* 58 (Dec. 1919–Feb. 1920), 37–39.

75. Edward L. Thorndike, *Education: A First Book* (Macmillan, 1912), 155–56.

76. In *Statistics of State School Systems, 1933–34,* U.S. Office of Education Bulletin no. 2 (1935), 66–67.

77. Perlmann & Margo fault reliance on census data in *Women's Work?* Ronald Butchart, Amy Rollen, & Kevin Williams found women teachers more often underreported than men in their Troy (NY), Louisiana, and South Carolina data; in "Method Matters: The GIGO Effect in Research on the History of Teachers" (paper presented at the Annual Meeting, American Educational Research Association, New Orleans, April 2002).

78. George W. Pierson, "A Restless Temper. . . . ,"*American Historical Review* 49, no. 4 (July 1964): 969–89.

79. Adolphine Fletcher Terry, typescript *Memoir,* as told to Carolyn Rose. Used by permission of William L. Terry, a son, and the Quapaw Quarter Association, owner of the manuscript.

80. For example, W. Lee Hansen, "Total and Private Rates of Return to Investment in Schooling," *Journal of Political Economy* 71 (April 1963): 128–40.

81. Ian Brice, "The Early Co-education Movement in English Secondary Education," in Stephen Murray-Smith (Ed.), *Melbourne Studies in Education* (Melbourne UP, 1980). See the 26-nation average in *Annuaire international de l'education et de l'enseignement* (Geneva: International Bureau of Education, 1936).

82. Christina Florin, "Social Closure as a Professional Strategy: Male and Female Teachers from Cooperation to Conflict in Sweden, 1860–1906," *History of Education* 20, no. 1 (1991): 17–26.

83. In 1935 women were 64% of elementary teachers and 57% of secondary teachers in France; in *Annuaire international de l'education et de l'enseignement*; U.S. Bureau of Education, Bulletin no. 10 (1933).

84. College figures in Mabel Newcomer, *A Century of Higher Education for American Women* (Harper, 1959), 49; high school coeducation in Thomas Woody, *A History of Women's Education in the United States* (Science Press, 1929).

85. Alison Prentice et al., *Canadian Women: A History* (Harcourt Brace Jovanovich, 1988), 68, 156.

86. Rollo Arnold, "Women in the New Zealand Teaching Profession, 1877–1920," in *New Zealand Journal of Educational Studies* 20, no 1 (May 1985): 70–81.

87. Some letters of immigrants appear in Lucy Frost, *No Place for a Nervous Lady: Voices from the Australian Bush* (McPhee Gribble, 1984), 189.

88. Martin Sullivan, *Men and Women of Port Phillip* (Hale & Iremonger, 1985), 254–61; Janina Trotman, "Women Teachers in Western Australian 'Bush' Schools, 1900–1939: Passive Victims of Oppressive Structures?," *History of Education Quarterly* 46, no. 2 (Summer 2006): 248–73.

89. James Albisetti, "Could Separate Be Equal? Helene Lange and Women's Education in Imperial Germany," *History of Education Quarterly* 22, no. 3 (Fall 1982): 301–18; & James C. Albisetti, "Between Unemployment Crisis and Government Regulation: Women Secondary School Teachers in Prussia Between the Wars," in Claudia Huerkamp, *Bildungsburgerinnen: Frauen im Studien und in akademischen Berufen, 1900–1945,* trans. Linda von Hoene (Vandenhoeck & Ruprecht, 1996).

90. I am indebted to Dr. Hannelore Faulstich-Wieland of Münster for her discussion of class, attitudes, and practices affecting coeducation.

91. In 1860 the U.S. total population figure is for the nonslave population; in Virginia Penny, *The Employment of Women: A Cyclopaedia of Women's Work* (Walker, Wise, 1863), 38.

92. Mary E. Kelly, *Adventures of an Exchange Teacher* (Vintage Books, 1954), 69–70.

93. "The most important structural feature of American society bearing on the participation of 19th century middle class women in the political life of the nation was the limited extent of State centralization and intervention in social services." In Shirley Carmichael Cartwright, "Blessed Drudgery: Womanly Virtue and Nineteenth Century Organizations" (Ph.D. diss., University of California, Davis, 1977), 408.

94. Renner, *Who Will Teach?*; Robert Church, *Education in the United States: An Interpretive History* (Free Press, 1976); William Reese, *The Origins of the American High School* (Yale UP, 1995).

95. The Michigan Supreme Court effectively foreclosed the issue nationally in 1874, ruling (in *Stuart & Others v. School District No. 1 of the Village of Kalamazoo*) that levying taxes to provide a free high school education was not unlawful. Court text in Cohen, *Education in the United States*, 2:1270–80.

96. B. T. Nichols to Amanda Stewart, May 18, 1885, in SLC. Spelling as in the original, some punctuation inserted for clarity.

Chapter 3 · "A Sisterhood of Instruction, Essential to the World's Progress"

1. Mrs. Federson in Belle Kearney, *A Slaveholder's Daughter* (Abbey Press, 1900), 31.

2. Nita Katharine Pyburn, "The Public School System of Charleston before 1860," *South Carolina Historical Magazine* 61 (April 1960): 86–98.

3. Oliver Johnson (1821–1907), *A Home in the Woods: Pioneer Life in Indiana* (Indiana UP, 1951).

4. Quotation from Fernand Braudel, *On History [Ecrites sur l'histoire]* (1969). English translation by Sarah Matthews (U Chicago P, 1982), 10, 20.

5. The following chapter develops a more individualistic, less macrosocial account, a division of emphases adopted for descriptive and analytical purposes.

6. Greenfield School Accounts, April 1, 1847, in William A. Tunnell Papers, Illinois State Historical Society Collections, Abraham Lincoln Presidential Library, Springfield. Cf. Kim Tolley & Nancy Beadie, "Socioeconomic Incentives to Teach in New York and North Carolina: Toward a More Complex Model of Teacher Labor Markets, 1800–1850,"*History of Education Quarterly* 46, no. 1 (Spring 2006): 36–72.

7. "The Confessions of a Successful Teacher by One of Them," *World's Work* 19, no. 1 (Nov. 1909): 12224–25.

8. A. Abram, "Women Trades in Medieval London," *Economic Journal* 26 (June 1916): 276–85; Fernand Braudel, *Civilization and Capitalism, 15–18th Century*, 3 vols. (Harper, 1984); Jean H. Quataert, "The Shaping of Women's Work in Manufacturing, Guilds, Households, and the State in Central Europe, 1648–1870," *American Historical Review* 90, no. 5 (Dec. 1985): 1122–48.

9. Arthur Schlesinger, *New Viewpoints in American History* (Macmillan, 1922), chap. 6; Elisabeth Anthony Dexter, *Colonial Women of Affairs* (Houghton Mifflin, 1924); Julia

Cherry Spruill, *Women's Life & Work in the Southern Colonies* (U North Carolina P, 1938); Patricia Cleary, "'She Merchants' of Colonial America: Women and Commerce on the Eve of the Revolution" (Ph.D. diss.: Northwestern University, 1989).

10. Eliza Barney to Mr. Higginson, quoted in Caroline Healey Dall, *The College, The Market, and the Court; Or, Women's Relation to Education, Labor, and Law* (Lee & Shepherd, 1867), 197–98.

11. Joan Jensen, *Loosening the Bonds: Mid-Atlantic Farm Women, 1750–1850* (Yale UP, 1968).

12. John Ise, *Sod and Stubble: The Story of a Kansas Homestead* (Wilson-Erickson, 1936).

13. Account by a "Miss Anonymous," cited in Mary Ormsbee Whitton, *These Were the Women: U.S.A. 1776–1860* (Hastings House, 1954), 168–69.

14. Preface to "Lights and Shadows of Factory Life in New England, by a Factory Girl" (1843) and *Voices of Industry* (Nov. 5, 1847), both in Philip Foner (Ed.), *The Factory Girls* (U Illinois P, 1977); Lucy Larcom in James, *Notable American Women*.

15. Nancy F. Cott, *Bonds of Womanhood: "Woman's Sphere" in New England, 1780–1835* (Yale UP, 1977).

16. Morton Hunt, "The Direction of Feminine Evolution," in Seymour M. Farber & Roger H. L. Wilson (Eds.), *The Potential of Woman* (McGraw-Hill, 1963), 258.

17. David Hogan, "'To Better Our Condition': Educational Credentialing and 'the Silent Compulsion of Economic Relations' in the United States, 1830 to the Present," *History of Education Quarterly* 36, no. 3 (Fall 1996): 243–70.

18. Emily Blackwell, "The Industrial Position of Women," *Popular Science Monthly* 23 (July 1883): 388–99; William Hard & Rheta Childe Dorr, "The Woman's Invasion," *Everybody's Magazine* 19, no. 5 (Nov. 1908): 579–91.

19. Eulalia Bourne, *Nine Months Is a Year, at Boboquévari School* (U Arizona P, 1968).

20. Elgar sisters in Tommy Boley (Ed.), *An Autobiography of a West Texas Pioneer: Ella Elgar Bird Dumont* (U Texas P, 1988).

21. Robert Bingham, *The New South: An Address*, 7–8, in Louis Harlan, *Separate and Unequal: Public School Campaigns and Racism in the Southern Seaboard States 1901–1915* (Atheneum, 1969), 31–32.

22. Mary Oates, "Organized Voluntarism: The Catholic Sisters in Massachusetts, 1870–1940," *American Quarterly* 30, no. 5 (Winter 1978): 652–81.

23. Eliot in Shirley Carmichael Cartwright, "'Blessed Drudgery': Womanly Virtue and Nineteenth Century Organizations" (Ph.D. diss.: University of California, Davis), 42.

24. Gamaliel Bradford, "Portraits of American Women: IV. Mary Lyon," *Atlantic Monthly* 122 (Dec. 1918): 785–96, esp. 787; Sister Mary Loretta Petit, O.P., "Samuel Lewis, Educational Reformer Turned Abolitionist" (Ed.D. diss.: Western Reserve University, 1966), 50; Thomas Rich, "The Western Literary Institute and College of Professional Teachers and the Common School Movement in the West, 1830–1849" (Ed. D., diss., Northern Illinois University, 1973), 66.

25. Miss Craft in Culver City (CA), "Schools," *Culver City History,* www.culvercity.org /en/Visitors/CulverCityHistory/Schools.aspx, accessed Nov. 6, 2013. Boston figures in National American Woman Suffrage Association, *Victory, How Women Won It* (H. W.

Wilson, 1940), 91. The maximum annual salary for Boston's women teachers ("assistants") was $450; in *The Boston Directory 1864–5* (Adams, Sampson, 1864); Susan Carter, "Incentives and Rewards in Teaching," in Donald Warren (Ed.), *American Teachers: Histories of a Profession at Work* (Macmillan, 1989), esp. 49.

26. Denver figures in Helen Sumner, *Equal Suffrage* (Harper, 1909).

27. Alison Oram, *Women Teachers and Feminist Politics, 1900–39* (Manchester UP, 1996), 16, 30.

28. Robert Lynd & Helen Merrell Lynd, *Middletown: A Study in Contemporary American Culture* (Harcourt, Brace, 1929); and *Middletown in Transition: A Study in Cultural Conflicts* (Harcourt, Brace, 1937).

29. Rush Welter, *Popular Education and Democratic Thought in America* (Columbia UP, 1962); J. A. Mangan (Ed.), *A Significant Social Revolution: Cross-Cultural Aspects of the Evolution of Compulsory Schooling* (Woburn Press, 1994).

30. Linda Kerber, *Women of the Republic: Intellect and Ideology in Revolutionary America* (U North Carolina P, 1980).

31. Horace Mann. "A Few Thoughts on the Powers and Duties of Woman: Two Lectures" (1853), quoted in Madeline Stern, *We the Women: Career Firsts of Nineteenth-Century America* (Schulte, 1965), 147–77.

32. Kathryn Sklar, "The Schooling of Girls and Changing Community Values in Massachusetts Towns, 1750–1820," *History of Education Quarterly* 33, no. 4 (Winter 1993): 511–42, esp. 528.

33. Michael Katz, *The Irony of Early School Reform* (Harvard UP, 1968).

34. Alonzo Potter & George Emerson, *The School and the Schoolmaster* (Harper, 1842), 204.

35. Kimberly Tolley, "The Science Education of American Girls" (Ph.D. diss., University of California, Berkeley, 1996).

36. Catharine Beecher, *The True Remedy for the Wrongs of Women* (Phillips, Sampson, 1851).

37. Carol Lopate, "Power and Authority in a Rural School: A History of the Green Valley Central School System" (Ph.D. diss., Columbia University, 1974).

38. Average annual attendance in Albert Fishlow, "The American Common School Revival; Fact or Fancy?" in Henry Rossovsky (Ed.), *Industrialization in Two Systems: Essays in Honor of Alexander Gershenkron* (Wiley, 1966), 62.

39. Before the 1890s, medical education was a two-year course. "Reading law" in a practitioner's office and an oral examination before a friendly judge was an alternative to a bachelor's degree and law courses.

40. Jared Willson in John R. Frisch, "To Be Seen and Not Heard: Drugs, Discipline, and a Diary, Three Aspects of Children's Lives in Nineteenth-Century America" (unpublished paper courtesy of Prof. Frisch, Morton College, Cicero, IL, 1978).

41. John Andrew Rice, *I Came Out of the Eighteenth Century* (Harper, 1942), 146.

42. Marcus Eli Ravage, *An American in the Making: The Life Story of an Immigrant* (Harper & Bros., 1917), 90.

43. Samuel Griswold Goodrich, *Recollections of a Lifetime* (Miller, Orton & Mulligan, 1856), vol. 1.

44. Clark Evan Lewis to Miriam Green, Jan. 25, 1867; & Rhoda Ann Davis (?) to "Cousin Mell," Mar. 21, 1867 (original spelling), both in Miriam Green Papers, Indiana Historical Society, by permission.

45. Kathryn Babb Vossler, "Women and Education in West Virginia, 1810–1909," *West Virginia History* 36, no. 4 (July 1975): 271–90.

46. Willard Elsbree, *The American Teacher: Evolution of a Profession in a Democracy* (American Book, 1939), 340, 473.

47. Willard Keyes cited in Lloyd Jorgensen, *The Founding of Public Education in Wisconsin* (Wisconsin State Historical Society, 1956), 12.

48. George Pettitt, *Berkeley: The Town and Gown of It* (Howell-North Books, 1973), 21–4, 139–40.

49. Houston in *Western Journal of Education,* n.s., no. 8 (Aug. 1900), 40.

50. John Outhouse in David Tyack, "Bureaucracy and the Common School: The Example of Portland, Oregon, 1851–1913," *American Quarterly* 19, no. 3 (Fall 1967): 475–98.

51. The pioneering work was Thomas Morain, "The Departure of Males from the Teaching Profession in Nineteenth-Century Iowa," *Civil War History* 26, no. 2 (June 1980): 160–70. Opportunity costs also include the potential earnings lost (forgone income) while meeting rising requirements or qualifying for a new occupation.

52. Wallace Boughton to May Stewart, May 14, 1885, in Stewart-Lockwood Family Collection, Kansas Collection, Spencer Research Library, University of Kansas (hereafter SLC).

53. Calvin Kendall, "The Training of High-School Teachers," *School Review* 21, no. 2 (Feb. 1913): 92. On New York City, Ruth Jacknow Markowitz, *My Daughter, The Teacher: Jewish Teachers in New York City Schools* (Rutgers UP, 1993), 88–89.

54. "In the limited extent of State centralization and intervention in social services . . . America followed a different path toward modernization than did other Western societies undergoing democratic and industrial revolution"; in Samuel P. Huntington, *Political Order in Changing Societies* (Yale UP, 1968).

55. Frederick Wells, *History of Newbury Vermont: From the Discovery of Coös Country to Present Time* (Caledonian, 1902), 209.

56. Reed Ueda, *Avenues to Adulthood: The Origins of the High School and Social Mobility in an American Suburb* (Cambridge UP, 1987), 37–38.

57. Marguerite Renner, "Who Will Teach? Changing Job Opportunities and Roles for Women in the Evolution of the Pittsburgh Public Schools" (Ph.D. diss., University of Pittsburgh, 1981), esp. 100–101.

58. Jabez Brown Collection, Wisconsin State Historical Society.

59. Mrs. Gloyd (later Carry Nation) turned her zeal to antisaloon crusades.

60. C. H. Brown, Dungannon, OH, to Amanda Stewart, Millwood, KS, Sept. 27, 1880; Willie King to Amanda Stewart, March 7 & 10, 1883, both in SLC.

61. Paul Peterson, *The Politics of School Reform, 1870–1940* (U Chicago P, 1985).

62. Mrs. Byars in Thad Sitton & Milam Rowold, *Ringing the Children In: Texas Country Schools* (Texas A&M UP, 1987), 4, 175.

63. Author's interview of Frances Slater (Institute of Education, University of London) at Monash University, Victoria, Australia, September 1981.

64. *Louisville Herald Post* (April 24, 1929).

65. Alexis Lange, *The Lange Book* (Trade, 1927), 278. Lange was the first dean of education at the University of California (hereafter UC), Berkeley.

66. Sitton & Rowold, *Ringing the Children In*, 163; William Link, *A Hard Country and a Lonely Place: Schooling, Society, and Reform in Rural Virginia, 1870–1920* (U North Carolina P, 1986).

67. Ellwood Patterson Cubberley quoted in Ervin Eugene Lewis, *Personnel Problems of the Teaching Staff* (Century, 1925), 255, esp. 160, 180–82.

68. Maude Frazier (1881–1963), unpublished memoir cited in A. D. Hopkins & K. J. Evans, *The First 100: Men and Women Who Shaped Las Vegas* (Huntington Press, 1999).

69. In 1910 Du Rocher (later Sister M. Domitilla) entered nursing; in Irene English, "Sister M. Domitilla," *Biographical Sketches* (National League of Nursing Education, 1939).

70. Jonathan Zimmerman, *Small Wonder: The Little Red Schoolhouse in History and Memory* (Yale UP, 2009).

71. Daniel Boorstin, *The Americans: The National Experience* (Random House, 1965), esp. 134.

72. Robert Wells, "Demographic Change and the Life Cycle of American Families," in Theodore Rabb & Robert Rotberg, *The Family in History: Interdisciplinary Essays* (Harper, 1973), 85–94; World Bank data in Mark Mather, "Fact Sheet: The Decline in U.S. Fertility," in Population Reference Bureau, *World Population Data Sheet 2012*, www.prb .org/Publications/Datasheets/2012/world-population-data-sheet/fact-sheet-us-popula tion.aspx, accessed Nov. 6, 2013.

73. A lucid, nontechnical review of the formative studies of demographers is Carl Degler, *At Odds: Women and Family in America from the Revolution to the Present* (Oxford UP, 1980), chap. 8.

74. Miriam David Colt, *Went to Kansas* (L. Ingells, 1862), 234–37.

75. Republished as Elaine Showalter, *These Modern Women: Autobiographical Essays from the Twenties* (Feminist Press, 1978), esp. 77, 111, 127. The term "feminists" was known and used in France and Holland by 1872.

76. "Statistics on Public High Schools, 1925–1926," *U.S. Bureau of Education Bulletin 1927*, no. 33 (1927).

77. Alexis de Tocqueville, *Democracy in America* (Knopf, 1963), 2:199, 201–3.

78. Effie Richardson interview in Pamela Clair Hronek, "Women and Normal Schools: Tempe Normal, a Case Study, 1885–1925" (Ph.D. diss.: Arizona State University, 1985), 106; Christiane Fischer, "A Profile of Women in Arizona in Frontier Days," *Journal of the West* 16, no. 3 (July 1977): 42–53.

79. Mary Hunter Austin, *A Woman of Genius* (Doubleday, 1912), 219.

80. Carolyn Heilbrun & Margaret Higonnet (Eds.), *The Representation of Women in Fiction* (Johns Hopkins UP, 1983), 152–79; Nina Baym, *Women's Fiction: A Guide to Novels by and about Women in America, 1820–1870* (Cornell UP, 1978).

81. Mary Nelson in Joyce Kinkead (Ed.), *A Schoolmarm All My Life: Personal Narratives from Frontier Utah* (Signature Books, 1996); Alice Louise Reynolds in Bruce A. Van Orden, "George Reynolds: Secretary, Sacrificial Lamb, and Seventy" (Ph.D. diss., Brigham Young University, 1986), esp. chap. 9.

82. Edward Clarke, *Sex in Education; Or, A Fair Chance for the Girls* (James R. Osgood, 1873); Arthur Lapthorn Smith, "Higher Education of Women and Race Suicide," *Popular Science Monthly*, 66 (1905): 466–73.

83. Sally McMillen, *Motherhood in the Old South: Pregnancy, Childbirth, and Infant Rearing* (Louisiana State UP, 1990); Gail Collins, *America's Women: Four Hundred Years of Dolls, Drudges, and Heroine* (William Morrow, 2003).

84. Like Grimké, Mary Chestnut condemned the presence of slave concubines among the planter aristocracy; in C. Vann Woodward (Ed.), *Mary Chestnut's Civil War* (Yale UP, 1981), 29.

85. Roberta Frankfort, *Collegiate Women: Domesticity and Career in Turn-of-the-Century America* (NYU P, 1977).

86. Frankfort, *Collegiate Women*, Daniel Scott Smith, "Family Limitation, Sexual Control, and Domestic Feminism in Victorian America," in Esther Katz & Anita Rapone (Eds.), *Women's Experience in America: An Historical Anthology* (Transaction Books, 1980), 235–57; Frank Stricker, "Cookbooks and Lawbooks: The Hidden History of Career Women in Twentieth Century America," *Journal of Social History* 10, no. 1 (Fall 1976): 1–19.

87. E. C. Hewitt editorial, *Public School Journal* 16 (Sept. 1896): 37.

88. Oscar Handlin in Bernard Weiss (Ed.), *American Education and the European Immigrant: 1840–1940* (U Illinois P, 1982), 14; Rebecca Mann Pennell Dean's journal, courtesy of Elizabeth Bull Waldhauer of Annandale (MN), descendant of Mrs. Dean's sister, Eliza Mann Pennell Blake; contact courtesy of Eleanor Waldhauer Dommerich of Cincinnati and San Francisco.

89. JoEllen McNergney Vinyard, "The Irish on the Urban Frontier: Detroit, 1850–1880" (Ph.D. diss., University of Michigan, 1972), 193.

90. Ann Douglas, *The Feminization of American Religion* (Knopf, 1977); Donald Hall (Ed.), *Muscular Christianity: Embodying the Victorian Age* (Cambridge UP, 1994).

91. *A Voice from the Roman Catholic Laity: The Parochial School Question—an Open Letter to Bishop Keane, Rector of the Catholic University at Washington, D.C.* (Arnold, 1890), 5. Quoted in Hasia R. Diner, *Erin's Daughters in America: Irish Immigrant Women in the Nineteenth Century* (Johns Hopkins UP, 1983), 97.

92. Janet Nolan, *Servants of the Poor: Teachers and Mobility in Ireland and Irish America* (U Notre Dame P, 2004); Sitton & Rowold, *Ringing the Children In*, 173.

93. G. P. Randle to Edgar Strain, Aug. 8 & Aug. 27, 1887, folder 1, Edgar Strain Collection, courtesy of Lincoln Presidential Library, Springfield, IL.

94. Euphemia Watson Strayer, "Our Social Advantages: Careful Resumé of Our Town and Surroundings," *Axtelle Anchor* (July 27, 1900); in City of Axtell (KS), "Careful Resume of Our Town and Surroundings: Our Business Men and What They Are Doing," *History of Axtell, Kansas*, www.marshallco.net/axtell/anchor1900.html, accessed Nov. 6, 2013.

95. Sharon Ordman Geltner, "The Common Schools of Los Angeles, 1850–1900: Variations on a National Pattern" (Ed.D. diss., University of California, Los Angeles, 1972).

96. Howard Rabinowitz, *Race Relations in the Urban South, 1865–1890* (Oxford, 1978), 94. The Yanceyville school in Vanessa Siddle Walker, *Their Highest Potential: An African American School Community in the Segregated South* (U North Carolina P, 1996);

Anthony Dillard, "Nicholas Longworth Dillard," in Jeannine Whitlow (Ed.), *The Heritage of Caswell County, North Carolina* (Caswell County Historical Association, 1985).

97. Raymond Wolters, *The Burden of Brown: Thirty Years of School Desegregation* (U Tennessee P, 1984).

98. Henriette Bruns to Heinrich Geisberg, July 30, 1868. In Adolf Schroeder and Carla Schulz-Geisberg (Eds.), *"Hold Dear, As Always": Jette, a German Immigrant Life in Letters,* trans. Adolf Schroeder (U Missouri P, 1988).

99. Estella Stevens' correspondence in James C. Christie Family Papers, courtesy of Minnesota Historical Society.

100. Deborah Dash Moore, *At Home in America: Second Generation New York Jews* (Columbia UP, 1981); Wendell Pritchett, *Brownsville Brooklyn: Blacks, Jews, and the Changing Face of the Ghetto* (U Chicago P, 2002), chap. 1.

101. In Miriam Cohen, "Changing Education Strategies among Immigrant Generations." *Journal of Social History* 15, no. 3 (Spring 1982): 443–66; Kelly Durand & Louis Sessa, *The Italian Invasion of the Ghetto* (New York, 1909?), 10, reprint in New York Public Library collections.

102. Newbern in Committee on Pioneer Women in Education, *Some Pioneer Women Teachers of North Carolina* (NC Delta Kappa Gamma Society, 1955). The phrase that heads this section was long and widely used, for example, in Lyman Cobb (Ed.), *The North American Reader: Containing a Great Variety of Pieces in Prose and Poetry....* (Cushing & Sons, 1836), 429.

103. Quoted in Christine Ladd Franklin, "The Education of Woman in the Southern States," in Annie Nathan Meyer (Ed.), *Woman's Work in America* (Henry Holt, 1891), 89.

104. Pyburn, "The Public School System of Charleston before 1860."

105. Kearney, *Slaveholder's Daughter,* 41, 71–72; Jane Turner Censer, *The Reconstruction of White Southern Womanhood, 1865–1895* (Louisiana State UP, 2003). Ida Stover Eisenhower in American Mothers Committee, *Mothers of Achievement in American History* (C. E. Tuttle, 1976), 206–7.

106. Eugenia Dunlap Potts, "Woman's Work in Kentucky," in Mary Eagle (Ed.), *The Congress of Women: Held in the Woman's Building, World's Columbian Exposition, Chicago 1893* (International, 1894), 566.

107. Margaret Hearn in Committee on Pioneer Women in Education, *Women Teachers of North Carolina*; Jennie Lines to Daisy Lines, Dec. 9, 1884, in Amelia Akehurst Lines Papers, Hargrett Library, University of Georgia, by permission.

108. Margaret Walker Weber's reminiscences, in Southern Historical Collection, Wilson Library, University of North Carolina, Chapel Hill, by permission.

109. Mary Susan Ker Papers, Wilson Library, University of North Carolina.

110. National Education Association, *Estimates of School Statistics 1973–74,* 28.

111. Elsbree, *American Teacher,* 206–8. Quotation from Clarence Aurner, *History of Education in Iowa* (State Historical Society of Iowa, 1914), 1:76; Virginia Penny, *Employments of Women: A Cyclopedia of Women's Work* (Walker, Wise, 1863), v.

112. Daniel Clark, *Creating the College Man: American Mass Magazines and Middle-Class Manhood, 1890–1915* (U Wisconsin P, 2010).

113. "Woman's Work for the Lowly," in James McPherson, *The Abolitionist Legacy: From Reconstruction to the NAACP* (Princeton UP, 1975), 165.

114. Philippe Ariès, *Centuries of Childhood: A Social History of Family Life,* trans. Robert Baldick (Knopf, 1962); Viviana Zelizer, *Pricing the Priceless Child: The Changing Social Value of Children* (Basic Books, 1985); David Kertzer & Marzio Barbagli (Eds.), *Family Life in the Long Nineteenth Century, 1789–1913* (Yale UP, 2002).

115. Committee in Samuel Randall, *History of the Common School System of the State of New York* (Norwood, 1871), 182, 185–86; Michigan superintendent in Hronek, "Women and Normal Schools," 52.

116. Anna Robeson Burr, *The Autobiography: A Critical and Comparative Study* (Houghton Mifflin, 1909), esp. 310–11.

117. Mary Laselle & Katherine Wiley, *Vocations for Girls* (Houghton Mifflin, 1913), 79–80.

118. Alice Kessler Harris, *Out to Work: A History of Wage-Earning Women in the United States* (Oxford UP, 1982), 225; Julia Kirk Blackwelder, *Now Hiring: The Feminization of Work in the United States, 1900–1995* (Texas A&M UP, 1997), esp. 124; Jennifer Diamond, "Caught between the Typewriter and the Toilet Bowl" (paper presented at the 14th Berkshire Conference of Women Historians, Minneapolis, MN, June 12–15, 2008).

119. W. Nikola-Lisa & Gail Burnaford, "A Mosaic: Contemporary Schoolchildren's Images of Teachers," in Pamela Joseph & Gail Burnaford (Eds.), *Images of Schoolteachers in America* (Lawrence Erlbaum, 2001), 121.

120. Jo Anne Preston, " 'He lives as a *Master*': Seventeenth-Century Masculinity, Gendered Teaching, and Careers of New England Schoolmasters," *History of Education Quarterly* 41, no. 1 (Fall 2003): 350–71.

121. Superintendent-elect Samuel T. Black, *Proceedings of the California State Teachers Association,* 28th Annual Meeting (Santa Cruz, Dec. 1894), 89, copy in Joseph LeConte Papers, Bancroft Library, UC Berkeley, by permission.

122. Jorgensen, *Founding of Public Education in Wisconsin,* 157.

123. Hershel Parker, *Herman Melville: A Biography,* vol. 1 (Johns Hopkins UP, 1996); Robert Frost in Walter Crockett (Ed.), *Vermonters: A Book of Biographies* (Stephen Daye, 1932); Justin Kaplan, *Walt Whitman: A Life* (Simon & Schuster, 1980).

124. Altgeld in Howard Fast, *The American: A Middle Western Legend* (Duell, Sloan & Pearce, 1946), 28. Five public university campuses in Illinois have an Altgeld Hall.

125. Chicago numbers in Kay Hodes Kamin, "The Woman Peril in American Public Schools: How Perilous?" (paper presented at the third Berkshire Conference of Women Historians, Bryn Mawr College, June 1976). On Boston, Barbara Beatty (Wellesley College) to Geraldine Clifford, April 24, 1991.

126. Edwin A. Lee (Ed.), *Teaching As a Man's Job* (Phi Delta Kappa, 1939), esp. 8, 13.

127. Leonard P. Ayres, *Laggards in Our Schools* (Survey, 1909), 7.

Chapter 4 · "Overflowing from the Domestic Circle"

1. Horace Mann, *Eighth Annual Report (1844),* in *Life and Complete Works of Horace Mann,* 5 vols. (Lee & Shepard, 1891); Edith Hoshino Altbach, *Women in America* (Heath, 1974), 41. The chapter title is from G. Stanley Hall, introduction to Johann Pestalozzi, *Leonard and Gertrude* (D. C. Heath, 1885).

2. M. Carey Thomas to Margaret Hicks, Aug. 30, 1880, in Marjorie Dobkin (Ed.), *The Making of a Feminist: Early Journals and Letters of M. Carey Thomas* (Kent State UP, 1979), 224.

3. *Report of Her Majesty's Commissioners.* . . . (1884), cited in Jane McDermid, "Gender and Geography: The Schooling of Poor Girls in the Highlands and Islands of Nineteenth-Century Scotland," *History of Education Review* 32, no. 2 (2003): 30–43.

4. Anonymous governess in Michael O'Brien (Ed.), *An Evening When Alone: Journals of Four Single Women in the South, 1827–67* (UP of Virginia, 1993), 135.

5. Unnamed teacher in David Hobson, "Across the Generations: Conversations with Retired Teachers," in Pamela Joseph & Gail Burnaford (Eds.), *Images of Schoolteachers in Twentieth-Century America* (St. Martin's Press, 1994), 82.

6. Laura Ellsworth Seiler in Sherna Gluck, *From Parlor to Prison: Five American Suffragists Talk about Their Lives* (Vintage Books, 1976), 189.

7. Libbie Burbank to Amanda Stewart, Mar. 6, 1881, in Stewart-Lockwood Family Collection, Kansas Collection, Spencer Research Library, University of Kansas (hereafter SLC).

8. Blanche Bettington in author's interview, Dec. 17, 1993, Los Angeles.

9. Rosetta Marantz Cohen, *A Lifetime of Teaching: Portraits of Five Veteran High School Teachers* (Teachers College P, 1991).

10. Quoted in Robert Emerson Treacy, "Progressivism and Corinne Seeds: UCLA and the University Elementary School" (Ph.D. diss., University of Wisconsin, 1972), 345. Heffernan was a statewide leader in rural and elementary education with the California State Department of Education.

11. Samantha Yeager in Val Daniels, *A Ranch, a Ring and Everything* (Harlequin, 1966), 51.

12. In a script by Claudia Levin (Smith College Project on Woman and Social Change) for *Only a Teacher,* a 3-part television documentary, PBS, 2000, www.pbs.org/onlyateacher.

13. Diana Natalicio, "Life Is a Team Sport," in Karen Doyle Walton (Ed.), *Against the Tide: Career Paths of Women Leaders in American and British Higher Education* (Phi Delta Kappa Educational Foundation, 1996), esp. 177.

14. Gladys Peterson Meyers in Diane Manning, *Hill Country Teacher* (Twayne, 1990), 65.

15. Author's telephone interviews with Rosemma "Rosie" Burney's sister, Anita Burney (Silver Spring, MD), Sept.–Nov. 1996.

16. Priscilla Tremper in Joseph Illick, *At Liberty: The Story of a Community and a Generation* (U Tennessee P, 1989), 239, 262.

17. Arnold Bennett, *Hilda Lessways* (Dutton, 1911), 6, 8–9.

18. Delia Bacon in Helen Beal Woodward, *The Bold Women* (Books for Libraries, 1953).

19. Villa Fender in Courtney Ann Vaughn-Roberson, "Sometimes Independent but Never Equal—Women Teachers, 1900–1950: The Oklahoma Example," *Pacific Historical Review* 53 (Feb. 1984): 39–58.

20. Adria Reich, "Teaching Is a Good Profession . . . for a Woman," in Judith Stacey, Susan Bereaud & Joan Daniels (Eds.), *"And Jill Came Tumbling After": Sexism in American Education* (Dell, 1974), 337–43.

21. "Sylvia" interview in Dee Ann Spencer, *Contemporary Women Teachers: Balancing Home and School* (Longman, 1986), 72–73.

22. "Cleo" interview in Petra Munro, "Resisting 'Resistance': Stories Women Teachers Tell" (unpublished paper courtesy of the author).

23. Maria Howland in Lina Mainiero (Ed.), *American Women Writers*, 5 vols. (Frederick Ungar, 1980); Bessie Van Vorst & Marie Van Worst, *The Woman Who Toils, Being the Experiences of Two Factory Girls* (Doubleday, 1903), 78.

24. Donna Littlejohn, "Bess Akerson, a longtime S.P. volunteer, dies," *San Pedro News Pilot* (Dec. 23, 1944). "Sally" interview in Claire Sylvan, "The Impact of Motherhood on Teacher Career Attitudes" (Ed.D. diss., Teachers College, 1988).

25. Jean Sarah Pond, *Bradford: A New England Academy* (Bradford Alumnae Association, 1930), 191.

26. Alice Kennedy Lynch in Alice Clare, *The Kennedy Clan and Tierra Redonda* (Marnell, 1935).

27. Lotus Delta Coffman, *The Social Composition of the Teaching Population* (Teachers College P, 1911), 66.

28. Alverson family history in Larry Glassco, *Preacher Afloat* (privately printed, 1992); copy in Archives Department, Urbana (IL) Free Library.

29. Mary Finnin in Peter Gronn, "Sister of an Educated Man: Margaret Robertson Darling," *History of Education Review* 20, no. 1 (1991): 4–21, esp. 8; Vera Brittain, *Women's Work in Modern England* (Noel Douglas, 1928), 60.

30. Ward S. Mason, *The Beginning Teacher: A Survey of New Teachers in the Public Schools 1956–57* (U.S. Department of Health, Education, and Welfare, 1961), 89.

31. Helen Hooven Santmyer, "... *And Ladies of the Club*" (Ohio State UP, 1982), 709.

32. Cohen, *Lifetime of Teaching*, 82.

33. Paul Conkin, *Peabody College: From a Frontier Academy to the Frontiers of Teaching and Learning* (Vanderbilt UP, 2002), esp. 143, 217.

34. Sketchy information on Miss Wims in the entry for Gwendolyn Brooks (b. 1917) in Elaine Showalter, Lea Baechler, & A. Walton Litz (Eds.), *Modern American Women Writers* (Scribner's Sons, 1991), 38–39.

35. Victor Rector to Professor Wardlaw, March 27, 1915, in Papers of Patterson Wardlaw, courtesy of South Caroliniana Library, University of South Carolina.

36. Parke Anderson to Nashville superintendent of schools (February 10, 1926) in Record Group 92, courtesy of Tennessee State Library and Archives.

37. Lillian Quinn in Bowman & Ryan, *Who's Who in Education*; David Riesman, "Teachers as a Counter-cyclical Influence," *School Review* 60 (Spring 1957): 78–91.

38. Ruth Appeldoorn Mead in Kenan Heise, "Artist, Teacher Ruth Appeldoorn Mead," *Chicago Tribune* (February 27, 1994), http://articles.chicagotribune.com/1994-02-27/news/9402270465_1_joseph-albers-longtime-art-teacher-one-person-show, accessed Nov. 6, 2013.

39. Chad Jones, "Verda Delp, Teacher," *Oakland Tribune* (Dec. 9, 1997).

40. Interview with "Lee" in Spencer, *Contemporary Women Teachers*, esp. 20, 26.

41. Mary Hunter Austin (1868–1934), *Earth Horizon* (Houghton Mifflin, 1932), 122; Charles Rosen, "The Future of Music," *New York Review of Books* 48, no. 20 (Dec. 20, 2001); Craig H. Roell, *The Piano in America, 1890–1940* (U North Carolina P, 1989).

42. Author's interview of Vincent Mustacich Jr., Santa Barbara (CA), n.d.

43. Mary Roger Madden, S.P., "This Noble Work; A Ministry of Christian Education for Women, 1840–1910" (paper presented at the History of Education Society Annual Meeting, Kansas City, Oct. 21–25, 1991), 6–7; Kim Tolley, "'A Comfortable Living for Herself and Her Children': The Gender and Wages of North Carolina Music Teachers in a Free Market, 1800–1840" (paper presented at the Annual Meeting, Social Science History Association, Chicago, Nov. 18–21, 2004).

44. Music education in Vermont, courtesy of Betty Bandel (University of Vermont, Burlington), letter to author, April 3, 1979.

45. Janet M. Hooks, *Women's Occupations through Seven Decades*, U.S. Women's Bureau Bulletin no. 218 (Department of Labor, 1947); Jacqueline Hoefer, "June Recital," in *Night in a White Wood* (Sunstone Press, 2003).

46. Carmen Sanabia de Figueroa in American Mothers Committee, *Mothers of Achievement in American History, 1776–1976* (C. E. Tuttle, 1976), 469–70.

47. Eliza Champ Gordon McCabe in Ruth Edmonds Hill & Patricia Miller King (Eds.), *Guide to the Transcripts of the Black Women Oral History Project* (Meckler, 1991).

48. Thad Sitton & Milam C. Rowold, *Ringing the Children In: Texas Country Schools* (Texas A&M UP, 1987), 139.

49. Mary Dalton, *The Hollywood Curriculum: Teachers and Teaching in the Movies* (Peter Lang, 1999), 23.

50. Patty Smith Hill (Ed.), *The Free Kindergarten* (Louisville Free Kindergarten Association, 1894–1895), 42–43.

51. Quoted in Zylpha S. Morton, "Harriet S. Bishop, Frontier Teacher," *Minnesota History* 23 (June 1947): 134, 139.

52. Nora Stewart to family, Oct. 31, 1886, in SLC.

53. Sarah Bigelow, Class of 1851 Records, Class Letter, 1879, Mount Holyoke College Archives and Special Collections, South Hadley (MA), by permission.

54. Alcott diary entry for Feb. 14, 1868, cited in Lee Virginia Chambers-Schiller, *Liberty, a Better Husband: Single Women in America; The Generations of 1780–1840* (Yale UP, 1984); Alcott quoted in Andrew Sinclair, *The Emancipation of the American Woman* (Harper & Row, 1965), 81. Also Nina Auerbach, "The Materfamilias: Power and Presumption," in Dana Hiller & Robin Ann Sheets (Eds.), *Women & Men: The Consequences of Power* (Office of Women's Studies, U of Cincinnati, 1977), 136–37.

55. Emma Dorothy Eliza Nevitt Southworth in J. C. Derby, *Fifty Years among Authors, Books and Publishers* (Carleton, 1884), 214; Mary Kelly, "The Unconscious Rebel: Studies in Feminist Fiction, 1820–1880" (Ph.D. diss., University of Iowa, 1974).

56. Miss Mayhew in Edith Layton, "Autumn Leaves," in *A Love for All Seasons* (Penguin Books, 1992), 177.

57. Sarah Stiles in Linda Auwers, "The Social Meaning of Female Literacy, Windsor Connecticut, 1660–1775," in Newberry Papers in Family and Community History (#77-4), Newberry Library, Chicago; Thomas Woody, *Early Quaker Education in Pennsylvania* (Teachers College P, 1920), 214–15.

58. On the novel *Ruth Hall*, see Ann Wood, "The 'Scribbling Women' and Fanny Fern: Why Women Wrote," *American Quarterly*, 23, no. 1 (Spring 1971): 3–24, esp. 21.

59. Isabelle Moodie Frost in Jay Parini, *Robert Frost: A Life* (Henry Holt, 1999). To support his family while establishing himself as a poet, Frost farmed and taught at Pinkerton Academy in Derry (NH) (1906–1911), the state normal school at Plymouth (NH), and intermittently at Amherst College.

60. Alice Pierce to Ira Benjamin Whitcomb (Feb. 7, 1882), in Ira Benjamin Whitcomb Collection in Oregon Historical Society Library, by permission.

61. Abiah Hiller in Linda Peavy & Ursula Smith, *Women in Waiting in the Westward Movement* (U Oklahoma P, 1994).

62. Lucille Ellison in Sheila Cavanagh, "Female-Teacher Gender and Sexuality in Twentieth-Century Ontario, Canada," *History of Education Quarterly* 45, no. 2 (Summer 2005): 254.

63. Mary Constance Lynn, "Some Aspects of the Changing Position of Women in America, 1920–1929" (Ph.D. diss., University of Rochester, 1975), 124, 136.

64. Laura Farnsworth Frampton Owen (b.1906) in Joyce Kinkead (Ed.), *A Schoolmarm All My Life: Personal Narratives from Frontier Utah* (Signature Books, 1996), 17–19.

65. Between 1867 and 1929, the population increased by 300%, marriage numbers by 400%, and divorce by 2,000%; in Alfred Cahan, *Statistical Analysis of American Divorce* (Columbia UP, 1932), 21.

66. Lella Secor Florence in Blain, *The Feminist Companion to Literature in English*.

67. Mae Harveson, *Catharine Esther Beecher, Pioneer Educator* (U Pennsylvania P, 1932), 29.

68. Diary entries for April 12, July 19 & 20, 1866, in Wayne E. Reilly (Ed.), *Sarah Jane Foster: Teacher of the Freedmen: A Diary and Letters* (U Virginia P, 1990), 91, 156–57.

69. George Gissing (1857–1903), *The Odd Women* (Norton, 1977; originally published 1893), vii, 2–3.

70. Linda Leavell, "Marianne Moore, Her Family and Their Language," *Proceedings of the American Philosophical Society* 147, no. 2 (June 2003): 140–49; James Fenton, "Becoming Marianne Moore," *New York Review of Books*, 44, no. 7 (April 24, 1997), 40–45.

71. Madge in Ruth Adams, *I'm Not Complaining* (Dial Press, 1938), 343.

72. Peter Petschauer, *The Education of Women in Eighteenth-Century Germany* (Edwin Mellen, 1989), 114.

73. The Berry sisters in Andrew Spaull & Martin Sullivan, *A History of the Queensland Teachers Union* (Allen & Unwin, 1989), 19.

74. Statistics on U.S. Catholic nuns in Susan Jonas & Marilyn Nissenson, *Going Going Gone: Vanishing Americana* (Chronicle Books, 1994), 100.

75. Edmonia Highgate in Ronald Butchart, " 'We Best Can Instruct Our Own People': New York African Americans in the Freedmen's Schools, 1861–1875," in Donald Nieman (Ed.), *African Americans and Education in the South, 1865–1900* (Garland, 1994), 39.

76. The fourth daughter, Hannah More, started several schools while writing poetry, plays, and religious tracts; Hannah More in Maureen Bell, George A. E. Parfitt, & Simon Shepherd, *Biographical Dictionary of English Women Writers, 1580–1720* (G. K. Hall, 1990).

77. Kathryn Sklar, "The Schooling of Girls and Changing Community Values in Massachusetts Towns, 1750–1820," *History of Education Quarterly* 33, no. 4 (Winter 1993): 511–42.

78. William Kinnis, "Propagating the Pestalozzian: The Story of William McClure's Involvement in Efforts to Affect Educational and Social Reforms in the Early Nineteenth Century" (Ph.D. diss., Loyola University, 1972), 196–97.

79. Mary Hoyt in Sharon Geltner, "The Common Schools of Los Angeles, 1850–1900" (Ed.D. diss., University of California, Los Angeles, 1972), 26–27. Bray family in Nevada Women's History Project, "Mildred Bray," *Women's Biographies,* www.unr.edu/nwhp/bios /women/bray.htm, accessed Nov. 6, 2013.

80. The Yandells in "Three Sisters," *Teacher Magazine* (Aug. 1990): 19.

81. Telephone interview of Elizabeth Bull Waldhauer of Annandale, MN, June 1, 2007, and the biographical notes she prepared, as E.B.W., for various public occasions.

82. Lida and Flora Dodd died in the 1930s, in Walter Vernon, "The Dodds: Southern Methodist Educators," *Methodist History* 28, no. 1 (Oct. 1989): 42–56.

83. Rachel Ann Rosenfeld & Aage Sørensen, *Sex Differences in Patterns of Career Mobility* (Institute for Research on Poverty, U Wisconsin P, 1977).

84. J. Gary Knowles, "Models for Understanding Pre-service and Beginning Teachers' Biographies: Illustrations from Case Studies," in Ivor Goodson (Ed.), *Studying Teachers' Lives* (Routledge, 1992), 99–152.

85. Zerwekh sisters in Joan Ryan, "Convent Life at Twilight," *San Francisco Chronicle Magazine* (June 17, 2007): 10–17, 27.

86. Ruskin quoted in Gissing, *Odd Women,* 153.

87. Anne Firor Scott, *The Southern Lady: From Pedestal to Politics, 1830–1930* (U Chicago P, 1970), 214.

88. I am indebted for the Brontë example to Peter Hollindale, University of York, Sept. 2004.

89. Kate B. Carter (Comp.), *Diary of Isaiah Moses Coombs* (Daughters of Utah Pioneers, n.d.), esp. 401–2. The academy was the forerunner of Brigham Young University.

90. Herriclia Elides in Julia Kirk Blackwelder, *Now Hiring: The Feminization of Work in the United States, 1900–1995* (Texas A&M UP 1997), 81.

91. Irene Shapiro Goldenberg in Ruth Jacknow Markowitz, *My Daughter, the Teacher: Jewish Teachers in the New York City Schools* (Rutgers UP, 1992) 135.

92. Marie Haggerty interview, WPA Federal Writers' Project, in Ann Banks (Ed.), *First-Person America* (Knopf, 1980), 173.

93. Pamela Claire Hronek, "Women and Normal Schools: Tempe Normal, a Case Study, 1885–1925" (Ph.D. diss: Arizona State University, 1985), 96, 106, 107.

94. George Bates Jr., "Winona Normal School Student Profile, 1860–1900," *Journal of the Midwest History of Education Society* 7 (1979): 17.

95. Gregg in Elaine Showalter (Ed.), *These Modern Women: Autobiographical Essays from the Twenties* (Feminist Press, 1978).

96. Anna Frucht in Judith E. Smith, *Family Connections: A History of Italian and Jewish Immigrant Lives in Providence, Rhode Island 1900–1940* (SUNY P, 1985), 74.

97. Sharon Harley, "Beyond the Classroom: Organizational Lives of Black Female Educators in the District of Columbia, 1890–1930," *Journal of Negro Education* 52, no. 3 (Summer 1982): 254–65.

98. Opal Seales in Vaughn-Roberson, "Sometimes Independent but Never Equal," esp. 44.

99. Isabella Godding in Class of 1857 Records, Class Letter, 1905. Mount Holyoke College Archives and Special Collections, South Hadley (MA), by permission.

100. John Modell, "Family and Fertility on the Indiana Frontier, 1820," *American Quarterly* 23, no. 5 (Dec. 1971): 615–34.

101. Geographic mobility in Stephan Thernstrom & Peter R. Knights, "Men in Motion: Some Data and Speculations about Urban Population Mobility in Nineteenth-Century America," *Journal of Interdisciplinary History* 1 (Fall 1970): 7–35.

102. George Pierson, "A Restless Temper. . . . ," *American Historical Review* 49, no. 4 (July 1964): 969–89, & "The M-Factor in American History," *American Quarterly,* no. 2 (Summer 1962): 275–89. See also Stanley Lebergott, "Migration Rates Within the U.S., 1800–1960," *Journal of Economic History* 30, no. 4 (Dec. 1970): 839–46.

103. Susan Griggs in Griggs-Bragg Family Letters, 1848–1938, in Vermont Historical Society; Richard Boone, *A History of Education in Indiana* (D. Appleton, 1892, 1909).

104. Laura Ingalls Wilder (1867–1957) in American Mother's Committee, *Mothers of Achievement,* 312–13.

105. Christine Ogren, "State Normal Schools in the United States" (paper presented at the Congress of the International Commission for the History of Universities, Montreal, Canada, Sept. 1995), courtesy of the author.

106. Robert Louis Stevenson, *The Silverado Squatters* (Scribner, 1905, 1923), 219–21.

107. Lucy Virginia Smith French in Blain, *Feminist Companion to Literature in English,* 398.

108. Stephen Cresswell (Ed.), *We Will Know What War Is: The Civil War Diary of Sirene Bunten* (West Virginia Wesleyan College P, 1993), 18–19, 21–22 (entry for Mar. 5, 1863).

109. Rev. Edward Hitchcock, *The Power of Christian Benevolence,* in Kathryn Sklar, "The Founding of Mount Holyoke College," in Carol Berkin & Mary Beth Norton, *Women of America: A History* (Houghton Mifflin, 1979), 193.

110. Gail Collins, *America's Women: Four Hundred Years of Dolls, Drudges, Helpmates, and Heroines* (William Morrow, 1998), iii.

111. Cited in Michael Berger, "Social Impact of the Automobile, 1893–1929: A Documentary History" (Ed.D. diss., Teachers College, 1972), 104.

112. Kathleen Lodwick, *Educating the Women of Hainan: The Career of Margaret Moninger in China, 1915–1942* (UP Kentucky, 1995), esp. 5; Alice A. Langer in Sibley, *Golden Book of California.*

113. Mrs. Brady's address is cited in Sylvia Hunt, "To Wed and to Teach: The Myth of the Single Teacher," in Fane Downs & Nancy Baker Jones (Eds.), *Women and Texas History* (Texas State Historical Association, 1993), 127–42.

114. William Hard (with Rheta Childe), "The Woman's Invasion," *Everybody's Magazine* 19, no. 5 (Oct. 1908): 589–91.

115. The women painstakingly traced by Polly Kaufman were intrepid pioneers, including the one-third who returned East after their expected stay was completed; in *Western Teachers on the Frontier* (Yale UP, 1984).

116. Ralph Waldo Emerson, "The Young American," *Dial* 4 (April 1844): 486–87; *Essays and Lectures* (Vintage-Library of America, 1983), 2:210–30.

117. Towne letters, esp. April 28 & July -, 1882, in Katherine Redington Morgan (Ed.), *My Ever Dear Daughter, My Own Dear Mother: The Correspondence of Julia Stone Towne and Mary Julia Towne, 1868–1882* (U Iowa P, 1996) 20, 146–47, 212.

118. Nellie Cronk in Gail Martin, "The Remarkable Young Women from Turkey Creek," *Voices, Kancoll's Online Magazine* (Winter 2000), www.kancoll.org/articles/martin/.

119. Laura Carman Bowles, "A Teacher Remembers," *Tales of Paradise Ridge* 19, no. 2 (Dec. 1978): 3–14; copy in California State Library, Sacramento.

120. The state of Victoria contracted with California State University at Hayward to coordinate and supervise the Victoria Teacher Selection Program. From interviews (Oct. 1987, Jan. 1988) by the author with Ethel Rumaker and Clair Peterson, participating teacher educators from CSU Hayward.

121. "Young People of the Graduating Class," in Sarah Catharine Warthen Searcy Papers, Kansas Collection, Spencer Research Library, University of Kansas Libraries.

122. Colin Bradley Burke, "The Quiet Influence: The American Colleges and Their Students, 1800–1860" (Ph.D. diss., Washington University, St. Louis, 1973), 153–54.

123. Josephine Ballard in Thad Sitton & Milam Rowold, *Ringing the Children In: Texas Country Schools* (Texas A&M UP, 1987), 155–56.

124. *Addresses at the Inauguration of Charles William Eliot as President of Harvard College* (Sever & Francis, 1869), 50; Barrett Wendell, "The Relations of Radcliffe with Harvard," *Harvard Monthly* (Oct. 1899): 7.

125. Seller, *Women Educators in the United States,* 503, 505; M. Carey Thomas, "Should the Higher Education of Women Differ from that of Men," *Educational Review* 21 (Sept. 1901): 1–10.

126. Alexis Lange, "The Problem of the Professional Training of Women," *School and Society* 3, no. 66 (April 1, 1916), 246, 247.

127. Frances Levy in Markowitz, *My Daughter, the Teacher,* 175.

128. John Folger & Charles Nam, *Education of the American Population* (U.S. Census Bureau, 1957), 91.

129. Arthur Conan Doyle, *The Naval Treaty* (1893), quoted in Dina Copelman, *London's Women Teachers: Gender, Class and Feminism, 1870–1930* (Routledge, 1966), 57.

130. Janie Richardson and Soleda Lujan obituaries in the *Oakland (CA) Tribune* (Sept. 4, 1998).

Chapter 5 · "An Honorable Breadwinning Weapon"

1. Madam Capron in Mary Ormsbee Whitton, *These Were the Women: U.S.A. 1776–1860* (Hastings House, 1954); Margaretta Bleecker Faugeres in Mainiero, *American Women Writers.* This chapter's title is from Frances Willard's challenge to the Woman's Christian Temperance Union c. 1874; in Miriam Gurko, *Ladies of Seneca Falls* (Macmillan, 1974), 261.

2. Emma Edwards Green in American Mothers Committee, *Mothers of Achievement in American History, 1776–1976* (C. E. Tuttle, 1976).

3. Mary Jane and Nancy Dawson (1858–1951) are pictured in Portrait File #1905.002, Bancroft Library, UC Berkeley.

4. Marina Chukaayef McCarthy, "The Anchor and the Wind: A Profile of Sacred Heart Schools in the U.S." (Ph.D. diss., Harvard University, 1990).

5. Cletus Pfeiffer, "The Art of Seed Throwing or Teacher Recruitment—Some Observations," *Lutheran Education* 125, no. 1 (Sept.–Oct. 1989): 35–42.

6. Caroline Eick, "Student Relationships across Social Markers of Difference in a Baltimore County, Maryland, Comprehensive High School, 1950–1969," *History of Education Quarterly* 50, no. 3 (Aug. 2010): 359–89.

7. "Chris" in Dee Ann Spencer, *Contemporary Women Teachers: Balancing Home and School* (Longman, 1986), 41.

8. Polly Bullard, "Iron Range Schoolmarm," *Minnesota History* 32, no. 4 (Dec. 1951): 193–201.

9. Marguerite Renner, "Who Will Teach? Changing Job Opportunity and Roles for Women in the Evolution of the Pittsburgh Public Schools, 1830–1900" (Ph.D. dissertation, University of Pittsburgh, 1981), 145–46.

10. Ella Gertrude Clanton Thomas Papers, Perkins Library, Duke University; Victoria-Marie MacDonald, "Paving the Way: A Comparative Analysis of the Role of Teachers' Social Class, Gender, and Race in Nineteenth Century Northern and Southern School Reform" (paper presented at the American Educational Research Association Annual Meeting, San Francisco, April 18–22, 1995).

11. Providence example cited in Victoria-Maria MacDonald, "The Paradox of Bureaucratization: New Views on Progressive Era Teachers and the Development of a Woman's Profession," *History of Education Quarterly* 39, no. 4 (Winter 1999): 427–53.

12. Career study in Mabel Robinson, *The Curriculum of the Women's Colleges,* Bulletin 1918, no. 6 (U.S. Bureau of Education, 1918).

13. Mary McCarthy (1912–1989), *Memories of a Catholic Girlhood* (Harcourt Brace Jovanovich, 1957), 102.

14. Luella Smith McWhirter in American Mothers Committee, *Mothers of Achievement.*

15. Biographical sketch of Miss Willie C. Johnson in Paul Coppock, *Memphis Memories* (Memphis State UP, 1980), 165–68.

16. Sarah (Sadie) (b. 1889?) & Annie Elizabeth (Bessie) Delany published a joint autobiography, *Having Our Say: The Delany Sisters' First 100 Years* (Kodansha', 1993). Mary Sanderson in Amy Hill Hearth & Rudolph Lapp, "Jeremiah B. Sanderson: Early California Negro Leader," *Journal of Negro History* 53, no. 4 (Oct. 1968): 321–33.

17. Edward Franklin Frazier, *Black Bourgeoisie* (Collier Books, 1962); John Wesley Dobbs reference courtesy of Anita Burney (Silver Springs, MD).

18. August Meier & Elliott Rudwick, "Early Boycotts of Segregated Schools: The East Orange (NJ), Experience, 1899–1906," *History of Education Quarterly* 7, no. 1 (Spring 1967): 22–35.

19. Sidney Ellwood interview in Carla O'Connor, "Black Women Beating the Odds from One Generation to the Next: How the Changing Dynamics of Constraint and Opportunity Affect the Process of Educational Resilience," *American Educational Research Journal* 19, no. 4 (Winter 2002): 855–903.

20. The James Snyder household is listed in the 13th (1910) federal manuscript census for Carbon County, WY.

21. Clyde Griffen & Sally Griffen, *Natives and Newcomers: The Ordering of Opportunity in Mid-nineteenth Century Poughkeepsie* (Harvard UP, 1977).

22. William Jackameit, "Negro Public Higher Education in West Virginia, 1890–1965," *West Virginia History* 37, no. 4 (July 1976): 309–24.

23. Lotus D. Coffman, *Social Composition of the Teaching Population* (Teachers College P, 1911), 57.

24. Ward Mason, *The Beginning Teacher: Status and Career Orientation* (U.S. Department of Health, Education, & Welfare, 1961).

25. Quotation from David Labaree, "Mutual Subversion: A Short History of the Liberal and Professional in American Higher Education," *History of Education Quarterly* 46, no. 1 (Spring 2006): 1–15.

26. Christine Ogren, "State Normal Schools in the United States: The Roots of Many State Colleges and Regional Universities" (paper presented Congress of the International Commission for the History of Universities, Montreal, Canada, Sept. 1995).

27. Dot Miller in Nancy Green & Mary Phillips Manke, "Good Women and Old Stereotypes," in Pamela Bolotin Joseph & Gail Burnaford, *Images of Schoolteachers in America* (Lawrence Erlbaum, 2001), 107, 121.

28. Ellen Skerrett in Thomas J. Meagher (Ed.), *From Paddy to Studs: Irish-American Communities in the Turn of the Century Era, 1880 to 1920* (Greenwood, 1986).

29. Jeff Gillenkirk, "Year 4702: A Reunion like No Other," *California Monthly* 117, no. 2 (March–Apr. 2006): 39–41.

30. Bessie Rayner Parkes, "The Profession of Teacher," in *Essays on Women's Work* (London: Alexander Strahan, 1865), cited in A. James Hammerton, *Emigrant Gentlewomen: Genteel Poverty and Female Emigration, 1830–1914* (Rowman & Littlefield, 1979), 32.

31. Annie Barnes, with Kate Harding & Caroline Gibbs, *Tough Annie. . . .* (Stepney Books, 1980), 7, cited in Dina Copelman's *London's Women Teachers: Gender, Class and Feminism, 1870–1930* (Routledge, 1996), 128, 262.

32. Carol Gold, *Educating Middle Class Daughters: Private Girls Schools in Copenhagen, 1790–1820* (Museum Tusculanum, 1994), esp. 18, 62–63.

33. Linda Clark, "The Primary Education of French Girls: Pedagogical Prescriptions and Social Realities, 1880–1940," *History of Education Quarterly* 21, no. 4 (Winter 1981): 411–28.

34. Rev. M. Mitchell, *HMI [Her Majesty's Inspector] in Privy Council Committee on Education Report* (1854–55), in Pamela Horn, *Education in Rural England, 1800–1914* (St. Martin's Press, 1978), 207.

35. In Copelman, *London's Women Teachers*, 35.

36. Christine Ruane, *Gender, Class, and the Professionalization of Russian City Teachers, 1860–1914* (U Pittsburgh P, 1994), esp. 66–67; Ben Eklof, *Russian Peasant Schools: Officialdom, Village Culture, and Popular Pedagogy, 1861–1914* (U California P, 1987).

37. Christina Florin, "Social Closure as a Professional Strategy: Male and Female Teachers from Cooperation to Conflict in Sweden, 1860–1906," *History of Education*, 20, no. 1 (1991): 17–26.

38. Author's interview of Marie Cermáková, Gender Studies Unit, Institute of Sociology, Academy of Sciences of the Czech Republic, Prague, Sept. 22, 1995; Gordon White,

Party and Professionals: The Political Role of Teachers in Contemporary China (M. E. Sharpe, 1981), esp. 5, 32.

39. W. E. Burghardt Du Bois, *Dusk of Dawn* (Harcourt, Brace, & World, 1940; Schocken Books, 1968), 3, 5. Given the large, multidisciplinary literature in education on African Americans, Native Americans, and immigrants, this survey focuses on an illustrative sample of individual women teachers representing these demographic groups.

40. Mary Bonzo Suzuki, "American Education in the Philippines, the Early Years: American Pioneer Teachers and the Filipino Response, 1890–1935" (Ph.D. diss., University of California, Berkeley, 1991).

41. Miriam King & Steven Ruggles, "American Immigration, Fertility Differentials, and Race Suicide at the Turn of the Century," *Journal of Interdisciplinary History* 20, no. 3 (Winter 1990): 347–69.

42. Coffman, *Social Composition of the Teaching Population,* 57.

43. Ruth Jacknow Markowitz, *My Daughter, the Teacher; Jewish Teachers in New York City Schools* (Rutgers UP, 1993).

44. U.S. Bureau of the Census, *Statistics of Women at Work* (U.S. Government Printing Office, 1907). Additional data from 30 of the 37 cities profiled in *Report of the Immigration Commission: The Children of Immigrants in Schools* (U.S. Government Printing Office, 1911).

45. Divine Providence history in "Divine Providence Parish: Westchester, Illinois," *Franzosenbusch Heritage Society,* www.franzosenbuschheritagesociety.org/churches/divine%20providence%20parish2.htm, accessed Nov. 6, 2013.

46. Committee of Graduate School of Education, University of Nebraska, *The Rural Teacher of Nebraska,* Bulletin no. 20 (U.S. Bureau of Education, 1919), 27–28; Cynthia Kendall, "Anglo-Saxonism and the Reaction of the American Public Schools, 1870–1915" (Ed.D. diss., Teachers College, Columbia University, 1975).

47. Stephen Fugita, *Altered Lives, Enduring Community: Japanese Americans Remember Their World War II Incarceration* (U Washington P, 2004), 28. Ada Mahon (1881–1951) is also noted in Yoon K. Pak, *Wherever I Go, I Will Always Be a Loyal American: Schooling Seattle's Japanese during World War II* (Routledge Falmer, 2002).

48. In 1982, Southeast Asians were 53% of all immigrants.

49. Laju Shaw in Charles Burress, "Groups Seeking Textbook Revisions," *San Francisco Chronicle* (Feb. 28, 2006).

50. Mary J. Oates, "The Professional Preparation of Parochial School Teachers, 1870–1940," in Michael Konig and Martin Kaufman (Eds.), *Education in Massachusetts: Selected Essays* (Institute for Massachusetts Studies, Westfield State College, 1989), 103–20.

51. The distinction between voluntary (immigrants) and involuntary (conquered) minorities and the consequences in John U. Ogbu, *Minority Education and Caste* (Academic Press, 1978)

52. In Estelle Reel Collection, Wyoming State Archives.

53. U.S. Bureau of the Census, *Census Statistics of Teachers,* Bulletin no. 23 (1905), 14–15; *Characteristics of American Indian and Alaska Native Education: Results from the 1990–91 and 1993–94 Staffing Surveys* (U.S. Department of Education, National Center for Education Statistics, n.d.), esp. 32.

54. Carol Locust, "Wounding the Spirit: Discrimination and Traditional American Indian Belief Systems," *Harvard Educational Review* 58, no. 3 (Aug. 1968): 315–30; Robert Rosson, "Values and American Indian Leadership Styles," in *Multicultural Education and the American Indian* (American Indian Studies Center, UCLA, 1979), 117–28.

55. Wendy Hopkins in *Indian Education, 2006,* Native News Project, U of Montana School of Journalism.

56. Elsie Itta in Bob Reiss, "The Mayor at the Top of the World," *Parade Magazine* (July 18, 2010).

57. Polingaysi Qöyawayma (b.1892?), also called Elizabeth Q. White, *No Turning Back: A Hopi Woman's Struggles to Live in Two Worlds,* as told to Vada F. Carlson (U New Mexico P, 1964), esp. 3, 23–26, 175, 190. For short biographies of Qöyawayma, Caroline Bushyhead Quarles (Cherokee), Janine Pease-Windy-Boy (Crow), and Martha Beulah Mann Yallup (Yakima), see Seller, *Women Educators in the United States.*

58. Sarah Mapps Douglass in Gerda Lerner, *The Grimké Sisters from South Carolina: Pioneers for Woman's Rights and Abolition* (Schocken Books, 1971), esp. 133; and Seller, *Woman Educators in the United States.*

59. Leon Litwack, *North of Slavery: The Negro in the Free States, 1790–1860* (U Chicago P, 1961); Graham Russell Hodges, *Root & Branch: African Americans in New York and East Jersey 1613–1863* (U North Carolina P, 1999).

60. Catto in Harry Silcox, "Nineteenth Century Philadelphia Black Militant: Octavius V. Catto (1839–1871)," *Pennsylvania History* 44, no. 1 (1977): 52–76; see also Silcox, "A Comparative Study in School Desegregation: Boston and Philadelphia, 1800–1881" (Ed.D. diss., Temple University, 1971).

61. A Philadelphia native, Forten was schooled in Salem and attended its state normal school; in Ray Allen Billington (Ed.), *The Journal of Charlotte L. Forten* (Dryden Press, 1953; Collier Books, 1961, 1967).

62. Albert Broussard, *African-American Odyssey: The Stewarts, 1853–1963* (UP Kansas, 1998).

63. Howard Rabinowitz, "Half a Loaf: The Shift from White to Black Teachers in the Negro Schools of the Urban South, 1865–1890," *Journal of Southern History* 40, no. 4 (Nov. 1974): 565–94, esp. 588n97.

64. J. B. Corbell to Mortimer Warren, Sept. 11, 1871, in Avery Institute Papers of Mortimer A. Warren, box 60: "South Carolina," AMA Archives, Amistad Research Center, Tulane University.

65. Teacher names from *Memphis City Directory* (Sholes, 1880, 1882; Harlow Dow, 1885). See, esp. 7:343,417; 9:22–23; 12:774–75. The Ida Brown incident in Victoria MacDonald Huntzinger, "The Intersection of Three Worlds: The Social Origins of Black Women Teachers in Columbus, Georgia" (unpublished paper, Harvard Graduate School of Education, 1992). Charlotte Hawkins Brown to F. P. Hobgood Jr. (Oct. 19, 1921) in Elaine Partnow (Ed.), *The Quotable Woman, 1800–1981* (Facts on File, 1982), 179.

66. Courtney Ann Vaughn-Roberson, "Sometimes Independent but Never Equal—Women Teachers, 1900–1950: The Oklahoma Example," *Pacific Historical Review* 53, no. 1 (Feb. 1984): 39–58.

67. Sara Jones in Delilah Beasley, *The Negro Trail Blazers of California* (Los Angeles Times Mirror, 1919), 175.

68. Charles Burress, "UC honors Louise Jackson, Class of '22," and Roberta Park, "Ida Louise Jackson, Class of '22," *Chronicles of the University of California* 1, no. 2 (Fall 1998): 95–98. Jackson is often but incorrectly identified as the first black woman certified to teach in California.

69. The quotation is from Claudia Roth Pierpont, "James Baldwin's Flight from America," *New Yorker* (Feb. 9 & 16, 2009). See also Linda Perkins, "The History of Blacks in Teaching," in Warren, *American Teachers,* 344–69; Michele Foster, "The Politics of Race: Through the Eyes of African-American Teachers," in Kathleen Weiler & Candia Mitchell, *What Schools Can Do* (SUNY P, 1992), 177–202.

70. Adolphine Fletcher Terry, *Charlotte Stephens, Little Rock's First Black Teacher* (Academic P Arkansas, 1973), copy courtesy of Terry's son, William Terry.

71. Albertina Andrade (1915–1997), obituary in *Oakland (CA) Tribune* (Aug. 5, 1997).

72. Victoria-Maria MacDonald, "Hispanic, Latino, Chicano, or 'Other'? Deconstructing the Relationship between Historians and Hispanic-American Educational History," *History of Education Quarterly* 41, no. 3 (Fall 2001): 365–413.

73. Yolanda Armijo and this author were colleagues at Escuela Bella Vista in Maracaibo, Venezuela in 1957–1958.

74. Ruth Galindo (b. 1910) obituary in *Contra Costa (CA) Times* (Dec. 29, 1999), courtesy of Zack Rogow, School of Education, UC Berkeley.

75. Guadelupe San Miguel, *Brown, Not White: School Integration and the Chicano Movement in Houston* (Texas A&M UP, 2001).

76. Manuela Cota in T. N. Snow, "Santa Barbara Educationally," *Santa Barbara News-Press* (n.d.) clipping; and Tulita de La Cuesta Scrapbook, both in Santa Barbara Historical Society.

77. "Public Schools of El Paso, Texas," *1928 Yearbook*; Mira Sovin, "Aoy School" (unpublished class paper, April 1994?, Graduate School of Education, UC Berkeley).

78. Leonor Villegas de Magnon & Jovita Idar in Barbara Beatty, *Preschool Education in America: The Culture of Young Children from the Colonial Era to the Present* (Yale UP, 1995).

79. "Roster of Class Room Teachers Employed by the Indian Service," in Estelle Reel Collection, Wyoming State Archives.

80. Maria Cristina Garcia, "Exiles, Immigrants, and Transnationals: Cubans in the United States," in David Gutiérrez (Ed.), *The Columbia Anthology of Latino History* (Columbia UP, 2004); California State Department of Education, "Certificated Staff by Ethnicity for 2010–11: State Summary, Number of Staff by Ethnicity," http://dq.cde.ca.gov/dataquest/Staff/StaffByEth.aspx?cYear=2010-11&cChoice=StateNum&cType=T&cGender=&Submit=1, accessed Nov. 6, 2013.

81. *Spotlight: A Newsletter of the Los Angeles City Schools* (June 18, 1969), in "California Ephemera Collection: Education," in UCLA Research Library.

82. Author's interview with Missoula (MT) resident John Wathen, Sept. 24, 1995; Claudia DeMonte, "The Whole World Was Italian," in Linda Brandi Cateura, *Growing Up Italian* (William Morrow, 1987), 51–62.

83. Robert Ostergren, *A Community Transplanted: The Trans-Atlantic Experience of a Swedish Immigrant Settlement in the Upper Middle West, 1836–1915* (U Wisconsin P, 1988), esp. 111.

84. Walter L. Fleming "Immigration to the Southern States," *Political Science Quarterly* 20, no. 2 (June 1905): 276–97.

85. U.S. Bureau of the Census, *Census Statistics of Teachers* (1905); Coffman, *Social Composition of the Teaching Population*, 55.

86. Margaret Knapple & Bertha Knemeyer in Bowman & Ryan, *Who's Who in Education* (1927).

87. Nancy Hoffman, *Woman's True Profession: Voices from the History of Teaching* (Feminist Press, 1981), 215; Joseph Newman, "A History of the Atlanta Public School Teachers' Association, Local 89 of the American Federation of Teachers, 1919–1956" (Ph.D. diss., Georgia State University, 1978), 67ff.

88. Ronald Cohen, *Children of the Mill: Schooling and Society in Gary, Indiana, 1906–1960* (Indiana UP, 1990), 143; Paul Peterson, *The Politics of School Reform, 1870–1940* (U Chicago P, 1985), 84–89.

89. Hannibal G. Duncan, *Immigration and Assimilation* (D. C. Heath, 1933), 725; Paul Knaplund, *Moorings Old and New: Entries in an Immigrant's Log* (State Historical Society of Wisconsin, 1963), 90.

90. "Many Tributes Received by Miss Esther Anderson," *Casper (WY) Tribune Herald* (Nov. 12, 1938).

91. Catharine Murphy in Ted Hinckley, *The Americanization of Alaska, 1867–97* (Pacific Books, 1972).

92. Mary McNamara Nevens in American Mothers Committee, *Mothers of Achievement*, 417–18.

93. Nora Joyce (b.1910), in Ide O'Carroll, *Models for Movers: Irish Women's Emigration to America* (Attic Press, 1990), 39.

94. Janet Nolan, *Servants of the Poor: Teachers and Mobility in Ireland and Irish America* (U Notre Dame P, 2004).

95. Polly Welts Kaufman, *Boston Women and City School Politics 1872–1905* (Garland, 1994).

96. Ann Marie Ryan, "Negotiating Assimilation: Chicago Catholic High Schools' Pursuit of Accreditation in the Early Twentieth Century," *History of Education Quarterly* 46, no. 3 (Fall 2006): 348–81.

97. Mildred Tudy quoted in Anne Witte Garland, *Women Activists: Challenging the Abuse of Power* (Feminist Press, 1988), xvii, 66.

98. Karen Kennelly, *American Catholic Women: A Historical Exploration* (Macmillan, 1989), 97; Noel Ignatiev, *How the Irish Became White* (Routledge, 1995).

99. May Stewart to family, Oct. 31, 1887, in Stewart-Lockwood Family Collection, Kansas Collection, Spencer Research Library, University of Kansas (hereafter SLC).

100. Correspondent's report, "German-American Teachers Convention," *California Teacher and Home Journal* 2, no. 1 (Aug. 1883): 31–36, in Peterson, *Politics of School Reform*, 201. Adolph Kraus, *Annual Report of the Chicago Board of Education* 30 (July 1884), 28, cited in Kay Hodes Kamin, "The Woman Peril in American Public Schools: How Perilous?" (unpublished paper, Rosary College, 1976, courtesy of the author).

101. W. G. Walker, "The Development of the Free Public High School in Illinois during the Nineteenth Century," *History of Education Quarterly* 4, no. 4 (Dec. 1964): 264–79.

102. Maude Schaeffer and Velma Augusta Shartle (Mrs. Harry Powell Jr.) and BIA teachers in Sibley, *Golden Book of California*.

103. Judith Rosenberg Raftery, *Land of Fair Promise: Politics and Reform in Los Angeles Schools, 1885–1941* (Stanford UP, 1991), 65, 222 n56.

104. Gertrude Pignol case cited in Patricia Howlett & Charles Howlett, "A Silent Witness for Peace: The Case of Schoolteacher Mary Stone McDowell and America at War," *History of Education Quarterly* 48, no. 1 (Aug. 2008): 371–96.

105. Anna Johnson, "Recollections of a Country School Teacher," *Annals of Iowa* 41 (1975): 485–505.

106. Mary Gospardarić in Sibley, *Golden Book of California*.

107. Angeline Bratich Mayall obituary in *San Francisco Examiner* (July 16, 2000).

108. Thad Sitton & Milam C. Rowold, *Ringing the Children In: Texas Country Schools* (Texas A&M UP, 1987), 4, 165.

109. Ryan, "Negotiating Assimilation," 368; John Bodnar, "The Slavic-American Family," in Bernard Weiss (Ed.), *American Education and the European Immigrant, 1840–1940* (U Illinois P, 1982), 87.

110. Samuel F. Vitone, "The Italian-Americans of San Francisco and Public Education," in *Columbus: A Publication of the Columbian Celebration* (Baccari, 1977): 115–20.

111. Mariana Bertola in *Historical Sketch of the State Normal School at San José, California* (State Printer, 1889), 279.

112. Mario Puzo, *The Fortunate Pilgrim* (Atheneum, 1965), esp. 87, 92, 148, 151. Italian census figures from *Encyclopædia Britannica*, vols. 15, 16 (1911).

113. Timothy O'Leary & Sandra Schoenberg, "Ethnicity and Social Class Convergence in an Italian Community: The Hill in St. Louis," *Missouri Historical Society Bulletin* 33 (Jan. 1977): 77–86; Rudolph Vecoli (Ed.), *Italian Immigrants in Rural and Small Town America* (American Italian Historical Association, 1987).

114. O'Leary & Schoenberg, "Ethnicity and Social Class Convergence in an Italian Community," 77–86; Joel Perlmann, *Ethnic Differences: Schooling and Social Structure among the Irish, Italians, Jews, and Blacks in an American City, 1880–1935* (Cambridge UP, 1988), esp. 145, 149.

115. Quoted in Louise Odenkrantz, *Italian Women in Industry: A Study of Conditions in New York City* (Russell Sage Foundation, 1919), 255–56.

116. Miriam Cohen, "Changing Education Strategies among Immigrant Generations: New York Italians in Comparative Perspective" *Journal of Social History* 15, no. 3 (Spring 1982): 443–66; Richard Alba, *Ethnic Identity: The Transformation of White America* (Yale UP, 1990), 8–9.

117. Alice Newberry to Mother, Oct. 11, 1909, Alice C. Newberry Collection (MSS 1202), History Colorado, Denver, Colorado, by permission.

118. Della Francone in Bowman & Ryan, *Who's Who in Education*.

119. Frank McCourt, *Teacher Man: A Memoir* (Scribner, 2005), 130.

120. Teacher and pupil numbers in Deborah Dash Moore, *At Home in America: Second Generation New York Jews* (Columbia UP, 1981), 95–99; Ruth Jacknow Markowitz, "Subway Scholars at Concrete Campuses: Daughters of Jewish Immigrants Prepared for the Teaching Profession, New York City, 1920–1940," *History of Higher Education*

Annual 10 (1990) 31–50; Selma Berrol, *Julia Richman, a Notable Woman* (Balch Institute Press, 1933), esp. 119, 125ff; Markowitz, *My Daughter, the Teacher.*

121. Elizabeth Bloomstein in Paul Conkin, *Peabody College: From Frontier Academy to the Frontiers of Teaching and Learning* (Vanderbilt UP, 2002): 118.

122. Marjorie Murphy, *Blackboard Unions: The AFT and the NEA, 1900–1980* (Cornell UP, 1990), esp. 238.

123. All named in Harriet Rochlin, "Riding High: Annie Oakley's Jewish Contemporaries," *Lilith,* no. 14 (Fall–Winter 1985–86): 14–18. Norton and Lazard also at www.jmaw.org/mina-norton-early-professional-teacher-of-los-angeles/.

124. Rasjidah Franklin, "Berta Rantz: Her Life and Legacy," *Teacher Education Quarterly* (California Council on Teacher Education), 28, no. 3 (Summer 2001), 19–28.

125. Florence Rosenfeld Howe, "Sexism and the Aspirations of Women," *Phi Delta Kappan* 55, no. 2 (Oct. 1973): 99–104.

126. Author's interview with Rena Margulies Chernoff, Valdivia, Chile, March 13, 2008.

127. Valerie Ooka Pang, "Ethnic Prejudice: Still Alive and Hurtful," *Harvard Educational Review* 58, no. 3 (Aug. 1988): 375–80. Online sources (e.g., Facebook) are a source for currently active teachers of various ethnic origins.

128. Interviews of Estella Yorozu Takahashi (1916–2011) by the author, San Francisco, March 25 & July 15, 2002.

129. Doris Hinson Pieroth, *Seattle's Women Teachers of the Interwar Years: Shapers of a Livable City* (U Washington P, 2004); Pak, *Wherever I Go, I Will Always Be a Loyal American.*

130. Interviews of Estella Yorozu Takahashi (1916–2011) by the author, San Francisco, March 25 & July 15, 2002.

131. Thomas James, *Exile Within: The Schooling of Japanese Americans, 1942* (Harvard UP, 1987); Gary Y. Okihiro, *Storied Lives: Japanese American Students and World War II* (U Washington P, 1999).

132. The histories of San Francisco's ethnic neighborhoods courtesy of Dr. Charles Wollenberg.

133. Marcelo M. Suarez-Orozco, "'Becoming Somebody': Central American Immigrants in U.S. Inner-City Schools," *Anthropology and Education Quarterly* 18, no. 4 (Dec. 1987): 287–99.

134. Mission High-School Teacher Ethnicity Research (1996), using a sample of Mission High School yearbooks from 1910 to 1990, by Colin Ormsby, with help from Patrick McComb of Mission High's science faculty; my thanks to both. Fernande de Ghetaldi in Sibley, *Golden Book of California.* Ethnicity is determined by surnames, photographs, or personal knowledge. Italian American teacher numbers from Vitone, "The Italian-Americans of San Francisco," 117.

135. All quotations are from Dorothy Bryant, *Miss Giardino* (Ata Books, 1978).

136. Lowell High teachers in "Class Notes," *California Monthly* 10, no. 3 (Dec. 2000): 50.

137. Mary Kay Zuravleff, *The Bowl Is Already Broken—A Novel* (Picador/Farrar, Straus & Giroux, 2005), 172.

138. Maude Alverson (b. 1886) and 1981 faculty, in *Rosemary: The Urbana High School Annual,* vols. 13 (1922), 14 (1923), & 72 (1981); Alverson obituary in *Champagne-*

Urbana (IL) News Gazette (Sept. 24, 1970). Both in Archives Department, Urbana (IL) Free Library.

139. Rosa Sonnenschein, "The American Jewess," *American Jewess* (Feb. 1898): 205–8.

140. Karen Leroux, "'Unpensioned Veterans': Women Teachers and the Politics of Public Service in the Late-Nineteenth-Century United States," *Journal of Women's History* 2, no. 1 (Spring 2009): 34–62.

Chapter 6 · "The Presiding Genius of His Home and Heart"

1. Emma Hart Willard (1841) quoted in Henry Fowler, "Educational Services of Mrs. Emma Willard," in Barnard, *Memoirs of Teachers and Educators,* 125–68, esp. 132–34. The epigraph is from Ronald Butchart, Amy Rollieri, & Kevin Williams, "Method Matters: The GIGO Effect in Research on the History of Teachers" (paper presented at the Annual Meeting, American Educational Research Association, April 1–5, 2002, New Orleans).

2. Anne Hardeman in Michael O'Brien, *An Evening When Alone: Four Journals of Single Women in the South, 1827–67* (UP Virginia, 1993), esp. 32, 224, 373.

3. Elizabeth Thompson East in American Mothers Committee, *Mothers of Achievement in American History, 1776–1976* (C. E. Tuttle, 1976).

4. The Markham sisters, Jackson (MS), in "Sisters Teachers," *Between the Gate Posts,* blog entry by LindaRe, Jan. 10, 2011, http://betweenthegateposts.blogspot.com/2011/01/sisters-teachers.html.

5. Gerda Lerner, *The Creation of Feminist Consciousness: From the Middle Ages to Eighteen-Seventy* (Oxford UP, 1993), esp. 15.

6. Mrs. O'Neal in Susie Powers Tompkins, *Cotton-Patch Schoolhouse* (U Alabama P, 1992), 3.

7. Ruth Jacknow Markowitz, *My Daughter, the Teacher: Jewish Teachers in the New York City Schools* (Rutgers UP, 1993).

8. One of many examples is Edna C. Karlinsey (b. 1908) in American Mothers Committee, *Mothers of Achievement.*

9. Mercer girls in Mary Ormsbee Whitton, *These Were the Women: USA 1776–1860* (Hastings House, 1954).

10. Joan M. Jensen & Darlis Miller, "The Gentle Tamers Revisited: New Approaches to the History of Women in the American West," *Pacific Historical Review* 49, no. 2 (May 1980): 173–213; T. B. Crisp to Edgar Strain (Sept. 11, 1885), folder 1 in Edgar W. Strain Papers, Illinois Historical Society Collections.

11. Andrew Gulliford, *America's Country Schools* (Preservation Press, 1984), 67.

12. Mary Street Arms in "All about the Schools and the People Who Made Them Successful," *Plumas County Historical Society Publications,* no. 16 (June 7, 1964): 20.

13. Edna Fay Kaiser (1873–1962) in American Mothers Committee, *Mothers of Achievement,* 323; Pearl Barker in Beth R. Kiteley to Geraldine Clifford, April 6, 1998; Corintha Bruce Croy in "Alumni Roster, 1917," *Bulletin of the First District Normal School* [formally Northeast Missouri State Teachers College] 17, no. 4 (April 1917), Pickler Memorial Library, Truman State University Archives, Kirksville, Missouri, library.truman.edu/archives

/alumni1917.asp). For an update see the 1924 alumni roster, library.truman.edu/archives
/alumni1924A.asp.

14. Lydia O'Hare Oldfield, *The O'Hare Women* (AAUW–IKG, 1978); Jennie O'Hare Riordan, "Capsules of the Past," in Unpublished Memoirs, Special Collections, U of Nevada Library.

15. J. B. Corbell to Motimer Warren, Sept. 1871; in Avery Institute Collection: Mortimer A. Warren Papers, box 160 (South Carolina materials) in American Missionary Association Archives, Amistad Research Center, Tulane University Library.

16. Unnamed Lassen County teacher in *Western Journal of Education* 5, no. 11 (May 1900), 43.

17. Rebecca Stuart Reed in Sylvia Hunt, "To Wed and to Teach: The Myth of the Single Teacher," in Fane Downs & Nancy Baker Jones (Eds.), *Women and Texas History: Selected Essays* (Texas State Historical Association, 1993), 127–43.

18. Marguerite Renner, "Who Will Teach? Changing Job Opportunities and Roles for Women in the Evolution of the Pittsburgh Public Schools 1830–1900" (Ph.D. diss., University of Pittsburgh, 1981), esp. 8.

19. Hunt, "To Wed and to Teach." The married were 20% of her sample of 250 Texas women who taught between 1850 and 1930.

20. Mary Nolan & Mrs. Wilson in Eulalia Bourne, *Ranch Schoolteacher* (U Arizona P, 1974); Ronald Butchart, "The Frontier Teacher: Arizona, 1875–1925," *Journal of the West* 16, no. 3 (July 1977): 54–67.

21. Zenobia Boyle Kissinger was Joleen Wessel's teacher in 1933. Author's interview with Dr. D. Joleen Wessel Bock (Boone, NC) in Riva di Garda, Italy, May 2006; Dr. Bock to author, July 20, 2006.

22. Lyman Henry Van Houten, "Length of Service of Pennsylvania High School Teachers" (Ph.D. diss., Teachers College, Columbia University, 1932), 41.

23. One-Room Schools: The Heart of Old Tehama County," *San Francisco Chronicle* (June 14, 1998); Mendocino County examples in *What Became of the Little Red Schoolhouse? Facts and Figures, Tales and Photos of Early Mendocino County Schools*, vol. 1, *Mendocino Area* (Mendocino Coast Genealogical Society, 1990). Ruddock family in Lyman Palmer, *History of Mendocino County, California: Comprising its Geography, etc.* (Alley, Bowen, 1880).

24. Details of Elizabeth Danner's life courtesy of her daughter, Margaret Mallette of Oroville (CA), from interview with author, March 12, 1998. Mrs. Danner's obituary in *Oakland (CA) Tribune* (March 6, 1998). Information on Shandon courtesy of Frank Armendariz, Santa Barbara (CA) Historical Society.

25. Ina Beauchamp Hall in American Mothers Committee, *Mothers of Achievement*; Elizabeth Qöyawayma, *No Turning Back: A Hopi Indian Woman's Struggle to Live in Two Worlds* (U New Mexico P, 1964).

26. Blanche V. Harris in Ellen Lawson & Marlene Merrill, "The Antebellum 'Talented Thousandth': Black College Students at Oberlin before the Civil War," *Journal of Negro History* 52, no. 2 (Spring 1983): 142–55. Jeanes teachers in Valina Littlefield, "'I Am Only One, but I Am One': Southern African-American Women Schoolteachers, 1884–1954," Spencer Foundation Winter Forum, Berkeley, CA, Feb. 19, 1999.

27. Ralph Richard Banks, *Is Marriage for White People? How the African American Marriage Decline Affects Everyone* (Dutton, 2011).

28. Ida Stornetta in *What Became of the Little Red Schoolhouse?*, vol. 5, *Anderson Valley-Point Arena; Ukiah (CA) Republican Press* (Dec. 29, 1916); and Sibley, *Golden Book of California.*

29. Willie Wilkinson, "Family Values," *San Francisco Chronicle* (May 5, 2004).

30. Emmeline Woodward Whitney Wells in American Mothers Committee, *Mothers of Achievement*, 525; Cynthia Fisher in Joyce Kinkead (Ed.), *A Schoolmarm All My Life: Personal Narratives from Frontier Utah* (Signature Books, 1996).

31. Seattle teacher quoted in Doris Hinson Pieroth, *Seattle's Women Teachers of the Interwar Years: Shapers of a Livable City* (U Washington P, 2004).

32. Anne Kunstler interviewed for Markowitz, *My Daughter, the Teacher.*

33. Lizzie Locke Collings in Katherine Redington Morgan (Ed.), *My Ever Dear Daughter, My Own Dear Mother: Correspondence of Julia Stone Towne & Mary Julia Towne* (U Iowa P, 1996).

34. Boston regulations in *Proceedings of the Boston School Committee*, Oct. 23, 1900 & Feb. 26, 1901; Polly Welts Kaufman, *Boston Women and City School Politics, 1872–1905* (Garland, 1994).

35. Mrs. Watkins in "County Items," *School Bulletin & New York State Educational Journal* 25, no. 295 (March 1899): 154; Margaret K. Nelson, "Using Oral Case Histories to Reconstruct the Experiences of Women Teachers in Vermont, 1900–50," in Ivor Goodson (Ed.), *Studying Teachers' Lives* (Teachers College P 1992), 167–86.

36. "Women Teachers of New York: What Is Required of Them," *California Teacher & Home Journal* 2, no. 3 (Oct. 1883): 163; Editors, "Discussions: Women as Teachers," *Educational Review* 2 (Nov. 1891): 361–62.

37. Markowitz, *My Daughter, the Teacher.* In 1974 the Supreme Court struck down mandatory maternity leaves for teachers—thereby allowing a woman to teach throughout her pregnancy.

38. Mrs. Lytle in Ronald Cohen, *Children of the Mill: Schooling and Society in Gary, Indiana, 1906–1960* (Indiana UP, 1990), 15; Gloria Hull (Ed.), *Give Us Each Day: The Diary of Alice Dunbar-Nelson* (Norton, 1984), 438–39.

39. Mrs. Terrell in Linda Perkins, "The Role of Education in the Development of Black Feminist Thought, 1860–1920," *History of Education* 22, no. 3 (Sept. 1993): 268.

40. Mrs. Lytle in Ronald Cohen, *Children of the Mill: Schooling and Society in Gary, Indiana, 1906–1960* (Indiana UP, 1990), 15.

41. Cincinnati in "Married School Teacher Question," *Chicago Daily Tribune* (Sept. 11, 1890).

42. Ruby Blanche Larson, "The Status of the Married Teacher in the Public Schools of the United States" (master's thesis, University of California, Berkeley, 1926); Leslie Gale Parr, *A Will of Her Own: Sarah Towles Reed and the Pursuit of Democracy in Southern Public Education* (U Georgia P, 1998). On Charleston, R. Scott Baker letter to author, Sept. 14, 1992.

43. "Married Women Teachers and Their Status in 1,500 Cities," *Nation's Schools* 8, no. 4 (Oct. 1932): 52.

44. Dutart v. Woodward, 99 Cal. Ct. App. Rptr., 736, 279 (1929), p. 493; Newton Edwards, "The Law Governing the Dismissal of Teachers—II," *Elementary School Journal* 33, no. 6 (Jan. 1932): 365–76.

45. Diane Manning, *Hill Country Teachers: Oral Histories from the One-Room School and Beyond* (Twayne, 1990); Jessie L. Embry, "The School Marms of San Juan County" (unpublished paper, Brigham Young University, courtesy of the author).

46. Claudia Goldin, "Marriage Bars: Discrimination against Married Woman Workers, 1920s to 1950s," Working Paper no. 2747 (National Bureau of Economic Research, 1988), 6.

47. Willard Ellsbree, *The American Teacher: Evolution of a Profession in a Democracy* (American Book, 1939), 537–38. Specialists in women's history have also extrapolated from limited data; see Nancy Cott, *The Grounding of Modern Feminism* (Yale UP, 1987).

48. Questionnaire responses from superintendents in *The Educational Research Bulletin of the Pasadena Schools* (Nov.–Dec. 1925); "Administrative Practices Affecting Classroom Teachers: Part I: The Selection and Appointment of Teachers," *Research Bulletin of the National Education Association*, 10, no. 1 (Jan. 1932), 4.

49. Larson, *Status of the Married Teacher in the Public Schools of the United States*; David Wilbur Peters, *The Status of the Married Woman Teacher* (Teachers College P, 1934).

50. In Adolphine Fletcher Terry, *Charlotte Stephens: Little Rock's First Black Teacher* (Academic P Arkansas, 1973), 102, 106–7. By permission.

51. Janet M. Hooks, *Women's Occupations through Seven Decades,* U.S. Women's Bureau Bulletin no. 218 (1947), 161.

52. Lois Scharf, *To Work and to Wed: Female Employment, Feminism, and the Great Depression* (Greenwood, 1980); Evan Warwick Roberts, "Her Real Sphere? Married Women's Labor Force Participation in the United States, 1860–1940" (Ph.D. diss., University of Minnesota, 1907), esp. 34; Julia Kirk Blackwelder, *Now Hiring: The Feminization of Work in the United States, 1900–1995* (Texas A&M UP, 1997).

53. Dina M. Copelman, *London's Women Teachers: Gender, Class and Feminism, 1870–1930* (Routledge, 1996), esp. 179; Hilda Kean, *Deeds Not Words: The Lives of Suffragette Teachers* (Pluto Press, 1990), 97–98; Miriam E. David, *The State, The Family, and Education* (Routledge & Kegan Paul, 1980).

54. Christine Ruane, *Gender, Class, and the Professionalization of Russian City Teachers, 1860–1914* (U Pittsburgh P, 1994), 79.

55. Leslie Page Moch, "Government Policy and Women's Experience: The Case of Teachers in France," *Feminist Studies* 14, no. 2 (Summer 1988): 301–24. M. Laird as quoted by Dorothy Canfield Fisher in a *New York Tribune* article (n.d.), "The Married Teacher in France," reproduced in *School and Society* 6, no. 143 (Sept. 22, 1917): 356–57.

56. Luise Zeitz in Susan Groag Bell & Karen M. Offen, *Women, the Family, and Freedom: The Debate in Documents*, vol. 2, *1880–1950* (Stanford UP, 1983), 297.

57. *La situation de la femme mariée dans l'enseignement* (Geneva: Bureau International d'Education, 1933).

58. Alison Oram, "A Master Should Not Serve under a Mistress: Women and Men Teachers 1900–1970," in Sandra Acker (Ed.), *Teachers, Gender and Careers* (Falmer Press, 1989), 21.

59. Author's interview of Jeannette Scholnick Urbas, Desenzano, Italy, May 14, 2006.

60. Author's interview of Beverley Craine DeWinter, San Francisco, April 2003 (courtesy of Jean Cardoza, San Francisco).

61. Ella Kahu & Mandy Morgan, "A Critical Discourse Analysis of New Zealand Government Policy: Women as Mothers and Workers," *Women's Studies International Forum* 30, no. 2 (March 2007): 134–46; Sue Middleton, *Educating Feminists: Life Histories and Pedagogy* (Teachers College P, 1993), 84; Tom Sheridan & Pat Stretton, "Mandarins, Ministers and the Bar on Married Women," *Journal of Industrial Relations* 46, no. 1 (Mar. 2004): 84–101.

62. Weaver in *Times Education Supplement* (Oct. 4, 1958) quoted in Geoffrey G. Partington, *Women Teachers in the Twentieth Century in England and Wales* (NFER, 1976), 85.

63. Author's interview of Sidney Lionel Waterson, Dec. 8, 1988, in Ringwood, Victoria. See also Shirley Sampson, "Teacher Careers and Promotion in Australia," in Patricia A. Schmuck (Ed.), *Women Educators: Employees of Schools in Western Countries* (SUNY P, 1987), 43–56.

64. Author's interviews with Dr. John Theobald, Monash University, Victoria, Dec. 1988.

65. Some indirect statistical support appears in John Folger & Charles Nam, *Education of the American Population* (U.S. Bureau of the Census, 1967), 91, 100. Also Winifred Wandersee Bolin, "The Economics of Middle-Income Family Life: Working Women during the Great Depression," *Journal of American History* 65, no. 1 (June 1978): 60–74.

66. Sallie Southall Cotton (1846–1929) in Lou Rogers, *Tar Heel Women* (Warren, 1949), 159–64.

67. Clara Hampson in James, *Notable American Women*; the Behrends in Ted Hinckley, *The Americanization of Alaska, 1867–1898* (Pacific Books, 1972), 236.

68. W. E. B. Du Bois, *Crisis* 9 (Aug. 1914): 179.

69. Georgia Camp Johnson, Sallie Wyatt, Clarissa Scott Delany, Rosa Dixon Bowser, & Dorothy Jemison (in Mae Jemison entry) all in Salem, *African American Women*.

70. Julia Reed, "Marriage and Fertility in Black Female Teachers," *Black Scholar* 1, nos. 3–4 (Jan.–Feb. 1970): 285–314.

71. Correspondence in McLean Family Papers, Bancroft Library, University of California, Berkeley, by permission.

72. Richard Quantz, "Teachers as Women: An Ethnohistory of the 1930s" (paper presented at the Annual Meeting, American Educational Research Association, New York, March 19–23, 1982).

73. "Bodie's Bad Man," in Mary Austin, *Earth Horizon: An Autobiography* (Literary Guild, 1932), 172.

74. Floy Lawrence Emhoff, "A Pioneer School Teacher in Central Iowa: Alice Money Lawrence," *Iowa Journal of History and Politics* 33, no. 4 (Oct. 1935): 376–95, esp. 395.

75. From a 1911 critique of employed women, cited in Robert Smuts, *Women and Work in America* (Columbia UP, 1959), 42.

76. WSTA incident in Edith Clark diary entry for Jan. 2, 1908, Agnes Wright Spring Collection, box 10, courtesy of American Heritage Center, University of Wyoming.

77. John Steinbeck, *East of Eden* (Viking, 1952); John Kenneth Galbraith, *The Scotch* (Houghton Mifflin, 1964), esp. 135–37.

78. Interview with Farrington Carpenter, *Saturday Evening Post* (1952), quoted in Dorothy Wickenden, "Roughing It: What Two Young Women Found in the Rockies," *New Yorker* (April 20, 2009): 56–67, esp. 57.

79. Mary Ann Hatten in American Mothers Committee, *Mothers of Achievement.*

80. Reed Ueda, *Avenues to Adulthood: The Origins of the High School and Social Mobility in an American Suburb* (Cambridge UP, 1987), 170–71.

81. Myrtle Sagan McFarlane, "Mrs. Amelia Lyon Hall, Pioneer Teacher," in *Biographies of Pioneer Women,* in Delta Kappa Gamma Manuscripts, on microfilm, in Wyoming State Archives.

82. Dorcas Calmes Cooper in Marguerite Tolbert, Irene Dillard Elliott, & Wil Lou Gray (Eds.), *South Carolina's Distinguished Women of Laurens County* (R. L. Bryan, 1972), 73–79, 113–20. 247–54.

83. Susan Purington Lloyd, *A Singular School: Abbot Academy* (Phillips Academy, 1979), 524n26; Austin, *Earth Horizon,* 172.

84. Amanda Reid in Helen Hooven Santmyer, *". . . And Ladies of the Club"* (Berkley Books, 1985), 405–6. The year was 1878.

85. Linda Perkins, "Heed Life's Demands: The Educational Philosophy of Fanny Jackson Coppin," *Journal of Negro Education* 51, no. 3 (1982): 181–90.

86. Josephine Leavell Allensworth (b. 1855) in Salem, *African American Women.* On Allensworth see Kathleen Weiler, *Country Schoolwomen: Teaching in Rural California 1850–1950* (Stanford UP, 1998).

87. Ronald Rayman, "The Winnebago Indian School Experiment in Iowa Territory, 1834–1848," *Annals of Iowa* 44, no. 5 (Summer 1978): 359–98, esp. 391–92.

88. Mary McKinlay in Marjorie Theobald, *Knowing Women: Origins of Women's Education in Nineteenth-Century Australia* (Cambridge UP, 1996), 102.

89. Zoé Penon Villin, quoted in Moch, "Government Policy and Women's Experience," 311.

90. Edgar MacDonald (Ed.), *The Education of the Heart: The Correspondence of Rachel Mordecai Lazarus and Maria Edgeworth* (U North Carolina P, 1977).

91. James H. Wilson, *Life of John A. Rawlins* (Neale, 1916), esp. 388; Mrs. Grant's account of his courtship in John Simon (Ed.), *Personal Memoirs of Julia Dent Grant* (Putnam's Sons, 1975), 121.

92. Priscilla White in Thad Sitton & Milan Rowold, *Ringing the Children In: Texas County Schools* (Texas A&M UP, 1987), 115.

93. Abia Warren Hiller in Linda Peavy & Ursula Smith, *Women in Waiting in the Westward Movement: Life on the Frontier* (U Oklahoma P, 1994), esp. 49.

94. Advertisement in Robert Francis Seybolt, *The Private Schools of Colonial Boston* (Harvard UP, 1935), 14–15; J. Emerick Nagy, "Wanted: A Teacher for the Nashville English School," *Tennessee Historical Quarterly* 21 (June 1962): 171–86.

95. Staffing report, "Filipinos and Americans in the Philippine Bureau of Education (1901–1906)," in Philippine Bureau of Education, Bulletin no. 25, http://rizal.lib.admu.edu .ph/ahc/guides/Bureau%20of%20Education%20(1901-1906).pdf, accessed Nov. 6, 2013.

96. Gilbert D. Kingsbury Papers [pseudonym F. F. Fenn], Dolph Briscoe Center for American History, University of Texas; Kingsbury Papers, Special Collections, University of Florida Library.

97. The temporary gender rebalancing of high school faculties after World War II increased workplace contacts between marriageable men and women.

98. Ethel L. Collins and Elias Jacobsen in "List of Our Field Workers," *American Missionary* 45, no. 2 (Feb. 1891): 48–73, esp. 69; Margaret Hines Roberts in "Margaret and J. M. Roberts: Companions in the Education of Thomas Wolfe," *Thomas Wolfe Review* 30, nos. 1–2 (2006): 56pp.

99. Folger & Nam, *Education of the American Population,* 99; Gerald J. Brunetti, "Why Do They Teach? A Study of Job Satisfaction among Long-Term High School Teachers," *Teacher Education Quarterly* (California Council on Teacher Education) 38, no. 3 (Summer 2001): 49–74, esp. 68.

100. Helen MacKnight Doyle, *A Child Went Forth: The Autobiography of Dr. Helen MacKnight Doyle* (Gotham House, 1934), 48, 92.

101. A son, Berry Gordy Jr. (b. 1888), became a music-business tycoon. His autobiography is *To Be Loved: The Music, the Magic, the Memories of Motown* (Harper & Row, 1979).

102. Mary Patterson McPherson, "Two Afternoons on the Job," in Karen Doyle Walton (Ed.), *Against the Tide: Career Paths of Women Leaders in American and British Higher Education* (Phi Delta Kappa Educational Foundation, 1996), 153–164, esp.154. The phrase heading this section is by Zoé Penon Villin, quoted in Leslie Page Moch, "Government Policy and Women's Experience: The Case of Teachers in France," *Feminist Studies* 14, no. 2 (Summer 1988): 301–24, esp. 311.

103. "Mr. Conner" in Erin McNamara Horvat, Elliot Weininger, & Annette Lareau, "From Social Ties to Social Capital: Class Differences in the Relations between Schools and Parent Networks," *American Educational Research Journal* 40, no. 2 (Summer 2003): 319–51, esp. 337.

104. Author's interview of Beverley Craine De Winter, San Francisco, April 2003.

105. Susan Isaacs, *Red, White and Blue* (HarperCollins, 1999), esp. 259–64.

106. The influence of national culture on a school's social climate is featured in Christina De Bellaigue, *Educating Women: Schooling and Identity in England and France, 1800–1867* (Oxford UP, 2007).

107. Andrea Turpin, "The Ideological Origins of the Women's College: Religion, Class, and Curriculum in the Educational Visions of Catharine Beecher and Mary Lyon," *History of Education Quarterly* 50, no. 2 (May 2010): 133–58.

108. Abilene example from author's interview May 11, 2006, with Charlotte Laing (Mrs. Robert Dahl) of Sun City West (AZ).

109. Alice Pierce in Ira Benjamin Whitcomb Collection, Manuscripts Division, Oregon Historical Society, by permission.

110. Janina Trotman, "Women Teachers in Western Australian 'Bush' Schools, 1900–1939: Passive Victims of Oppressive Structures?," *History of Education Quarterly* 46, no. 2 (Summer 2006): 248–73.

111. Arthur Gray, "The Teacher's Home," *Elementary School Journal,* 17, no. 3 (Nov. 1916): 201–8, esp. 205.

112. Nellie Purle Cronk in Gail Martin, "The Remarkable Young Woman from Turkey Creek," *Voices: KanColl Online Magazine* (Winter 2000); Alice Newberry Papers, History Colorado.

113. Polly Bullard, "Iron Range Schoolmarm," *Minnesota History* 32, no. 4 (Dec. 1951): 193–201; Jane M. Bernhardt in Sibley, *Golden Book of California*.

114. Coral Adams Kube in Kirksville Alumni Roster, 1917 and 1924.

115. Mrs. Sullivan in Gray, "The Teacher's Home," 202; Eleanor Hasenkamp "Memoir," in Wells Chamber of Commerce, Metropolis entry, *Trail of the 49ers*, www.trailofthe49ers .org/memoir.shtml, accessed Nov. 6, 2013.

116. "Washington State Schools History Timeline," in Mary Jane Honegger, *Washington State Historic School: Status 2002* (Washington Trust for Historic Preservation), www .dahp.wa.gov/sites/default/files/2002WTHP%20Historic%20Schools%20Status%20Report1 .pdf. Hall County (NE) had the first known teacherage in a U.S. school district in 1894, built for "$1,000 in gold"; in Gray, "Teacher's Home," 202.

117. When Marianne Barton taught at Ramstein Air Base in Germany in 1952, teachers were billeted in the officers' barracks. Author's interview with Marianne Barton, San Francisco, July 9, 2010.

118. Elissa Gootman, "City Will Help Pension Plans Build Housing for Teachers," *New York Times* (Oct. 5, 2007).

119. Sarah Lawrence Lightfoot, "The Lives of Teachers," in Lee Shulman & Gary Sykes (Eds.), *Handbook of Teaching and Policy* (Longman, 1983), 256.

120. Gertrude Thomas journal entry for Oct. 26, 1880, Thomas Papers, Duke University Library.

121. Effie Decker in Adolf E. Schroeder & Carla Schulz-Geisberg (Eds.), *"Hold Dear, As Always": Jette, a German Immigrant Life in Letters* (U Missouri P, 1988), 197, 236, 240; Mrs. Sullivan in Gray, "Teacher's Home," 202.

122. Martha Spence Heywood and Eunice Harris in Kinkead, *Schoolmarm All My Life*, 20–31, esp. 26, 29.

123. Judith Smith, "City and Family: Italians and Jews in Industrial Rhode Island" (unpublished paper presented at the Annual Meeting of the American Historical Association, Washington, DC, Dec. 26–29, 1976); author's interview of Jessie Lai Young's granddaughter, Gail Oshiro, in San Francisco, Dec. 2010.

124. Emily Feistritzer, *The American Teacher* (Feistrizer, 1983).

125. Oliver Wendell Holmes, *The Autocrat of the Breakfast-Table* (Phillips, Sampson, 1859). The phrase in the heading to this section is from Rayman, "Winnebago Indian School Experiment."

126. Bart Stanley in *Parade* magazine (June 30, 1991): 17.

127. Self-assessments of New York City teacher-mothers from interviews in Claire Elaine Sylvan, *Impact of Motherhood on Teacher Career Attitudes* (Teachers College P, 1988), 263–74.

128. On changing pedagogical views among black leaders see Daniel Perlstein, "Minds Stayed on Freedom: Politics and Pedagogy in the African-American Freedom Struggle," *American Educational Research Journal* 39, no. 2 (Summer 2002): 249–77.

Chapter 7 · "In the Mind's Eye"

1. Wardlaw Sisters Collection, Tennessee State Library and Archives; James S. Angle, "The Black Sisters: Evolution of a Folk Tale," Vanderbilt University English paper, May

1969; Eugene Sloan, "Soule College," *Rutherford County Historical Society,* no. 11 (Summer 1978): 58–103, courtesy of Alicia Rae Crowe, Vanderbilt University; *Wellesley College Calendar,* 1881–1882, courtesy of Wellesley archivist Wilma Slaight and Professor Barbara Beatty. Epigraph from Phyllis McGinley, "A Garland of Precepts," *New Yorker* (Feb. 6, 1954): 28.

2. Dennis Carlson, "Teachers as Political Actors: From Reproductive Theory to the Crisis of Schooling," *Harvard Educational Review* 57, no. 3 (Aug. 1987): 283–307; Robert Everhard (Ed.), *The Public School Monopoly: A Critical Analysis of Education and the State in American Society* (Ballinger Books, 1981).

3. Heather Weaver, "The Celluloid Schoolhouse: Early Film Depictions of Schooling in the U.S., 1910–1940" (paper presented at the Annual Meeting of the American Educational Research Association, San Francisco, April 7–11, 2006). Quotation from Director Gregory La Cava.

4. Susan Griffin, "Letter to the Outside," in *Dear Sky* (Shameless Hussy Press, 1971).

5. Only one woman teacher, a female assistant in an infant school, is pictured in Paul Monroe, *A Text-Book in the History of Education* (Macmillan, 1905, 1922), a well-illustrated classic. On the shift from goddesses of learning to "country louts" in depictions of teachers elsewhere in art, see Jeroen J. H. Dekker, "A Republic of Educators: Educational Messages in Seventeenth-Century Dutch Genre Paintings," *History of Education Quarterly* 36, no. 2 (Summer 1996): 155–82.

6. Adeline Ireson in *Historical Sketches of the Framingham State Normal School* (Alumnae Association, 1914), 103.

7. Winslow Homer in Geoffrey O'Brien, "The Great Prose Painter," *New York Review of Books* 43, no. 4 (Feb. 29, 1996): 15–19, esp. 16.; Deborah Solomon, *American Mirror: The Art and Life of Norman Rockwell* (Farrar, Straus & Giroux, 2013).

8. Gail Drago, *Etta Place: Her Life and Times with Butch Cassidy and the Sundance Kid* (Republic of Texas Press, 1996).

9. Jean Brodie is based on Christina Kay, who taught Muriel Spark (1918–2006) at Edinburgh's James Gillespie High School for Girls.

10. Monica Sullivan, *Movie Magazine International* (2002). www.shoestring.org/mmi _alpha.html. Early, serious works on movies in American culture include Henry James Forman, *Our Movie Made Children* (Macmillan, 1934); & Margaret Farrand Thorp, *America at the Movies* (Yale UP, 1939).

11. Adam Farhi, "Hollywood Goes to School: Recognizing the Superteacher Myth in Film," *Clearing House* 72 (Jan. 1999): 157–59.

12. Anthony Lane, "Academic Questions," *New Yorker* (July 4, 2011), 78.

13. Mont Hawthorne in Martha Ferguson McKeown, *Them Was the Days: An American Saga of the '70s* (Macmillan, 1950; U Nebraska P, 1961), 54–55, 59.

14. Harriet Williams Russell (1844–1926) to dear friends at home, Feb. 6, 1859, in Harriet Russell Strong Papers, Henry E. Huntington Library.

15. Wihelmine Cordt to May Stewart, April 15, 1883, in Stewart-Lockwood Family Collection, Kansas Collection, Spencer Research Library, University of Kansas Libraries (hereafter SLC), original spelling and punctuation. By permission.

16. Kathleen Jett Schwarzschild (White Plains, NY) to author, correspondence, 2004, 2005.

17. Joyce Carol Oates, *Foxfire: Confessions of a Girl Gang* (Penguin-Dutton, 1993).

18. Arethusa Hall in Paul Monroe (Ed.), *A Cyclopedia of Education* (Macmillan, 1912).

19. George Sturt, *A Small Boy in the 'Sixties* (Cambridge, 1927), cited in E. Stuart Bates, *Inside Out: An Introduction to Autobiography* (Blackwell, 1936), 71.

20. Jodi Picoult, *Vanishing Acts* (Washington Square Press, 2005), 246.

21. Susan Nash, "Wanting a Situation: Governesses and Victorian Novels" (Ph.D. diss., Rutgers University, 1980); Dina M. Copelman, *London's Women Teachers: Gender, Class and Feminism, 1870–1930* (Routledge, 1996).

22. Miss Read [Dora Jessie Gunnis Saint], *Village School* (Houghton Mifflin, 1956), 9. See also her *Emily Davis* (Magna Print Books, 1971); & *Miss Clare Remembers* (Michael Joseph, 1962).

23. Henry Handel Richardson [Ethel Florence Lindesay Richardson], *The Getting of Wisdom* (London: William Heinemann, 1910), esp. 49, 99. See Germaine Greer's introduction to the Virago edition (Dial Press, 1981).

24. Analyses of popular culture include Jan Cohn, *Romance and the Erotics of Property: Mass-Market Fiction for Women* (Duke UP, 1988); Jayne Ann Krentz (Ed.), *Dangerous Men and Adventurous Women: Romance Writers on the Appeal of the Romance* (U Pennsylvania P, 1992); Jane Tompkins, *West of Everything: The Inner Life of Westerns* (Oxford UP, 1992).

25. Frances Allard in Mary Balogh, *Simply Unforgettable* (Bantam Dell, 2006).

26. Anne Jewell in Mary Balogh, *Simply Love* (Dell, 2007), 159–60.

27. Ted Sennett, *Great Hollywood Movies* (Harry N. Abrams, n.d.), 77; Fred Erisman, introduction to Judy Alter & A. T. Row, *Unbridled Spirits: Short Fiction about Women in the Old West* (Texas Christian UP, 1994), x.

28. Allison Hayes, *Spellbound* (Avon Books, 1990), esp. 6, 17, 113.

29. In Dorothy Wickenden, "Roughing It: What Two Young Women Found in the Rockies," *New Yorker* (April 20, 2009), 56–67; and Wickenden, *Nothing Daunted: The Unexpected Education of Two Society Girls in the West* (Scribner, 2011).

30. S. F. Smith, "Mrs. Sarah Davis Comstock," in Hamilton Wilcox Pierson (Ed.), *American Missionary Memorial* (Harper, 1853), 162–82, esp. 272.

31. Mary Jane Walker, normal school journal entry for Jan. 17, 1849, in Schlesinger Library, Radcliffe College.

32. *California State Examination Board Reports,* California State Library, Sacramento.

33. William Kritek & Delbert Clear, "Teachers and Principals in the Milwaukee Public Schools," in John Rury & Frank Cassell (Eds.), *Seeds of Crisis: Public School in Milwaukee Since 1920* (U Wisconsin P, 1993), 145–92.

34. Carol Coburn, "Spirited Lives: The Religious Community as Educator of American Women, 1870–1918" (paper presented at the History of Education Society Annual Meeting, Nov. 4, 1994, Chapel Hill, North Carolina).

35. Arturo Pérez-Reverte, *The Seville Communion* (Harcourt, Brace, 1999), 270, 271.

36. Susan Isaacs, *After All These Years* (HarperCollins, 1993), 18, 70, 98, 254, 272.

37. Jesse Petherbridge to Amanda Stewart, April 6, 1887, in SLC (emphasis in the original).

38. *The Memoirs of Herbert Hoover: Years of Adventure, 1874–1920* (Macmillan, 1951), 5.

39. Walker, normal school journal entry for Jan. 11, 1849.

40. Leo Rosten (b. 1908), *People I Have Loved, Known or Admired* (McGraw-Hill, 1970), 53–58.

41. Weaver, "Celluloid Schoolhouse."

42. Octavia Angelluzi in Mario Puzo's novel, *The Fortunate Pilgrim* (Atheneum, 1965), 13, 26.

43. Catherine Ford Rea, "Childhood Memories," *Mendocino Historical Review* 5, no. 1 (Winter 1972): 11.

44. Callen Taylor in Heather Knight, "Machiavelli's Stories at Bedtime Set a Child on a Teacher's Path," & "The Saturday Morning Dante Club," *San Francisco Chronicle* (March 20, 2006).

45. Patricia Howlett & Charles F. Howlett, "A Silent Witness for Peace: The Case of Schoolteacher Mary Stone McDowell and America at War," *History of Education Quarterly* 48, no. 3 (Aug. 2008): 371–96.

46. Charles Robinson, letter to the editor, *Oakland (CA) Tribune* (Aug. 24, 1998).

47. "Wanda" was one of 32 teachers interviewed for Claire Sylvan, "The Impact of Motherhood on Teacher Career Attitudes" (Ed.D. diss., Teachers College, Columbia University, 1988), esp. 332, 356. See also Sterling Brown, "Negro Character as Seen by White Authors," *Journal of Negro Education* 2, no. 2 (April 1933): 179–203.

48. Letter of Dec. 18, 1852, in Ruth Newcomb Hastings Papers, Clements Library, University of Michigan, by permission.

49. Willard Waller, *The Sociology of Teaching* (Russell & Russell, 1932; Wiley & Sons, 1965), 49ff.

50. In Lyman L. Palmer, *History of Mendocino County, California: Comprising Its Geography, etc.* (Alley, Bowen, 1880).

51. Frank McCourt, *Teacher Man* (Scribner, 2005), 75.

52. Christine Zajac in Tracy Kidder, *Among Schoolchildren* (Avon Books, 1989), 8, 71.

53. Frances Mayes, *Under the Tuscan Sun* (Broadway Books, 1997), 190.

54. Hayes, *Spellbound*.

55. Phyllis Bottome, *Search for a Soul* (Faber & Faber, 1947), 187–88, by permission.

56. David Tyack, "Bureaucracy and the Common School: The Example of Portland, Oregon, 1851–1913," *American Quarterly* 19, no. 3 (Fall 1967): 475–98, esp. 477.

57. James Purdy, *The Nephew* (Farrar, Straus & Cudahy, 1960; Penguin Books, 1980), 79.

58. The phrase is from Glyn Hughes, *Brontë* (St. Martin's Press, 1996).

59. Citations in Pamela Horn, *Education in Rural England 1800–1914* (St. Martin's Press, 1978), 319nn19, 20.

60. Ray Allen Billington (Ed.), *The Journal of Charlotte L. Forten* (Dryden Press, 1953; Collier Books, 1961, 1967), entries for May 30, 1855, Mar. 5, 1864, May 18, 1864.

61. Jeanne Noble, *The Negro Woman's College Education* (Columbia University P, 1956), 21; Karen Anderson, "Brickbats and Roses: Lucy Diggs Slowe, 1883–1937," in Geraldine Jonçich Clifford (Ed.), *"Lone Voyagers": Academic Women in Coeducational Institutions 1883–1937* (Feminist Press, 1989), 287.

62. In Karen Leroux, "'Lady Teachers' and the Genteel Roots of Teacher Organization in Gilded Age Cities," *History of Education Quarterly* 46, no. 2 (Summer 2006): 164–191, esp. 188n60.

63. Eulalia Bourne, *Ranch Schoolteacher* (University of Arizona P, 1974).

64. Teacher rules posted in the schoolhouse at Bannack State Park, Montana.

65. Mary J. Oates, "Organized Voluntarism: The Catholic Sisters in Massachusetts, 1870–1940," *American Quarterly* 30, no. 5 (Winter 1978): 652–80, esp. 678, 679.

66. Tyack, "Bureaucracy and the Common School," esp. 489–90.

67. Maude Frazier (1881–1963) in A. D. Hopkins & K. J. Evans, *The First 100: Men and Women Who Shaped Las Vegas* (Huntington Press, 1999).

68. James Runciman, *School Board Idylls* (Chatto & Windus, 1887), 76–77, as quoted in Copelman, *London's Women Teachers,* 109.

69. Adria Reich, "Teaching Is a Good Profession . . . for a Woman," in Judith Stacey, Susan Bereaud, & Joan Daniesl (Eds.), *"And Jill Came Tumbling After": Sexism in American Education* (Dell, 1974), 337–43; Nicholas Hoppe, "Many Children Left Behind," May 23, 2006, www.hoppecolumns.com/columns/kellyfollowup.htm, accessed Nov. 6, 2013. Used by permission.

70. Stockwell College cited in Horn, *Education in Rural England,* 94. The expression in the title of this section comes from www.newworldencyclopedia.org/entry/Walter_Bagehot.

71. David Weigand, "'Mr. Chips' adaptation refreshingly sentimental," *San Francisco Chronicle* (Nov. 18, 2003); Sandra Weber & Claudia Mitchell, *That's Funny, You Don't Look like a Teacher* (Falmer Press, 1995); Mary Dalton, *The Hollywood Curriculum: Teachers and Teaching in the Movies* (Peter Lang, 1995).

72. Waller, *Sociology of Teaching,* 220.

73. Helen Mirren interview in Edward Guthmann, *San Francisco Chronicle* (Oct. 12, 2006).

74. Joseph Fichter, S.J., *Parochial School: A Sociological Study* (Doubleday, 1964), 319.

75. Mary S. Edwards, "Sign of the Times," *Journal of Social Hygiene,* 16, no. 1 (Jan. 1930), 13.

76. Marianne Costantinou, "56 Years after Class Was Dismissed, Miss Bricoe Visits Her Fourth-Graders," *San Francisco Chronicle* (Jan. 27, 2005).

77. Erma Bombeck, "Dressing for Duty," *Oakland (CA) Tribune* (Mar. 14, 1986), LA Times Syndicate. Washington (DC) teacher interviews in Antoinette Mitchell, "Work Lives of Urban Teachers, 1960–1990" (Ph.D. diss., University of California, Berkeley, 1996), esp. 73, 250.

78. John Berger, *Ways of Seeing* (British Broadcasting Association / Penguin Books, 1978), 47.

79. Margaret Fuller journal entry, quoted in Judith Strong Albert, *Minerva's Circle: Margaret Fuller's Women* (Paper Mill Press, 2010), 78.

80. Rachel Brownstein, *Becoming a Heroine: Reading about Women in Novels* (Penguin Books, 1984). Also see Andrea Wyman, "Representations of U.S. Rural Women Teachers (1760–1940)" (Ph.D. project, Graduate School of the Union Institute, Cincinnati, 1991).

81. Sarah Halprin, *Look at My Ugly Face! Myths and Musings on Beauty and Other Perilous Obsessions with Women's Appearance* (Penguin Books, 1995), 77.

82. "Full Text of 'Abstract of the Proceedings of the Massachusetts Teachers Association 1845–80,'" (typescript volume in UCLA Library).

83. Cited in Eugene Lee (Ed.), *Teaching as a Man's Job* (Phi Delta Kappa, 1939).

84. Dorothy Bryant, *Miss Giardino* (Ata Books, 1978), 40–41.

85. McCourt, *Teacher Man*, 12.

86. Mary B. Thomas, diary entry, University of Georgia Library, Athens. Courtesy of Hargrett Rare Book and Manuscript Library, University of Georgia Libraries.

87. Mary Balogh, *Simply Magic* (Delacorte Press, 2007), 25–26.

88. Quoted in John Hurt, *Education in Evolution: Church, State, Society, and Popular Education 1800–1870* (Hart-Davis, 1971), 140–41.

89. Rasjidah Franklin, "Berta Rantz: Her Life and Legacy," *Teacher Education Quarterly* (California Council on Teacher Education) 28, no. 3 (Summer 2001): 19–28, esp. 24.

90. In Estelle Reel Papers, Wyoming State Archives, Cheyenne. Also cited in Patricia Carter, " 'Completely Discouraged': Women Teachers' Resistance in the Bureau of Indian Affairs Schools, 1900–1919," *Frontiers: A Journal of Women Studies* 15, no. 3 (Spring 1995): 53–86, esp. 76.

91. Sarah Fielding, *The Little Governess; or, Little Female Academy* (Pandora Press / Routledge, 1987): 2.

92. Monica Kiefer, *American Children through Their Books, 1700–1835* (U Pennsylvania P, 1948), 79.

93. In Christina de Bellaigue, "The Development of Teaching as a Profession for Women Before 1870," *Historical Journal* 44, no. 4 (2001): 967.

94. Typescript memoir of Adolphine Fletcher Terry, as told to Carolyn Rose. The copy in the University of North Carolina Library is attributed to the Oral History Project (1974), University of Arkansas, and is catalogued as a holding of the University of Arkansas, Fayetteville. Used here by permission of William L. Terry, a son, and the Quapaw Quarter Association, owner of the manuscript.

95. In Lillian Faderman, "Female Same-Sex Relationships in Novels by Longfellow, Holmes, and James," *New England Quarterly* 61, no. 3 (Sept. 1978): 309–32.

96. In Úna Ni Bhrolméll, "A Borderland Pedagogy: Using Image and Text in a Historical Inquiry into the Formation of Female Elementary Teachers in Early 20th Century Ireland" (paper presented at the Annual Meeting of the American Educational Research Association, San Francisco, April 7, 2006).

97. Waller, *Sociology of Teaching*, esp. 143; Alan W. Trelease, *North Carolina Literate: The University of North Caroline at Greensboro from Normal School to Metropolitan University* (Carolina Academic Press, 2004); Pauline Galvarro, "A Study of Certain Emotional Problems of Women Teachers" (Ph.D. diss., Northwestern University, 1943).

98. Author's interview with Dorothy Weisselberg Berson, Albany, California, November 4, 1997; Karen L. Graves, "Developmental Delay: Toward a Historiography of Lesbian and Gay Educational History" (paper presented at the Annual Meeting of the American Educational Research Association, San Francisco, April 8, 2006).

99. Karen L. Graves, *And They Were Wonderful Teachers: Florida's Purge of Gay and Lesbian Teachers* (U Illinois P, 2009); Kathleen Weiler, "The Case of Martha Deane: Sexuality and Power at Cold War UCLA," *History of Education Quarterly* 47, no. 4 (Nov. 2007): 471–96.

100. Ronald Philip Dore, *Education in Tokugawa Japan* (U California P, 1965), 255.

101. Carlos Slafter, *A Record of Education: The School and Teachers of Dedham, Massachusetts, 1644–1940* (Dedham Transcript Press, 1905), 114.

102. "Conditions of Masters," quoted in Foster Watson, *The English Grammar Schools to 1600: Their Curriculum and Practice* (Cambridge UP, 1908).

103. William Faulkner, *The Hamlet* (Random House, 1940), 220–21; Frank McCourt, *Teacher Man,* 104.

104. John Noyes Mead, journal entry for Dec. 7, 1849, cited in John R. Frisch, "To Be Seen and Not Heard: Drugs, Discipline, and a Diary, Three Aspects of Children's Lives in Nineteenth-Century America" (unpublished paper courtesy of the author, Morton College, Cicero, IL, 1978).

105. David Wiggins in Kenneth Wiggins Porter (Ed.), "Catharine Emma Wiggins, Pupil and Teacher in Northwest Kansas, 1888–1895," *Kansas History* 1, no. 1 (Spring 1978): 16–38; Kansas teachers in SLC.

106. Bob Greene, *Be True to Your School: A Diary of 1964* (Atheneum, 1987), 281, 27, 31, 49, 95.

107. Robin M. Williams, *American Society* (Knopf, 1963), quoted in Patricia Cayo Sexton, *The Feminized Male: Classrooms, White Collars and the Decline of Manliness* (Vintage Books, 1970), 190; Albert John Miles, "The Image of the Teacher in the Nineteenth-Century American Novel" (Ph.D. diss., Temple University, 1977).

108. Douglas Edgar Gosse, "Queer Theory and the Educational Novel" (paper presented at the Annual Meeting of the American Educational Research Association, San Francisco, April 7, 2006).

109. Edna L. Furness, "Portrait of the Pedagogue in Eighteenth Century England," *History of Education Quarterly* 2, no. 1 (Mar. 1963): 62–70.

110. Foster Watson (Comp.), *English Writers on Education, 1480–1603: A Sourcebook* (Scholars' Facsimiles & Reprints, 1967), 498, was first published as reports of the U.S. Commissioner of Education (1902–1906), offering many classic observations on teachers.

111. Mont Hawthorne quoted in *Them Was the Days,* 147–48, 165, 215.

112. "Class Prophecy," *Yearbook, San Francisco Polytechnic High School,* 1915.

113. Rachel Van Dyke, diary entries for May 24, June 14, & Nov. 29, 1810, Special Collections and University Archives, Rutgers University Libraries.

114. Journal entry for July 11, 1862, in Gertrude Clanton Thomas Papers, David M. Rubenstein Rare Book & Manuscript Library, Duke University, by permission (spelling in the original).

115. Mary Richardson Walker, journal (1833–1837) entry for Aug. 7, 1833, copy in Henry E. Huntington Library, original in Washington State University Library, by permission.

116. Faulkner, *The Hamlet.*

117. Donal O'Donoghue, "'Crossing Over': Re/Searching the Troubled Relationships between the Socially Constructed Categories of 'Men' and 'Teacher' through A/R/Topography" (session 18.041 at the Annual Meeting of the American Educational Research Association, San Francisco, April 7, 2006).

118. Teacher quoted in Mitchell, "Work Lives of Urban Teachers," 158.

119. Steve Kink and John Cahill, *Class Wars: The Story of the Washington Education Association 1965–2001* (U Washington P, 2005).

120. Diane Ravitch, *The Death and Life of the Great American School System: How Testing and Choice Undermine Education* (Basic Books, 2010).

121. Sister M. Domitilla, "Daisy Dean Urch," *Biographical Sketches* (National League of Nursing Education, 1940?).

122. Garret Keizer, "Why We Hate Teachers," *Harpers* 303, no. 1816 (Sept. 2001): 37–44.

123. Marjorie Housepian Dobkin (Ed.), *The Making of a Feminist: Early Journals and Letters of M. Carey Thomas* (Kent State UP, 1979), 63, 103, 271.

124. Judith McNaught, *Perfect* (Simon & Schuster, 1993), 156, also 67.

125. Psychoanalytic theory and the myth of Narcissus are used to claim that perfectionism and expertness are personally damaging to teachers and contribute to pedagogical formalism and rigidity; in Edward Pajak, "Willard Waller's Sociology of Teaching Reconsidered: What Does Teaching Do to Teachers?" *American Educational Research Journal* 49, no. 6 (Dec. 2012): 1182–1213.

126. Harmon L. Zeigler, *The Political Life of American Teachers* (Prentice Hall, 1967).

127. Rep. Berman in Blanche Wadleigh Bettington obituary, *Los Angeles Times* (Mar. 3, 2001).

128. The student was Franklin Nofziger, later press secretary to President Ronald Reagan. Author's interview with Frances Eisenberg, Los Angeles, Dec. 22, 1993; Frances R. Eisenberg Los Angeles City Loyalty Oath Collection (Collection 1078) Special Collections, C. R. Young Research Library, University of California, Los Angeles, by permission.

129. In Los Angeles Board of Education, Committee Report, December 30, 1946. In Eisenberg Papers, box 1, folder 4.

130. Guy H. Raner Jr. to Blanche Bettington and Frances Eisenberg, August 20, 1950. In Eisenberg Papers, box 1, folder 6. Raner was another teacher of courage and intelligence, according to his obituary in the *Los Angeles Times* (July 26, 2009).

131. Zeigler, *Political Life of American Teachers,* 17.

132. Ann Harrigan diary entries for Jan. 30 and Feb. 1, 2, 9, 28, 1940, Ann Harrigan Makletzoff Papers, folder 1, box 1, in University of Notre Dame Archives. By permission.

133. Leah Garchik, courtesy of David Bye, in *San Francisco Chronicle* (Nov. 20, 2006).

Chapter 8 · "Higher Prospects for a Useful Life"

1. In Irving Hendrick, "Academic Revolution in California: A History . . . ," *Southern California Quarterly* 47, no. 2 (June 1967): 130–34.

2. Editorial, *Alta California* (Dec. 6, 1878): 2; also Jan. 3, 4, & 8, 1879.

3. Henry C. Johnson Jr. & Erwin Johanningmeier, *Teachers for the Prairie: The University of Illinois and the Schools, 1868–1945* (U Illinois P, 1972).

4. "Texas," in Monroe, *Cyclopedia of Education*; see also Diane Manning, *Hill Country Teacher: Oral Histories from the One-Room School and Beyond* (Twayne, 1990); Joyce Thompson, *Marking a Trail: A History of the Texas Woman's University* (Texas Woman's UP, 1982).

5. In Judith R. Joyner, *Beginnings: Education in Colonial South Carolina* (Museum of Education, U of South Carolina, 1985), 5.

6. Merle Borrowman, *The Liberal and the Technical in Teacher Education* (Teachers College P, 1956).

7. J. B. Harrison to Miriam Green, Sept. 1, 1864, Miriam Wilson Green Papers, box 1, Indiana State Historical Society, by permission. See "Indiana" in Jim Pearson & Edgar Fuller (Eds.), *Education in the States: Historical Development and Outlook* (National Education Association, 1969), 373–97.

8. Lizzie Parker to Mell Green, Oct. 27, 1867, with original spelling and punctuation. Unless otherwise noted, the source on nineteenth-century Indiana is Richard Boone, *History of Education in Indiana* (D. Appleton, 1892).

9. Mary Stevens Wescott in Floy Lawrence Emhoff, "A Pioneer School Teacher in Central Iowa: Alice Money Lawrence," *Iowa Journal of History and Politics*, 33, no. 4 (Oct. 1935): 376–95.

10. C. Evan Lewis to Berdie Green, esp. April 25, 1867; & S. W. Wiatt to Cousin Mell, May 12, 1867, both in Green Papers.

11. William Alcott, *Confessions of a School Master* (Gould, Newman and Saxton, 1839; Arno Press, 1969), 191.

12. Virgil Monroe Young, "The Development of Education in Territorial Idaho: 1863–1880" (Ed.D. diss., University of Idaho, 1967), esp. 26–28.

13. Lucia Downing, "Teaching in the Keeler 'Deestrict' School," *Vermont Quarterly*, n.s., 14, no. 4 (Oct. 1951): 233–40.

14. J. Morgan to Miss Stewart, Aug. 8, 1883; & W. C. McBride to Miss Stewart, Aug. 17, 1883, both in Stewart-Lockwood Family Collection, Kansas Collection, Spencer Research Library, University of Kansas (hereafter SLC).

15. Nellie [Helen] Miller to Mrs. Mary Jane Miller Stewart, Mar. 3, 1875, in SLC; Thad Sitton & Milam Rowold, *Ringing the Children In: Texas Country Schools* (Texas A&M UP, 1987), 162.

16. Ellen Eten Farrer in *What Became of the Little Red Schoolhouse? Facts and Figures—Tales and Photos of Early Mendocino County Schools* (Mendocino Coast Genealogical Society, 1990).

17. Robert Louis Stevenson, *The Silverado Squatters* (Scribner, 1905), 202.

18. Address to the National Education Association (NEA), 1872, in John Swett, *History of the Public School System of California* (Bancroft, 1876), 175.

19. John Swett, in State Board of Examination, minutes, esp. Aug. 15 & Nov. 7, 1868, in California State Archives.

20. Kathleen Cruikshank, "Centralization, Competition, and Racism: Teacher Education in Georgia," in John Goodlad, Roger Soder, & Kenneth Sirotnik (Eds.), *Places Where Teachers Are Taught* (Jossey-Bass, 1990), 330–81.

21. Atkinson in Richard Gerry Durnin, "New England's Eighteen-Century Incorporated Academies: Their Origin and Development to 1850" (Ed.D. diss., University of Pennsylvania, 1986), 171; Committee on Pioneer Women in Education, *Some Pioneer Women Teachers of North Carolina* (North Carolina Delta Kappa Gamma Society, 1955).

22. Amory Dwight Mayo, quoted in Victoria-Maria MacDonald, "Paving the Way: A Comparative Analysis of the Role of Teachers' Social Class, Gender, and Race in Nineteenth Century Northern and Southern School Reform" (paper presented at the Annual

Meeting of the American Educational Research Association, San Francisco, April 18–22, 1995).

23. Susan McIntosh Lloyd, *A Singular School: Abbot Academy 1828–1973* (Phillips Academy, 1979).

24. Chicago, *Annual Report of the Board of Education* 2 (1855): 6, as cited in Kay Kamin, "The Woman Peril in American Public Schools: How Perilous?" (unpublished paper, Rosary College, 1976, courtesy of the author); William Septimus Taylor, *The Development of the Professional Education of Teachers in Pennsylvania* (Lippincott, 1924), 171.

25. In R. McLaran Sawyer, "No Teacher for the School: The Nebraska Junior Normal School Movement," *Nebraska History* 52, no. 3 (Summer 1971): 191–203.

26. *The Telegraph and Texas Register* (May 9, 1850) cited in Anita White, *The Teacher in Texas: 1836–1879* (Baylor UP, 1972), 94.

27. Monia Cook Morris, "Teacher Training in Missouri Before 1871," *Missouri Historical Review* 43, no. 1 (Oct. 1948): 18–19.

28. "Samuel Read Hall," in Barnard, *Memoirs of Teachers*, 169–81; Mason Stone, "The First Normal School in America," *Teachers College Record* 24, no. 3 (May 1923): 263–71.

29. Response to Victor Cousin's *Report on the Condition of Public Instruction in Germany, and Particularly Prussia* (1831) in Gregory Wegner, "Prussia Volksschulen through American Eyes," in Henry Geitz, Jürgen Heideking, & Jürgen Herbst (Eds.), *German Influences on Education in the United States to 1917* (Cambridge UP, 1995), 85–102.

30. Christine Ogren, *The American State Normal School: "An Instrument of Great Good"* (Palgrave, Macmillan, 2005); Arthur Norton (Ed.), *The First State Normal School in America: The Journals of Cyrus Peirce and Mary Swift* (Harvard UP, 1926), xxxv.

31. Peirce's report from his journal entry for July 3, 1840, in Norton, *The First State Normal School*, 47; Samuel May, "Cyrus Peirce," in Barnard, *Memoirs of Teachers*, 426, 434–35.

32. Blue Mound students in Wallace Boughton to May Stewart, Oct. 16, 1884, & Feb. 5, 1885, in SLC.

33. Colin Burke, "The Quiet Influence, 1800–1860" (Ph.D. diss., Washington University, St. Louis, 1973), 247–50; Nashville Normal and Theological Institute students in Tennessee State Board of Education Records, Tennessee State Library & Archives.

34. George Brown, "Some of the Obstructions, Natural and Interposed, That Resist the Formation and Growth of the Pedagogic Profession," *Addresses and Proceedings of the National Education Association, 1880* (NEA, 1880), 190.

35. Albany's early students in Mary Alpern, "Gender, Class, and the Historiography of Antebellum Normal Schools" (paper presented at the Annual Meeting of the American Educational Research Association, Chicago, March 1997); Sally Thatcher in "Alumni Roster, 1917," *Bulletin of the First District Normal School* [formally Northeast Missouri State Teachers College] 17, no. 4 (April 1917), Pickler Memorial Library Archives, Truman State University, library.truman.edu/archives/alumni1917.asp, accessed Nov. 6, 2013.

36. *Historical Sketch of the State Normal School at San José, California, with a Catalogue of Its Graduates and a Record of Their Work for Twenty-Seven Years* (State Printing Office, 1889), 16. For the full fourth class list and graduates' whereabouts in 1889, see 152–53.

37. Catherine Ford Rea, "Childhood Memories," *Mendocino Historical Review* 5, no. 1 (Winter 1972): 11.

38. Ferol Slotte, *School Bell Memories: Horse and Buggy to Space Age* (Del Monte Press, 1986), 3.

39. Marguerite Tolbert, interview by Constance Myers (June 1974), Southern Oral History Program Collection (#4007), Louis Round Wilson Special Collections Library, University of North Carolina at Chapel Hill.

40. George Bates Jr., "Winona Normal School Student Profile, 1860–1900," *Journal of the Midwest History of Education Society* 7 (1879): 10–22.

41. Lyman Henry Van Houten, "Length of Service of Pennsylvania High School Teachers" (Ph.D. diss., Teachers College, Columbia University, 1932), 142.

42. Elizabeth Quiroz Gonzalez, "The Education and Public Career of Maria L. Urquides" (Ed.D. diss., University of Arizona, 1986), esp. 43–45.

43. Quotation printed in *Grant County (WI) Witness* (Aug. 16, 1866), cited in Jeff Wasserman, "Wisconsin Normal Schools and the Educational Hierarchy, 1860–1890," *Journal of the Midwest History of Education Society* 7 (1979): 1–9.

44. On the uncommitted student in Eastern and Midwestern normal schools, see Jurgen Herbst, *And Sadly Teach: Teacher Education and Professionalization in American Culture* (U Wisconsin P, 1991).

45. Janina Trotman, "Women Teachers in Western Australian 'Bush' Schools, 1900–1939: Passive Victims of Oppressive Structures?," *History of Education Quarterly* 46, no. 2 (Summer 2006): 248–73.

46. Robert T. Brown, *The Rise and Fall of the People's Colleges: The Westfield Normal School, 1839–1914* (Westfield State College, 1988).

47. On Colorado, see Kathleen Underwood, "The Pace of Their Own Lives: Teacher Training and the Life Course of Western Women," *Pacific Historical Review*, 55, no. 4 (Nov. 1986): 513–30.

48. The school and teaching experiences of Barker descendants are from the author's interview of the daughters of Amelia Turner Devenny Rathbun (Ruth Devenny Rose and Beth Rathbun Kiteley), in Cortona, Italy, Mar. 24, 1996; also Beth R. Kiteley to author, April 6, 1998.

49. Case studies, organized by institutional types, in Goodlad et al., *Places Where Teachers Are Taught*.

50. Christine Ogren's study of seven normal schools is "Education for Women in the United States: The Normal School Experience, 1870–1920" (Ph.D. diss., University of Wisconsin, 1996). A contrary view is Jo Ann Preston, "Gender and the Formation of a Woman's Profession: The Case of Public School Teaching," in Jerry A. Jacobs (Ed.), *Gender Inequality at Work* (Sage, 1995), 379–407.

51. Helen Cole to Agnes McLean, Jan. 6, 1891, in Helen Erskine file; & Agnes McLean to Sarah Chester McLean, May 11, 1894, both in McLean Family Papers, Bancroft Library, UC Berkeley, by permission.

52. Agnes McLean to Sarah Chester McLean, undated (1896?), McLean Family Papers.

53. George Deyoe, *Certain Trends in Curriculum Practices and Policies in State Normal Schools,* Teachers College Contributions to Education 606 (Teachers College P, 1934).

54. Polly Welts Kaufman, *Boston Women and City School Politics, 1872–1905* (Garland, 1994), esp. 232, 257.

55. Herbst, *And Sadly Teach.*

56. Steel, Tall, and Earhart named in "Reunion and Conferences of the Alumni Association," *Teachers College Record* 14, no. 3 (May 1923): 181.

57. Thomas Hill, "Remarks on the Study of Didactics in Colleges," *American Journal of Education* 15, no. 38 (March 1865): 179.

58. Annie Nathan Meyer (Ed.), *Woman's Work in America* (Henry Holt, 1891), 73.

59. Quoted in Louis Harlan, *Separate and Unequal: Public School Campaigns and Racism in the Southern Seaboard States 1901–1915* (Atheneum, 1969), 27.

60. Nathan Bell, *CGS/GRE Graduate Enrollment and Degrees: 2000 to 2010* (Council of Graduate Schools & Graduate Record Examination Board, 2011), esp. 46, 86.

61. Mabel Newcomer, *A Century of Higher Education for American Women* (Harper, 1959).

62. Paul Woodring, "The Development of Teacher Education," in Kevin Ryan (Ed.), *Teacher Education,* 74th Yearbook of the National Society for the Study of Education, part 2 (U of Chicago P, 1975), 1–24.

63. Burke, *Quiet Influence.*

64. Roger Geiger, "The Era of Multipurpose Colleges in American Higher Education, 1850–1890," *History of Higher Education Annual* 15 (1995): 51–92.

65. George Male, "A Century of Efforts to Improve the Salaries of Teachers in Michigan," *History of Education Journal* 10 (1959): 47–54.

66. Kathleen Weiler, *Country Schoolwomen: Teaching in Rural California, 1850–1950* (Stanford UP, 1998).

67. Emma McVicker, *Third Report of the Superintendent of Public Instruction of the State of Utah, for the Biennial Period Ending June 30, 1900* (State Board of Education, 1900), 20–21.

68. Marguerite Renner, "Who Will Teach? Changing Job Opportunity and Roles for Women in the Evolution of the Pittsburgh Public Schools, 1830–1900" (Ph.D., diss., University of Pittsburgh, 1981), esp. 285–86, 312ff.

69. Horace Mann, *Twelfth Annual Report of the Secretary of the Board* (Dutton & Wentworth, 1849): 48–49.

70. *Annual Report of the State Superintendent of Public Instruction, 1858,* 6. In Andrew Johnson Moulder Papers, Bancroft Library, UC Berkeley, by permission.

71. Everett Dick, *The Sod-House Frontier, 1854–1890* (Johnson, 1954), 327–28.

72. Oregon institute in Henry Cummins to Oliver Applegate (Feb. 17, 1863), cited in David B. Tyack, "The Tribe and the Common School: Community Control in Rural Education," *American Quarterly* 24, no. 1 (March 1972): 11–12. For Kansas, Amanda Stewart to all the dear ones, July 29, 1875, in SLC.

73. Recollections composed c. 1940 by Sarah Brown DeBra, *Sweet Memories of "Old Indianie" in 1870* (Indiana Historical Society, 1970), 112.

74. John Ware, Oct. 26, 1887, in Edgar W. Strain Collection, Illinois State Historical Collections; "Thoughts on Institutes," *Journal of Education* 6 (Aug. 9, 1877): 51; Mindy Spearman, "The Peripatetic Normal School: Teacher Institutes in the Southwestern

United States, 1880–1920" (paper presented at the Annual Meeting of the American Educational Research Association, San Francisco, April 7–11, 2006).

75. For example, the criticism of the suggestions made by the president of the San Jose Normal School "as to primary instruction," in "Sonoma County Institute," *California Teacher and Home Journal* (California State Department of Public Instruction, 1883), 141.

76. John W. Payne, "Poor-Man's Pedagogy: Teachers' Institutes in Arkansas," *Arkansas Historical Quarterly* 14, no. 3 (Autumn 1955): 195–206.

77. W. H. Wells to Henry Barnard, Nov. 26, 1845, in Edith Nye Macmullen, *In the Cause of True Education: Henry Barnard & Nineteenth-Century School Reform* (Yale UP, 1991); Dick Bryan Clough, "Teacher Institutes in Tennessee, 1870–1900," *Tennessee Historical Quarterly* (Spring 1972): 61–73.

78. John Swett, *American Public Schools: History and Pedagogics* (American Book, 1900), 200–201.

79. Oregon cited in David Tyack, "The Tribe and the Common School," *American Quarterly* 24, no. 1 (May 1972): 3–19; Kay Graber (Ed.), *Sister to the Sioux: The Memoirs of Elaine Goodale Eastman, 1885–91* (U Nebraska P, 1978), 127.

80. Dick Bryan Clough, "A History of Teachers' Institutes in Tennessee, 1875–1915" (Ed.D. diss., Memphis State University, 1972), esp. 65ff., 139, 173, 176; Harlan, *Separate and Unequal*, 89.

81. Jesse Newlon & A. J. Threlkeld, "The Denver Curriculum Revision Program," in Harold Rugg (Ed.), *Curriculum Making: Past and Present*, 26th Yearbook, part 1, National Society for the Study of Education (U Chicago P, 1927), 229–40; Frances Doull in Bowman & Ryan, *Who's Who in Education*.

82. Gerald Grow, "The Woman Who Became County School Superintendent" (Jan. 15, 1996), based on his conversations with Elva White Grow Clark, www.longleaf.net/elva/superintendent.html, accessed Nov. 6, 2013; and an obituary at www.legacy.com/obituaries/tallahassee/obituary.aspx?n=elva-white-grow-clark&pid=1770622&fhid=4647. Copyrighted material used by permission.

83. Bruce Kimball, *The "True Professional Ideal" in America: A History* (Blackwell, 1992), 193.

84. In Adolphene Fletcher Terry, *Charlotte Stephens: Little Rock's First Black Teacher* (Academic P Arkansas, 1973), 79. Used by permission of William L. Terry.

85. William Graebner, "Retirement in Education: The Economic and Social Functions of the Teacher's Pension," *History of Education Quarterly* 18, no. 4 (Summer 1978): 397–417.

86. Elizabeth Allen in Karen Leroux, "'Unpensioned Veterans': Women Teachers and the Politics of Public Service in the Late-Nineteenth-Century United States," *Journal of Women's History* 21, no. 1 (Spring 2009): 34–62.

87. Karen Leroux, "'Lady Teachers' and the Genteel Roots of Teacher Organization in Gilded Age Cities," *History of Education Quarterly* 46, no. 2 (Summer 2006): 164–91.

88. Alice Pierce letters in Ira Benjamin Whitcomb Collection, Oregon Historical Society, by permission.

89. Supt. Faber in "Programme: Leavenworth County Teachers Association for 1887–8," in SLC.

90. Kaufman, *Boston Women and City School Politics*, 274–77.

91. Courtney A. Vaughn-Roberson, "Sometimes Independent but Never Equal—Women Teachers, 1900–1950: The Oklahoma Example," *Pacific Historical Review* 53, no. 1 (Feb. 1984): 39–58.

92. Laurence Block, "The History of the Public School Teachers Association of Baltimore City: A Study of the Internal Politics of Education" (Ph.D. diss.: Johns Hopkins University, 1972).

93. Geraldine Clifford & Lynne Wiley, "'An Association—Serious, Restricted, Diminutive': A History of the Cleveland Conference as an Elite Organization in American Education" (unpublished report to the Spencer Foundation and the Cleveland Conference, 1994).

94. Dennis Carlson, "Teachers as Political Actors: From Reproductive Theory to the Crisis of Schooling," *Harvard Educational Review* 57, no. 3 (August 1987): 283–307.

95. Robert Reid (Ed.), *Battleground: The Autobiography of Margaret A. Haley* (U Illinois P, 1982). This section relies on Wayne Urban, *Gender, Race, and the National Education Association: Professionalism and Its Limitations* (Routledge Falmer, 2000).

96. Sarah Douglass in Harry Silcox, "A Comparative Study in School Desegregation: The Boston and Philadelphia Experience, 1800–1881" (Ed.D. diss., Temple University, 1971), esp. 54–55n; Leslie Gale Parr, *A Will of Her Own: Sarah Towles Reed and the Pursuit of Democracy in Southern Education* (U Georgia P, 2010), esp. 101–4.

97. Parr, *Will of Her Own*; Cynthia Stokes Brown, *Ready from Within: Septima Clark and the Civil Rights Movement* (Wild Trees Press, 1986), 124. On teachers organizations' responses to the civil rights movement, see Marjorie Murphy, *Blackboard Unions: The AFT & the NEA, 1900–1990* (Cornell UP, 1990).

98. Frank McCourt, *Teacher Man: A Memoir* (Scribner, 2005), 108–9.

99. Robin Heimos, "Organizing at Catholic Schools," *Education Week* 11, no. 2 (Spring 1997): 19.

100. C. B. Gilbert, "The Professional Spirit of the Teachers," *Education* 20, no. 7 (March 1900): 397–99; Leroux, "'Lady Teachers' and the Genteel Roots of Teacher Organization," 176.

101. Ruth Jacknow Markowitz, *My Daughter, the Teacher: Jewish Teachers in New York City Schools* (Rutgers UP, 1993), 155.

102. "Bertha C. Knemeyer," Nevada Women's History Project, *Women's Biographies*, www.unr.edu/nwhp/bios/women/knemeyer.htm, accessed Nov. 6, 2013; Patricia Geuder, *Pioneer Women of Nevada* (American Association of University Women, 1976).

103. *Biennial Report of the Illinois Superintendent of Public Instruction* 8 (1869–1870), 489, in Kamin, "Woman Peril in American Public Schools," 6.

104. Jennifer Monaghan, "Gender and Textbooks: Women Writers of Elementary Readers, 1880–1950," *Publishing Research Quarterly* 10 (1994): 28–46.

105. William Payne, in *Contributions to the Science of Education* (Harper, 1887). See Peter Woods, "Cold Eyes and Warm Hearts: Changing Perspectives on Teachers' Work and Careers," *British Journal of Sociology of Education* 11, no. 1 (1990): 101–17.

106. Helen Foss Weeks reference in Davis Y. Paschall (president emeritus of the College of William and Mary) to the author, Nov. 25, 1996. Copies of college newspaper articles on Helen Foss Weeks (b. 1923) courtesy of Sharon Garrison, archives assistant at the College of William and Mary.

107. Arthur Bestor, *The Restoration of Learning* (Knopf, 1955), 269.

108. Sara Freedman, "Weeding Woman out of 'Woman's True Profession,'" in Joyce Antler & Sari Knopp Biklen (Eds.), *Changing Education: Women as Radicals and Conservators* (SUNY P, 1990), 239–56.

109. Dina Copelman, *London's Women Teachers: Gender, Class and Feminism, 1870–1930* (Routledge, 1996), 9.

110. Richard Simpson & Ida Harper Simpson, "Women and Bureaucracy in the Semi-professions," in Amitai Etzioni (Ed.), *The Semi-professions and Their Organization: Teachers, Nurses, Social Workers* (Free Press, 1969), 196–265.

111. Kimball, *"True Professional Ideal,"* 220–21; Joan Jacobs Brumberg & Nancy Tomes, "Women in the Professions: A Research Agenda for American Historians," *Reviews in American History* 10, no. 2 (June 1982): 287.

112. Douglas Klegon, "Women in the Professions and Semi-professions: A Question of Power," in Dana Hiller & Robin Ann Sheets (Eds.), *Women and Men: The Consequences of Power* (Office of Women's Studies, U of Cincinnati, 1977), 231–38; Penina Glazer & Miriam Slater, *Unequal Colleagues: The Entrance of Women into the Professions, 1890–1940* (Rutgers UP, 1987).

113. Administrator quoted in Daniel Thompson, *Private Black Colleges at the Crossroads* (Greenwood, 1973), 124.

114. Author's 1998 correspondence and interview with Ruth Devenny Rose & Beth Rathbun Kiteley.

115. Travel reports (c. 1913), in Amanda Stoltzfus Papers, Dolph Briscoe Center for American History Archives, University of Texas Library.

116. Jennie Hubbard Lloyd in Joyce Kinkead, *A Schoolmarm All My Life: Personal Narratives from Frontier Utah* (Signature Books, 1996), xlv.

117. Jackie Blount, *Destined to Rule the Schools: Women and the Superintendency, 1873–1995* (SUNY P, 1998).

118. Burrows in "Alumni Roster, 1924," *Bulletin of the First District Normal School* [formally Northeast Missouri State Teachers College] 17, no. 4 (April 1917), Pickler Memorial Library, Truman State University Archives, Kirksville, Missouri, library.truman.edu /archives/alumni1917.asp and http://library.truman.edu/archives/alumni1924A.asp.

119. Zonia Baber in Bowman & Ryan, *Who's Who in Education*; Agnes Stowell in *Directory of Graduates of the University of California, 1864–1905* (U of California P, 1905).

120. Nellie Angel Smith in Paul R. Coppock, *Memphis* (Memphis State UP, 1980), 161–65.

121. Charlotte Smith to H. S. Thompson, Aug. 7, 1882, in Hugh Smith Thompson Papers, Manuscripts Collection, South Caroliniana Library, U of South Carolina, by permission.

122. Hattie Stewart (Brook Haven, MS) to unknown addressee, Nov. 19, 1923, in Hugh Smith Thompson Papers (copy of original in Papers of Robert Means Davis), by permission.

123. Anne Walker Daniels in *What Became of the Little Red Schoolhouse?*, 111.

124. Hilda Kean, *Deeds Not Words: The Lives of Suffragette Teachers* (Pluto Press, 1990), esp. 47.

125. Ellen Richardson in Rosetta Marantz Cohen, *A Lifetime of Teaching: Portraits of Five Veteran High School Teachers* (Teachers College P, 1991).

126. Magdalene Lampert, "How Do Teachers Manage to Teach? Perspectives on Problems in Practice," *Harvard Educational Review* 55, no. 2 (May 1985): 178–94.

127. Willard Waller, *The Sociology of Teaching* (Russell & Russell, 1932), 457.

128. Bruce Brousseau, Donald Freeman, & Cassandra Book, "Comparing Educational Beliefs of Teacher Candidates and Their Non-teaching Counterparts"; & "Comparing Academic Backgrounds, Career Decisions, and Educational Beliefs of Elementary and Secondary Teacher Education Candidates" (papers presented at the Annual Meetings of American Educational Research Association, New Orleans, April 23–27, 1984, and Chicago, March 31–April 5, 1985).

129. Mary Ritter Beard, *Women's Work in Municipalities* (Appleton, 1915), 3.

130. Howard Stevenson, "Restructuring Teachers' Work and Trade Union Responses in England: Bargaining for Change?" *American Educational Research Journal* 44, no. 2 (June 2007): 224–31.

131. Susan Faludi, *Backlash: The Undeclared War against American Women* (Crown, 1991); Andrea Dworkin, *Life and Death: Unapologetic Writings on the Continuing War against Women* (Free Press, 1997); Nicholas Kristof & Sheryl WuDunn, *Half the Sky: Turning Oppression into Opportunity for Women and Girls Worldwide* (Knopf, 2009).

132. Madeline Grumet, *Bitter Milk: Women and Teaching* (U Massachusetts P, 1988), 25.

133. Teacher quoted in Gerald J. Brunetti, "Why Do They Teach? A Study of Job Satisfaction among Long-Term High School Teachers," *Teacher Education Quarterly* (California Council on Teacher Education) 28, no. 3 (Summer 2001): 49–74.

Chapter 9 · "Laboring Conscientiously, Though Perhaps Obscurely"

1. "Mindy" interview in Claire Elaine Sylvan, "The Impact of Motherhood on Teacher Career Attitudes" (Ed.D. diss., Teachers College, Columbia University, 1988), 139–40. The title of chap. 9 is drawn from John Orville Taylor (Ed.), *Lord Brougham on Education* (Taylor & Clement, 1839), 87. The chapter epigraph is from Virginia Penny, *The Employments of Women: A Cyclopaedia of Woman's Work* (Walker, Wise, 1863), 35.

2. Cynthia Stokes Brown (Ed.), *Ready from Within: Septima Clark and the Civil Rights Movement* (Wild Trees Press, 1986), 106.

3. "To stand behind several teachers and see the first day of school through their eyes!" is the approach taken in Thad Sitton & Milam C. Rowold, *Ringing the Children In: Texas County Schools* (Texas A&M UP, 1989), 48.

4. James Patterson, *Mary, Mary* (Warner, 2005), 313–14.

5. Entry for Dec. 15, 1862, in Ray Allen Billington (Ed.), *The Journal of Charlotte L. Forten* (Dryden Press, 1953; Collier Books, 1961, 1967), 165. Cited passages from the 1967 edition.

6. Ella Gertrude Clanton Thomas, journal entry for Feb. 9, 1881, in Ella Gertrude Clanton Thomas Papers, Perkins Library, Duke University, by permission.

7. Billington, *Journal of Charlotte L. Forten,* entry for May 7, 1857, 98.

8. Mary Stewart to family, Sept. 20, 1887; & May Stewart to Mary J. Stewart, Oct. 10, 1887, both in Stewart-Lockwood Collection, Spencer Research Library, University of Kansas (hereafter SLC), by permission.

9. George Herbert Palmer, *The Life of Alice Freeman Palmer* (Houghton Mifflin, 1908), 67, 70, from a letter to her parents.

10. E. May Stewart to Amanda Stewart, June 10, & July 16, 1864, & May 23, 1866, in SLC; Stephen Cresswell, *We Will Know What War Is: The Civil War Diary of Sirene Bunten* (West Virginia Wesleyan College P, 1993).

11. William A. Alcott, *Confessions of a Schoolmaster* (Gould, Newman & Saxton, 1839), 3.

12. Polly Bullard, "Iron Range Schoolmarm," *Minnesota History* 32, no. 4 (Dec. 1951): 193–201.

13. Lucia B. Downing, "Teaching in the Keeler 'Deestrict' School," *Vermont Quarterly,* n.s., 14, no. 4 (Oct. 1951): 233, 237–38.

14. Kenneth Wiggins Porter (Ed.), "Catharine Emma Wiggins, Pupil and Teacher in Northwest Kansas, 1888–1895," *Kansas History* 1, no. 1 (Spring 1978): 16–38, esp. 22.

15. Susie Powers Tompkins, *Cotton-Patch Schoolhouse* (U. Alabama P, 1992), esp. 1, 46.

16. Charles Dorn, "'I Had All Kinds of Kids in My Classes, and It Was Fine': Public Schools in Richmond, California, during World War II," *History of Education Quarterly* 45, no. 4 (Winter 2005): 538–64, esp. 548–49.

17. Frank McCourt, *Teacher Man: A Memoir* (Scribner, 2005), 12, 15–16.

18. Barbara Finkelstein, "Pedagogy as Intrusion: Teaching Values in Popular Primary Schools in Nineteenth-Century America," *History of Childhood Quarterly* 2, no. 3 (Winter 1975): 349–78.

19. Kate Warthen diary entry for Jan. 28, 1886, in Sarah Catharine Warthen Searcy Papers, Kansas Collection, Spencer Library, University of Kansas, by permission.

20. Belle Kearney, *A Slaveholder's Daughter* (Abbey Press, 1900), 78, 79.

21. John Swett, *American Public Schools: History and Pedagogics* (American Book, 1900), 292. A forerunner to a raft of books on school bureaucracies in the 1970s was Raymond E. Callahan, *Education and the Cult of Efficiency* (U Chicago P, 1962).

22. Horace Mann quoted in Samuel Findley, editorial, *Ohio Educational Monthly and the National Teacher* 34, no. 11 (Nov. 1885): 556–57; Horace Mann, *Ninth Annual Report of the Board of Education* (Dutton & Wentworth, 1846), 34.

23. Kennedy in Alvin F. Harlow, *Schoolmaster of Yesterday: A Three-Generation Story, 1820–1919* (Whittlesey House / McGraw-Hill, 1940), 20.

24. Mary Ellen Chase, *A Goodly Heritage* (Henry Holt, 1932), 288–89.

25. Quotation in Deborah Fitts, "Una and the Lion," in Barbara Finkelstein (Ed.), *Regulated Children / Liberated Children* (Psychohistory Press, 1979), 149.

26. Examples from Carlos Slafter, *A Record of Education: The School Teachers of Dedham, Massachusetts, 1644–1904* (Dedham Transcript Press, 1905), 97, 111. This section's heading is credited to a former California teacher and rural superintendent, Paul Henderson (1956), in "One-Room Schools: The Heart of Old Tehama County," *San Francisco Chronicle* (June 13, 1998).

27. "Willie's Essay" in unidentified newspaper clipping pasted in Edith K. O. Clark diary entry for Sept. 28, 1908, in Clark Papers, American Heritage Center, University of Wyoming, by permission.

28. Louisa Barnes Pratt in Joyce Kinkead (Ed.), *A Schoolmarm All My Life: Personal Narratives from Frontier Utah* (Signature Books, 1996), xxxix, 5.

29. Tubbs sisters in John Chadbourne Irwin, "Reminiscences," Irwin Papers, Southwest Collection, Texas Tech University, Lubbock, Texas.

30. Kinkead, *Schoolmarm All My Life,* esp. 89.

31. Mary ? to May Stewart, Dec. 4, 1883; & Mary Petherbridge to Amanda Stewart, Feb. 21, 1886, both in SLC.

32. American International School Alumni Association of Manila, *The American School—History,* chaps. 2 & 4, www.aisaam.org/History/historyintro.htm, accessed Nov. 6, 2013.

33. Joseph Fichter, S.J., *Parochial School: A Sociological Study* (Doubleday, 1958), 159, 163.

34. Peter Meyer, "Can Catholic Schools Be Saved?," *Education Next* 7, no. 2 (Spring 2007): 12–20.

35. Jill Eisenstadt, *From Rockaway* (Knopf, 1987; Vintage Books, 1988), 133.

36. Rütlinger in Robert Billigmeier & Fred Altschuler Picard (Eds.), *The Old Land and the New: The Journals of Two Swiss Families in America in the 1820s* (U Minnesota P, 1965), 236.

37. In Lyman Cobb, *The Evil Tendencies of Corporal Punishment: As a Means of Moral Discipline in Families and Schools, Examined and Discussed* (M. H. Newman, 1847), 261.

38. Ovid Lockwood to dear friend [Nora Stewart], Nov. 19, 1886, in SLC.

39. C. J. Wimer to May Stewart, Nov. 20, 1881, in SLC.

40. Tarbox incident from *The Jamestown* (NY) *Journal* (Feb. 14, 1879), reported in "The Trials of School-Teaching," *New York Times* (Feb. 16, 1879).

41. Cobb, *Evil Tendencies of Corporal Punishment,* 261.

42. Emma Shirley in Sitton & Rowold, *Ringing the Children In,* 115.

43. Lockwood to dear friend [Nora Stewart], Nov. 19, 1886, in SLC; Marshall Baker to Nora Stewart, April 4, 1881, both in SLC.

44. Peter Gay, *Schnitzler's Century: The Making of Middle-Class Culture, 1815–1914* (Norton, 2002): 125–26. The heading of this section is attributed to Cyrus Peirce, in Barnard, *Memoirs of Teachers,* 405–38.

45. "Cyrus Peirce," in Barnard, *Memoirs of Teachers,* esp. 433, 435–36.

46. Queensland school in Peter Meadmore, "In the Cause of Governance: Disciplinary Practices and Women Teachers between the Wars," *History of Education Review* 25, no. 2 (1996): 18–33, esp. 20.

47. Bullard, "Iron Range Schoolmarm," 197–98; Bullard Papers, Minnesota Historical Society, St. Paul.

48. Author's interview of Judith Alper Udall, daughter of Eve Alper, San Francisco, May 2003.

49. Sister Mary Loretta Petit, O.P., "Samuel Lewis, Educational Reformer Turned Abolitionist" (Ed.D. diss., Western Reserve University, 1966), 50.

50. John Martin Vincent (1857–1939), papers in Henry E. Huntington Library, San Marino, California.

51. Kate B. Carter (Comp.), *Diary of Isaiah Moses Coombs* (Daughters of Utah Pioneers, n.d.), esp. 325–26.

52. Lloyd P. Jorgenson, *Founding of Public Education in Wisconsin* (State Historical Society of Wisconsin, 1956), 11, 141; Mary Stewart to Nora Stewart, April 12, 1885, in SLC.

53. Mary Richardson Walker, journal (1833–1837) entries for June 13 & 14, 1833, in Huntington Library. Spelling and punctuation are as in the original.

54. Gertrude Clanton Thomas, journal entry for Jan. 5, 1881, in Thomas Papers, Duke University.

55. Libby Burbank to Amanda Stewart, June 11, 1882; Amanda Stewart to Mrs. M. J. Stewart and dear sisters, April 30, May 8, & May 31, 1883, all in SLC.

56. Mary Wills in Porter, "Catharine Emma Wiggins," esp. 19.

57. Item from the *Jamestown (NY) Journal* (Feb. 14, 1879), in "The Trials of School-Teaching," *New York Times* (Feb. 16, 1879).

58. Charles Stokes, diary (1851–1922) entries for Sept. 9, 1867, & Jan. 11–19, 1870, in Special Collections and University Archives, Rutgers University Library, New Brunswick, New Jersey. Misspellings in the original.

59. G. P. Randle to Edgar Strain, Sept 11, 1887, folder 1, Edgar W. Strain Collection, Illinois State Historical Library, Springfield.

60. McCourt, *Teacher Man*, 91–92.

61. Richard Coe, *When the Grass Was Taller: Autobiography and the Experience of Childhood* (Yale UP, 1984); Fitts, in Finkelstein, *Regulated Children/Liberated Children,* 149.

62. G. Bull to Moses Waddel, May 1, 1806, in Waddel letterbook, Manuscripts Division, Library of Congress, Washington, DC.

63. Jennie Lines (1827?-1886) to Daisy Lines, Dec. 9, 1884, in Amelia Akehurst Lines Papers, University of Georgia Library, by permission. Also Daisy Lines to Jennie Lines, Jan. 15, 1882, in Amelia Akehurst Lines, *"To Raise Myself a Little": The Diaries and Letters of Jennie, a Georgia Teacher, 1851–1886,* Thomas Dyer (Ed.) (U Georgia, P 1982), 261.

64. Letter of Nellie O'Donald (Mrs. George T. Knott), 1931, quoted in Charles Tennyson, "History of Education in Wichita County" (master's thesis, East Texas State Teachers College, 1925), chap. 2.

65. Frederick P. Wells, *History of Newbury, Vermont* (Caledonian, 1902), 151.

66. Merlin R. Hovey, "An Early History of Cache County," as printed in the *Logan Journal,* 1923–1925, typescript in Utah State Historical Society, Salt Lake City.

67. Merrill in R. H. Watlington Memoirs, Briscoe Center for American History, University of Texas Library.

68. Agnes Morley Cleaveland (1874–1958), *No Life for a Lady* (Houghton Mifflin, 1941), 121–26.

69. Mrs. M. J. Griswold to Amanda Stewart, Jan. 6, 1888, SLC.

70. Anna Dakin from author's interview of Charlotte Laing (Mrs. Robert Dahl) of Sun City West (AZ), interviewed May 2006 in Riva di Garda, Italy. Dakin family data from the 1900 U.S. Census, Microfilm T623 478: Flora Township, Dickinson County, Kansas, p. 84.

71. Robert Weibe, "The Social Functions of Public Education," *American Quarterly* 21, no. 2 (Summer 1969): 147–64.

72. Moses Waddel diary entry for Aug. 13, 1834, in Manuscripts Division, Library of Congress.

73. Mary Richardson Walker, journal entry for Aug. 7, 1833.

74. Mendocino County superintendent's report, 1879–1880 in Lyman Palmer, *History of Mendocino County, California: Comprising Its Geography, etc.* (Alley, Bowen & Son, 1880).

75. Ella Gertrude Clanton Thomas, journal entry for Dec. 12, 1864, in Thomas Papers, Duke University.

76. Journal of Catherine Van Schaack (36), Research Library, New York Historical Society, New York City; Theodore Sizer, Nancy Sizer, et al., *To Ornament Their Minds: Sarah Pierce's Litchfield Female Academy* (Litchfield Historical Society, 1993).

77. Lucy Forsyth Townsend, *The Best Helpers of One Another: Anna Peck Sill and the Struggle for Women's Education* (Educational Studies Press, 1988), 62.

78. Dowling, "Teaching in the Keeler 'Deestrict' School," 239–40.

79. Tommy Boley (Ed.), *An Autobiography of a West Texas Pioneer: Ella Elgar Bird Dumont* (U Texas P, 1988), 91, 101.

80. Madeleine Grumet, "Restaging the Civil Ceremonies of Schooling," *Review of Education/Pedagogy/Cultural Studies* 19, no. 1 (Jan.–Mar. 1997): 39–54.

81. Kay Graber (Ed.), *Sister to the Sioux: The Memoirs of Elaine Goodale Eastman 1885–91* (U Nebraska P, 1978), 43.

82. Janis Price Greenough, "Resistance to the Institutionalization of Schooling in Antebellum Southern Highlands" (Ph.D. diss., University of California, Berkeley, 1999), esp. 150; Finkelstein, "Pedagogy as Intrusion," 374nn74, 75.

83. Miss Duke in *The Dresden Enterprise* (May 1, 1903), item from Martin (Weakley County), TN.

84. Horace Bushnell, *Woman Suffrage; Reform against Nature* (Scribner, 1869), esp. 352.

85. Sallie Bethune (1851–1928) in Charlotte (NC) Chapter, American Association of University Women, *Making a Difference: Women of Mecklenburg* (Charlotte Branch, AAUW, 1980), 17–19, copy in Public Library of Charlotte and Mecklenburg County.

86. Seth Koven, "Borderlands: Women, Volunteer Action, and Child Welfare in Britain, 1840–1914," in Seth Koven & Sonya Michel (Eds.), *Mothers of a New World: Maternalist Politics and the Origins of Welfare States* (Routledge, 1993), 103.

87. "Irish tough" Ada Mahon in Yoon K. Pak, *Wherever I Go, I Will Always Be a Loyal American: Schooling Seattle's Japanese Americans during World War II* (Routledge Falmer, 2002).

88. The large and growing literature on Michelle Rhee includes Clay Risen, "The Lightning Rod," *Atlantic* (Nov. 2008): 78–87; Ben Nuckols, "D.C. Teacher Firings," *Huffington Post* (Sept. 21, 2012), www.huffingtonpost.com/2012/09/21/dc-teachers-firing_n_1904072.html.

89. Jettie Felps (1889–1964) in Sylvia Oates Hunt, "To Wed and To Teach: The Myth of the Single Teacher," in Fane Downs & Nancy Baker Jones (Eds.), *Women and Texas History: Selected Essays* (Texas State Historical Association, 1993): 127–42.

90. David Tyack & Elizabeth Hansot, *Managers of Virtue: Public School Leadership in America, 1820–1980* (Basic Books, 1982), 183.

91. Ronald Gould in Harry L. V. Fletcher, *Portrait of the Wye Valley* (Hale, 1968), 56.

92. A[nson] O[vid] Lockwood to Nora Stewart, Oct. 30, 1885, in SLC.

93. Alice Newberry to Edna Mitchell, n.d. (fall term 1909), in Alice Newberry Papers, History Colorado, Denver, by permission.

94. Rasjidah Franklin, "Berta Rantz: Her Life and Legacy"; & James A. Muchmore, "The Story of 'Anna,'" both in *Teacher Education Quarterly* (California Council on Teacher Education) 28, no. 3 (Summer 2001): 19–28 (esp. 21–22) & 89–110 (esp. 97).

95. May Stewart to Mary Stewart, Nov. 24, 1887; Robert Lee, director, to Miss May Stewart, Dec. 14, 1887; May Stewart to home folks, May 6, 1888; M. J. Faber, reference letter (no addressee), June 26, 1888; all in SLC.

96. Rightsell in Adolphene Fletcher Terry, *Charlotte Stephens: Little Rock's First Black Teacher* (Academic P of Arkansas, 1973), 104.

97. Elaine Goodale in Graber, *Sister to the Sioux*, 125.

98. Rebecca Akin, "On My Knees Again," *Teacher Education Quarterly* (California Council on Teacher Education) 28, no. 3 (Summer 2001): 7–10, esp. 8.

99. For example, the suburban New York high school teachers featured in Janet C. Goodman, "In Their Own Words: An Examination of the Ways Teachers View Their Work Life" (Ed.D. diss., Hofstra University, 1989).

100. Sister Roberta in Fichter, *Parochial School*, 314–15.

101. Author interviews with Rosemma Wallace's sister, Anita Burney of Silver Spring, Maryland (chiefly by telephone), Sept.–Nov. 1996; then–Oakland superintendent Dr. Ruth Love, Jan. 21 & 23, 1997, and Dorothy Kakamoto, Jan. 17 & Feb. 3, 1997.

102. "Annual Report to the Community on Oakland Public Schools," *Oakland Tribune* (Nov. 9, 1997). My thanks to Della Piretti, Thea Maestre, & Virginia Johnson for help in organizing and analyzing the original data, where administrators were not identified by race. Emma Willard's term, "spoiled and petted misses" in Anne Firor Scott, *Making the Invisible Woman Visible* (U Illinois P, 1987), 46.

103. Jozef E. Verheyen, *De moderne school* (1927), trans. from Flemish, in Kristof Dams, Marc Depaepe, & Frank Simon, "Sneaking into the School: Dealing with the Source Problem of Classroom History, Belgium: 1880–1970" (unpublished paper presented to Second International Conference, "Silences and Images: The Social History of the Classroom," Toronto, November 1995). Used with permission of the authors.

104. Diane Bjorklund, "School as a Waste of Time? Complaints about Schooling in American Autobiographies," *Journal of American Culture* 27, no. 3 (Sept. 2004): 290–302.

105. Isobel Osborne Strong Field, *This Life I've Loved* (Longmans, Green, 1938), 58.

106. Florence Kelley, *Some Ethical Gains through Legislation* (Macmillan, 1905), 96.

107. Quoted in Harry L. Miller & Roger Woock, *Social Foundations of Urban Education* (Dryden Press, 1970), esp. 70, 108, 281. Responses of Chicago teachers dissatisfied with their careers were traced in Howard Becker, "Social Class Variations in the Teacher-Pupil Relationship," *Journal of Educational Sociology* 25, no. 8 (April 1952): 451–65.

108. Nick Hoppe, "Many Children Left Behind," May 23, 2006, www.hoppecolumns .com/columns/kellyfollowup.htm; "Have You Hugged a Teacher Today," Nov. 21, 2006, www.hoppecolumns.com/columns/kelly.htm; & "Eating Up the Latin Culture," Nov. 3, 2009, www.hoppecolumns.com/columns/buenos.htm.

109. J. B. E. Jonas, "Intra-national Exchange of Teachers," *Educational Review* 42, no. 1 (June 1911): 66.

110. Anna Sill in Townsend, *Best Helpers of One Another,* 43.

111. Richard M. Ingersoll, "Teacher Turnover and Teacher Shortages: An Organizational Analysis," *American Educational Research Journal* 38, no. 3 (Fall 2001): 499–534.

112. Vera Summers, oral history (1981) by Jesse Embry, cited in Embry, "'Separate and Unequal'": Schoolmarms of Utah, 1900–1950," in John Sillito (Ed.), *From Cottage to Market: The Professionalization of Women's Sphere* (papers presented at Third Annual Meeting of Utah Women's History Association, March 13, 1982, Salt Lake City, UT), 64–76, esp. 69.

113. Sitton & Rowold, *Ringing the Children In,* 183–84.

114. Samuel Ervin Shideler, "Qualifications, Salary, and Tenure of the Teachers in the Commissioned High Schools of Indiana," *School Review* 21, no. 7 (Sept. 1913): 446–60.

115. Maud Pritchard (b. 1875) in Bowman & Ryan, *Who's Who in Education.*

116. Candace H. Lacey, Amaney Saleh, & Reita Gorman, "Teaching Nine to Five: A Study of the Teaching Styles of Male and Female Professors" (paper presented at the Annual Women in Education Conference, Lincoln, NE, Oct. 11–12, 1998).

117. Patricia Cayo Sexton, *The Feminized Male: Classrooms, White Collars and the Decline of Manliness* (Vintage Books, 1969).

118. Quotations from Leonard Ayres, "What Educators Think about the Need for Employing Men Teachers in Our Public Schools," *Journal of Educational Psychology* 2, no. 2 Jan. 1911): 89–93; Alice Duer Miller, "The Protected Sex," in *Are Women People? A Book of Rhymes for Suffrage Times* (G. H. Doran, 1915), 34–35.

119. Lionel Tiger, *The Decline of Males* (Golden Books, 1999); Michelle Conlin, "The New Gender Gap: From Kindergarten to Grad School, Boys Are Becoming the Second Sex," *Business Week* (May 26, 2003): 75–84; Hanna Rosin, "The End of Men: How Women Are Taking Control of Everything," *Atlantic* (July/Aug. 2010), 56–62.

120. Sexton, *Feminized Male,* 113.

121. Redding Sugg, *Motherteacher: The Feminization of American Education* (U Virginia P, 1978).

122. Franklin, "Berta Rantz," esp. 21–22.

Chapter 10 · "The Great Perplexities of the Teacher-Life"

1. Mary E. Gamble to Amanda Stewart, Oct. 16, 1872; Jan. 8, 1876; Feb. 3, 1877; Nov. 17, 1879; & Mary E. Presby to Amanda, Mar. 25, 1882, in Stewart-Lockwood Family Collection, Kansas Collection, Spencer Library, University of Kansas (hereafter SLC).

2. This chapter's title borrows from David P. Page, Lecture 7, "On the Mutual Duties of Parents and Teachers," in *The Lectures Delivered before the American Institute of Instruction, at Lowell (Mass), August 1838, Including the Journal of Proceedings and a List of the Officers* (Ticknor, 1839), vii. Paul Veyne, *Writing History: Essays on Epistemology,* trans. by Mina Moore-Rinvolucri (Wesleyan UP, 1984), 220.

3. Louis Menand, "Woke Up This Morning: Why Do We Read Diaries?," *New Yorker* (Dec. 10, 2007): 106–11.

4. Journal of Mary Richardson Walker, 1833–1837, Manuscripts, Archives, and Special Collections, Washington State University Libraries, by permission. Typescript copy in Huntington Library, San Marino, CA. Except where indicated, spelling and punctuation are as in the original.

5. With three other newly married missionary couples, Rev. Elkanah and Mary Richardson Walker went west to open new outposts of the Oregon Mission, to minister to the Spokane people in what became Washington Territory.

6. Mary Jane Walker, normal school journal, in Schlesinger Library, Radcliffe Institute, Cambridge, MA, by permission. Spelling and punctuation are as in the original.

7. "Conversations" were discussions among the students, on some specified subject. "Exercises" were teaching lessons (demonstrations) by the normal school students, with their classmates acting as the pupils.

8. In the unedited and voluminous Ella Gertrude Clanton Thomas Papers, David M. Rubenstein Rare Book & Manuscript Library, Duke University, Durham, NC, by permission. Spelling is as in the original.

9. All in SLC, by permission. While the Collection Inventory identifies Amanda M. Stewart as the sister of Thomas Stewart, who came to Kansas about 1859 and settled in Millwood, internal evidence places her as his daughter.

10. A never-met cousin, Susannah M. Garner (1848–1927) was a modest aspiring teacher. Her dates and marriage in 1877 to Lewis Dodge in "Descendants of Lewis Phillip Burgess Garner," Generation no. 4, http://familytreemaker.genealogy.com/users/c/r/a/Bronwyn-Craig-WV/BOOK-0001/0004-0005.html.

11. Chalmers H. Brown (d. 1928?) may have been the person speculated to be Amanda's suitor.

12. Hattie was one of a number of Baker cousins who taught.

13. Mary Eva Braman (1855–1939) married Ernest Arthur Beebe (1855–1909), a marble cutter, in Wyandotte (KA) in 1878 and continued teaching, retiring in 1930; "Descendants of Clement Minor: Eighth Generation," http://tmsociety.org/thomas/clement/aqwg135.htm, accessed Nov. 6, 2013.

14. Libbie Burbank finished her course at the Normal Department, University of Kansas in 1877.

15. The four-story, grade 1–12 Morris School opened in 1867 to 900 scholars. A high school was organized in 1868 from the upper grades. In J. H. Johnston III, *Leavenworth: Beginning to Bicentennial* (privately printed, 1976), 103.

16. Alice Pierce's letters are addressed to Ira, his are signed Ben; in Ira Benjamin Whitcomb Collection, Manuscripts Division, Oregon Historical Society, Portland, by permission. Spelling and punctuation are as in originals.

17. Alice spent her weekends at the home of her married sister, Mary.

18. Alice Pierce and Ira Whitcomb were married in Monmouth and had one daughter, Susie Ann Whitcomb Cottrill (b.1895).

19. Phyllis Bottome [Phyllis Forbes Dennis], *Search for a Soul: Fragment of an Autobiography* (Reynal & Hitchcock, 1948). Used by permission of David Higham firm, literary agents.

20. This narrative by Kathleen Jett Schwarzschild was written at the author's request, between Oct. 2004 and Feb. 2005. Reorganized for clarity and condensed for brevity, it is presented without ellipses and used with her permission. After her Union City schooling, Kathleen Jett attended Berea College and the Cincinnati Conservatory of Music, married Henry Schwarzschild, and settled in New York.

21. Miss Cora's final year of teaching was 1960–1961; in Teachers' Retirement System to Cora Dunbar, April 17, 1962; professional courses at Eastern Kentucky State Teachers College in Registrar M. E. Mattox to J. D. Hamilton, Madison County superintendent, Aug. 24, 1935. Originals in Richmond (KY) Board of Education archives, copies courtesy of Kathleen Schwarzschild.

Chapter 11 · "That Our Daughters May Be as Cornerstones"

1. Betsey Stockton's journal (1822–1823), in David Wills & Albert Roboteau (Eds.), *African-American Religion: A Historical Interpretation with Representative Documents,* portions accessed on Nov. 6, 2013, at www3.amherst.edu/~aardoc/Betsey_Stockton_Jour nal_1.html. Stockton's shipboard journal was printed as "Religious Intelligence: Sandwich Islands," Ashbel Green (Ed.), *Christian Advocate* 2, 3, 4 (May & Dec. 1824, Jan. 1825). Epigraph in *Report of the Commissioner of Education for Porto Rico [Puerto Rico]* (U.S. War Dept. Bureau of Insular Affairs, 1910, 1926), 43.

2. Annie Scoville in Isabelle C. Barrows (Ed.), *Proceedings of the Nineteenth Annual Meeting of the Lake Mohonk Conference, 1901* (Lake Mohonk Conference, 1902), 17–18.

3. Committee on Pioneer Women in Education, *Some Pioneer Women Teachers of North Carolina* (North Carolina Delta Kappa Gamma Society, 1955).

4. In Edward Hitchcock, *The Power of Christian Benevolence Illustrated in the Life and Labors of Mary Lyon,* 9th ed. (Hopkins, Bridgman, 1851), esp. 232–35.

5. In "Songs of Labor" (1850), *The Poetical Works of John Greenleaf Whittier: Complete in Two Volumes* (Ticknor & Fields, 1857).

6. In Clyde Griffen, "Workers Divided: The Effect of Craft and Ethnic Differences in Poughkeepsie, New York, 1850–1880," in Stephan Thernstrom and Richard Sennett (Eds.), *Nineteenth-Century Cities: Essays in the New Urban History* (Yale UP, 1969), 49–93.

7. In Mother M. Benedict Murphy, "Pioneer Roman Catholic Girls' Academies: Their Growth, Character, and Contributions to American Education" (Ph.D.: diss., Columbia University, 1958), esp. 24–31.

8. Oscar Handlin, *Boston's Immigrants, 1790–1880: A Study in Acculturation* (Harvard UP, 1959; Atheneum, 1968), esp. 185–86; James Sanders, *The Education of an Urban Minority: Catholics in Chicago, 1833–1965* (Oxford UP, 1977); Janet Miller, "Urban Education and the New City: Cincinnati's Elementary Schools, 1870–1914," *Ohio History* 88, no. 2 (Spring 1979): 152–72.

9. Mary Beth Fraser, "Devoted to the Interest of the Italians: The Sisters of Charity and the Santa Maria Institute in Cincinnati, Ohio, 1890–1930" (Ph.D. diss., Catholic University of America, 2006).

10. Immaculate Conception Academy in Joan Ryan, "Convent Life at Twilight: The Younger Sisters of Mission San Jose," *San Francisco Chronicle* (June 17, 2007). Parochial schools enrollments (est.) in U.S. Bureau of the Census, *Historical Statistics,* 207.

11. Mary J. Oates, "Organized Voluntarism: The Catholic Sisters in Massachusetts, 1870–1940," *American Quarterly* 30, no. 5 (Winter 1978): 652–80.

12. Ann Marie Ryan, "Negotiating Assimilation: Chicago's Catholic High Schools' Pursuit of Accreditation in the Early Twentieth Century," *History of Education Quarterly* 46, no. 3 (Fall 2006): 348–81.

13. Robert Cross, *The Emergence of Liberal Catholicism in America* (Harvard UP, 1958); Fayette Veverka, *For God and Country: Catholic School in the 1920s* (Garland, 1988); Paula Fass, *Outside In: Minorities and the Transformation of American Education* (Oxford UP, 1989).

14. Ryan, "Negotiating Assimilation," 360.

15. Nanette Asimov, "Marguerite Ann Costello—Middle-School Teacher," *San Francisco Chronicle* (May 14, 2004).

16. City of Axtell (KS), "Churches," *History of Axtell, Kansas,* www.marshallco.net /axtell/church.html. National 2012 data in Christina Hoag, "Catholic Schools See Marketing Helps Aid Enrollment," *Seattle Post Intelligencer* (July 29, 2012).

17. Sisters Rodriguez and Shinas in Ryan, "Convent Life at Twilight," esp. 14; Mary Lawrence McKenna, SCMM, *Women of the Church: Role and Renewal* (P. J. Kenedy, 1967).

18. Associated Press, "Nuns Pledge Not to 'Compromise Mission,'" *San Francisco Chronicle* (Aug. 11, 2012).

19. Geoffrey D. Borman & N. Maritza Dowling, "Teacher Attrition and Retention: A Meta-analytic and Narrative Review of the Literature," *Review of Educational Research* 78, no. 3 (Sept. 2008): 367–409.

20. St. Luke's (a pseudonym) in Joseph Fichter, *Parochial School: A Sociological Study* (U. Notre Dame P. 1958, 1964), esp. 301–2, 319n25, 321, 454.

21. "Catholics and the Public Schools," *School Bulletin and New York State Education Journal* 16 (Sept. 1889): 3, cited in Cynthia Kendall, "Anglo-Saxonism and the Reaction of the American Public School, 1870–1915" (Ed.D. diss., Teachers College, Columbia, 1975), 128.

22. Edward Callahan (prof. emeritus, Boston College) who knew Ellen Buttomer, an elderly relation, in boyhood. Interviewed by the author in Riva del Garda, Italy, May 2006.

23. James Iverne Dowie, "Luther Academy, from 1883–1903: A Facet of Swedish Pioneer Life in Nebraska" (Ph.D. diss., University of Minnesota, 1957); Carol K. Coburn, *Life at Four Corners: Religion, Gender, and Education in a German-Lutheran Community, 1868–1945* (UP Kansas, 1992).

24. Susan Mumm, *Stolen Daughters, Virgin Mothers: Anglican Sister in Victorian Britain* (Continuum International, 1999). History of St. Helens Hall in Oregon Episcopal School, "History," www.oes.edu/alumni/history.html, accessed Nov. 6, 2013.

25. Quoted in John William Buys, "Quakers in Indiana in the Nineteenth Century" (Ph.D. diss.: University of Florida, 1973), 52–53, 246.

26. Rosa Kinsey Young, *Light in the Dark Belt* (Concordia, 1950); Julieanna Frost, "Teaching the Pure Gospel: The Life of Rosa Jinsey Young" (Ph.D. diss., Union Institute and University, 2007).

27. Mary Goldsmith Prag in Reda Davis, *California Women: A Guide to Their Politics, 1885–1911* (California Scene, 1967), 168.

28. Fannie Neumann, "A Modern Jewish Experimental School—in Quest of a Synthesis," *Jewish Education* 4, no. 1 (Jan–March 1932): 26–27; Beth Wenger, *New York Jews and the Great Depression* (Yale UP, 1996).

29. Thomas Laqueur, "The English Sunday School and the Formation of a Respectable Working Class, 1780–1850" (Ph.D. diss., Princeton University, 1973).

30. Cary Wimer to Maude Stewart, Oct. 3, 1883, in Stewart-Lockwood Family Collection, Kansas Collection, Spencer Research Library, University of Kansas (hereafter SLC), by permission.

31. Pearl Allen Williams, "History of the Kindergarten Movement in Louisville, Kentucky, 1887–1930," typescript in Archives and Records Retention Center, Jefferson County Public Schools, Louisville, Kentucky, courtesy of Amy E. Wells. Paul Conkin, *Peabody College: From Frontier Academy to the Frontiers of Teaching and Learning* (Vanderbilt UP, 2002).

32. Karen Phoenix, "The YWCA and Americanization at Home and Abroad, 1900–1941" (paper for the 13th Berkshire Conference on the History of Women, Scripps College, June 2–5, 2005).

33. Van Schaak cited in Lloyd P. Jorgenson, *The Founding of Public Education in Wisconsin* (State Historical Society of Wisconsin, 1956), 129. The expression heading this section, widely used since colonial times, is from the Bible, 2 Timothy 3:15.

34. Christine Ogren, *The American Normal School: "An Instrument of Great Good"* (Palgrave, Macmillan, 2005); Conkin, *Peabody College.*

35. Mother [May Jane Miller Stewart] to May Stewart, Nov. 26, 1883, in SLC.

36. Peter A. Soderbergh, "'Old School Days' on the Middle Border, 1849–1859: The Mary Payne Beard Letters," *History of Education Quarterly* 8 (Winter 1968): 497–504.

37. Ann S. Chirhart, *Torches of Light: Georgia Teachers and the Coming of the Modern South* (U Georgia P, 2005).

38. Joan Marie Johnson, *Southern Women at the Seven Sister Colleges: Feminist Values and Social Activism, 1875–1915* (U Georgia P, 2008).

39. Flannery O'Connor, "Some Aspects of the Grotesque in Southern Fiction," in Sally & Robert Fitzgerald (Eds.), *Mystery and Manners: Occasional Prose* (Farrar, Straus & Giroux, 1969), 36–50.

40. Timothy L. Smith, "Righteousness and Hope: Christian Holiness and the Millennial Vision in America, 1800–1900," *American Quarterly* 31, no. 1 (Spring 1979): 21–46, esp. 21, 24; Ernest Lee Tuveson, *Redeemer Nation: The Idea of America's Millennial Role* (U Chicago P, 1968).

41. Frances Louisa Goodrich in Lou Rogers, *Tar Heel Women* (Warren, 1949), 180–86; Annie Kennedy Bidwell in Margaret D. Jacobs, "Resistance to Rescue: The Indians of Bahapki and Mrs. Annie E. K. Bidwell," in Elizabeth Jameson & Susan Armitage (Eds.), *Writing the Range: Race, Class, and Culture in the Women's West* (U Oklahoma P, 1997), 230–51.

42. *The Earnest Worker* (Dec. 1883) and "Minutes of the Synod of Utah" (Feb. 1877), quoted in Joyce Kinkead (Ed.), *A Schoolmarm All My Life: Personal Narratives from Frontier Utah* (Signature Books, 1996).

43. In Thomas Edgar Lyons, "Evangelical Protestant Missionary Activities in Mormon Dominated Areas: 1869–1900" (Ph.D. diss., University of Utah, 1962); *Annual Report of the New West Education Commission* (C. E. Southard, 1881), esp. 69.

44. Melinda Rankin entry in Seymour V. Connor, *The Handbook of Texas* www.tsha online.org/handbook/online/articles/fra39.

45. E. Jennifer Monaghan, "'She Loved to Read in Good Books': Literacy and the Indians of Martha's Vineyard, 1643–1725." *History of Education Quarterly* 30, no. 4 (Winter 1990): 493–522.

46. K. Tsianina Lomawaima, *They Called It Prairie Light: The Story of Chilocco Indian School* (U Nebraska P. 1994) 2, 6; Merrill Gates, U.S. Board of Indian Commissioners, quoted in David Wallace Adams, "Fundamental Considerations: The Deep Meaning of Native American Schooling, 1880–1900,"*Harvard Educational Review* 58, no. 1 (Feb. 1980): 1–28.

47. Lomawaima, *They Called It Prairie* Light, xi.

48. Mary Richardson Walker diary entry for Feb. 17, 1842, in Clifford Drury, *Elkanah and Mary Walker: Pioneers among the Spokanes* (Caxton, 1945).

49. Lucy Smith in Kinkead, *Schoolmarm All My Life*, 14.

50. Lomawaima, *They Called It Prairie Light*; Buys, "Quakers in Indiana," 85, 196.

51. Edwin L. Chalcraft, *Assimilation's Agent: My Life as a Superintendent in the Indian Boarding School System* (U Nebraska P, 2004).

52. *The Red Man* (Carlisle school newspaper), Feb. 1900, quoted in Barbara Landis, "Carlisle Indian Industrial School History," http://home.epix.net/~landis/histry.html, accessed Nov. 6, 2013.

53. Narcissa Whitman to Jane Prentis, March 31, 1836, in Letters and Journals of Narcissa Whitman, 1836–1847, www.pbs.org/weta/thewest/resources/archives/two/whitmano.htm, accessed Nov. 6, 2013; Julie Roy Jeffrey, *Converting the West: A Biography of Narcissa Whitman* (U Oklahoma P, 1991).

54. Marcus Whitman to Stephen Prentiss, her father, Oct. 9, 1844; & Marcus Whitman to Edward Prentiss, her brother, May 27, 1843; both in "Letters and Journals of Narcissa Whitman." Daily life and instruction in Catherine Sager Pringle memoir, "Across the Plains in 1844," in *Archives of the West* (Kessinger, 2004).

55. Helen Rezatto, "Mary Collins—Missionary to the Sioux," National Museum of the American Indian. Also the Mary Collins Family Papers, South Dakota State Historical Society and State Archives, Pierre.

56. Buys, "Quakers in Indiana," 161. The phrase "useful in my Master's Vineyard" is from Mary Bowers, Northern missionary teacher; quoted in Ronald Butchart, *Schooling the Freed People: Teaching, Learning, and the Struggle for Black Freedom, 1861–1876* (U North Carolina P, 2010), 16.

57. Bessy L. Canedy, March 15, 1865, printed in the *Freedman's Record* (May 1865).

58. Anna Julia Cooper, *A Voice from the South* (Aldine, 1892; Oxford, 1988), 25; Derrick P. Alridge, "Of Victorianism, Civilization, and Progressivism: The Educational Ideas of Anna Julia Cooper and W. E. B. Du Bois, 1892–1940," *History of Education Quarterly* 47, no. 4 (Nov. 2007): 426–46, esp. 439.

59. In Butchart, *Schooling the Freed People*, 12, 13.

60. Harriette Pike in Roberta Sue Alexander, "Hostility and Hope: Black Education in North Carolina during Presidential Reconstruction, 1865–1867," *North Carolina Historical Review* 53, no. 2 (April 1976): 113–32, esp. 128.

61. Theresa Rector, "Black Nuns as Educators," *Journal of Negro Education* 51, no. 3 (Summer 1982): 238–53; Charles Conrad Di Mechele, "The History of the Roman Catholic Educational System in Mississippi" (Ed.D. diss., Mississippi State University, 1973).

62. Mrs. Williams to Rev. C. Kennedy, May 1, 1867, quoted in "Letters from St. Augustine," in *Dr. Bronson's St. Augustine History Page,* www.drbronsontours.com/bronsonlet tersfromstaugustinereconstructioneducation.html, accessed Nov. 6, 2013.

63. Col. H. N. Frisbee et al. to Gen. N. P. Banks, May 25, 1864; typed biographical sketch of Wheelock, 5; both in Edwin M. Wheelock Papers, Dolph Briscoe Center for American History, University of Texas Library, by permission.

64. Typescript 3, Ann Harrigan Makletzoff Manuscript, Feb.–Dec. 1937 (CMAK 3/05), Makletzoff Papers in University Archives, University of Notre Dame, by permission; Albert Schorsch III, "Uncommon Women and Others: Memoirs and Lessons from Radical Catholics at Friendship House," *U.S. Catholic Historian* 9, no. 4 (Fall 1990): 371–86.

65. Typescript 3, Makletzoff Papers.

66. From a 1938 public lecture, in Composition Book in Makletzoff Collection (CMAK folder 3/18). The Baroness is quoted in Makletzoff (typescript 3).

67. Lecture to Friendship House staff, Makletzoff Collection (CMAK folder 3/18).

68. "Just a Brooklyn School Teacher," typescript memoir with diary entries (August 17, 1942, entry), in Makletzoff Papers.

69. Adams, "Fundamental Considerations," 4; Michael Hunt & Steven Levine, *Arc of Empire: America's Wars in Asia from the Philippines to Vietnam* (U. North Carolina P, 2012).

70. Sarah Josepha Hale, *Woman's Record; or, Sketches of All Distinguished Women, from "the Beginning" till A.D. 1850* (Harper, 1853), 868 (quotation), 870.

71. Henry Fowler's brief account of the Athens school is in Barnard, *Memoirs of Teachers,* 157–58; Henry D. Gilpin, "The American Missionaries in Greece," *Address Delivered at St. Luke's Church, Philadelphia, October 13, 1856* (King & Baird, 1856), n.p. The Hills in *Appleton's Cyclopedia of American Biography* (D. Appleton, 1887–1889).

72. *American Missionary* 44, no. 2 (Feb. 1890).

73. Betsey Stockton's journal; Eileen Moffett, "Stockton, Betsey," in Gerald H. Anderson (Ed.), *Biographical Dictionary of Christian Missions* (Macmillan, 1998), 643; Mary Zweip, *Pilgrim Path: The First Company of Women Missionaries to Hawaii* (U Wisconsin P, 1991).

74. Ann White, "Counting the Cost of Faith: America's Early Female Missionaries," *Church History* 57, no. l (Mar. 1988): 19–30; Charlotte White in William H. Brackney, *Baptists in North America in Historical Perspective* (Blackwell, 2006), 236–37.

75. Marjorie Dawes, "Henrietta Hall Shuck," in Albert Samuel Clement (Ed.), *Great Baptist Women* (Carey Knightsgate, 1955), 72–83.

76. Adele M. Fielde in Marilyn Ogilvie & Joy Harvey, *A Biographical Dictionary of Women in Science* (Taylor & Francis, 2000), 444; Ruth A. Tucker, *From Jerusalem to Irian Jaya: A Biographical History of Christian Missions* (Academie, 1983), 292.

77. Philomela Thurston & companions in *The American Baptist Magazine and Missionary Intelligence* (Loring & Lincoln & Edmands, 1817), 1:415; Thurston in Bela Bates Edwards & Charles Williams, *The Missionary Gazetteer: Comprising a Geographical and Statistical Account. . . .* (W. Hyde, 1832), esp. 46, 82–83.

78. Lucy Lyon Lord in Barbara Welter, "She Hath Done What She Could: Protestant Women's Missionary Careers in Nineteenth-Century America," *American Quarterly* 30,

no. 5 (Winter 1978), 624–38, esp. 627. More generally see Marguerite Kraft & Meg Crossman, "Women in Mission," in Ralph Winter & Steven Hawthorne, *Perspectives on the World Christian Movement: A Reader,* 3rd ed. (William Carey Library, 2002).

79. Rosemary Keller & Rosemary Ruether (Eds.), *Encyclopedia of Women and Religion in North America* (Harper, 1981–1986).

80. Dana L. Robert, "The Influence of American Missionary Women on the World Back Home," *Religion and American Culture* 12, no. 1 (Winter 2002): 59–89.

81. Sarah Stow, *History of Mount Holyoke Seminary, South Hadley, Mass., during Its First Half Century, 1837–1887* (Springfield, 1887); Robert S. Fletcher, *A History of Oberlin College from Its Foundation through the Civil War* (Oberlin, 1943), esp. 1:214, 423.

82. Lucy Forsyth Townsend, *The Best Helpers of One Another: Anna Peck Sill and the Struggle for Women's Education* (Educational Studies Press, 1988).

83. Helen Albee Monsell, *Her Own Way: The Story of Lottie Moon* (Broadman, 1958).

84. Eva Robert Coles-Boone in Raymond Hylton, "University History," Virginia Union University website, www.vuu.edu/about_vuu/history.aspx, accessed Nov. 6, 2013; Rev. Clinton Caldwell Boone, *Congo as I Saw It* (Little Ives, 1927).

85. "Illiteracy," in Monroe, *Cyclopedia of Education.*

86. Emma Latimer, "Martha Linda Franks," in Marguerite Tolbert, Irene Elliott, & Wil Lou Gray, *South Carolina's Distinguished Women of Laurens County* (R. L. Bryan, 1972), 246–54.

87. *Reports of the Board of Foreign Missions of the Presbyterian Church USA* (1881), 12, cited in Welter, "She Hath Done What She Could," 631n28; Dana Lee Robert, *American Women in Mission: A Social History of Their Thought and Practice* (Mercer UP, 1997), 88.

88. Alice Houston Luiggi, *65 Valiants* (U Florida P, 1965); Julyan G. Peard, "Making Connections: U.S. Teachers, the Education of Argentine Women, and Social Change, 1869–1900" (presentation at the 13th Berkshire Conference on the History of Women, Scripps College, June 2005).

89. Mary Anne Hastings in Ruth Newcomb Hastings Papers, Clemens Library, University of Michigan, by permission.

90. Obituary of Sara C. Eccleston, *Kindergarten Primary Magazine* 29, no. 4 (Dec. 1916): 89; http://es.wikipedia.org/wiki/Sara_Eccleston.

91. Dorothy Dee Bailey, "Early History of the Argentine Normal Schools," *Peabody Journal of Education* 35, no. 1 (July 1958): 16–26.

92. Irene Da Rold, "Teachers That Made a Difference" (Sept. 10, 2006), http://lcbttc educators.blogspot.com/2006/09/role-of-women-in-education.html, accessed Nov. 6, 2013, a blog kept by teacher trainees and their teachers at Profesorado de Inglés del Liceo Cultural Británico.

93. "Fortune of the Republic," in *The Selected Lectures of Ralph Waldo Emerson,* Ronald Bosco & Joel Myerson (Eds.) (U Georgia P, 2005), 310–26, esp. 325.

94. Mary Helen Fee's *A Woman's Impressions of the Philippines* (Cornell UP, 1912) is available at www.readanybook.com/ebook/a-woman-s-impression-of-the-philippines -12160.

95. See James D. Anderson, "Race-Conscious Educational Policies versus a 'Color-Blind Constitution': A Historical Perspective," *Educational Researcher* 36, no. 5 (June–

July 2007): 249–57; Funie Hsu, "Colonial Articulations: English Instruction and the 'Benevolence' of U.S. Overseas Expansion in the Philippines, 1898–1916" (Ph.D. diss., University of California, Berkeley, 2013).

96. Jonathan Zimmerman, *Innocents Abroad: American Teachers in the American Century* (Harvard UP, 2006), 2.

97. Agnes Crary Weaver & P. L. Weaver Jr. in *Directory of Graduates of the University of California, 1864–1905*. Genealogy in "Missionary Album: Descendants of New England Protestant Missionaries to the Sandwich Islands (Hawaiian Islands) 1820–1900," Hawaiian Mission Children's Society Library, Honolulu.

98. President William McKinley's instructions quoted in Prescott Ford Jernegan, *The Philippine Citizen: A Test-Book of Civics* (Philippine Education, 1907), 56.

99. Hamilton Mercer Wright, "American Ideals and Schools in the Philippines," *A Handbook of the Philippines* (McClurg, 1907).

100. Wright, "American Ideals and Schools in the Philippines," 3, 81, 170 (Taft quotation).

101. Kingsley M. de Silva, "Religion and Nationalism in Nineteenth Century Sri Lanka: Christian Missionaries and their Critics," *Ethnic Studies Report* (International Center for Ethnic Studies, Kandy, Sri Lanka) 16, no. 1 (Jan. 1998): esp. 127–28.

102. Dolores Machado (B.Lit. 1900) in *University of California Directory of Graduates,* 1905 & 1911 editions.

103. "Opening the Manila Schools," *Chicago Tribune* (July 5, 1899).

104. Juan Pimontel (1904) quoted in Wright, "American Ideals and Schools in the Philippines," 83.

105. Wright, "American Ideals and Schools in the Philippines," 45, 46, 50.

106. Staffing report—Filipinos and Americans in the Philippine Bureau of Education (1901–1905) drawn from Philippine Bureau of Education, Bulletin no. 25: Official Roster of the Bureau of Education (Manila Bureau of Printing, 1906); & Bureau of Public Schools, Department of Education, *Annual School Reports* 1901–1905 (repr. 1954). http://rizal.lib .admu.edu.ph/ahc/guides/Bureau%20of%20Education%20(1901-1906).pdf. Most Filipino teachers were, however, employees of municipalities or provinces, not the bureau.

107. Philinda R. Anglemyer (1876–1972), Anglemyer Papers, Schlesinger Library, Radcliffe Institute. Salaries from *Official Roster of Officers and Employees in the Civil Service, Bureau of Education* (Philippine Government, 1908), 61, 64.

108. Wright, "American Ideals and Schools in the Philippines."

109. Sally Inguito (Gardena, CA) interviewed by author, Dec. 1997.

110. The U.S. government and many American educational publications used the variant spelling, Porto Rico, especially before the island was officially renamed in 1932. Booker T. Washington quoted in Sonia M. Rosa, "The Puerto Ricans of Carlisle Indian School," *Kacike: The Journal of Caribbean Amerindian History and Anthropology,* http:// archive.org/stream/KacikeJournal_34/soniarosa_djvu.txt, accessed Nov. 6, 2013.

111. David Rodriguez Sanfiorenso, "Problems in the Recruitment of English Teachers from the United States by the Department of Education of Puerto Rico: 1900–1910" (Ph.D. diss., University of Puerto Rico, 2010).

112. Rosario Andraca de Timothee in American Mothers Committee, *Mothers of Achievement in American History, 1776–1976* (C. E. Tuttle, 1976), 468–70; Anna Roque in

Ronald Fernandez, Serin Méndez Méndez, & Gail Cueto, *Puerto Rico, Past and Present: An Encyclopedia* (Greenwood, 1998).

113. Juan José Osuna Papers, 1905–1977, Bloomsburg University Library; the Duchesne sisters in Rosa, "The Puerto Ricans of Carlisle Indian School."

114. Teresa Amott and Julie Mattbaei, *Race, Gender, and Work: A Multicultural Economic History of Women in the United States* (South End Press, 1991), 266.

115. Maria Cadilla de Martínez (b. 1886) and Julia de Burgos (b. 1914) in Sicherman, *Notable American Women*. List of commissioners and secretaries of education for Puerto Rico in *Estudion historico relacionado con la evolucion de los superintendentes de escuela . . .* (Puerto Rican Department of Public Education, 1982).

116. Lucy Wilcox Adams in "Miscellaneous Obituaries of Anthropologists," http://archive.is/atbKp, accessed Nov. 6, 2013.

117. "Marie" interview in Dee Ann Spencer, *Contemporary Women Teachers: Balancing Home and School* (Longman, 1986), 59, 72–73; Elizabeth Rodman Shuey obituary, *San Francisco Chronicle* (Jan. 29, 2007).

118. Helene Maxwell Brewer, interview of Lulu H. Holmes, "Education for Women in Japan," Regional History Office, Bancroft Library, University of California, Berkeley, Aug. 1968.

119. James Trent, *Mission on the Rhine: Reeducation and Denazification in American-Occupied Germany* (U Chicago P, 1982); James Albisetti, "Symposium: German Education after 1945: Introduction," *History of Education Quarterly* 45, no. 4 (Winter 2005): 593–96.

120. Karl-Hans Füssl & Christian Kubina, "Educational Reform between Politics and Pedagogics—the Development of Education in Berlin after World War II," *History of Education Quarterly* 25, no. 1–2 (Spring–Summer 1985): 133–54.

121. Unless otherwise noted, the sources for this section are the Department of Defense Education Activity (DoDEA) website, www.dodea.edu; Wikipedia, en.wikipedia.org/wiki/Department_of_Defense_Education_Activity; American Overseas Schools Historical Society, www.aoshs.org; and linked websites.

122. Obituary of Mary Meniktas Thodos in *San Francisco Chronicle* (July 9, 2012).

123. Marlene Koenig in "In Memoriam: Marlene Knudson Koenig," *BRATS: Our Journey Home,* www.bratsourjourneyhome.com/marlene.htm, accessed Nov. 6, 2013; Ellen Minette in DoDEA press release, www.dodea.edu/newsroom/20060911.cfm, Sept. 11, 2006.

124. Ohman in "UW Profiles," University of Wyoming website, www.uwyo.edu/pro files/notable-alumni/ohman.html, July 19, 1999; Bridges in DoDEA press release, www .dodea.edu/newsroom/pressreleases/20060823.cfm, Aug. 23, 2006.

125. Betty Nichols quoted in *BRATS: Our Journey Home.*

126. "Stories of the Fall of the Berlin Wall," American Overseas Schools Historical Society, www.aoshs.org/WallStories.htm; www.aoshs.org/memories/index.asp.

127. *Community Strategic Plan: Summary of Volume 1; School Years 2013/14—2017/18,* brochure, www.dodea.edu/CSP/upload/DoDEA-CSP-Brochure.pdf.

128. United Church of Christ, "Education and Mission," United Church of Christ website, www.ucc.org/about-us/short-course/education-and-mission.html, accessed Nov. 6, 2013.

129. Conkin, *Peabody College,* 219.

130. Emily Rosenberg, *Spreading the American Dream* (Hill & Wang, 1982); Liping Bu, "International Activism and Comparative Education: Pioneering Efforts of the International Institute of Teachers College, Columbia University," *Comparative Education Review* 41, no. 4 (Nov. 1997): 413–34.

131. Francis Little [Fannie Macaulay], *The Lady and Sada San* (Century, 1912), 96, 108, 110–11, 124–25. In 1907 a fictionalized account of Macaulay's overseas experiences, *The Lady of the Decoration,* was published under the pen name of Frances Little. Macaulay research courtesy of Amy Wells.

132. Peter James Tarr, "The Education of the Thomasites: American School Teachers in Philippine Colonial Society, 1901–1913" (Ph.D. diss., Cornell University, 2006); Zimmerman, *Innocents Abroad.*

133. Isabella Hall in Marjorie Dawes, "Henrietta Hall Shuck," in Albert Clement (Ed.), *Great Baptist Women* (Carey Knightsgate, 1955), 72–83; Motoe Sasaki-Gayle, "Entangles with Empire: American Women and the Creation of the 'New Woman' in China, 1898–1937" (Ph.D. diss.: Johns Hopkins University, 2009).

134. Tucker, *From Jerusalem to Irian Jaya,* 290.

Chapter 12 · "The Feast of Reason and Flow of Soul"

1. Elizabeth Stewart Boyd in Clarice Wittenburg, "Portrait of an 'Ordinary' Woman," *Biographies of Pioneer Women,* Delta Kappa Gamma manuscripts on microfilm in Wyoming State Archives. Epigraph from John Hyde Braly, *Memory Pictures: An Autobiography* (Neuner, 1912), 249–50.

2. E-mail to author, March 12, 2012, from an unnamed source.

3. Stone in Mary Beard (Ed.), *America through Women's Eyes* (Macmillan, 1933; Greenwood, 1969).

4. The term *feminisme* first appeared in France in the 1880s and was taken up, in Anglicized form, in the United States only around 1910, decades after American and other women articulated its principles. I employ "feminist" and "feminism" without the proliferating adjectives that historians have coined to distill the intellectual and strategic variability present in women's consciousness and women's movements. See Nancy F. Cott, "What's in a Name: The Limits of 'Social Feminism'; or, Expanding the Vocabulary of Women's History," *Journal of American History* 76, no. 3 (Dec. 1989): 809–29.

5. Phillip Earl, "The Story of the Woman Suffrage Movement in Northeastern Nevada, 1869–1914," *Northeastern Nevada Historical Society Quarterly* 6, no. 4 (1986). The phrase in the title of this section if from The Declaration of Sentiments drafted at the Seneca Falls conference in 1848: http://www.fordham.edu/halsall/mod/senecafalls.asp.

6. Lucretia Mott quoted in Parton, *Eminent Women of the Age,* 373–76. See Olive Banks, *Becoming a Feminist: The Social Origins of "First Wave" Feminism* (U Georgia P, 1986), 2.

7. Sarah Jane Christie to James C. Christie, Nov. 11, 1862, in James Christie and Family Papers, Historical Society Library (hereafter Christie Papers), by permission.

8. Frances Merritt, diary entries for Nov. 10, 1856, & Sept. 26, 1858, in Frances Merritt Quick Papers, Schlesinger Library, Radcliffe Institute, by permission.

9. William O'Neill, *Everyone Was Brave: The Rise and Fall of Feminism in America* (Quadrangle Books, 1968); Gerda Lerner, "Women's Rights and American Feminism," *American Scholar* 40, no. 2 (Spring 1971): 235–48; Pauline Maier, *American Scripture: Making the Declaration of Independence* (Knopf, 1997).

10. Miriam Gurko, *Ladies of Seneca Falls: The Birth of the Woman's Rights Movement* (Macmillan, 1974; Schocken Books, 1976), 296–97; Blanche Glassman Hersh, *The Slavery of Sex: Feminist-Abolitionists in America* (U Illinois P, 1978), 106.

11. Pauline Maier, *American Scripture: Making the Declaration of Independence* (Knopf, 1997).

12. Iowa resolution in Katherine Redington Morgan (Ed.), *My Ever Dear Daughter, My Own Dear Mother: Correspondence of Julia Stone Towne & Mary Julia Towne* (U Iowa P, 1996), 147; Isabel Kelren in Karen Leroux, "'Lady Teachers' and the Genteel Roots of Teacher Organization in Gilded Age Cities," *History of Education Quarterly* 45, no. 2 (Summer 2008): 164–81, esp. 179.

13. Robert Riegel, *American Feminists* (U Kansas P, 1963), esp. 114; Andrew Sinclair, *The Emancipation of the American Woman* (Harper & Row, 1965), 40.

14. Nancy F. Cott, *The Grounding of Modern Feminism* (Yale UP, 1987), 27; Louise M. Young, "Women's Place in American Politics: The Historical Perspective," *Journal of Politics* 36, no. 3 (Aug. 1976): 295–335.

15. Gordon sisters in Marjorie Spruill Wheeler, *New Women of the New South: The Leaders of the Woman Suffrage Movement in the Southern States* (Oxford UP, 1993), xvi, 62.

16. Fannie McLean, "Address on Suffrage for Teachers"; and "Equal Suffrage and the Teacher," typescript in McLean Family Papers, box 9, Bancroft Library, University of California, Berkeley, by permission.

17. Walter Lippmann, "The Vote as a Symbol," *New Republic* 4, no. 49 (Oct. 9, 1915): 4.

18. Hilda L. Smith, "Woman's History & Social History: An Untimely Alliance," *Organization of American Historians Newsletter* (Nov. 1984): 5.

19. Patricia Smith Butcher, *Education for Equality: Women's Rights Periodicals and Higher Education, 1849–1920* (Greenwood, 1989).

20. Riegel, *American Feminists,* 192. Phrase in section title from Margaret S. McNaught, "The Enfranchised Woman Teacher: Her Opportunity" (paper given to Department of Elementary Education of the National Education Association, Portland (OR), July 1917), printed in *School and Society* 6, no. 137 (Aug. 11, 1917): 155–60, and in *Journal of Education* 86, no. 6 (Aug. 1917): 143.

21. Frances Knox to Sarah Jane Christie, June 30, 1882. In Christie Papers.

22. Lizzie Wilkinson in Marguerite Renner, "Who Will Teach? Changing Job Opportunities and Roles for Women in the Evolution of the Pittsburgh Public Schools, 1830–1900" (Ph.D. diss., University of Pittsburgh, 1981), esp. 326–27, 350; Patricia Lowry, "Bessie Bramble: A Force for Change," *Post-Gazette* (Pittsburg), Mar. 4, 2007.

23. McNaught, "Enfranchised Woman Teacher."

24. Lucy Smith in Joyce Kinkead, *A Schoolmarm All My Life: Personal Narratives from Frontier Utah* (Signature Books, 1996), 39–42; Joan Iverson, "The Mormon-Suffrage Relationship: Personal and Political Quandaries," *Frontiers* 11, nos. 2 & 3 (1990): 8–16, esp. 9.

25. Teachers' anti-Hughes campaign in newspaper clipping (n.d., n.p.) in Edson Papers, box 6, folder 2, Young Research Library, University of California at Los Angeles. New York campaign quoted in Hersh, *Slavery of Sex*, 136; Ellen Carol Dubois, *Feminism and Suffrage: The Emergence of an Independent Women's Movement in America, 1848–1869* (Cornell UP, 1978).

26. Florence Hope Luscomb, Oral History Project, University of Rhode Island, 1972, 73, quoted in Elaine Partnow (Ed. & Comp.), *The Quotable Woman, 1800–1981*, 2nd ed. (Facts on File, 1982), 462.

27. Gerda Lerner, *The Female Experience: An American Documentary* (Bobbs-Merrill, 1977), 216. While this is a valuable collection of primary sources, I disagree with some of her commentaries.

28. Kennedy & Goggins in Hasia Diner, *Erin's Daughters in America: Irish Immigrant Women in the Nineteenth Century* (Johns Hopkins UP, 1983), esp. 101.

29. Patricia Wittberg, "Feminist Consciousness among American Nuns: Patterns of Ideological Diffusion," *Women's Studies International Forum* 12, no. 3 (1989): 529–37.

30. Belle Kearney, *A Slaveholder's Daughter* (Abbey Press, 1900), 77–78, 134.

31. In Louisville Free Kindergarten Association, "Report and Catalogue, 1900–1901," 51, copy in Archives and Records Retention Center, Jefferson County Public Schools, Louisville, Kentucky. Courtesy of Amy Wells.

32. William R. Taylor and Christopher Lasch, "Two 'Kindred Spirits': Sorority and Family in New England, 1839–1846," *New England Quarterly* 36, no. 1 (March 1963): 23–41; Anne Firor Scott, "The Ever-Widening Circle: The Diffusion of Feminist Values from the Troy Female Seminary, 1822–1872," *History of Education Quarterly* 19, no. 1 (Spring 1979): 3–26.

33. Abigail Scott Duniway, *Path Breaking: An Autobiographical History of the Equal Suffrage Movement in Pacific Coast States* (James, Kerns & Abbott, 1914; Schocken Books, 1971, 2nd ed.); esp., 10, 11, 28, 84; Ruth Barnes Moynihan, *Rebel for Rights: Abigail Scott Duniway* (Yale UP, 1983), esp. 10.

34. Alice S. Pierce to Ira Whitcomb, n.d. [Nov. 1881], in Ira Benjamin Whitcomb Collection, Oregon Historical Society, by permission.

35. Quotation from Wheeler, *New Women of the New South*, 16.

36. Sarah Grimké, *Letters on the Equality of the Sexes* (1838), as quoted in Judith Papachristou, *Women Together: A History of Documents of the Women's Movement in the United States* (Knopf, 1976), 147; Anne Firor Scott & Andrew MacKay Scott, *One Half the People: The Fight for Woman Suffrage* (U Illinois P, 1975), 8. Alma Lutz broke the ground in *Crusade for Freedom: Women of the Antislavery Movement* (Beacon, 1968).

37. Chapman and Gibbons in James, *Notable American Women*.

38. John Updike, review of *Fear of Flying*, by Erica Jong, *New Yorker* (Dec. 17, 1973); Edmund Morgan, "Subject Women," *New York Review of Books* (Oct. 31, 1996): 69; Rebeca [or Rebecca] Latimer Felton, "Why I Am a Suffragist," in *Country Life in Georgia in the Days of My Youth* (Index, 1919), 251–52.

39. Felton, *Country Life in Georgia*, 188, 253–55; Latimer, *The Subjection of Women and the Enfranchisement of Women* (Cartersville, GA: 1915), n.p.

40. Anna H. Jones, "Woman Suffrage and Social Reform," *Crisis* 10, no. 4 (Aug. 1915): 189; Frances Ellen Watkins Harper (b. 1825) in James, *Notable American Women*.

41. Adella Hunt Logan in Salem, *African American Women.*

42. Mary Ann Shadd and Ida B. Wells in Jessie Carney Smith (Ed.), *Notable Black American Women* (Gale Research, 1992); Wells is highlighted in Petra Munro, "Educators as Activists: Five Women from Chicago," *Social Education* 59, no. 5 (Sept. 1995): 274–78.

43. Josephine Pearson, "President's Message to Anti-suffrage Leaders of Tennessee," Sept. 30, 1920, in Pearson Papers, Tennessee State Library and Archives, by permission.

44. Linda K. Lewis, "Julia Brown Asplund and New Mexico Library Service," in Suzanne Hildenbrand (Ed.), *Rewriting the American Library Past: Writing the Women In* (Ablex, 1994). This section's title is from Fannie McLean, "Address on Suffrage for Teachers," and "Equal Suffrage and the Teacher," Typescripts in McLean Family Papers, Box 9, Bancroft Library. University of California, Berkeley.

45. Stanton in Parton, *Eminent Women of the Age,* 398; Elizabeth Cady Stanton, *Eighty Years: Reminiscences, 1815–1897* (Schocken Books, 1971; first published in 1898), 162; Anthony in James, *Notable American Women.*

46. The two women met at an antislavery meeting in 1850 or a temperance convention in 1851; the sources disagree.

47. Bertha-Monica Stearns, "Reform Periodicals and Female Reformers 1830–1860," *American Historical Review* 37, no. 4 (July 1932): 693–94.

48. Duniway, *Path Breaking*; Mary Evelyn Dobbs and Kansas WCTU collection in Kansas Historical Society, Topeka; Mrs. Crane in Ollie [Olive Maude Stewart] to Eliza M. Stewart, Dec. 17, 1887, in Stewart-Lockwood Family Collection, Kansas Collection, Spencer Research Library, University of Kansas (hereafter SLC).

49. The quotation is from Thomas Wentworth Higginson, "Margaret Fuller Ossoli," in Parton, *Eminent Women of the Age.*

50. Quotation from Jacqueline Van Voris, *Carrie Chapman Catt: A Public Life* (Feminist Press, 1987); Young, "Women's Place in American Politics," 334.

51. Catt to Mrs. Park in Ida Husted Harper (Ed.), *History of Woman Suffrage* (J. J. Little and Ives, 1922), 5:753. Reprinted in Scott & Scott, *One-Half the People.*

52. Mary Austin, *Earth Horizon: An Autobiography* (Literary Guild, 1932): 137–50.

53. Frances Willard, *Glimpses of Fifty Years: The Autobiography of an American Woman* (H. J. Smith, 1889); Ruth Bordin, *Frances Willard: A Biography* (U North Carolina P, 1986).

54. Willard in Kathy Owen Sorenson et al., *Illinois Women: 75 Years of the Right to Vote* (Performance Media, Chicago Sun-Times, 1996), 10–11.

55. Paul C. Nagel, *The Adams Women: Abigail and Louisa Adams, Their Sisters and Daughters* (Oxford UP, 1987). Williams in Downs, *Women and Texas History,* 137–39.

56. Young, "Women's Place in American Politics," esp. 312–13. Mary Emma Smith Holmes in Francis E. Willard & Mary Livermore (Eds.), *A Woman of the Century* (Charles Wells Moulton, 1893; Gale Research, 1967), 389–90.

57. Mont Hawthorne in Martha Ferguson McKeown, *Them Were the Days: An American Saga of the '70's* (Macmillan, 1950; U Nebraska P, 1961), 183, 236.

58. Carol D. Spencer, "Evangelism, Feminism and Social Reform: The Quaker Woman Minister and the Holiness Revival," *Quaker History* 80, no. 1 (Spring 1991): 24–48.

59. Austin, *Earth Horizon,* 144.

60. Kearney, *Slaveholder's Daughter,* esp. 266; Della Haydn in Cynthia Neverdon-Morton, *Afro-American Women of the South and the Advancement of the Race* (U Tennessee P, 1989), 206–7.

61. This signed copy of *Woman Suffrage* (Scribner, 1869) in Doe Library, UC Berkeley, was a gift from Bushnell to Dr. Francis Lieber (1800–1872). The verse is from Sir Walter Scott's 1808 *Marmion* (canto 6).

62. Minnie Bronson, *The Wage-Earning Woman and the State* (NAOWS, 1914), copy in Pearson Papers, Tennessee State Library.

63. Sarah B. Cooper, "Woman Suffrage—Cui Bono?" *Overland Monthly,* o.s., 8, no. 2 (Feb. 1872): 159, 161–62.

64. Sarah B. Cooper, "Woman's Work," in Nora A. Smith (Ed.), *A History of Our Beginnings* (1883) cited in Barbara Beatty, *Preschool Education in America: The Culture of Young Children from the Colonial Era to the Present* (Yale UP, 1995), 113–14.

65. Elizabeth Gillespie McRae, "Caretakers of Southern Civilization: Georgia Women and the Anti-Suffrage Campaign, 1914–1920," *Georgia Historical Quarterly* 82 (Winter 1998): 801–28.

66. See "Sketch of Rev. Philip A. Pearson," 1938 MS, in Pearson Papers, by permission. Except where noted, these papers are the source materials for this section, especially the manuscript "My Story," which appears in several iterations.

67. Josephine Pearson, "President's Message," Sept. 30, 1920, in Pearson Papers.

68. Josephine Pearson to President Wilson, quoted in *Chattanooga Times,* n.d. Clipping in Pearson Papers.

69. "Support Messages Sent Miss Williams," clipping from unidentified Indiana newspaper in Pearson Papers, box 1. For Williams's activities within the NEA, see Wayne Urban, *Gender, Race, and the National Education Association* (Routledge Falmer, 2000).

70. Joan Marie Johnson, *Southern Women at the Seven Sister Colleges: Feminist Values and Social Activism 1875–1915* (U Georgia P, 2008).

71. D. B. Johnson, interview by Marguerite Tolbert, June 1974, 15–16, in Southern Oral History Project, University of North Carolina Library, Chapel Hill, by permission.

72. Fannie McLean, MS speech to College Equal Suffrage League, May 2, 1908; "Suffrage Luncheon Talk" MS, June 1913, in McLean Family Papers, UC Berkeley. Emmeline Pankhurst founded the Women's Franchise League (1889) and the more militant Women's Social and Political Union (1903).

73. Katharine [or Katherine] Susan Anthony (1877–1965), *Feminism in Germany and Scandinavia* (Henry Holt, 1915), 3–4.

74. Helen Jones, *Nothing Seemed Impossible: Women's Education and Social Change in South Australia, 1875–1915* (U Queensland P, 1985).

75. Sarah King, "Feminists in Teaching: The National Union of Women Teachers, 1920–1945," in Martin Lawn & Gerald Grace (Eds.), *Teachers: The Culture and Politics of Work* (Falmer, 1987), 31–49; Hilda Kean, *Deeds Not Words: The Lives of Suffragette Teachers* (Pluto Press, 1990); Dina M. Copelman, *London's Women Teachers: Gender, Class and Feminism, 1870–1930* (Routledge, 1996); Alison Oram, *Women Teachers and Feminist Politics, 1900–1939* (Manchester UP, 1996).

76. All in Agness G. Gilman & Gertrude M. Gilman, *Who's Who in Illinois: Women-Makers of History* (Eclectic, 1927), 109, 134, 221.

77. Data from 1923–1928 received on 893 teachers, one-third of them not rehired. In Joseph McElhannon, "The Social Failure of Teachers," *Journal of Educational Sociology* 2 (May 1929): 536, 542–43. Cited in Maureen A. Reynolds, "Moral Restrictions on the Private Lives of Teachers between World War I and World War II" (unpublished paper, College of Education, Indiana University, 1993).

78. Florence Greenhoe, *Community Contacts and Participation of Teachers* (American Council on Public Affairs, 1941).

79. Eulalia Bourne, *Ranch Schoolteacher* (U Arizona P, 1974), 147.

80. Mary Beard, *Woman's Work in Municipalities* (D. Appleton, 1915).

81. This is a personal observation based on the author's years of regularly reading obituary columns in local newspapers of whatever community she was in. While family members may be more likely to mention community involvements in the obituaries of women teachers than of men, this possible explanation for the differences noted appears weak.

82. Department of Defense Education Activity (DoDEA), press release, April 26, 2004, http://www.dodea.edu/newsroom/pressreleases/26042004.cfm.

83. Austin, *Earth Horizon,* 142–43.

84. Fiona MacCarthy, "The Power of Chastity," review of *Sisters in Arms: Catholic Nuns Through Two Millennia,* by Jo Ann Kay McNamara, *New York Review of Books* (Dec. 19, 1996).

85. Mary Hunter Austin, *A Woman of Genius* (Doubleday, 1912), 218.

86. Mary Burnett Talbert in Darlene Clark Hine (Ed.), *Black Women in America: An Historical Encyclopedia* (Carlson, 1993), 1138.

87. Anne Firor Scott & William H. Chaafe, "What We Wish We Knew about Women: A Dialogue," in Mabel Deutrich & Virginia Purdy (Eds.), *Clio Was a Woman: Studies in the History of American Women* (Howard UP 1980), 10.

88. Lucy Worthington Blackman, *The Women of Florida* (Southern Historical, 1940), 1:viii.

89. Barbara Stuhler & Gretchen Kreuter, *Women of Minnesota: Selected Biographical Essays* (Minnesota Historical Society Press, 1977), 265–67. A conspiracy theory is noted in Hope Chamberlin, *A Minority of Members: Women in the U.S. Congress* (Praeger, 1973), 264–66.

90. Frank C. Lockwood, "School Teaching in Yuma Co., Arizona," *Pittsburgh Christian Advocate* (Oct. 4, 1917): 6–7. Clipping in Special Collections, University of Arizona Library.

91. Lippmann, "The Vote as a Symbol," 4.

92. Individual reports from incumbent state superintendents or commissioners to the author (1995, 1998).

93. Amanda Stewart to dear sisters, Sept. 6, 1886; Nora Stewart to family, Sept. 24, 1886; Mary Petherbridge Hull to Nora Stewart, July 7, 1887, all in SLC.

94. Alice Newberry to family, Dec. 8, 1895, Newberry Collection, History Colorado, by permission; John Morris, "The Women and Governor Waite," *Colorado Magazine* 44 (Winter 1967): 111–19. Also Helen L. Sumner, *Equal Suffrage: The Results of an Investigation in Colorado Made for the Collegiate Equal Suffrage League of New York State* (Harper & Brothers, 1909), 143.

95. Editorial, *Western Journal of Education* 5, no. 10 (1900), 33.

96. Unnamed Oregon legislator, 1933, in Sophonisba Breckinridge, *Women in the Twentieth Century: A Study of Their Political, Social and Economic Activities* (McGraw-Hill, 1933), 329.

97. Cornell in Charles Lincoln (Ed.), *Messages from the Governors,* vol. 8 (J. B. Lyon, State Printers, 1909).

98. Sarah Christie Stevens, "To the Women of Blue Earth County," 1894 MS, box 35, Christie Papers.

99. Undated draft manuscript in Sarah Catharine Warthen Searcy Papers, University of Kansas Library, by permission; Rosalind Urbach Moss, "Educated and Ambitious Women: Kate Warthen on the Kansas Frontier," in Janet Sharistanian (Ed.), *Gender, Ideology and Action: Historical Perspectives on Women's Public Lives* (Greenwood, 1986), 121–55.

100. "All about the Schools and the People Who Made Them Successful," *Plumas County Historical Society,* publication no. 16 (June 7, 1964), copy in California State Library, Sacramento.

101. Kellie McGarrh, "Hanging Tough: Mildred E. Doyle, School Superintendent, and the Negotiation of Gender Constructs" (paper presented at the Annual Meeting of the, Southern History of Education Society, Atlanta, March 18, 1995.)

102. Summarized in Robert Dinkin, *Before Equal Suffrage: Women in Partisan Politics from Colonial Times to 1920* (Greenwood, 1995), esp. 136–38. See also the 60 biographies in Esther Stineman, *American Political Women: Contemporary and Historical Profiles* (Libraries Unlimited, 1981).

103. K–12 teachers were 16% of women state senators in the 1970 and 13% of assembly members; the corresponding figures for attorneys were 10% and 11%, and for college teachers 9% and 6%. Courtesy of Nina Gabelko, who analyzed data drawn primarily from Rutgers University's Center for the American Women and Politics.

104. Susan Carroll & Wendy Strimling, *Women's Routes to Elective Office: A Comparison with Men's* (Center for the American Woman and Politics, 1983), tables 1.9 & 1.11.

105. Marilyn Johnson & Susan Carroll, *Women in Public Office: A Biographical Directory and Statistical Analysis,* 2nd ed. (Scarecrow Press, 1978), table 9.

106. Irene Diamond, *Sex Roles in the State House* (Yale UP, 1977), 1; "Women Make Historic Gains in Congress, the States," *Emily's List Newsletter,* Dec. 2008.

107. Georgia Lusk in Joan M. Jensen & Darlis A. Miller, *New Mexico Women: Intercultural Perspectives* (U New Mexico P, 1986), esp. 309, 322.

108. Carroll & Strimling, *Women's Routes to Elective Office,* esp. table 5.11.

109. Cecil Harden in Chamberlin, *Minority of Members,* 209–12. Hardin exemplified what was reported more generally in Johnson & Carroll, *Women in Public Life,* 1A–64A.

110. Irwin Gertzog, "The Matrimonial Connection: The Nomination of Congressmen's Widows for the House of Representatives," *Journal of Politics* 42 (1980): 820–31.

111. Diane D. Kincaid (Ed.), *Silent Hattie Speaks: The Personal Journal of Senator Hattie* (Greenwood, 1979), 4–8.

112. Two-thirds of congresswomen through 1964 had held one or more paid occupation. To approach the full extent of teachers' presence among political women, add those hidden in the category of "housewife," and among the lawyers, farmers and ranchers,

journalists, businesswomen, and social service workers elected to office; see Emmy Werner, "Women in Congress: 1917–1964," *Western Political Quarterly* 19, no. 1 (March 1966): 16–30.

113. Chisholm in Partnow, *Quotable Woman*, 377. Compared to whites, higher percentages of black women were lawyers and smaller percentages were teachers; in *Bringing More Women into Public Office* (Center for the American Woman and Politics, Jan. 1986).

114. From a 1981 study reported in Susan Carroll, Debra Dodson, & Ruth Mandel, *The Impact of Women in Public Office* (Center for the American Woman and Politics, 1991), 8.

115. May Sewall's own writings and biographical sketches are referenced in her biography in James, *Notable American Women*.

116. Mary Yeargin, *Cornell Era* 26, no. 7 (Nov. 11, 1893): 76–77; Miss M. H. Connor, *Cornell Era* 26, no. 9 (Nov. 25, 1893): 100–101; *Cornell Daily Sun* 14, no. 61 (Jan. 4, 1894). For Yeargin's Cornell activities and the circumstances and aftermath of her death, I am indebted to David Long, who searched the Cornell University Archives and Ithaca and other newspaper files.

117. Yeargin correspondence in Mary Little Yeargin Collection, South Caroliniana Library, University of South Carolina; R. Wright Spears, "Mary Yeargin" in Marguerite Tolbert, Irene Dillard Elliott, & Wil Lou Gray, *South Carolina's Distinguished Women of Laurens County* (L. R. Bryan, 1972), 55–61.

118. The phrase is from a Columbia (SC) news dispatch, in *Boston Globe* (Nov. 21, 1893), 12.

119. In Florence Howe, "Sexism and the Aspirations of Women," *Phi Delta Kappan* 55, no. 2 (Oct. 1973): 94–104.

120. Alice Money in Floy Lawrence Emhoff, "A Pioneer School Teacher in Central Iowa," *Iowa Journal of History and Politics* 33, no. 4 (Oct. 1935): 376–95; Geraldine Joncich Clifford, "Alice, How Could You!," review of *Alice Freeman Palmer: Evolution of a New Woman*, by Ruth Bordin, *History of Education Quarterly* 35, no. 3 (Fall 1995): 312–15.

121. Quoted in Elizabeth Brown Pryor, *Clara Barton, Professional Angel* (U Pennsylvania P, 1987), 6. Also see Clara Barton's autobiography written for children, *The Story of My Childhood* (Baker & Taylor, 1907), esp. 99.

122. Sinclair, *Emancipation of the American Woman*, 100; Kathryn Kish Sklar, *Catharine Beecher: A Study in American Domesticity* (Yale UP, 1973), esp. 267–69.

123. Joan Jensen, *Loosening the Bonds: Mid-Atlantic Farm Women, 1750–1850* (Yale UP, 1986), 182–83.

Chapter 13 · "A Lady Well Qualified to Show the Way"

1. "Concerning All Co-Eds," *Daily Californian* (May 19, 1943), 4, in Charles Dorn, "'A Woman's World': The University of California, Berkeley, during the Second World War," *History of Education Quarterly* 48, no. 4 (Nov. 2008): 534–64. The epigraph is from Virginia Penny, *The Employments of Women: A Cyclopaedia of Woman's Work* (Walker, Wise, 1863), vii.

2. Marjorie Stinson in Sylvia Oates Hunt, "To Wed and to Teach: The Myth of the Single Teacher," in Fane Downs & Nancy Baker Jones (Eds.), *Women and Texas History:*

Selected Essays (Texas State Historical Association, 1993): 127–42; Gussie Nettleton Whitcomb (b. 1886) in Bowman & Ryan, *Who's Who in Education.*

3. Andrew Hacker, "Women at Work," *New York Review of Books* 33, no. 13 (Aug. 14, 1986), 30, 31.

4. Sarah Stow, *History of Mount Holyoke Seminary, South Hadley, Mass., during Its First Half Century,* 1837–1887 (Springfield, 1887), 318.

5. Charles Thwing, "What Becomes of College Women," *North American Review* 161 (Nov. 1895): 546–53.

6. John Folger & Charles Nam, *Education of the American Population* (U.S. Commerce Department, 1967); John Parrish, "Women in Professional Training," *Monthly Labor Review* 97 (May 1974): 38, chart 3 (Women in selected professions as percent of all professional workers).

7. Sue Zschoche, "Seduced and Abandoned by Objectivity: The Home Economist and the Woman Question, 1890–1920" (paper presented at the Annual Meeting of the American Educational Research Association, San Francisco, April 20–24, 1992).

8. Ellen Gates Starr Papers in Sophia Smith Collection, Smith College; Matilda Evans in Katherine Smedley, *Martha Schofield and the Re-education of the South* (Edwin Mellen, 1987).

9. Harriot Hunt quoted in Blanche Glassman Hersh, *The Slavery of Sex: Feminist-Abolitionists in America* (U Illinois P, 1978), 136.

10. "Lucy Montz," in National Library of Medicine website, www.nkyviews.com/gallatin/text/txt_lucy_montz.htm, accessed Nov. 6, 2013.

11. Pearl L'Heureux in Harold C. Place, "Unusual Kansas Women," *Progress in Kansas Magazine* (Nov. 1935), at www.kancoll.org/articles/progress/kswomen.htm, accessed Nov. 6, 2013.

12. Alice Echols, *"Scars of Sweet Paradise": The Life and Times of Janis Joplin* (Metropolitan-Henry Holt, 1999), 25, 305. Reference courtesy of Dr. Suzanne Hildenbrand.

13. Karen Elliott House in Ken Auletta, "Family Business," *New Yorker* (Nov. 3, 2003): 54–67.

14. Jeff Bailey, "These Millionaires May Pass Out Peanuts," *New York Times* (May 15, 2006).

15. David H. Burton, *Clara Barton: In the Service of Humanity* (Greenwood, 1995), 163.

16. Patricia Okker, *Our Sister Editors: Sarah J. Hale and the Tradition of Nineteenth-Century American Women Editors* (U Georgia P, 1995).

17. "Library Service," in Monroe, *Cyclopedia of Education*; "Enrollment Statistics for 32 Accredited Library Schools," *Journal of Education for Librarianship* 1, no. 1 (Summer 1960): 38–46.

18. Louisa (Van Vleet) Wright in Angela Redinger, "The Early Years of Camas, Washington," Spring 2000, www.ccrh.org/comm/camas/student%20papers/camas%20paper.htm, accessed Nov. 6, 2013.

19. Unnamed Indiana woman in "The Moral Qualifications of a Candidate for Teacher in Our Public Schools," one of a series of 40 letters on early California published in an unidentified Sacramento newspaper in the 1860s. Clipping in Miscellaneous Education Collection, Research Library University of California, Los Angeles.

20. Anna Finch quoted in James Fitzmaurice & Josephine Roberts (Eds.), *Major Women Writers of Seventeenth Century England* (U Michigan P, 1997), 336.

21. Sylvia Ashton-Warner, *I Passed This Way* (Knopf, 1979), 196; Dale Spender, *Mothers of the Novel: 100 Good Women Writers before Jane Austen* (Pandora, 1986), 3.

22. Mary Balfour & Alice Flowerdew entries in Blain et al., *Feminist Companion to Literature.*

23. Ann Douglass, *The Feminization of American Culture* (Knopf, 1977), 113.

24. Kate Douglas Wiggin in E. F. Harkins & C. H. L. Johnston, *Little Pilgrimages: Among the Women Who Have Written Famous Books* (Page, 1901), 191–203; and standard reference works.

25. Mary Abigail Dodge in Denise Knight (Ed.), *Nineteenth-Century American Women Writers* (Greenwood, 1997).

26. Brenda Morrissey (Ed.), *Abby Hemenway's Vermont* (Stephen Greene, 1972).

27. Beth Timson, "Rachel Jones Holton," in Charlotte (NC) Chapter, American Association of University Women, *Making a Difference: Women of Mecklenburg* (1980), 7–8, copy in Public Library of Charlotte and Mecklenburg County.

28. Gilson Willets, *Workers of the Nation* (Collier & Son, 1903), 2:934–35. Annie Louise Brown Leslie in Mainiero, *American Women Writers.*

29. Jessie Fauset in Lee Edwards & Arlyn Diamond, *American Voices, American Women* (Avon Books, 1973), 383–84; Salem, *African American Women.* Alice Dunnigan in Ruth Edmonds Hill & Patricia Miller King (Eds.), *Guide to the Transcripts of the Black Women Oral History Project* (Meckler, 1991), 23.

30. George Gissing, *The Odd Women* (repr., Norton, 1977), 35–36.

31. Mary Laselle & Katherine Wiley, *Vocations for Girls* (Houghton Mifflin, 1913), 79.

32. McGill, "Elizabeth Conrad," in American Association of University Women, *Making a Difference,* 34–35.

33. Eleanor Marie Reser in Courtney Ann Vaughn Roberson, "Having a Purpose in Life: Western Women Teachers in the Twentieth Century," *Great Plains Quarterly* 5 (Spring 1985): 107–24, esp. 112, 122.

34. Robert Smuts, *Women and Work in America* (Columbia UP, 1959; Schocken, 1971), 65; *Handbook of Women Workers* (U.S. Labor Department, 1975), esp. 89.

35. Alison Lurie, *New York Review of Books* 53, no. 13 (Aug. 10, 2006), 4–5.

36. Patricia Hummer, *The Decade of Elusive Promise: Professional Women in the United States, 1920–1930* (UMI Research, 1979); Willystine Goodsell, "The Educational Opportunities of American Women—Theoretical and Actual," *Annals of the American Academy of Political and Social Science* 143 (May 1929): 6.

37. Author's interview with Judith Alper Udall, San Francisco, May 2003.

38. Penina Grazer & Miriam Slater, *Unequal Colleagues: The Entrance of Women into the Professions, 1890–1940* (Rutgers UP, 1987), 232; Janet M. Hooks, *Women's Occupations through Seven Decades,* Women's Bureau Bulletin no. 218 (U.S. Labor Department, 1947), 154–89.

39. Sophie Drinker, "Women Attorneys of Colonial Times," *Maryland Historical Magazine* 56, no. 4 (Dec. 1961).

40. Louis Haselmayer, "Belle A. Mansfield," *Women Lawyers Journal* 55, no. 2 (Spring 1969): 46.

41. Jean Norris, "Law," in Doris Fleischman (Ed.), *An Outline of Careers for Women: Practical Guide to Achievement* (Doubleday, 1928), 271.

42. Sandra Epstein, *Law at Berkeley: The History of Boalt Hall* (Institute of Governmental Studies, University of California, 1997), 310–11.

43. Smuts, *Women and Work in America,* 110–11; Karen Morello, *The Invisible Bar* (Random House, 1986).

44. Charlotte Ray (b. 1850) in Salem, *African American Women.*

45. Mary Ann Shadd in Joan M. Jensen, *Loosening the Bonds: Mid-Atlantic Farm Women, 1750–1850* (Yale UP, 1986), 181–82. Emma Mellinda Gillett in James, *Notable American Women.*

46. Nancy Ellen Barr, "A Profession for Women: Education, Social Service Administration, and Feminism in the Life of Sophonisba Preston Breckinridge, 1866–1948" (Ph.D. diss., Emory University, 1993).

47. Sarah Hughes in Sylvia Oates Hunt, "To Wed and to Teach," in Fane Downs & Nancy Baker Jones (Eds.), *Women and Texas History: Selected Essays* (Texas State Historical Association, 1993): 127–42.

48. Lynne Kawamoto in John McCormick, "Chicago Hope," *Newsweek* (March 24, 1997): 68–71.

49. Laurel Thatcher Ulrich, *A Midwife's Tale: The Life of Martha Ballard, Based on Her Diary, 1785–1812* (Knopf, 1990).

50. Nancy Theriot, *The Biosocial Construction of Femininity: Mothers and Daughters in Nineteenth-Century America* (Greenwood, 1988); Katherine Arnup, Andrée Lévesque, & Ruth Roach Pierson (Eds.), *Delivering Motherhood: Maternal Ideologies and Practices in the Nineteenth and Twentieth Centuries* (Routledge, 1990).

51. In Julia Cherry Spruill, *Women's Work & Life in the Southern Colonies* (U North Carolina P, 1938), esp. 267–69, 275; Lamar Riley Murphy, *Enter the Physician: The Transformation of Domestic Medicine, 1760–1860* (U Alabama P, 1991).

52. Boston physician quoted in Victor Robinson, *White Caps: The Story of Nursing* (Lippincott, 1946), 139.

53. Mary Roth Walsh *"Doctors Wanted, No Women Need Apply": Sexual Barriers in the Medical Profession, 1835–1975* (Yale UP, 1977).

54. Martha Hughes Cannon in *Women of the West Museum,* http://theautry.org/explore/exhibits/suffrage/cannon_full.html, accessed Nov. 6, 2013; Constance Lieber & John Sillito, *Letters from Exile: The Correspondence of Martha Hughes Cannon and Angus M. Cannon, 1886–1888* (Signature Books, 1989).

55. Annie Wells Williams in *Historical Sketch of the State Normal School at San José.* . . . (State Printing Office, 1889), 239, 279; Franklin Harper (Ed.), *Who's Who on the Pacific Coast* (Harper, 1913).

56. Alice Hamilton, *Exploring the Dangerous Trades: The Autobiography of Alice Hamilton* (Little, Brown, 1943).

57. Benson Tong, *Susan La Flesche Picotte, M.D.: Omaha Indian Leader and Reformer* (U Oklahoma P, 1999).

58. Carolina Healey Dall's lectures were published as *The College, the Market, and the Court; or, On Women's Relation to Education, Labor, and Law* (Lee & Shepherd, 1867, 1914), esp. 441.

59. *Journal of Addresses and Proceedings*, National Education Association, Topeka, 1886 (Observer Book & Job Printing, 1887).

60. Barbara Welter, "She Hath Done What She Could: Protestant Women's Missionary Careers in Nineteenth-Century America," *American Quarterly* 30, no. 5 (Winter 1978): 624–38.

61. Horace Bushnell, *Women's Suffrage: Reform against Nature* (Scribner, 1869), 21, 57.

62. Sarah Sentilles, *A Church of Her Own: What Happens When a Woman Takes the Pulpit* (Harcourt, 2008).

63. Antoinette Brown Blackwell, *The Sexes throughout Nature* (Putnam, 1875).

64. In Henry Born & Frederick A. Williams (Eds.), *The Diary of James A. Garfield* (Michigan State UP, 1967); diary of Lucretia Rudolph in L. R. Garfield Papers, Library of Congress.

65. Rev. Ada Bowles in *California Women: A Guide to Their Politics, 1885–1911* (California Scene, 1967?); Otis G. Hammond, "Rev. Benjamin Boles," *Granite State Monthly*, 14, no. 2 (Feb. 1892): 62; Bowles correspondence in Helen Lyman Papers, Schlesinger Library, Radcliffe College.

66. Glen T. Miller, *Piety and Profession: American Protestant Theological Education, 1870–1970* (Eerdmans, 2007).

67. Alexis Lange, "The Problem of the Professional Training for Women," *School and Society* 3, no. 66 (April 1, 1916): 242–50. Lange was dean of education at UC Berkeley.

68. Kathryn Kish Sklar, *Catharine Beecher: A Study in American Domesticity* (Yale UP, 1973).

69. Goldthwaite in Carole Shmurak & Bonnie Handler, "'Castle of Science': Mount Holyoke College and the Preparation of Women in Chemistry, 1837–1941," *History of Education Quarterly* 32, no. 3 (Fall 1992): 315–42.

70. Louis Booker Wright, "Dr. Christine South Gee," in Marguerite Tolbert, Irene Dillard Elliott, & Wil Lou Gray, *South Carolina's Distinguished Women of Laurens County* (Bryan, 1972), 129–36.

71. Sue Zschoche, "Seduced and Abandoned by Objectivity: The Home Economist and the Woman Question, 1890–1992"; & Anne Knupfer, "Educating Female Students for 'Useful Womanhood': Midwestern Female Presidents and Their Colleges, 1885–1920" (papers presented at the Annual Meeting of the American Educational Research Association, San Francisco, April 7–11, 2006).

72. Madge Reese in "Alumni Roster, 1917," *Bulletin of the First District Normal School* [formally Northeast Missouri State Teachers College] 17, no. 4 (April 1917), Pickler Memorial Library, Truman State University Archives, Kirksville, Missouri, library.truman.edu /archives/alumni1917.asp.

73. Barbara Sicherman, "College and Careers: Historical Perspectives on the Lives and Work Patterns of Women College Graduates," in John Faragher & Florence Howe (Eds.), *Women and Higher Education in American History* (Norton, 1988), 154; Gladys Branegan, *Home Economics Teacher Training under the Smith-Hughes Act, 1917–1927* (Teachers College P, 1929).

74. Joyce Antler, *The Educated Woman and Professionalization: The Struggle for a New Feminine Identity, 1890–1920* (Garland, 1987), 381.

75. Arthur Reed Taylor, "From the Ashes: Atlanta during Reconstruction, 1865–1876" (Ph.D. diss.: Emory University, 1973), 303–4.

76. Lora Dee Garrison, *Apostles of Culture: The Public Librarian and American Society, 1876–1920* (U Wisconsin P, 1979).

77. Joanne Passet, *Cultural Crusaders: Women Librarians in the American West, 1900–1917* (U New Mexico P, 1994); & Passet, "Entering the Professions: Women Library Educators and the Placement of Female Students, 1887–1912," *History of Education Quarterly* 31, no. 2 (Summer 1991): 207–28.

78. Anne Brugh & Benjamin Beede, "Review Essay: American Librarianship," *Signs: Journal of Women in Culture and Society* 1, no. 4 (Summer 1971): 943–55.

79. Mary Niles Maack, "No Philosophy Carries So Much Connection as the Personal Life: Mary Wright Plummer as an Independent Woman," *Library Quarterly* 70, no. 1 (Jan. 2000): 1–46.

80. Stuart Stotts, "A Thousand Little Libraries: Lutie Stearns, the Johnny Appleseed of Books," *Wisconsin Magazine of History* 90, no. 2 (2006–2007): 38–49.

81. Clara Sitter, "Fannie Elizabeth Ratchford," in Susanne Hildenbrand (Ed.), *Reclaiming the American Library Past: Writing the Women In* (Ablex, 1996), 135–63.

82. Melville Dewey quoted in Laurel Grotzinger, "Remarkable beginnings," in W. C. Allen & R. F. Delzell (Eds.), *Ideas and Standards: The History of the University of Illinois Graduate School of Library and Information Science* (Graduate School of Library and Information Science, 1992), 5.

83. Mary Niles Maach, "Women in Library Education: Down the Up Staircase," *Library Trends* 34, no. 3 (Winter 1986): 401–32; Phyllis Wetherby et al. in *Sixteen Reports on the Status of Women in the Professions* (Professional Women's Caucus, 1970).

84. Suzanne Hildenbrand, "The Information Age vs. Gender Equity," *Library Journal* 124, no. 7 (April 15, 1999): 44–47.

85. Roma Harris, *Librarianship: The Erosion of a Woman's Profession* (Ablex, 1992).

86. James Govan, "The Creeping Invisible Hand: Entrepreneurial Librarianship," *Library Journal* 113, no. 1 (Jan. 1988), 38.

87. In Smuts, *Women and Work in America*, 29.

88. Frances Abigail Goodale, *The Literature of Philanthropy* (Harper, 1893), 2; Lori Ginzberg, *Women and the Work of Benevolence: Morality, Politics, and Class in the Nineteenth Century United States* (Yale UP, 1990); Sherri Broder, *Tramps, Unfit Mothers, and Neglected Children: Negotiating the Family in Nineteenth-Century Philadelphia* (U Pennsylvania P, 2002).

89. Ellen Fitzpatrick, *Endless Crusade: Women Social Scientists and Progressive Reform* (Oxford UP, 1990).

90. Julia Short, "Kate Barnard: Liberated Woman" (master's thesis, University of Oklahoma, 1972); Keith Bryant Jr., "Kate Barnard, Organized Labor and Social Justice in Oklahoma," *Journal of Social History* 35 (1969): 143–64.

91. Emelia Martinez-Brawley, "From Countrywoman to Federal Emergency Relief Administrator: Josephine Chapin Brown, A Biographical Study," *Journal of Sociology and Social Welfare* 14, no. 2 (June 1987), 153–85.

92. Esther E. Peterson, recorded interview by Ann M. Campbell, Feb. 11, 1970, in John F. Kennedy Library Oral History Program, Washington, DC.

93. Mary Elizabeth McDowell in *Illinois Women: 75 Years of the Right to Vote* (Chicago Sun-Times Features, 1996), 25, 34–35.

94. Mrs. John Van Vorst, with Marie Van Vorst, *The Woman Who Toils: Being the Experiences of Two Gentlewomen as Factory Girls* (Doubleday, Page, 1903), 3–4.

95. Anna Beach Pratt is one of many social work figures in James, *Notable American Women*.

96. Linda Shoemaker, "The Gendered Foundations of Social Work Education in Boston, 1904–1930," in Susan Porter (Ed.), *Women of the Commonwealth; Work, Family, and Social Change in Nineteenth-Century Massachusetts* (U Massachusetts P, 1996), 99–120.

97. Cited in Barbara Melosh, *"The Physician's Hand": Work Culture and Conflict in American Nursing* (Temple UP, 1982), 3.

98. Smuts, *Women and Work in America*; Alfred Worcester, *Nurses and Nursing* (Harvard UP, 1927), 37–38.

99. Linda Richards, *America's First Trained Nurse* (Whitcom & Barrows, 1915), 5.

100. Isabel Maitland Stewart, *The Education of Nurses: Historical Foundations and Modern Trends* (Macmillan, 1953).

101. Persis Mary Hamilton, *Realities of Contemporary Nursing*, 2nd ed. (Addison Wesley, 1996), 33–37; Peggy Anderson, *Nurse* (Berkley Books, 1979), 36.

102. Mary M. Roberts, *American Nursing: History and Interpretation* (Macmillan, 1961).

103. Bellevue report cited in Shirley Carmichael Cartwright, "'Blessed Drudgery': Womanly Virtue and Nineteenth Century Organizations" (Ph.D. diss., University of California, Davis, 1977), 340. A number of erstwhile teachers appear in *Biographical Sketches* (National League of Nursing Education, 1939), including Lydia Anderson, Sister M. Domitilla, Mary Gladwin, Carolyn Gray, Marion G. Howell, Sally Johnson, Louise Powell, Isabel Stewart, Daisy Urch, and Helen Young.

104. Mary Lewis Wyche in Lou Rogers, *Tar Heel Women* (Warren, 1949), 187–92; Mary Lewis Wyche, *The History of Nursing in North Carolina* (U North Carolina P, 1938, 1977), completed and published posthumously.

105. "Mary Benjamin" (the pseudonym of a 27-year-old head nurse in a big-city hospital) in Anderson, *Nurse*, vii.

106. Quotation in Lavinia R. Dock & Isabel Maitland Stewart, *A Short History of Nursing from the Earliest Times to the Present Day* (Putnam, 1931), 9–10.

107. Gissing, *Odd Women*, 135–36.

108. Lois Mathews, "Report of the Dean of Women," 1912, cited in Jana Nidiffer, *Pioneering Deans of Women: More Than Wise and Pious Matrons* (Teachers College P, 2000).

109. David Clark and Gerald Marker, "The Institutionalization of Teacher Education," in Kevin Ryan (Ed.), *Teacher Education*, 74th Yearbook of the National Society for the Study of Education, part 2 (U Chicago P, 1975), 204–29; William Graybeal, "Status and Trends in Public School Teacher Supply and Demand," *Journal of Teacher Education* 25 (Summer 1974): 200–209.

110. Rael Jean Isaac, "American Women in the Great Society," *Colorado Quarterly* 16, no. 1 (1967): 87.

111. Canadian teacher ("Geraldine") quoted in Cecelia Reynolds, "Hegemony and Hierarchy: Becoming a Teacher in Toronto, 1930–1980," *Historical Studies in Education / Revue d'Histoire de l'Éducation* 1, no. 2 (Spring 1990): 95–118, esp. 99.

112. As summarized in Andrew Hacker, "Goodbye to Affirmative Action?," *New York Review of Books* 43 (July 11, 1996), 26. Whites includes Hispanics who so identified themselves.

113. *Business Week* (May 26, 2003); Constance Penley, *NASA/TREK Popular Science and Sex in America* (Verso, 1997).

114. Ruth Lebowitz, "Women Elementary-School Teachers and the Feminist Movement," *Elementary School Journal* 80, no. 5 (May 1980): 239–45. See also, Patti Laffer, "Reclaiming Our Profession: Towards a Feminist Theory of Public Education" (unpublished paper, April 1981, courtesy of the author).

115. Florence Howe (Ed.), *Women and the Power to Change* (McGraw-Hill, 1975), 166.

116. Meg Richards (Associated Press), "Boomer Women Still Growing Strong," *San Francisco Chronicle* (June 12, 2003); Judith Havemann, "Great Expectations," *Wilson Quarterly* 31, no. 3 (Summer 2007): 46–66.

117. In Sam Yarger, Kenneth Howey, & Bruce Joyce, "Reflections on Preservice Preparation: Impressions from the National Survey," *Journal of Teacher Education* 28, nos. 5 & 6 (Sept.–Oct. & Nov.–Dec. 1977): 14, 24; Graybeal, "Status and Trends," 208.

118. Sandra Acker, "Women and Teaching: A Semi-detached Sociology of a Semi-profession," in Stephen Walker & Len Barton (Eds.), *Gender, Class & Education* (Falmer, 1983), 132.

119. Richard Freeman, *The Overeducated American* (Academic Press, 1976), 168.

120. Janeen Richards's deferred dream in David Boxer, "Two Paths to Social Justice," *TC Today* (Fall 2005): 24–27.

121. Richard Freeman, *The Overeducated American* (Academic Press, 1976), 168; for shifts in college majors see *Trends in Educational Equity of Girls & Women* (National Center for Education Statistics, 2000).

122. Penelope Trunk, *Brazen Careers: The New Rules for Success* (Warner, 2007).

123. The spending disparity between the wealthiest and poorest U.S. school districts approaches 10–1 ratios; in Linda Darling-Hammond, "The Flat Earth and Education: How America's Commitment to Equity Will Determine Our Future," *Educational Researcher* 36, no. 6 (Aug.–Sept. 2007): 318–34.

124. "Teachers Are in Trouble," *Newsweek* (April 27, 1981).

125. Raymond Wolters, *The Burden of "Brown": Thirty Years of School Desegregation* (U Tennessee P, 1984); Mary Anne Fowlkes, "A Hundred Years of Kentucky Kindergartens: A Rich Legacy, a New Hope 1887–1987," in Archives & Records Retention Center, Jefferson County Public Schools, Louisville, Kentucky, courtesy of Amy E. Wells.

126. Antoinette Mitchell, "The Work Lives of Teachers, 1960-1990" (Ph.D. diss., University of California, Berkeley, 1996), 16. A 28-year veteran of teaching, "Berta" was interviewed for Claire Elaine Sylvan, "The Impact of Motherhood on Teacher Career Attitudes" (Ed.D. diss., Teachers College, Columbia University, 1988), 175.

127. Evelyn Weiss in Ruth Jacknow Markowitz, *My Daughter, the Teacher: Jewish Teachers in the New York City Schools* (Rutgers UP, 1993), 174.

128. Carol A. Langdon, "Third Phi Delta Kappa Poll of Teachers' Attitudes toward the Public Schools," *Phi Delta Kappan* 78, no. 3 (Nov. 1996), 244–50.

129. Cited in Harry L. Miller & Roger Woock, *Social Foundations of Urban Education* (Dryden Press, 1970), 110.

130. The chief source for this section is Michael Fultz, "The Displacement of Black Educators Post-*Brown*: An Overview and Analysis," *History of Education Quarterly* 44, no. 1 (Spring 2004): 11–45. See also Amy Stuart Wells, Jennifer Jellison Holme, Anita Tijerina Revilla, & Awo Korantemaa Atanda, *Both Sides Now: The Story of School Desegregation's Graduates* (U California P, 2009).

131. Gloria Ladson Billings, "Landing on the Wrong Note: The Price We Paid for *Brown*," *Educational Researcher* 23, no. 7 (Oct. 2004): 3–13.

132. Caroline Eick, "Student Relationships across Social Markers of Difference in a Baltimore County, Maryland, Comprehensive High School, 1950–1969," *History of Education Quarterly* 50, no. 3 (Aug. 2010): 359–89, esp. 364n7, 372.

133. Miller & Woock, *Social Foundations of Urban Education*, 290; St. Clair Drake, "The Black University in the American Social Order," *Dædalus* 100, no. 3 (Summer 1971): 833–97, esp. 851.

134. Boyd Bosma, "The Role of Teachers in School Desegregation," *Integrated Education* 15, no. 6 (1977): 108.

135. John Roden & Diane Truscott, "Entry into Teacher Education 12 Years Later: A Longitudinal Perspective on Gender and Ethnicity in Teacher Supply" (paper presented at the Annual Meeting of the American Educational Research Association, San Francisco, April 8, 2006).

136. Mary Roth Walsh, "The Rediscovery of the Need for a Feminist Medical Education," *Harvard Educational Review* 49, no. 4 (Nov. 1979): 447–66.

137. From interviews in Sylvan, "Impact of Motherhood on Teacher Career Attitudes."

138. Prof. Joseph E. Illick, San Francisco State University, e-mail to author, Sept. 3, 2000.

139. Vincent Coppola, "A Vocation Dies in Brooklyn," *Newsweek* (April 27, 1981): 81.

140. Quotation from Walter Benjamin, letter (Dec. 9, 1923), quoted in Susan Sontag, "Under the Sign of Saturn," Introduction to Walter Benjamin, *One-Way Street and Other Writings*, trans. Edmund Jephcott & Kingsley Shorter (Harcourt Brace Jovanovich,1978), 7–28.

141. *Statistical Yearbook, Fifty-Fifth Issue 2010* (United Nations, 2012): 71–86.

142. Usha Nayar, *Women Teachers in South Asia: Continuities, Discontinuities, and Change* (Chanakya, 1988), 182; P. V. L. Rammana, *Modernity and Role Performance of Women Teachers* (Kanti, 1992); Jill Ker Conway & Susan Bourque (Eds.), *The Politics of Women's Education: Perspectives from Asia, Africa, and Latin America* (U Michigan P, 1993).

143. *Statistics Yearbook, 1975* (UNESCO, 1976).

144. *Annual Demographic Supplement to the March 2002 Current Population Survey* (U.S. Bureau of the Census, 2002).

145. Jayne Williams in "More Children Growing Up with Parents Working, Census Shows," *San Francisco Chronicle* (May 22, 2002).

146. Commission on Women in the Profession, *Elusive Equality: The Experiences of Women in Legal Education* (American Bar Association, 1996); Mary Wasiak in "Class Acts," *O, The Oprah Magazine* (Sept. 2009): 48.

147. In Fred Davis, Virginia Olesen, & Elvi Whittaker, "Problems and Issues in Collegiate Nursing Education," in Fred Davis (Ed.), *The Nursing Profession: Five Sociological Essays* (Wiley & Sons, 1966), 165.

148. Vivian Gussin Paley, *Kwanzaa and Me: A Teacher's Story* (Harvard UP, 1995), 88–89.

149. A 2003 study of those teaching 9th- or 10th-grade math in Dade County (Miami) found women were 57% of teachers but 76% of National Board Certified teachers, in Linda Cavalluzzo, *Is National Board Certification an Effective Signal of Teacher Quality?* (CNA, 2004); Cavalluzzo to author, Dec. 17, 2004.

150. Langdon, "Third Phi Delta Kappa Poll of Teachers' Attitudes," 246.

151. Nathan Bell, "CGS Enrollment & Degrees, 2000 to 2010," Council of Graduate Schools (Sept. 2011), available at www.cgsnet.org/ckfinder/userfiles/files/R_ED2010.pdf, accessed Nov. 6, 2013. Also Sicherman, "College and Careers," 154; Nancy Woloch, *Women and the American Experience* (Knopf, 1984), 222–24.

152. Annie M. Brainard, *The Evolution of Public Health Nursing* (1922), in Melosh, "*Physician's Hand*," 23.

153. Dorothy Bryant, *Miss Giardino* (Ata Books, 1978), 36–37.

154. Walt Whitman, *Leaves of Grass* (Rees Welsh, 1882), 308.

John H. Garrity & Mark C. Carnes (Eds.), *American National Biography* (Oxford University Press, 1990) is the overarching work, but the following sources are more useful in locating and learning about the mostly unknown women who taught in America, their antecedents, essentials of their lives, and circumstances—often leading to other individuals. Despite its title, most of the entries in Edward T. James, Janet Wilson James, & Paul Boyer (Eds.), *Notable American Women: A Biographical Dictionary*, vols. 1–3, *1607–1950* (Harvard UP, 1971) would be unfamiliar to most readers. The companion volume is Barbara Sicherman & Carol Hurd Green (Eds.), *Notable American Women: A Biographical Dictionary*, vol. 4, *The Modern Period* (Harvard UP, 1980). Dorothy C. Salem (Ed.) includes 300, mostly twentieth-century, figures in *African American Women: A Biographical Dictionary* (Garland, 1993).

The following compilations reveal the large overlap between teachers and published authors: Janet Todd (Ed.), *A Dictionary of British and American Women Writers* (London: Routledge, 1989); Elaine Showalter, Lea Baechler, & Liz Walton (Eds.), *Modern American Women Writers* (Scribner's Sons, 1991); Virginia Blaine, Patricia Clements, & Isobel Grundy, (Eds.), *The Feminist Companion to Literature in English: Women Writers from the Middle Ages to the Present* (Yale University Press, 1990); and Lina Mainiero (Ed.), *American Women Writers*, 5 vols. (Frederick Ungar, 1980).

For some persons, biographical detail may be confirmed in the multiple editions of *Who's Who in Education* (Marquis) or the separately published *Who's Who in Education* (Who's Who, 1927) compiled by George E. Bowman & Nellie C. Ryan; it focuses on Colorado and adjacent states, with women well represented. Other useful sources are Richard Altenbaugh (Ed.), *Historical Dictionary of American Education* (Greenwood, 1999); James McKeen Cattell (Ed.), *Leaders in Education: A Biographical Directory* (Science Press, 1932, 1940) with Jaques Cattell & E. E. Ross, (1941), & Jaques Cattell & E. E. Ross (1948); and John F. Ohles (Ed.), *Biographical Dictionary of American Educators* (Greenwood, 1978).

Among nineteenth-century reference works that have themselves become primary sources for that period are James Parton (Ed.), *Eminent Women of the Age* (S. M. Betts, 1868, 1873) and Henry Barnard (Ed.), *Memoirs of Teachers, Educators, and Promoters and Benefactors of Education, Literature, and Science* (F. C. Brownell, 1861; Arno Press & New York Times, 1969). Modern sensibilities are reflected in the "feminized" and ethnically inclusive Maxine Schwartz Seller (Ed.), *Women Educators in the United States, 1820–1903: A Bio-Bibliographical Sourcebook* (Greenwood, 1994) that features longer, more interpretive biographies of generally better-known women. A comprehensive, topical survey of scholarship on teachers is Donald Warren (Ed.), *American Teachers: Histories of a Profession at Work* (McGraw-Hill, 1999)—an essential for newcomers to the subject.

Even if lacking context or interpretation, normal school and college alumni directories and other publications can be an invaluable resource in providing perspective on career trajectories and longevity, as well as marital and family factors. See, for example, the "Alumni Roster" (1917 & 1924 editions) in the *Bulletin of the First District Normal School, Kirksville, Missouri* (subsequently Northeast Missouri State Teachers College), available online, and class letters from various of the women's colleges' alumnae associations. This study relies heavily on several editions of the University of California's alumni directories, the most comprehensive being Robert Sibley (Ed.), *Golden Book of California* (California Alumni Association, 1937). While college and university histories are only beginning to attend to women's presence as students and faculty and, more important, their formative effects, they are worth perusing.

Apart from biographical searches, standard background sources include Sol Cohen (Ed.), *Education in the United States: A Documentary History*, 5 vols. (Random House, 1974) and Paul Monroe (Ed.), *A Cyclopedia of Education in Five Volumes* (Macmillan, 1911–1913). Many insights on schools, students, and, most relevant, the immigrant backgrounds of teachers (and university students who might become teachers) can be gleaned from *The Children of Immigrants in Schools*, vols. 29–33 of the 41-volume *Report of the United States Immigration Commission* (U.S. Government Printing Office, 1911). A reprint, with an introduction by Francesco Cordasco is *The Children of Immigrants in Schools* (Scarecrow Press, 1970.)

The basic references for quantifiable trends in education are *Historical Statistics of the United States, Colonial Times to 1957* (U.S. Bureau of the Census, 1960), *Continuation to 1962 and Revisions* (U.S. Bureau of the Census, 1965), and *120 Years of American Education: A Historical Portrait* (U.S. Department of Education, 1993). The National Center for Education Statistics (*Digest of Education Statistics*), Bureau of Labor Statistics (*Current Population Survey*), and UNESCO (*Statistics* or *Statistical Yearbook*) all issue periodic reports, many available online.

United States of America

Arizona
   Arizona State Historical Society (Research Library), Tucson
   Tucson Public Library (Special Collections), Tucson
   University of Arizona Library (Special Collections), Tucson

California
   California State Archives, Sacramento (Roseville Depository)
   California State Library, Sacramento
   Henry E. Huntington Library (Manuscripts Department), San Marino
   Santa Barbara Historical Society, Santa Barbara
   University of California, Berkeley (Bancroft Library)
   University of California, Los Angeles (Charles E. Young Research Library)

Colorado
   History Colorado, Denver
   Denver Public Library (Western History Room), Denver

Florida
   Sisters of Saint Joseph of St. Augustine Archives, St. Augustine
   St. Augustine Historical Society (Research Library), St. Augustine
   University of Florida Library (Special Collections), Gainesville

Georgia
   Atlanta History Center Library, Atlanta
   Emory University Library (Manuscript, Archives, & Rare Book Library) Atlanta
   Georgia Historical Society (Research Center) Savannah
   University of Georgia Libraries (Hargrett Rare Book & Manuscript Library), Athens

Idaho
   Boise Public Library, Boise
   Idaho State Historical Society Library (Archives), Boise
   Idaho State University Library (Special Collections), Pocatello

Illinois
   Illinois State Historical Library Collections, Abraham Lincoln Presidential Library,
      Springfield

Newberry Library (Special Collections), Chicago
University of Illinois (Rare Book & Manuscript Library), Urbana
Urbana Free Library (Archives), Urbana

Indiana
Indiana State Historical Society Library (Glick History Center), Indianapolis
Indiana University (Lilly Library), Bloomington
St. Mary's College Library (College Archives and Sisters' Archives), Notre Dame
University of Notre Dame Libraries (Rare Books & Special Collections and University Archives), Notre Dame

Kansas
Kansas State Historical Society Library, Topeka
University of Kansas (Kenneth Spencer Research Library), Lawrence

Louisiana
Tulane University (Amistad Research Center), New Orleans
Tulane University Library (Special Collections), New Orleans

Maine
Maine Historical Society (Research Library), Portland

Massachusetts
American Antiquarian Society Library, Worcester
Beverly Historical Society, Beverly
Forbes Library, Northampton
Harvard University Archives (Pusey Library), Cambridge
Harvard University (Houghton Library), Cambridge
Mount Holyoke College Library (Archives & Special Collections), South Hadley
New England Historic Genealogical Society Library, Boston
The Schlesinger Library on the History of Women, Radcliffe Institute, Harvard University, Cambridge
Smith College (Sophia Smith Library), Northampton

Michigan
University of Michigan (Special Collections Library), Ann Arbor

Minnesota
Minnesota Historical Society, Minnesota History Center Library, St. Paul
University of Minnesota (Immigration History Research Center & Archives), Minneapolis
University of Minnesota (University Archives), Minneapolis

Missouri
University of Missouri (Joint Collection: Western Historical Manuscript Collection and State Historical Society of Missouri Manuscripts), Kansas City

Montana
University of Montana (Mansfield Library) Archives & Special Collections, Missoula

New Jersey
Center for American Women and Politics, Eagleton Institute, Rutgers University
Rutgers University Library (Special Collections & University Archives), New Brunswick

New Mexico
  University of New Mexico (Zimmerman Library), Center for Southwest Research &
    Special Collections), Albuquerque
New York
  Columbia University Library (Rare Book & Manuscript Library), New York City
  New-York Historical Society (Klingenstein Research Library), New York City
  New York Public Library (Manuscripts & Archives Division), New York City
  Vassar College Libraries (Archives & Special Collections), Poughkeepsie
North Carolina
  Duke University Libraries (David M. Rubinstein Rare Book & Manuscript Library),
    Durham
  Public Library of Charlotte & Mecklenburg County (Carolina Room), Charlotte
  University of North Carolina Library (Wilson Special Collections Library), Chapel Hill
Ohio
  Cincinnati Historical Society (Research Library), Cincinnati
Oklahoma
  Oklahoma State Historical Society (History Center), Oklahoma City
  University of Oklahoma Library (Western History Collections), Norman
Oregon
  Curry (County) Historical Society, Gold Beach
  Oregon Historical Society Research Library, Portland
  University of Oregon Library (Special Collections & University Archives), Eugene
Pennsylvania
  American Philosophical Society Library, Philadelphia
  Historical Society of Pennsylvania Library, Philadelphia
South Carolina
  University of South Carolina (South Caroliniana Library), Columbia
  Winthrop College (Dacus Library, Archives & Special Collections), Rock Hill
Tennessee
  Tennessee State Library and Archives, Nashville
Texas
  University of Texas at Brownsville (Arnulfo Oliveira Library), Brownsville
  University of Texas (Dolph Briscoe Center for American History Archives), Austin
Utah
  Utah Pioneers Memorial Museum (Manuscript Room), Salt Lake City
  Utah State Historical Society Library, Salt Lake City
Vermont
  Vermont Historical Society (Leahy Library, Vermont History Center), Barre
Washington
  University of Washington Library (Special Collections), Seattle
Washington, DC
  Howard University (Moorland-Spingarn Research Center)
  Library of Congress (Manuscript Division)

Wisconsin
  Swiss Historical Village and Museum, New Glarus
  State Historical Society of Wisconsin (Library & Archives), Madison
Wyoming
  University of Wyoming (American Heritage Center), Laramie
  Wyoming State Archives, Cheyenne

Australia

ACT (Australian Capital Territory)
  Manuscript Branch, National Library of Australia, Canberra
New South Wales
  State Library of New South Wales (Mitchell Library), Sydney
South Australia
  State Library (Mortlock Library of South Australiana), Adelaide
Tasmania
  Furneaux Historical Research Association Museum, Emita, Flinders Island
Victoria
  Ballarat Public Library (Australiana Research Room), Ballarat
  Geelong Heritage Centre, Geelong
  Royal Historical Society of Victoria Library, Melbourne
  Sovereign Hill Gold Museum Library Sovereign Hill
  Swan Hill Regional Library (Local History Section), Swan Hill

Canada

The Ontario Institute for Studies in Education (Special Collections), University of
  Toronto

An annotated list of collections, arranged by state and by archive, can be accessed through a link at the Johns Hopkins University Press website: www.press.jhu.edu/books.